Southern Italy

Naples &
Campania
p36

Puglia,
Basilicata &
Calabria
p100

Sicily
p160

Contents

PLAN YOUR TRIP

Welcome to
Southern Italy 4

Southern Italy Map 6

Southern Italy's Top 11 . . . 8

Need to Know 14

First Time
Southern Italy 16

If You Like... 18

Month by Month 20

Itineraries 22

Eat & Drink
Like a Local 26

Travel with Children 31

Regions at a Glance 33

CATANIA P194

COFFEE GRANITE P252

ON THE ROAD

NAPLES &
CAMPANIA 36

Naples 37

Bay of Naples 60

Capri 60

Ischia 66

Procida 69

South of Naples 70

Ercolano
& Herculaneum 70

Mt Vesuvius 72

Pompeii 72

Sorrento 78

West of Sorrento 82

Amalfi Coast 83

Positano 83

Praiano & Furore 87

Amalfi 87

Ravello 89

South of Amalfi 91

Costiera Cilentana 96

Agropoli 96

Parco Nazionale
del Cilento e Vallo
di Diano 96

PUGLIA, BASILICATA
& CALABRIA 100

Puglia 101

Bari 101

Around Bari 107

Promontorio
del Gargano 110

Isole Tremiti 115

Valle d'Itria 116

Lecce 122

Brindisi 127

Southern &
Western Salento 130

Basilicata 135

Matera 135

Metaponto 142

Potenza 143

Appennino Lucano 143

Basilicata's Western
Coast 144

Calabria 145

Northern Tyrrhenian
Coast 146

Cosenza 148

Parco Nazionale
della Sila 149

Ionian Coast 150

Parco Nazionale
dell'Aspromonte 151

Reggio di Calabria 152

Southern Tyrrhenian
Coast 154

Contents

VIESTE P110

UNDERSTAND

Southern Italy
Today 226

History 228

The Southern
Way of Life 241

The Mafia 246

The Southern Table . . . 248

Art & Architecture 256

SURVIVAL GUIDE

Directory A–Z 262

Transport 273

Language 281

Index 288

Map Legend 295

SICILY 160

Palermo 164
Tyrrhenian Coast 176
Cefalù 176
Aeolian Islands 178
Lipari 179
Vulcano 183
Salina 184
Stromboli 188
Ionian Coast 190
Taormina 190
Catania 194
Mt Etna 200
Syracuse &
the Southeast 201

Syracuse 201
Noto 208
Modica 211
Ragusa 212
Central Sicily & the
Mediterranean Coast . . 214
Agrigento 214
Western Sicily 217
Marsala 218
Selinunte 219
Trapani 219
Erice 222
Segesta 223

SPECIAL FEATURES

Pompeii in 3D 74
Historical Riches 98
Surprises
of the South 158
Delightful Desserts . . . 186

Welcome to Southern Italy

Italy's north may have the euros, but the south has the soul. Beautifully sun-bleached, weathered and worn, this is Italy at its most ancient and complex.

Cultural Riches

At the crossroads of civilisations for millennia, southern Italy is littered with the detritus of diverse and gilded ages, from Greek and Roman to Saracen, Norman and Spanish. Every carved stone and every frescoed palace tells a story, from fiery Carthaginian invasions and power-hungry kings, to the humble hopes of Roman slaves and gladiators. Here, ancient Greek temples are older than Rome, Byzantine mosaics attest to cosmopolitan encounters and royal palaces outsize Versailles. Southern Italy is home to no less than 13 Unesco World Heritage cultural sites, each laced with tales of victory, failure and timeless humanity.

Endless Feasting

Italy's south is a belt-busting, mouthwatering feast: bubbling, wood-fired pizza and sucker-punch espresso in Naples; long, lazy lunches at vine-framed Pugliese farmhouses; just-caught sardines on a Tyrrhenian island; and lavish pastries in chintzy Palermo *pasticcerie* (pastry shops). Should you go mushroom hunting in the wilds of Calabria? Taste-test your first red eggplant (aubergine) at an heirloom trattoria in Basilicata? Feast on fresh sea urchin on an Adriatic beach? Or just kick back with a glass of crisp local Falanghina as you debate who has the creamiest buffalo mozzarella: Caserta, Paestum or Foggia?

A Warm Benvenuto

You'll rarely be short of a conversation south of Rome. Southern Italians are naturally curious, famously affable and quick to share their opinion. Family and friends are sacred, and time spent laughing, arguing or gossiping is as integral to southern life as lavish Sunday lunches and long, hot summers. One minute you're picking produce at a street market, the next you're in the middle of a feverish discussion about the in-laws or who grows Italy's sweetest *pomodori* (tomatoes) – Sicily or Campania? No one is a stranger for long, and a casual *chiacchiera* (chat) could easily land you at the dining table of your new best friend.

Natural Highs

Rugged mountains, fiery volcanoes and glittering coastal grottoes – southern Italy feels like one giant playground waiting to be tackled. Crank up the heart rate rafting down Calabria's river Lao, scaling Europe's most active volcano, Stromboli, or diving into prehistoric sea caves on Puglia's Promontorio del Gargano. If you need to bring it down a notch, consider slow pedalling across Puglia's gentle countryside, sailing along the Amalfi Coast or simply soaking in Vulcano's healing geothermal mud. The options may be many, but there is one constant: a landscape that is beautiful, diverse and just a little ethereal.

Why I Love Southern Italy

By Cristian Bonetto, Writer

Southern Italy is like the Slow Food of travel. While much of Europe marches to an increasingly homogenised beat, this raffish corner of the continent dances to its own hypnotic tune. Melancholy folk songs still fill the air, eyeshadow is applied thick and bright, and hearts are proudly worn on sleeves. Many of my fondest travel memories have been formed here: epic Sunday lunches to the sound of Pino Daniele; hot winds whistling through ancient temples; quiet swims in milky blue Tyrrhenian waters. I might hail from the north, but my heart belongs to the Mezzogiorno.

For more about our writers, see page 296.

Above: Positano (p83)

Southern Italy

ELEVATION

2500m
2000m
1500m
1000m
500m
300m
100m
0

100 km
50 miles

42°N
18°E
17°E
16°E
15°E
13°E
41°N
40°N

Matera
An eerie and ancient townscape (p135)

Alberobello
Italy's kookiest-looking town (p117)

Leece
The Florence of the south (p122)

Naples
Glorious art, architecture and street life (p37)

Pompeii
A town frozen in time (p72)

Adriatic Sea

ROME

LAZIO

ABRUZZO
Pescara
Chieti

Vasto

Termoli

Isole Tremiti

Peschici
Vieste

Trani

Campobasso

Isernia

Volturno

Caserta

Naples
Procida
Ischia
Ponza

Golfo di Gaeta

Mt Vesuvius (1281m)
Pompeii
Ercolano
Sorrento
Amalfi
Amalfi Coast
Capri

CAMPANIA

Salerno

Agropoli

Paestum

Potenza

BASILICATA

Maratea

Parco Nazionale del Cilento e Vallo di Diano

Sele

Basento

Bradano

Agri

Sinni

Matera

Polignano a Mare
Locorotondo
Valle d'Itria
Alberobello
Martina Franca
Ostuni
Oria

PUGLIA

Taranto

Golfo di Taranto

Brindisi

Lecce
Otranto
Galatina

PUGLIA

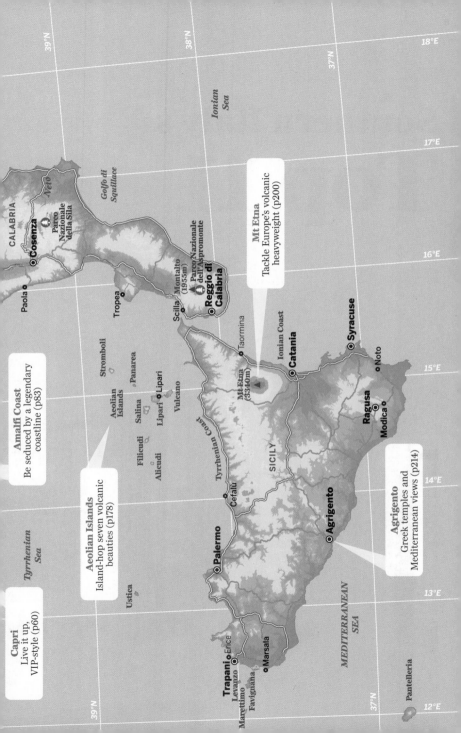

Capri
Live it up,
VIP-style (p60)

Amalfi Coast
Be seduced by a legendary
coastline (p83)

Aeolian Islands
Island-hop seven volcanic
beauties (p178)

Mt Etna
Tackle Europe's volcanic
heavyweight (p200)

Agrigento
Greek temples and
Mediterranean views (p214)

*Tyrrhenian
Sea*

*Ionian
Sea*

*MEDITERRANEAN
SEA*

CALABRIA

Cosenza
Parco
Nazionale
della Sila

Neto

*Golfo di
Squillace*

Paola

Tropea

Scilla

Montalto
(1955m)
Parco Nazionale
dell'Aspromonte

**Reggio di
Calabria**

Stromboli

Panarea

Aeolian
Islands

Salina

Lipari Lipari

Vulcano

Filicudi

Alicudi

Tyrrhenian Coast

Ustica

Palermo

Cefalù

Ionian Coast

Taormina

Catania

Mt Etna
(3340m)

SICILY

Syracuse

Noto

Ragusa

Modica

Agrigento

Trapani Erice
Levanzo
Marettimo
Favignana
Marsala

Pantelleria

39°N
38°N
37°N

18°E
17°E
16°E
15°E
14°E
13°E
12°E

Southern Italy's
Top 11

Ghostly Pompeii

1 Frozen in its death throes, the sprawling, time-warped ruins of Pompeii (p72) hurtle you 2000 years into the past. Wander through chariot-grooved Roman streets, lavishly frescoed villas and bathhouses, food stores and markets, theatres, even an ancient brothel. Then, your eye on ominous Mt Vesuvius, ponder Pliny the Younger's terrifying account of the town's final hours: 'Darkness came on again, again ashes, thick and heavy. We got up repeatedly to shake these off; otherwise we would have been buried and crushed by the weight'. Foro (p73)

Naples

2 Refined and rough, tough and tender, Naples (p37) is a contradictory, complex beast. Gritty alleyways hit palm-fringed boulevards, crumbling facades mask baroque ballrooms, and cultish shrines flank fashionable bars. Intensity underlines the details, from the muscular strength of Neapolitan espresso to the high-octane rush of the city's markets and streets. Add to this a jumble of castles, royal palaces and superlative art, and you have yourself one of southern Italy's most unexpected thrills. Quartieri Spagnoli (p46)

Temples in Agrigento

3 Few archaeological sites evoke the past like Agrigento's Valley of the Temples (p214). Located on a ridge overlooking the Mediterranean, its temples belonged to Akragas, a once-great city settled by the Greeks. The scars of ancient battles endure in the Tempio di Hera, while the Tempio della Concordia's state of preservation inspired Unesco's own logo. To conjure the ghosts of the past, roam the ruins late in the afternoon, when the crowds have thinned and the wind whistles hauntingly between the columns.

Fallen Icarus by Igor Mitoraj, Tempio della Concordia

Matera

4 The best time to explore Matera (p135) is before it gets up. The town is tinged gold by the morning sun and the scent of the day's first coffee lingers in the air. Matera is an extraordinary place: its Unesco World Heritage–listed *sassi* (former cave dwellings) developed from caves that pock a dizzying ravine. In no other place do you come face to face with such powerful images of Italy's lost peasant culture; these cavernous dwellings echo a level of poverty difficult to fathom in an affluent, modern G8 country.

3

4

Capri

5 Even the summer hordes can't quite dilute the ethereal magic of Capri (p60). Described as 'one of the magnetic points of the earth' by the writer and painter Alberto Savinio, Italy's most fabled island has been seducing mere mortals for millennia. Emperor Tiberius reputedly threw his lovers off its cliffs, travellers on the Grand Tour waxed lyrical about its electric-blue grotto and celebrities continue to moor their yachts in its turquoise waters. For a view you won't forget, head to the summit of Monte Solaro. Isole Faraglioni (p61)

Alberobello

6 Imagination runs riot in Alberobello (p117), famed for its kooky, one-of-a-kind architecture. We're talking *trulli* – whitewashed circular dwellings with cone-shaped roofs. Looking like they're straight out of a Disney cartoon, these sunbaked dwellings tumble down the slopes like armies of hatted dwarves. You can dine in some of them and sleep in others. Just don't be surprised if you feel the need to pinch yourself... Was that Snow White? Are you even on Earth? Unesco seems to thinks so; they're World Heritage treasures.

Aeolian Island–Hopping

7 The Greeks don't have a monopoly on Mediterranean island-hopping. Sicily's Aeolian Islands (p178) might be a little less famous than their Aegean Sea rivals, but they are no less stunning. Mix and match from seven volcanic outcrops, among them thermal hot-spot Vulcano, vine-laced Salina and lava-oozing Stromboli. But don't just take our word for it. The islands are one of only four Italian natural landscapes on Unesco's World Heritage list (the others being Sicily's Mt Etna, the Dolomites and Monte San Giorgio). Stromboli (p188)

DEA / R. CARNOVALINI/GETTY IMAGES ©

Scaling Mt Etna

8 Known to the Greeks as the 'column that holds up the sky', Mt Etna (p200) is Europe's largest volcano and one of the world's most active. It's also the highest mountain south of the Alps. The ancients believed the giant Tifone (Typhoon) lived in its crater and lit up the sky with regular pyrotechnics. At 3330m it towers above Sicily's Ionian Coast, and since 1987 its slopes have been part of the Parco dell'Etna, an area that encompasses both alpine forests and the black summit. Whether scaled on foot or on wheels, the magnitude of its power, presence and otherworldly vistas are strictly unforgettable.

Southern Flavours

9 Southern Italy's food (p248) obsession is utterly forgivable. After all, this is the country's gastronomic showcase, a sun-drenched platter of produce and flavours. The options are as gut-rumbling as they are overwhelming. Should you succumb to perfectly charred pizza on an ancient Neapolitan street or luscious *burrata* (cream-filled buffalo mozzarella) by Puglian seas? Perhaps you're hankering for chilli-fuelled *salsiccie* (sausages) in the wilds of Basilicata and Calabria? Or couscous in the shadow of a Sicilian *palazzo*? Whatever you choose, we know you'll beg for seconds.

Amalfi Coast

10 The Amalfi Coast (p83) bewitches with its astounding beauty and gripping geology: coastal mountains plunge into blue sea in a scene of precipitous crags, sun-bleached villages and lush forest. Between sea and sky, mountain-top hiking trails deliver Tyrrhenian panoramas. While some may argue that Italy's most beautiful coast is Liguria's Cinque Terre or Calabria's Costa Viola, it was the Amalfi Coast that prompted American writer John Steinbeck to describe it as a 'dream place that isn't quite real when you are there and beckoningly real after you have gone'.
Positano (p83)

10

11

GREG ELMS/GETTY IMAGES ©

Baroque Lecce

11 The extravagant architectural character of many Puglian towns is due to the local style of *barocco leccese* (Lecce baroque). The stone here is so soft, art critic Cesare Brandi claimed 'it can be carved with a penknife'. Local craftsmen vied for ever-greater heights of creativity, crowding facades with swirling vegetal designs, gargoyles and strange zoomorphic figures. Lecce's Basilica di Santa Croce (p122) is the high point of the style, so outrageously busy the Marchese Grimaldi said it made him think a lunatic was having a nightmare.

Need to Know

For more information, see Survival Guide (p261)

Currency
Euro (€)

Language
Italian

Visas
Generally not required for stays of up to 90 days (or at all for EU nationals); some nationalities need a Schengen visa.

Money
ATMs at every airport, most train stations and widely available in towns and cities. Credit cards accepted in most hotels and restaurants.

Mobile Phones
Local SIM cards can be used in European, Australian and some unlocked US phones. Other phones must be set to roaming.

Time
Central European Time (GMT/UTC plus one hour)

Room Tax
Visitors may be charged an extra €1 to €5 per night 'room occupancy tax'.

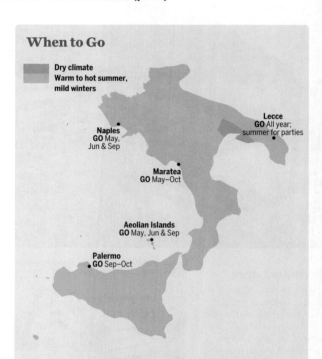

When to Go

Dry climate
Warm to hot summer, mild winters

Lecce
GO All year; summer for parties

Naples
GO May, Jun & Sep

Maratea
GO May–Oct

Aeolian Islands
GO May, Jun & Sep

Palermo
GO Sep–Oct

High Season
(Jul & Aug)

➡ Queues and crowds at big sights and beaches, especially in August.

➡ High levels of traffic congestion in tourist areas, including the Amalfi Coast.

➡ A good period for cultural events and festivals in tourist areas.

Shoulder Season (Apr–Jun, Sep & Oct)

➡ Good deals on accommodation.

➡ Spring is best for wildflowers and local produce, with numerous festivals too.

➡ Autumn offers warm weather without the crowds, and the grape harvest.

Low Season
(Nov–Mar)

➡ Prices can be 30% lower than high season (except major holidays).

➡ Many sights, hotels and restaurants close in coastal and mountainous areas.

➡ Christmas feasting and colourful Carnevale.

Websites

Lonely Planet (www.lonely planet.com/italy) Destination information, hotel bookings, traveller forum and more.

Trenitalia (www.trenitalia.com) Italian railways website.

Agriturismi (www.agriturismi. it) Farm accommodation guide.

Enit Italia (www.italiantourism. com) Italy's official tourism website.

The Local (www.thelocal.it) English-language news from Italy, including travel-related stories.

Important Numbers

From outside Italy, dial your international access code, Italy's country code (☑39) then the number (including the '0').

Italy country code	☑39
International access code	☑00
Ambulance	☑118
Police	☑113
Fire	☑115

Exchange Rates

Australia	A$1	€0.66
Canada	C$1	€0.70
Japan	¥100	€0.76
New Zealand	NZ$1	€0.61
Switzerland	Sfr1	€0.93
UK	UK£1	€1.42
US	US$1	€0.93

For current exchange rates see www.xe.com

Daily Costs

Budget: Less than €100

➡ Dorm bed: €15–€30

➡ Double room in a budget hotel: €50–€110

➡ Pizza or pasta: €6–€12

➡ Excellent markets and delis for self-catering

Midrange: €100–€250

➡ Double room in a hotel: €100–€220

➡ Local restaurant dinner: €25–€50

➡ Admission to museum: €4–€15

Top End: More than €250

➡ Double room in a four- or five-star hotel: €200–€450

➡ Top restaurant dinner: €50–€150

➡ Opera ticket: €40–€200

Opening Hours

Opening hours vary throughout the year. We've provided high-season opening hours; hours will generally decrease in the shoulder and low seasons. In this guide, 'summer' times generally refer to the period from April to September or October, while 'winter' times generally run from October or November to March.

Banks 8.30am–1.30pm & 2.45–3.45pm or 4.15pm Monday to Friday

Restaurants noon–3pm & 7.30–11pm or midnight

Cafes 7.30am–8pm or later

Clubs 11pm–5am

Shops 9am–1pm & 3.30–7.30pm (or 4–8pm) Monday to Saturday, some close Monday morning and some in large cities and tourist areas open Sunday

Arriving in Southern Italy

Capodichino airport (Naples) A shuttle bus to the centre of Naples will cost €3 (€4 if ticket bought on-board); they run every 20 minutes from 6.30am to 11.40pm. Taxis have a €19 set fare and take 30 minutes.

Karol Wojtyła airport (Palese airport; Bari) A shuttle bus to the centre of Bari will cost €4; they run hourly from 5.35am to 12.10am. A taxi will cost about €24 and will take 15 minutes.

Falcone-Borsellino airport (Palermo) A shuttle bus to the centre of Palermo will cost €6.30; they run half-hourly from 5am to midnight. Trains cost €5.80; they run once to twice hourly from 5.58am to 10.05pm. A taxi will cost about €40 to €45 and take 30 minutes.

Getting Around

Transport in southern Italy is reasonably priced and usually efficient.

Train Affordable, with extensive coverage and frequent departures.

Car Handy for travelling at your own pace or for visiting areas with minimal public transport. Not a good idea for travelling within major urban areas.

Bus Cheaper and slower than trains. Useful for more remote villages not serviced by trains.

Ferries & Hydrofoils Large ferries *(navi)* service Campania and Sicily. Smaller ferries *(traghetti)* and hydrofoils *(aliscafi)* service the Bay of Naples islands, the Amalfi Coast, Puglia's Isole Tremiti and Sicily's Aeolian Islands. Most services are pared back in winter.

For much more on **getting around**, see p276

First Time Southern Italy

For more information, see Survival Guide (p261)

Checklist

➡ Ensure your passport is valid for at least six months past your arrival date

➡ Check airline baggage restrictions

➡ Organise travel insurance

➡ Make bookings (for accommodation and entertainment)

➡ Inform your credit/debit card company of your travels

➡ Check you can use your mobile (cell) phone

➡ Check requirements for hiring a car

What to Pack

➡ Hat, sunglasses, sunscreen and comfortable walking shoes

➡ Electrical adapter and phone charger

➡ A detailed driving map for southern Italy's rural backroads

➡ Smart threads for higher-end restaurants

➡ Patience: for coping with inefficiency

➡ Phrasebook: for ordering and charming

Top Tips for Your Trip

➡ Visit in the shoulder season (spring and autumn).

➡ If driving, get off the main roads where possible: some of the most stunning scenery is on secondary or tertiary roads.

➡ Avoid restaurants with touts and the mediocre *menu turistico* (tourist menu).

➡ Queue-jumping is common: be polite but assertive.

What to Wear

Appearances matter in Italy. In general, trousers (pants), jeans, shirts and polo shirts for men and skirts or trousers for women will serve you well in the city. Shorts, T-shirts and sandals are fine in summer and at the beach, but long sleeves are required for dining out. Come evening, think smart casual. A light sweater or waterproof jacket is useful in spring and autumn, and sturdy shoes are good for visiting archaeological sites.

Sleeping

Book ahead if travelling in the high season, especially if visiting popular coastal areas. Also consider booking ahead if visiting cities or towns during major events.

➡ **Hotels** All prices and levels of quality, from cheap-and-charmless to sleek-and-exclusive boutique.

➡ **Farm Stays** Perfect for families and for relaxation, *agriturismi* range from rustic farmhouses to luxe country estates.

➡ **B&Bs** Often great value, options span rooms in family houses to self-catering studio apartments.

➡ **Pensions** Similar to hotels, though *pensioni* are generally of one- to three-star quality and family-run.

➡ **Hostels** You'll find both official HI-affiliated and privately run *ostelli* (hostels), many also offering private rooms with bathroom.

Money

Credit and debit cards can be used almost everywhere with the exception of some rural towns and villages.

Visa and MasterCard are widely recognised. American Express is only accepted by some major chains and big hotels, and few places take Diners Club.

ATMs (known as Bancomat) are everywhere, but be aware of transaction fees. Some ATMs in Italy reject foreign cards. If this happens, try a few before assuming your card is the problem.

For more information, see p267.

Bargaining

Gentle haggling is common in markets. Haggling in stores is generally unacceptable, though good-humoured bargaining at smaller artisan or craft shops is not unusual if making multiple purchases.

Tipping

Tipping is customary in restaurants, but optional elsewhere.

➡ **Taxis** Most people round up to the nearest euro.

➡ **Hotels** Tip porters about €4 at high-end hotels.

➡ **Restaurants** Service (*servizio*) is generally included in restaurants – if it's not, a euro or two is fine in pizzerias, 10% in restaurants.

➡ **Bars** Many Italians leave small change (€0.10 or €0.20) on the bar when ordering coffee. If drinks are brought to your table, a small tip is generally appreciated.

Language

Unlike many other European countries, English is not widely spoken in Italy. Of course, you can get by in the main tourist centres, but in the countryside and off the tourist track, you'll need to master a few basic phrases. This will improve your experience no end, especially when ordering in restaurants, some of which have no written menu. It's also a good way of connecting with the locals, leading to a richer, more personable experience of the region and its people. For more on language, see p281.

 What's the local speciality?
Qual'è la specialità di questa regione?
kwa·le la spe·cha·lee·ta dee kwes·ta re·jo·ne

A bit like the rivalry between medieval Italian city-states, these days the country's regions compete in speciality foods and wines.

 Which combined tickets do you have?
Quali biglietti cumulativi avete?
kwa·lee bee·lye·tee koo·moo·la·tee·vee a·ve·te

Make the most of your euro by getting combined tickets to various sights; they are available in all major Italian cities.

 Where can I buy discount designer items?
C'è un outlet in zona? che oon owt·let in zo·na

Discount fashion outlets are big business in major cities – get bargain-priced seconds, samples and cast-offs for *la bella figura*.

 Let's meet at 6pm for pre-dinner drinks.
Ci vediamo alle sei per un aperitivo.
chee ve·dya·mo a·le say per oon a·pe·ree·tee·vo

At dusk, watch the main piazza get crowded with people sipping colourful cocktails and snacking the evening away: join your new friends for this authentic Italian ritual!

Etiquette

Italy is a surprisingly formal society; the following tips will help you avoid any awkward moments.

➡ **Greetings** Shake hands and say *buongiorno* (good day) or *buonasera* (good evening) to strangers; kiss both cheeks and say *come stai* (how are you) for friends. Use *lei* (you) in polite company; use *tu* (you) with friends and children. Only use first names if invited.

➡ **Asking for help** Say *mi scusi* (excuse me) to attract attention; use *permesso* (permission) when you want to pass by in a crowded space.

➡ **Religion** Dress modestly (cover shoulders, torso and thighs) and show respect when visiting religious sites.

➡ **Eating & Drinking** When dining in an Italian home, bring a small gift of *dolci* (sweets) or wine and dress well. Let your host lead when sitting and starting the meal. When dining out, summon the waiter by saying *mi scusi* (excuse me).

➡ **Gestures** Maintain eye contact during conversation.

If You Like...

Food, Glorious Food

Southern Italy's rich soil, produce-packed hillsides and turquoise seas are a giant natural larder. Traditions are fiercely protected and eating well is a given. Tuck in!

Pizza Chow down Italy's top export in its spiritual home, Naples. (p53)

Buffalo mozzarella Swoon over Italy's silkiest cheese in Campania. (p36)

Seafood So fresh it's eaten *crudo* (raw) in Campania (p36), Puglia (p101) and Sicily (p160).

Street food From *pizza fritta* (deep-fried pizza) in Naples (p53) to *panelle* (chickpea fritters) in Palermo (p172), fast food comes with culinary cred.

Markets Lip-smacking produce and street life collide at markets such as Porta Nolana (p43), Ballarò (p165) and La Pescheria (p195).

Medieval Towns

Cobbled streets snake up hillsides to sculpted fountains, the scent of *ragù* (meat and tomato sauce) wafts from shuttered windows and washing hangs like holiday bunting.

Ravello Romantic gardens, dreamy Tyrrhenian views and a world-class music festival above the Amalfi Coast. (p89)

Taormina A chic summertime favourite, with secret gardens and a panoramic ancient amphitheatre. (p190)

Cefalù Lapping waves, enchanting narrow streets and an imposing Arab-Norman cathedral. (p176)

Maratea A 13th-century *borgo* (medieval town) with pint-sized piazzas and startling views across the Gulf of Policastro. (p135)

Erice Ancient walls, a brooding castle and views to kill for. (p222)

Baroque Architecture

Southern Italy found its soulmate in the baroque architecture of the 17th and 18th centuries. Enter a world of outrageous palaces and bling-tastic churches.

Val di Noto A valley adorned with baroque towns, including best-of-the-lot Noto. (p208)

Lecce This hallucinogenic city is to the baroque what Florence is to the Renaissance. (p122)

Reggia di Caserta Caserta's royal pad could put Versailles to shame. (p60)

Catania The city's Piazza del Duomo is a World Heritage pin-up. (p195)

The Great Outdoors

Saunter between sea and sky in Campania, slip into silent forests in Basilicata and Calabria or come face to face with Mother Nature's wrath in lava-spewing Sicily.

Sentiero degli Dei Hit the 'Path of the Gods' for a different take on the stunning Amalfi Coast. (p85)

Mt Etna Hike the picturesque slopes of Europe's tallest active volcano. (p200)

IF YOU LIKE... HIDDEN TREASURES

Subterranean Naples is a thrilling, silent sprawl of ancient cisterns, wartime hideouts and royal escape routes. For a sneak peek, descend into the remarkably restored Tunnel Borbonico (p51).

Parco Nazionale del Gargano
Explore an enchanted world of
Aleppo pines, springtime orchids
and sacred pilgrimage sites.
(p110)

Islands & Beaches

Northern Italy would sell
its soul for a coastline this
alluring. From bijou islands
to crystal-clear grottoes, the
south's offerings are as varied as they are beautiful.

Puglia The region's beaches
include Baia dei Turchi and the
cliff-backed beaches of the
Gargano. (p101)

Aeolian Islands Sicily's seven
volcanic island gems. (p178)

Capri Golden light and a
mesmerising grotto lure A-list
jet-setters. (p60)

Maratea This Basilicata beauty
gives the Amalfi Coast a serious
run for its money. (p135)

Vivid History

Southern Italy's past comes
to life in its art and architecture. Lose yourself in
frescoed scenes of classical
mythology or ponder the
glories of Constantinople in
Byzantine mosaics.

Villa Romana del Casale Sicily's
top Roman site is home to the
finest Roman floor mosaics in
existence. (p213)

Museo Archeologico Nazionale
Showstopping sculptures and
frescoes from Pompeii, Herculaneum and beyond at Naples' top
museum. (p43)

Herculaneum From frescoed
homes to time-warped changing
rooms, Roman life lives on in its
original setting. (p70)

Cattedrale di Monreale Twelfth-
century mosaics bring the Old
Testament to life in this Arab-
Norman wonder. (p175)

Top: Waterfront dining, Lecce (p122), Puglia
Bottom: Enjoy tomato and mozzarella pizza in Naples (p53), the city where
pizza was created

Month by Month

TOP EVENTS

Settimana Santa, March & April

Maggio dei Monumenti, May

Ravello Festival, June to September

Festival della Valle d'Itria, July & August

La Notte della Taranta, August

February

Short and accursed is how Italians describe February. It might still be chilly down south, but almond trees start to blossom and Carnevale season brightens things up with confetti, costumes and sugar-dusted treats.

Carnevale

In the period leading up to Ash Wednesday, many southern towns stage pre-Lenten carnivals. One of the most flamboyant is the Carnevale di Acireale (www.carnevaleacireale. com), the elaborate and whimsical floats of which are famous throughout the country.

March

The weather in March is capricious: sunny, rainy and windy all at once. Understandably, the Italians call it *Marzo pazzo* (Crazy March). The official start of spring is 21 March, but the main holiday season starts with Easter week.

Settimana Santa

Processions and passion plays mark Easter Holy Week across the south. On Good Friday and the Thursday preceding it, hooded penitents walk through the streets of Sorrento (p80). On Procida, Good Friday sees wooden statues and life-size tableaux carted across the island for the Procession of the Misteri. (p69)

May

The month of roses and early summer produce makes May a perfect time to travel, especially for walkers. The weather is warm but not too hot and prices throughout the south are good value. It's also patron-saint season.

Festa di San Gennaro

As patron-saint days go, Naples' Festa di San Gennaro has a lot riding on it, namely securing the city from volcanic disaster. Held on the first Saturday in May, it sees the faithful gather in the Duomo to witness San Gennaro's blood liquefy. If it does, the city is safe. The miraculous event is repeated on 19 September and 16 December.

Maggio dei Monumenti

As the weather warms up, Naples rolls out a mammoth, month-long program of art exhibitions, concerts, performances and tours around the city. Many historical and architectural treasures usually off-limits to the public are open and free to visit.

Wine & The City

A two-week celebration of regional vino in Naples (www.wineandthecity.it), with free wine degustations, *aperitivo* sessions, theatre, music and exhibitions. Venues span museums, castles and galleries to restaurants, shops and yachts.

☆ Ciclo di Rappresentazioni Classiche

Classical intrigue in an evocative Sicilian setting, the Festival of Greek Theatre (www.indafondazione. org), held from mid-May to mid-June, brings Syracuse's 5th-century-BC amphitheatre to life with performances from Italy's acting greats.

June

The summer season kicks off in June. The temperature cranks up quickly, beach lidos start to open in earnest and some of the big summer festivals commence. There's a national holiday on 2 June, the Anniversary of the Republic.

☆ Ravello Festival

Perched high above the Amalfi Coast, Ravello draws world-renowned artists during its summer-long Ravello Festival (www.ravellofestival.com). Covering everything from music and dance to film and art exhibitions, several events take place in the exquisite Villa Rufolo gardens from late June to early September.

☆ Napoli Teatro Festival Italia

For three weeks in June, Naples celebrates all things performative with the Napoli Teatro Festival Italia (www.napoliteatrofestival. it). Using both conventional and unconventional venues, the program ranges from classic works to specially commissioned pieces from both local and international acts.

July

School is out and Italians everywhere are heading out of the cities and to the mountains or beaches for their summer holidays. Prices and temperatures rise. The beach is in full swing, but many cities host summer art festivals.

☆ Taormina Arte

Ancient ruins and languid summer nights set a seductive scene for Taormina Arte (www.taormina-arte. com), a major arts festival held through July and September. Events include film, theatre, opera and concerts.

☆ Festival della Valle d'Itria

Between mid-July and early August, the town of Martina Franca holds its esteemed music festival (www.festival dellavalleditria.it). The focus is on classical music and opera, including obscure pieces and more famous works performed in their original form.

August

August in southern Italy is hot, expensive and crowded. Everyone is on holiday and while it may no longer be true that everything is shut, many businesses and restaurants do close for part of the month.

☆ Ferragosto

After Christmas and Easter, Ferragosto is Italy's biggest holiday. While it now marks the Feast of the Assumption, even the ancient Romans honoured their pagan gods on Feriae Augusti.

☆ La Notte della Taranta

Puglia celebrates its hypnotic *pizzica* dance with the Night of the Taranta (www.lanottedellataranta. it), a two-week festival held in and around the Puglian town of Melpignano.

September

This is a glorious month in the south. As summer wanes into autumn, the grape harvest begins. Adding to the culinary excitement are the many local *sagre* (food festivals), celebrating regional produce and traditions.

☆ Couscous Fest

The Sicilian town of San Vito celebrates its famous fish couscous at this six-day festival (www.couscousfest. it). Highlights include an international couscous cook-off, workshops and free world-music concerts.

December

The days of alfresco living are at an end. Yet, despite the cooler days and longer nights, looming Christmas festivities warm things up with festive street lights, nativity scenes and Yuletide specialities.

☆ Natale

The weeks preceding Christmas are studded with religious events. Many churches set up nativity scenes known as *presepe*. While Naples is especially famous for these, you'll find impressive tableaux in many southern towns, including Erice in Sicily.

Itineraries

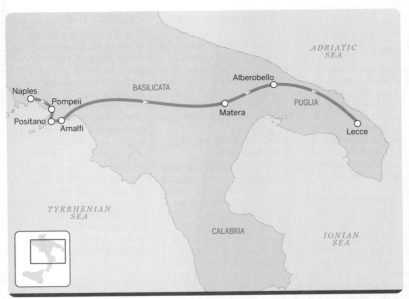

Southern Highlights

An easy introduction to some of southern Italy's must-see wonders, this 10-day overview delivers everything from cosmopolitan city culture to ancient ruins, breathtaking coastal scenery and World Heritage–listed architecture.

Pique your appetite with two heady days in **Naples**, an urban wild child bursting with glorious art, architecture, street life and flavours. Spend day three roaming time-warped **Pompeii** before continuing to **Positano**, the Amalfi Coast's pin-up town. Lap up two days here, hiring a boat for a spot of coastal cruising or hiking the breathtaking Sentiero degli Dei (Path of the Gods). On day six, continue east along the Amalfi Coast, stopping briefly in atmospheric **Amalfi** on your way to **Matera** in time for dinner, then spend the following day exploring the town's extraordinary, Unesco-lauded *sassi* (former cave dwellings). Swap *sassi* for *trulli* (conical-roofed abodes) in **Alberobello** the following day. Spend the night, then hit the road one last time to vibrant **Lecce**. Dubbed the 'Florence of the South', the town's quixotic baroque buildings make for an extravagant epilogue to your southern overview.

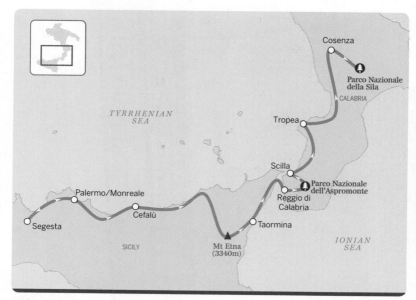

2 WEEKS Sicily to Calabria

Ancient cultures and natural beauty collide in this two-week adventure. From Greek temples and Norman cathedrals to rugged mountains and coveted coastal resorts, expect a gripping journey through Italy's southern extremes.

Fly into **Palermo** and take two days to savour the city's cross-cultural food and architecture, detouring to **Monreale** to view Sicily's finest Norman cathedral. On day three, take a day trip west to the World Heritage ruins of **Segesta** before shooting east to eye-candy **Cefalù** on day four. Spend a night – just enough time to admire its commanding Arab-Norman cathedral and crystalline sea. Come day five, shoot through to VIP-favourite **Taormina**, a long-time haunt of poets, painters and hopeless romantics. The town was once Sicily's Byzantine capital and its sweeping ancient Greek theatre is the island's second largest. Allow two nights of elegant slumming and consider tackling nearby **Mt Etna** on one of your days.

Day seven sees you catching a ferry from Messina to **Reggio di Calabria** in time to see the *Bronzi di Riace* at the Museo Nazionale della Magna Grecia. The finest examples of ancient Greek sculpture in existence, the bronze sculptures are southern Italy's answer to Florence's *David*. Rest your head in tiny Gambarie, using the town as your base as you explore the wild beauty of the **Parco Nazionale dell'Aspromonte** over the next two days.

Come day 10, head back down to the Tyrrhenian coast. Lunch on fresh swordfish in castle-capped **Scilla**, continuing through to dazzling **Tropea**, Calabria's coastal darling. Spend a night recharging your weary bones, then continue north to the gritty yet erudite city of **Cosenza** on day 11. After taking in its impressively preserved medieval core on day 12, hit Camigliatello Silano for two nights, concluding your adventure with soul-lifting hikes through the alpine beauty of the **Parco Nazionale della Sila**.

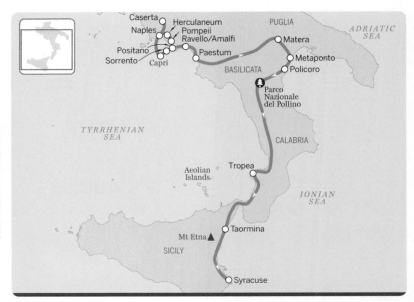

Grand Southern Tour

3 WEEKS

Covering Campania, Basilicata, Calabria and Sicily, this three-week trip is rich in both blockbuster sights and off-the-beaten-track treasures.

Commence with a trio of days in **Naples**, day-tripping it to the formidable royal palace of **Caserta** or the ill-fated ancient towns of **Pompeii** or **Herculaneum**. Whichever you choose, treat yourself to two romantic days on **Capri**, making time for quiet hikes, the spectacular Grotta Azzurra and the mesmerising views from atop Monte Solaro. Sail across to **Sorrento** for a night then hit the fabled Amalfi Coast on day six, allowing two days in see-and-be-seen **Positano** and a further night in **Amalfi** or **Ravello**. Explore ancient Greek temples in **Paestum** on day nine before continuing to fellow World Heritage marvel **Matera** and its otherworldly abodes.

Come day 12, drop into ancient **Metaponto**. The hometown of number-crunching Pythagoras, it's also where you'll find the so-called Palatine Tables, a reputed pit stop for Crusade-bound knights. Close by is **Policoro**, its oldest cultural artefacts dating back some 9000 years. Its ancient booty appreciated, it's time to escape to the wilds of the **Parco Nazionale del Pollino**. With Terranova di Pollino as your base, spend three days hiking through invigorating woods and exploring the curious Albanian villages of San Paolo Albanese and San Costantino Albanese.

Slide down to Calabria's Tyrrhenian coastline on day 16, home to seaside show-off **Tropea**. Allow two nights of waterside *dolce vita* (sweet life) before catching a ferry from Villa San Giovanni to Sicily on day 18. Allow yourself another two days of coastal bliss in gorgeous **Taormina**, home to a world-class summertime arts festival. If you can pull yourself away on day 20, wrap things up with a couple of days exploring evocative ruins in **Syracuse**, described by Roman philosopher Cicero as the 'greatest Greek city and the most beautiful of them all'.

 Perfect Puglia

Puglia is one of Italy's most underrated regions. Start your revelation in dynamic **Bari**, exploring its ancient historic centre and huge Romanesque basilica. Strike out south, via **Polignano a Mare**, to the famous **Grotte di Castellana**, Italy's longest network of subterranean caves. From here, a two- to three-day drive south will take you through some of the finest Valle d'Itria towns, including **Alberobello**, with its hobbitlike *trulli* houses, wine-producing **Locorotondo**, beautiful baroque **Martina Franca** and chic, whitewashed **Ostuni**. Next up is **Lecce**, dubbed 'Florence of the South' for its operatic architectural ensembles and scholarly bent. Hire a bike and spend at least three or four days here before moving on to **Galatina**, its basilica awash with astounding frescoes. Head east to the fortified port of **Otranto** and the inviting beaches of the Baia dei Turchi, then push south along the wild, vertiginous coastline to **Santa Maria di Leuca**, the very tip of the Italian stiletto. Conclude your adventure in the island city of **Gallipoli**, feasting on raw sea urchin and octopus in its elegant town centre.

The Deep South

Start your soulful saunter in the cave city of **Matera**. Spend a couple of days exploring its famous *sassi,* as well as the *chiese rupestri* (cave churches) on a hike along the Gravina. From here, continue south to the Parco Nazionale del Pollino for a serious nature fix. Base yourself in **Terranova di Pollino** for four days, hiking through pine woods and beech forest to Basilicata's highest peak, Monte Pollino, and dancing to the *zampogne* (double-chantered pipes) in the Albanian villages of **San Paolo Albanese** and **San Costantino Albanese**. Don't leave the park without spotting the rare Bosnian pine tree, *pino loricato.* Lungs filled with mountain air, it's time to head west to the gorgeous coastal gem of **Maratea**. Pass a couple of days soothing your muscles in the town's crystalline Tyrrhenian waters, kicking back at local bars and feasting on fresh seafood. From here, head south to Calabria on the SS18 coastal road. If it's September, you might catch a chilli-eating competition in **Diamante**. Otherwise, keep moving until you reach Calabria's most arresting coastal town, **Tropea**, where your journey ends with piercing views and sunsets.

Plan Your Trip

Eat & Drink Like a Local

Italy is a gastronomic powerhouse and the country's south claims many of its most lauded exports, from Gragnano pasta and San Marzano tomatoes, to buffalo mozzarella and *cannoli* (pastry shells with a sweet filling of ricotta or custard). Here, businesses still close for lunch, and Sunday *pranzo* (lunch) remains a long, sacred family affair. Famished? You've come to the right place.

The Year in Food

While *sagre* (local food festivals) go into overdrive in autumn, there's never a bad time to raise your fork in southern Italy.

Spring (Mar–May)
Come for asparagus, artichokes and Easter specialities like Naples' *casatiello:* rustic-style bread stuffed with Neapolitan salami, pancetta and hard cheeses.

Summer (Jun–Aug)
Eggplants, peppers, berries and fresh seafood by the sea. Beat the heat with Sicilian *granite* (ices made with coffee, fresh fruit, pistachios or almonds).

Autumn (Sep–Nov)
Hearty chestnuts, mushrooms and game. In September, celebrate fish couscous at San Vito's famous Couscous Fest.

Winter (Dec–Feb)
Time for festive treats like Campania's *raffioli* (sponge and marzipan biscuits) and Sicily's *co-baita* (hard, sesame-seed confectionery).

Food Experiences

So much produce, so many specialities, so little time! Fine-tune your culinary radar with the following edible musts.

Meals of a Lifetime

➡ **Il Frantoio, Ostuni** Legendary 10-course lunches at an olive grove–fringed *masseria* (working farm). (p118)

➡ **Il Focolare, Ischia** A carnivorous, Slow Food stalwart, especially famous for its *coniglio all'ischitana* (Ischian-style rabbit). (p68)

➡ **President, Pompeii** A rising Michelin star, serving whimsical reinterpretations of Campanian cuisine. (p78)

➡ **Pizzeria Starita, Naples** More than 60 types of perfectly wood-fired pizza in a historic Neapolitan pizzeria. (p55)

➡ **Soul Kitchen, Matera** Bold, contemporary takes on Basilicatan flavours and traditions. (p141)

➡ **Trattoria Ai Cascinari, Palermo** A traditional neighbourhood trattoria serving authentic, lip-smacking Sicilian flavours. (p172)

➡ **Osteria La Bettolaccia, Trapani** Savour Trapani's famous fish couscous and other Slow Food seafood classics. (p221)

Cheap Treats

➡ **Arancini** Deep-fried rice balls stuffed with *ragù* (meat sauce), tomato and vegetables.

➡ **Crocchè** Deep-fried, mozzarella-filled potato croquettes.

➡ **Pizza fritta** Neapolitan fried pizza dough stuffed with salami, dried lard cubes, smoked *provola* (provolone) cheese, ricotta and tomato.

➡ **Sgagliozze** Deep-fried polenta cubes served street-side in Bari.

➡ **Pane e panelle** Palermo chickpea fritters on a sesame roll.

➡ **Mozzarella di bufala** Silky, snow-white mozzarella made with local buffalo milk.

➡ **Gelato** The best Italian gelato uses seasonal ingredients and natural colours.

Dare to Try

➡ **Pani ca meusa** A Palermo sandwich of beef spleen and lungs dipped in boiling lard.

➡ **Sanguinaccio** Hearty pig's blood sausage, particularly popular in Calabria and Basilicata.

➡ **Cavallo** Puglia's Salento region is famous for its horse meat. Taste it in dishes like *pezzetti di cavallo* (horse-meat casserole with tomato, celery, carrot and bay leaf).

➡ **Stigghiola** A classic Sicilian dish of grilled sheep's or goat's intestines stuffed with onions and parsley, and seasoned with salt or lemon.

➡ **'Mpanatigghiu** A traditional Sicilian pastry from Modica, filled with minced meat, almonds and the town's famous chocolate.

Local Specialities

The Italian term for civic pride is *campanilismo*, but a more accurate word would be *formaggismo*: loyalty to the local cheese. Clashes among medieval duchies and principalities involving castle sieges and boiling oil have been replaced by competition in speciality foods and wine. Keep reading for a gut-rumbling overview of southern Italy's culinary nuances.

Naples & Campania

Explosions of flavour come with the territory in Campania, where intensely sweet tomatoes and superlative citrus thrive in volcanic soil. In Naples, tuck into Italy's

WHAT TO BOOK

Avoid disappointment with the following simple tips:

➡ Book high-end and popular restaurants, especially for Friday and Saturday evenings and Sunday lunch.

➡ In major tourist centres, always book restaurants in the summer high season and during Easter and Christmas.

➡ Book culinary and wine courses, such as Lecce's popular Awaiting Table (p125) cooking course, at least two months in advance.

best pizza, a wood-fired masterpiece of thin charred crust and slightly chewy dough. Its on-the-go sibling is the surprisingly light *pizza fritta:* fried pizza dough stuffed with salami, dried lard cubes, smoked *provola* cheese, ricotta and tomato.

Vegetarian decadence comes in the form of *parmigiana di melanzana* (fried eggplants layered with hard-boiled eggs, mozzarella, onion, tomato sauce and basil), while the city's signature *spaghetti alla puttanesca* (whore's spaghetti) blends tomatoes and black olives with capers, anchovies and (in some cases) a dash of red chilli. Altogether more virtuous is Campania's unique *friarielli,* a bitter vegetable similar to broccoli rabe, *saltata in padella* (pan-fried), spiked with *peperoncino* (red chilli) and often served with rustic *salsiccia di maiale* (pork sausage).

At the sweeter end of the spectrum are the *sfogliatella* (sweetened ricotta–filled pastry), *babà* (rum-soaked sponge cake) and *pastiera* (latticed tart filled with ricotta, cream, candied fruits and cereals flavoured with orange-blossom water).

Both Caserta and the Cilento region produce Italy's finest *mozzarella di bufala* (buffalo mozzarella), a star ingredient in Capri's refreshing *insalata caprese* (mozzarella, tomato and basil salad). The neighbouring island of Ischia is famed for its succulent *coniglio all'ischitana,* claypot-cooked local rabbit with garlic, chilli, tomato, basil, thyme and white wine.

Back on the mainland, Sorrento peddles sizzling *gnocchi alla sorrentina* (oven-baked gnocchi drizzled with mozzarella and *parmigiano reggiano* cheese) and ricotta-stuffed cannelloni, while the Amalfi Coast has no shortage of fish and seafood-based dishes. This star-studded coast is also famous for two larder essentials: Cetara's *colatura di alici* (an intense anchovy essence) and Salerno's Colline Salernitane DOP olive oil.

Puglia, Basilicata & Calabria

Head southeast to Puglia for peppery olive oil, crunchy *pane* (bread), and honest *cucina povera*. Carbolicious snacks include *puccia* (bread with olives) and ring-shaped *taralli* (pretzel-like biscuits), while breadcrumbs lace everything from *strascinati con la mollica* (pasta with breadcrumbs and anchovies) to *tiella di verdure* (baked vegetable casserole). Vegetables play a leading role in Puglian cuisine, with herbivorous classics including *maritata,* a dish of boiled chicory, escarole, celery and fennel layered alternatively with *pecorino* (sheep's milk cheese) and pepper and covered in broth.

> ### THE CAFFÈ LOWDOWN
>
> Great *caffè* (coffee) in Italy is not a hipster novelty, it's an old-school tradition. Sip like a local with the following basics.
>
> ➡ Caffè latte and cappuccino are considered morning drinks, with espresso and macchiato the preferred post-lunch options.
>
> ➡ Baristas may offer a glass water, either *liscia* (still) or *frizzante* (sparkling), with your espresso. Most southern Italians drink it before their coffee to cleanse the palate. If you are not offered a glass of water and would like one, simply say *Mi da un bicchiere di acqua, per piacere?* (Could I please have a glass of water?)
>
> ➡ Take the edge off with a *caffè corretto,* a shot of espresso spiked with liqueur (usually grappa).
>
> ➡ Coffee with dessert is fine, but ordering one with your main meal is a travesty.

Puglia's coastline delivers spiky *ricci di mare* (sea urchins), caught south of Bari in spring and autumn. They might be a challenge to crack open, but once you've dipped your bread into the delicate, dark-red roe, chances are you'll be glad that you persisted. Easier to slurp is *zuppa di pesce* (fish soup), *riso cozze e patate* (baked rice, mussels and potatoes) and *polpo in umido* or *alla pignata* (steamed octopus teamed with garlic, onion, tomatoes, parsley, olive oil, black pepper, bay leaves and cinnamon).

Basilicata and Calabria have a knack for salami and sausages – pigs here are prized and fed on natural foods such as acorns. Basilicata's *lucanica* or *lucanega* sausage is seasoned with fennel, pepper, *peperoncino* and salt, and eaten fresh – roasted on a coal fire – or dried, or preserved in olive oil. The drooling continues with *soppressata,* the pork sausage from Rivello made from finely chopped pork grazed in pastures, dried and pressed and kept in extra-virgin olive oil, and *pezzenta* ('beggars' – probably a reference to their peasant origins) made from pork scraps and spicy Senise peppers. Across the border, the Calabrians turn pig's fat, organ meats and hot *peperoncino* into spicy, cured *'nduja* sausage.

In August, look out for red eggplants (aubergines), unique to Rotonda, Basilicata, and originally from Africa. Spicy and bitter, they're often dried, pickled or preserved in oil and served as antipasti. Come autumn and the mountains yield delicious *funghi* (mushrooms) of all shapes and sizes. A favourite of the ancient Romans was the small, wild umbel oyster, eaten fried with garlic and parsley or accompanying lamb or vegetables. One of the best spots for a little mushroom hunting is Calabria's Parco Nazionale della Sila, which even hosts a *fungo*-focussed *sagra* (local festival).

For a year-round treat, nibble on provolone, a semi-hard, wax-rind cheese. Though now commonly produced in the northern Italian regions of Lombardy and the Veneto, its roots lie firmly in Basilicata. Like mozzarella, the cheese is made using the *pasta filata* method, which sees the curd heated until it becomes stringy (*filata*). Aged two to three months, *provolone dolce* is milder and sweeter than the more piquant *provolone piccante*, itself aged for over four months.

Sicily

Sicily's history as a cultural crossroad shines through in its sweet and sour flavours. The Saracens brought the eggplant and spiced up dishes with saffron and sultanas. These ancient Arab and North African influences live on in western Sicily's fragrant fish couscous, as well as the island's spectacular sweets. Sink your teeth into *cannoli, cuccia* (grain, honey and ricotta cake) and the queen of Sicilian desserts, the *cassata* (made with ricotta, sugar, vanilla, diced chocolate and candied fruits). Almonds are put to heavenly use in *pasta di mandorle* (almond cookies) and *frutti della Martorana,* marzipan sweets shaped to resemble fruits or vegetables. Both Arab and New World influences flavour Modica's lauded chocolate, spiked with anything from cinnamon to fiery red chilli.

Sicily's Norman invaders live on in *pasta alla Norma* (pasta with basil, eggplant, ricotta and tomato), while the island's bountiful seafood shines in staples like *pasta con le sarde* (pasta with sardines, pine nuts, raisins and wild fennel), Palermo's *sarde a beccafi co alla Palermitana* (sardines stuffed with anchovies, pine nuts, currants and parsley) and Messina's *agghiotta di pesce spada* (swordfish flavoured with pine nuts, sultanas, garlic, basil and tomatoes). Swordfish also gets top billing in *involtini di pesce spada* (thinly sliced swordfish fillets rolled up and filled with breadcrumbs, capers, tomatoes and olives).

Then there are Sicily's finger-licking *buffitieri* (hot street snacks), among them *sfincione* (spongy, oily pizza made with *caciocavallo* cheese, tomatoes, onions and occasionally anchovies) and Palermo's *pane e panelle* (fried chickpea-flour fritters, often served in a roll). Other doughy morsels include calzone (a pocket of pizza-like dough baked with ham, cheese or other stuffings), *impanata* (bread-dough snacks stuffed with meat, vegetables or cheese) and *scaccie* (discs of bread dough spread with a filling and rolled up into a crêpe). Queen of the street scene, however, is the ubiquitous *arancino* (rice ball stuffed with meat or cheese, coated with breadcrumbs and fried).

TABLE MANNERS

➡ Cardinal sins: skipping or being late for lunch.

➡ *Buon appetito* is what you say before eating. *Salute!* (cheers!) is the toast used for alcoholic drinks – always make eye contact when toasting.

➡ Eat spaghetti with a fork, not a spoon.

➡ Don't eat bread with your pasta; using it to wipe any remaining sauce from your plate is fine.

➡ Unless you have hollow legs, don't accept a second helping of that delicious *primo* – you might not have room for the *secondo, dolce, sopratavola* and fruit.

➡ Whoever invites usually pays. Splitting *il conto* (the bill) is common enough, itemising it is not.

➡ If invited to someone's house, bring flowers, wine or a tray of *dolcetti* from a local *pasticceria* (pastry shop).

How to Eat & Drink Like a Local

Now that your appetite is piqued, it's time for the technicalities of eating *all'italiana*.

When to Eat

➡ **Colazione (breakfast)** A continental affair, often little more than a pre-work espresso, accompanied by a *cornetto* (Italian croissant) or *brioche* (breakfast pastry). In Sicily, your brioche might be filled with gelato or *granita* (flavoured crushed ice).

➡ **Pranzo (lunch)** A sacred time, with most businesses closing for *la pausa* (afternoon break). Traditionally the main meal of the day, lunch usually consists of a *primo* (first course), *secondo* (second course) and *dolce* (dessert). Standard restaurant times are noon to 2.30pm, though most locals don't lunch before 1pm.

➡ **Aperitivo** Popular in larger cities like Naples, Palermo and Catania, post-work drinks usually take place between 7pm and 9pm, when the price of your drink includes a buffet of tasty morsels.

➡ **Cena (dinner)** Traditionally lighter than lunch, though still a main meal. Standard restaurant times are 7.30pm to around 11pm, though many southern Italians don't have dinner until 9pm or later.

Where to Eat

➡ **Ristorante (restaurant)** Formal service and refined dishes.

➡ **Trattoria** Cheaper than a restaurant, with more-relaxed service and home-style classics.

➡ **Osteria** Historically a tavern focused on wine, the modern version is often an intimate trattoria or wine bar offering a handful of dishes.

➡ **Enoteca** Wine bars often serve snacks to accompany your tipple.

➡ **Agriturismo** A working farmhouse offering food made with farm-grown produce.

➡ **Pizzeria** Cheap grub, cold beer and a convivial vibe. The best pizzerias are often crowded: be patient.

➡ **Tavola calda** Cafeteria-style spots serving cheap pre-made food like pasta and roast meats.

➡ **Friggitoria** Simple, take-away businesses specialising in deep-fried street snacks like *arancini, crocchè* and tempura-style vegetables.

➡ **Mercato** The market is an integral part of southern Italian life and a great place to pick up picnic provisions like crunchy bread, local cheeses, salami, antipasti, fruit and vegetables.

Menu Decoder

➡ **Menù a la carte** Choose whatever you like from the menu.

➡ **Menù di degustazione** Degustation menu, usually consisting of six to eight 'tasting size' courses.

➡ **Menù turistico** The 'tourist menu' usually signals mediocre fare – steer clear!

➡ **Piatto del giorno** Dish of the day.

➡ **Antipasto** A hot or cold appetiser. For a tasting plate of different appetisers, request an *antipasto misto* (mixed antipasto).

➡ **Primo** First course, usually a substantial pasta, rice or *zuppa* (soup) dish.

➡ **Secondo** Second course, often *carne* (meat) or *pesce* (fish).

➡ **Contorno** Side dish, usually *verdura* (vegetable).

➡ **Dolce** Dessert, including *torta* (cake).

➡ **Sopratavola** Raw vegetables such as fennel or chicory eaten after a meal.

➡ **Frutta** Fruit, usually the epilogue to a meal.

➡ **Nostra produzione** Made in-house.

➡ **Surgelato** Frozen, usually used to denote fish or seafood that's not freshly caught.

Plan Your Trip

Travel with Children

Southern Italy is a dangerous place for children's cheeks. Locals adore *bambini* (children) and acts of face pinching are as common as Vespas, espresso and olive groves. On the flipside, the country's southern regions offer few special amenities for little ones, which makes a little planning go a long way.

Southern Italy for Kids

Southern Italy bursts with extraordinary archaeological sites and museums. But while Pompeian frescoes might thrill mum or dad, a youngster unversed in the wonders of history and art might not be quite as keen. Kids' books or films about the places you visit can help bring these sights to life.

If you're travelling with young children, punctuate museum visits with plenty of rest stops – gelaterie (ice-cream shops), parks and beaches are always good back-ups – and always ask tourist offices about any special family activities or festivals, especially in summer.

Discounted admission for children is available at most Italian tourist attractions, though age limits can vary. Most government-run museums and archaeological sites offer free entry to EU citizens under the age of 18, though some staffers may extend this discount to all under-18s.

For more information, see Lonely Planet's *Travel with Children* book, and check out the useful websites Italia Kids (www.italiakids.com), Context Travel (www.contexttravel.com) and Ciao Bambino (http://ciaobambino.com).

The Regions

Naples & Campania Children aged five and over will enjoy roaming subterranean ruins, secret catacombs and otherworldly cemeteries in Naples, a city famous for cheap, scrumptious pizza and pastries. Kids under 10 may need a piggyback for part of the walk up Mt Vesuvius, though most young ones will enjoy playing gladiators among the ruins of Pompeii, Herculaneum and Pozzuoli. Both young kids and teens will appreciate Ischia's bubbling beach and thermal pools.

Puglia, Basilicata & Calabria Puglia's Valle d'Itria and Basilicata's Matera will catapult young minds into a fantastical other-world of storybook abodes, while all ages will indulge in a little toilet humour at Puglia's Castel del Monte. Puglia's countless soft, sandy beaches suit all ages, while its relatively flat terrain makes for easy cycling adventures. The national parks of Basilicata and Calabria offer older teens some serious thrills, from hikes and skiing to white-water rafting.

Sicily Fire up the imagination of older primary (elementary) and high-school students with ancient temples and theatres, as well as glittering Byzantine mosaics. Younger kids will love Sicilian puppet shows, while older kids and teens will get a kick from climbing a volcano. Young and old will appreciate Sicily's superlative sweet treats.

MANGIA! MANGIA! (EAT! EAT!)

Kids are more than welcome at most eateries. Highchairs are often available and though kids' menus are rare, it's perfectly acceptable to order a *mezzo piatto* (half portion).

Arancini (rice balls), *crocchè* (potato croquettes) and *pizza al taglio* (pizza by the slice) are great on-the-run snacks, as are *panini* from little grocery stores.

You can buy baby formula in powder or liquid form, as well as sterilising solutions such as Milton, at pharmacies. Fresh cow's milk is sold in cartons in supermarkets and in bars with a 'Latteria' sign. UHT milk is popular and in many out-of-the-way areas, it is the only kind available.

Children's Highlights
History Was Here

➡ **Tunnel Borbonico** Escape routes, hideouts and vintage smugglers' cars bring wartime Naples to life. (p51)

➡ **Herculaneum** Smaller and better-preserved than Pompeii, Herculaneum is easier to visit in a shorter time. (p70)

➡ **Valley of the Temples** Agrigento's astounding Greek temples come with picnic-friendly grounds and space to move. (p214)

➡ **Castel del Monte** Puglia's octagonal 13th-century castle boasts Europe's very first flush toilet. (p110)

Alfresco Thrills

➡ **Aeolian Islands** Seven tiny volcanic islands off Sicily with everything from spewing lava to black-sand beaches. (p178)

➡ **Mt Vesuvius** Play 'spot the landmark' from the summit of Naples' formidable volcano. (p72)

➡ **Ischia** Catch a water taxi to a bubbling thermal beach or pool hop at a spa resort. (p66)

➡ **Maratea** Shallow, sandy beaches and a very walkable town centre. (p144)

Kooky Kicks

➡ **Cimitero delle Fontanelle** `FREE` Tour Naples' bizarre Fontanelle Cemetery, stacked with skulls, shrines and fantastical tales. (p50)

➡ **Alberobello** Imagination runs riot in this World Heritage–listed town in Puglia, famous for its cone-roofed *trulli* abodes. (p117)

➡ **Matera** Relive the Flintstones exploring Matera's Unesco-protected *sassi* (stone houses carved out of caves and cliffs). (p135)

➡ **Museo Internazionale delle Marionette** Palermo's ode to the art of puppetry. (p170)

Planning
Where to Stay

Hostels and apartments are sound options for families, offering multibed rooms, guest kitchens, lounge facilities and, often, washing machines. In summer (July and August), many camping grounds offer activities for kids. Italy's *agriturismi* (farm stays) are fantastic for green space and outdoor activities, whether it's swimming and horse riding, or feeding animals and olive picking.

Book accommodation in advance whenever possible. In hotels, some double rooms can't accommodate an extra bed for kids, so check. If your toddler is small enough to share your bed, some hotels will let you do so for free. The website www.booking. com specifies the 'kid policy' for each hotel listed and any extra charges incurred.

Getting Around

Arrange car rental before leaving home. Car seats for infants and children are available from most car-rental agencies, but should be booked in advance.

Public transport discounts are available for children. In some cases, young children travel free if accompanied by a paying adult. Check details in specific destination coverage or ask at the tourist office. Intercity trains and buses are safe, convenient and relatively inexpensive.

Cobbled stones and potholes can make stroller use challenging. Consider purchasing an ergonomic baby carrier before leaving home.

Regions at a Glance

Home to A-list coastal hot spots like Capri and the Amalfi Coast, not to mention the cultural riches of Naples, it's not surprising that Campania has traditionally been southern Italy's blockbuster region.

Puglia and Basilicata have become the darlings of the in-the-know set, famed for their gorgeous beaches, fantastic food, architectural quirks and authentic festivals. While off-the-radar Calabria may lack big-hitter sights and cosmopolitan cities, it's well compensated by its rugged natural beauty, outdoor thrills and spicy rustic grub.

Like Campania, Sicily offers an enviable repertoire of landscapes, from volcanic peaks and vine-laced slopes to irresistible beaches. It's also home to some of Italy's greatest Graeco-Roman temples and amphitheatres, baroque architecture and culinary traditions.

Naples & Campania

History
Food & Wine
Scenery

Ancient Ruins

Sitting beneath Mt Vesuvius, the Neapolitans abide by the motto *Carpe diem* (Seize the day). And why not? All around them – at Pompeii, Herculaneum and the Campi Flegrei – they have reminders that life is short. Further afield, Paestum's Greek temples defy the test of time.

Pizza & Mozzarella

Campania claims some of Italy's most iconic bites: pizza, pasta, San Marzano tomatoes, *sfogliatelle* (sweet ricotta pastries) and vibrant Falanghina wine. Head to the Cilento for buffalo mozzarella and up Ischia's hills for pit-reared *coniglio* (rabbit), slow-cooked with wild herbs.

Cliffs & Coves

From the Amalfi Coast's panoramas to Ischia's subtropical gardens and Capri's dramatic cliffs, the views from this coastline are as famous as its holidaying celebrities. Add thermal beaches and enchanted grottoes, and the appeal is as crystal clear as the sea itself.

p36

Puglia, Basilicata & Calabria

Beaches
Outdoor Activities
Food & Wine

Coastal Bliss

Italy's northern shores may have all the drama, but the south has all the sand. Lounge beneath white cliffs in the Gargano, gaze at the violet sunsets in Tropea and spend summer on the golden beaches of Otranto and Gallipoli.

Wild Places

With its crush of spiky mountains, Basilicata and Calabria are top spots to go wild. Burst through the clouds in mountaintop Pietrapertosa, white-water raft down the Lao river, pick bergamot in the Aspromonte and keep an eye out for Apennine wolves.

Honest Flavours

Puglia has turned its poverty into a culinary art: sample vibrant, vegetable-based pasta dishes like *orecchiette con le cime di rape* ('little ears' pasta with turnip greens), taste-test creamy *burrata* (cheese made from mozzarella and cream) and toast with a rustic Salento red.

p100

Sicily

Food & Wine
History
Outdoor Activities

Culinary Highs

Sicilian cuisine seduces seafood lovers and sets sweet tooths on edge. Tuna, sardines, swordfish and shellfish come grilled, fried or seasoned with mint or wild fennel. Desserts, laden with citrus fruits, ricotta and nuts, include Arab-Italian dishes such as *cannoli* (pastry shells with a sweet filling of ricotta or custard), while libations span luscious Nero d'Avola to silky Marsala.

Cultural Hybrid

A Mediterranean crossroads for centuries, Sicily spoils history buffs with windswept Greek temples, Roman and Byzantine mosaics, Phoenician statues and sun-bleached Arab-Norman churches.

Volcanoes & Islands

Sicily's restless geology gives outdoor activities a thrilling kick. Pamper weary muscles in warm volcanic waters, hike the Aeolian Islands' dramatic coastlines or take in the thrill of the natural fireworks of Stromboli and Etna.

p160

On the Road

Naples & Campania
p36

Puglia, Basilicata & Calabria
p100

Sicily
p160

Naples & Campania

Includes ➡

Naples 37
Capri 60
Ischia 66
Procida 69
Ercolano &
Herculaneum 70
Mt Vesuvius 72
Pompeii 72
Sorrento 78
Positano 83
Amalfi 87
Ravello 89
Parco Nazionale
del Cilento e
Vallo di Diano 96

Best Places to Eat

➡ L'Ebbrezza di Noè (p55)
➡ President (p78)
➡ Il Focolare (p68)
➡ Donna Rosa (p86)

Best Places to Stay

➡ Hotel Palazzo Murat (p85)
➡ Hotel Luna Convento (p89)
➡ Hotel Caruso (p90)
➡ Hotel Piazza Bellini (p52)

Why Go?

Campania could be a multi–Academy Award winner, scooping up everything from Best Cinematography to Best Original Screenplay. Strewn with temples, castles and palaces, the region bursts with myths, legends and anecdotes – Icarus plunged to his death in the Campi Flegrei, sirens lured sailors off Sorrento, and Wagner put quill to paper in lofty Ravello.

Campania's cast includes some of Europe's most fabled destinations, from haunting Pompeii and Herculaneum to celebrity-studded Capri and Positano. At its heart thumps bad-boy Naples, a love-it-or-loathe-it sprawl of operatic *palazzi* (mansions) and churches, mouthwatering markets and art-crammed museums. Beyond its hyperactive streets lies a wonderland of lush bay islands, faded fishing villages and wild mountains. Seductive, vivacious and often contradictory – welcome to Italy at its passionate best.

When to Go
Naples

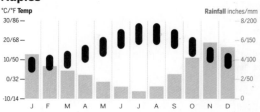

Easter Follow the faithful at mystical Easter processions in Sorrento and Procida.

May Naples celebrates culture with its event-packed Maggio dei Monumenti festival.

Sep Hit the coast for warm, languid days without the maddening August crowds.

NAPLES

POP 989,110

Italy's most misunderstood city is also one of its most intriguing – an exhilarating mess of bombastic baroque interiors, cocky baristas and subterranean ruins. Contradiction is the catchphrase here, a place where anarchy and grit sidle up beside glorious churches, tranquil cloisters and dignified seaside castles. Naples' *centro storico* (historic centre) is a Unesco World Heritage Site, its museums lay claim to some of Europe's finest archaeology and art, and its gilded royal palaces make Rome look positively provincial.

History

According to legend, traders from Rhodes established the city on the island of Megaris (where Castel dell'Ovo now stands) in about 680 BC. Originally called Parthenope, in honour of the siren whose body had earlier washed up there (she drowned herself after failing to seduce Ulysses), it was eventually incorporated into a new city, Neapolis, founded by Greeks from Cumae (Cuma) in 474 BC. However, within 150 years it was in Roman hands, becoming something of a VIP resort favoured by emperors Pompey, Caesar and Tiberius.

After the fall of the Roman Empire, Naples became a duchy, originally under the Byzantines and later as an independent dukedom, until it was captured in 1139 by the Normans and absorbed into the Kingdom of the Two Sicilies. The Normans, in turn, were replaced by the German Swabians, whose charismatic leader Frederick II injected the city with new institutions, including its university.

The Swabian period came to a violent end with the victory of Charles I of Anjou at the 1266 battle of Benevento. The Angevins did much for Naples, promoting art and culture, building Castel Nuovo and enlarging the port, but they were unable to stop the Spanish Aragons taking the city in 1442. However, Naples continued to prosper. Alfonso I of Aragon, in particular, introduced new laws and encouraged the arts and sciences.

In 1503 Naples was absorbed by Spain, which sent viceroys to rule as virtual dictators. Despite Spain's heavy-handed rule, Naples flourished artistically and acquired much of its splendour. Indeed, it continued to bloom when the Spanish Bourbons reestablished Naples as the capital of the Kingdom of the Two Sicilies in 1734. Aside from a Napoleonic interlude under Joachim Murat (1806–15), the Bourbons remained until they were unseated by Garibaldi and the Kingdom of Italy in 1860.

Modern Struggles & Achievements

Naples was heavily bombed in WWII, and the effects can still be seen on many monuments around the city. Since the war, Campania's capital has continued to suffer. Endemic corruption and the re-emergence of the Camorra have plagued much of the city's postwar resurrection, reaching a nadir in the years following a severe earthquake in 1980. In 2011 the city's sporadic garbage-disposal crisis flared up again, leading frustrated residents to set fire to uncollected rubbish in the streets.

Despite these tribulations, the winds of change are blowing. In recent years, Naples' young and visionary mayor, Luigi de Magistris, has introduced numerous schemes aimed at making Italy's third-largest city cleaner and greener. Among these is the pedestrianisation of Naples' famous Lungomare (seafront). New ideas and innovation are driving a growing number of youth-run enterprises and businesses, while the city's famous art-themed metro launched another two show-stopping, starchitect-designed stations in 2015.

◉ Sights

◉ Centro Storico

The three east–west *decumani* (main streets) of Naples' *centro storico* follow the original street plan of ancient Neapolis. Most of the major sights are grouped around the busiest two of these classical thoroughfares: 'Spaccanapoli' (consisting of Via Benedetto Croce, Via San Biagio dei Librai and Via Vicaria Vecchia) and Via dei Tribunali. North of Via dei Tribunali, Via della Sapienza, Via Anticaglia and Via Santissimi Apostoli make up the quieter third *decumanus*.

★**Complesso Monumentale di Santa Chiara**   BASILICA, MONASTERY
(Map p44; ☑ 081 551 66 73; www.monasterodisantachiara.eu; Via Santa Chiara 49c; basilica free, Complesso Monumentale adult/reduced €6/4.50; ⊗ basilica 7.30am-1pm & 4.30-8pm, Complesso Monumentale 9.30am-5.30pm Mon-Sat, 10am-2.30pm Sun; Ⓜ Dante) Vast, Gothic and cleverly deceptive, the mighty **Basilica di Santa Chiara** stands at the heart of this tranquil

Naples & Campania Highlights

1 Channelling the ancients on the ill-fated streets of **Pompeii** (p72).

2 Being bewitched by Capri's ethereal **Grotta Azzurra** (p64).

3 Walking with the gods on the **Amalfi Coast** (p85).

4 Re-evaluating artistic ingenuity in Naples' **Cappella Sansevero** (p40).

5 Lunching by lapping waves on pastel-hued **Procida** (p69).

6 Indulging in a little thermal therapy on **Ischia** (p66).

7 Attending a concert at Ravello's dreamy **Villa Rufolo** (p90).

8 Exploring Naples' underworld on a **Tunnel Borbonico** (p51) tour.

9 Pretending you're royalty at the **Reggia di Caserta** (p60).

10 Admiring ancient Hellenic ingenuity in **Paestum** (p94).

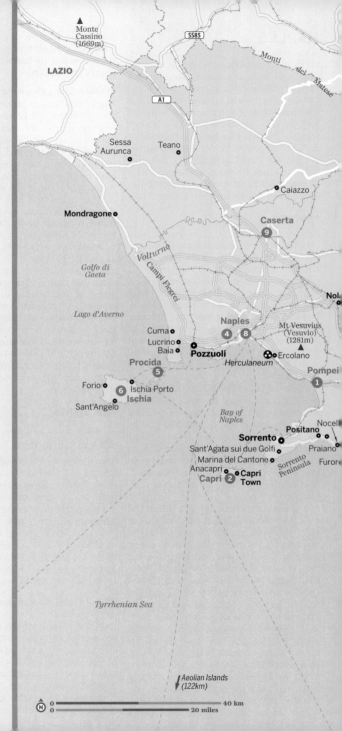

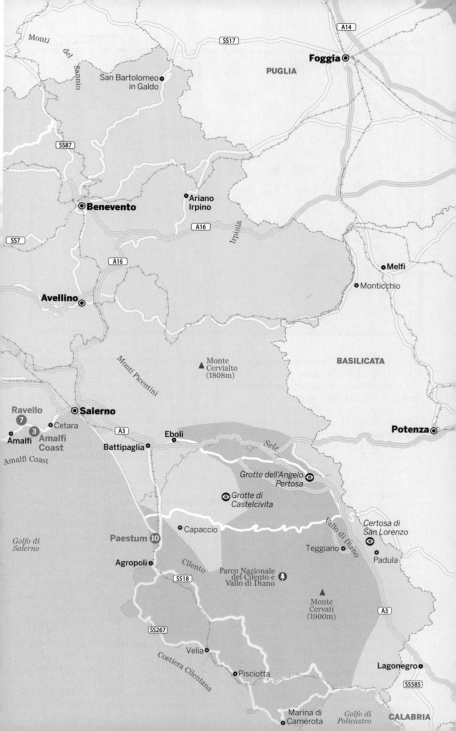

Naples

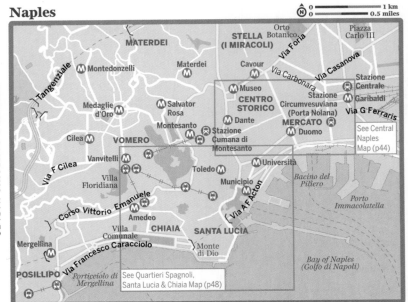

monastery complex. The church was severely damaged in WWII: what you see today is a 20th-century recreation of Gagliardo Primario's 14th-century original. Adjoining it are the basilica's cloisters, adorned with brightly coloured 17th-century majolica tiles and frescoes.

While the Angevin porticoes date back to the 14th century, the cloisters took on their current look in the 18th century thanks to the landscaping work of Domenico Antonio Vaccaro. The walkways that divide the central garden of lavender and citrus trees are lined with 72 ceramic-tiled octagonal columns connected by benches. Painted by Donato e Giuseppe Massa, the tiles depict various rural scenes, from hunting sessions to vignettes of peasant life. The four internal walls are covered with soft, whimsical 17th-century frescoes of Franciscan tales.

Adjacent to the cloisters, a small and elegant museum of mostly ecclesiastical props also features the excavated ruins of a 1st-century spa complex, including a remarkably well-preserved *laconicum* (sauna).

Commissioned by Robert of Anjou for his wife Sancia di Maiorca, the monastic complex was built to house 200 monks and the tombs of the Angevin royal family. Dissed as a 'stable' by Robert's ungrateful son Charles

of Anjou, the basilica received a luscious baroque makeover by Domenico Antonio Vaccaro, Gaetano Buonocore and Giovanni Del Gaizo in the 18th century before taking a direct hit during an Allied air raid on 4 August 1943. Its reconstruction was completed in 1953. Features that did survive the fire include part of a 14th-century fresco to the left of the main door and a chapel containing the tombs of the Bourbon kings from Ferdinand I to Francesco II.

★ **Cappella Sansevero** CHAPEL
(Map p44; ☎ 081 551 84 70; www.museo sansevero.it; Via Francesco de Sanctis 19; adult/reduced €7/5; ⊙ 9.30am-6.30pm Mon & Wed-Sat, to 2pm Sun; Ⓜ Dante) It's in this Masonic-inspired baroque chapel that you'll find Giuseppe Sanmartino's incredible sculpture, *Cristo velato* (Veiled Christ), its marble veil so realistic that it's tempting to try to lift it and view Christ underneath. It's one of several artistic wonders that include Francesco Queirolo's sculpture *Disinganno* (Disillusion), Antonio Corradini's *Pudicizia* (Modesty) and riotously colourful frescoes by Francesco Maria Russo, the latter untouched since their creation in 1749.

Originally built around the end of the 16th century to house the tombs of the di

Sangro family, the chapel was given its current baroque fit-out by Prince Raimondo di Sangro, who, between 1749 and 1766, commissioned the finest artists to adorn the interior. In Queirolo's *Disinganno,* the man trying to untangle himself from a net represents Raimondo's father, Antonio, Duke of Torremaggiore. After the premature death of his wife, Antonio abandoned the young Raimondo, choosing instead a life of travel and hedonistic pleasures. Repentant in his later years, he returned to Naples and joined the priesthood. His attempt to free himself from sin is represented in Queirolo's masterpiece.

Even more poignant is Antonio Corradini's *Pudicizia,* whose veiled female figure pays tribute to Raimondo's mother, Cecilia Gaetani d'Aquila d'Aragona. Raimondo was only 11 months old when she died, and the statue's lost gaze and broken plaque represent a life cruelly cut short.

The chapel's original polychrome marble flooring was badly damaged in a major collapse involving the chapel and the neighbouring Palazzo dei di Sangro in 1889. Designed by Francesco Celebrano, the flooring survives in fragmentary form in the passageway leading off from the chapel's right side. The passageway leads to a staircase, at the bottom of which you'll find two meticulously preserved human arterial systems – one of a man, the other of a woman. Debate still circles the models: are the arterial systems real or reproductions? And if they are real, just how was such an incredible state of preservation achieved? More than two centuries on, the mystery surrounding the alchemist prince lives on.

Chiesa del Gesù Nuovo
CHURCH

(Map p44; ☑ 081 551 86 13; Piazza del Gesù Nuovo; ⏱ 7.15am-12.45pm & 4-8pm Mon-Sat, 7am-2pm & 4-9pm Sun; Ⓜ Dante) The extraordinary Chiesa del Gesù Nuovo is an architectural Kinder Surprise. Its shell is the 15th-century, Giuseppe Valeriani–designed facade of Palazzo Sanseverino, converted to create the 16th-century church. Inside, piperno-stone sobriety gives way to a gob-smacking blast of baroque that could make the Vatican blush: a vainglorious showcase for the work of top-tier artists such as Francesco Solimena, Luca Giordano and Cosimo Fanzago.

Chiesa e Chiostro di San Gregorio Armeno
CHURCH, CLOISTER

(Map p44; ☑ 081 420 63 85; Via San Gregorio Armeno 44; ⏱ 9.30am-noon Mon-Fri, to 1pm Sat & Sun; ☐ C55 to Via Duomo) Overstatement knows no bounds at this richly ornamented 16th-century monastic complex. The church packs a visual punch with its lavish wood and papier-mâché choir stalls, sumptuous altar by Dionisio Lazzari, and Luca Giordano's masterpiece fresco *The Embarkation, Journey and Arrival of the Armenia Nuns with the Relics of St Gregory.* Excess gives way to soothing tranquillity in the picture-perfect cloisters, accessible through the gate on Vico Giuseppe Maffei.

NAPLES IN...

Two Days

Start with a burst of colour in the cloister of the **Basilica di Santa Chiara** (p37), get breathless over the astounding *Cristo velato* (Veiled Christ) in the **Cappella Sansevero** (p40), then head underground on a **Napoli Sotterranea** tour (p51). After lunch, take in Lanfranco's dome fresco in the Duomo, meditate on a Caravaggio masterpiece at **Pio Monte della Misericordia** (p42), then simply kick back in bohemian Piazza Bellini. Next morning, explore ancient treasures at the **Museo Archeologico Nazionale** (p43), then head up to the **Certosa e Museo di San Martino** (p45), for extraordinary baroque interiors, Neapolitan art and a sweeping panorama. Cap the night on the fashionable, bar-packed streets of Chiaia.

Four Days

Spend the morning of day three cheek-to-crater with **Mt Vesuvius** (p72), then ponder its bone-chilling fury at **Herculaneum** (p70) or **Pompeii** (p72). Alternatively, spend the day at Caserta's mammoth royal pad **Reggia di Caserta** (p60). On day four, head up to the **Palazzo Reale di Capodimonte** (p47) to eye up the bounty of artistic masterpieces inside, then head underground on a guided tour of the otherworldly **Catacomba di San Gennaro** (p52). Top it all off with a romantic evening shouting 'bravo' at the luscious **Teatro San Carlo** (p56).

ⓘ BEFORE YOU EXPLORE

If you're planning to blitz the sights, the **Campania Artecard** (☑800 60 06 01; www.campaniartecard.it) is an excellent investment. A cumulative ticket that covers museum admission and transport, it comes in various forms. The Naples three-day ticket (adult/reduced €21/12) gives free admission to three participating sites, a 50% discount on others and free use of public transport in the city. Other handy options include a 7-day 'Tutta la Regione' ticket (€34), which offers free admission to five sites and discounted admission to others in areas as far afield as Caserta, Ravello (Amalfi Coast) and Paestum. The latter does not cover transport. Cards can be purchased online, at the dedicated Artecard booth inside the tourist office at Stazione Centrale, or at participating sites and museums.

Complesso Monumentale di San Lorenzo Maggiore ARCHAEOLOGICAL SITE

(Map p44; ☑081 211 08 60; www.sanlorenzo maggiorenapoli.it; Via dei Tribunali 316; church admission free, excavations & museum adult/reduced €9/7; ⊙9.30am-5.30pm; ☐C55 to Via Duomo) Architecture and history buffs shouldn't miss this richly layered religious complex, its commanding basilica deemed one of Naples' finest medieval buildings. Aside from Ferdinando Sanfelice's petite facade, the Cappella al Rosario and the Cappellone di Sant'Antonio, its baroque makeover was stripped away last century to reveal its austere, Gothic elegance. Beneath the basilica, a sprawl of extraordinary ruins will transport you back two millennia.

Pio Monte della Misericordia CHURCH, MUSEUM

(Map p44; ☑081 44 69 44; www.piomontedella misericordia.it; Via dei Tribunali 253; adult/reduced €7/5; ⊙9am-2pm Thu-Tue; ☐C55 to Via Duomo) The 1st floor of this octagonal, 17th-century church delivers a small, satisfying collection of Renaissance and baroque art, including works by Francesco de Mura, Giuseppe de Ribera, Andrea Vaccaro and Paul van Somer. It's also home to contemporary artworks by Italian and foreign artists, each inspired by Caravaggio's masterpiece *Le Sette Opere di Misericordia* (The Seven Acts of Mercy), considered by many to be the most important painting in Naples. You'll find it above the main altar in the ground-floor chapel.

★ Duomo CATHEDRAL

(Map p44; ☑081 44 90 65; Via Duomo 149; baptistry €1.50; ⊙cathedral 8.30am-1.30pm & 2.30-8pm Mon-Sat, 8.30am-1.30pm & 4.30-7.30pm Sun, baptistry 8.30am-1pm Mon-Sat, 8.30am-12.30pm & 5-6.30pm Sun; ☐C55 to Via Duomo) Whether you go for Giovanni Lanfranco's fresco in the **Cappella di San Gennaro** (Chapel of St Janarius), the 4th-century mosaics in the baptistry, or the thrice-annual miracle of San Gennaro, do not miss Naples' cathedral. Kick-started by Charles I of Anjou in 1272 and consecrated in 1315, it was largely destroyed in a 1456 earthquake, with copious nips and tucks over the subsequent centuries.

Among these is the gleaming neo-Gothic facade, only added in the late 19th century. Step inside and you'll immediately notice the central nave's gilded coffered ceiling, studded with late-mannerist art. The high sections of the nave and the transept are the work of baroque overachiever Luca Giordano.

Off the right aisle, the 17th-century Cappella di San Gennaro (also known as the Chapel of the Treasury) was designed by Giovanni Cola di Franco and completed in 1637. The most sought-after artists of the period worked on the chapel, creating one of Naples' greatest baroque legacies. Highlights here include Giuseppe de Ribera's gripping canvas *St Gennaro Escaping the Furnace Unscathed* and Giovanni Lanfranco's dizzying dome fresco. Hidden away in a strongbox behind the altar is a 14th-century silver bust in which sit the skull of San Gennaro and the two phials that hold his miraculously liquefying blood.

The next chapel eastwards contains an urn with the saint's bones and a cupboard full of femurs, tibias and fibulas. Below the high altar is the **Cappella Carafa**, a Renaissance chapel built to house yet more of the saint's remains.

Off the left aisle lies the 4th-century **Basilica di Santa Restituta**, subject to an almost complete makeover after the earthquake of 1688. From it you can access the **Battistero di San Giovanni in Fonte**. Western Europe's oldest baptistry, it's encrusted with fragments of glittering 4th-century mosaics. Alas, the Duomo's subterranean archaeological zone, which includes fascinating remains of Greek and Roman buildings and roads, remains closed indefinitely.

MADRE   GALLERY
(Museo d'Arte Contemporanea Donnaregina; ☑ 081 1931 3016; www.madrenapoli.it; Via Settembrini 79; adult/reduced €7/3.50, Mon free; ☉ 10am-7.30pm Mon & Wed-Sat, to 8pm Sun; Ⓜ Piazza Cavour) When *Madonna and Child* overload hits, reboot at Naples' museum of modern and contemporary art. Start on level three – the setting for temporary exhibitions – before hitting the permanent collection of painting, sculpture and installations from prolific 20th- and 21st-century artists on level two. Among these are Olafur Eliasson, Shirin Neshat and Julian Beck, as well as Italian heavyweights Mario Merz and Michelangelo Pistoletto. Specially commissioned installations from the likes of Francesco Clemente, Anish Kapoor and Rebecca Horn cap things off on level one.

★ Museo Archeologico Nazionale   MUSEUM
(Map p44; ☑ 081 442 21 49; http://cir.campania.beniculturali.it/museoarcheologiconazionale; Piazza Museo Nazionale 19; adult/reduced €8/4; ☉ 9am-7.30pm Wed-Mon; Ⓜ Museo, Piazza Cavour) Naples' National Archaeological Museum serves up some of the world's finest collections of Graeco-Roman artefacts. Originally a cavalry barracks and later a seat of the city's university, the museum was established by the Bourbon king Charles VII in the late 18th century to house the antiquities he inherited from his mother, Elisabetta Farnese, as well as treasures looted from Pompeii and Herculaneum. Star exhibits include the celebrated *Toro Farnese* (Farnese Bull) sculpture and a series of awe-inspiring mosaics from Pompeii's Casa del Fauno.

Before tackling the collection, consider investing in the *National Archaeological Museum of Naples* (€12), published by Electa; if you want to concentrate on the highlights, audioguides (€5) are available in English. It's also worth calling ahead to ensure that the galleries you want to see are open, as staff shortages often mean that sections of the museum close for part of the day.

The basement houses the Borgia collection of Egyptian relics and epigraphs (closed indefinitely on our last visit). The ground-floor Farnese collection of colossal Greek and Roman sculptures features the *Toro Farnese* and a muscle-bound *Ercole* (Her-

cules). Sculpted in the early 3rd century AD and noted in the writings of Pliny, the *Toro Farnese,* probably a Roman copy of a Greek original, depicts the humiliating death of Dirce, Queen of Thebes. Carved from a single colossal block of marble, the sculpture was discovered in 1545 near the Baths of Caracalla in Rome and was restored by Michelangelo, before eventually being shipped to Naples in 1787. *Ercole* was discovered in the same Roman excavations, albeit without his legs. When they turned up at a later dig, the Bourbons had them fitted.

If you're short on time, take in both these masterpieces before heading straight to the mezzanine floor, home to an exquisite collection of mosaics, mostly from Pompeii. Of the series taken from the Casa del Fauno, it is *La battaglia di Alessandro contro Dario* (The Battle of Alexander against Darius) that really stands out. The best-known depiction of Alexander the Great, the 20-sq-metre mosaic was probably made by Alexandrian craftsmen working in Italy around the end of the 2nd century BC.

Beyond the mosaics, the **Gabinetto Segreto** (Secret Chamber) contains a small but much-studied collection of ancient erotica. Pan is caught in the act with a nanny goat in the collection's most famous piece – a small and surprisingly sophisticated statue taken from the Villa dei Papiri in Herculaneum. You'll also find a series of nine paintings depicting erotic positions – a menu for brothel patrons.

Originally the royal library, the enormous **Sala Meridiana** (Great Hall of the Sundial) on the 1st floor is home to the *Farnese Atlante,* a statue of Atlas carrying a globe on his shoulders, as well as various paintings from the Farnese collection. Look up and you'll find Pietro Bardellino's riotously colourful 1781 fresco depicting the (short-lived) triumph of Ferdinand IV of Bourbon and Marie Caroline of Austria in Rome.

The rest of the 1st floor is largely devoted to fascinating discoveries from Pompeii, Herculaneum, Boscoreale, Stabiae and Cuma. Among them are whimsical wall frescoes from the Villa di Agrippa Postumus and the Casa di Meleagro, extraordinary bronzes from the Villa dei Papiri, as well as ceramics, glassware, engraved coppers and Greek funerary vases.

Mercato di Porta Nolana   MARKET
(Porta Nolana; ☉ 8am-6pm Mon-Sat, to 2pm Sun; Ⓜ Garibaldi) Naples at its most vociferous and

Central Naples

Piazza Museo
Nazionale 4
Museo
Archeologico
Nazionale

Catacomba di Gennaro (1km);
Palazzo Reale di Capodimonte (2km)

Via Tommasi

Via G Brombeis

Via Broggia

Via Santa Maria di Costantinopoli

Via Bellini

Via Enrico Pessina

MADRE (50m)

Ceraniello B&B
(350m)

Via Duomo

Via Santissimi Apostoli

Via S Gaudioso

Via S Pisanelli

Via di Anticaglia

Vico Giganti

Via S San Paolo

Via Atri

Via F del Giudice

Via del Sole

Piazza
Luigi
Miraglia

Piazza
Bellini

Via Port'Alba

Dante

Piazza
Dante

Piazza del
Gesù
Nuovo

Via San Sebastiano

Vico San
Domenico
Maggiore

Piazza San
Domenico
Maggiore

Via B Croce

Via Santa Chiara

Complesso
Monumentale
di Santa Chiara

Via S Anna dei Lombardi

Via D Lioy

Via Toledo

Piazza
Carità

Via Pignasecca

Vico San Geronimo

Largo
Giusso

Via Mezzocannone

Vico S Nicola al Nilo

Vico S Severino

Piazza
San Gennaro

Via San
Gregorio Armeno

Via San Biagio dei Librai

Vico della Pace

Via della Zite

Vico Zuroli

Vicolo Sedil
Capuano

Via S Nicola
dei Caserti

Via del Tribunali

Duomo

CENTRO
STORICO

Via Vicaria Vecchia

Via del
Cimbri

Via d'Alagno

Piazza
Duomo

Nicola
Amore

Via Duomo

Via Scialoia

Corso Umberto I

Piazzetta
Orefici

See Quartieri Spagnoli, Santa Lucia & Chiaia Map (p48)

Via B Capasso

Via G Paladino

Vico
Donnaromita

Via C Muzy

MADRE

Via P Colletta

Via dell'Annunziata

Corso Umberto I

Via Carbonara

Via Duchesca

Via PS Mancini

Via Ranieri

Via A de Pace

Vico Barre

Via Nolana

Via Lavinaio

Via G Pica

Via S Cosmo Fuori Porta Nolana

Via Sopramuro

Corso G Garibaldi

Via C Carmignano

Via G Savarese

Piazza del
Mercato

Via Sant'Eligio

MERCATO

Via Duca di San Donato

Piazza
Masaniello

Piazza
Santa Maria del
Carmine

Chiesa di
Santa Maria del
Carmine

Via D Carmine

Piazza
G Pepe

Via E Cosenz

Vico S Giovanni

Via Amerigo Vespucci

Via Nuova Marina

Calata della Marinella

Calata Villa del Popolo

SITA Sud
Bus Stop (180m)

Piazza
Firenze

Corso Novara

Stazione
Centrale

Garibaldi

Piazza
Garibaldi

Garibaldi

Stazione
Circumvesuviana
(Piazza Garibaldi)
Terminal Bus
Metropark

Eccellenze Campane
(1km)

Stazione
Circumvesuviana
(Porta Nolana)

Piazza
Principe
Umberto

Cappella
Sansevero

Via del Popolo

Scale: 0 — 400 m / 0 — 0.2 miles

20
3
9
21
7
6 10
8 22
11
14 16
19
13
5
18
15 17
2
1
12

Central Naples

◉ **Top Sights**
1	Cappella Sansevero	B3
2	Complesso Monumentale di Santa Chiara	B3
3	Duomo	D1
4	Museo Archeologico Nazionale	A1

◎ **Sights**
5	Chiesa del Gesù Nuovo	B3
6	Chiesa e Chiostro di San Gregorio Armeno	C2
7	Complesso Monumentale di San Lorenzo Maggiore	C2
8	Napoli Sotterranea	C2
9	Pio Monte della Misericordia	D2
10	Via San Gregorio Armeno	C2

⬤ **Sleeping**
11	Casa Latina	C2

12	Decumani Hotel de Charme	B3
13	Hotel Piazza Bellini	B2

⊗ **Eating**
14	La Campagnola	C2
15	La Taverna di Santa Chiara	B3
16	Pizzeria Gino Sorbillo	C2
17	Salumeria	B3

◉ **Drinking & Nightlife**
18	Galleria 19	B3
19	Spazio Nea	B2

⊕ **Entertainment**
20	Lanificio 25	E1

⬤ **Shopping**
21	Ars Neapolitana	C2
22	La Scarabattola	C2

intense, the Mercato di Porta Nolana is a heady, gritty street market where bellowing fishmongers and greengrocers collide with fragrant delis and bakeries, industrious Chinese traders and contraband cigarette stalls. Dive in for anything from buxom tomatoes and mozzarella to golden-fried street snacks, cheap luggage and bootleg CDs.

The market's namesake is medieval city gate **Porta Nolana**, which stands at the head of Via Sopramuro. Its two cylindrical towers, optimistically named Faith and Hope, support an arch decorated with a bas-relief of Ferdinand I of Aragon on horseback.

◉ Vomero

Visible from all over Naples, the stunning Certosa di San Martino is the one compelling reason to take the funicular up to middle-class Vomero (*vom*-e-ro).

★ Certosa e Museo di San Martino

MONASTERY, MUSEUM

(Map p48; ☐ 081 229 45 68; www.polomusealenapoli.beniculturali.it; Largo San Martino 5; adult/reduced €6/3; ⊙ 8.30am-7.30pm Thu-Tue; Ⓜ Vanvitelli, ☐ Montesanto to Morghen) The high point (quite literally) of the Neapolitan baroque, this charterhouse-turned-museum was founded as a Carthusian monastery in the 14th century. Centred on one of the most beautiful cloisters in Italy, it has been decorated, adorned and altered over the centuries by some of Italy's finest talent, most importantly Giovanni Antonio Dosio in the 16th century and baroque master Cosimo

Fanzago a century later. Nowadays, it's a superb repository of Neapolitan artistry.

The monastery's church and the rooms that flank it contain a feast of frescoes and paintings by some of Naples' greatest 17th-century artists, among them Francesco Solimena, Massimo Stanzione, Giuseppe de Ribera and Battista Caracciolo. In the nave, Cosimo Fanzago's inlaid marble work is simply extraordinary.

Adjacent to the church, the **Chiostro dei Procuratori** is the smaller of the monastery's two cloisters. A grand corridor on the left leads to the larger **Chiostro Grande** (Great Cloister). Originally designed by Dosio in the late 16th century and added to by Fanzago, it's a sublime composition of Tuscan-Doric porticoes, marble statues and vibrant camellias. The skulls mounted on the balustrade were a light-hearted reminder to the monks of their own mortality.

Just off the Chiostro dei Procuratori, the small **Sezione Navale** documents the history of the Bourbon navy from 1734 to 1860, and features a small collection of beautiful royal barges. The **Sezione Presepiale** houses a whimsical collection of rare Neapolitan *presepi* (nativity scenes) from the 18th and 19th centuries, including the colossal 18th-century Cuciniello creation, which covers one wall of what used to be the monastery's kitchen. The **Quarto del Priore** in the southern wing houses the bulk of the picture collection, as well as one of the museum's most famous pieces, Pietro Bernini's tender *Madonna col Bambino e San Giovannino*

THE ART OF THE NEAPOLITAN PRESEPE

Christmas nativity cribs may not be exclusive to Naples, but none match the artistic brilliance of the *presepe napoletano* (Neapolitan nativity crib). What sets the local version apart is its incredible attention to detail, from the lifelike miniature *prosciutti* (hams) in the tavern to the lavishly costumed *pastori* (crib figurines or sculptures) adoring the newborn Christ.

For the nobility and bourgeoisie of 18th-century Naples, the *presepe* provided a convenient marriage of faith and ego, becoming as much a symbol of wealth and good taste as a meditation on the Christmas miracle. The finest sculptors were commissioned and the finest fabrics used. Even the royals got involved: Charles III of Bourbon consulted the esteemed *presepe* expert, Dominican monk Padre Rocco, on the creation of his 5000-*pastore* spectacular, still on show at the Palazzo Reale. Yet even this pales in comparison to the up-sized Cuciniello crib on display at the Certosa e Museo di San Martino (p45), considered the world's greatest.

Centuries on, the legacy continues. The craft's epicentre is the *centro storico* street of Via San Gregorio Armeno (Map p44; C55 to Via Duomo), its clutter of shops and workshops selling everything from doting donkeys to kitsch celebrity caricatures. Serious connoisseurs, however, will point you towards the very few workshops that completely handcraft their *pastori* the old-fashioned way. Among the latter are Ars Neapolitana (Map p44; 392 537 71 16; Via dei Tribunali 303; 10am-6.30pm Mon-Fri, to 3pm Sat, plus 10am-6.30pm Sat & Sun late Oct-early Jan; C55 to Via Duomo) and La Scarabattola (p57), both in the *centro storico*.

(Madonna and Child with the Infant John the Baptist).

A pictorial history of Naples is told in **Immagini e Memorie di Napoli** (Images and Memories of Naples). Here you'll find portraits of historic characters; antique maps, including a 35-panel copper map of 18th-century Naples in Room 45; and rooms dedicated to major historical events such as the Revolt of the Masaniello (Room 36) and the plague (Room 37). Room 32 boasts the beautiful *Tavola Strozzi* (Strozzi Table); its fabled depiction of 15th-century maritime Naples is one of the city's most celebrated historical records.

You will need to book in advance to access the Certosa's imposing **Sotterranei Gotici** (Gothic basement), open to the public on Saturday and Sunday at 11.30am (with guided tour in Italian) and 4.30pm (without guided tour). The austere vaulted space is home to about 150 marble sculptures and epigraphs, including a statue of St Francis of Assisi by 18th-century master sculptor Giuseppe Sanmartino. To book a visit, email accoglienza.sanmartino@beniculturali.it at least two weeks in advance.

Castel Sant'Elmo   CASTLE, MUSEUM
(Map p48; 081 558 77 08; www.coopculture.it; Via Tito Angelini 22; adult/reduced €5/2.50; castle 8.30am-7.30pm Wed-Mon, museum 9am-7pm

Wed-Mon; Vanvitelli, Montesanto to Morghen) Star-shaped Castel Sant'Elmo was originally a church dedicated to St Erasmus. Some 400 years later, in 1349, Robert of Anjou turned it into a castle before Spanish viceroy Don Pedro de Toledo had it further fortified in 1538. Used as a military prison until the 1970s, it's now famed for its jaw-dropping panorama, and for its **Museo del Novecento**, dedicated to 20th-century Neapolitan art.

Via Toledo & Quartieri Spagnoli

Galleria di Palazzo Zevallos Stigliano   GALLERY
(Map p48; 081 42 50 11; www.palazzozevallos. com; Via Toledo 185; adult/reduced €5/3; 10am-6pm Tue-Fri, to 8pm Sat & Sun; Municipio) Built for a Spanish merchant in the 17th century and reconfigured in belle époque style by architect Luigi Platania in the early 20th century, Palazzo Zevallos Stigliano houses a compact yet stunning collection of Neapolitan and Italian art spanning the 17th- to early-20th centuries. Star attraction is Caravaggio's mesmerising swan song, *The Martyrdom of St Ursula* (1610). Completed weeks before the artist's lonely death, the painting depicts a vengeful king of the Huns piercing the heart of his unwilling virgin bride-to-be, Ursula.

☉ Santa Lucia & Chiaia

Palazzo Reale PALACE, MUSEUM
(Royal Palace; Map p48; ☑ 081 40 05 47; www.
sbapsae.na.it/cms; Piazza del Plebiscito 1; adult/
reduced €4/3; ☺ 9am-8pm Thu-Tue; ☐ R2 to Via
San Carlo, Ⓜ Municipio) Envisaged as a 16th-
century monument to Spanish glory (Naples
was under Spanish rule at the time), the
magnificent Palazzo Reale is home to the
Museo del Palazzo Reale, a rich and eclectic collection of baroque and neoclassical
furnishings, porcelain, tapestries, sculpture
and paintings, spread across the palace's
royal apartments.

Among the many highlights is the Teatri-
no di Corte, a lavish private theatre created
by Ferdinando Fuga in 1768 to celebrate the
marriage of Ferdinand IV and Marie Caroline of Austria. Incredibly, Angelo Viva's statues of Apollo and the Muses set along the
walls are made of papier mâché.

In Sala (Room) XII, there's the 16th-
century canvas *Gli esattori delle imposte*
(The Tax Collectors) by Dutch artist Marinus
Claesz Van Raymerswaele. Sala XIII used to
be Joachim Murat's study in the 19th century but was used as a snack bar by Allied
troops in WWII. Meanwhile, what looks like
a waterwheel in Sala XXIII is actually a nifty
rotating reading desk made for Marie Caroline by Giovanni Uldrich in the 18th century.

The Cappella Reale (Royal Chapel) houses an 18th-century *presepe napoletano* (Neapolitan nativity crib). Fastidiously detailed,
its cast of *pastori* (crib figurines) were
crafted by a series of celebrated Neapolitan
artists, including Giuseppe Sanmartino,
creator of the *Cristo velato* (Veiled Christ)
sculpture in the Cappella Sansevero.

The palace is also home to the **Biblioteca
Nazionale** (National Library; Map p48; ☑ 081 781
91 11; www.bnnonline.it; ☺ 8.30am-7pm Mon-Fri,
to 2pm Sat, papyri exhibition closes 2pm Mon-Sat;
☐ R2 to Via San Carlo, Ⓜ Municipio) **FREE**, its
own priceless treasures including at least
2000 papyri discovered at Herculaneum and
fragments of a 5th-century Coptic Bible. The
National Library's beautiful **Biblioteca Lucchesi Palli** (Lucchesi Palli Library; closed
Saturday), designed by some of Naples'
most celebrated 19th-century craftspeople,
is home to numerous fascinating artistic
artefacts, including letters by composer Giuseppe Verdi. Bring photo ID to enter the
Biblioteca Nazionale.

MeMus MUSEUM
(Museum & Historical Archive of the Teatro San
Carlo; Map p48; http://memus.squarespace.com;
Palazzo Reale, Piazza del Plebiscito; adult/reduced
€6/5, incl Palazzo Reale €10/5; ☺ 9.30am-5pm
Mon, Tue & Thu-Sat, to 2pm Sun; ☐ R2 to Via San
Carlo, Ⓜ Municipio) Located inside the Palazzo
Reale (purchase tickets at the palace ticket
booth), modern museum MeMus documents the history of Europe's oldest working opera house, the Teatro San Carlo (p56).
The collection includes costumes, sketches,
instruments and memorabilia, displayed in
annually changing themed exhibitions. One
interactive, immersive exhibit allows visitors
to enjoy the music of numerous celebrated
composers with accompanying visuals by
artists who have collaborated with the opera
house, among them William Kentridge.

Castel Nuovo CASTLE, MUSEUM
(Map p48; ☑ 081 795 77 22; Piazza Municipio;
admission €6; ☺ 9am-7pm Mon-Sat, last entry
6pm; Ⓜ Municipio) Locals know this 13th-
century castle as the Maschio Angioino
(Angevin Keep) and its Cappella Palatina
is home to fragments of frescoes by Renaissance maverick Giotto; they're on the splays
of the Gothic windows. You'll find Roman
ruins under the glass-floored Sala dell'Ar-
meria (Armoury Hall), and a collection of
mostly 17th- to early-20th-century Neapolitan paintings on the upper floors. The top
floor houses the more interesting works, including landscape paintings by Luigi Crisco-
nio and a watercolour drawing by architect
Carlo Vanvitelli.

Castel dell'Ovo CASTLE
(Map p48; ☑ 081 795 45 93; Borgo Marinaro;
☺ 8am-6.45pm Mon-Sat, to 1.45pm Sun; ☐ 128 to
Via Santa Lucia) **FREE** Built by the Normans in
the 12th century, Naples' oldest castle owes
its name (Castle of the Egg) to Virgil. The
Roman scribe reputedly buried an egg on
the site where the castle now stands, warning that when the egg breaks, the castle
(and Naples) will fall. Thankfully, both are
still standing, and walking up to the castle's
ramparts will reward you with a breathtaking panorama.

☉ Capodimonte & La Sanità

★**Palazzo Reale di Capodimonte** MUSEUM
(☑ 081 749 91 11; www.polomusealenapoli.beni
culturali.it; Via Miano 2; adult/reduced €7.50/3.75;
☺ 8.30am-7.30pm Thu-Tue; ☐ R4, 178 to Via

Quartieri Spagnoli, Santa Lucia & Chiaia

VOMERO

Via Tito Angelini

Largo
San Martino

1 Certosa e Museo
di San Martino

5

M
Vanvitelli

16

Piazza
Fuga

Via Annibale
Caccavello

Via Gaetano Donizetti

Via G Puccini

Via Luigia Sanfelice

Via G Toma

Via F Palizzi

Corso Vittorio Emanuele

Via de Deo

QUARTIERI
SPAGNOLI

Piazzetta
Cariati

26

Via Santa Caterina da Siena

Via G Nicotera

Corso Vittorio Emanuele

Funicolare
di Chiaia

Via del Parco Margherita

Amedeo
M

Piazza
Amedeo

Via Vittorio Colonna

Via F Crispt

Via G Martucci

Via G Piscicelli

Via Santa
Teresa a Chiaia

Via Ascensione

Via G Bausan

Via dei Mille

17

Vico Vetriera

Via G Filangieri

Vico Sergente
Maggiore

Vico Cario
de Cesare

15

Piazza
Amendola

Via S Pasquale a Chiaia

Via V Imbriani

Via V Cuoco

Vico Belledonne a
Chiaia

Via Cavalerizza a Chiaia

23

Via Ferrigni

CHIAIA

Via C Poerio

29

18

Via Alabardieri

Piazza dei
Martiri

Piazza Santa
Maria degli
Angeli

Vico Santo
Spirito

Via Egiziaca a Pizzofalcone

9

Via Monte di Dio

24

10

Monte
Echia

Vico Santa Maria a
Cappella Vecchia

Largo
Principessa
R Pignatelli

Riviera di Chiaia

Via
Calabritto

Vico
Satriano

28

Vico
Ischitella

Villa
Comunale

Piazza
Vittoria

Via G Arcoleo

Largo
Nunziatella

Viale Anton Dohrn

Via Francesco Caracciolo

←
Mergellina Ferry
Terminal (600m)

Via Partenope

PIZZOFALCONE

Monte
di Dio

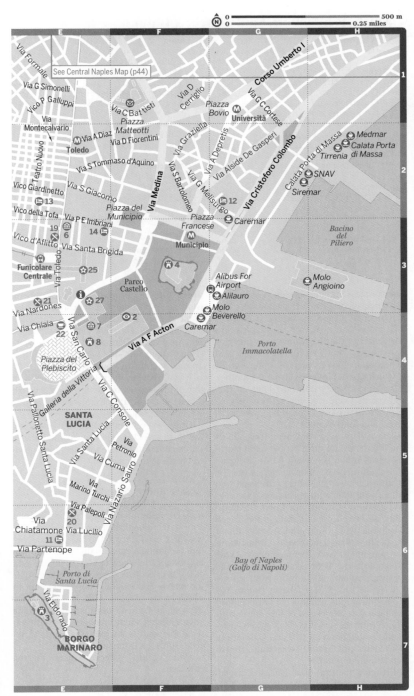

N 0 ————————————— 500 m
0 ————————————— 0.25 miles

Via Formale

See Central Naples Map (p44)

Corso Umberto I

Via G Simonelli

Vico P Galluppi

Via Montecalvario

Via C Battisti

Via D Cerriglio

Piazza Bovio

Via G C Cortese

M Università

Piazza Matteotti

Via A Diaz

M Toledo

Via D Fiorentini

Via S Tommaso d'Aquino

Via Graziella

Via A Depretis

Via Alside De Gasperi

Medmar

Calata Porta di Massa

Tirrenia

Via Cristoforo Colombo

Calata Porta di Massa

Via S Giacomo

Via Medina

Via S Bartolomeo

Via G Melisurgo

SNAV

Vico Giardinetto

13

Vico della Tofa

Piazza del Municipio

12

Siremar

Via P E Imbriani

19

6

14

Piazza Francese

Caremar

Bacino del Piliero

Vico d'Afflitto

Via Santa Brigida

M Municipio

Funicolare Centrale

25

4

Parco Castello

Alibus For Airport

Molo Angioino

21

Alilauro

Via Nardones

i

27

Molo Beverello

Via Chiaia

2

Caremar

22

7

Porto Immacolatella

8

Via A F Acton

Piazza del Plebiscito

SANTA LUCIA

Via C Console

Galleria della Vittoria

Via Santa Lucia

Via Petronio

Via Curna

Via Marino Turchi

Via Nazario Sauro

Via Palepoli

20

Via Chiatamone

Via Lucilio

Bay of Naples
(Golfo di Napoli)

11

Via Partenope

Porto di Santa Lucia

Via Eldorado

3

BORGO MARINARO

Quartieri Spagnoli, Santa Lucia & Chiaia

◎ Top Sights
1 Certosa e Museo di San Martino C1

◎ Sights
2 Biblioteca Nazionale...............................F4
3 Castel dell'Ovo E7
4 Castel Nuovo..F3
5 Castel Sant'Elmo....................................C1
6 Galleria di Palazzo Zevallos
    Stigliano E3
7 MeMus...E4
8 Palazzo Reale E4
9 Tunnel Borbonico D4

◎ Sleeping
10 B&B Cappella Vecchia D4
11 Grand Hotel Vesuvio E6
12 Hostel of the Sun G2
13 Hotel Il Convento E2
14 La Ciliegina Lifestyle Hotel E3
15 Nardones 48..D4

◎ Eating
16 Friggitoria Vomero A1
17 L'Ebbrezza di Noè C3
18 Muu Muzzarella Lounge C4
19 Pintauro E3
20 Ristorantino dell'Avvocato....................E6
21 Trattoria San Ferdinando.......................E3

◎ Drinking & Nightlife
22 Caffè Gambrinus E4
23 Enoteca Belledonne C4

◎ Entertainment
24 Azzurro Service C4
25 Box Office E3
26 Centro di Musica Antica Pietà
    de' Turchini...D3
27 Teatro San Carlo E3

◎ Shopping
28 E. Marinella...C5
29 Tramontano C4

Capodimonte) Originally designed as a hunting lodge for Charles VII of Bourbon, this monumental palace was begun in 1738 and took more than a century to complete. It's now home to the **Museo Nazionale di Capodimonte**, southern Italy's largest and richest art gallery. Its vast collection – much of which Charles inherited from his mother, Elisabetta Farnese – was moved here in 1759 and ranges from exquisite 12th-century altarpieces to works by Botticelli, Caravaggio, Titian and Andy Warhol.

The gallery is spread over three floors and 160 rooms; for most people, a full morning or afternoon is enough for an abridged best-of tour. The 1st floor includes works by greats such as Michelangelo, Raphael and Titian, with highlights including Masaccio's *Crocifissione* (Crucifixion; Room 3), Botticelli's *Madonna col Bambino e due angeli* (Madonna with Child and Angels; Room 6), Bellini's *Trasfigurazione* (Transfiguration; Room 8) and Parmigianino's *Antea* (Room 12). The floor is also home to the royal apartments, a study in regal excess. The **Salottino di Porcellana** (Room 52) is an outrageous example of 18th-century chinoiserie, its walls and ceiling dense with whimsically themed porcelain 'stucco'. Originally created between 1757 and 1759 for the Palazzo Reale in Portici, it was transferred to Capodimonte in 1867.

Upstairs, the 2nd-floor galleries display work by Neapolitan artists from the 13th to the 19th centuries, including de Ribera, Giordano, Solimena and Stanzione. It's also home to some spectacular 16th-century Belgian tapestries. The piece that many come to see, however, is Caravaggio's *Flagellazione* (Flagellation; 1607-10), which hangs in reverential solitude in Room 78.

If you have any energy left, the small gallery of modern art on the 3rd floor is worth a quick look, if for nothing else than Andy Warhol's poptastic *Mt Vesuvius*.

Once you've finished in the museum, the **Parco di Capodimonte** – the palace's 130-hectare estate – provides a much-needed breath of fresh air.

Cimitero delle Fontanelle   CEMETERY
(☑ 081 1970 3197; cimiterofontanelle.com; Via Fontanelle 80; ☉9am-4pm; ☐C51 to Via Fontanelle) **FREE** Holding about eight million human bones, the ghoulish Fontanelle Cemetery was first used during the 1656 plague, before becoming Naples' main burial site during the 1837 cholera epidemic. At the end of the 19th century it became a hot spot for the *anime pezzentelle* (poor souls) cult, in which locals adopted skulls and prayed for their souls. Lack of information at the site makes joining a tour much more rewarding; reputable outfits include Cooperativa Sociale Onlus 'La Paranza' (p52).

Avoid guides offering tours at the entrance.

☞ Tours

Tunnel Borbonico HISTORIC SITE
(Map p48; ☏ 081 764 58 08, 366 2484151; www.
tunnelborbonico.info; Vico del Grottone 4; 75min
standard tour adult/reduced €10/5; ⊘ standard
tour 10am, noon, 3.30pm & 5.30pm Fri-Sun; ☐ R2
to Via San Carlo) Traverse five centuries along
Naples' engrossing Bourbon Tunnel. Con-
ceived by Ferdinand II in 1853 to link the
Palazzo Reale to the barracks and the sea,
the never-completed escape route is part
of the 17th-century Carmignano Aqueduct
system, itself incorporating 16th-century
cisterns. An air-raid shelter and military
hospital during WWII, this underground
labyrinth rekindles the past with evocative
wartime artefacts. The standard tour doesn't
require booking, though the Adventure Tour
(80 minutes; adult/reduced €15/10) and
adults-only Speleo Tour (2½ hours; €30) do.
Tours also depart from Tunnel Borbonico's
second entrance, reached through the Par-
cheggio Morelli (Via Domenico Morelli 40)
parking complex in Chiaia.

Napoli Sotterranea ARCHAEOLOGICAL SITE
(Underground Naples; Map p44; ☏ 081 29 69 44;
www.napolisotterranea.org; Piazza San Gaetano
68; adult/reduced €10/8; ⊘ English tours 10am,
noon, 2pm, 4pm & 6pm; ☐ C55 to Via Duomo) This
evocative guided tour leads you 40m below

street level to explore Naples' ancient labyrinth of aqueducts, passages and cisterns.

Kayak Napoli KAYAKING
(☏ 331 9874271; www.kayaknapoli.com; tours €20-
30; ☐ 140 to Via Posillipo) ✐ Popular kayak
tours along the Neapolitan coastline, gliding
past often-inaccessible ruins, neoclassical
villas and luscious gardens, as well as into
secret sea grottoes. Tours cater to rookie and
experienced paddlers, with day and night
options. Meet at Via Posillipo 68 (Baia delle
Rocce Verdi) in the Posillipo neighbourhood.
Tours are subject to weather and should be
booked ahead.

✵ Festivals & Events

Festa di San Gennaro RELIGIOUS
The faithful flock to the Duomo to witness
the miraculous liquefaction of San Gennaro's blood on the Saturday before the first
Sunday in May. Repeat performances take
place on 19 September and 16 December.

Maggio dei Monumenti CULTURAL
(⊘ May) A month-long cultural feast, with
concerts, performances, exhibitions, guided
tours and other events across Naples.

Wine & The City WINE
(www.wineandthecity.it; ⊘ May) A two-week
celebration of regional *vino,* with free wine

THE SUBTERRANEAN CITY

Mysterious shrines, secret passageways, forgotten burial crypts: it might sound like the
set of an Indiana Jones film, but it's actually what lurks beneath Naples' loud and greasy
streets. Subterranean Naples is one of the world's most thrilling urban wonderlands;
a silent, mostly undiscovered sprawl of cathedral-like cisterns, pin-thin conduits, catacombs and ancient ruins.

Speleologists (cave specialists) estimate that about 60% of Neapolitans live and work
above this network, known in Italian as the *sottosuolo* (underground). Since the end
of WWII, some 700 cavities have been discovered, from original Greek-era grottoes to
palaeo-Christian burial chambers and royal Bourbon escape routes. According to the
experts, there are over 3 million square feet of caves, caverns and tunnels under the
modern city.

Naples' dedicated caving geeks are quick to tell you that their underworld is one of the
largest and oldest on earth. Sure, Paris might claim a catacomb or two, but its subterranean offerings don't come close to this giant's 2500-year history.

And what a history it is. Naples' most famous saint, San Gennaro, was interred in the
Catacomba di San Gennaro in the 5th century. A century later, in 536, Belisario and his
troops caught Naples by surprise by storming the city through the city's ancient tunnels.
According to legend, Alfonso of Aragon used the same trick in 1442, undermining the
city walls by using an underground passageway leading into a tailor's shop and straight
into town. Even the city's dreaded Camorra has got in on the act. In 1992 the notorious
Stolder clan was busted for running a subterranean drug lab, with escape routes heading
straight to the pad of the clan boss.

DON'T MISS

CATACOMBA DI SAN GENNARO

An evocative otherworld of tombs, corridors and broad vestibules, the **Catacomba di San Gennaro** (☏081 744 37 14; www.catacombedinapoli.it; Via Capodimonte 13; adult/reduced €8/5; ⊙1hr tours every hour 10am-5pm Mon-Sat, to 1pm Sun; ☐R4, 178 to Via Capodimonte) are Naples' oldest and most sacred catacombs. Not only home to 2nd-century Christian frescoes and 5th-century mosaics, they harbour the oldest known image of San Gennaro as the protector of Naples. Indeed, it was the interment of the saint's body here in the 5th century that turned this city of the dead into a Christian pilgrimage site.

Tours of the catacomb are run by the **Cooperativa Sociale Onlus 'La Paranza'** (☏081 744 37 14; www.catacombedinapoli.it; Via Capodimonte 13; ⊙information point 10am-5pm Mon-Sat, to 1pm Sun; ☐R4 to Via Capodimonte), the ticket office of which is to the left of the **Chiesa di Madre di Buon Consiglio** (☏081 741 00 06; Via Capodimonte 13; ⊙8am-12.30pm & 5-7pm Mon-Sat, 9am-1pm & 5-7pm Sun; ☐R4 to Via Capodimonte), a snack-sized replica of St Peter's in Rome completed in 1960. The cooperative also runs a fascinating walking tour called *Il Miglio Sacro* (The Holy Mile), which explores the neighbouring Sanità district. See its website for details.

tastings and cultural events in palaces, museums, boutiques and eateries throughout the city.

Napoli Teatro Festival　THEATRE
(www.napoliteatrofestival.it; ⊙Jun) Three weeks of local and international theatre and performance art, staged in conventional and unconventional venues.

🛏 Sleeping

From funky B&Bs and cheery hostels to old-school seafront luxury piles, slumber options in Naples are varied, plentiful and relatively cheap. For maximum atmosphere, consider the *centro storico,* where you'll have many of the city's sights on your doorstep.

🛏 Centro Storico

Cerasiello B&B　B&B €
(☏338 9264453, 081 033 09 77; www.cerasiello.it; Via Supportico Lopez 20; s €40-60, d €55-80, tr €70-95, q €85-105; ✳🖥; ⓜPiazza Cavour, Museo) This gorgeous B&B consists of four rooms with private bathroom, an enchanting communal terrace and an ethno-chic look melding Neapolitan art with North African furnishings. The stylish kitchen offers a fabulous view of the Certosa di San Martino, a view shared by all rooms (or their bathroom) except Fuoco (Fire), which looks out at a beautiful church cupola.

Although technically in the Sanità district, the B&B is a short walk from Naples' *centro storico.* Bring €0.20 for the lift.

Casa Latina　B&B €
(Map p44; ☏338 9264453; www.bbcasalatina.it; Vico Cinquesanti 47; s €40-55, d €55-75, tr €70-90, q €85-100; ✳🖥; ⓜPiazza Cavour) Creativity and style flow through this crisp new B&B, accented with eclectic lighting, boho photography, a fully equipped kitchen and a tranquil terrace. All four rooms are soothing and contemporary, with original architectural detailing and fetching bathrooms with recycled terracotta basins. One upper-level room features a tatami-style bed and banquettes, the latter transforming into extra bed space (ideal for young families).

Hostel of the Sun　HOSTEL €
(Map p48; ☏081 420 63 93; www.hostelnapoli.com; Via G Melisurgo 15; dm €18-22, s €30-35, d €60-80; ✳@🖥; ⓜMunicipio) HOTS is an ultra-friendly hostel near the hydrofoil and ferry terminals. Located on the 7th floor (have €0.05 for the lift), it's a bright, sociable place with multicoloured dorms, a casual in-house bar (with cheap cocktails between 8pm and 11pm) and – a few floors down – a series of hotel-standard private rooms, seven with en suite bathrooms.

★**Hotel Piazza Bellini**　BOUTIQUE HOTEL €€
(Map p44; ☏081 45 17 32; www.hotelpiazzabellini.com; Via Santa Maria di Costantinopoli 101; d from €100; ✳@🖥; ⓜDante) Only steps from buzzing Piazza Bellini, this sharp, contemporary hotel occupies a 16th-century *palazzo,* its mint white spaces spiked with original majolica tiles and the work of emerging artists. Rooms offer pared-back cool, with designer fittings,

chic bathrooms and mirror frames drawn straight onto the wall. Rooms on the 5th and 6th floors have panoramic terraces.

Decumani Hotel de Charme   BOUTIQUE HOTEL €€
(Map p44; ☑ 081 551 81 88; www.decumani.it; Via San Giovanni Maggiore Pignatelli 15; s €99-124, d €99-164; 🕸 @ 🛜; Ⓜ Università) This classic boutique hotel occupies the former *palazzo* of Cardinal Sisto Riario Sforza, the last bishop of the Bourbon kingdom. Simple, stylish rooms feature high ceilings, parquet floors, 19th-century furniture, and modern bathrooms with spacious showers. Deluxe rooms crank up *la dolce vita* with personal hot tubs. The *pièce de résistance*, however, is the property's breathtaking baroque salon.

🛏 Via Toledo & Quartieri Spagnoli

Nardones 48   APARTMENT €
(Map p48; ☑ 338 8818998; www.nardones48.it; Via Nardones 48; small apt €60-72, large apt €80-120; 🕸 🛜; 🚇 R2 to Via San Carlo) White-on-white Nardones 48 serves up seven smart mini-apartments in a historic Quartieri Spagnoli building. The five largest apartments, each with mezzanine bedroom, accommodate up to four; the two smallest, each with a sofa bed, accommodate up to two. Three apartments boast a panoramic terrace, and all have modern kitchenette, flat-screen TV and contemporary bathroom with spacious shower.

La Ciliegina Lifestyle Hotel   BOUTIQUE HOTEL €€
(Map p48; ☑ 081 1971 8800; www.cilieginahotel.it; Via PE Imbriani 30; d €150-250, junior ste €200-350; 🕸 @ 🛜; Ⓜ Municipio) An easy walk from the hydrofoil terminal, this chic, contemporary slumber spot is a hit with fashion-conscious urbanites. Spacious white rooms are splashed with blue and red accents, each with top-of-the-range Hästens bed, flat-screen TV and marble-clad bathroom with water-jet Jacuzzi shower (one junior suite has a Jacuzzi tub).

Hotel Il Convento   HOTEL €€
(Map p48; ☑ 081 40 39 77; www.hotelilconvento.com; Via Speranzella 137a; s €50-93, d €65-140; 🕸 🛜; Ⓜ Municipio) This lovely hotel in the Quartieri Spagnoli is a soothing blend of antique Tuscan furniture, well-stocked bookshelves and candle-lit stairs. Rooms are cosy and elegant, combining creamy

tones and dark woods with patches of 16th-century brickwork. For €80 to €180 you get a room with a private roof garden. The hotel is wheelchair accessible.

🛏 Santa Lucia & Chiaia

B&B Cappella Vecchia   B&B €
(Map p48; ☑ 081 240 51 17; www.cappellavecchia11.it; Vico Santa Maria a Cappella Vecchia 11; s €50-80, d €75-110, tr €90-140; 🕸 🛜; 🚇 C24 to Piazza dei Martiri) Run by a super-helpful young couple, this B&B is a first-rate choice in the smart, fashionable Chiaia district. Rooms are simple and upbeat, with funky bathrooms, vibrant colours, and Neapolitan themes. There's a spacious communal area for breakfast, and free internet available 24/7. Check the website for special offers.

Grand Hotel Vesuvio   HOTEL €€€
(Map p48; ☑ 081 764 00 44; www.vesuvio.it; Via Partenope 45; s/d €280/310; 🕸 @ 🛜; 🚇 128 to Via Santa Lucia) Known for hosting legends – past guests include Rita Hayworth and Humphrey Bogart – this five-star heavyweight is a decadent mélange of dripping chandeliers, period antiques and opulent rooms. Count your lucky stars while drinking a martini at the rooftop restaurant.

🍴 Eating

Pizza and pasta are the staples of Neapolitan cuisine. Pizza was created here and nowhere will you eat it better. Seafood is another local speciality and you'll find mussels and clams served in many dishes. Neapolitan street food is equally delicious. *Misto di frittura* – zucchini flowers, deep-fried potato and aubergine – makes for a great snack, especially if eaten from paper outside a tiny streetside stall. It's always sensible to book a table if dining at a restaurant on a Friday or Saturday night. Also note that many eateries close for two to four weeks in August, so check before heading out.

🍴 Centro Storico

★ **Pizzeria Gino Sorbillo**   PIZZA €
(Map p44; ☑ 081 44 66 43; www.accademiadellapizza.it; Via dei Tribunali 32; pizzas from €3.30; ⊙ noon-3.30pm & 7pm-1am Mon-Sat; Ⓜ Dante) Day in, day out, this cult-status pizzeria is besieged by hungry hordes. While debate may rage over whether Gino Sorbillo's pizzas are the best in town, there's no doubt that his giant, wood-fired discs – made using

organic flour and tomatoes – will have you licking finger tips and whiskers. Head in super early or prepare to queue.

Salumeria
BISTRO €

(Map p44; ☑ 081 1936 4649; www.salumeria upnea.it; Via San Giovanni Maggiore Pignatelli 34/35; sandwiches from €3.70, charcuterie platters from €5.90; ⊗ 10am-midnight, closed Wed Sep-May; ⊛; Ⓜ Dante) The latest project for UpNea, a dynamic team known for hip arts events, this bistro-bar covers all bases, from coffee and house-baked morning muffins, to soups, salads, charcuterie boards and insanely good *panini* and hamburgers. The menu focuses on top-quality local produce; even the ketchup is made in-house using DOP Piennolo tomatoes from Vesuvius. Libations include Petragnola craft beers.

La Campagnola
NEAPOLITAN €

(Map p44; ☑ 081 45 90 34; Via dei Tribunali 47; meals €18; ⊗ 12.30-4pm & 7-11.30pm; ⊛; Ⓜ Dante) Boisterous and affable, this spruced-up Neapolitan stalwart dishes unfussed, soul-coaxing classics. Daily specials include a killer *genovese* (pasta with a slow-cooked lamb, tomato and onion *ragù*) on Thursday, while week-round classics include hearty *salsiccia con friarielli* (pork sausage with Neapolitan bitter greens). If there's still room to move, conclude with the rum-soaked *babà*.

La Taverna di Santa Chiara
NEAPOLITAN €€

(Map p44; ☑ 339 8150346; Via Santa Chiara 6; meals €25; ⊗ 12.30-3pm & 7-11pm Wed-Mon; ⊛; Ⓜ Dante) Gragnano pasta, Agerola pork, Benevento *latte nobile:* this intimate, two-level eatery is healthily obsessed with small, local producers and Slow Food ingredients. The result is a beautiful, seasonal journey across Campania. For an inspiring overview, order the *antipasto misto* (mixed antipasto), then tuck into lesser-known classics like *zuppa di soffritto* (spicy meat stew) with a glass of smooth house *vino*.

★ Eccellenze Campane
NEAPOLITAN €€

(☑ 081 20 36 57; www.eccellenzecampane.it; Via Benedetto Brin 49; pizza from €6, meals €30; ⊗ 7am-11pm Sun-Fri, to midnight Sat; ☐ 116, 192, 460, 472, 475) This is Naples' answer to Turin-based food emporium Eataly, an impressive, contemporary showcase for top-notch Campanian comestibles. The sprawling space is divided into various dining and shopping sections, offering everything from beautifully charred pizzas and light *fritture* (fried snacks) to finer-dining seafood, coveted Sal

Da Riso pastries, craft beers and no shortage of take-home pantry treats. A must for gastronomes.

✗ Via Toledo & Quartieri Spagnoli

Pintauro
PASTRIES €

(Map p48; ☑ 348 7781645; Via Toledo 275; sfogliatelle €2; ⊗ 9am-8pm Mon-Sat, 9.30am-2pm Sun, closed mid-Jul–early Sep; Ⓜ Municipio) Of Neapolitan *dolci* (sweets), the cream of the crop is the *sfogliatella,* a shell of flaky pastry stuffed with creamy, scented ricotta. This local institution has been selling *sfogliatelle* since the early 1800s, when its founder supposedly brought them to Naples from their culinary birthplace on the Amalfi Coast.

Trattoria San Ferdinando
NEAPOLITAN €€

(Map p48; ☑ 081 42 19 64; Via Nardones 117; meals €27; ⊗ noon-3pm Mon-Sat, 7.30-11pm Tue-Fri; ☐ R2 to Via San Carlo, Ⓜ Municipio) Hung with theatre posters, cosy San Ferdinando pulls in well-spoken theatre types and intellectuals. For a Neapolitan taste trip, ask for a rundown of the day's antipasti and choose your favourites for an *antipasto misto* (mixed antipasto). Seafood standouts include a delicate *seppia ripieno* (stuffed squid), while the homemade desserts make for a satisfying dénouement.

✗ Vomero

Friggitoria Vomero
FAST FOOD €

(Map p48; ☑ 081 578 31 30; Via Domenico Cimarosa 44; snacks from €0.20; ⊗ 9.30am-2.30pm & 5-9.30pm Mon-Fri, to 11pm Sat; ☐ Centrale to Piazza Fuga) The stuff of legend, this spartan snack bar makes some of the city's most scrumptious *fritture* (deep-fried snacks). Crunch away on tempura-style aubergines and spinach, *zeppole* (doughnuts), *frittatine di maccheroni* (fried pasta and egg) and *supplì di riso* (rice balls). Located opposite the funicular, it's a handy pit stop before legging it to the Certosa di San Martino.

✗ Santa Lucia & Chiaia

Muu Muzzarella Lounge
NEAPOLITAN €

(Map p48; Vico II Alabardieri 7; dishes €7-14; ⊗ 12.30pm-1.30am Tue-Sat, 6.30am-1.30am Sun; ⊛; ☐ C24 to Riviera di Chiaia) Pimped with milking-bucket lights and cow-hide patterned cushions, playful, contemporary Muu is all about super-fresh Campanian mozzarella, from cheese and charcuterie platters to creative dishes like buffalo bocconcini with creamy pesto and crunchy apple. Leave room for the chef's secret-recipe white-chocolate cheesecake, best paired with a glass of Guappa (buffalo-milk liqueur).

★ **L'Ebbrezza di Noè** NEAPOLITAN €€
(Map p48; ☑ 081 40 01 04; www.lebbrezzadinoe. com; Vico Vetriera 9; meals €37; ☉ 8.30pm-midnight Tue-Sun; M Piazza Amedeo) A wine shop by day, 'Noah's Drunkenness' transforms into an intimate culinary hot spot by night. Slip inside for *vino* and conversation at the bar, or settle into one of the bottle-lined dining rooms for seductive, market-driven dishes like house special *paccheri fritti* (fried pasta stuffed with aubergine and served with fresh basil and a rich tomato sauce).

Ristorantino dell'Avvocato NEAPOLITAN €€
(Map p48; ☑ 081 032 00 47; www.ilristorantino dellavvocato.it; Via Santa Lucia 115-117; meals €40; ☉ noon-3pm & 7.30-11pm, lunch only Mon & Sun; ☎; ☐ 128 to Via Santa Lucia) This elegant yet welcoming restaurant has quickly won the respect of Neapolitan gastronomes. Apple of their eye is affable lawyer turned head chef Raffaele Cardillo, whose passion for Campania's culinary heritage merges with a knack for subtle, refreshing twists – think gnocchi with fresh mussels, clams, crumbed pistachio, lemon, ginger and garlic.

✖ Capodimonte & La Sanità

Pizzeria Starita PIZZA €
(☑ 081 557 36 82; Via Materdei 28; pizzas from €3.50; ☉ noon-4pm & 7pm-midnight Mon-Sat, 7pm-midnight Sun; M Materdei) The giant fork and ladle hanging on the wall at this historic pizzeria were used by Sophia Loren in *L'Oro di Napoli,* and the kitchen made the *pizze fritte* sold by the actress in the film. While the 60-plus pizza varieties include a tasty *fiorilli e zucchine* (zucchini, zucchini flowers and *provola*), our allegiance remains to its classic marinara.

🍷 Drinking & Nightlife

The city's student and alternative drinking scene is around the piazzas and alleyways of the *centro storico*. For a something more chic hit the cobbled lanes of upmarket Chiaia. While some bars operate from 8am, most open from around 5.30pm and close around 2am.

Clubs usually open at 10.30pm or 11pm but don't fill up until after midnight. Many close in summer (July to September), some transferring to out-of-town beach locations. Admission charges vary, but expect to pay between €5 and €30, which may or may not include a drink.

Caffè Gambrinus CAFE
(Map p48; ☑ 081 41 75 82; www.grancaffe gambrinus.com; Via Chiaia 12; ☉ 7am-1am Sun-Thu, to 2am Fri, to 3am Sat; ☐ R2 to Via San Carlo, M Municipio) Grand, chandeliered Gambrinus is Naples' oldest and most venerable cafe. Oscar Wilde knocked back a few here and Mussolini had some of the rooms shut to keep out left-wing intellectuals. The prices may be steep, but the *aperitivo* nibbles are decent and sipping a *spritz* or a luscious *cioccolata calda* (hot chocolate) in its belle époque rooms is something worth savouring.

Spazio Nea CAFE
(Map p44; ☑ 081 45 13 58; www.spazionea.it; Via Constantinopoli 53; ☉ 9am-2am; ☎; M Dante) Aptly skirting bohemian Piazza Bellini, this whitewashed gallery features its own cafe-bar speckled with books, flowers, cultured crowds and alfresco seating at the bottom of a baroque staircase. Eye up exhibitions of contemporary Italian and foreign art, then kick back with a *caffé* or a Cynar *spritz*. Check Nea's Facebook page for upcoming readings, live music gigs or DJ sets.

Enoteca Belledonne BAR
(Map p48; ☑ 081 40 31 62; www.enoteca belledonne.com; Vico Belledonne a Chiaia 18; ☉ 10am-2pm & 4.30pm-2am Tue-Sat, 6.30pm-1am Mon & Sun; ☎; ☐ C24 to Riviera di Chiaia) Exposed-brick walls, ambient lighting and bottle-lined shelves set a cosy scene at Chiaia's best-loved wine bar – just look for the evening crowd spilling out onto the street. Swill, sniff and eavesdrop over a list of well-chosen, mostly Italian wines, including 30 by the glass. The decent grazing menu includes charcuterie and cheese (€16), crostini (from €6) and *bruschette* (€7).

Galleria 19 CLUB
(Map p44; www.galleria19.it; Via San Sebastiano 19; ☉ 11pm-5am Tue-Sat; M Dante) Set in a long, cavernous cellar scattered with chesterfields and industrial lamps, this popular *centro storico* club draws a uni crowd early in the week and 20- and 30-somethings on Friday and Saturday. Tunes span electronica,

ⓘ TICKETS, PLEASE

If travelling on public transport in Naples and Campania, you will most likely be using TIC (Ticket Integrato Campania) tickets. Available from newspaper kiosks and *tabaccai* (tobacconists), these integrated tickets are valid on bus, tram, funicular, metro and sub-urban train services in Naples, on regional Circumvesuviana and Cumana trains, as well as on EAV and SITA Sud buses across Campania. They are not valid on ferry and hydrofoil services. Ticket types and prices vary depending on where you want to travel.

The cheapest option is a *corsa semplice* (one-trip) ticket, valid for one trip within one travel zone only. The *biglietto orario* (multi-trip ticket) allows for multiple trips within a specified time period and across any number of zones. Daily and multi-day tickets are also available in some areas. Prices listed in this chapter are generally for *biglietto orario* tickets. Check the TIC website (www.tic-campania.net, in Italian) for exact details.

commercial and house. Check the website for upcoming events.

☆ Entertainment

Options run the gamut from nail-biting football games to world-class opera. For cultural listings check www.incampania.it. Tickets for most cultural events are available from ticket agency **Box Office** (Map p48; ☏ 081 551 91 88; www.boxofficenapoli.it; Galleria Umberto I 17; ☺ 9.30am-8pm Mon-Fri, 9.30am-1.30pm & 4.30-8pm Sat; 🚌 R2 to Piazza Trieste e Trento) or the box office inside bookshop **Feltrinelli** (Map p48; ☏ 081 032 23 62; www.azzurro service.net; Piazza dei Martiri 23; ☺ 11am-2pm & 3-8pm Mon-Sat; 🚌 C24 to Piazza dei Martiri).

Teatro San Carlo   OPERA, BALLET
(Map p48; ☏ 081 797 23 31; www.teatrosan carlo.it; Via San Carlo 98; ☺ box office 10am-5.30pm Mon-Sat, to 2pm Sun; 🚌 R2 to Via San Carlo) One of Italy's top opera houses, the San Carlo stages opera, ballet and concerts. Bank on €50 for a place in the sixth tier, €100 for a seat in the stalls or – if you're under 30 and can prove it – €30 for a place in a side box. Ballet tickets range from €35 to €80, with €20 tickets for those under 30.

**Centro di Musica Antica
Pietà de' Turchini**   CLASSICAL MUSIC
(Map p48; ☏ 081 40 23 95; www.turchini.it; Via Santa Caterina da Siena 38; funicularCentrale to Corso Vittorio Emanuele) Classical-music buffs are in for a treat at this beautiful deconsecrated church, an evocative setting for concerts of mostly 17th- to 19th-century Neapolitan works. Tickets usually cost €10 (reduced €7).

Lanificio 25   LIVE MUSIC
(Map p44; www.lanificio25.it; Piazza Enrico De Nicola 46; admission €5-10; ☺ 9pm-late Fri & Sat; 🚇 Garibaldi) This Bourbon-era wool facto-ry and 15th-century cloister is now a burgeoning party and culture hub, strung with coloured lights and awash with video projections. Live music (usually from 10pm) is the mainstay, with mostly Italian outfits playing indie, rock, world music, electronica and more to an easy, arty, cosmopolitan crowd.

Football

Naples' football team, Napoli, is the third-most supported in the country after Juventus and Milan, and watching it play at the **Stadio San Paolo** (Piazzale Vincenzo Tecchio; 🚇 Napoli Campi Flegrei) is a highly charged rush. The season runs from late August to late May, with seats costing between €20 and €100. Book tickets at Azzurro Service in bookshop Feltrinelli, at Box Office or from some tobacconists, and don't forget your photo ID. On match days, tickets are also available at the stadium itself.

🛍 Shopping

Tramontano   ACCESSORIES
(Map p48; ☏ 081 41 48 37; www.tramontano.it; Via Chiaia 143-144; ☺ 10am-1.30pm & 4-8pm Mon-Sat; 🚌 C24 to Piazza dei Martiri) Tramontano has a solid rep for its exquisitely crafted Neapolitan leather goods, from glam handbags and preppy satchels to duffels and totes. Each year, a new bag is added to the Rock Ladies' Collection, inspired by a classic song, whether it's Patti Smith's 'Kimberley' or Creedence Clearwater Revival's 'Proud Mary'.

E. Marinella   FASHION
(Map p48; ☏ 081 764 42 14; www.marinellana poli.it; Via Riviera di Chiaia 287; ☺ 8am-8pm Mon-Sat, 9am-1pm Sun; 🚌 C25 to Riviera di Chiaia, C24 to Piazza dei Martiri) One-time favourite of Luchino Visconti and Aristotle Onassis, this pocket-sized, vintage boutique is the place for prêt-à-porter and made-to-measure silk ties in

striking patterns and hues. Match them with an irresistible selection of luxury accessories, including shoes, vintage colognes, and scarves for female style queens.

La Scarabattola CRAFTS
(Map p44; ☑ 081 29 17 35; www.lascarabattola.it; Via dei Tribunali 50; ⊗ 10.30am-2pm & 3.30-7.30pm Mon-Fri, 10am-6pm Sat; ☑ C55 to Via Duomo) Not only do La Scarabattola's handmade sculptures of *magi* (wise men), devils and Neapolitan folk figures constitute Jerusalem's official Christmas crèche, the artisan studio's fans include fashion designer Stefano Gabbana and Spanish royalty. Figurines aside, sleek ceramic creations (think Pulcinella-inspired place-card holders) refresh Neapolitan folklore with contemporary style.

ⓘ Information

Loreto-Mare Hospital (Ospedale Loreto-Mare; ☑ 081 254 27 01, emergency 081 254 27 43; Via A Vespucci 26; ☑ 154, ☑ 1, 2, 4) Central-city hospital with an emergency department.

Pharmacy (Stazione Centrale; ⊗ 7am-9pm Mon-Sat, to 8pm Sun) Inside the train station.

Police Station (Questura; ☑ 081 794 11 11; Via Medina 75; Ⓜ Università) Has an office for foreigners. To report a stolen car, call ☑ 081 79 41 43.

TOURIST OFFICES

Head to the following tourist bureaux for information and a map of the city:

Tourist Information Office (Map p44; ☑ 081 551 27 01; Piazza del Gesù Nuovo 7; ⊗ 9am-5pm Mon-Sat, to 1pm Sun; Ⓜ Dante) Tourist office in the *centro storico*.

Tourist Information Office (Map p44; ☑ 081 26 87 79; Stazione Centrale; ⊗ 8.30am-7.30pm; Ⓜ Garibaldi) Tourist office inside Stazione Centrale (Central Station).

Tourist Information Office (Map p48; ☑ 081 40 23 94; Via San Carlo 9; ⊗ 9am-5pm Mon-Sat, to 1pm Sun; ☑ R2 to Via San Carlo, Ⓜ Municipio) Tourist office at Galleria Umberto I, directly opposite Teatro San Carlo.

WEBSITES

In Campania (www.incampania.com) Campania's official tourist website.

Napoli Unplugged (www.napoliunplugged. com) Informative website covering sights, events, news and practicalities.

ⓘ Getting There & Away

AIR

Capodichino, 7km northeast of the city centre, is southern Italy's main airport, linking Naples with most Italian and several European cities, as well as New York. Budget carrier Easyjet operates several routes to/from Capodichino, including London, Paris, Brussels and Berlin.

BOAT
Ferry Terminals

Naples, the bay islands and the Amalfi Coast are served by a comprehensive ferry network. There are several ferry and hydrofoil terminals in central Naples.

Molo Beverello (Map p48) Right in front of Castel Nuovo; services fast ferries and hydrofoils for Capri, Sorrento, Ischia (both Ischia Porto and Forio) and Procida. Some hydrofoils for Capri, Ischia, Procida and Sicily's Aeolian Islands also leave from Mergellina, 5km west.

Molo Angioino (Map p48) Right beside Molo Beverello; services slow ferries for Sicily, the Aeolian Islands and Sardinia.

Calata Porta di Massa (Map p48) Beside Molo Angioino; services slow ferries to Ischia, Procida and Capri.

FERRIES

DESTINATION (FROM NAPLES – CALATA PORTA DI MASSA & MOLO ANGIOINO)	FERRY COMPANY	PRICE (€)	DURATION	DAILY FREQUENCY (HIGH SEASON)
Capri	Caremar	12.70	80 min	3
Ischia (Ischia Porto)	Caremar	11.20 / 11.30	80/75 min	6/6
Procida	Caremar	12.20	60 min	6
Aeolian Islands	Siremar / SNAV (summer only)	from 50 to 150	10½/4½ hr	2 weekly/1 daily
Milazzo (Sicily)	Siremar	from 57	17 hr	2 weekly
Palermo (Sicily)	SNAV / Tirrenia	from 50 / from 32	10¼–11¾ hr	1 to 2/1 daily
Cagliari (Sardinia)	Tirrenia	from 49	16¼ hr	2 weekly

HYDROFOILS & HIGH-SPEED FERRIES

DESTINATION (FROM NAPLES – MOLO BEVERELLO)	FERRY COMPANY	PRICE (€)	DURATION (MIN)	DAILY FREQUENCY (HIGH SEASON)
Capri	Caremar/Navigazione Libera del Golfo/SNAV	17.80/19/ 20.10	45–50	4/8/17
Ischia (Casamicciola Terme & Forio)	Caremar/Alilauro/ SNAV	17.60/18.70/ 18.60	50–65	4/7/8
Procida	Caremar/SNAV	13.20/15.90	40	8/4
Sorrento	Alilauro/Navigazione Libera del Golfo	12.30/12.30	35–40	5/1

Ferry Services

Ferry services are pared back considerably in the winter, and adverse sea conditions may affect sailing schedules.

The tables list hydrofoil and ferry destinations from Naples. The fares, unless otherwise stated, are for a one-way, high-season, deck-class single.

Tickets for shorter journeys can be bought at the ticket booths on Molo Beverello, Calata Porta di Massa or at Mergellina. For longer journeys try the offices of the ferry companies or a travel agent.

Hydrofoil and ferry companies are:
Caremar (☑081 551 38 82; www.caremar.it)
Alilauro (☑081 497 22 01; www.alilauro. it) Runs up to five daily hydrofoils between Naples and Sorrento (€12.30, 40 minutes).
SNAV (☑081 428 55 55; www.snav.it)
Medmar (☑081 333 44 11; www.medmar group.it)
Siremar (☑081 497 29 99; www.siremar.it)
Tirrenia (☑892 123; www.tirrenia.it)

BUS

Most national and international buses now leave from **Terminal Bus Metropark** (Map p44; ☑800 650006; Corso Arnaldo Lucci; Ⓜ Garibaldi), located on the south side of Stazione Centrale. The bus station is home to **Biglietteria Vecchione** (☑081 563 03 20; Corso Arnaldo Lucci, Terminal Bus Metropark; ☉6.30am-7.30pm Mon-Sat; Ⓜ Garibaldi), a ticket agency selling national and international bus tickets.

Terminal Bus MetroPark serves numerous bus companies offering regional services, the most useful of which is SITA Sud. Connections from Naples include Amalfi and Positano.

CAR & MOTORCYCLE

Naples is on the Autostrada del Sole, the A1 (north to Rome and Milan) and the A3 (south to Salerno and Reggio di Calabria). The A30 skirts Naples to the northeast, while the A16 heads across the Apennines to Bari.

On approaching the city, the motorways meet the Tangenziale di Napoli, a major ring road around the city. The ring road hugs the city's northern fringe, meeting the A1 for Rome in the east and continuing westwards towards the Campi Flegrei and Pozzuoli.

TRAIN

Naples is southern Italy's rail hub and on the main Milan–Palermo line, with good connections to other Italian cities and towns.

National rail company **Trenitalia** (☑892021; www.trenitalia.com) runs regular services to Rome (2nd class €11.80 to €43, 70 minutes to 2¾ hours, up to 49 daily).

High-speed private rail company **Italo** (☑06 07 08; www.italotreno.it) also runs daily services to Rome (2nd class €15 to €39, 70 minutes, up to 15 daily). Not all Italo services stop at Roma Termini, with many stopping at Roma Tiburtina instead.

Circumvesuviana (☑800 211388; www.eavs rl.it) operates frequent train services to Sorrento (€4.50, 66 minutes) via Ercolano (€2.50, 16 minutes), Pompei (€3.20, 35 minutes) and other towns along the coast, departing from Naples' Porta Nolana and stopping at Piazza Garibaldi station, adjacent to Stazione Centrale.

From late May to October, express tourist train Campania Express runs three times daily between Porta Nolana and Piazza Garibaldi stations in Naples and Sorrento. The only stops en route are Ercolano and Pompei. One-day return tickets (€15, €10 for Artecard holders) can be purchased at the stations, online at www.eavs rl.it or www.campaniartecard/grandtour, or by phone on 800 600 601.

Ferrovia Cumana (www.sepsa.it) trains leave from Stazione Cumana di Montesanto on Piazza Montesanto, 500m southwest of Piazza Dante, running to Pozzuoli (€1.30, 22 minutes, every 20 minutes) and other Campi Flegrei locations beyond, including Lucrino (€2.50, 29 minutes) and Fusaro (€3.20, 33 minutes).

CAMPI FLEGREI

Stretching west of Posillipo Hill to the Tyrrhenian Sea, the Campi Flegrei (Phlegraean or 'Fiery' Fields) is home to some of Campania's most remarkable – and overlooked – Graeco-Roman ruins. Gateway to the area is the port town of Pozzuoli. Established by the Greeks around 530 BC, its most famous resident is the **Anfiteatro Flavio** (☑ 848 80 02 88; Via Nicola Terracciano 75; adult/reduced €4/2; ⊘ 9am-1hr before sunset Wed-Mon; Ⓜ Pozzuoli, � Cumana to Pozzuoli), Italy's third-largest ancient Roman amphitheatre.

A further 6km west, Baia was once a glamorous Roman holiday resort frequented by sun-seeking emperors. Fragments of this opulence linger among the 1st-century ruins of the **Parco Archeologico di Baia** (☑ 081 868 75 92; www.coopculture.it; Via Sella di Baia; adult/reduced €4/2 Sat & Sun, Tue-Fri free; ⊘ varied; 🚊 EAV to Baia, � Cumana to Fusaro), its mosaics, stuccoed *balneum* (bathroom) and imposing Tempio di Mercurio once part of a sprawling palace and spa complex. While the ruins are free on weekdays, weekend visitors need to purchase their tickets at the fascinating **Museo Archeologico dei Campi Flegrei** (Archaeological Museum of the Campi Flegrei; ☑ 081 523 37 97; cir.campania.beniculturali.it/museoarcheologicocampiflegrei; Via Castello 39; admission Sat & Sun €4, Tue-Fri free; ⊘ 9am-2pm Tue-Sun, last entry 1pm; 🚊 EAV to Baia), a further 2km south along the coast.

Yet another 2km south, in the sleepy town of Bacoli, lurks the magical **Piscina Mirabilis** (Marvellous Pool; ☑ 333 6853278; Via Piscina Mirabilis; donation appreciated; ⊘ varied, closed Mon; � Cumana to Fusaro, then EAV bus to Bacoli), the world's largest Roman cistern. You'll need to call the custodian to access the site, but it's well worth the effort. Bathed in an eerie light and featuring 48 soaring pillars and a barrel-vaulted ceiling, the so-called 'Marvellous Pool' is more subterranean cathedral than giant water tank. While entrance is free, show your manners by offering the custodian a €2 or €3 tip.

Both the Ferrovia Cumana and Naples' metro line 2 serve Pozzuoli, and the town is also connected to Ischia and Procida by frequent car and passenger ferries. To reach Baia, take the Ferrovia Cumana train to Fusaro station, walk 150m north, turning right into Via Carlo Vanvitelli (which eventually becomes Via Bellavista). The ruins are 750m to the east. To reach Bacoli, catch a Bacoli-bound EAV Bus from Fusaro.

Unfortunately, the Campi Flegrei's second-rate infrastructure and unreliable public transport, plus the fickle opening times of its sites, make pre-trip planning a good idea. Contact the **tourist office** (☑ 081 526 14 81; www.infocampiflegrei.it; Largo Matteotti 1a; ⊘ 9am-3pm Mon-Fri; Ⓜ Pozzuoli, � Cumana to Pozzuoli) in Pozzuoli for updated information on the area's sights and opening times, or consider exploring the area with popular local tour outfit **Yellow Sudmarine** (p73).

ⓘ Getting Around

TO/FROM THE AIRPORT

Airport shuttle bus Alibus connects the airport to Piazza Garibaldi (Stazione Centrale) and Molo Beverello (€3 from selected tobacconists, €4 on board; 45 minutes; every 20 minutes).

Official taxi fares from the airport are as follows: €23 to a seafront hotel or to Mergellina hydrofoil terminal, €19 to Piazza Municipio or Molo Beverello ferry terminal, and €16 to Stazione Centrale.

BUS

In Naples, buses are operated by city transport company **ANM** (☑ 800 639525; www.anm.it). There's no central bus station, but most buses pass through Piazza Garibaldi.

CAR & MOTORCYCLE

Vehicle theft, anarchic traffic and illegal parking 'attendants' make driving in Naples a bad option. Furthermore, much of the city centre is closed to nonresident traffic for much of the day.

East of the city centre, there's a 24-hour car park at Via Brin (€1.30 for the first four hours, €7.20 for 24 hours).

FUNICULAR

Three services connect central Naples to Vomero, while a fourth connects Mergellina to Posillipo.

METRO

Line 1 Runs from Garibaldi (Stazione Centrale) to Vomero and the northern suburbs via the city centre. Useful stops include:

WORTH A TRIP

REGGIA DI CASERTA

The one compelling reason to stop at the otherwise nondescript town of Caserta, 30km north of Naples, is to gasp at the colossal, World Heritage-listed **Reggia di Caserta** (Palazzo Reale; ☑ 0823 27 71 11; www.reggiadicaserta.beniculturali.it; Viale Douhet 22, Caserta; adult/reduced €12/6; ☺ palace 8.30am-7.30pm Wed-Mon, park 8.30am-1hr before sunset Wed-Mon, Giardino Inglese 8.30am-2hr before sunset Wed-Mon Jun-Aug, reduced hours rest of year; ⓡ Caserta). With film credits including *Mission: Impossible 3* and the interior shots of Queen Amidala's royal residence in *Star Wars Episode 1: The Phantom Menace* and *Star Wars Episode 2: Attack of the Clones*, this former royal residence is Italy's monumental swan song to the baroque. The complex began life in 1752 after Charles VII ordered a palace to rival Versailles. Neapolitan Luigi Vanvitelli was commissioned for the job and built a palace bigger than its French rival. With its 1200 rooms, 1790 windows, 34 staircases and 250m-long facade, it was reputedly the largest building in 18th-century Europe.

Vanvitelli's immense staircase leads up to the royal apartments, lavishly decorated with frescoes, art, tapestries, period furniture and crystal. The apartments are also home to the Mostra Terrea Motus, an underrated collection of international modern art commissioned after the region's devastating earthquake in 1980.

To clear your head afterwards, explore the elegant landscaped park, which stretches for some 3km to a waterfall and fountain of Diana. Within the park is the famous Giardino Inglese (English Garden), a romantic oasis of intricate pathways, exotic flora, pools and cascades. Bicycle hire (€4) is available at the back of the palace building, as are pony and trap rides (€50 per 30 minutes, up to five people).

If you're feeling peckish, consider skipping the touristy palace cafeteria for local cafe **Martucci** (☑ 0823 32 08 03; Via Roma 9, Caserta; pastries from €1.50, sandwiches from €3.50, salads €7.50; ☺ 5am-10.30pm Sun-Thu, to midnight Fri & Sat). Located 250m east of the palace. it has great coffee freshly made *panini* and substantial cooked-to-order meals.

Regular trains connect Naples to Caserta (€3.90, 35 to 50 minutes) from Monday to Saturday, with reduced services on Sunday. Caserta train station is located directly opposite the palace grounds. If you're driving, follow the signs for the Reggia.

Duomo and Università (southern edge of the *centro storico*), Municipio (hydrofoil and ferry terminals), Toledo (Via Toledo and Quartieri Spagnoli), Dante (western edge of the *centro storico*) and Museo (National Archaeological Museum).

Line 2 Runs from Gianturco to Garibaldi (Stazione Centrale) and on to Pozzuoli. Useful stops include: Piazza Cavour (La Sanità and northern edge of *centro storico*), Piazza Amedeo (Chiaia) and Mergellina (Mergellina ferry terminal). Change between lines 1 and 2 at Garibaldi or Piazza Cavour (known as Museo on Line 1).

Line 6 A light-rail service running between Mergellina and Mostra.

TAXI

Official taxis are white and have meters; always ensure the meter is running. There are taxi stands at most of the city's main piazzas or you can call one of the following taxi cooperatives. See the taxi company websites for a comprehensive list of fares.

Consortaxi (☑ 081 22 22; www.consortaxi. com)

Consorzio Taxi Napoli (☑ 081 88 88; www. consorziotaxinapoli.it)

Radio Taxi Napoli (☑ 081 556 44 44; www. radiotaxinapoli.it)

BAY OF NAPLES

Capri

POP 12,200

A stark mass of limestone rock rising sheerly through impossibly blue water, Capri (*capri*) is the perfect microcosm of Mediterranean appeal – a smooth cocktail of vogueish piazzas and cool cafes, Roman ruins, rugged seascapes and holidaying VIPs. While it's also a popular day-trip destination, consider staying a couple of nights to explore beyond Capri Town and its uphill rival Anacapri. It's here, in Capri's hinterland, that the island really seduces with its overgrown vegetable plots, sun-bleached stucco and indescribably beautiful walking trails.

◉ Sights

◉ Capri Town & Around

Whitewashed buildings, labyrinthine lane-ways, and luxe boutiques and cafes: Capri Town personifies upmarket Mediterranean chic.

Piazza Umberto I   PIAZZA
Located beneath the clock tower and framed by see-and-be-seen cafes, this showy, open-air salon is central to your Capri experience, especially in the evening when the main activity in these parts is dressing up and hanging out. Be prepared for the cost of these front-row seats – the moment you sit down for a drink, you're going to pay handsomely for the grand-stand views (around €6 for a coffee and €16 for a couple of glasses of white wine).

Chiesa di Santo Stefano   CHURCH
(Piazza Umberto I; ⊘8am-8pm) Overlooking Piazza Umberto I, this baroque 17th-century church boasts a well-preserved marble floor (taken from Villa Jovis) and a statue of San Costanzo, Capri's patron saint. Note the pair of languidly reclining patricians in the chapel to the south of the main altar, who seem to mirror some of the mildly debauched folk in the cafes outside. Beside the northern chapel is a reliquary with a saintly bone that reputedly saved Capri from the plague in the 19th century.

★ Villa Jovis   RUIN
(Jupiter's Villa; Via A Maiuri; admission €2; ⊘11am-3pm, closed Tue 1st-15th of month, closed Sun rest of month) A 45-minute walk east of Capri along Via Tiberio, Villa Jovis was the largest and most sumptuous of the island's 12 Roman villas and Tiberius' main Capri residence. A vast pleasure complex, now reduced to ruins, it famously pandered to the emperor's debauched tastes, and included imperial quarters and extensive bathing areas set in dense gardens and woodland.

The villa's spectacular location posed major headaches for Tiberius' architects. The main problem was how to collect and store enough water to supply the villa's baths and 3000-sq-metre gardens. The solution they eventually hit upon was to build a complex canal system to transport rainwater to four giant storage tanks, whose remains you can still see today.

The stairway behind the villa leads to the 330m-high **Salto di Tiberio** (Tiberius' Leap), a sheer cliff from where, as the story goes, Tiberius had out-of-favour subjects hurled into the sea. True or not, the stunning views are real enough; if you suffer from vertigo, tread carefully.

A shortish but steep walk from the villa, down Via Tiberio and Via Matermània, is the **Arco Naturale** – a huge rock arch formed by the pounding sea; you can time this walk to take in lunch at cave restaurant **Le Grotelle** (⊘081 837 57 19; Via Arco Naturale 13; meals around €28; ⊘noon-2.30pm & 7-11pm Jul & Aug, noon-2.30pm & 7-11pm Fri-Wed Jun & Sep, noon-2.30pm Fri-Wed Apr, May & Oct).

Certosa di San Giacomo   MONASTERY
(⊘081 837 62 18; Viale Certosa 40; admission €4; ⊘9am-2pm Tue-Sun, plus 5-8pm summer) Founded in 1363, this picturesque monastery is generally considered to be the finest remaining example of Caprese architecture and today houses a school, a library, a temporary exhibition space and a museum with some evocative 17th-century paintings. Be sure to look at the two cloisters, which have a real sense of faded glory (the smaller is 14th century, the larger 16th century).

To get here take Via Vittorio Emanuele, east of Piazza Umberto I, which meanders down to the monastery.

Giardini di Augusto   GARDENS
(Gardens of Augustus; admission €1; ⊘9am-1hr before sunset) Escape the crowds by seeking out these colourful gardens near the Certosa di San Giacomo. Founded by Emperor Augustus, they rise in a series of flowered terraces to a lookout point offering breathtaking views over to the **Isole Faraglioni**, a group of three limestone stacks that rise out of the sea.

◉ Anacapri & Around

Delve beyond the Villa San Michele di Axel Munthe and the souvenir stores and you'll discover that Capri Town's more subdued sibling is, at heart, the laid-back rural village that it's always been.

★ Seggiovia del Monte Solaro   CABLE CAR
(⊘081 837 14 38; www.capriseggiovia.it; single/return €7.50/10; ⊘9.30am-5pm summer, to 3.30pm winter) A fast and painless way to reach Capri's highest peak, Anacapri's Seggiovia del Monte Solaro chairlift whisks you

Capri

Enlargement

Piazza
Umberto I

Via Vittorio
Emanuele III

Vico Sella
Orta

Via Roma

Via Longano

20 17
15
5 23
22

100 m
0.05 miles

Punta del
Capo

Villa
Jovis

Salto di
Tiberio

Punta
Massullo

Pizzolungo

Porto di
Tragara

Scoglio del
Monacone

Punta di
Tragara

Monte
Tuoro (261m)

19

3

Via Tiberio

Marina di
Cuterola

Via
Camerelle

Via Tuoro

Via Tragara

Gulf of Naples
(Golfo di Napoli)

See Enlargement

CAPRI
TOWN

14
18 24
4
6

Isole
Faraglioni

La Fontelina

Scoglio
dell'Unghia Marina

Gulf of Salerno
(Golfo di Salerno)

Bagno di
Tiberio

Via Marina Grande

Via Roma

Via Marina Piccola

Torre
Saracena

Bagni di
Gioia

Scoglio
delle Sirene

Punta di
Mulo

10

11

Via Provinciale Anacapri

Monte
Santa Maria
(498m)

Santa
Maria a Cetrella

Monte
Cappello
(514m)

Monte Solaro
(589m)

Tyrrhenian Sea

Punta
Ventroso

Via Seggiovia del Monte Solaro

Via de Tommaso

Seggiovia (Funicular)

Piazzetta
Cimitero

Bagno di
Tiberio

25 9
12
1

ANACAPRI

Piazza
Giuseppe
Vittoria

Via Giuseppe
Orlandi

Piazza
Diaz

Via Tuoro

21
13

Via Pagliaro

Via La Fabbrica

16

Via Miglera

Migliera
(304m)

Punta del
Tuono

Cala
Marmolata

Punta del'Arcera

Via Grotta Azzurra

7

Sentiero dei Fortini

Via Nuove del Faro

Cala del
Rio

Cala del
Tombosiello

Lido del
Faro

Punta Carena

Tyrrhenian Sea

1 km
0.5 miles

N

Capri

◎ Top Sights
1 Seggiovia del Monte Solaro...................C2
2 Villa Jovis G1

◎ Sights
3 Arco Naturale F2
4 Certosa di San Giacomo E3
5 Chiesa di Santo Stefano G4
6 Giardini di Augusto E3
7 Grotta Azzurra B1
8 Piazza Umberto I G4
9 Villa San Michele di Axel Munthe C1

◉ Activities, Courses & Tours
10 Banana Sport E1
11 Sercomar E1

◎ Sleeping
12 Capri Palace C1
13 Casa Mariantonia......................................C2

14 Grand Hotel Quisisana............................E2
15 Hotel Gatto Bianco G4
16 Hotel Villa Eva B1

◎ Eating
17 È Divino G4
18 Il Geranio E2
La Rondinella..................................(see 13)
19 Le Grottelle..F2
20 Raffaele Buonacore G4

◎ Drinking & Nightlife
21 Caffè Michelangelo C2
22 Pulalli..G4
23 Taverna Anema e Core G4

◎ Shopping
24 Carthusia I Profumi di Capri E2
25 Limoncello di Capri C1

to the top of the mountain in a beautiful ride of just 12 minutes. The views from the top are outstanding – on a clear day, you can see the entire Bay of Naples, the Amalfi Coast and the islands of Ischia and Procida.

Villa San Michele di Axel Munthe
MUSEUM, GARDENS

(☑081 837 14 01; www.villasanmichele.eu; Via Axel Munthe 34; admission €7; ☺9am-6pm summer, reduced hours rest of year) The former home of Swedish doctor, psychiatrist and animal-rights advocate Axel Munthe, San Michele di Axel Munthe should be included on every visitor's itinerary. Built on the site of the ruins of a Roman villa, the gardens make a beautiful setting for a tranquil stroll, with pathways flanked by immaculate flowerbeds. There are also superb views from here, plus some fine photo props in the form of Roman sculptures.

If you are here between July and September, you may be able to catch one of the classical concerts that take place in the gardens. Check the Axel Munthe Foundation website (www.sanmichele.org) for the current program and reservation information.

🏃 Activities

★ Banana Sport
BOATING

(☑081 837 51 88; Marina Grande; 2hr/day rental €90/200; ☺May-Sep) Located on the eastern edge of the waterfront, Banana Sport hires out five-person motorised dinghies, allowing you to explore secluded coves and grottoes. You can also visit the popular swimming spot **Bagno di Tiberio** (€10), a small inlet west of Marina Grande; it's said that Tiberius once swam here.

Sercomar
DIVING

(☑081 837 87 81; www.capriseaservice.com; Via Colombo 64, Marina Grande; ☺Apr-Oct; ⚑) Sercomar offers various diving packages costing from €100 for a single dive (maximum of three people) to €150 for an individual dive and €350 for a four-session beginner's course. It also organises children's snorkelling classes from €35 for 30 minutes (12 years and over).

🛌 Sleeping

Capri's accommodation is top-heavy, with plenty of four- and five-star hotels and fewer budget options. As a general rule, the further you go from Capri Town, the less you'll pay. Camping is forbidden.

Always book ahead. Hotel space is at a premium during the summer, and many places close in winter, typically between November and March.

★ Hotel Villa Eva
HOTEL €€

(☑081 837 15 49; www.villaeva.com; Via La Fabbrica 8; d €110-180, tr €160-210, apt per person €55-70; ☺Easter-Oct; ❈@🛜🏊⚑) Nestled amid fruit and olive trees in the countryside near Anacapri, Villa Eva is an idyllic retreat, complete with swimming pool, lush gardens and

GROTTA AZZURRA

Glowing in an ethereal blue light, the bewitching **Grotta Azzurra** (Blue Grotto; admission €13; ⊗9am-1hr before sunset) is Capri's most famous single attraction.

The grotto had long been known to local fishermen when it was rediscovered by two Germans – writer Augustus Kopisch and painter Ernst Fries – in 1826. Subsequent research, however, revealed that Emperor Tiberius had built a quay in the cave around AD 30, complete with a nymphaeum. Remarkably, you can still see the carved Roman landing stage towards the rear of the cave.

Measuring 54m by 30m and rising to a height of 15m, the grotto is said to have sunk by up to 20m in prehistoric times, blocking every opening except the 1.3m-high entrance. And this is the key to the magical blue light. Sunlight enters through a small underwater aperture and is refracted through the water; this, combined with the reflection of the light off the white sandy seafloor, produces the vivid blue effect to which the cave owes its name.

The easiest way to visit is to take a **tour** (☑081 837 56 46; www.motoscafisticapri.com; Private Pier 0, Marina Grande; tickets online €12, in person €14) from Marina Grande; tickets include the return boat trip and a rowing boat into the cave, with the admission fee paid separately. Allow a good hour.

The grotto is closed if the sea is too choppy and swimming in it is forbidden, although you can swim outside the entrance – get a bus to Grotta Azzurra, take the stairs down to the right and dive off the small concrete platform. When visiting, keep in mind that the singing 'captains' are included in the price, so don't feel any obligation if they push for a tip.

sunny rooms and apartments. Whitewashed domes, terracotta floors, stained-glass windows and vintage fireplaces add character, while the location ensures peace and quiet.

The only drawback is that it's tricky to get to: take the Grotta Azzurra bus from Anacapri and ask the driver where to get off, or cough up for a taxi.

Hotel Gatto Bianco   HOTEL €€

(☑081 837 51 43; www.gattobianco-capri.com; Via Vittoria Emanuele III 32; s €100-170, d €150-230; ⊗Apr-Nov; ✴@🛜) This gracious hotel dates from 1953 and boasts leafy courtyards and terraces and a fluffy white cat – presumably from a long lineage. The light-filled rooms are decorated in traditional style with stunning blue-and-yellow majolica tiling, a tasteful colour scheme and verdant views.

Casa Mariantonia   BOUTIQUE HOTEL €€

(☑081 837 29 23; www.casamariantonia.com; Via Guiseppe Orlandi 80; d €120-280; ⊗Apr-Oct; P✴🛜🏊) This fabulous boutique retreat counts Jean-Paul Sartre and Alberto Moravia among its past guests, which may well give you something to muse over while you are enjoying the tranquil beauty of the surroundings. Rooms deliver restrained elegance in soothing tones and there are

private terraces with garden views. The in-house restaurant is set in a lemon grove.

Grand Hotel Quisisana   HOTEL €€€

(☑081 837 07 88; www.quisi.com; Via Camerelle 2; r/ste from €330/850; ⊗Easter-Oct; ✴🛜🏊) Boasting a five-star luxury rating, the Quisisana is Capri's most prestigious address and just few espadrille-clad steps from La Piazzetta (Piazza Umberto I). A hotel since the 19th century, it's a bastion of unapologetic opulence, with two swimming pools, a fitness centre and spa, restaurants, bars and subtropical gardens. Rooms are suitably palatial, with cool colour schemes and classy furniture.

Capri Palace   HOTEL €€€

(☑081 978 01 11; www.capripalace.com; Via Capodimonte 2b; d/ste from €500/1000; ⊗Apr-Oct; ✴🛜🏊) A VIP favourite (Gwyneth Paltrow, Liz Hurley and Naomi Campbell have all chilled here), the super-slick Capri Palace is the hotel of the moment. Its stylish Mediterranean interior is enlivened with eye-catching contemporary art and its guest rooms are never less than lavish – some even have their own terraced garden and private plunge pool.

For stressed guests, the health spa is said to be the island's best. Note that there's a three-night minimum stay in high season.

Eating

Many restaurants, like the hotels, close over winter.

Raffaele Buonacore FAST FOOD €
(☑081 837 78 26; Via Vittorio Emanuele III 35; snacks €1-6; ⓢ6am-5pm Mar-Oct; ♠) Ideal for a quick fill-up, this popular and down-to-earth snack bar does a roaring trade in savoury and sweet treats, including frittatas, *panini* (sandwiches), pastries, waffles and legendary ice cream. Hard to beat, though, are the delicious *sfogliatelle* (cinnamon-infused ricotta in a puff-pastry shell, €1) and the feather-light speciality *caprilu al limone* (lemon and almond cakes).

★ È Divino ITALIAN €
(☑081 837 83 64; Vico Sella Orta; meals €20; ⓢ1-3pm & 7.30pm-midnight Tue-Sun) Look hard for the sign: this slow-food restaurant is a well-kept secret. Step inside and you find yourself in what resembles a traditional sitting room; the only hints that this is a restaurant are the tantalising aromas and the distant tinkle of glasses. The menu changes daily, according to whatever is fresh from the garden or market.

La Rondinella ITALIAN €€
(☑081 837 12 23; www.ristorantepizzerialarondinella.com; Via Guiseppe Orlandi 295; meals €30; ⓢnoon-2.30pm & 7-11.30pm Fri-Mon) La Rondinella has a relaxed, rural feel and remains one of Anacapri's better restaurants; apparently Graham Greene had a favourite corner table here. The menu features a number of Italian classics such as *saltimbocca alla romana* (veal slices with ham and sage).

Il Geranio SEAFOOD €€€
(☑081 837 06 16; www.geraniocapri.com; Via G Matteotti 8; meals €50; ⓢnoon-3pm & 7-11.30pm Apr-Oct) Time to pop the question, celebrate an anniversary or quell those pre-departure blues? The terrace here has stunning views over the pine trees to the sea and beyond to the extraordinary Isole di Faraglioni rocks. Seafood is the house speciality, particularly the salt-baked fish. Other good choices include octopus salad and linguini with saffron and mussels. Dress to impress.

NAPLES & CAMPANIA CAPRI

OFF THE BEATEN TRACK

SOOTHING ISLAND HIKES

Away from the boutiques, yachts and bikinis, Capri offers some soul-lifting hikes. Favourite routes include from Arco Naturale to the Punta dell'Arcera (1.2km, 1¼ hours), best tackled in this direction to avoid a final climb up to Arco Naturale. Another popular route is from Anacapri to Monte Solaro (2km, two hours), the island's highest point. If you don't fancy an upward trek, take the *seggiovia* (chairlift) up and walk down.

Running along the island's oft-over-looked western coast, the Sentiero dei Fortini (Path of the Small Forts; 5.2km, three hours), which connects Punta dell'Arcera near the Grotta Azzurra to Punta Carena, promises more bucolic bliss. For the best effect, start at Punta dell'Arcera so you can end your hike with sunset drinks at Punta Carena. Capri's tourist offices can provide information and maps of the island's various trails.

🍷 Drinking & Nightlife

Capri's nightlife is a showy business. The main activity is dressing up and hanging out, ideally at one of the cafes on La Piazzetta (Piazza Umberto 1). Aside from the cafes, the nightlife here is fairly staid, with surprisingly few nightclubs, given the penchant for the locals to glitz up and strut their stuff.

Pulalli WINE BAR
(☑081 837 41 08; Piazza Umberto I, Capri Town; ⓢnoon-3pm & 7pm-11.30pm daily Aug, closed Tue Sep-Jul) Climb the clock-tower steps to the right of the tourist office and your reward is this lofty local hang-out where fabulous wine meets a discerning selection of cheese, charcuterie, and more substantial fare such as *risotto al limone* (lemon risotto). Try for a seat on the terrace or, best of all, the coveted table on its own balcony.

Caffè Michelangelo CAFE
(Via Giuseppe Orlandi 138, Anacapri; ⓢ8am-1am) It's not that flashy, but the position of the delightful Caffè Michelangelo, on a street flanked by tasteful shops and near two lovely piazzas, makes it a perfect spot for indulging in a little people-watching-and-cocktail-sipping time. Large, cushioned chairs and a raised terrace add to the kick-back appeal.

Taverna Anema e Core
CLUB

(☑ 081 837 64 61; www.anemaecore.com; Vico Sella Orta 39E, Capri Town; ☺noon-11pm Apr-Oct) Lying beyond a humble exterior is one of the island's most famous nightspots, run by the charismatic Guido Lembo. This smooth and sophisticated bar-club attracts an appealing mix of super-chic and casually dressed punters, here for the relaxed atmosphere and regular live music, including unwaveringly authentic Neapolitan guitar strumming and singing.

 Shopping

If you're not in the market for a new Rolex or Prada bag, look out for ceramic work, lemon-scented perfume and *limoncello* (lemon liqueur). For perfume don't miss **Carthusia I Profumi di Capri** (☑081 837 53 35; www. carthusia.it; Via F Serena 28, Capri Town; ☺9am-6pm) in Capri Town; for *limoncello* head up to Anacapri and **Limoncello di Capri** (☑081 837 29 27; www.limoncello.com; Via Capodimonte 27, Anacapri; ☺9am-7.30pm).

If you *are* in the market for a new Rolex or Prada bag, head to Via Vittorio Emanuele and Via Camerelle.

ℹ **Information**

Post Office (Via Roma 50; ☺8am-6.30pm Mon-Fri, to 12.30pm Sat)
Tourist Office (☑081 837 06 34; www. capritourism.com; Banchina del Porto, Marina Grande) Can provide a map of the island (€1) with town plans of Capri and Anacapri. For hotel listings and other useful information, ask for a free copy of *Capri è*.

RESOURCES

Capri (www.capri.com) User-friendly site covering everything from hotel bookings and attractions to ferry times.
Capri Tourism (www.capritourism.com) Official website of Capri's tourist office.

ℹ **Getting There & Away**

See Naples, Sorrento and specific Amalfi Coast towns for details of ferries and hydrofoils to the island.

Note that some companies require you to pay a small supplement for luggage, typically around €2.

ℹ **Getting Around**

BUS

Sippic (☑081 837 04 20; Bus Station, Via Roma, Capri Town; tickets €1.80) Runs regular buses to/from Marina Grande, Anacapri and Marina Piccola. It also operates buses from Marina Grande to Anacapri and from Marina Piccola to Anacapri.

Staiano Autotrasporti (☑081 837 24 22; www.staianotourcapri.com; Bus Station, Via Tommaso, Anacapri; tickets €1.80, day tickets €8.60) Buses serve the Grotta Azzurra and Faro of Punta Carena.

SCOOTER

Ciro dei Motorini (☑081 837 80 18; www. capriscooter.com; Via Marina Grande 55, Marina Grande; per 2/24hr €30/65) For scooter hire at Marina Grande, stop here.

FUNICULAR

Funicular (tickets €1.80; ☺6.30am-12.30am) Connects Marina Grande to Capri Town. Single tickets cost €1.80.

TAXI

From Marina Grande, a **taxi** (☑ in Anacapri 081 837 11 75, in Capri Town 081 837 66 57) costs around €20 to Capri and €25 to Anacapri; from Capri to Anacapri costs about €20.

Ischia

POP 62,200

Sprawling over 46 sq km, Ischia (iss-*kyah*) is the biggest and busiest island in the bay. It's a lush concoction of sprawling spa towns, mud-wrapped Germans and ancient relics. Also famous for its thermal waters, it has some fine beaches and spectacular scenery.

Most visitors stay on the touristy north coast, but go inland and you'll find a rural landscape of chestnut forests, dusty farms and earthy hillside villages.

◎ **Sights**

★**Castello Aragonese**
CASTLE

(Aragon Castle; ☑081 991 959, 081 992 834; Rocca del Castello, Ischia Ponte; adult/reduced €10/6; ☺9am-90min before sunset) The elegant 15th-century Ponte Aragonese connects Ischia Ponte to Castello Aragonese, a sprawling, magnificent castle perched high and mighty on a rocky islet. While Syracusan tyrant Gerone I built the site's first fortress in 474 BC, the bulk of the current structure dates from the 1400s, when King Alfonso of Aragon gave the older Angevin fortress a thorough makeover, building the fortified bastions, current causeway and access ramp cut into the rock.

★**La Mortella**   GARDENS

(Place of the Myrtles; ☑ 081 98 62 20; www.lamor
tella.it; Via F Calese 39, Forio; adult/reduced €12/7;
☺ 9am-7pm Tue, Thu, Sat & Sun Apr-early Nov) Designed by Russell Page and inspired by the
Moorish gardens of Spain's Alhambra, La
Mortella is recognised as one of Italy's finest
botanical gardens and is well worth a couple
of hours of your time. Stroll among terraces, pools, palms, fountains and more than
1000 rare and exotic plants from all over
the world. The lower section of the garden
is humid and tropical, while the upper level
features Mediterranean plants.

Activities

Unlike Capri, Ischia has some great beaches.
From chic Sant'Angelo on the south coast,
water taxis reach the sandy **Spiaggia dei
Maronti** and the intimate cove of **Il Sorgeto**
(Via Sorgeto; ☺ Apr-Oct), with its steamy thermal spring. Sorgeto can also be reached on
foot down a poorly signposted path from the
village of Panza.

★**Negombo**   SPA

(☑ 081 98 61 52; www.negombo.it; Baia di San
Montano, Lacco Ameno; admission all day €32, from
2pm €20; ☺ 8.30am-7pm late Apr-Oct) This is the
place to come for a dose of pampering. Part
spa resort, part botanical wonderland, with
more than 500 exotic plant species, Negombo's combination of Zen-like thermal pools,
hammam, contemporary sculpture and
private beach on the Baia di San Montano
tends to draw a younger crowd than many
other Ischian spa spots.

Geo-Ausfluge   HIKING

(Geo-Ausfluge; ☑ English spoken 081 90 30 58;
www.eurogeopark.com; walks €17-26) Unlike
Capri and Procida, Ischia is not easily accessible to hikers. If you're interested in exploring the hinterland, Italian geologist Aniello
Di Lorio conducts a selection of walks
throughout the island ranging from three to
five hours, including lunch, with various collection points in Ischia; pick up in Casamicciola and Panza costs a further €9 return.

Ischia Diving   DIVING

(☑ 081 98 18 52; www.ischiadiving.net; Via Iasolino
106, Ischia Porto; single dive €40) This well-
established diving outfit offers some attrac-
tively priced dive packages, like five dives
including equipment for €185.

Sleeping

Most hotels close in winter and prices normally drop considerably among those that
stay open.

Hotel Noris   HOTEL €

(☑ 081 99 13 87; www.norishotel.it; Via A Sogliuzzo 2, Ischia Ponte; d €50-85; ☺ Easter-Oct; ✳ 🛜)
This place has a great price and a great position within easy strolling distance of the
Ponte sights. The comfy, decent-size rooms
have small balconies and are decked out
in fresh colours. Breakfast is the standard,
albeit slightly more expansive, Continental
buffet. Bonus points are due for the special
parking deal with the public car park across
the way.

Camping Mirage   CAMPGROUND €

(☑ 081 99 05 51; www.campingmirage.it; Via
Maronti 37, Spiaggia dei Maronti, Barano d'Ischia;
camping per 2 people, car & tent €45; ☺ Easter-Oct;
🅿 🚿) Located on Spiagga dei Maronti, one
of Ischia's best beaches, and within walking
distance of Sant'Angelo, this shady campground offers 50 places, showers, laundry
facilities, a bar and a restaurant dishing
up local special *tubettoni, cozze e pecorino*
(pasta with mussels and sheep's cheese).

Albergo il Monastero   HOTEL €€

(☑ 081 99 24 35; www.albergoilmonastero.it; Castello Aragonese, Rocca del Castello, Ischia Ponte; s
€90, d €135-190; ☺ Easter-Oct; ✳) The former
monks' cells still have a certain appealing
sobriety about them, featuring dark-wood
furniture, white walls, vintage terracotta
tiles and no TV (don't worry – the views are
sufficiently prime time). Elsewhere there
is a pleasing sense of space and style, with
vaulted ceilings, chic plush sofas and antiques. The hotel restaurant has an excellent
reputation.

★**Hotel Semiramis**   HOTEL €€

(☑ 081 90 75 11; www.hotelsemiramisischia.it;
Spiaggia di Citara, Forio; d €140-180; ☺ late Apr-
Oct; 🅿 ✳ 🛜 🏊) A few minutes' walk from the
Poseidon spa complex, this bright hotel has
a tropical-oasis feel with its central pool surrounded by lofty palms. Rooms are large and
beautifully tiled in the traditional yellow-
and-turquoise pattern, and the garden is
glorious, featuring fig trees, vineyards and
distant sea views.

WORTH A TRIP

IL FOCOLARE: A SLOW FOOD WONDER

Tucked away in the hills above Casamicciola Terme is one restaurant verified foodies cannot afford to miss – Il Focolare (☑ 081 90 29 44; www.trattoriailfocolare.it; Via Creajo al Crocefisso 3, Barano d'Ischia; meals €30; ⊙12.30-2.45pm & 7.30-11.30pm Jun-Oct, 12.30-2.45pm Wed, 7.30-11.30pm Sat & Sun Nov-May). Forget *spaghetti alle vongole* (spaghetti with clams) – this proud Slow Food stalwart celebrates all things turf. Indeed, it's one of the best spots to savour the island's legendary *coniglio all'Ischitana* (a claypot-cooked local rabbit with garlic, onion, tomatoes, wild thyme and white wine), a dish that needs to be booked two days in advance.

If you haven't pre-ordered the rabbit, don't fret – the daily menu brims with beautiful, seasonal dishes, from *tagliatelle al ragù di cinghiale* (ribbon-shaped pasta with wild boar ragout) to a sublime *antipasto misto*, where you might get anything from *rotolino di zucchini* (fried, bread-crumbed zucchini filled with buffalo mozzarella) to *terrina di parmigiano tartufata con i funghi* (think porcini-mushroom crème brûlée).

To get here, catch bus 16 from Piazza Marina in Casamicciola Terme and ask the driver to let you off at the restaurant (it's the last stop). From June to November, the last bus back to town departs at around 12.40am; from December to May the last service departs at 7.30pm.

✖ Eating

Seafood aside, Ischia is famed for its rabbit, which is bred on inland farms. Another local speciality is *rucolino* – a green liquorice-flavoured liqueur made from *rucola* (rocket).

★ Montecorvo   ITALIAN €€

(☑ 081 99 80 29; www.montecorvo.it; Via Montecorvo 33, Forio; meals €30; ⊙12.30-3.30pm & 7.30pm-1am, closed lunch Jul & Aug) At this extraordinary place part of the dining room is tunnelled into a cave and the terrace looks as though it belongs in a jungle. Owner Giovanni prides himself on the special dishes he makes daily, with an emphasis on grilled meat and fish, and the menu also includes a good range of pasta and vegetable antipasti.

You will need more than a good compass to find this spot, hidden amid lush foliage outside Forio and fronted by pines, a waterfall and steep steps. Fortunately, it is well signposted.

Ristorante da Ciccio   ITALIAN €€

(☑ 081 99 16 86; Via Luigi Mazzella 32, Ischia Ponte; meals €25; ⊙noon-3.30pm & 7.30-11.30pm, closed Tue Dec-Feb) Sublime seafood and charming host Carlo make this atmospheric place a winner. Highlights include *tubattone* pasta with clams and pecorino cheese, a zesty mussel soup topped with fried bread and *peperoncino* (chilli), and a delicious chocolate and almond cake. Tables spill out onto the pavement in summer, from where there are fabulous castle views.

Ristorante Pietratorcia   ITALIAN €€

(☑ 081 90 72 32; www.ristorantepietratorcia. it; Via Provinciale Panza 267, Forio; set menu from €28; ⊙11am-11pm Tue-Sun Apr-Oct) Enjoying a bucolic setting among tumbling vines, wild fig trees and rosemary bushes, this A-list winery is a foodie's nirvana. Tour the old stone cellars, sip a local drop and eye up the delectable degustation menu. Offerings include fragrant bruschetta and cheeses, hearty Campanian sausages and spicy *salumi* (charcuterie).

❶ Information

Ischia Online (www.ischiaonline.it) Good all-around website including sights, hotels and ferry times.

Tourist Office (☑ 081 507 42 11; www.infoischiaprocida.it; Corso Sogliuzzo 72, Ischia Porto; ⊙9am-2pm & 3-8pm Mon-Sat) A slim selection of maps and brochures.

❶ Getting There & Away

Regular hydrofoils and ferries run to/from Naples. You can also catch hydrofoils direct to Capri (€19.80, 50 minutes). Ischia is also connected to Procida by hydrofoil (€8 to €9.20, 15 minutes) and ferry (€7.10, 15 to 30 minutes).

❶ Getting Around

The island's main bus station is located in Ischia Porto. There are two principal lines: the CS (Circolo Sinistro, or Left Circle), which circles the island anticlockwise, and the CD line (Circolo Destro, or Right Circle), which travels in a clockwise direction, passing through each town and departing every 30 minutes. Buses pass near all hotels and campsites. A single ticket, valid for 90 minutes, costs €1.90; an all-day, multi-use ticket is €6; a two-day ticket €10; three days €13; and one week €26. Taxis and micro-taxis (scooter-engined three-wheelers) are also available.

You can do this small island a favour by not bringing your car. If you want to hire a car or a scooter for a day, there are plenty of hire companies. **Balestrieri** (081 98 56 91; www.autonoleggiobalestrieri.it; Via Iasolino 35, Ischia Porto) hires out cars and scooters (per day/week €20/140) and they also have mountain bikes (€15 per day). You can't take a hired vehicle off the island.

Procida

POP 10,800

Dig out your paintbox: the Bay of Naples' smallest island (and its best-kept secret) is a soulful blend of hidden lemon groves, weathered fishing folk and pastel-hued houses. August aside – when beach-bound mainlanders flock to its shores – its narrow sun-bleached streets are the domain of the locals.

Sights & Activities

The best way to explore the island (a mere 4 sq km) is on foot or by bike. However, the island's narrow roads can be clogged with cars – one of its few drawbacks.

From panoramic Piazza dei Martiri, the village of **Corricella** tumbles down to its marina in a riot of pinks, yellows and whites. Further south, a steep flight of steps leads down to **Chiaia** beach, one of the island's most beautiful.

All pink, white and blue, little **Marina di Chiaiolella** has a yacht-stocked marina, old-school eateries and a languid disposition. Nearby, the **Lido** is a popular beach.

Abbazia di San Michele Arcangelo   CHURCH, MUSEUM
(334 8514028, 334 8514252; associazionemillennium@virgilio.it; Via Terra Murata 89, Terra Murata; admission €3; ⊙10am-1pm & 3-6pm) Soak in the dizzying bay views at the belvedere before exploring the adjoining Abbazia di San Michele Arcangelo. Built in the 11th century and remodelled between the 17th and 19th centuries, this one-time Benedictine abbey houses a small museum with some arresting pictures done in gratitude by shipwrecked sailors, plus a church with a spectacular coffered ceiling and an ancient Greek alabaster

basin converted into a font, and a maze of catacombs that leads to a tiny secret chapel.

Barobe & Gommoni   BICYCLE RENTAL
(339 7163303; Via Roma 134, Marina Grande; per day €10;) The bicycles for hire here are one of the best ways to explore the island. Small, open micro-taxis can also be hired for two to three hours for around €35, depending on your bargaining prowess.

Blue Dream Yacht Charter Boating BOATING
(339 5720874, 081 896 05 79; www.bluedreamcharter.com; Via Vittorio Emanuele 14, Marina Grande; per week from €1500) If you have 'champagne on the deck' aspirations, you can always charter your very own yacht from here. Sleeps six.

Festivals & Events

Procession of the Misteri   RELIGIOUS
Good Friday sees a colourful procession when a wooden statue of Christ and the Madonna Addolorata, along with life-size plaster and papier-mâché tableaux illustrating events leading to Christ's crucifixion, are carted across the island. Men dress in blue tunics with white hoods, while many of the young girls dress as the Madonna.

Sleeping

Bed & Breakfast La Terrazza   B&B €
(081 896 00 62; Via Faro 26, Marina Grande; s €50-70, d €75-90; ⊙Easter-Oct) An extremely attractive budget option, where the rooms are decked out with paintings, metal lamps, tiles and antiques. Take time out on the terracotta-floored terrace – thus the B&B's name – where you can lie back on a lounger and enjoy the sunset. Homemade breakfasts are served up here.

★Hotel La Vigna   BOUTIQUE HOTEL €€
(081 896 04 69; www.albergolavigna.it; Via Principessa Margherita 46, Terra Murata; d €150-180, ste €180-230; ⊙Easter-Oct; ❀@⊛) Enjoying a fabulous cliff-side location with a delightful garden and in-house spa, this 18th-century villa is a delight. Five of the spacious, simply furnished rooms offer direct access to the garden. Superior rooms (€180 to €200) feature family-friendly mezzanines, while the main perk of the suite is the bedside hot tub: perfect for romancing couples.

Casa Sul Mare   HOTEL €€
(081 896 87 99; www.lacasasulmare.it; Salita Castello 13, Marina Corricella; r €125-170;

⊙ Easter-Oct; ❀ 🛜) A fabulous place with the kind of evocative views that helped make *The Talented Mr Ripley* such a memorable film. Overlooking the picturesque Marina Corricella, near the ruined Castello d'Avalos, the rooms are elegant, with exquisite tiled floors, wrought-iron bedsteads and a warm Mediterranean colour scheme.

Eating

Da Giorgio
TRATTORIA €

(☑ 081 896 79 10; Via Roma 36, Marina Grande; meals €18; ⊙ noon-3pm & 7-11.30pm Mar-Oct; 🖟) These folks try hard to please, with a reasonably priced menu, welcoming window boxes and inexpensive beer. The menu holds few surprises, but the ingredients are fresh; try the *antipasto di mare* (€10) or *gnocchi alla sorrentina* (gnocchi in a tomato, basil and pecorino cheese sauce).

Fammivento
SEAFOOD €€

(☑ 081 896 90 20; Via Roma 39, Marina Grande; meals €25; ⊙ noon-12.30am Tue-Sat, noon-3pm Sun Apr-Oct) Get things going with the *frittura di calamari* (fried squid), then try the *fusilli carciofi e calamari* (pasta with artichokes and calamari). For a splurge, go for the house speciality of *zuppa di crostaci e moluschi* (crustacean and mollusc soup).

❶ Information

Pro Loco (☑ 081 810 19 68; www.proloco procida.it; Via Roma, Stazione Marittima, Marina Grande; ⊙ 9.30am-6pm) Located at the Ferry & Hydrofoil Ticket Office, this modest office has sparse information but should be able to advise on activities and the like.

❶ Getting There & Around

Procida is linked to Ischia by ferry (€7.10, 15 to 30 minutes) and hydrofoil (€8 to €9.20, 15 minutes). Ferries run to Pozzuoli (€7, 20 minutes) and both ferries and hydrofoils sail to Naples.

There is a limited bus service (€1), with four lines radiating from Marina Grande. Bus L1 connects the port and Via Marina di Chiaiolella.

SOUTH OF NAPLES

Ercolano & Herculaneum

Ercolano is an uninspiring Neapolitan suburb that's home to one of Italy's best-preserved ancient sites: Herculaneum. A superbly conserved Roman fishing town, Herculaneum is smaller and less daunting than Pompeii, allowing you to visit without that nagging itch that you're bound to miss something.

⊙ Sights

★ Ruins of Herculaneum
ARCHAEOLOGICAL SITE

(☑ 081 732 43 27; www.pompeiisites.org; Corso Resina 187, Ercolano; adult/reduced €11/5.50, incl Pompeii €20/10; ⊙ 8.30am-7.30pm summer, to 5pm winter; ☒ Circumvesuviana to Ercolano-Scavi) Upstaged by its larger rival, Pompeii, Herculaneum harbours a wealth of archaeological finds, from ancient advertisements and stylish mosaics to carbonised furniture and terror-struck skeletons. Indeed, this superbly conserved Roman fishing town of 4000 inhabitants is easier to navigate than Pompeii, and can be explored with a map and audioguide (€6.50).

From the site's main gateway on Corso Resina, head down the walkway to the ticket office (at the bottom on your left). Ticket purchased, follow the walkway to the actual entrance to the ruins (*scavi*).

Herculaneum's fate runs parallel to that of Pompeii. Destroyed by an earthquake in AD 62, the AD 79 eruption of Mt Vesuvius saw it submerged in a 16m-thick sea of mud that essentially fossilised the city. This meant that even delicate items, such as furniture and clothing, were discovered remarkably well preserved. Tragically, the inhabitants didn't fare so well; thousands of people tried to escape by boat but were suffocated by the volcano's poisonous gases. Indeed, what appears to be a moat around the town is in fact the ancient shoreline. It was here in 1980 that archaeologists discovered some 300 skeletons, the remains of a crowd that had fled to the beach only to be overcome by the terrible heat of clouds surging down from Vesuvius.

The town itself was rediscovered in 1709 and amateur excavations were carried out intermittently until 1874, with many finds carted off to Naples to decorate the houses of the well-to-do or ending up in museums. Serious archaeological work began again in 1927 and continues to this day, although with much of the ancient site buried beneath modern Ercolano it's slow going. Indeed, note that at any given time some houses will invariably be shut for restoration.

➡ Casa d'Argo

(Argus House) This noble house would originally have opened onto Cardo II (as yet unearthed). Onto its porticoed, palm-treed garden open a *triclinium* (dining room) and other residential rooms.

➡ Casa dello Scheletro

(House of the Skeleton) The modest Casa dello Scheletro features five styles of mosaic flooring, including a design of white arrows at the entrance to guide the most disorientated of guests. In the internal courtyard, don't miss the skylight, complete with the remnants of an ancient security grill. Of the house's mythically themed wall mosaics, only the faded ones are originals; the others now reside in Naples' Museo Archeologico Nazionale (p43).

➡ Terme Maschili

(Men's Baths) The Terme Maschili were the men's section of the **Terme del Foro** (Forum Baths). Note the ancient latrine to the left of the entrance before you step into the *apodyterium* (changing room), complete with bench for waiting patrons and a nifty wall shelf for sandal and toga storage.

While those after a bracing soak would pop into the *frigidarium* (cold bath) to the left, the less stoic headed straight into the *tepadarium* (tepid bath) to the right. The sunken mosaic floor here is testament to the seismic activity preceding Mt Vesuvius' catastrophic eruption. Beyond this room lies the *caldarium* (hot bath), as well as an exercise area.

➡ Decumano Massimo

Herculaneum's ancient high street is lined with shops, and fragments of advertisements – listing everything from the weight of goods to their price – still adorn the walls. Note the one to the right of the Casa del Salone Nero. Further east along the street, a crucifix found in an upstairs room of the Casa del Bicentenario (Bicentenary House) provides possible evidence of a Christian presence in pre-Vesuvius Herculaneum.

➡ Casa del Bel Cortile

(House of the Beautiful Courtyard) Inside the Casa del Bel Cortile lie three of the 300 skeletons discovered on the ancient shore by archaeologists in 1980. Almost two millennia later, it's still poignant to see the forms of what are understood to be a mother, father and young child huddled together in the last, terrifying moments of their lives.

➡ Casa di Nettuno e Anfitrite

(House of Neptune and Amphitrite) This aristocratic pad takes its name from the extraordinary mosaic in the *nymphaeum* (fountain and bath). The warm colours in which the sea god and his nymph bride are depicted hint at how lavish the original interior must have been.

➡ Casa del Tramezzo di Legno

(House of the Wooden Partition) Unusually, this house features two atria, which likely belonged to two separate dwellings that were merged in the 1st century AD. The most famous relic here is a wonderfully well-preserved wooden screen, separating the atrium from the *tablinum*, where the owner talked business with his clients. The second room off the left side of the atrium features the remains of an ancient bed.

➡ Casa dell'Atrio a Mosaico

(House of the Mosaic Atrium; ⊘ closed for restoration) An ancient mansion, the House of the Mosaic Atrium harbours extensive floor tilework, although time and nature have left the floor buckled and uneven. Particularly noteworthy is the black-and-white chessboard mosaic in the atrium.

➡ Casa del Gran Portale

(House of the Large Portal) Named after the elegant brick Corinthian columns that flank its main entrance, the House of the Large Portal is home to some well-preserved wall paintings.

➡ Casa dei Cervi

(House of the Stags) Closed indefinitely on our last visit, the Casa dei Cervi is an imposing example of a Roman noble family's house that, before the volcanic mud slide, boasted a seafront address. Constructed around a central courtyard, the two-storey villa contains murals and some beautiful still-life paintings. Waiting for you in the courtyard is a diminutive pair of marble deer assailed by dogs, and an engaging statue of a drunken, peeing Hercules.

Terme Suburbane   ARCHAEOLOGICAL SITE

(Suburban Baths; ⊘ closed for restoration) Marking Herculaneum's southernmost tip is the 1st-century-AD Terme Suburbane, one of the best-preserved Roman bath complexes in existence, with deep pools, stucco friezes and bas-reliefs looking down upon marble seats and floors. This is also one of the best places to observe the soaring volcanic deposits that smothered the ancient coastline.

MAV   MUSEUM
(Museo Archeologico Virtuale; ☎081 1980 6511;
www.museomav.com; Via IV Novembre 44; adult/
reduced €7.50/6, optional 3D documentary €4;
☻9am-5.30pm daily Mar-Sep, reduced hours rest
of year;🚈Circumvesuviana to Ercolano-Scavi)
Using high-tech holograms and computer-
generated recreations, this 'virtual archaeological museum' brings ruins like Pompeii's
forum and Capri's Villa Jovis back to virtual
life. Especially fun for kids, it's a useful place
to comprehend just how impressive those
crumbling columns once were. The museum
is on the main street linking Ercolano-Scavi
train station to the ruins of Herculaneum.

✖ Eating

Viva Lo Re   NEAPOLITAN €€
(☎081 739 02 07; www.vivalore.it; Corso Resina 261;
meals €35; ☻noon-4pm & 8.30-late Tue-Sat, noon-
4pm Sun; 🚈Circumvesuviana to Ercolano-Scavi)
Located 500m southeast of the ruins of Herculaneum on Corso Resina – dubbed the Miglio d'oro (Golden Mile) for its once-glorious
stretch of 18th-century villas – Viva Lo Re
is a stylish, inviting osteria, where vintage
prints and bookshelves meet a superb wine
list, gracious staff and gorgeous, revamped
regional cooking.

❶ Information

Tourist Office (Via IV Novembre 44; ☻9am-
5.30pm Mon-Sat; 🚈Circumvesuviana to
Ercolano-Scavi) Ercolano's new tourist office is
located in the same building as MAV, between
the Circumvesuviana Ercolano-Scavi train
station and the Herculaneum ruins.

❶ Getting There & Away

You can reach Ercolano by Circumvesuviana
train, which run frequently from Naples (€2.50,
17 minutes) and Sorrento (€3.40, 48 minutes).
Alight at Ercolano-Scavi station, from where
the ruins are an 800m walk southwest on Via IV
Novembre.

By car take the A3 from Naples, exit at Ercolano Portico and follow the signs to car parks
near the site's entrance.

Mt Vesuvius

Looming over the Bay of Naples, stratovol-
cano **Mt Vesuvius** (☎081 239 56 53; adult/
reduced €10/8; ☻9am-6pm Jul & Aug, to 5pm Apr-
Jun & Sep, to 4pm Mar & Oct, to 3pm Nov-Feb, ticket
office closes 1hr before the crater) has blown its
top more than 30 times. Its violent outburst

in AD 79 not only drowned Pompeii in pumice and pushed the coastline back several
kilometres but also destroyed much of the
mountain top, creating a huge caldera and
two new peaks. The most destructive explosion after that of AD 79 was in 1631, while
the most recent was in 1944.

What redeems this slumbering menace
is the spectacular panorama from its crater,
which takes in Naples, its world-famous bay,
and part of the Apennine mountains. From
Piazzale Stazione Circumvesuviana, outside
Ercolano-Scavi train station, **Vesuvio Express** (☎081 739 36 66; www.vesuvioexpress.it;
Piazzale Stazione Circumvesuviana, Ercolano; return incl admission to summit €20; ☻every 40min,
9.30am to 4pm) runs shuttle buses up to the
summit car park. From here, an 860m path
(best tackled in trainers, with sweater in tow)
leads up to the crater (roughly a 25-minute
climb). From Pompeii, **Busvia del Vesuvio**
(☎340 9352616; www.busviadelvesuvio.com; Via
Villa dei Misteri, Pompeii; return incl entry to summit
adult/reduced €22/7; ☻9am-4pm) runs hourly
shuttle services between Pompei-Scavi-Villa
dei Misteri train station (steps away from
the Ruins of Pompeii) and Boscoreale Terminal Interchange, from where a 4WD-style
bus continues the journey up the slope to
the summit car park.

Vesuvius itself is the focal point of the
Parco Nazionale del Vesuvio (Vesuvius
National Park; www.epnv.it), which offers nine
nature walks around the volcano. A simple map of the trails can be downloaded
from the park's website. Alternatively, **Naples Trips & Tours** (☎349 7155270; www.
naplestripsandtours.com; guided tour €50) runs a
daily horse-riding tour of the park (weather permitting). Running for three to four
hours, the tour includes transfers to/from
Naples or Ercolano-Scavi Circumvesuviana
station, helmet, saddle, guide and (most importantly) coffee.

If travelling by car, exit the A3 at Ercolano
Portico and follow signs for the Parco Nazionale del Vesuvio.

Note that when weather conditions are
bad the summit path is shut and bus departures are suspended.

Pompeii

POP 25,365
Each year about 2.5 million people pour in
to wander the eerie shell of ancient Pompeii,
a once thriving commercial centre. Not only

an evocative glimpse into Roman life, the ruins provide a stark reminder of the malign forces that lie deep inside Mt Vesuvius.

⊙ Sights

★ Ruins of Pompeii   ARCHAEOLOGICAL SITE

(☑ 081 857 53 47; www.pompeiisites.org; entrances at Porta Marina, Piazza Esedra & Piazza Anfiteatro; adult/reduced €11/5.50, incl Herculaneum €20/10; ⊙ 8.30am-7.30pm summer, to 5pm winter) The ghostly ruins of ancient Pompeii (Pompei in Italian) make for one of the world's most engrossing archaeological experiences. Much of the site's value lies in the fact that the town wasn't simply blown away by Vesuvius in AD 79 but buried under a layer of *lapilli* (burning fragments of pumice stone). The result is a remarkably well-preserved slice of ancient life, where visitors can walk down Roman streets and snoop around millennia-old houses, temples, shops, cafes, amphitheatres, and even a brothel.

The origins of Pompeii are uncertain, but it seems likely that it was founded in the 7th century BC by the Campanian Oscans. Over the next seven centuries the city fell to the Greeks and the Samnites before becoming a Roman colony in 80 BC.

In AD 62, a mere 17 years before Vesuvius erupted, the city was struck by a major earthquake. Damage was widespread and much of the city's 20,000-strong population was evacuated. Fortunately, many had not returned by the time Vesuvius blew, but 2000 men, women and children perished nevertheless.

After its catastrophic demise, Pompeii receded from the public eye until 1594, when the architect Domenico Fontana stumbled across the ruins while digging a canal. Exploration proper, however, didn't begin until 1748. Of Pompeii's original 66 hectares, 44 have now been excavated. Of course that doesn't mean you'll have unhindered access to every inch of the Unesco-listed site – expect to come across areas cordoned off for no apparent reason, a noticeable lack of clear signs, and the odd stray dog. Audio guides are a sensible investment (€6.50, cash only) and a good guidebook will also help – try *Pompeii*, published by Electa Napoli.

In recent years, the site has suffered a number of high-profile incidents due to bad weather. Most recently, heavy rain caused the wall of an ancient shop to collapse in March 2014. Maintenance work is ongoing,

but progress is beset by political, financial and bureaucratic problems.

➡ **Terme Suburbane**

Just outside ancient Pompeii's city walls, this 1st-century-BC bathhouse is famous for several erotic frescoes that scandalised the Vatican when they were revealed in 2001. The panels decorate what was once the *apodyterium* (changing room). The room leading to the colourfully frescoed *frigidarium* (cold-water bath) features fragments of stuccowork, as well as one of the few original roofs to survive at Pompeii. Beyond the *tepadarium* (tepid bath) and *caldarium* (hot bath) rooms are the remains of a heated outdoor swimming pool.

➡ **Porta Marina**

The ruins of Pompeii's main entrance is at Porta Marina, the most impressive of the seven gates that punctuated the ancient town walls. A busy passageway now, as it was then, it originally connected the town with the nearby harbour, hence the gateway's name. Immediately on the right as you enter the gate is the 1st-century-BC **Tempio di Venere** (Temple of Venus), formerly one of the town's most opulent temples.

➡ **Foro**

(Forum) A huge grassy rectangle flanked by limestone columns, the *foro* was ancient Pompeii's main piazza, as well as the site of gladiatoral battles before the Anfiteatro was constructed. The buildings surrounding the forum are testament to its role as the city's hub of civic, commercial, political and religious activity.

➡ **Basilica**

The basilica was the 2nd-century-BC seat of Pompeii's law courts and exchange. Their

Tragedy in Pompeii

24 AUGUST AD 79

8am Buildings including the **Terme Suburbane** ❶ and the **foro** ❷ are still undergoing repair after an earthquake in AD 63 caused significant damage to the city. Despite violent earth tremors overnight, residents have little idea of the catastrophe that lies ahead.

Midday Peckish locals pour into the **Thermopolium di Vetutius Placidus** ❸. The lustful slip into the **Lupanare** ❹, and gladiators practise for the evening's planned games at the **anfiteatro** ❺. A massive boom heralds the eruption. Shocked onlookers witness a dark cloud of volcanic matter shoot some 14km above the crater.

3pm–5pm Lapilli (burning pumice stone) rains down on Pompeii. Terrified locals begin to flee; others take shelter. Within two hours, the plume is 25km high and the sky has darkened. Roofs collapse under the weight of the debris, burying those inside.

25 AUGUST AD 79

Midnight Mudflows bury the town of Herculaneum. Lapilli and ash continue to rain down on Pompeii, bursting through buildings and suffocating those taking refuge within.

4am–8am Ash and gas avalanches hit Herculaneum. Subsequent surges smother Pompeii, killing all remaining residents, including those in the **Orto dei Fuggiaschi** ❻. The volcanic 'blanket' will safeguard frescoed treasures like the **Casa del Menandro** ❼ and **Villa dei Misteri** ❽ for almost two millennia.

TOP TIPS

» Visit in the afternoon
» Allow three hours
» Wear comfortable shoes and a hat
» Bring drinking water
» Don't use flash photography

Terme Suburbane
The *laconicum* (sauna), *caldarium* (hot bath) and large, heated swimming pool weren't the only sources of heat here; scan the walls of this suburban bathhouse for some of the city's raunchiest frescoes.

Villa di Diomede

Casa del Poeta Tragico

Porta Ercolano

Casa de Fauno

Tempio di Apollo

Basilica

Porta Marina

Terme del Foro

Macellum

Teatro Grande

Quadriportico dei Teatri

Porta di Stabia

Teatro Piccolo

Foro
An ancient Times Square of sorts, the forum sits at the intersection of Pompeii's main streets and was closed to traffic in the 1st century AD. The plinths on the southern edge featured statues of the imperial family.

Villa dei Misteri
Home to the world-famous *Dionysiac Frieze* fresco. Other highlights at this villa include *trompe l'oeil* wall decorations in the *cubiculum* (bedroom) and Egyptian-themed artwork in the *tablinum* (reception).

Lupanare
The prostitutes at this brothel were often slaves of Greek or Asian origin. Mattresses once covered the stone beds and the names engraved in the walls are possibly those of the workers and their clients.

Thermopolium di Vetutius Placidus
The counter at this ancient snack bar once held urns filled with hot food. The *lararium* (household shrine) on the back wall depicts Dionysus (the god of wine) and Mercury (the god of profit and commerce).

Casa dei Vettii

Porta del Vesuvio

Porta di Nola

EYEWITNESS ACCOUNT

Pliny the Younger (AD 61–c 112) gives a gripping, first-hand account of the catastrophe in his letters to Tacitus (AD 56–117).

Casa della Venere in Conchiglia

Porta di Sarno

Grande Palestra

Tempio di Iside

Orto dei Fuggiaschi
The Garden of the Fugitives showcases the plaster moulds of 13 locals seeking refuge during Vesuvius' eruption – the largest number of victims found in any one area. The huddled bodies make for a moving scene.

Anfiteatro
Magistrates, local senators and the games' sponsors and organisers enjoyed front-row seating at this veteran amphitheatre, home to gladiatorial battles and the odd riot. The parapet circling the stadium featured paintings of combat, victory celebrations and hunting scenes.

Casa del Menandro
This dwelling most likely belonged to the family of Poppaea Sabina, Nero's second wife. A room to the left of the atrium features Trojan War paintings and a polychrome mosaic of pygmies rowing down the Nile.

Old Pompeii

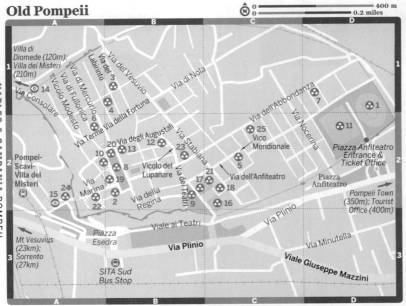

Old Pompeii

◎ Sights

1 Anfiteatro		D1
2 Basilica		B2
3 Casa dei Vettii		B1
4 Casa del Fauno		B1
5 Casa del Menandro		C2
6 Casa del Poeta Tragico		A2
7 Casa della Venere in Conchiglia		D1
8 Foro		B2
9 Foro Triangolare		B2
10 Granai del Foro		A2
11 Grande Palestra		D2
12 Lupanare		B2
13 Macellum		B2
14 Porta Ercolano		A1
15 Porta Marina		A2
16 Quadriportico dei Teatri		C2
17 Teatro Grande		B2
18 Teatro Piccolo		C2
19 Tempio di Apollo		B2
20 Tempio di Giove		B2
21 Tempio di Iside		C2
22 Tempio di Venere		A2
23 Terme Stabiane		B2
24 Terme Suburbane		A2
25 Via dell'Abbondanza		C2

semicircular apses would later influence the design of early Christian churches.

➡ Tempio di Apollo

(Temple of Apollo) The oldest and most important of Pompeii's religious buildings, the Tempio di Apollo largely dates to the 2nd century BC, including the striking columned portico. Fragments remain of an earlier version dating to the 6th century BC.

➡ Tempio di Giove

(Temple of Jupiter) One of the two flanking triumphal arches of the Tempio di Giove still remains.

➡ Granai del Foro

(Forum Granary) The Granai del Foro is now used to store hundreds of amphorae and a number of body casts that were made in the late 19th century by pouring plaster into the hollows left by disintegrated bodies. Among these casts is a pregnant slave; the belt around her waist would have displayed the name of her owner.

➡ Macellum

The *macellum* was the city's main produce market. The circular area in the centre was the *tholos*, a covered space in which fish and seafood were sold. Surviving market frescoes reveal some of the goods for sale, including prawns.

➡ Lupanare

Ancient Pompeii's only dedicated brothel, Lupanare is a tiny two-storey building with five rooms on each floor. Its collection of raunchy frescoes was a menu of sorts for clients. The walls in the rooms are carved with graffiti – including declarations of love and hope written by the brothel workers – in various languages.

➡ Foro Triangolare

The verdant Foro Triangolare would originally have overlooked the sea.

➡ Teatro Grande

The 2nd-century-BC Teatro Grande was a huge 5000-seat theatre carved into the lava mass on which Pompeii was originally built.

➡ Quadriportico dei Teatri

Behind the Teatro Grande's stage, the porticoed Quadriportico dei Teatri was initially used for the audience to stroll between acts, and later as a barracks for gladiators.

➡ Teatro Piccolo

Also known as the Odeion, the Teatro Piccolo was once an indoor theatre renowned for its acoustics.

➡ Tempio di Iside

(Temple of Isis) The pre-Roman Tempio di Iside was a popular place of cult worship.

➡ Casa del Menandro

Better preserved than the larger Casa del Fauno, luxurious Casa del Menandro has an outstanding, elegant peristyle (a colonnade-framed courtyard) beyond its beautifully frescoed atrium. On the peristyle's far right side a doorway leads to a private bathhouse, lavished with exquisite frescoes and mosaics. The central room off the far end of the peristyle features a striking mosaic of the ancient Greek dramatist Menander, after which the rediscovered villa was named.

➡ Via dell'Abbondanza

(Street of Abundance) The Via dell'Abbondanza was ancient Pompeii's Main Street. The elevated stepping stones allowed people to cross the street without stepping into the waste that washed down the thoroughfare.

➡ Terme Stabiane

At this typical 2nd-century-BC bath complex, bathers would enter from the vestibule, stop off in the vaulted *apodyterium* (changing room), and then pass through to the *tepidarium* (warm room) and *caldarium* (hot room). Particularly impressive is the stuccoed vault in the men's changing room, complete with whimsical images of *putti* (winged babies) and nymphs.

➡ Casa della Venere in Conchiglia

(House of the Venus Marina) Casa della Venere in Conchiglia harbours a lovely peristyle looking onto a small, manicured garden. It's here in the garden that you'll find the striking Venus fresco after which the house is named.

➡ Anfiteatro

(Amphitheatre) Gladiatorial battles thrilled up to 20,000 spectators at the grassy *anfiteatro*. Built in 70 BC, it's the oldest known Roman amphitheatre in existence.

➡ Grande Palestra

Lithe ancients kept fit at the Grande Palestra, an athletics field with an impressive portico dating to the Augustan period. At its centre, and closed off to public access, lie the remains of a swimming pool.

➡ Casa del Fauno

(House of the Faun) Covering an entire *insula* (city block) and boasting two atria at its front end (humbler homes had one), Pompeii's largest private house is named after the delicate bronze statue in the *impluvium* (rain tank). It was here that early excavators found Pompeii's greatest mosaics, most of which are now in Naples' Museo Archeologico Nazionale (p43). Valuable on-site survivors include a beautiful, geometrically patterned marble floor.

➡ Casa del Poeta Tragico

(House of the Tragic Poet) Hidden behind scaffolding when we visited, the Casa del Poeta Tragico features the world's first known 'beware of the dog' (*cave canem*) warnings.

➡ Casa dei Vettii

The Casa dei Vettii is home to a famous depiction of Priapus with his gigantic phallus balanced on a pair of scales...much to the anxiety of many a male observer.

Villa dei Misteri ARCHAEOLOGICAL SITE

This recently restored, 90-room villa is one of the most complete structures left standing in Pompeii. The dionysiac frieze, the most important fresco still on site, spans the walls of the large dining room. One of the biggest and most arresting paintings from the ancient world, it depicts the initiation of a bride-to-be into the cult of Dionysus, the Greek god of wine.

A farm for much of its life, the villa's *vino*-making area is still visible at the northern end.

Follow Via Consolare out of the town through **Porta Ercolano**. Continue past **Villa di Diomede**, turn right, and you'll come to Villa dei Misteri.

🛏 Sleeping & Eating

The ruins are best visited on a day trip from Naples, Sorrento or Salerno; once the excavations close for the day, the area around the site becomes decidedly seedy. Most of the restaurants near the ruins are characterless affairs set up for feeding busloads of tourists. Down in the modern town are a few decent restaurants serving excellent local food.

If you'd rather eat at the ruins, the onsite cafeteria peddles the standard choice of *panini*, pizza slices, salads, hot meals and gelato.

★ **President**   CAMPANIAN €€
(☑ 081 850 72 45; www.ristorantepresident.it; Piazza Schettini 12; meals €35; ☻noon-4pm & 7pm-midnight, closed Mon Oct-Apr; ▣FS to Pompei, ▣Circumvesuviana to Pompei Scavi-Villa dei Misteri) With its dripping chandeliers and gracious service, the Michelin-starred President feels like a private dining room in an Audrey Hepburn film. At the helm is charming owner-chef Paolo Gramaglia, whose passion for local produce, history and culinary creativity translates into bread made to ancient Roman recipes, slow-cooked snapper paired with tomato puree and sweet-onion gelato, and deconstructed *pastiera* (sweet Neapolitan tart).

❶ Information

Tourist Office (☑ 081 850 72 55; Via Sacra 1; ☻8.30am-3.30pm Mon-Fri) Located in the centre of the modern town.

❶ Getting There & Away

To reach the ruins by Circumvesuviana train from either Naples (€3.20, 36 minutes) or Sorrento (€2.80, 30 minutes), alight at Pompeii-Scavi-Villa dei Misteri station, located beside the main entrance at Porta Marina.

Busvia del Vesuvio (p72) shuttle buses to Vesuvius depart from outside the Pompeii-Scavi-Villa dei Misteri train station.

To get here by car, take the A3 from Naples. Use the Pompeii exit and follow signs to Pompei Scavi. Car parks (approximately €5 per hour) are clearly marked and vigorously touted.

Sorrento

POP 16,500

On paper, cliff-straddling Sorrento is a place to avoid – a package-holiday centre with few must-see sights and no beach to speak of. In reality, it's a strangely appealing place, its laid-back southern Italian charm resisting all attempts to swamp it in graceless development.

Dating to Greek times and known to Romans as Surrentum, it's ideally situated for exploring the surrounding area: to the west, the best of the peninsula's unspoiled countryside and, beyond that, the Amalfi Coast; to the north, Pompeii and the archaeological sites; offshore, the fabled island of Capri.

According to Greek legend, it was in Sorrento's waters that the mythical sirens once lived. Sailors of antiquity were powerless to resist the beautiful song of these charming maidens-cum-monsters, who would lure them and their ships to their doom. Homer's Ulysses escaped by having his oarsmen plug their ears with wax and by strapping himself to his ship's mast as he sailed past.

◉ Sights

Museo Correale   MUSEUM
(☑ 081 878 18 46; www.museocorreale.it; Via Correale 50; admission €7; ☻9.30am-6.30pm Tue-Sat, to 1.30pm Sun) East of the city centre, this museum is well worth a visit, whether you're a clock collector, an archaeological egghead or into embroidery. In addition to the rich assortment of 17th- to 19th-century Neapolitan art and crafts, there are Japanese, Chinese and European ceramics, clocks, furniture and, on the ground floor, Greek and Roman artefacts.

Chiesa di San Francesco   CHURCH
(Via San Francesco; ☻8am-1pm & 2-8pm) Located next to the Villa Comunale Park, this is one of Sorrento's most beautiful churches. Surrounded by bougainvillea and birdsong, the evocative cloisters have an Arabic portico and interlaced arches supported by octagonal pillars. The church is most famous, however, for its summer program of concerts featuring world-class performers from the classical school. If this strikes a chord, check out the schedule at the tourist office. There are also regular art exhibitions.

Museo Bottega della Tarsia Lignea   MUSEUM
(☑ 081 877 19 42; www.museomuta.it; Via San Nicola 28; adult/reduced €8/5; ☻10am-6.30pm

Sorrento

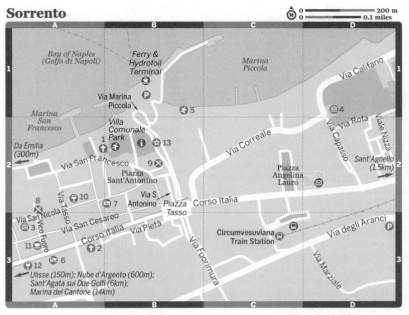

N 0 ————— 200 m
0 ————— 0.1 miles

Sorrento

◎ Sights
1 Chiesa di San Francesco	A2
2 Duomo	A3
3 Museo Bottega della Tarsia Lignea	A3
4 Museo Correale	D1

⚘ Activities, Courses & Tours
5 Sic Sic	B1

🛏 Sleeping
6 Casa Astarita	A3
7 Hotel Astoria	B2

✕ Eating
8 Inn Bufalito	A2
9 Ristorante il Buco	B2

◉ Drinking & Nightlife
10 Bollicine	A2
11 Cafè Latino	A3
12 English Inn	A3

✪ Entertainment
13 Teatro Tasso	B2

Apr-Oct, to 5pm Nov-Mar) Since the 18th century, Sorrento has been famous for its *intarsio* furniture, made with elaborately designed inlaid wood. Some wonderful examples can be found in this museum, housed in an 18th-century palace, complete with beautiful frescoes. There's also an interesting collection of paintings, prints and photographs depicting the town and surrounding area in the 19th century.

Duomo   CATHEDRAL
(Corso Italia; ⊙8am-12.30pm & 4.30-9pm) To get a feel for Sorrento's history, stroll down Via Pietà from Piazza Tasso and past two medieval palaces en route to the cathedral, with its striking exterior fresco, triple-tiered bell tower, four classical columns and elegant majolica clock. Take note of the striking marble bishop's throne (1573) and the beautiful wooden choir stalls decorated in the local *intarsio* style.

🏃 Activities

★ **Sic Sic**   BOATING
(📞081 807 22 83; www.nauticasicsic.com; Marina Piccola; ⊙May-Oct) Seek out the best beaches by rented boat, with or without a skipper. This outfit rents a variety of motor boats, starting at around €40 per hour or €100 per day. It also organises boat excursions, wedding shoots and similar.

Bagni Regina Giovanna SWIMMING

Sorrento lacks a decent beach, so consider heading to Bagni Regina Giovanna, a rocky beach with clear, clean water about 2km west of town, set among the ruins of the Roman Villa Pollio Felix. It's possible to walk here (follow Via Capo), although you'll save your strength if you get the SITA bus headed for Massa Lubrense.

Festivals & Events

Sant'Antonino RELIGIOUS

(⊙14 Feb) The city's patron saint, Sant'Antonino, is remembered annually with processions and huge markets. The saint is credited with having saved Sorrento during WWII when Salerno and Naples were heavily bombed.

Settimana Santa RELIGIOUS

Famed throughout Italy; the first procession of Holy Week takes place at midnight on the Thursday preceding Good Friday, with robed and hooded penitents in white; the second occurs on Good Friday, when participants wear black robes and hoods to commemorate the death of Christ.

🛏 Sleeping

Most accommodation is in the town centre or clustered along Via Capo, the coastal road west of the centre. Be sure to book early for the summer season.

Ulisse HOSTEL €

(📞081 877 47 53; www.ulissedeluxe.com; Via del Mare 22; dm €30, d €60-120; P✳🌐) Although it calls itself a hostel, the Ulisse is about as far from a backpackers' pad as a hiking boot from a stiletto. Most rooms are plush, spacious affairs with swish if rather bland fabrics, gleaming floors and large en suite bathrooms. There are two single-sex dorms, and quads for sharers. Breakfast is included in some rates but costs €10 with others.

Casa Astarita B&B €

(📞081 877 49 06; www.casastarita.com; Corso Italia 67; d €90-130, tr €110-150; ✳🌐) Housed in a 16th-century *palazzo* on Sorrento's main strip, this charming B&B has a colourful, eclectic look with original vaulted ceilings, brightly painted doors and majolica-tiled floors. Its six simple but well-equipped rooms surround a central parlour, where breakfast is served on a large rustic table.

Nube d'Argento CAMPGROUND €

(📞081 878 13 44; www.nubedargento.com; Via Capo 21; camping per 2 people, car & tent €38, 2-person bungalows €60-85, 4-person bungalows €90-120; ⊙Mar-Dec; @✳🌐🏧) This inviting campground is an easy 1km drive west of the Sorrento city centre. Pitches and wooden chalet-style bungalows are spread out beneath a canopy of olive trees – a source of much-needed summer shade – and the facilities are excellent. Kids in particular will enjoy the open-air swimming pool, table-tennis table, slides and swings.

★ Hotel Cristina HOTEL €€

(📞081 878 35 62; www.hotelcristinasorrento.it; Via Privata Rubinacci 6, Sant'Agnello; s €130, d €150, tr €180, q €200; ⊙Mar-Oct; ✳🌐🏧) Located high above Sant'Agnello, this hotel has superb views, particularly from the swimming pool. The spacious rooms have sea-view balconies and combine inlaid wooden furniture with contemporary flourishes like Philippe Starck chairs. There's an in-house restaurant and a free shuttle bus to/from Sorrento's Circumvesuviana train station.

La Tonnarella HOTEL €€

(📞081 878 11 53; www.latonnarella.com; Via Capo 31; d €120-140, ste €240-350; ⊙Apr-Oct & Christmas; P✳@🌐) A splendid choice – but not for minimalists – La Tonnarella is a dazzling canvas of majolica tiles, antiques, chandeliers and statues. Rooms, most with their own balcony or small terrace, continue the sumptuous classical theme with traditional furniture and discreet mod cons. The hotel also has its own private beach, accessible by lift, and a highly regarded terrace restaurant.

Hotel Astoria HOTEL €€

(📞081 807 40 30; www.hotelastoriasorrento.com; Via Santa Maria delle Grazie 24; s €50-110, €70-170; ✳🌐) This renovated classic has the advantage of being located in the heart of the *centro storico*. Overall, it's an excellent choice. The interior sparkles with colourful glossy tiles and blue and buttercup-yellow paintwork. The large enclosed back terrace is a delight, with seats set under orange and lemon trees and colourful tiled murals lining the back wall.

Eating

A local speciality to look out for is *gnocchi alla sorrentina* (gnocchi baked in tomato sauce with mozzarella).

★ Da Emilia
TRATTORIA €

(☑ 081 807 27 20; Via Marina Grande 62; meals €20; ☺ noon-2.30pm & 7pm-midnight; 🚸) Founded in 1947 and still run by the same family, this is a homely yet atmospheric joint overlooking the fishing boats in Marina Grande. There's a large informal dining room, complete with youthful photos of former patron Sophia Loren, a scruffily romantic terrace and a menu of straightforward, no-fail dishes such as mussels with lemon.

Inn Bufalito
ITALIAN €€

(☑ 081 365 69 75; www.innbufalito.it; Vico Fuoro 21; meals €25; ☺ 11am-midnight; 🛜 🚸) 🍽 Owner Franco Coppola (no relation to the movie man) exudes a real passion for showcasing local produce – the restaurant is a member of the Slow Food Movement. A mozzarella bar as well as a restaurant, this effortlessly stylish place boasts a menu including delights such as Sorrento-style cheese fondue and buffalo-meat *carpaccio*.

Ristorante il Buco
ITALIAN €€€

(☑ 081 878 23 54; www.ilbucoristorante.it; Rampa Marina Piccola 5; meals €60; ☺ 12.30-2.30pm & 7.30-11pm Thu-Tue Feb-Dec) Housed in a former monks' wine cellar, this dress-up restaurant offers far-from-monastic cuisine. The emphasis is on innovative regional cooking, so expect modern combos such as pasta with rockfish sauce, or *treccia* (local cheese) and prawns served on capers with tomato and olive sauce. In summer there's outdoor seating near one of the city's ancient gates. Reservations recommended.

🍷 Drinking & Nightlife

Cafè Latino
CAFE, BAR

(☑ 081 878 37 18; Vico Fuoro 4a; ☺ 10am-1am summer) Think locked-eyes-over-cocktails time. This is the place to impress your date with cocktails (from €7) on the terrace, surrounded by orange and lemon trees. Sip a Mary Pickford (rum, pineapple, *grenadino* and maraschino) or a glass of chilled white wine. If you can't drag yourselves away, you can also eat here (meals around €30).

Bollicine
WINE BAR

(☑ 081 878 46 16; Via Accademia 9; ☺ 7.30pm-2am) The wine list at this unpretentious bar with a dark, woody interior includes all the big Italian names and a selection of interesting local labels. If you can't decide what to go for, the amiable bar staff will advise you.

There's also a small menu of *panini*, bruschettas and one or two pasta dishes.

English Inn
PUB

(☑ 081 807 43 57; www.englishinn.it; Corso Italia 55; ☺ 9am-2am) The vast upstairs garden terrace, with its orange trees and dazzle of bougainvillea, is a delight and attracts a mainly expat crowd, who head here for the disco beats and karaoke nights, accompanied by Guinness on tap. The party atmosphere continues late into the night, while the bacon-and-eggs breakfast is a suitable reviver.

☆ Entertainment

Teatro Tasso
THEATRE

(☑ 081 807 55 25; www.teatrotasso.it; Piazza Sant'Antonino; incl a cocktail €25; ☺ Sorrento Musical 9.30pm summer) The southern-Italian equivalent of a London old-time music hall, Teatro Tasso is home to the *Sorrento Musical,* a sentimental 75-minute revue of Neapolitan classics such as 'O Sole Mio' and 'Trona a Sorrent'.

ℹ Information

Main Tourist Office (☑ 081 807 40 33; www. sorrentotourism.com; Via Luigi de Maio 35; ☺ 8.30am-8pm Mon-Sat, 9am-1pm Sun Jul-Sep) In the Circolo dei Forestieri (Foreigners' Club). Ask for the useful publication *Surrentum*.

Post Office (Corso Italia 210)

ℹ Getting There & Away

BOAT

Sorrento is the main jumping-off point for Capri and also has good ferry connections to Naples, Ischia and Amalfi coastal towns. All ferries and hydrofoils depart from the port at Marina Piccola, where you buy your tickets.

Caremar (p58) Runs ferries to Capri (€14.70, 25 minutes, 4 daily).

Alilauro (p58) Runs up to five daily hydrofoils between Naples and Sorrento (€12.30, 40 minutes).

BUS

Curreri (☑ 081 801 54 20; www.curreriviaggi. it) Runs eight daily services to Sorrento from Naples Capodichino airport (75 minutes). Buses depart from outside the arrivals hall and arrive in Piazza Angelina Lauro. Buy tickets (€10) on board.

SITA Sud (p83) Buses serve Naples, the Amalfi Coast and Sant'Agata, leaving from the bus stop across from the entrance of the Circumvesuviana train station. Buy tickets at the station bar or from shops bearing the SITA sign.

TRAIN

Sorrento is the last stop on the Circumvesuviana (p58) train line from Naples. Trains run every half-hour for Naples (one hour 10 minutes; €4.50), via Pompeii (30 minutes; €2.80) and Ercolano (50 minutes; €3.40).

❶ Getting Around

Local bus lines B and C run to/from the port at Marina Piccola (€1).

For a **taxi**, call ☑ 081 878 22 04 or ☑ 081 877 24 84.

West of Sorrento

The countryside west of Sorrento is the very essence of southern Italy. Tortuous roads wind their way through hills covered in olive trees and lemon groves, passing through sleepy villages and tiny fishing ports. There are magnificent views at every turn, the best being from Sant'Agata sui Due Golfi and the high points overlooking Punta Campanella, the westernmost point of the Sorrento Peninsula.

Sant'Agata sui Due Golfi

Perched high in the hills above Sorrento, sleepy Sant'Agata sui due Golfi commands spectacular views of the Bay of Naples on one side and the Bay of Salerno on the other (hence its name, Saint Agatha on the Two Gulfs). The best viewpoint is the **Convento del Deserto** (☑ 081 878 01 99; Via Deserto; ⊙ gardens 8am-7pm, lookout 10am-noon & 5-7pm summer, 10am-noon & 3-5pm winter), a Carmelite convent 1.5km uphill from the village centre.

Agriturismo La Tore (☑ 081 808 06 37; www.letore.com; Via Pontone 43; s €60-70, d €90-130, dinner €25-35; ⊙ Easter-early Nov; P@🛜🖫) is a wonderful organic farm with seven barnlike rooms that sleep six. In the winter, a self-contained apartment is also available. A short drive (or a long walk) from the village, the rustic farmhouse hidden among fruit trees and olive groves has a lovely setting. Conveniently, the owners can also organise a shuttle-bus pick-up from Naples' Capodichino airport or Stazione Centrale.

From Sorrento, there's a pretty 3km (approximately one hour) trail up to Sant'Agata. SITA Sud buses leave roughly every hour to two hours from the Circumvesuviana train station.

Marina del Cantone

From Sorrento, follow the coastal road round to **Termini**. Stop a moment to admire the views before continuing on to **Nerano**, from where a beautiful hiking trail leads down to the stunning **Bay of Ieranto**, one of the coast's top swimming spots, and the tranquil, unassuming village of **Marina del Cantone**.

◉ Sights & Activities

A popular diving destination, the protected waters here are part of an 11-sq-km marine reserve called the **Punta Campanella**, its underwater grottoes lush with flora and fauna.

Nettuno Diving   DIVING
(☑ 081 808 10 51; www.sorrentodiving.com; Via Vespucci 39; 🖫) Dive the depths of this marine reserve with a PADI-certified outfit that runs underwater activities for all ages and abilities. These include snorkelling excursions, beginner's courses, cave dives and immersions off Capri and the Li Galli islands. Costs start at €25 (children €15) for a day-long outing to the Baia de Ieranto. It can also organise reasonably priced accommodation.

🛏 Sleeping & Eating

Villaggio Residence Nettuno   CAMPGROUND, APARTMENT €
(☑ 081 808 10 51; www.villaggionettuno.it; Via A Vespucci 39; camping per 2 people, tent & car €41, bungalows €130-185, apt €190; ⊙ Mar-early Nov; P❄@🛜🖫) Marina's campground, in the terraced olive groves by the entrance to the village, offers an array of accommodation options, including campsites, mobile homes and (best of all) apartments in a 16th-century tower for two to five people. It's a friendly, environmentally sound place with excellent facilities and a comprehensive list of activities.

Lo Scoglio   ITALIAN €€€
(☑ 081 808 10 26; www.hotelloscoglio.com; Piazza delle Sirene 15, Massa Lubrense; meals €60; ⊙ 12.30-5pm & 7.30-11pm) The only marina restaurant directly accessible from the sea, Lo Scoglio is a favourite of visiting celebs. The food is top notch (and priced accordingly). Although you can eat *fettucine al bolognese* and steak here, you'd be sorry to miss the superb seafood. Options include a €30 antipasto of raw seafood and *spaghetti al riccio* (spaghetti with sea urchins).

🛈 Getting There & Around

SITA Sud runs regular buses between Sorrento and Marina del Cantone from the Circumvesuviana train station in Sorrento.

AMALFI COAST

Stretching about 50km along the southern side of the Sorrento Peninsula, the Amalfi Coast (Costiera Amalfitana) is one of Europe's most breathtaking. Cliffs terraced with scented lemon groves sheer down into sparkling seas; sherbet-hued villas cling precariously to unforgiving slopes while sea and sky merge in one vast blue horizon.

Yet its stunning topography has not always been a blessing. For centuries after the passing of Amalfi's glory days as a maritime superpower (from the 9th to the 12th centuries), the area was poor and its isolated villages were regular victims of foreign incursions, earthquakes and landslides. But it was this very isolation that first drew visitors in the early 1900s, paving the way for the advent of tourism in the latter half of the century. Today the Amalfi Coast is one of Italy's premier tourist destinations, a favourite of cashed-up jet-setters and love-struck couples.

The best time to visit is in late spring or early autumn. In summer the coast's single road (SS163) gets very busy and prices are inflated; in winter much of the coast simply shuts down.

🛈 Getting There & Away

BOAT

Boat services to the Amalfi Coast towns are generally limited to the summer tourist season, from April/May to October. In July and August, it's a good idea to book tickets in advance, especially if travelling between the Amalfi Coast and Capri.

BUS

SITA Sud (☑ 089 40 51 45; www.sitasud trasporti.it) operates a frequent, year-round service along the SS163 between Sorrento and Amalfi via Positano, and from Amalfi to Salerno.

CAR & MOTORCYCLE

If driving from the north, exit the A3 autostrada at Vietri sul Mare and follow the SS163 along the coast. From the south, leave the A3 at Salerno and head for Vietri sul Mare and the SS163.

TRAIN

From Naples you can take either the Circumvesuviana to Sorrento or a Trenitalia train to Salerno, then continue along the Amalfi Coast, eastwards or westwards, by SITA Sud bus.

Positano

POP 3900

The pearl in the pack, Positano is the coast's most photogenic and expensive town. Its steeply stacked houses are a medley of peaches, pinks and terracottas, and its near-vertical streets (many of which are, in fact, staircases) are lined with vogueish shop displays, jewellery stalls, elegant hotels and smart restaurants. Look closely, though, and you'll find reassuring signs of everyday reality – crumbling stucco, streaked paintwork and even, on occasion, a faint whiff of drains.

An early visitor, John Steinbeck, wrote in May 1953 in *Harper's Bazaar*: 'Positano bites deep. It is a dream place that isn't quite real when you are there and becomes beckoningly real after you have gone.' More than 60 years on, his words still ring true.

⊙ Sights

Chiesa di Santa Maria Assunta   CHURCH
(Piazza Flavio Gioia; ⊙ 8am-noon & 4-9pm) This church, with its colourful majolica-tiled dome, is the most famous and, let's face it, pretty much the only sight in Positano. If you are visiting at a weekend you will probably have the added perk of seeing a wedding; it's one of the most popular churches in the area for exchanging vows.

Step inside to see a delightful classical interior, with pillars topped with gilded Ionic capitals and winged cherubs peeking from above every arch.

Above the main altar is a 13th-century Byzantine Black Madonna and Child. During restoration works of the square and the crypt, a Roman villa was discovered; still under excavation, it is closed to the public.

🏃 Activities

Although Spiaggia Grande is no one's dream beach, with greyish sand covered by legions of brightly coloured umbrellas, the water's clean and the setting is striking. Hiring a chair and umbrella in the fenced-off areas costs around €20 per person per day, but the crowded public areas are free.

Positian

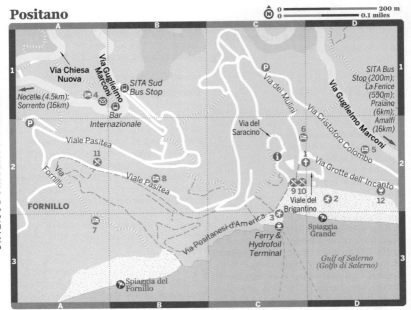

Positano

◉ Sights
1 Chiesa di Santa Maria Assunta C2

⊕ Activities, Courses & Tours
2 Blue Star D2
3 L'Uomo e il Mare C3

⊝ Sleeping
4 Hostel Brikette A1
5 Hotel California D2
6 Hotel Palazzo Murat C2

7 Pensione Maria Luisa.............................. A3
8 Villa Nettuno B2

⊗ Eating
9 La Brezza..C2
10 La Cambusa..C2
11 Next2...A2

⊙ Drinking & Nightlife
12 Music on the Rocks.................................D2

★ **Blue Star**   BOATING
(📞089 81 18 88; www.bluestarpositano.it; Spiaggia
Grande; ☺8.30am-9pm) Operating out of a kiosk on Spiaggia Grande, Blue Star hires out
small motorboats for €60 per hour (€200
for four hours). Consider heading for the archipelago of Li Galli, the four small islands
where, according to Homer, the sirens lived.
The company also organises popular and
fun yacht excursions to Capri and the Grotta
dello Smeraldo (€60).

L'Uomo e il Mare   BOATING
(📞089 81 16 13; www.gennaroesalvatore.it;
☺9am-8pm) An Italian-English couple offers
a range of tours, including Capri and Amalfi day trips (from €55), out of a kiosk near

the ferry terminal. They also run a romantic sunset cruise to Li Galli, complete with
champagne (€30).

🛏 Sleeping

Positano is a glorious place to stay, but be
aware that prices are, overall, high. Like
everywhere on the Amalfi Coast it gets very
busy in summer, so book ahead, particularly
on weekends and in July and August. Ask at
the tourist office about rooms or apartments
in private houses.

Villa Nettuno   HOTEL €
(📞089 87 54 01; www.villanettunopositano.it; Viale
Pasitea 208; s/d €70/85; ☺year-round) Hidden
behind a barrage of perfumed foliage, Vil-

la Nettuno oozes charm. Go for one of the original rooms in the 300-year-old part of the building with heavy rustic decor and a communal terrace. Rooms in the renovated part of the villa lack the same character.

Hostel Brikette
HOSTEL €

(☎089 87 58 57; www.hostel-positano.com; Via Marconi 358; dm €24-50, d €65-145, apt €80-220; ⊙year-round; ✳🔊) The Brikette is a bright, cheerful place with wonderful views and a range of sleeping options, from dorms to doubles and apartments. Conveniently, it also offers a daily hostelling option that allows day trippers use of the hostel's facilities, including showers, wi-fi and left luggage, for €10. Breakfast isn't included.

Pensione Maria Luisa
PENSION €

(☎089 87 50 23; www.pensionemarialuisa.com; Via Fornillo 42; d €70-80, with sea view €95; ⊙Mar-Oct; @🔊) The Maria Luisa is a friendly old-school *pensione*. Rooms feature shiny blue tiles and simple, no-frills decor; those with private balconies are well worth the extra €15 for the bay views. If you can't bag a room with a view, there's a small communal terrace offering the same sensational vistas. Breakfast is an additional €5.

La Fenice
B&B €€

(☎089 87 55 13; www.lafenicepositano.com; Via Guglielmo Marconi 4; d €140; ⊙Easter-Oct; ❄) With hand-painted Vietri tiles, white walls and high ceilings, the rooms here are simple but stylish; most have their own balcony or terrace. The views are stunning, but it feels very homely and not super posh. As with everywhere in Positano, you'll need to be good at stomping up and down steps to stay here.

Hotel California
HOTEL €€

(☎089 87 53 82; www.hotelcaliforniapositano.it; Via Cristoforo Colombo 141; d €160-195; ⊙Easter-Oct; P✳🔊) Ignore the incongruous name: this Hotel California is housed in a grand 18th-century palace, its facade washed in soothing pinks and yellows. The rooms in the older part of the house are magnificent, with original ceiling friezes; new rooms are spacious and luxuriously decorated. Breakfast is served on a glorious and leafy front terrace.

★Hotel Palazzo Murat
HOTEL €€€

(☎089 87 51 77; www.palazzomurat.it; Via dei Mulini 23; d €180-270; ⊙May–mid-Jan; ✳@🔊) Hidden behind an ancient wall from the tourists who surge along its pedestrian thoroughfare daily, this magnificent hotel occupies the 18th-century *palazzo* that the one-time king of Naples used as his summer residence. Rooms – five (more expensive) in the original part of the building, 25 in the newer section – are decorated with sumptuous antiques, original oil paintings and glossy marble.

WALK THE COAST

Rising steeply from the coast, the densely wooded Lattari mountains provide some stunning walking opportunities. An extraordinary network of paths traverses the craggy, precipitous peaks, climbing to remote farmhouses through wild and beautiful valleys. It's tough going, though – long ascents up seemingly endless flights of steps are almost unavoidable.

The best-known walk, the 12km Sentiero degli Dei (Path of the Gods; three to six hours), follows the steep, often rocky paths linking Positano to Praiano. Marked by red-and-white stripes daubed on rocks and trees, it's a spectacular, mountain-top trail punctuated by caves, dizzying terraces and deep valleys framed by the brilliant blue of the sea. The walk starts in the centre of Praiano, where the tourist office can provide maps and guidance. Just downhill and on the same side is Alimentari Rispoli, where you can buy bread, cheeses, meat, drinks and fruit for the hike (tip: bring a pen knife as sandwiches aren't made on site). Also, don't forget to bring plenty of water and comfortable walking shoes for the journey.

Hiking maps can be downloaded at www.amalficoastweb.com. Another reliable regional hiking map is the CAI (Club Alpino Italiano; Italian Alpine Club) *Monti Lattari, Peninsola Sorrentina, Costiera Amalfitana: Carta dei Sentieri* (€9) at 1:30,000. If you prefer a guided hike, there are a number of reliable local guides including American **Frank Carpegna** (www.positanofrankcarpegna.com), a longtime resident here, and **Zia Lucy** (www.zialucy.it).

🍴 Eating

Most restaurants, bars and trattorias, many of which are unashamedly touristy, close over winter, making a brief reappearance for Christmas and New Year.

La Brezza CAFE €
(☑089 87 58 11; www.labrezzapositano.it; Via Regina Giovanna 2; snacks around €6; ⊙9am-1am; 🛜) With a steely grey-and-white interior, free internet and wi-fi, and a terrace with views over the sea and quay, this is the best beachfront place for *panini* or snacks. There are regular art exhibitions and a daily 'happy hour' (6pm to 8pm), with drinks accompanied by complimentary light eats.

⭐Donna Rosa ITALIAN €€
(☑089 81 18 06; www.drpositano.com; Via Montepertuso 97-99, Montepertuso; meals from €40; ⊙noon-2.30pm & 7-11.30pm Mon, Tue & Thu-Sun Apr-Dec, closed lunch Aug) This is one of the Amalfi Coast's most reputable restaurants, located in mountainside Montepertuso, above Positano. Once a humble trattoria and now run by Rosa's daughter Raffaella, the lineage is set to continue with Raffaella's daughter Erika, who studied with Jamie Oliver in London. The celebrity chef dined here on his honeymoon and declared it one of his favourite restaurants.

Next2 RISTORANTE €€
(☑089 812 35 16; www.next2.it; Viale Pasitea 242; meals €45; ⊙6.30-11.30pm) Understated elegance meets creative cuisine at this contemporary set-up. Local and organic ingredients are put to impressive use in beautifully presented dishes such as ravioli stuffed with aubergine, and prawns or sea bass with tomatoes and lemon-scented peas. Desserts are wickedly delicious, and the alfresco sea-facing terrace is summer perfection.

La Cambusa SEAFOOD €€
(☑089 81 20 51; www.lacambusapositano.com; Piazza A Vespucci 4; meals €40; ⊙noon-midnight Mar-Nov) This restaurant, run by amiable Luigi, is on the front line, which, given the number of cash-rich tourists in these parts, could equal high prices for less than average food. Happily, that is not the case here. The locals still rate La Cambusa as a top place for seafood. Go for simple spaghetti with clams, oven-baked sea bass or splash out with the Mediterranean lobster. There is a good selection of side dishes, like roasted artichokes, and the position is Positano at its best.

🍸 Drinking & Nightlife

Generally speaking, Positano's nightlife is genteel, sophisticated and safe.

Music on the Rocks CLUB
(☑089 87 58 74; www.musicontherocks.it; Via Grotte dell'Incanto 51; cover €10-30; ⊙10pm-late) This is one of the town's few genuine nightspots and one of the best clubs on the coast. Music on the Rocks is dramatically carved into the tower at the eastern end of Spiaggia Grande. Join the flirty, good-looking crowd and some of the region's top DJs spinning mainstream house and reliable disco.

ℹ️ Information

Post Office (Via Marconi 318)
Tourist Office (☑089 87 50 67; Via del Saracino 4; ⊙9am-7pm Mon-Sat, to 2pm Sun summer, 9am-4pm Mon-Sat winter) Can provide lots of information; expect to pay for walking maps and similar.

RESOURCES
Positano (www.positano.com) Information on sights, activities, accommodation, transport and more in Positano and along the Amalfi Coast.

ℹ️ Getting There & Away

BOAT
Positano has excellent ferry connections to the coastal towns and Capri from April to October.
Alicost (☑089 87 14 83; www.alicost.it) Operates three daily services to Amalfi (€8, 20 minutes), with one continuing to Salerno (€12, 75 minutes). It also runs one daily service to Capri (€19.20, 50 minutes) and two daily services to Sorrento (€16, 40 minutes).
TraVelMar (☑089 87 29 50; www.travelmar.it) Runs six daily ferries to Amalfi (€8, 25 minutes) and Salerno (€12, 70 minutes).
Lucibello (☑089 87 50 32; www.lucibello.it) Operates three daily services to Capri (€18.50, 50 minutes).
NLG (☑081 552 07 63; www.navlib.it) Sails once daily service to Capri (€19.20, 30 minutes).

BUS
SITA Sud (p83) runs frequent buses to/from Amalfi (€2.50, 40 to 50 minutes) and Sorrento (€2.50, one hour). Buses drop you off at one of two main bus stops: arriving from Sorrento and the west, opposite Bar Internazionale; arriving from Amalfi and the east, at the top of Via Cristoforo Colombo. To get into town from the former, follow Viale Pasitea; from the latter (a far shorter route), take Via Cristoforo Colombo. When de-

parting, buy bus tickets at Bar Internazionale or, if headed east, from the *tabaccheria* (tobacconist) at the bottom of Via Colombo.

ⓘ Getting Around

Getting around Positano is largely a matter of walking. If your knees can handle it, there are dozens of narrow alleys and stairways that make walking relatively easy and joyously traffic-free.

Otherwise, **Flavio Gioia** (☑ 089 81 18 95; www.flaviogioia.com; Via Cristoforo Colombo 49) local buses follow the lower ring road every half-hour. Stops are clearly marked and you can buy your ticket (€1.20) on board. The Flavio Gioia buses pass by both SITA bus stops. There are also around 14 daily buses up to Montepertuso and Nocelle.

Praiano & Furore

An ancient fishing village, **Praiano** has one of the coast's most popular beaches, Marina di Praia. From the SS163 (next to the Hotel Continental), take the steep path that leads down the side of the cliffs to a tiny inlet with a small stretch of coarse sand and deep-blue water.

Respected local dive outfit **Centro Sub Costiera Amalfitana** (☑ 089 81 21 48; www.centrosub.it; Via Marina di Praia; dives from €80; ⬦) runs lessons for adults and children over eight, as well as night dives and full diving days exploring the area's coral, marine life and grottoes.

Stunningly set on a cliffside overlooking Marina di Praia, **Hotel Onda Verde** (☑ 089 87 41 43; www.hotelondaverde.com; Via Terramare 3, Praiano; d €110-230; ◷ Apr-Nov; ❄ 🛜) is a sound slumber option, its rooms a smart, soothing combo of satin bedheads, elegant Florentine-style furniture and majolica-tiled floors. The restaurant also comes highly recommended.

A few kilometres further on, **Marina di Furore** sits at the bottom of what's known as the fjord of Furore, a giant cleft that cuts through the Lattari mountains. The main village, however, stands 300m above, in the upper Vallone del Furore. A one-horse place that sees few tourists, it breathes a distinctly rural air despite the colourful murals and unlikely modern sculpture.

To get to upper Furore by car follow the SS163 and then the SS366 signposted to Agerola; from Positano, it's 15km. Otherwise, regular SITA Sud buses depart from the bus terminus in Amalfi (€1.60, 25 minutes, at least three daily).

Amalfi

POP 5430

Believe it or not, pretty little Amalfi, with its sun-filled piazzas and small beach, was once a maritime superpower with a population of more than 70,000. For one thing, it's not a big place – you can easily walk from one end to the other in about 20 minutes. For another, there are very few historical buildings of note. The explanation is chilling – most of the old city, and its populace, simply slid into the sea during an earthquake in 1343.

Just around the headland, neighbouring Atrani is a picturesque tangle of whitewashed alleys and arches centred on a lively, lived-in piazza and popular beach.

◉ Sights

★ **Cattedrale di Sant'Andrea**　CATHEDRAL
(☑ 089 87 10 59; Piazza del Duomo; ◷ 7.30am-7.45pm) A melange of architectural styles, Amalfi's cathedral, one of the few relics of the town's past as an 11th-century maritime superpower, makes a striking impression at the top of its sweeping flight of stairs. Between 10am and 5pm entrance is through the adjacent **Chiostro del Paradiso** (☑ 089 87 13 24; Piazza del Duomo; adult/reduced €3/1; ◷ 9am-7pm), a 13th-century cloister.

The cathedral dates in part from the early 10th century and its stripey facade has been rebuilt twice, most recently at the end of the 19th century. Although the building is a hybrid, the Sicilian Arabic-Norman style predominates, particularly in the two-tone masonry and the 13th-century bell tower. The huge bronze doors also merit a look; the first of their type in Italy, they were commissioned by a local noble and made in Syria before being shipped to Amalfi. Less impressive is the baroque interior, although the altar features some fine statues and there are some interesting 12th- and 13th-century mosaics.

Museo della Carta　MUSEUM
(☑ 089 830 45 61; www.museodellacarta.it; Via delle Cartiere 23; admission €4; ◷ 10am-6.30pm daily Mar-Oct, 10am-3.30pm Tue, Wed & Fri-Sun Nov-Feb) Amalfi's paper museum is housed in a rugged, cave-like 13th-century paper mill (the oldest in Europe). It lovingly preserves the original paper presses, which are still in full working order, as you'll see during the 15-minute guided tour (in English), which explains the original cotton-based paper

OFF THE BEATEN TRACK

NOCELLE

A world apart from self-conscious Positano, the tiny, left-alone mountain village of Nocelle (450m) affords some of the most spectacular views on the entire coast. A stop on the Sentiero degli Dei hiking route, it's a sleepy, silent place where not much ever happens, much to the delight of its very few residents. If you can't pull yourself away, consider checking in at **Villa della Quercia** (☑089 812 34 97; www.villadellaquercia.com; Via Nocelle 5; r €70-80; ☺Apr-Oct; ☜), a former monastery with a heavenly panorama. If peckish, tuck into delicious, regional dishes at **Trattoria Santa Croce** (www.ristorantesantacrocepositano.com; Via Nocelle 19; ☺noon-2.30pm & 7-11pm Apr-Oct), a reliable low-key nosh spot in the main part of the village.

The easiest way to get to Nocelle is by local bus from Positano (€1.20, 30 minutes, 14 daily). If you're driving, follow the signs from Positano. Hikers tackling the Sentiero degli Dei might want to stop off as they pass through.

production and the later wood-pulp manufacturing. Afterwards you may well be inspired to pick up some of the stationery sold in the gift shop, alongside calligraphy sets and paper pressed with flowers.

Grotta dello Smeraldo　　　　CAVE
(admission €5; ☺9.30am-4pm) Four kilometres west of Amalfi, this grotto is named after the eerie emerald colour that emanates from the water. Stalactites hang down from the 24m-high ceiling, while stalagmites grow up to 10m tall. Buses regularly pass the car park above the cave entrance (from where you take a lift or stairs down to the rowing boats). Alternatively, **Coop Sant'Andrea** (☑089 87 29 50; www.coopsantandrea.com; Lungomare dei Cavalieri 1) runs boats from Amalfi (€10 return, plus cave admission). Allow 1½ hours for the return trip.

🏃 Activities

Amalfi Marine　　　　　　　BOATING
(☑329 2149811; www.amalfiboats.it; Spiaggia del Porto, Lungomare dei Cavalieri) Run by American local resident Rebecca Brooks, Amalfi Marine hires out boats (without a skipper

from €250 per day, per boat; maximum six passengers). It also organises day-long excursions along the coast and to the islands (from €45 per person).

🎉 Festivals & Events

Every 24 December and 6 January, divers from all over Italy make a pilgrimage to the ceramic *presepe* (nativity scene) submerged in the Grotta dello Smeraldo.

The **Regatta of the Four Ancient Maritime Republics**, which rotates between Amalfi, Venice, Pisa and Genoa, is held on the first Sunday in June. Amalfi's turn comes round again in 2017.

🛌 Sleeping

Albergo Sant'Andrea　　　　HOTEL €
(☑089 87 11 45; www.albergosantandrea.it; Via Duca Mansone I; s/d €60/90; ☺Mar-Oct; ❄☜) Enjoy the atmosphere of busy Piazza del Duomo from the comfort of your own room. This modest two-star has basic rooms with brightly coloured tiles and coordinating fabrics. Double glazing has helped cut down the piazza hubbub, which can reach fever pitch in high season – this is one place to ask for a room with a (cathedral) view.

Residenza del Duca　　　　HOTEL €€
(☑089 873 63 65; www.residencedelduca.it; Via Duca Mastalo II 3; s €70, d €130; ☺Mar-Oct; ❄) This family-run hotel has just six rooms, all of them light, sunny, and prettily furnished with antiques, majolica tiles and the odd chintzy cherub. The jacuzzi showers are excellent. Call ahead if you are carrying heavy bags, as it's a seriously puff-you-out-climb up some steps to reach here and a luggage service is included in the price. Room 2 is a particular winner, with its French windows and stunning views.

Hotel Lidomare　　　　　HOTEL €€
(☑089 87 13 32; www.lidomare.it; Largo Duchi Piccolomini 9; s/d €65/145; ☺year-round; ❄☜) Family run, this old-fashioned hotel has real character. The large, luminous rooms have an air of gentility, with their appealingly haphazard decor, vintage tiles and fine antiques. Some have jacuzzi bathtubs, others have sea views and a balcony, some have both. Rather unusually, breakfast is laid out on top of a grand piano.

Hotel Centrale　　　　　HOTEL €€
(☑089 87 26 08; www.amalfihotelcentrale.it; Largo Duchi Piccolomini 1; d €100-120; ☺Easter-Oct;

❄@⊚) This is one of the best-value hotels in Amalfi. The entrance is on a tiny little piazza in the *centro storico*, but many of the small but tastefully decorated rooms overlook Piazza del Duomo. The aquamarine ceramic tiling lends it a vibrant, fresh look and the views from the rooftop terrace are magnificent.

★ Hotel Luna Convento HOTEL €€€

(✒ 089 87 10 02; www.lunahotel.it; Via Pantaleone Comite 33; s €250-300, d €270-320, ste €460-620; ⊙ Easter-Oct; P ❄@⊚▧) This former convent was founded by St Francis in 1222 and has been a hotel for some 170 years. Rooms in the original building are in the former monks' cells, but there's nothing poky about the bright tiles, balconies and seamless sea views. The newer wing is equally beguiling, with religious frescoes over the bed. The cloistered courtyard is magnificent.

✕ Eating

La Pansa CAFE €

(✒ 089 87 10 65; www.pasticceriapansa.it; Piazza del Duomo 40; cornetti & pastries from €1.50; ⊙ 8am-10pm Wed-Mon) A marbled and mirrored 1830 cafe on Piazza del Duomo where black-bow-tied waiters serve a great Italian breakfast: freshly made *cornetti* and deliciously frothy cappuccino.

Il Teatro TRATTORIA €€

(✒ 089 87 24 73; Via E Marini 19; meals €25; ⊙ 11.30am-3pm & 6.30-11pm, closed Wed; 🌿) Superb no-fuss trattoria tucked away in the atmospheric backstreets of the *centro storico* (Via E Marini is reached via Salita delgi Orafi). Seafood specialities include *pesce spada il teatro* (swordfish in a tomato, caper and olive-oil sauce), plus there are good vegetarian options, including *scialatielli al teatro* (pasta with tomatoes and aubergines).

Le Arcate ITALIAN €€

(✒ 089 87 13 67; www.learcate.net; Largo Orlando Buonocore, Atrani; pizzas from €6, meals €25; ⊙ 12.30-3pm & 7.30-11.30pm Tue-Sun Sep-Jun, daily Jul & Aug) On a sunny day, it's hard to beat the dreamy location: at the far eastern point of the harbour overlooking the beach, with Atrani's ancient rooftops and church tower behind you. Huge white parasols shade the sprawl of tables, while the dining room is a stone-walled natural cave. Pizzas are served at night; daytime fare includes risotto with seafood and grilled swordfish.

The food is good, but it's a step down from the setting.

★ Marina Grande SEAFOOD €€€

(✒ 089 87 11 29; www.ristorantemarinagrande.com; Viale Delle Regioni 4; tasting menu lunch/dinner €25/60, meals €45; ⊙ noon-3pm & 6.30-11pm Tue-Sun Mar-Oct) 🍴 Run by the third generation of the same family, this beachfront restaurant serves fish so fresh it's almost flapping. It prides itself on its use of locally sourced organic produce, which, in Amalfi, means high-quality seafood.

ℹ Information

Post Office (Corso delle Repubbliche Marinare 31) Next door to the tourist office.

Tourist Office (✒ 089 87 11 07; www.amalfi touristoffice.it; Corso delle Repubbliche Marinare 33; ⊙ 9am-1pm & 2-6pm Mon-Sat)

ℹ Getting There & Away

BOAT

Between April and October there are daily sailings to/from Amalfi.

Alicost (p86) Operates three daily services to Positano (€8, 20 minutes), with two stopping in Capri (€20.80, 80 minutes) and Sorrento (€17, 60 minutes).

TraVelMar (p86) Runs ferries to Positano (€8, 25 minutes, seven daily), Minori (€3, 10 minutes, six daily), Maiori (€3, 15 minutes, six daily) and Salerno (€8, 35 minutes, seven daily).

NLG (p86) Sails once daily service to Positano (€8, 15 minutes) and Capri (€21.30, 80 minutes).

BUS

SITA Sud (p83) runs frequent daily services from Piazza Flavio Gioia to Sorrento (€3.40, 100 minutes) via Positano (€2.20, 50 minutes), as well as to Ravello (€1.60, 25 minutes) and Salerno (€2.80, 1¼ hours). Buy tickets and check current schedules at Bar Il Giardino delle Palme, opposite the bus stop.

Ravello

POP 2500

Sitting high in the hills above Amalfi, refined Ravello is a polished town almost entirely dedicated to tourism. Boasting impeccable bohemian credentials (Wagner, DH Lawrence and Virginia Woolf all lounged here), it's today known for its ravishing gardens and stupendous views, the best in the world according to former resident Gore Vidal.

Most people visit on a day trip from Amalfi – a nerve-tingling 7km drive up the Valle del Dragone – although to best enjoy Ravello's romantic other-worldly atmosphere you'll need to stay overnight.

The **tourist office** (☏089 85 70 96; www.ravellotime.it; Via Roma 18; ☺9am-7pm) has information on the town and its walking trails.

◉ Sights & Activities

Cathedral
CATHEDRAL

(Piazza Duomo; museum €3; ☺8.30am-noon & 5.30-8.30pm) Forming the eastern flank of Piazza Duomo, the cathedral was built in 1086 but has since undergone various makeovers. The facade is 16th century, but the central bronze door, one of only about two dozen in the country, dates from 1179; the interior is a late-20th-century interpretation of what the original must once have looked like.

Of particular interest is the striking pulpit, supported by six twisting columns set on marble lions and decorated with flamboyant mosaics of peacocks and other birds. Note also how the floor is tilted towards the square – a deliberate measure to enhance the perspective effect. Entry is via the cathedral museum.

★Villa Rufolo
GARDENS

(☏089 85 76 21; www.villarufolo.it; Piazza Duomo; adult/reduced €5/3; ☺9am-5pm) To the south of Ravello's cathedral, a 14th-century tower marks the entrance to this villa, famed for its beautiful cascading gardens. Created by a Scotsman, Scott Neville Reid, in 1853, they are truly magnificent, commanding divine panoramic views packed with exotic colours, artistically crumbling towers and luxurious blooms. Note that the gardens are at their best from May till October; they don't merit the entrance fee outside those times.

The villa was built in the 13th century for the wealthy Rufolo dynasty and was home to several popes as well as king Robert of Anjou. Wagner was so inspired by the gardens when he visited in 1880 that he modelled the garden of Klingsor (the setting for the second act of the opera *Parsifal*) on them. Today the gardens are used to stage concerts during the town's classical-music festival.

Villa Cimbrone
GARDENS

(☏089 85 80 72; www.villacimbrone.com; Via Santa Chiara 26; adult/reduced €7/4; ☺9am-7.30pm summer, to sunset winter) Some 600m south of Piazza Duomo, the Villa Cimbrone is worth a wander, if not for the 11th-century villa itself (now an upmarket hotel), then for the fabulous views from the delightful gardens. They're best admired from the Belvedere of Infinity, an awe-inspiring terrace lined with classical-style statues and busts.

⁂ Festivals & Events

★Ravello Festival
PERFORMING ARTS

(☏089 85 83 60; www.ravellofestival.com; ☺Jun-Sep) Between late June and early September, the Ravello Festival – established in 1953 – turns much of the town centre into a stage. Events range from orchestral concerts and chamber music to ballet performances; film screenings and exhibitions are held in atmospheric outdoor venues, most notably the famous overhanging terrace in the Villa Rufolo gardens.

⊨ Sleeping

Agriturismo Monte Brusara
AGRITURISMO €

(☏089 85 74 67; www.montebrusara.com; Via Monte Brusara 32; s/d €45/90; ☺year-round) An authentic working farm, this mountainside *agriturismo* is located a tough half-hour walk of about 1.5km from Ravello's centre (call ahead to arrange to be picked up). It is especially suited to families – children can feed the pony while you sit back and admire the views – or to those who simply want to escape the crowds. The three rooms are comfy but basic, the food is fabulous and the owner is a charming, garrulous host. Half-board is also available.

Hotel Villa Amore
PENSION €€

(☏089 85 71 35; www.villaamore.it; Via dei Fusco 5; s/d €65/120; ☺May-Oct; @) This welcoming family-run *pensione* is the best choice in town by price. Tucked down a quiet lane, it has modest, homey rooms and sparkling bathrooms. All rooms have a balcony and some have bathtubs. The restaurant is a further plus, its terrace boasting (still more) fabulous views: the food's good and prices are reasonable (around €25 for a meal).

★Hotel Caruso
HOTEL €€€

(☏089 85 88 01; www.hotelcaruso.com; Piazza San Giovanni del Toro 2; s €575-720; d €757-976; ☺Apr-Nov; ᴾ✳ি⩩) There can be no better place to swim than the Caruso's sensational infinity pool. Seemingly set on the edge of a precipice, its blue waters merge with sea and sky to magical effect. Inside, the sublimely restored 11th-century *palazzo* is no less impressive, with Moorish arches doubling as window frames, 15th-century vaulted ceilings and high-class ceramics.

Eating

Babel
CAFE €€

(☑089 85 86 215; Via Trinità 13; meals €20; ⊗11am-11pm) A cool little white-painted deli-cafe serving high-quality, affordable salads, bruschetta, cheese and meat boards and an excellent range of local wines. There's a jazz soundtrack, and a little gallery selling unusually stylish ceramic tiles.

Da Salvatore
ITALIAN €€

(☑089 85 72 27; www.salvatoreravello.com; Via della Republicca 2; meals €28; ⊗noon-3pm & 7.30-10pm Tue-Sun) Located just before the bus stop, Da Salvatore has nothing special by way of decor, but the view, from both the dining room and the large terrace, is very special indeed. Dishes include creative options like tender squid on a bed of pureed chickpeas with spicy *peperoncino*.

In the evening, part of the restaurant is transformed into an informal pizzeria, serving some of the best wood-fired pizza you will taste anywhere this side of Naples.

❶ Getting There & Away

SITA Sud (p83) operates regular daily buses from Piazza Flavio Gioia in Amalfi (€1.60, 25 minutes).

By car, turn north about 2km east of Amalfi. Vehicles are not permitted in Ravello's pedestrianised town centre and the metered parking around it is costly: €5 an hour and only payable by credit card.

South of Amalfi

From Amalfi to Salerno

The 26km drive to Salerno, though less exciting than the 16km stretch westwards to Positano, is exhilarating and dotted with a series of small towns, each with their own character and each worth a brief look.

Three and a half kilometres east of Amalfi, or a steep 1km-long walk down from Ravello, **Minori** is a small workaday town, popular with holidaying Italians. If you're a sweet tooth, pit stop at **Gambardella** (☑089 87 72 99; www.gambardella.it; Piazza Cantilena 7; pastries from €1.50), a *pasticceria* (pastry shop) peddling exemplary treats, including *torta di ricotta e pera* (ricotta and pear tart).

Further along, **Maiori** is the coast's biggest resort, a brassy place full of large seafront hotels, restaurants and beach clubs.

Just beyond **Erchie** and its beautiful beach, **Cetara** is a picturesque tumbledown fishing village with a reputation as a gastronomic highlight. Tuna and anchovies are the local specialities, appearing in various guises at **Al Convento** (☑089 26 10 39; www.alconvento.net; Piazza San Francesco 16; meals €25; ⊗12.30-3pm & 7-11pm summer, closed Wed winter), a sterling seafood restaurant near the small harbour. Particularly delicious is the spaghetti served with anchovies and wild fennel.

Shortly before Salerno, the road passes through **Vietri sul Mare**, the ceramics capital of Campania. Pop into **Ceramica Artistica Solimene** (☑089 21 02 43; www.ceramicasolimene.it; Via Madonna degli Angeli 7; ⊗9am-7pm Mon-Fri, 10am-1pm & 4-7pm Sat), a vast ceramics factory outlet with an extraordinary glass-and-ceramic facade by Italian architect Paoli Soleri, a former student of American architect Frank Lloyd Wright.

Salerno

POP 139,000

Upstaged by the glut of postcard-pretty towns along the Amalfi Coast, Campania's second-largest city is actually a pleasant surprise. A decade of civic determination has turned this major port and transport hub into one of southern Italy's most liveable cities, and its small but buzzing *centro storico* is a vibrant mix of medieval churches, tasty trattorias and good-spirited, bar-hopping locals.

Originally an Etruscan and later a Roman colony, Salerno flourished with the arrival of the Normans in the 11th century. Robert Guiscard made it the capital of his dukedom in 1076 and, under his patronage, the Scuola Medica Salernitana was renowned as one of medieval Europe's greatest medical institutes. More recently, it was left in tatters by the heavy fighting that followed the 1943 landings of the American 5th Army, just south of the city.

◉ Sights

★Duomo
CATHEDRAL

(Piazza Alfano; ⊗9am-6pm Mon-Sat, 4-6pm Sun) You can't miss the looming presence of Salerno's impressive cathedral, widely considered to be the most beautiful medieval church in Italy. Built by the Normans in the

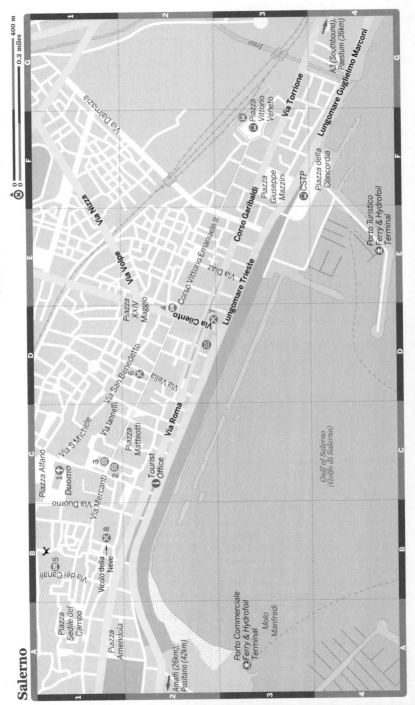

Salerno

Piazza Sedile del Campo

Piazza Amendola

Via del Canali

Piazza Alfano

Via Duomo

Duomo

Via Mercanti

Via S Michele

Vicolo della Neve

Via Iannelli

Piazza Matteotti

Tourist Office

Via San Benedetto

Piazza XXIV Maggio

Via Volpe

Via Nizza

Via Dalmazia

Via Vella

Via Roma

Via Cilento

Corso Vittorio Emanuele II

Via Diaz

Corso Garibaldi

Lungomare Trieste

Piazza Giuseppe Mazzini

CSTP

Piazza della Concordia

Piazza Vittorio Veneto

Via Torrione

Lungomare Guglielmo Marconi

A3 (Southbound); Paestum (36km)

Porto Turistico Ferry & Hydrofoil Terminal

Gulf of Salerno (Golfo di Salerno)

Porto Commerciale Ferry & Hydrofoil Terminal

Molo Manfredi

Amalfi (26km); Positano (42km)

Irno

400 m
0.2 miles

Salerno

◎ **Top Sights**
1 Duomo..................................C1

◎ **Sights**
2 Museo Pinacoteca Provinciale............C1
3 Museo Virtuale della Scuola
Medica Salernitana..........................C1

🛏 **Sleeping**
4 Hotel Montestella....................D2
5 Ostello Ave Gratia Plena.................B1

🍴 **Eating**
6 La Cantina del Feudo....................D2
7 Pizza Margherita........................D2
8 Vicolo della Neve........................B1

11th century and later aesthetically remodelled in the 18th century, it sustained severe damage in a 1980 earthquake. It is dedicated to San Matteo (St Matthew), whose remains were reputedly brought to the city in 954 and now lie beneath the main altar in the vaulted crypt.

Take special note of the magnificent main entrance, the 12th-century **Porta dei Leoni**, named after the marble lions at the foot of the stairway. It leads through to a beautiful, harmonious courtyard, surrounded by graceful arches and overlooked by a 12th-century bell tower. Carry on through the huge bronze doors (similarly guarded by lions), which were cast in Constantinople in the 11th century. When you come to the three-aisled interior, you will see that it is largely baroque, with only a few traces of the original church. These include parts of the transept and choir floor and the two raised pulpits in front of the choir stalls. Throughout the church you can see extraordinarily detailed and colourful 13th-century mosaic work.

In the right-hand apse, don't miss the **Cappella delle Crociate** (Chapel of the Crusades), containing stunning frescoes and more wonderful mosaics. It was so named because crusaders' weapons were blessed here. Under the altar stands the tomb of 11th-century pope Gregory VII.

Castello di Arechi   CASTLE
(☑089 296 40 15; www.ilcastellodiarechi.it; Via Benedetto Croce; adult/reduced €5/2.50; ☉9am-7pm Tue-Sat, to 6.30pm Sun summer, to 5pm Tue-Sun winter) Hop on bus 19 from Piazza XXIV Maggio to visit Salerno's most famous landmark, the forbidding Castello di Arechi, dramatically positioned 263m above the city. Originally a Byzantine fort, it was built by the Lombard duke of Benevento, Arechi II, in the 8th century and subsequently modified by the Normans and Aragonese, most recently in the 16th century.

The views of the Gulf of Salerno and the city rooftops are spectacular; you can also visit a permanent collection of ceramics, arms and coins. If you are here during summer, ask the tourist office for a schedule of the annual series of concerts staged here.

Museo Virtuale della Scuola
Medica Salernitana   MUSEUM
(☑089 257 61 26; www.museovirtualescuola medicasalernitana.beniculturali.it; Via Mercanti 74; adult/reduced €3/1; ☉9.30am-1pm Tue-Wed, 9.30am-1pm & 5-8pm Thu-Sat, 10am-1pm Sun; 🖐) Slap bang in Salerno's historic centre, this engaging museum deploys 3D and touchscreen technology to explore the teachings and wince-inducing procedures of Salerno's once-famous, now-defunct medical institute. Established around the 9th century, the school was the most important centre of medical knowledge in medieval Europe, reaching the height of its prestige in the 11th century. It was closed in the early 19th century.

Museo Pinacoteca Provinciale   MUSEUM
(☑089 258 30 73; www.museibiblioteche. provincia.salerno.it; Via Mercanti 63; adult/reduced €3/1.50; ☉9am-7.45pm Tue-Sun) **FREE** Art enthusiasts should seek out the Museo Pinacoteca Provinciale, located deep in the heart of the historic quarter. Spread throughout six galleries, the museum houses a collection dating from the Renaissance right up to the first half of the 20th century.

🛏 Sleeping

Ostello Ave Gratia Plena   HOSTEL €
(☑089 23 47 76; www.ostellodisalerno.it; Via dei Canali; dm/s/d €16/45/65; ☉year-round; @🖥) Housed in a 16th-century convent, Salerno's excellent HI hostel is right in the heart of the *centro storico*. Inside there's a charming central courtyard and a range of bright rooms, from dorms to great bargain doubles with private bathroom. The 2am curfew is for dorms only.

Hotel Montestella   HOTEL €€
(☑089 22 51 22; www.hotelmontestella.it; Corso Vittorio Emanuele II 156; s/d/tr €75/100/110;

year-round; ✱@☎) Within walking distance of just about anywhere worth going to, the Montestella is on Salerno's main pedestrian thoroughfare, halfway between the *centro storico* and train station. The rooms are spacious and comfortable, with blue carpeting and patterned wallpaper, while the public spaces have a fresh, modern look. It's one of the best midrange options in town.

✖ Eating

★ **Vicolo della Neve**   ITALIAN €
(☎089 22 57 05; www.vicolodellaneve.it; Vicolo della Neve 24; meals €20; ⊙7-11.30pm Thu-Tue) A city institution on a scruffy street, this is the archetypal *centro storico* trattoria, with brick arches, fake frescoes and walls hung with works by local artists. The menu is, similarly, unwaveringly authentic, with pizzas and *calzones, peperoni ripieni* (stuffed peppers) and a top-notch *parmigiana di melanzane* (baked aubergine). It can get incredibly busy: book well in advance.

Pizza Margherita   ITALIAN €
(☎089 22 88 80; Corso Garibaldi 201; pizzas/ buffet from €5/6.50, lunch menu €8.50; ⊙12.30-3.30pm & 7.30pm-midnight; 👶) It looks like a bland, modern canteen, but this is, in fact, one of Salerno's most popular lunch spots. Locals regularly queue for the lavish lunchtime buffet that, on any given day, might include buffalo mozzarella, salami, mussels in various guises and a range of salads.

If that doesn't appeal, the daily lunch menu (pasta, main course, salad and half a litre of bottled water) is chalked up on a blackboard, or there's the regular menu of pizzas, pastas, salads and main courses.

La Cantina del Feudo   ITALIAN €€
(☎089 25 46 96; Via Velia 45; meals €28; ⊙noon-2pm & 7-11pm Tue-Sun; 🖋) Frequented by locals in the know, this restaurant is tucked up a side street off the pedestrian *corso*. The menu changes daily, but the emphasis is on vegetable dishes like white beans with chicory, noodles and turnip tops, and ravioli stuffed with cheese. The interior has a rural trattoria feel and there's a terrace for alfresco dining.

❶ Information

Post Office (Corso Garibaldi 203)
Tourist Office (☎089 23 14 32; Lungomare Trieste 7; ⊙9am-1pm & 3-7pm Mon-Sat) Has limited information.

❶ Getting There & Away

BOAT
Between April and October there are daily sailings to/from Salerno.
Caremar (Map p48; ☎02 577 65 871; www. caremar.it) Runs a daily hydrofoil to/from Capri (€18.30, 50 minutes).
Alicost (p86) Runs several daily hydrofoils to/ from Capri (€21, 50 minutes), Amalfi (€8, 20 minutes) and Positano (€12, 30 minutes). Departures are from the Porto Turistico, 200m down the pier from Piazza della Concordia. You can buy tickets from the booths by the embarkation point.

Departures for Capri leave from Molo Manfredi at the Porto Commerciale.

BUS
SITA Sud (p83) Buses for Amalfi (€2.80, 1¼ hours, at least hourly) depart from Piazza Vittorio Veneto, beside the train station, stopping en route at Vietri sul Mare, Cetara, Maiori and Minori. Tickets are available inside the train station.
CSTP (☎089 48 70 01; www.cstp.it) Bus 50 runs from Piazza Vittorio Veneto to Pompeii (€2.80, 70 minutes, 15 daily). For Paestum take bus 34 from the CSTP bus stop on Piazza della Concordia (€3.40, one hour and 20 minutes, 12 daily).

CAR & MOTORCYCLE
Salerno is on the A3 between Naples and Reggio di Calabria; the A3 is toll-free from Salerno south. If you want to hire a car, there's a **Europcar** (☎089 258 07 75; www.europcar.com; Via Clemente Mauro 18) agency between the train station and Piazza della Concordia.

TRAIN
Salerno is a major stop on southbound routes to Calabria, and the Ionian and Adriatic Coasts. From the station in Piazza Vittorio Veneto there are regular trains to Naples (€9, 35 minutes, half-hourly) and Rome (Intercity, from €21, three hours, hourly).

❶ Getting Around
Walking is the most sensible option; from the train station it's a 1.2km walk along Corso Vittorio Emanuele II to the historic centre.

Paestum

Paestum, or Poseidonia as the city was originally called (in honour of Poseidon, the Greek god of the sea), was founded in the 6th century BC by Greek settlers and fell under Roman control in 273 BC. It became an important trading port and remained so until the fall of the Roman Empire, when periodic outbreaks of malaria and savage Saracen raids led its weakened citizens to abandon the town.

Its ancient temples are utterly unmissable, not to mention an easy day trip from Salerno or Agropoli. For more information on Paestum and the Costiera Cilentana, drop into the local **tourist office** (☑0828 81 10 16; www.infopaestum.it; Via Magna Crecia 887; ☺9am-1.30pm & 2.30-7pm Mon-Sat).

◉ Sights

Paestum's Temples ARCHAEOLOGICAL SITE
(☑0828 81 10 23; incl museum adult/reduced €10/5; ☺8.45am-7.45pm, last entry 7pm Jun & Jul, as early as 3.35pm Nov) A Unesco World Heritage Site, these temples are among the best-preserved monuments of Magna Graecia, the Greek colony that once covered much of southern Italy. Rediscovered in the late 18th century, the site as a whole wasn't unearthed until the 1950s. Lacking the tourist mobs that can sully better-known archaeological sites, the place has a wonderful serenity. Take sandwiches and prepare to stay at least three hours. In spring the temples are particularly stunning, surrounded by scarlet poppies.

Buy your tickets in the museum, just east of the site, before entering from the main entrance on the northern end. The first structure is the 6th-century-BC **Tempio di Cerere** (Temple of Ceres); originally dedicated to Athena, it served as a Christian church in medieval times.

As you head south, you can pick out the basic outline of the large rectangular forum, the heart of the ancient city. Among the partially standing buildings are the vast domestic housing area and, further south, the amphitheatre; both provide evocative glimpses of daily life here in Roman times. In the former houses you'll see mosaic floors, and a marble *impluvium* that stood in the atrium and collected rainwater.

The **Tempio di Nettuno** (Temple of Neptune), dating from about 450 BC, is the largest and best preserved of the three temples at Paestum; only parts of its inside walls and roof are missing. Almost next door, the so-called basilica (in fact, a temple to the goddess Hera) is Paestum's oldest surviving monument. Dating from the middle of the 6th century BC, it's a magnificent sight, with nine columns across and

18 along the sides. Ask someone to take your photo next to one of the columns: it's a good way to appreciate the scale.

Save time for the **museum** (☑0828 81 10 23; ☺8.30am-7.30pm, last entry 6.45pm, closed 1st & 3rd Mon of month), which covers two floors and houses a collection of fascinating, if weathered, metopes (bas-relief friezes). This collection includes 33 of the original 36 metopes from the Tempio di Argiva Hera (Temple of Argive Hera), situated 9km north of Paestum, of which virtually nothing else remains. The star exhibit is the 5th-century-BC fresco Tomba del Truffatore (Tomb of the Diver), thought to represent the passage from life to death with its frescoed depiction of a diver in mid-air. The fresco was discovered in 1968 inside the lid of the tomb of a young man, alongside his drinking cup and oil flasks, which he would perhaps have used to oil himself for wrestling matches. Rare for the period in that it shows a human form, the fresco expresses pure delight in physicalilty, its freshness and grace eternally arresting. Below the diver, a symposium of men repose languidly on low couches and brandish drinking cups.

🛏 Sleeping & Eating

★**Casale Giancesare** B&B €
(☑333 1897737, 0828 72 80 61; www.casale-giancesare.it; Via Giancesare 8; s €65-120, d €65-120, apt per week €600-1300; ☺year-round; 🅿✳@☎☺) A 19th-century former farmhouse, this elegantly decorated stone-clad B&B is run by the delightful Voza family, who will happily ply you with their homemade wine and *limoncello*. It's located 2.5km from the glories of Paestum and surrounded by vineyards and olive and mulberry trees; views are stunning, particularly from the swimming pool.

Nonna Sceppa ITALIAN €€
(☑0828 85 10 64; Via Laura 53; meals €35; ☺12.30-3pm & 7.30-11pm Fri-Wed; 🍴) Seek out the superbly prepared, robust dishes at Nonna Sceppa, a family-friendly restaurant that's gaining a reputation throughout the region for excellence. Dishes are firmly seasonal and, during summer, concentrate on fresh seafood like the refreshingly simple grilled fish with lemon. Other popular choices include risotto with zucchini and artichokes, and spaghetti with lobster.

ⓘ Getting There & Away

The best way to get to Paestum by public transport is to take **CSTP** (☑ 089 48 70 01; www.cstp.it) bus 34 from Piazza della Concordia in Salerno.

Regular trains link Salerno with Paestum (€2.70, 32 minutes). From Paestum station, walk straight ahead through the stone arch and up Via Porta Sirena; it's a pleasant 10-minute walk.

If you're driving, you could take the A3 from Salerno and exit for the SS18 at Battipaglia. More pleasant is the Litoranea, the minor road that hugs the coast. From the A3 take the earlier exit for Pontecagnano and follow the signs for Agropoli and Paestum.

COSTIERA CILENTANA

Southeast of the Gulf of Salerno, the coastal plains begin to give way to wilder, jagged cliffs and unspoilt scenery, a taste of what lies further on in the stark hills of Basilicata and the wooded peaks of Calabria. Inland, dark mountains loom over the remote highlands of the Parco Nazionale del Cilento e Vallo di Diano, one of Campania's best-kept secrets.

Several destinations on the Cilento coast are served by the main rail route from Naples to Reggio di Calabria. Check Trenitalia (p58) for fares and times.

By car take the SS18, which connects Agropoli with Velia via the inland route, or the SS267, which hugs the coast.

Agropoli

POP 20,700

Located just south of Paestum, Agropoli is a busy summer resort, but otherwise a pleasant, tranquil town that makes a good base for exploring the Cilento coastline and park. While the shell is a fairly faceless grid of shop-lined streets, the kernel, the historic city centre, is a fascinating tangle of narrow cobbled streets with ancient churches, venerable residents and a castle with superb views.

◉ Sights

Il Castello CASTLE
(⊙10am-8pm) **FREE** Built by the Byzantines in the 5th century, the castle was strengthened during the Angevin period, the time of the Vespro War bloodbath. It continued to be modified, and only part of the original defensive wall remains. It's an enjoyable walk here through the historic centre, and you can wander the ramparts and enjoy magnificent views of the coastline and town.

🛏 Sleeping & Eating

Anna B&B, APARTMENT €
(☑ 0974 82 37 63; www.bbanna.it; Via S Marco 28-30, Agropoli; d €75-90; ⊙year-round; P❄) A great location, across from the town's sweeping sandy beach, this trim budget choice is known locally for its restaurant, where you can salivate over homemade morning *cornetti*. The rooms are large and plain with small balconies; specify a sea view to enjoy the sun setting over Sorrento. Sunbeds and bicycles can be hired for a minimal price.

Anna PIZZA €
(☑ 0974 82 37 63; www.ristorantepizzeriaanna.it; Lungomare San Marco 32; meals from €15, pizzas from €4; ⊙11am-midnight) At the city-centre end of the promenade, this has been a locals' favourite for decades. Family run, with a small B&B upstairs, Anna is best known for its pizzas, especially since a British broadsheet named Anna's *sorpresa* the best pizza in Italy in 2010, its seven-slice selection including mussels, aubergines, zucchini, marinated pork, ham, prawns and spicy sausage.

ⓘ Getting There & Away

CSTP (☑ 089 48 70 01; www.cstp.it) operates several buses daily to Agropoli from Salerno (€3.90, 75 to 80 minutes) and Paestum (€2.20, 20 minutes). If driving from Paestum, head south along the SS18.

Parco Nazionale del Cilento e Vallo di Diano

Stretching from the coast up to Campania's highest peak, Monte Cervati (1900m), and beyond to the regional border with Basilicata, the Parco Nazionale del Cilento e Vallo di Diano is Italy's second-largest national park. A little-explored area of barren heights and empty valleys, it's the perfect antidote to the holiday mayhem on the coast.

For further information stop by the tourist office (p95) in Paestum. For guided hiking opportunities, contact **Gruppo Escursionistico Trekking** (☑ 0975 7 25 86; www.get-vallodidiano.it; Via Provinciale 29, Silla di Sassano) or **Associazione Trekking Cilento** (☑ 0974 84 33 45; www.trekkingcilento.it; Via Cannetiello 6, Agropoli).

⊙ Sights & Activities

★ Grotte di Castelcivita
CAVE

(☑ 0828 77 23 97; www.grottedicastelcivita.com; Piazzale N Zonzi, Castelcivita; adult/reduced €10/8; ☺ standard tours 10.30am, noon, 1.30pm & 3pm Mar-Oct, plus 4.30pm & 6pm Apr-Sep; ℗ ♿) The grottoes are fascinating otherworldly caves that date from prehistoric times: excavations have revealed that they were inhabited 42,000 years ago, making them the oldest known settlement in Europe. Take a jacket, and leave the high heels at home, as paths are wet and slippery. Hard hats, and a certain level of fitness and mobility, are required. Located 40km southeast of Salerno, the complex is refreshingly non-commercial.

Although it extends over 4800m, only around half of the complex is open to the public. The one-hour tour winds around extraordinary stalagmites and stalactites, and a mesmerising play of colours, caused by algae, calcium and iron that tint the naturally sculpted rock shapes. The tour culminates in a cavernous lunar landscape – think California's Death Valley in miniature – called the Caverna di Bertarelli (Bertarelli Cavern). The caves are still inhabited – by bats – so no flash photos for fear of blinding them.

Grotte di Pertosa
CAVE

(☑ 0975 39 70 37; www.grottedipertosa-auletta.it; Pertosa; guided visits adult/reduced 100min €20/15, 75min €16/13, 60min €13/10; ☺ 9am-7pm Apr & May, 10am-7pm Jun-Aug, 10am-6pm Sep, reduced hours rest of year; ℗ ♿) (Re)discovered in 1932, the Grotte di Pertosa date back 35 million years. Used by the Greeks and Romans as places of worship, the caves burrow for some 2500m, with long underground passages and lofty grottoes filled with stalagmites and stalactites. The first part of the tour takes part as a boat (or raft) ride on the river; you disembark just before the waterfall (phew!) and continue on foot for around 800m, surrounded by marvellous rock formations and luminous crystal accretions.

Certosa di San Lorenzo
MONASTERY

(☑ 0975 77 74 45; Padula; adult/reduced €4/2; ☺ 9am-7pm Wed-Mon) One of the largest monasteries in southern Europe, the Certosa di San Lorenzo dates from 1306 and covers 250,000 sq metres. Numerologists can swoon at the following: 320 rooms and halls, 2500m of corridors, galleries and hallways, 300 columns, 500 doors, 550 windows, 13 courtyards, 100 fireplaces, 52 stairways and 41 fountains – in other words, it is *huge*.

You won't have time to see everything, be sure to visit the highlights, including the vast central courtyard (a venue for summer classical-music concerts), the magnificent wood-panelled library, frescoed chapels, and the kitchen with its grandiose fireplace and famous tale: apparently this is where the legendary 1000-egg omelette was made in 1534 for Charles V. Unfortunately, the historic frying pan is not on view!

Within the monastery you can also peruse the modest collection of ancient artefacts at the **Museo Archeologico Provinciale della Lucania Occidentale** (☑ 0975 7 71 17; ☺ 8am-1.15pm & 2-3pm Tue-Sat, 9am-1pm Sun) FREE .

🛏 Sleeping & Eating

★ Agriturismo i Moresani
AGRITURISMO €

(☑ 0974 90 20 86; www.imoresani.com; Località Moresani; d €90-110; ☺ Mar-Oct; ❀ 🐕 ≋) If you are seeking utter tranquility, head to this *agriturismo* 1.5km west of Casal Velino. The setting is bucolic: rolling hills in every direction, interspersed with grapevines, grazing pastures and olive trees. Family run, the 18-hectare farm produces its own *caprino* goat's cheese, wine, olive oil and preserves. Rooms have cream- and earth-coloured decor and surround a pretty private garden.

Trattoria degli Ulivi
ITALIAN €

(☑ 334 2595091; www.tavolacaldadegliulivi.it; Viale Certosa, Padula; menus from €12; ☺ Sun-Sat 11am-4pm) If you've worked up an appetite walking the endless corridors of the Certoza de San Lorenzo then this restaurant – located just 50m to the west – is the place to come. The decor is canteen-like, but the daily specials are affordable, tasty and generously proportioned. It serves snacks as well as four-course blow-out lunches.

Vecchia Pizzeria Margaret
PIZZA €

(☑ 0975 33 00 00; Via Luigi Curto, Pollo; pizza from €3) Fabulous wheels of pizza, cooked in a wood-fired oven; it also dishes up antipasti and pasta dishes. Service is fast and friendly, and prices are low. You'll find the restaurant just east of the river, near the hospital.

ℹ Getting There & Away

Public transport in the area is lacking and inconvenient. To get the best out of the park and the surrounding region, you will need a car. Car rental companies include Europcar (p94) in Salerno and **Alba Rent Car** (☑ 0974 82 80 99; Via A De Gasperi 82; per day from €50) in Agropoli.

1. Parco Archeologico di Baia (p59), Campi Flegrei **2.** Remains of a statue in Pompeii (p72) **3.** Tempio di Nettuno (p95), Paestum **4.** Ancient mosaic in Casa di Nettuno e Anfitrite (p71), Herculaneum

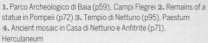

Historical Riches

Few Italian regions can match Campania's historical legacy. Colonised by the ancient Greeks and loved by the Romans, it's a sun-drenched repository of A-list antiquities, from World Heritage wonders to lesser-known archaeological gems.

Paestum

Great Greek temples never go out of vogue and those at Paestum (p94) are among the greatest outside Greece itself. With the oldest structures stretching back to the 6th century BC, this place makes Rome's Colosseum feel positively modern.

Herculaneum

A bite-sized Pompeii, Herculaneum (p71) is even better preserved than its nearby rival. This is the place to delve into the details, from once-upon-a-time shop advertisements and furniture, to vivid mosaics, even an ancient security grille.

Pompeii

Short of stepping into the Tardis, Pompeii (p72) is your best bet for a little time travel. Locked in ash for centuries, its excavated streetscapes offer a tangible, encounter with the ancients and their daily lives, from luxury homes to a racy brothel.

Subterranean Naples

Eerie aqueducts, mysterious burial crypts and ancient streetscapes: beneath Naples' hyperactive streets lies a wonderland of Graeco-Roman ruins. For a taste, head below the Complesso Monumentale di San Lorenzo Maggiore (p42) or follow the leader on a tour of the evocative Catacombe di San Gennaro.

Campi Flegrei

The Phlegraean Fields (p59) simmer with ancient clues. Roam where emperors bathed at the Parco Archeologico di Baia, sneak into a Roman engineering marvel at the Piscina Mirabilis, or spare a thought for doomed martyrs at the Anfiteatro Flavio.

Puglia, Basilicata & Calabria

Includes ➡

Bari.............................101
Promontorio del
Gargano 110
Isole Tremiti 115
Valle d'Itria................116
Lecce..........................122
Brindisi......................127
Matera.......................135
Appennino Lucano.....143
Cosenza 148
Parco Nazionale
della Sila....................149
Parco Nazionale
dell'Aspromonte 151
Reggio di Calabria......152

Why Go?

The Italian boot's heel (Puglia), instep (Basilicata) and toe (Calabria) are where you can witness the so-called Mezzogiorno (southern Italy) in all its throbbing intensity. This is a land of drying washing on weather-worn balconies, speeding scooters and dilapidated *centro storicos* (historic centres) that haven't yet qualified for a Unesco listing. Though the south's more down-to-earth cities lack the extensive tourist infrastructure of northern Italy, there's prettiness amid the grittiness.

Head to Lecce for an eye full of baroque magnificence, or soon-to-be European Capital of Culture Matera and its remarkable cave houses. Other southern secrets have yet to seep out: the intricate mosaic floor of Otranto cathedral and the Amalfi-like luminescence of Maratea have figured little in most travellers' itineraries to date. Equally underplayed is the simple yet epic *cucina povera* (peasant food) and the wild national parks (including Pollino, Italy's largest).

Best Unesco World Heritage Sites

➡ Matera (p135)

➡ Monte Sant'Angelo (p113)

➡ Castel del Monte (p110)

Best Magna Graecia Museums

➡ Museo Nazionale di Reggio Calabria (p152)

➡ Tavole Palatine (p142)

➡ Museo Nazionale Archeologico di Taranto (p133)

When to Go
Bari

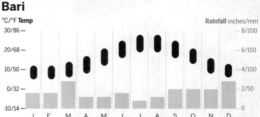

Apr–Jun Spring wildflowers are blooming: a perfect time for hiking in the mountains.

Jul & Aug Summer is beach weather and the best party time for festivals and events.

Sep & Oct No crowds, mild weather and wild mushrooms galore.

PUGLIA

Puglia is Italy's ascendant region, a place where savvy travellers bored or worn down by the crowds of Campania and Tuscany escape for something a bit less frenetic and manicured. Top of the list for prospective newcomers is the food. Puglia's *cucina povera* is about as earthy as Italian cuisine gets without eating it straight out of the soil. Then there's the exuberant architecture, best summarised by the word 'baroque' and exhibited in all its finery in the glittering 'Florence of the South', Lecce, and its smaller sibling, Gallipoli.

With the longest coastline of any region in mainland Italy, Puglia is larger than many people realise. In the north, the spur of land sticking out into the Adriatic is occupied by the balmy microclimates of the Gargano peninsula, a kind of miniature Amalfi with fewer poseurs. The Italian boot's 'stiletto' hosts the land of Salento, a dry scrubby region famous for its wines, and bloodthirsty Greek and Turkish history. In between lies the Valle d'Itria, a karstic depression populated by vastly contrasting medieval towns that have little in common apart from their haunting beauty.

Of the larger cities, Brindisi, an erstwhile Roman settlement, is one of the major departure points for Greece (by ferry), while Puglia's largest metropolis, Bari, has a university and trendier inclinations.

History

At times Puglia feels and looks Greek – and for good reason. This tangible legacy dates from when the Greeks founded a string of settlements along the Ionian coast in the 8th century BC. A form of Greek dialect (Griko) is still spoken in some towns southeast of Lecce. Historically, the major city was Taras (Taranto), settled by Spartan exiles who dominated until they were defeated by the Romans in 272 BC.

The long coastline made the region vulnerable to conquest. The Normans left their fine Romanesque churches, the Swabians their fortifications and the Spanish their flamboyant baroque buildings. No one, however, knows exactly the origins of the extraordinary 16th-century conical-roofed stone houses, the *trulli,* unique to Puglia.

Apart from invaders and pirates, malaria was long the greatest scourge of the south, forcing many towns to build away from the coast and into the hills. After Mussolini's seizure of power in 1922, the south became the frontline in his 'Battle for Wheat'. This initiative was aimed at making Italy self-sufficient when it came to food, following the sanctions imposed on the country after its conquest of Ethiopia. Puglia is now covered in wheat fields, olive groves and fruit arbours.

Bari

POP 320,200

If Lecce is the south's Florence, Bari is its Bologna, a historic but youthful town with a high percentage of students lending it a cooler and hipper edge. More urban than its neighbours Lecce and Brindisi, with grander boulevards and a more active nightlife, Bari supports a large university, a recently renovated opera house and municipal buildings that sparkle with a hint of northern grandiosity.

Some time-poor travellers skip over Bari on their way to Puglia's big-hitter, Lecce (the towns have a long-standing rivalry, especially over soccer), but Bari doesn't lack history or culture. The slower-paced old town contains the bones of St Nicholas (aka Santa Claus) in its Basilica di San Nicola, along with a strapping castle and plenty of unfussy trattorias that arguably plug the delicious local nosh – *cucina barese* – better than anywhere else in Puglia.

As the second-largest town in southern Italy, Bari is a busy port with connections to Greece, Albania and Croatia, and sports an international airport used by popular budget airlines.

ℹ️ Dangers & Annoyances

Once notorious for petty crime, Bari has cleaned up its act of late. Nonetheless, take all of the usual precautions: don't leave anything in your car; don't display money or valuables; and watch out for bag-snatchers on scooters. Be particularly careful in Bari Vecchia's dark streets at night.

◉ Sights

Most sights are in or near the atmospheric old town, Bari Vecchia, a medieval labyrinth of tight alleyways and graceful piazzas. It fills a small peninsula between the new port to the west and the old port to the southeast, cramming in 40 churches and more than 120 shrines.

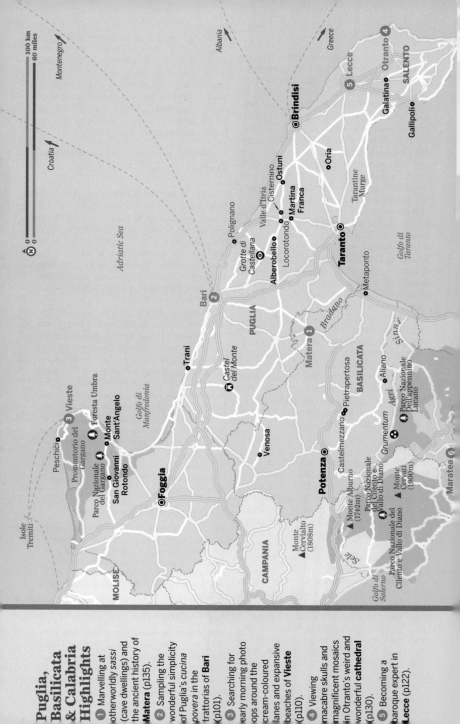

Puglia, Basilicata & Calabria Highlights

1 Marvelling at otherworldly *sassi* (cave dwellings) and the ancient history of **Matera** (p135).

2 Sampling the wonderful simplicity of Puglia's *cucina povera* in the trattorias of **Bari** (p101).

3 Searching for early morning photo ops around the cream-coloured lanes and expansive beaches of **Vieste** (p110).

4 Viewing macabre skulls and magnificent mosaics in Otranto's weird and wonderful **cathedral** (p130).

5 Becoming a baroque expert in **Lecce** (p122).

100 km
60 miles

Montenegro

Croatia

Albania

Greece

Isole
Tremiti

Adriatic Sea

Peschici **3** Vieste
Promontorio del Foresta Umbra
Gargano **4** Monte
Parco Nazionale Sant'Angelo
del Gargano San Giovanni
  Rotondo

*Golfo di
Manfredonia*

⊙Foggia

●Trani

CAMPANIA

Bari **2**

PUGLIA

Castel
del Monte

Polignano

Grotte di
Castellana

Alberobello ●
Locorotondo

Valle d'Itria
Cisternino
Ostuni

Martina
Franca

⊙Brindisi

5 Lecce

Otranto **4**

Galatina ●

SALENTO

Galipoli ●

Oria

Tarantine
Murge

Taranto ◉

Metaponto

*Golfo di
Taranto*

Venosa

Matera **1**

Castelmezzano

Monte
▲Cervialto
(1808m)

Monte Alburno
(1742m)

Seu

Parco Nazionale
del Cilento e
Vallo di Diano

*Golfo di
Salerno*

Parco Nazionale del
Cilento e Vallo di Diano

Potenza ◉

Pietrapertosa

Pietrapertosa

BASILICATA

Bradano

Agri

Sinn

Aliano

Grumentum

Parco Nazionale
Dell'appennino
Lucano

Monte
Cervati
(1900m)

Maratea **6**

MOLISE

6 Hiking on sinuous paths through vibrant Mediterranean foliage up to a massive statue of Jesus in the hills above **Maratea** (p144).

7 Admiring 2500-year-old Greek statues fashioned in bronze in the **Museo Nazionale di Reggio Calabria** (p152).

8 Enjoying walking and solitude in the wilds of the mysterious **Parco Nazionale dell'Aspromonte** (p151).

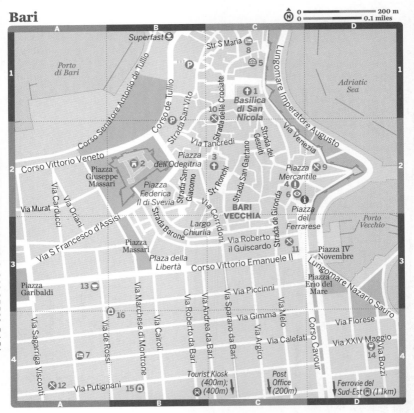

Bari

◉ Top Sights
1 Basilica di San Nicola	C1

◉ Sights
2 Castello Svevo	B2
3 Cathedral	C2
4 Colonna della Giustizia	C2
Museo del Succorpo della Cattedrale	(see 3)
5 Museo Nicolaiano	C1
6 Piazza Mercantile	C2

⊜ Sleeping
7 B&B Casa Pimpolini	A4
8 Santa Maria del Buon Consiglio	C1

⊗ Eating
9 La Locanda di Federico	D2
10 Maria delle Sgagliozze	C1
11 Paglionico Vini e Cucina	C3
12 Terranima	A4

◉ Drinking & Nightlife
13 Caffè Borghese	A3
14 Nessun Dorma	D4

⊜ Shopping
15 Enoteca Vinarius de Pasquale	B4
16 Il Salumaio	B4

Castello Svevo CASTLE
(Swabian Castle; ☑ 083 184 00 09; Piazza Federico II di Svevia; adult/reduced €3/1.50; ☺ 8.30am-7.30pm Thu-Tue) **FREE** The Normans originally built over the ruins of a Roman fort, then Frederick II built over the Norman castle, incorporating it into his design – the two towers of the Norman structure still stand. The bastions, with corner towers overhanging the moat, were added in the 16th centu-

ry during Spanish rule, when the castle was a magnificent residence.

★ Basilica di San Nicola
BASILICA

(www.basilicasannicola.it; Piazza San Nicola; ⊙7am-8.30pm Mon-Sat, to 10pm Sun) Bari's signature basilica was one of the first Norman churches to be built in southern Italy, and is a splendid example of Puglian-Romanesque architecture. Dating to the 12th century, it was originally constructed to house the relics of St Nicholas (better known as Father Christmas), which were stolen from Turkey in 1087 by local fishing folk. Today, it is an important place of pilgrimage for both Catholics and Orthodox Christians.

St Nicholas' remains, which are said to emanate a miraculous manna liquid with special powers, are ensconced in a shrine in the beautiful vaulted crypt. Above, the interior is huge and simple with a decorative 17th-century wooden ceiling. The magnificent 13th-century ciborium over the altar is Puglia's oldest. Other items related to the basilica, including chalices, vestments and crests, are displayed in the new-ish **Museo Nicolaiano** (Strada Vanese 1; ⊙11am-6pm Thu-Tue) FREE nearby.

Cathedral
CATHEDRAL

(Piazza dell'Odegitria; ⊙8am-12.30pm & 4-7.30pm Mon-Sat, 5-8.30pm Sun) Built over the original Byzantine church, the 11th-century Romanesque cathedral, dedicated to San Sabino, is technically Bari's most important church, although its fame pales alongside San Nicola. Inside, the plain walls are punctuated with deep arcades and the eastern window is a tangle of plant and animal motifs. The highlight lies in the subterranean **Museo del Succorpo della Cattedrale** (admission €1; ⊙9.30am-4pm Sun-Wed), where recent excavations have revealed remnants left over from an ancient Christian basilica and various Roman ruins. These include parts of a 2nd-century Roman road, the floor mosaic from a 5th-century palaeo-Christian basilica featuring octopuses, fish and plant motifs, and elements of a 9th-century Byzantine church. Talk about history in layers!

Piazza Mercantile
PIAZZA

This beautiful piazza is fronted by the Sedile, the headquarters of Bari's Council of Nobles. In the square's northeast corner is the **Colonna della Giustizia** (Column of Justice; Piazza Mercantile), where debtors were once tied and whipped.

★ Festivals & Events

Festa di San Nicola
RELIGIOUS

(⊙7-9 May) The Festival of St Nicholas is Bari's biggest annual shindig, celebrating the 11th-century arrival of St Nicholas' relics from Turkey. On the first evening a procession leaves Castello Svevo for the Basilica di San Nicola. The next day there's a deafening fly-past and a fleet of boats carries the statue of St Nicholas along the coast.

That evening – and the next – ends with a massive fireworks display. It's a jolly, crowded family affair, attended by many Russian visitors who come to view the relics.

⮞ Sleeping

Most hotel accommodation here tends to be bland and overpriced, aimed at business clientele. B&Bs are generally a better option.

Santa Maria del Buon Consiglio
B&B $

(⌨388 2227366; www.santamariadelbuon consiglio.com; Via Forno Santa Scolastica 1-3; s €35-70, d €60-100, tr €85-90; ✱ 🛜) A graciously hosted B&B in the heart of old Bari near the port. Rooms have rough-cast stone walls and four-poster beds with drapes.

B&B Casa Pimpolini
B&B $

(⌨080 521 99 38; www.casapimpolini.com; Via Calefati 249; s €45-60, d €70-80; ✱ @) This lovely B&B in the new town is within easy walking distance to shops, restaurants and Bari Vecchia. The rooms are warm and welcoming, and the homemade breakfast is a treat. Great value.

Villa Romanazzi Carducci
HOTEL $

(⌨080 542 74 00; www.villaromanazzi.com; Via Capruzzi 326; s/d from €59/69; 🅿 ✱ 🛜 ≋) The one hotel in Bari daring to show some flair, the Villa Romanazzi near the train station is run by the French Accor group. Businesslike rooms are modern and clean-lined, but the real bonuses are in the extras: gardens embellished with statues, a picturesque swimming pool (summer only), an enormous fitness centre, a spa and a decent restaurant with excellent breakfasts.

✗ Eating

★ Paglionico Vini e Cucina
OSTERIA $

(⌨338 2120391; Strada Vallisa 23; meals €20; ⊙noon-3pm & 7-11pm Mon-Sat, noon-3pm Sun) Run by the Paglionico family for more than a century, this 100% Italiano *osteria* (casual tavern) is an absolute classic. There's no menu, just a chalkboard displaying what's cooking that day. It's all fine salt-of-the-earth Puglian cuisine – the *riso, patate e cozze* (oven-baked rice, potatoes and mussels) is particularly good. The owners and waiters are brusque but brilliant.

Maria delle Sgagliozze   PUGLIAN $
(Strada delle Crociate; snacks €1; ⊙from 5pm) Octogenarian Maria dispenses the legendary Barese street food *sgagliozze* (deep-fried polenta cubes) from the front of her house. Sprinkle them with a pinch of salt and Bob's your uncle!

Terranima   PUGLIAN $$
(☑080 521 97 25; www.terranima.com; Via Putignani 213/215; meals €25-30; ⊙11.30am-3.30pm & 6.30-10.30pm Mon-Sat, 11.30am-3.30pm Sun) Peep through the lace curtains into the cool interior of this rustic trattoria where worn flagstone floors and period furnishings make you feel like you're dining in someone's front room. The menu features fabulous regional offerings such as veal, lemon and caper meatballs, and *sporcamuss*, a sweet flaky pastry.

La Locanda di Federico   PUGLIAN $$
(☑080 522 77 05; www.lalocandadifederico.com; Piazza Mercantile 63-64; meals €30; ⊙10.30am-3.30pm & 7pm-midnight) With domed ceilings, archways and medieval-style artwork on the walls, this restaurant oozes atmosphere. The menu is typical Puglian, starring dishes such as *orecchiette con le cime di rape* ('little ears' pasta with turnip tops) and prawns with pancetta. The people-watching is equally good – if you can take your eyes off the food.

🍷 Drinking & Nightlife

Nessun Dorma   COCKTAIL BAR
(www.nessundormabari.it; Via Fiume 3; ⊙11am-midnight Sun-Thu, 11am-3am Fri & Sat) This new aptly named bar (*nessun dorma* means 'nobody sleeps') behind the Teatro Petruzzelli stays open late at weekends with live music and DJ sets. The interior is mega-chic with plush sofas and fashionable furnishings. It also serves American-style food.

Caffè Borghese   CAFE
(☑080 524 21 56; Corso Vittorio Emanuele II 22; ⊙8am-2am Tue-Sun) You'll experience genuine hospitality and friendly service at this small refined cafe that has a faintly Parisian air. With an all-day menu, it serves some pretty good food starting with breakfast, but, with its casual tables and bustling bar,

it works best for a morning coffee, an afternoon *pausa* (break) or an evening cocktail.

🛍 Shopping

Designer shops and the main Italian chains line Via Sparano da Bari, while delis and gourmet food shops are located throughout the city.

Il Salumaio   FOOD
(☑080 521 93 45; www.ilsalumaio.it; Via Piccinni 168; ⊙8.30am-2pm & 4.30-9pm Mon-Sat) Breathe in the delicious smell of fine regional produce at this venerable delicatessen.

Enoteca Vinarius de Pasquale   WINE
(☑080 521 31 92; Via Marchese di Montrone 87; ⊙8am-2pm & 4-8.30pm Mon-Sat) Stock up on Puglian wines such as Primitivo di Manduria at this gorgeous old shop, founded in 1911.

ℹ Information

From Piazza Aldo Moro, in front of the main train station, streets heading north will take you to Corso Vittorio Emanuele II, which separates the old and new parts of the city.

Hospital (☑080 559 11 11; Piazza Cesare)
Morfimare Travel Agency (☑080 578 98 15; www.morfimare.it; Corso de Tullio 36-40) For ferry bookings.
Police Station (☑080 529 11 11; Via Murat 4)
Post Office (Piazza Umberto I 33/8)
Tourist Office (☑080 524 22 44; Piazza del Ferrarese 29; ⊙10am-1pm & 4-7pm) New office opened in 2014. There are also kiosks at the train station and airport.

ℹ Getting There & Away

AIR

Bari's **Palese airport** (www.aeroportidipuglia. it), 10km northwest of the city centre, is served by a host of international and budget airlines, including easyJet, Alitalia and Ryanair.

Pugliairbus (http://pugliairbus.aeroporti dipuglia.it) connects Bari airport with Foggia airport and Brindisi airport. It also has a service from Bari airport to Matera (€6, 1¼ hours, five daily), Vieste (€20, 2¾ hours, four daily) and Taranto (€9.50, 1¼ hours, two daily).

BOAT

Ferries run from Bari to Albania, Croatia, Greece and Montenegro. All boat companies have offices at the ferry terminal, accessible on bus 20 from the main train station. Fares vary considerably among companies and it's easier to book with a travel agent such as Morfimare The main companies and their routes are as follows:

Jadrolinija (☑080 527 54 39; www.jadrolinija. hr; Nuova Stazione Marittima di Bari) Ferries to Dubrovnik in Croatia. Up to six times a week in summer.

Montenegro Lines (☑382 3031 1164; www. montenegrolines.net; Corso de Tullio 36) To Bar in Montenegro.

Superfast (☑080 528 28 28; www.superfast. com; Corso di Tullio 6) To Corfu, Igoumenitsa and Patras in Greece. Departs at 7.30pm.

Ventouris Ferries (☑for Albania 080 521 27 56, for Greece 080 521 76 99; www.ventouris. gr; Nuova Stazione Marittima di Bari) Regular ferries to Corfu, Cephalonia and Igoumenitsa (Greece) and daily ferries to Durrës (Albania).

BUS

Intercity buses leave from two main locations. From Via Capruzzi, south of the main train station, **SITA** (☑080 579 01 11; www.sitabus.it) covers local destinations. **Ferrovie Appulo-Lucane** (☑080 572 52 29; http://ferrovie appulolucane.it) buses serving Matera (€4.90, 1¼ hours, six daily) also depart from here, plus **Marozzi** (☑080 556 24 46; www.marozzivt.it) buses for Rome (from €34.50, six hours, eight daily – note that the overnight bus departs from Piazza Moro) and other long-distance destinations.

Buses operated by **Ferrovie del Sud-Est** (FSE; ☑080 546 21 11; www.fseonline.it) leave from Largo Ciaia, south of Piazza Aldo Moro and service the following locations:

Alberobello (€4.90, 1¼ hours, hourly); continues to Locorotondo (€5.60, 1 hour 35 minutes) and Martina Franca (€5.60, 1 hour 50 minutes)

Grotte di Castellana (€2.80, one hour, five daily)

Taranto (€8.40, 1¾ to 2¼ hours, frequent)

TRAIN

A web of train lines spreads out from Bari. Note that there are fewer services on the weekend.

From the **main train station** (☑080 524 43 86), Trenitalia trains go to Puglia and beyond:

TO	FARE	DURATION (HRS)	FREQUENCY
Brindisi	€8.40	1	frequent
Foggia	€9	1	frequent
Milan	€66.50	7-10	every 4hrs
Rome	€54	4	every 4hrs

Ferrovie Appulo-Lucane serves two main destinations:

TO	FARE	DURATION (HRS)	FREQUENCY
Matera	€4.90	1½	12 daily
Potenza	€10.50	4	4 daily

Ferrovie del Sud-Est trains leave from the southern side of the station where they have their own separate ticket office.

TO	FARE	DURATION (HRS)	FREQUENCY
Albero-bello	€4.90	1½	hourly
Martina Franca	€5.60	2	hourly
Taranto	€8.40	2½	9 daily

❶ Getting Around

Central Bari is compact – a 15-minute walk will take you from Piazza Aldo Moro to the old town. For the ferry terminal, take bus 20 (tickets €1.50) from Piazza Moro.

Street parking is migraine-inducing. There's a large parking area (€1) south of the main port entrance; otherwise, there's a large multistorey car park between the main train station and the FSE station. Another car park is on Via Zuppetta opposite Hotel Adria.

TO/FROM THE AIRPORT

For the airport, take the **Tempesta shuttle bus** (www.autoservizitempesta.it) from the main train station (€4, 30 minutes, hourly), with pick-ups at Piazza Garibaldi and the corner of Via Andrea da Bari and Via Calefati. Alternatively, normal city bus 16 covers the same route and a trip is much cheaper (€1), though marginally slower (40 minutes). A taxi trip from the airport to town costs around €24.

Around Bari

The *Terra di Bari* (land of Bari') surrounding the capital is rich in olive groves and orchards, and the region has an impressive architectural history with some magnificent cathedrals, an extensive network of castles along its coastline, charming seaside towns like Trani and the mysterious inland Castel del Monte.

Trani

POP 53,900

Known as the 'Pearl of Puglia', beautiful Trani has a sophisticated feel, particularly

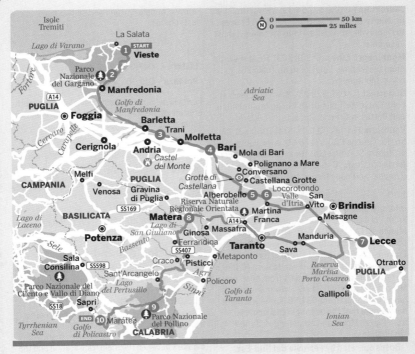

Driving Tour
Italy's Authentic South

START VIESTE
END MARATEA
LENGTH 650KM TO 700KM; ONE WEEK

Consider a gentle start in lovely, laid-back **1 Vieste** with its white sandy beaches and medieval backstreets, but set aside half a day to hike or bike in the lush green forests of the **2 Parco Nazionale del Gargano** (p110). Follow the coastal road past dramatic cliffs, salt lakes and flat farming land to **3 Trani**, with its impressive seafront cathedral and picturesque port, before spending a night in **4 Bari**, where you'll find hip bars and salt-of-the-earth trattorias. The next day head to **5 Alberobello**, home to a dense neighbourhood of extraordinary cone-shaped stone homes called *trulli*; consider an overnight *trulli* stay.

Stroll around one of the most picturesque *centro storico* (historic centres) in southern Italy at **6 Locorotondo**. Hit the road and cruise on to lively baroque **7 Lecce**, where you can easily chalk up a full day exploring the sights, shops and flamboyantly fronted *palazzi* and churches, including the Basilica di Santa Croce.

Day five will be one to remember. Nothing can prepare you for Basilicata's **8 Matera**, where *sassi* (former cave dwellings) are a dramatic reminder of the town's poverty-stricken past. After days of pasta, *fave* beans and *cornetti* (Italian croissants), it's high time for some exercise on the trails of the spectacular **9 Parco Nazionale del Pollino**. Finally, wind up the trip with more walking or a day of beach slothing at the spread out coastal town of **10 Maratea** with its surrounding seaside resorts, medieval village and cosmopolitan harbour offset by a thickly forested and mountainous interior.

in summer when well-heeled visitors pack the array of marina-side bars. The marina is the place to promenade and watch the white yachts and fishing boats in the harbour, while the historic centre, with its medieval churches, glossy limestone streets and faded yet charming *palazzi* is an enchanting area to explore. But it's the cathedral, pale against the deep-blue sea, that is the town's most arresting sight.

🔘 Sights

Cathedral
CATHEDRAL

(Piazza del Duomo; campanile €3; ⊘8.30am-12.30pm & 3.30-7pm Mon-Sat, 9am-12.30pm & 4-9pm Sun) The dramatic seafront cathedral is dedicated to St Nicholas the Pilgrim, famous for being foolish. The Greek Christian wandered through Puglia, crying *'Kyrie eleison'* (Greek for 'Lord, have mercy'). First thought to be a simpleton, he was revered after his death (aged 19) after several miracles attributed to him occurred. Below the church is the crypt, a forest of ancient columns where the bones of St Nicholas are kept beneath the altar. You can also visit the campanile (bell tower).

Construction of the cathedral started in 1097 on the site of a Byzantine church and was completed in the 13th century. The magnificent original bronze doors (now displayed inside) were cast by Barisano da Trani, an accomplished 12th-century artisan.

The interior of the cathedral reflects typical Norman simplicity and is lined by colonnades. Near the main altar are the remains of a 12th-century floor mosaic, stylistically similar to that in Otranto.

Castle
CASTLE

(☎0883 50 66 03; www.castelloditrani.benicultur ali.it; Piazza Manfredi 16; admission €3; ⊘8.30am-7pm) Two hundred metres north of the cathedral is Trani's other major landmark, the vast, almost modernist Swabian castle built by Frederick II in 1233. Charles V later strengthened the fortifications; it was used as a prison from 1844 to 1974.

Ognissanti Church
CHURCH

(Via Ognissanti; ⊘hours vary) Built by the Knights Templar in the 12th century, this church is where Norman knights swore allegiance to Bohemond I of Antioch, their leader, before setting off on the First Crusade.

ℹ️ TRAVELLING EAST

Puglia is the main jumping-off point for onward travel to Greece, Croatia and Albania. The two main ports are Bari and Brindisi, from where you can catch ferries to Vlorë and Durrës in Albania, Bar in Montenegro, and Cephalonia, Corfu, Igoumenitsa and Patras in Greece. Fares from Bari to Greece are generally more expensive than those from Brindisi. Taxes are usually from €9 per person and €12 per car. High season is generally the months of July and August, with reduced services in low season. Tariffs can be up to one-third cheaper in low season.

Scolanova Church
CHURCH

(☎0883 48 17 99; Via Scolanova 23; ⊘hours vary) This church was one of four former synagogues in the ancient Jewish quarter, all of which were converted to churches in the 14th century. Inside is a beautiful Byzantine painting of Madonna dei Martiri.

🛏️ Sleeping

Albergo Lucy
HOTEL **$**

(☎0883 48 10 22; www.albergolucy.com; Piazza Plebiscito 11; d/tr/q from €75/95/115; ✳🖥) Located in a restored 17th-century *palazzo* overlooking a leafy square and close to the shimmering port, this family run place oozes charm and is great value. Bike hire and guided tours are available. Breakfast isn't served, but there are plenty of cafes a short stroll away.

B&B Centro Storico Trani
B&B **$**

(☎0883 50 61 76; www.bbtrani.it; Via Leopardi 28; s €35-50, d €50-70, tr €70-80) This simple, old-fashioned B&B inhabits an old backstreet monastery and is run by an elderly couple. It's basic, but the rooms are large and 'Mama' makes a mean *crostata* (jam tart).

Hotel Regia
HOTEL **$$**

(☎0883 58 44 44; www.hotelregia.it; Piazza del Duomo 2; s €120-130, d €130-150; ✳🖥) A lone building facing the cathedral, the 18th-century Palazzo Filisio houses this charming hotel with understated grandeur. Rooms are sober and stylish, and the location is stupendous.

✕ Eating

★ Corteinfiore
SEAFOOD $$

(☑ 0883 50 84 02; www.corteinfiore.it; Via Ognissanti 18; meals €30; ⊙ 12.30-2.15pm & 8-10.15pm Tue-Sun) Romantic, urbane, refined. The wooden decking, buttercup-yellow tablecloths and marquee-conservatory setting are refreshing, while the wines are excellent and the cooking delicious. It also has modern and attractive rooms (from €100) decked out in pale colours.

La Darsena
SEAFOOD $$

(☑ 0883 48 73 33; Via Statuti Marittimi 98; meals €30; ⊙ noon-3pm & 8-11.30pm Tue-Sun) Renowned for its seafood, swish La Darsena is housed in a waterfront *palazzo*. Outside tables overlook the port while inside, photos of old Puglia cover the walls beneath a huge wrought-iron dragon chandelier.

❶ Information

From the train station, Via Cavour leads through Piazza della Repubblica to Piazza Plebiscito and the public gardens. Turn left at Piazza della Repubblica for the harbour and cathedral.

Tourist Office (☑ 0883 58 88 30; www.traniweb.it; 1st fl, Palazzo Palmieri, Piazza Trieste 10; ⊙ 8.30am-1.30pm Mon, Wed & Fri, 8.30am-1.30pm & 3.30-5.30pm Tue & Thu) Located 200m south of the cathedral. Offers free guided walking tours most days at 8pm.

❶ Getting There & Away

STP (☑ 0883 49 18 00; www.stpspa.it) has frequent bus services to Bari (€4.20, 45 minutes). Services depart from **Bar Stazione** (Piazza XX Settembre 23), which also has timetables and tickets.

Trani is on the main train line between Bari (€3.10, 30 to 45 minutes, frequent) and Foggia (€6.30, 40 to 50 minutes, frequent).

Castel del Monte

★ Castel del Monte
CASTLE

(☑ 0883 56 99 97; www.casteldelmonte.beniculturali.it; adult/reduced €5/2.50; ⊙ 9am-6.30pm Oct-Mar, 10.15am-7.45pm Apr-Sep) You'll see Castel del Monte, an unearthly geometric shape on a hilltop, from miles away. Mysterious and perfectly octagonal, it's one of southern Italy's most talked-about landmarks and a Unesco World Heritage Site.

No one knows why Frederick II built it – there's no nearby town or strategic crossroads. It was not built to defend anything, as it has no moat or drawbridge, no arrow slits, and no trapdoors for pouring boiling oil on invaders.

Some theories claim that, according to mid-13th-century beliefs in geometric symbolism, the octagon represented the union of the circle and square, of God-perfection (the infinite) and human-perfection (the finite). The castle was therefore nothing less than a celebration of the relationship between humanity and God.

The castle has eight octagonal towers. Its interconnecting rooms have decorative marble columns and fireplaces, and the doorways and windows are framed in corallite stone. Many of the towers have washing rooms with what are thought to be Europe's first flushing loos – Frederick II, like the Arab world he admired, set great store by cleanliness.

To get to the castle without a car, take the Ferrovia Bari-Nord train from Bari to Andria, then bus number 6 from Andria station to the castle (35 minutes, five daily, April to October only). The castle is about 35km from Trani.

Promontorio del Gargano

The coast surrounding this expansive promontory seems permanently bathed in a pink-hued, pearly light, providing a painterly contrast to the sea, which softens from intense to powder blue as the evening draws in. It's one of Italy's most beautiful areas, encompassing white limestone cliffs, fairy-tale grottoes, sparkling sea, ancient forests, rare orchids and tangled, fragrant maquis (dense scrub vegetation).

Once connected to what is now Dalmatia (in Croatia), the 'spur' of the Italian boot has more in common with the land mass across the sea than with the rest of Italy. Creeping urbanisation was halted in 1991 by the creation of the **Parco Nazionale del Gargano** (www.parcogargano.gov.it) FREE. Aside from its magnificent national park, the Gargano is home to pilgrimage sites and the lovely seaside towns of Vieste and Peschici.

Vieste

POP 13,900

Like a young belle who's beautiful without even realising it, the town of Vieste clings modestly to a spectacular promontory on the Gargano peninsula resembling a cross between Naples and Dubrovnik with a bit of Puglian magic mixed in. The narrow alleys of the old town, decorated with lines of drying clothes and patrolled by slinking cats and the odd friendly dog, are an atmospheric place day or night, off-season or on. Wedged up against the old town is the equally unpretentious new town, ghostly in winter, but packed with holidaying humanity in summer, especially during the *passeggiata* (evening stroll).

Vieste is strategically placed atop the steep Pizzomunno cliffs between two sweeping sandy beaches. The gritty harbour offers water sports, while the surrounding Parco Nazionale del Gargano is revered for cycling and hiking. All things considered, it's one of the south's most complete all-in-one destinations.

◉ Sights

Vieste is primarily a beach resort, but the steep, skinny alleys of the old town are your ticket for entry to another, more tranquil world. The castle built by Frederick II is occupied by the military and closed to the public.

Chianca Amara HISTORIC SITE
(Bitter Stone; Via Cimaglia) Vieste's most gruesome sight is this worn and polished stone where thousands were beheaded when Turks sacked Vieste in the 16th century.

Museo Malacologico MUSEUM
(🗷0884 70 76 88; Via Pola 8; ⊘9.30am-12.30pm & 4-8pm Apr-Oct) FREE This esoteric shell museum has four rooms of fossils and molluscs, some enormous and all beautifully patterned and coloured. Note the seasonal opening hours.

Cathedral CATHEDRAL
(Via Duomo; ⊘7.30am-noon & 4-11pm) Built by the Normans on the ruins of a Vesta temple, the cathedral is in Puglian-Romanesque style with a fanciful tower that resembles a cardinal's hat. Of note are its beautiful paintings, swirling interior columns and Latin-inscribed altar.

La Salata HISTORIC SITE
(🗷0854 70 66 35; adult/child €5/free; ⊘5.30pm & 8.15pm Mon-Fri Jun-Sep, by appointment Oct-May) This palaeo-Christian graveyard dating from the 4th to 6th centuries AD is 9km out of town. Inside the cave, tier upon tier of narrow tombs are cut into the rock wall; others form shallow niches in the cave floor. Guided tours are mandatory.

🏃 Activities

Superb sandy beaches surround the town: in the south are **Spiagga del Castello**, **Cala San Felice** and **Cala Sanguinaria**; due north, head for the area known as **La Salata. Diving** is popular around the promontory's rocky coastline, which is filled with marine grottoes.

From May to September fast boats zoom to the Isole Tremiti. For hiking ideas, pick up a *Guida al Trekking sul Gargano* brochure from the tourist office. A section of walk 4 is doable from Vieste. It starts 2.5km south of town off the Lungomare Enrico Mattei, where a track cuts up through olive groves into increasingly wild terrain.

Centro Ormeggi e Sub BOATING
(🗷0884 70 79 83; Lungomare Vespucci) Offers diving courses and rents out sailing boats and motorboats.

👉 Tours

Several companies offer tours of the caves that pock the Gargano coast – a three-hour tour costs around €13.

Explora Gargano CYCLING
(🗷0884 70 22 37; www.exploragargano.it; Vieste-Peschici km 5.5; hiking and mountain biking half-day from €70, quad tours and jeep safari per day from €50) To get off the beach for a day or two, take one of the many tours on offer at Explora Gargano. As well as hiking and mountain biking in the Foresta Umbra, it offers quad tours and jeep safaris.

Motobarca Desirèe BOAT TOUR
(www.grottemarinegargano.com; Lungomare Vespucci; adult/child €15/7; ⊘Apr-Oct) Boat tours of the various caves, arches and *trabucchi* (Puglian fishing structures) that characterise the Gargano coast. Trips are spectacular, though the boats can get crowded. Two departures a day (9am and 2.30pm); buy tickets port-side.

🛏 Sleeping

⭐ **B&B Parallelo 41** B&B **$**
(🗷0884 35 50 09; www.bbparallelo41.it; Via Forno de Angelis 3; r from €70; ❄@☎) Beautiful small B&B in the midst of the old town where four recently renovated rooms have been decorated with hand-painted ceilings, luxurious beds and super-modern bathrooms. Breakfasts consist of a substantial buffet, and the reception area acts as a mini-information centre for a slew of local activities.

THE RICH FLAVOURS OF CUCINA POVERA

In Italy's less wealthy 'foot', traditional recipes have been born out of economic necessity rather than through celebrity chefs with fancy ideas. Local people used whatever ingredients were available to them, plucked directly from the surrounding soil and seas, and kneaded and blended using recipes passed down through generations. The result is called *cucina povera* (literally 'food of the poor'), which, thanks to a recent global obsession with farm-to-table purity, has become increasingly popular.

If there is a mantra for *cucina povera*, it is 'keep it simple'. Pasta is the south's staple starch. Made with durum wheat rather than eggs, it is most commonly sculpted into *orecchiette* or 'little ears' and doused with various toppings, many of which include a mixture of readily available vegetables. Aubergine, mushrooms, tomatoes, artichokes and olives grow abundantly in southern climes and they're all put to good use in the dishes.

Meat, though present in southern cooking, is used more sparingly than in the north. Lamb and horse meat predominate and are usually heavily seasoned. Unadulterated fish is more common, especially in Puglia, which has a longer coastline than any other mainland Italian region. Popular fish dishes incorporate mussels, clams, octopus (in Salento), swordfish (in northern Calabria), cod and prawns.

A signature Puglian *primi* (first course) is *orecchiette con cima di rape*, a gloriously simple blend of rapini (a bitter green leafy veg with small broccoli-like shoots) mixed with anchovies, olive oil, chilli peppers, garlic and *pecorino*. Another popular *orecchiette* accompaniment is *ragù di carne di cavallo* (horse meat), sometimes known as *ragù alla barese*. Bari is known for its starch-heavy *riso, patate e cozze*, a surprisingly delicious marriage of rice, potatoes and mussels that is baked in the oven. Another wildly popular vegetable is wild chicory, which, when combined with a broad bean purée, is reborn as *fave e cicorie*.

Standard cheeses of the south include *burrata*, which has a mozzarella-like shell and a gooey centre, and *pecorino di filiano*, a sheep's-milk cheese from Basilicata. There are tons of bread recipes, but the horn-shaped crusty bread from Matera is king.

Campeggio Capo Vieste　　CAMPGROUND **$**
(☑ 0884 70 63 26; www.capovieste.it; Vieste-Peschici km 8; camping 2 people, car & tent €33, 1-bedroom bungalow €77-164; ☉ Mar-Oct; ▣) This tree-shaded campground is right by a sandy beach at La Salata, around 8km from Vieste and accessible by bus. Activities include tennis and a sailing school.

Hotel Seggio　　HOTEL **$$**
(☑ 0884 70 81 23; www.hotelseggio.it; Via Veste 7; d €120, half-board €150; ☉ Apr-Oct; ▣▣@☎▣) A butter-coloured, 17th-century, family-run *palazzo* in the town's historic centre. Steps spiral down to a dreamy pool and sunbathing terrace with an ocean backdrop. The 30 rooms are plain but modern.

✖ Eating

★ **Vecchia Vieste**　　PUGLIAN **$**
(☑ 0884 70 70 83; Via Mafrolla 32; meals €20-25, tasting menu €25; ☉ noon-3pm & 7-11pm) The best in Vieste can be found in the stony cavernous interior of this modest restaurant that sells what is possibly the best home-made, hand-shaped *orecchiette* in Puglia (and that's saying something). Try it topped with the obligatory *cima di rape* (rapini – a bitter green leafy veg – with anchovies, olive oil, chilli peppers, garlic and *pecorino*). The very reasonably priced *menù degustazione* comes with four courses.

Osteria Al Duomo　　OSTERIA **$$**
(☑ 0884 70 82 43; www.osterialduomo.it; Via Alessandro III 23; meals €25; ☉ noon-3pm & 7-11pm Mar-Nov) Tucked away in a picturesque narrow alley in the heart of the old town, this welcoming *osteria* has a cosy cave-like interior and outdoor seating under a shady arbour. Homemade pastas with seafood sauces feature prominently.

Taverna Al Cantinone　　TRADITIONAL ITALIAN **$$**
(☑ 0884 70 77 53; Via Mafrolla 26; meals €25-30; ☉ noon-3pm & 7-11pm Wed-Mon) Run by a charming Italian-Spanish couple who have a passion for cooking. The food is exceptional and exquisitely presented, and the menu changes with the seasons.

ℹ️ Information

Post Office (Via Vittorio Veneto)
Tourist Office (📞 0884 70 88 06; Piazza Kennedy; ⊗ 8am-8pm Mon-Sat) You can weigh yourself down with useful brochures here.

ℹ️ Getting There & Around

BOAT

Vieste's port is to the north of town, about a five-minute walk from the tourist office. In summer, several companies, including Linee Marittime Adriatico (p115), head to the Isole Tremiti (€27 to €30, 1½ hours). Tickets can be bought port-side.

BUS

From Piazzale Manzoni, where intercity buses terminate, a 10-minute walk east along Viale XXIV Maggio, which becomes Corso Fazzini, brings you into the old town and the Marina Piccola's attractive promenade. In summer buses terminate at Via Verdi, a 300m walk from the old town down Via Papa Giovanni XXIII.

SITA (📞 0881 35 20 11; www.sitabus.it) buses run between Vieste and Foggia (€7, 2¾ hours, four daily) via Manfredonia. There are also services to Monte Sant'Angelo (€5) via Manfredonia, but **Ferrovie del Gargano** (📞 0881 58 72 11; www.ferroviedelgargano.com) buses have a direct daily service to Monte Sant'Angelo (€6.30, two hours) and frequent services to Peschici (€1.70, 35 minutes).

From May to September, **Pugliairbus** (📞 080 580 03 58; http://pugliairbus.aeroportidipuglia.it) runs a service to the Gargano, including Vieste, from Bari airport (€20, 3½ hours, four daily).

Monte Sant'Angelo

POP 13,300 / ELEV 796M

One of Europe's most important pilgrimage sites, this isolated mountain-top town has an extraordinary atmosphere. Pilgrims have been coming here for centuries – and so have the hustlers, pushing everything from religious kitsch to parking spaces.

The object of devotion is the Santuario di San Michele. Here, in AD 490, St Michael the Archangel is said to have appeared in a grotto to the Bishop of Siponto. He left behind his scarlet cloak and instructions not to consecrate the site as he had already done so. During the Middle Ages, the sanctuary marked the end of the Route of the Angel, which began in Mont St-Michel (in Normandy) and passed through Rome. In 999 the Holy Roman Emperor Otto III made a pilgrimage to the sanctuary to pray that

prophecies about the end of the world in the year 1000 would not be fulfilled. His prayers were answered, the world staggered on and the sanctuary's fame grew. The sanctuary has been a Unesco World Heritage Site since 2011.

⊙ Sights

The town's serpentine alleys and jumbled houses are perfect for a little aimless ambling. Look out for the different shaped *cappelletti* (chimney stacks) on top of the neat whitewashed houses.

⭐ **Santuario di San Michele**   CAVE
(Via Reale Basilica; ⊗ 7am-8pm Jul-Sep, 7am-1pm & 2.30-8pm Apr-Jun & Oct, 7am-1pm & 2.30-7pm Nov-Mar) **FREE** Over the centuries this sanctuary has expanded to incorporate a large complex of religious buildings that overlay its original shrine. The double-arched entrance vestibule at street level stands next to a distinctive octagonal bell tower built by Carlo I of Naples in 1282. As you descend the staircase inside, look for the 17th-century pilgrims' graffiti. The grotto/shrine where St Michael is said to have left a footprint in stone is located at the bottom of the staircase. Because of St Michael's footprint it became customary for pilgrims to carve outlines of their feet and hands into the stone. Etched Byzantine bronze and silver doors, cast in Constantinople in 1076, open into the grotto itself. Inside, a 16th-century statue of the Archangel Michael covers the site of St Michael's footprint.

Tomba di Rotari   HISTORIC SITE
(admission €1; ⊗ 10am-1pm & 3-7pm Apr-Oct) A short flight of stairs opposite the Santuario di San Michele leads to a 12th-century baptistry with a deep sunken basin for total immersion. You enter the baptistry through the facade of the Chiesa di San Pietro with its intricate rose window squirming with serpents – all that remains of the church, destroyed in a 19th-century earthquake. The Romanesque portal of the adjacent 11th-century Chiesa di Santa Maria Maggiore has some fine bas-reliefs.

Castle   HISTORIC SITE
(Largo Roberto Giuscardo 2; admission €2; ⊗ 9.30am-1pm & 2.30-7pm) At the highest point of Monte Sant-Angelo is this rugged bijou, a Norman castle with Swabian and Aragonese additions as well as panoramic views.

TRABUCCHI

Hang around the coastal towns and villages of Abruzzo, Molise and northern Puglia and you'll soon become adept at spotting *trabucchi*. These old-fashioned wooden fishing platforms that jut out into the sea have a long history, possibly stretching back to Phoenician times. Made entirely of local pine wood they are located on rocky promontories where their complex nets trap fish swimming close to the shoreline.

There are two types of *trabucchi* on Italy's Adriatic coast. Those in Abruzzo and Molise usually inhabit shallow waters, necessitating a narrow wooden walkway to connect the platform (usually equipped with a small wooden hut) with the shore. The *trabucchi* on the Gargano peninsula in Puglia, on the other hand, are sited over deeper drop-offs meaning the platforms are generally connected directly to the shoreline.

Trabucchi are protected as historic monuments in Parco Nazionale del Gargano, where numerous examples embellish the shore between Vieste and Peschici. Most are still used by fishers and some have been turned into fish restaurants where – if you're lucky – you can watch your meal being caught before you eat it. A good *trabucco* to try is **Il Trabucco da Mimi** in Peschici.

Sleeping & Eating

Hotel Michael   HOTEL **$**

(✆0884 56 55 19; www.hotelmichael.com; Via Basilica 86; s/d €60/80; 🛜) A small hotel with shuttered windows, located on the main street across from the Santuario di San Michele, this traditional place has spacious rooms with extremely pink bedspreads. Ask for a room with a view.

Casa li Jalantuúmene   TRATTORIA **$$**

(✆0884 56 54 84; www.li-jalantuumene.it; Piazza de Galganis 5; meals €40; ⊗12.30-2.15pm & 7.30-10.30pm Wed-Mon) This renowned restaurant has an entertaining and eccentric chef, Gegè Mangano, and serves excellent fare. It's intimate, there's a select wine list and, in summer, tables spill onto the piazza. There are also four suites on site (€130), decorated in traditional Puglian style.

Getting There & Away

Ferrovie del Gargano (✆0882 22 89 60; www.ferroviedelgargano.com) Has a direct bus service from Vieste (€6.30, two hours, five daily). Buy your tickets from Bar Esperia next to Santuario di San Michele; buses leave from Corso Vittorio Emanuele.

SITA (✆0881 35 20 11; www.sitasudtrasporti.it) Buses run from Foggia (€4.90, 1¾ hours, four daily) and Vieste via Manfredonia. They leave from Corso Vittorio Emanuele in Monte Sant'Angelo.

Peschici

POP 4400

Perched above a turquoise sea and tempting beach, Peschici, like Vieste, is another cliff-clinging Amalfi lookalike. Its tight-knit old walled town of Arabesque whitewashed houses acts as a hub to a wider resort area. The small town gets crammed in summer, so book in advance. Boats zip across to the Isole Tremiti in high season.

Sleeping & Eating

Locanda al Castello   B&B **$**

(✆0884 96 40 38; www.peschicialcastello.it; Via Castello 29; s €35-70, d €70-120; 🅿❋🛜) Staying here is like entering a large, welcoming family home. It's by the cliffs with fantastic views. Enjoy hearty home cooking in the restaurant (meals €18) while the owners' kids run around playing football – indoors!

Baia San Nicola   CAMPGROUND **$**

(✆0884 96 42 31; www.baiasannicola.it; Localita Punta San Nicola; adult €7-10, tent €6-11, 2-person bungalow per week €420-720; ⊗mid-May–mid-Oct) The best campground in the area, 2km south of Peschici towards Vieste, Baia San Nicola is on a pine-shaded beach, offering camping, bungalows, apartments and myriad amenities.

⭐**Il Trabucco da Mimi**   SEAFOOD **$$**

(✆0884 96 25 56; www.altrabucco.it; Localita Punta San Nicola; meals €30-40; ⊗12.30-2.30pm & 7.30-10.30pm Easter-Oct) For the ultimate in fresh fish you can't beat eating at a *trabucco* (the traditional wooden fishing platforms lining the coast). Watch the fishing process in operation – you can even help out – and dine on the catch. The decor here is simple and rustic and you'll pay for the experience – but it's worth it. It also hosts live jazz.

Porta di Basso SEAFOOD **$$**
(☑ 0884 91 53 64; www.portadibasso.it; Via Colombo 38; meals €30-40; ⊙ noon-2.30pm & 7-11pm Fri-Wed) 🍴 Superb views of the ocean drop away from the floor-to-ceiling windows beside intimate alcove tables at this elegant clifftop restaurant. The menu of fresh local seafood changes daily. Close to the restaurant, two extremely stylish suites with fantastic sea views offer *albergo-diffuso*-style accommodation (€110 to €120).

ℹ Information

Tourist Office (☑ 0884 91 53 62; Via Magenta 3; ⊙ 8am-2pm & 5-9pm Mon-Sat Apr-Oct, 8am-2pm Mon-Fri, 9am-noon & 4-7pm Sat Nov-Mar)

ℹ Getting There & Away

The bus terminal is beside the sportsground, uphill from the main street, Corso Garibaldi.

Ferrovie del Gargano (p113) buses run frequent daily services between Peschici and Vieste (€1.70, 35 minutes).

From April to September, ferry companies, including **Linee Marittime Adriatico** (☑ 0884 96 20 23; www.collegamentiisoletremiti.com; Corso Garibaldi 32), serve the Isole Tremiti (adult €24 to €27, child €14 to €16, one to 1½ hours, one daily).

Foresta Umbra

The 'Forest of Shadows' is the Gargano's enchanted interior – thickets of tall, epic trees interspersed with picnic spots bathed in dappled light. It's the last remnant of Puglia's ancient forests: Aleppo pines, oaks, yews and beech trees shade the mountainous terrain. More than 65 different types of orchid have been discovered here, and the wildlife includes roe deer, wild boar, foxes, badgers and the increasingly rare wild cat. Walkers and mountain bikers will find plenty of well-marked trails within the forest's 5790 sq km.

◉ Sights & Activities

The small visitor centre in the middle of the forest houses a museum and nature centre (SP52bis; admission €1.20; ⊙ 9am-7pm mid-Apr–mid-Oct) with fossils, photographs, and stuffed animals and birds. Half-day guided hikes (per person €10), bike hire (per hour/day €5/25) and walking maps (€2.50) are available here. The centre is on SP52bis, close to the junction with SP528.

There are 15 official trails in the park ranging from 0.5km to 13.5km in length. Several of them start near the visitor centre and the adjacent Laghetto Umbra, including path 9, which can be done as a loop returning on a military road. A park leaflet provides a map and trail descriptions.

🛏 Sleeping

Rifugio Sfilzi B&B **$**
(☑ 340 6315260; www.rifugiosfilzi.com; SP528; adult/child €35/17) In the middle of the Foresta Umbra a few kilometres north of the visitor centre towards Vico di Gargano, this cosy *rifugio* (mountain hut) offers eight rooms with three- and four-bed configurations, making them ideal for groups or families. It also has a small shop selling locally made products such as jams and oils, and a cafe-restaurant with fantastic homemade cake and coffee.

La Chiusa delle More B&B **$$$**
(☑ 330 543766; www.lachiusadellemore.it; r €200-240; ⊙ May-Oct; P ❈ 🛜 🏊) La Chiusa delle More offers an escape from the cramped coast. An attractive stone-built *agriturismo* (farm stay accommodation), only 1.5km from Peschici, it's set in a huge olive grove, and you can dine on home-grown produce, borrow mountain bikes and enjoy panoramic views from your poolside lounger. Note there is a three-night minimum stay.

Isole Tremiti

POP 500

This beautiful archipelago of three islands, 36km offshore, is a picturesque sight of raggedy cliffs, sandy coves and thick pine woods, surrounded by the glittering dark-blue sea.

Unfortunately the islands are no secret, and in July and August some 100,000 holidaymakers descend on the archipelago. At this time it's noisy, loud and hot. If you want to savour the islands' tranquillity, visit during the shoulder season. In the low season most tourist facilities close down and the few permanent residents resume their quiet and isolated lives.

The islands' main facilities are on San Domino, the largest and lushest island, which was formerly used to grow crops. It's ringed by alternating sandy beaches and limestone cliffs, while the inland is covered in thick maquis flecked with rosemary and foxglove. The centre harbours a nondescript small town with several hotels.

Small San Nicola island is the traditional administrative centre; a castle-like cluster of medieval buildings rises up from its rocks. The third island, Capraia, is uninhabited.

Most boats arrive at San Domino. Small boats regularly make the brief crossing to San Nicola (€6 return) in high season; from October to March a single boat makes the trip after meeting the boat from the mainland.

◎ Sights & Activities

San Domino   ISLAND
Head to San Domino for walks, grottoes and coves. It has a pristine, marvellous coastline and the islands' only sandy beach, **Cala delle Arene**. Alongside the beach is the small cove **Grotta dell'Arene**, with calm clear waters for swimming.

You can also take a boat trip (€12 to €15 from the port) around the island to explore the grottoes: the largest, **Grotta del Bue Marino**, is 70m long. A tour around all three islands costs €15 to €17. Diving in the translucent sea is another option with **Tremiti Diving Center** (☑ 337 648917; www. tremitidivingcenter.com; Via Federico 2). There's an undemanding, but enchanting, walking track around the island, starting at the far end of the village.

San Nicola   ISLAND
Medieval buildings thrust out of San Nicola's rocky shores, the same pale-sand colour as the barren cliffs. In 1010, Benedictine monks founded the **Abbazia e Chiesa di Santa Maria** here; for the next 700 years the islands were ruled by a series of abbots who accumulated great wealth.

Although the church retains a weather-worn Renaissance portal and a fine 11th-century floor mosaic, its other treasures have been stolen or destroyed throughout its troubled history, which has seen various religious orders come and go, including the Benedictines, the Cistercians and the Lateran Canons. The only exceptions are a painted wooden Byzantine crucifix brought to the island in AD 747 and a black Madonna, probably transported here from Constantinople in the Middle Ages.

Capraia   ISLAND
The third of the Isole Tremiti, Capraia (named after the wild caper plant) is uninhabited. Bird life is plentiful, with impressive flocks of seagulls. There's no organised transport, but trips can be negotiated with local fishing folk.

🛏 Sleeping & Eating

In summer you'll need to book well ahead and many hotels insist on full board. Camping is forbidden.

La Casa di Gino   B&B $$
(☑ 0882 46 34 10; www.hotel-gabbiano.com; Piazza Belvedere; s/d €100/150; ❉) A tranquil accommodation choice on San Nicola, away from the frenzy of San Domino, this B&B run by the Hotel Gabbiano has stylish white-on-white rooms.

Hotel Gabbiano   HOTEL $$
(☑ 0882 46 34 10; www.hotel-gabbiano.com; Piazza Belvedere; r €100-130; ❉ 🤶) An established icon on San Nicola and run for more than 30 years by a Neapolitan family, this smart hotel has pastel-coloured rooms with balconies overlooking the town and the sea. It also has a seafood restaurant, spa and gym.

Architiello   SEAFOOD $$
(☑ 0882 46 30 54; www.ristorantearchitiello carolina.com; Via Salita delle Mura, San Nicola; meals €25; ⊙ Apr-Oct) A class act with a sea-view terrace, this place specialises in – what else? – fresh fish.

❶ Getting There & Away

Boats for the Isole Tremiti depart from several points on the Italian mainland: Manfredonia, Vieste and Peschici in summer, and Termoli in nearby Molise year-round.

Valle d'Itria

Between the Ionian and Adriatic coasts rises the great limestone plateau of the Murgia (473m). It has a strange karst geology: the landscape is riddled with holes and ravines through which small streams and rivers gurgle, creating what is, in effect, a giant sponge. At the heart of the Murgia lies the idyllic Valle d'Itria. Here you will begin to spot curious circular stone-built houses dotting the countryside, their roofs tapering up to a stubby and endearing point. These are *trulli,* Puglia's unique rural architecture. It's unclear why the architecture developed in this way; one popular story says that it was so the dry-stone constructions could be quickly dismantled, to avoid payment of building taxes.

The rolling green valley is criss-crossed by dry-stone walls, vineyards, almond and olive groves, and winding country lanes. This is the part of Puglia most visited by foreign tourists and is the best served by hotels and luxury *masserias* (working farms) or manor farms. Around here are also many of Puglia's self-catering villas; to find them, try websites such as www.tuscanynow.com, www.ownersdirect.co.uk, www.holidayhomesinitaly.co.uk and www.trulliland.com.

Grotte di Castellana

Grotte di Castellana CAVE
(✑080 499 82 21; www.grottedicastellana.it; Piazzale Anelli; admission €15; ◷9am-6pm Mar-Oct, by prior appointment Nov-Feb) Don't miss these spectacular limestone caves, 40km southeast of Bari and Italy's longest natural subterranean network. The interlinked galleries, first discovered in 1938, contain an incredible range of underground landscapes, with extraordinary stalactite and stalagmite formations – look out for the jellyfish, the bacon and the stocking. The highlight is the **Grotta Bianca** (White Grotto), an eerie white alabaster cavern hung with stiletto-thin stalactites.

There are two tours in English: a 1km, 50-minute tour that doesn't include the Grotta Bianca (€10, on the half-hour); and a 3km, two-hour tour (€15, on the hour) that does include it. The temperature inside the cave averages 18°C so take a light jacket.

Visit, too, the **Museo Speleologico Franco Anelli** (✑080 499 82 30; ◷9.30am-1pm & 3.30-6.30pm mid-Mar–Oct, 10am-1pm Nov–mid-Mar) FREE or the **Osservatorio Astronomico Sirio** (✑080 499 82 13; admission €4; ◷guided visits only by appointment), with its telescope and solar filters allowing for maximum solar-system visibility.

❶ Getting There & Away

The grotto can be reached by rail from Bari on the FSE Bari–Taranto train line, but not all trains stop at Grotte di Castellana. However, all services stop at Castellana Grotte (€2.80, 50 minutes, roughly hourly), 2km before the grotto, from where you can catch a local bus (€1.10) to the caves.

Alberobello

POP 11,000
Unesco World Heritage Site Alberobello resembles an urban sprawl – for gnomes. The Zona dei Trulli on the western hill of town is a dense mass of 1500 beehive-shaped houses, white-tipped as if dusted by snow. These dry-stone buildings are made from local limestone; none are older than the 14th century. Inhabitants do not wear pointy hats, but they do sell anything a visitor might want, from miniature *trulli* to woollen shawls.

The town is named after the primitive oak forest Arboris Belli (beautiful trees) that once covered this area. It's an amazing place, but also something of a tourist trap – from May to October busloads of tourists pile into *trullo* homes, drink in *trullo* bars and shop in *trullo* shops.

If you park in Lago Martellotta, follow the steps up to Piazza del Popolo, where the Belvedere Trulli lookout offers fabulous views over the whole higgledy-piggledy picture.

◉ Sights

Rione Monti NEIGHBOURHOOD
Within the old town quarter of Rione Monti more than 1000 *trulli* cascade down the hillside, most of which are now souvenir shops. The area is surprisingly quiet and atmospheric in the late evening, once the gaudy stalls have been stashed away.

Rione Aia Piccola NEIGHBOURHOOD
On the eastern side of Via Indipendenza is Rione Aia Piccola. This neighbourhood is much less commercialised than Rione Monti, with 400 *trulli*, many still used as family dwellings. You can climb up for a rooftop view at many shops, although most do have a strategically located basket for donations.

Trullo Sovrano MUSEUM
(✑080 432 60 30; Piazza Sacramento; admission €1.50; ◷10am-6pm) In the modern part of town, the 18th-century Trullo Sovrano is the only two-floor *trullo*, built by a wealthy priest's family. It's a small museum providing an insight into *trullo* life, with sweet, rounded rooms that include a re-created bakery, bedroom and kitchen. The souvenir shop here has a wealth of literature on the town and surrounding area, plus Alberobello recipe books.

🛏 Sleeping

It's a unique experience to stay in your own *trullo*, though some people might find Alberobello too touristy to use as a base.

MASSERIAS: LUXURY ON THE FARM

Masserias are unique to southern Italy. Modelled on the classical Roman villa, these fortified farmhouses – equipped with oil mills, cellars, chapels, storehouses and accommodation for workers and livestock – were built to function as self-sufficient communities. These days, they still produce the bulk of Italy's olive oil, but many have been converted into luxurious hotels, *agriturismi* (farm stay accommodation), holiday apartments or restaurants. Staying in a *masseria* is a unique experience, especially when you can dine on home-grown produce.

Il Frantoio (☑0831 33 02 76; www.masseriailfrantoio.it; SS16, km 874; d €180-240, ste €250; **P @**) Stay at this charming, whitewashed farmhouse, where the owners still live and work producing high-quality organic olive oil. (Or else book yourself in for one of the marathon eight-course lunches – the food is superb.) Owner Armando takes guests for a tour of the farm each evening in his 1949 Fiat. Il Frantoio lies 5km outside Ostuni along the SS16 in the direction of Fasano. You'll see the sign on your left-hand side when you reach the km 874 sign.

Masseria Torre Coccaro (☑080 482 93 10; www.masseriatorrecoccaro.com; Contrada Coccaro 8; d €430-520, ste €614-1365; **❅ @ ☎ ☎**) For pure luxury, stay at this superchic yet countrified *masseria*. There's a glorious spa set in a cave, a beach-style swimming pool, cooking courses on offer and a restaurant (meals €90) dishing up home-grown produce. It's around 10km from Locorotondo.

Masseria Maizza (www.masseriatorremaizza.com; d €460-558, ste €678-1522; **❅ @ ☎ ☎**) Around 10km from Locorotondo is Masseria Maizza. It is a luxurious farm-complex conversion but is contemporary and glamorous, and aimed at couples. There is a balmy beach club (about 4km away) and neighbouring golf course. It also runs cookery courses.

Borgo San Marco (☑080 439 57 57; www.borgosanmarco.it; Contrada Sant'Angelo 33; d from €165; **P ❅ ☎ ☎**) Once a *borgo* (medieval town), this *masseria* has 16 rooms, a spa in the orchard and is traditional with a bohemian edge. Nearby are some frescoed rock churches. It's 8km from Ostuni; to get here take the SS379 in the direction of Bari, exiting at the sign that says 'SC San Marco–Zona Industriale Sud Fasano', then follow the signs. Note: there's a four-night minimum stay in July, and seven-night minimum in August.

Casa Albergo Sant'Antonio HOTEL $
(☑080 432 29 13; www.santantonioalbergo.it; Via Isonzo 8a; s/d/tr/q €50/76/95/110; ☎) Excellent value right in the heart of the Rione Monti neighbourhood, this simple hotel is in an old monastery and located next to a unique *trulli*-style church with a conical roof. Rooms are relatively monastic and spartan, but will do the trick for the unfussy.

Camping dei Trulli CAMPGROUND $
(☑080 432 36 99; www.campingdeitrulli.com; Via Castellana Grotte; camping 2 people, car & tent €26.50, bungalows per person €25-40, trulli €30-60; **P @ ☎**) This campground, 1.5km out of town, has some nice tent sites, a restaurant, a market, two swimming pools, tennis courts and bicycle hire. You can also rent *trulli* off the grounds.

Trullidea TRULLO $$
(☑080 432 38 60; www.trullidea.it; Via Monte San Gabriele 1; 2-person trullo €99-150; ☎) Fifteen renovated, quaint, cosy and atmospheric *trulli* in Alberobello's *trulli* zone available on a self-catering, B&B, or half- or full-board basis.

✖ Eating

Trattoria Terra Madre ITALIAN $
(☑080 432 38 29; www.trattoriaterramadre.it; Piazza Sacramento 17; meals €18.50; ⊙8-11pm Tue-Sun; ☎) ✦ Run by the charming people from Charming Tours, this ambitious venture slavishly honours the farm-to-table ethos – most of what you eat will have been plucked within sight of your plate from the organic garden outside. The vegetable antipasto is epic, ditto the chickpea soup and stuffed artichokes. The place is educational

too: various alcoves in the restaurant explain the harvesting and processing techniques.

La Cantina
TRADITIONAL ITALIAN $$

(✍ 080 432 34 73; www.ilristorantelacantina.it; cnr Corso Vittorio Emanuele & Vico Lippolis; meals €25; ⊙ noon-3pm & 8-11.30pm Wed-Mon) Although tourists have discovered this place, located to the side of a little Doric temple, it has maintained the high standards established back in 1958. There are just seven tables (book ahead), and staff serve delicious meals made with fresh seasonal produce.

Il Poeta Contadino
TRADITIONAL ITALIAN $$$

(✍ 080 432 19 17; www.ilpoetacontadino.it; Via Indipendenza 21; meals €65; ⊙ noon-2.30pm & 7-10.30pm Tue-Sun Feb-Dec) Located just outside the main throng, the dining room here has a medieval banquet feel with its sumptuous decor and chandeliers. Dine on a poetic menu that includes the signature dish, broad bean purée with *cavatelli* (rod-shaped pasta) and seafood.

❶ Information

Tourist Office (✍ 080 432 51 71; Via Garibaldi; ⊙ 8am-1pm Mon, Wed & Fri, 8am-1pm & 3-6pm Tue & Thu) Just off the main square. There is another tourist information office (✍ 080 432 28 22; www.prolocoalberobello.it; Monte Nero 1; ⊙ 9am-7.30pm) in the Zona dei Trulli.

❶ Getting There & Away

Alberobello is easily accessible from Bari (€4.90, 1½ hours, hourly) on the FSE Bari–Taranto train line. From the station, walk straight ahead along Via Mazzini, which becomes Via Garibaldi, to reach Piazza del Popolo.

Locorotondo
POP 14,200

Locorotondo is endowed with a whisper-quiet pedestrianised *centro storico,* where everything is shimmering white aside from the blood-red geraniums that tumble from the window boxes. Situated on a hilltop on the Murge Plateau, it's a *borgo più bella d'Italia* (www.borghitalia.it) – that is, it's rated as one of the most beautiful towns in Italy. There are few 'sights' as such – rather, the town itself is a sight. The streets are paved with smooth ivory-coloured stones, with the church of **Santa Maria della Graecia** as their sunbaked centrepiece.

From **Villa Comunale**, a public garden, you can enjoy panoramic views of the surrounding valley. You enter the historic quarter directly across from here.

Not only is this deepest *trulli* country, it's also the liquid heart of the Puglian wine region. Sample some of the local *spumante* at **Cantina del Locorotondo** (✍ 080 431 16 44; www.locorotondodoc.com; Via Madonna della Catena 99; ⊙ 9am-1pm & 3-7pm).

🛏 Sleeping

Truddhi
TRULLO $

(✍ 080 443 13 26; www.trulliresidence.it; Contrada da Trito 292; d €65-80, apt €100-150, per week from €450-741; P⊛) This charming cluster of 10 self-catering *trulli* in the hamlet of Trito near Locorotondo is surrounded by olive groves and vineyards. It's a tranquil place and you can take cooking courses (per day €80) with Mino, a lecturer in gastronomy.

★ Sotto le Cummerse
APARTMENT $$

(✍ 080 431 32 98; www.sottolecummerse.it; Via Vittorio Veneto 138; apt incl breakfast €82-298; ❋⊛) At this *albergo diffuso* you'll stay in tastefully furnished apartments scattered throughout the *centro storico*. The apartments are traditional buildings that have been beautifully restored and furnished. Excellent value and a great base for exploring the region.

🍴 Eating

★ Quanto Basta
PIZZA $

(✍ 080 431 28 55; Via Morelli 12; pizza €6-7; ⊙ 7.30-11.30pm Tue-Sun) Craft beer and pizza make an excellent combination, no more so than at Quanto Basta in the old town with its wooden tables, soft lighting and stone floors.

La Taverna del Duca
TRATTORIA $$

(✍ 080 431 30 07; www.tavernadelducascatigna. it; Via Papadotero 3; meals €35; ⊙ noon-3pm & 7.30pm-midnight Tue-Sat, noon-3pm Sun & Mon) In a narrow side street off Piazza Vittorio Emanuele, this well-regarded trattoria serves local classics such as *orecchiette* with various vegetable sidekicks.

❶ Information

Tourist Office (✍ 080 431 30 99; www.prolo colocorotondo.it; Piazza Vittorio Emanuele 27; ⊙ 10am-1pm & 3-6pm Mon-Fri, 10am-1pm Sat) Offers free internet access.

PUGLIA, BASILICATA & CALABRIA VALLE D'ITRIA

ℹ Getting There & Away

Locorotondo is easily accessible via frequent trains from Bari (€5.60, 1½ to two hours) on the FSE Bari–Taranto train line.

Martina Franca

POP 49,800

The old quarter of this town is a picturesque scene of winding alleys, blinding white houses and blood-red geraniums. There are graceful baroque and rococo buildings here too, plus airy piazzas and curlicue ironwork balconies that almost touch above the narrow streets.

This town is the highest in the Murgia, and was founded in the 10th century by refugees fleeing the Arab invasion of Taranto. It only started to flourish in the 14th century when Philip of Anjou granted tax exemptions (*franchigie,* hence Franca); the town became so wealthy that a castle and defensive walls, complete with 24 solid bastions, were built.

◎ Sights & Activities

The best way to appreciate Martina Franca's beauty is to wander around the narrow lanes and alleyways of the *centro storico.*

Passing under the baroque **Arco di Sant'Antonio** at the western end of pedestrianised Piazza XX Settembre, you emerge into Piazza Roma, dominated by the imposing, 17th-century rococo **Palazzo Ducale** (Piazza Roma 32; ◎9am-1pm Mon-Fri, 9.30am-12.30pm Sat & Sun) **FREE**, whose upper rooms have semi-restored frescoed walls and host temporary art exhibitions.

From Piazza Roma, follow the fine Corso Vittorio Emanuele, with baroque townhouses, to reach Piazza Plebiscito, the centre's baroque heart. The piazza is overlooked by the 18th-century **Basilica di San Martino,** its centrepiece a statue of city patron, St Martin, swinging a sword and sharing his cloak with a beggar.

Walkers can ask for the free *Carta dei Sentieri del Bosco delle Pianelle* brochure at the tourist office, which maps out 10 walks in the nearby **Bosco delle Pianelle** (around 10km west of town). This lush woodland is part of the larger 1206-hectare **Riserva Naturale Regionale Orientata,** populated with lofty trees, wild orchids, and a rich and varied bird life, including kestrels, owls, buzzards, hoopoe and sparrow hawks.

✯ Festivals & Events

Festival della Valle d'Itria   MUSIC
This annual music festival (late July to early August) features international performances of opera, classical music and jazz. For information, contact the **Centro Artistico Musicale Paolo Grassi** (✆080 480 51 00; www.festivaldellavalleditria.it; ◎10am-1pm Mon-Fri) in the Palazzo Ducale.

⌱ Sleeping

B&B San Martino   B&B $
(✆080 48 56 01; http://xoomer.virgilio.it/bed-and-breakfast-sanmartino; Via Abate Fighera 32; d €40-120; ❄) A stylish B&B in a historic palace with rooms overlooking gracious Piazza XX Settembre. The rooms have exposed stone walls, shiny parquet floors, wrought-iron beds and small kitchenettes.

Villaggio In   APARTMENT $$
(✆080 480 59 11; www.villaggioincasesparse.it; Via Arco Grassi 8; apt €75-170, per week €420-1050; ❄🖤) These charming apartments with arched ceilings are located in original *centro storico* homes. The rooms are large, painted in pastel colours and decorated with antiques and country frills. A variety of apartments are on offer, sleeping from two to six people.

✗ Eating

Gran Caffè   CAFE $
(Piazza XX Settembre 7; snacks €1-4; ◎7am-2am) Quintessential Italian cafe. Sit. People-watch. Sip coffee. Nibble croissants. Repeat.

La Piazzetta Garibaldi   OSTERIA $$
(✆080 430 49 00; Piazza Garibaldi; meals €24-28; ◎noon-3pm & 7.30pm-midnight Thu-Tue) A highly recommended green-shuttered *osteria* in the *centro storico.* Delicious aromas entice you into the cave-like interior and the *cucina tipica* menu of typical Pugliese food doesn't disappoint. Worthy of a long lunch.

Ciacco   PUGLIAN $$
(✆080 480 04 72; Via Conte Ugolino; meals €30; ◎12.30-2.30pm & 8-11pm Tue-Sun) Dive into the historic centre to find Ciacco, a traditional restaurant with white-clad tables and a cosy fireplace, serving up Puglian cuisine in a modern key. It's tucked down a narrow pedestrian lane a couple of streets in from the Chiesa del Carmine.

ℹ️ Information

Tourist Office (☑ 080 480 57 02; Piazza XX Settembre 3; ⊙ 9am-1pm Mon-Fri, plus 4.30-7pm Tue & Thu, 9am-12.30pm Sat) The tourist office is to the right of the Arco di Sant'Antonio just before you enter the old town.

ℹ️ Getting There & Around

The FSE train station is downhill from the historic centre. From the train station, go right along Viale della Stazione, continue along Via Alessandro Fighera to Corso Italia, then continue to the left along Corso Italia to Piazza XX Settembre.

FSE (☑ 080 546 21 11) trains run to/from the following destinations:

Bari €5.60, two hours, hourly

Lecce €7.70, two hours, five daily

Taranto €2.40, 40 minutes, frequent

FSE buses run to Alberobello (€1, 30 minutes, five daily Monday to Saturday).

Ostuni

POP 32,500

Chic Ostuni shines like a pearly white tiara, extending across three hills with the magnificent gem of a cathedral as its sparkling centrepiece. It's the end of the *trulli* region and the beginning of the hot, dry Salento. With some excellent restaurants, stylish bars and swish yet intimate places to stay, it's packed in summer.

👁️ Sights

Ostuni is surrounded by olive groves, so this is the place to buy some of the region's DOC 'Collina di Brindisi' olive oil – either delicate, medium or strong – direct from producers.

Cathedral CATHEDRAL
(Via Cattedrale; admission €1; ⊙ 9am-1pm & 3-7pm) Ostuni's dramatic 15th-century cathedral has an unusual Gothic-Romanesque facade with a frilly rose window and an inverted gable.

Museo di Cività Preclassiche della Murgia MUSEUM
(☑ 0831 33 63 83; Via Cattedrale 15; ⊙ 10am-1pm Tue-Fri, 10am-1pm & 4-7pm Sat & Sun) FREE Located in the Convento delle Monacelle, the museum's most famous exhibit is the 25,000-year-old star of the show: Delia. She was pregnant at the time of her death and her well-preserved skeleton was found in a local cave. Many of the finds here come from the Palaeolithic burial ground, now the **Parco Archeologico e Naturale di Arignano**

(☑ 0831 30 39 73), which can be visited by appointment.

🏃 Activities

The surrounding countryside is perfect for cycling. **Ciclovagando** (☑ 330 985255; www.ciclovagando.com; Via di Savoia 19, Mesagne; half-/full-day €30/40), based in Mesagne, 30km south of Ostuni, organises guided tours. Each tour covers approximately 20km and departs daily from various towns in the district, including Ostuni and Brindisi. For an extra €15 you can sample typical Puglian foods on the tour.

⭐ Festivals & Events

La Cavalcata RELIGIOUS
Ostuni's annual feast day is held on 26 August, when processions of horsemen dressed in glittering red-and-white uniforms (resembling Indian grooms on their way to be wed) follow the statue of Sant'Oronzo around town.

🛏️ Sleeping

Le Sole Blu B&B $
(☑ 0831 30 38 56; www.webalice.it/solebluostuni; Corso Vittorio Emanuele II 16; s €30-40, d €60-80) Located in the 18th-century (rather than medieval) part of town, Le Sole Blu only has one room available: it's large and has a separate entrance, but the bathroom is tiny. However, the two self-catering apartments nearby are excellent value.

⭐ **La Terra** HOTEL $$
(☑ 0831 33 66 51; www.laterrahotel.it; Via Petrarolo; d €130-170; P ❄ 🛜) This former 13th-century palace offers atmospheric and stylish accommodation with original niches, dark-wood beams and furniture, and contrasting light stonework and whitewash. The result is a cool contemporary look. The bar is as cavernous as they come – it's tunnelled out of a cave.

🍴 Eating

Osteria Piazzetta Cattedrale OSTERIA $$
(☑ 0831 33 50 26; www.piazzettacattedrale.it; Via Arcidiacono Trinchera 7; meals €30-40; ⊙ 12.30-3pm & 7pm-12.30am Wed-Mon) Just beyond the arch opposite Ostuni's cathedral is this tiny little hostelry serving up magical food in an atmospheric setting. The menu includes plenty of vegetarian options.

PUGLIA, BASILICATA & CALABRIA VALLE D'ITRIA

Osteria del Tempo Perso OSTERIA $$
(📋0831 30 33 20; www.osteriadeltempoperso.
com; Gaetano Tanzarella Vitale 47; meals €30;
☉12.30-3pm & 7.30-11pm Tue-Sun) A sophisti-
cated rustic restaurant in a cave-like former
bakery, this laid-back place serves great Pug-
lian food, specialising in roasted meats. To
get here, face the cathedral's south wall and
turn right through the archway into Largo
Giuseppe Spennati, then follow the signs.

Porta Nova MODERN ITALIAN $$$
(📋0831 33 89 83; www.ristoranteportanova.com;
Via G Petrarolo 38; meals €45; ☉1-3.30pm &
7-11pm) This restaurant has a wonderful location on the old city wall. Revel in the rolling
views from the terrace or relax in the elegant
interior while you feast on top-notch local
cuisine, with seafood the speciality.

ⓘ Information

Tourist Office (📋0831 30 12 68; Corso
Mazzini 8; ☉9am-1pm & 5-9pm Mon-Fri, 5.30-
8.30pm Sat & Sun) Located off Piazza della
Libertà; can organise guided visits of the town
in summer, and bike rental.

ⓘ Getting There & Around

STP Brindisi (p129) buses run to Brindisi (€3.10,
50 minutes, six daily) and to Martina Franca
(€2.10, 45 minutes, three daily), leaving from
Piazza Italia in the newer part of Ostuni.

Trains run frequently to Brindisi (€4, 25 minutes) and Bari (€9, 50 minutes). A half-hourly
local bus covers the 2.5km between the station
and town.

Lecce

POP 95,000

If Puglia were a movie, Lecce would be
cast in the starring role. Bequeathed with
a generous stash of baroque buildings by
its 17th-century architects, the city has a
completeness and homogeneity that other
southern Italian metropolises lack. Indeed,
so distinctive is Lecce's architecture that
it has acquired its own moniker, *barocco
leccese* (Lecce baroque), an expressive and
hugely decorative incarnation of the genre
replete with gargoyles, asparagus columns
and cavorting gremlins. Swooning 18th-
century traveller Thomas Ashe thought
it 'the most beautiful city in Italy', but the
less-impressed Marchese Grimaldi said the
facade of Basilica di Santa Croce made him
think a lunatic was having a nightmare.

Either way, it's a lively, graceful but relaxed university town with some decent
Puglian restaurants, and a strong tradition
for papier-mâché making. Both the Adriatic
and Ionian Seas are within easy access and
it's a great base from which to explore the
Salento.

◉ Sights

Lecce has more than 40 churches and at
least as many *palazzi*, all built or renovated
between the 17th and 18th centuries, giving
the city an extraordinary cohesion. Two of
the main proponents of *barocco leccese* were
brothers Antonio and Giuseppe Zimbalo,
who both had a hand in the fantastical Basilica di Santa Croce.

★**Basilica di Santa Croce** CHURCH
(📋0832 24 19 57; www.basilicasantacroce.eu; Via
Umberto I; ☉9am-noon & 5-8pm) It seems that
hallucinating stonemasons have been at
work on the basilica. Sheep, dodos, cherubs and beasties writhe across the facade.
Throughout the 16th and 17th centuries, a
team of artists under Giuseppe Zimbalo la-
boured to work the building up to this pitch.
Look for Zimbalo's profile on the facade. The
interior is more conventionally Renaissance
and deserves a look, once you've drained
your camera batteries outside. Zimbalo also
left his mark in the former Convento dei
Celestini, just north of the basilica, which
is now the **Palazzo del Governo**, the local
government headquarters.

Piazza del Duomo PIAZZA
Piazza del Duomo is a baroque feast, the
city's focal point and a sudden open space
amid the surrounding enclosed lanes. During times of invasion the inhabitants of
Lecce would barricade themselves in the
square, which has conveniently narrow entrances. The 12th-century **cathedral** (crypt
€1; ☉8.30am-12.30pm & 4-8.30pm) is one of Giuseppe Zimbalo's finest works; he was also
responsible for the 68m-high bell tower.

The cathedral is unusual in that it has
two facades, one on the western end and
the other, more ornate, facing the piazza.
It's framed by the 15th-century **Palazzo
Vescovile** (Episcopal Palace; Piazza del Duomo)
and the 18th-century Seminario, designed
by Giuseppe Cino. The latter hosts a library
of old books and the **Museo Diocesano di
Arte Sacra** (Piazza del Duomo; admission €1;
☉9.30am-12.30pm & 5.30-8.30pm), home to
religious art.

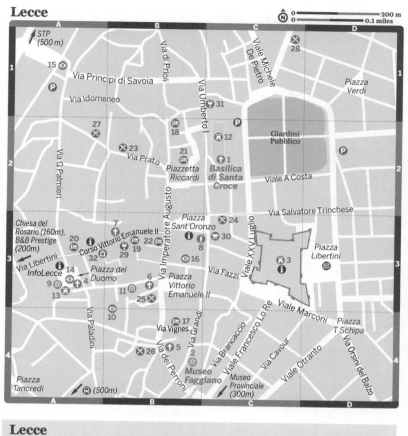

Lecce

PUGLIA, BASILICATA & CALABRIA LECCE

◎ Top Sights
- 1 Basilica di Santa Croce C2
- 2 Museo Faggiano B4

◎ Sights
- 3 Castello di Carlo V C3
- 4 Cathedral A3
- 5 Chiesa di San Matteo B4
- 6 Chiesa di Santa Chiara B3
- 7 Chiesa di Sant'Irene B3
- 8 Colonna di Sant'Oronzo B3
- 9 Museo Diocesano di Arte Sacra A3
- 10 Museo Teatro Romano B4
- 11 MUST B3
- 12 Palazzo del Governo C2
- 13 Palazzo Vescovile A3
- 14 Piazza del Duomo A3
- 15 Porta Napoli A1
- 16 Roman Amphitheatre B3

⬚ Sleeping
- 17 Azzurretta B&B B4
- 18 B&B Idomeneo 63 .... B2

- Centro Storico B&B .... (see 17)
- 19 Palazzo Belli B&B B3
- 20 Palazzo Rollo A3
- 21 Patria Palace Hotel B2
- 22 Risorgimento Resort B3

⊗ Eating
- 23 Alle due Corti B2
- 24 Gelateria Natale C3
- 25 La Torre di Merlino B3
- 26 Trattoria di Nonna Tetti B4
- 27 Trattoria Il Rifugio della Buona Stella ... A2
- 28 Trattoria le Zie – Cucina Casareccia ... C1

◎ Drinking & Nightlife
- 29 All'Ombra del Barocco B3
- 30 Caffè Alvino C3
- 31 Enoteca Mamma Elvira C1

◎ Shopping
- 32 La Cartapesta di Claudio Riso A3

LECCE'S NOTABLE CHURCHES

Lecce's unique baroque style is perhaps best seen in its churches; the city harbours dozens of them.

Chiesa di Sant'Irene (Corso Vittorio Emanuele II; ⊘ 7.30-11am & 4-6pm) The interior of 17th-century Chiesa di Sant'Irene contains a magnificent pair of mirror-image baroque altarpieces facing each other across the transept.

Chiesa di Santa Chiara (Piazza Vittorio Emanuele II; ⊘ 9.30-11.30am daily, plus 4.30-6.30pm Mon-Sat) A notable baroque church with every niche a swirl of twisting columns and ornate statuary. The ceiling is classic Leccese papier-mâché.

Chiesa di San Matteo (Via dei Perroni 29; ⊘ 7.30-11am & 4-6pm) Located 200m to the south of Chiesa di Santa Chiara. It's the last work of Giuseppe Zimbalo.

Chiesa del Rosario (Via Libertini; ⊘ 8am-1pm & 4-8pm) Instead of the intended dome roof, this church ended up with a quick-fix wooden one following architect Zimbalo's death before the building was completed.

Chiesa dei SS Nicolò e Cataldo (Via San Nicola; ⊘ 9am-noon Sep-Apr) The Chiesa dei SS Nicolò e Cataldo, near the main city gate Porta Napoli, was built by the Normans in 1180. It got caught up in the city's baroque frenzy and was revamped in 1716 by the prolific Cino, who retained the Romanesque rose window and portal.

★ **Museo Faggiano**   MUSEUM
(☑ 360 722448; www.museofaggiano.it; Via Grandi 56/58; admission €3; ⊘ 9.30am-1pm & 4-8pm) Breaking the floor to replace sewer pipes led the owner of this private home to the chance discovery of an archaeological treasure trove. Layers of history are revealed beneath the floors starting with the Messapii culture in around the 5th century BC and progressing through Roman crypts, medieval walls, Jewish insigna and Knights Templar symbolism in a rooftop tower. You have to see it to believe it!

Museo Provinciale   MUSEUM
(☑ 0832 68 35 03; Viale Gallipoli 28; ⊘ 8.30am-7.30pm Mon-Sat, to 1.30pm Sun) **FREE** This museum stylishly covers 10,000 years of history, from Palaeolithic and Neolithic bits and bobs to a handsome display of Greek and Roman jewels, weaponry and ornaments. The stars of the show are the Messapians, whose jaunty Mycenaean-inspired jugs and bowls date back 2500 years.

Roman Amphitheatre   HISTORIC SITE
(Piazza Sant'Oronzo; ⊘ 10am-noon & 5-7pm May-Sep) Below the ground level of the piazza is this restored 2nd-century-AD amphitheatre, discovered in 1901 by construction workers. It was excavated in the 1930s to reveal a perfect horseshoe with seating for 15,000. It was closed and a little overgrown at last visit.

MUST   GALLERY
(www.mustlecce.it; Via degli Ammirati 11; admission €3; ⊘ 10am-1.30pm & 2.30-7.30pm) This beautiful conversion of the Monastery of Santa Chiara houses the work of local artists and has a great view of a Roman amphitheatre from the back window. It was being renovated at last visit but should have reopened by the time you read this, with an extended remit to cover local history.

Colonna di Sant'Oronzo   MONUMENT
(Piazza Sant'Oronzo) Two Roman columns once marked the end of the Appian Way in Brindisi. When one of them crumbled in 1582 some of the pieces were rescued and subsequently donated to Lecce (the base and capital remain in Brindisi). The old column was rebuilt in 1666 with a statue of Lecce's patron saint placed on top. Sant'Oronzo is venerated for supposedly saving the city of Brindisi from a 1656 plague.

Museo Teatro Romano   HISTORIC SITE
(☑ 0832 27 91 96; Via degli Ammirati; adult/reduced €3/2; ⊘ 9.30am-1.30pm & 5-7.30pm Mon-Fri, 9.30am-1.30pm Sat) Uncovered in the 1930s, this small Roman theatre has well-preserved russet-coloured Roman mosaics and frescoes.

Castello di Carlo V   CASTLE
(☑ 0832 24 65 17; admission €5; ⊘ 9am-8.30pm Mon-Fri, 9.30am-8.30pm Sat & Sun) This 16th-century castle was built around a

12th-century Norman tower to the orders of Spain's Charles V and consists of two concentric trapezoidal structures. It's been used as a prison, a court and a military headquarters; now you can wander around the baronial spaces and visit the on-site papier-mâché museum.

🍽 Courses

Awaiting Table   COOKING
(www.awaitingtable.com; day/week course €195/1895) Silvestro Silvestori's splendid culinary and wine school provides day or weeklong courses with market shopping, tours, tastings, noteworthy lecturers – and lots of hands-on cooking. Book well in advance as courses fill up rapidly.

🛏 Sleeping

★Palazzo Rollo   APARTMENT $
(☑ 0832 30 71 52; www.palazzorollo.it; Corso Vittorio Emanuele II 14; s/d €65/85; P❋@) Stay in a 17th-century palace – the Rollo family seat for more than 200 years. The three grand B&B suites (with kitchenettes) have high curved ceilings and chandeliers. Downstairs, contemporary-chic studios open onto an ivy-hung courtyard. The rooftop garden has wonderful views.

Palazzo Belli B&B   B&B $
(☑ 380 7758456; www.palazzobelli.it; Corso Vittorio Emanuele II 33; s/d €60/80; 🛜) A wonderfully central, elegant and well-priced option located in a fine mansion near the cathedral. Rooms have marbled floors and wrought-iron beds. Breakfast is served in the nearby All'Ombra del Barocco bar.

Azzurretta B&B   GUESTHOUSE $
(☑ 0832 24 22 11; www.hostelecce.com; Via Vignes 2; d/tr €70/85; P🛜) The friendly brother of the owner of Centro Storico B&B runs this artier version located within the same building; ask for the large double with a balcony, wooden floors and a vaulted ceiling. Massage is available in your room or on the roof terrace. You get a cafe voucher for breakfast.

The brothers also have a tiny studio flat, which is a little dark but a good option if you're self-catering on a budget.

B&B Idomeneo 63   B&B $
(☑ 333 9499838; www.bebidomeneo63.it; Via Idomeneo 63; s/d/tr €50/80/95; 🛜) You'll be looked after like a VIP at this wonderfully curated B&B in the midst of Lecce's marvellous baroque quarter, complete with six colour-coded rooms and a funky entrance lounge. Decked out boutique-hotel style, but incorporating some older baroque features (stone ceiling arches), the real treat here is in the little extras such as breakfast, which is delivered on a tray to your room every morning. The upper suite has a roof terrace.

Centro Storico B&B   B&B $
(☑ 328 8351294, 0832 24 27 27; www.centrostorico lecce.it; Via A Vignes 2; s/d €40/60; P❋🛜) This friendly and efficient B&B located in a historic palace features big rooms, double-glazed windows and pleasantly old-fashioned decor. The huge rooftop terrace has sun loungers and views. Cafe vouchers are provided for breakfast, and there are also coffee-and-tea-making facilities.

B&B Prestige   B&B $
(☑ 349 7751290; www.bbprestige-lecce.it; Via Libertini 7; s/d/tr €70/80/110; P@🛜) On the corner of Via Santa Maria del Paradiso in the historic centre, the rooms at this lovely B&B are light, airy and beautifully finished. The communal sun-trap terrace has views over San Giovanni Battista church.

Risorgimento Resort   HOTEL $$
(☑ 0832 24 63 11; www.risorgimentoresort.it; Via Imperatore Augusto 19; d €115-220, ste €215-355; P❋@🛜) A warm welcome awaits at this stylish five-star hotel in the centre of Lecce. The rooms are spacious and refined with high ceilings, modern furniture and contemporary details reflecting the colours of the Salento, and the bathrooms are enormous. There's a restaurant, wine bar and rooftop garden.

Patria Palace Hotel   HOTEL $$
(☑ 0832 24 51 11; www.patriapalacelecce.com; Piazzetta Riccardi 13; r from €155; P❋@🛜) This sumptuous hotel is traditionally Italian with large mirrors, dark-wood furniture and wistful murals. The location is wonderful, the bar gloriously art deco with a magnificent carved ceiling, and the shady roof terrace has views over the Basilica di Santa Croce.

🍴 Eating

**★Trattoria Il Rifugio della
Buona Stella**   PUGLIAN $
(☑ 366 4373192; www.ilrifugiodellabuonastella.it; Via Prato 28; meals €14-20; ⊙12.15-3pm & 7.15-11.30pm Wed-Mon) A third-generation family restaurant in a gorgeous Leccese building with sandy stone walls and medieval decor, this wonderful trattoria serves fine food at

PAPIER-MÂCHÉ ART

Lecce is famous for its papier-mâché art (cartapesta). Statues and figurines are sculpted out of a mixture of paper and glue before being painted and used to adorn churches and other public buildings. Lecce's cartapesta culture originated in the 17th century when glue and paper offered cheap raw materials for religious artists who couldn't afford expensive wood or marble. Legend has it that the first exponents of the art were Leccese barbers who shaped and chiseled their morphing statues in between haircuts.

These days the art is still practiced in Lecce and you'll see a number of traditional workshops such as **La Cartapesta di Claudio Riso** (☑0832 24 34 10; Corso Vittorio Emanuele II 27) scattered around the old town centre. Also worth perusing is the papier-mâché museum inside the **Castello di Carlo V** (p124) and the decorative papier-mâché ceiling inside the **Chiesa di Santa Chiara** (p124).

sale-of-the-century prices (*secondi* from €6.50!). Start off with the homemade bread, proceed to pasta with swordfish and rapini, and it the jackpot with the grilled sausages.

A bottle of Salentino red wine should satisfy most alcohol cravings.

Gelateria Natale   GELATERIA **$**
(www.natalepasticceria.it; Via Trinchese 7a; ⊙7am-11pm Mon-Fri, 7.30am-1am Sat & Sun) Lecce's best ice-cream parlour also has an array of fabulous confectionery.

Trattoria di Nonna Tetti   TRATTORIA **$**
(☑0832 24 60 36; Piazzetta Regina Maria 28; mains €8-12; ⊙11am-2pm & 7-11pm Mon-Sat) A warmly inviting restaurant, popular with all ages and budgets, this trattoria serves a wide choice of traditional dishes. Try the most emblematic Puglian dish here – braised wild chicory with a purée of boiled dried broad beans, along with *contorni* (side dishes) like *patate casarecce* (homemade thinly sliced fries).

Trattoria le Zie – Cucina Casareccia   TRATTORIA **$**
(☑0832 24 51 78; Viale Costadura 19; meals €20-23; ⊙noon-3pm & 7-11pm Tue-Sat, 7-11pm Sun) Ring the bell to gain entry to this place that feels like a private home, with its patterned cement floor tiles, desk piled high with papers, and charming owner Carmela Perrone. In fact, it's known locally as simply le Zie (the aunts). Here you'll taste true *cucina povera*, including horse meat done in a *salsa piccante* (spicy sauce). Booking is a must.

La Torre di Merlino   PIZZA, ITALIAN **$$**
(☑0832 24 20 91; Via Giambattista del Tufo 10; meals €30-38; ⊙12.30-3pm & 8pm-1am Tue-Sun) It's hard to imagine that anyone couldn't be satisfied by the Merlino's all-encompassing

menu, which includes the best pizza in Lecce washed down with craft beer, some stalwart Puglian pasta dishes, and innovative modern main courses (involving black truffles, rabbit and raw red prawns marinated in lemon). Creative but not pretentious.

Alle due Corti   PUGLIAN **$$**
(☑0832 24 22 23; www.alleduecorti.com; Via Prato 42; meals €20-23; ⊙12.45-2.15pm & 7.45-11pm Mon-Sat) For a taste of sunny Salento, check out this no-frills, fiercely traditional restaurant. The seasonal menu is classic Puglian, written in a dialect that even some Italians struggle with. Go for the real deal with a dish of *ciceri e tria* (crisply fried pasta with chickpeas).

 Drinking

Via Imperatore Augusto is full of bars, and on a summer's night it feels like one long party. Wander along to find somewhere to settle.

★**Enoteca Mamma Elvira**   WINE BAR
(Via Umberto I 19; ⊙11am-midnight) All you need to know about emerging Salento wine will be imparted by the hip but friendly staff at this cool new joint near the Santa Croce church. Taster glasses are dispatched liberally if you order a few snacks.

All'Ombra del Barocco   WINE BAR
(www.allombradelbarocco.it; Corte dei Cicala 9; ⊙8am-1am) This cool restaurant-cafe-wine bar, next door to the Liberrima bookshop, has a range of teas, cocktails and *aperitivi*. It's open for breakfast and also hosts musical events; the modern cooking is well worth a try. Tables fill the little square outside, an ideal place from which to watch the *passeggiata*.

Caffè Alvino · CAFE
(Piazza Sant'Oronzo; ◷7am-8pm Wed-Mon; 🛜)
Treat yourself to great coffee and *pasticciotto* (custard pie) at this iconic chandeliered cafe in Lecce's main square; it has a hard-to-ignore display of cakes.

ⓘ Information

The historic centre's twin main squares are Piazza Sant'Oronzo and Piazza del Duomo, linked by pedestrianised Corso Vittorio Emanuele II.

Puglia Blog (www.thepuglia.com) An informative site run by Fabio Ingrosso with articles on culture, history, food, wine, accommodation and travel in Puglia.

Hospital (☑0832 66 11 11; Via San Cesario) About 2km south of the centre on the Gallipoli road.

InfoLecce (☑0832 52 18 77; www.infolecce.it; Piazza del Duomo 2; ◷9.30am-1.30pm & 3.30-7.30pm Mon-Sat, from 10am Sun) Independent and helpful tourist information office. Has guided tours and bike rental (per hour/day €3/15).

Police Station (☑0832 69 11 11; Viale Otranto 1)

Post Office (Piazza Libertini)

Tourist Office (☑0832 68 29 85; Corso Vittorio Emanuele II 16; ◷9am-1pm & 4-8pm) One of three main government-run offices. The others are in Castello di Carlo V (☑0832 24 65 17; Castello di Carlo V; ◷9am-8.30pm Mon-Fri, 9.30am-8.30pm Sat & Sun) and Piazza Sant'Oronzo (☑0832 24 20 99; Piazza Sant'Oronzo; ◷9.30am-1.30pm & 3.30-7.30pm).

ⓘ Getting There & Away

BUS

The city bus terminal is located to the north of Porta Napoli.

Pugliairbus (http://pugliairbus.aeroportidi puglia.it) Runs to Brindisi airport (€7.50, 40 minutes, nine daily).

STP (☑0832 35 91 42; www.stplecce.it) Runs buses to Brindisi (€6.30, 35 minutes, nine daily), Gallipoli (€2.80, 1¼ hours, frequent) and Otranto (€2.80, two hours, frequent) from the **STP bus station** (☑800 430346; Viale Porta D'Europa).

TRAIN

The main train station, 1km southwest of Lecce's historic centre, runs frequent services.

TO	FARE	DURATION
Bari	€9	1½ -2 hr
Bologna	€59.50	7½-9½ hr
Brindisi	€2.80	30 mins
Naples	€53.10	5½ hr (transfer in Caserta)
Rome	€66	5½-9 hr

FSE trains head to Otranto, Gallipoli and Martina Franca; the ticket office is located on platform 1.

Brindisi

POP 89,800

Like all ports, Brindisi has its seamy side, but it's also surprisingly slow-paced and balmy, particularly the palm-lined Corso Garibaldi, which links the port to the train station, and the promenade stretching along the interesting seafront.

The town was the end of the ancient Roman road Via Appia, down whose length trudged weary legionnaires and pilgrims, crusaders and traders, all heading to Greece and the Near East. These days little has changed except that Brindisi's pilgrims are now sun-seekers rather than soul-seekers.

⦿ Sights

Museo Archeologico Provinciale Ribezzo · MUSEUM
(☑0831 56 55 08; Piazza del Duomo 8; adult/reduced €5/3; ◷9.30am-1.30pm Tue-Sat, plus 3.30-6.30pm Tue, Thu & Sat) This superb museum covers several floors with well-documented exhibits (in English), including some 3000 bronze sculptures and fragments in Hellenistic Greek style. There are also terracotta figurines from the 7th century, underwater archaeological finds, and Roman statues and heads (not always together).

Roman Column · MONUMENT
(Via Colonne) The gleaming white column above a sweeping set of sun-whitened stairs leading to the waterfront promenade marks the imperial Via Appia terminus at Brindisi. Originally there were two columns, but one was presented to the town of Lecce back in 1666 as thanks to Sant'Oronzo for having relieved Brindisi of the plague.

Brindisi

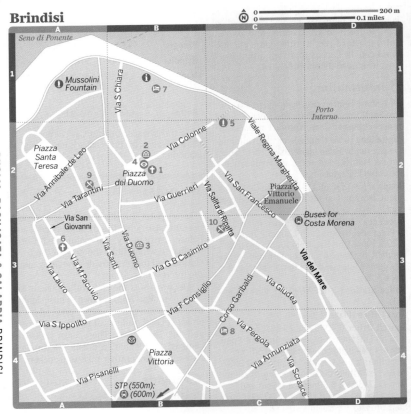

Brindisi

Sights

1 Cathedral B2
2 Museo Archeologico Provinciale
   Ribezzo B2
3 Palazzo Granafei-Nervegna B3
4 Porta dei Cavalieri Templari B2
5 Roman Column C2
6 Tempio di San Giovanni al
   Sepolcro A3

Sleeping

7 Grande Albergo Internazionale B1
8 Hotel Orientale C4

Eating

9 Il Giardino A2
10 Trattoria Pantagruele C3

Cathedral   CATHEDRAL
(Piazza del Duomo; ⊙8am-9pm Mon-Fri & Sun, to noon Sat) This 11th-century cathedral was substantially remodelled after an earth-quake in 1743. You can see how the original Romanesque structure may have looked by studying the nearby Porta dei Cavalieri Templari, a fanciful portico with pointy arches – all that remains of a medieval Knights Templar's church that once also stood here.

**Tempio di San Giovanni
al Sepolcro**   CHURCH
(Via San Giovanni) The Knights Templar's secondary church is a square brown bulk of Norman stone conforming to the circular plan the Templars so loved.

Palazzo Granafei-Nervegna   MUSEUM
(Via Duomo 20; ⊙10am-1pm & 5-8pm Tue-Sun) FREE A 16th-century Renaissance-style palace named for the two different families who owned it. The building is of interest because it houses the huge ornate capital that used to sit atop one of the Roman columns that marked the end of the Appian Way (the rest of the column is in Lecce). Also on site

is a salubrious cafe and the archaeological remains of a Roman *domus* (house).

Sleeping

Grande Albergo Internazionale   HOTEL $$

(☑ 0831 52 34 73; www.albergointernazionale.it; Viale Regina Margherita 23; s/d €100/160; ℙ❀☎) Built in 1870 for English merchants en route to Bombay and the Raj, the Internazionale offers grandeur, albeit of the rather faded variety. It has great harbour views, large rooms with grandly draped curtains, and stately common areas, but modern gadgetry takes second place to history here. Look out for off-season online room deals.

Hotel Orientale   HOTEL $$

(☑ 0831 56 84 51; www.hotelorientale.it; Corso Garibaldi 40; s/d €75/130; ℙ❀☎) This sleek, modern hotel overlooks the long palm-lined *corso*. Rooms are pleasant, the location is good and it has a small fitness centre, private car park and (rare) cooked breakfast option.

Eating

Trattoria Pantagruele   TRATTORIA $$

(☑ 0831 56 06 05; Via Salita di Ripalta 1; meals €30; ☉noon-3pm & 7.30-11.30pm Mon-Fri, 7.30-11.30pm Sat) Named after French writer François Rabelais' satirical character, this charming trattoria three blocks from the waterfront serves up excellent fish and grilled meats.

Il Giardino   PUGLIAN $$

(☑ 0831 56 40 26; Via Tarantini 14-18; meals €30; ☉12.30-2.30pm & 7.30-10.30pm Tue-Sat, 12.30-2.30pm Sun) Established more than 40 years ago in a restored 15th-century *palazzo,* sophisticated Il Giardino serves refined seafood and meat dishes in a delightful garden setting.

❶ Information

The new port is east of town, across the Seno di Levante at Costa Morena, in a bleak industrial wilderness.

The old port is about 1km from the train station along Corso Umberto I, which leads into Corso Garibaldi where there are numerous cafes, shops, ferry companies and travel agencies.

Antono Perrino Hospital (☑ 0831 53 71 11) Southwest of the centre; take the SS7 for Mesagne.

Post Office (Piazza Vittoria)

Tourist Office (☑ 0831 52 30 72; www.viaggia reinpuglia.it; Viale Regina Margherita 44; ☉9am-8.30pm Tue-Sun) Has a wealth of infor-

mation and brochures on the area. If you are interested in pedal power, pick up *Le Vie Verdi* map, which shows eight bicycling routes in the Brindisi area, ranging from 6km to 30km.

❶ Getting There & Away

AIR

From **Salento Airport** (BDS; ☑ 0831 411 74 06; www.aeroportidipuglia.it), Brindisi's small airport, there are domestic flights to Rome, Naples and Milan. Airlines include Alitalia and easyJet. There are also direct flights from London Stansted with Ryanair.

BOAT

Ferries, all of which take vehicles, leave Brindisi for Greece and Albania.

Ferry companies have offices at Costa Morena (the newer port), which is 4km from the train station. A free bus connects the two.

Grimaldi Lines (☑ 0831 54 81 16; www.grimaldi-lines.com; Costa Morena Terminal) Daily ferries to Igoumenitsa and Patras in Greece.

Red Star Ferries (☑ 0831 57 52 89; www.directferries.co.uk/red_star_ferries.htm; Costa Morena Terminal) To Vlorë in Albania.

BUS

There are regular SITA buses to Lecce (€6.30, 35 minutes, nine daily).

Pugliairbus (http://pugliairbus.aeroportidi puglia.it) Has services to Bari airport (€10, 1¾ hours) and Lecce (€7.50, 40 minutes) from Brindisi's airport.

Ferrovie del Sud-Est buses serving local towns leave from Via Bastioni Carlo V, in front of the train station.

Marozzi (☑ 0831 52 16 84) Runs to Rome's Stazione Tiburtina (€37.50 to €40, six to seven hours, four daily) from Viale Arno.

STP Brindisi (www.stpbrindisi.it) Buses go to Ostuni (€3.10, 50 minutes, six daily) and Lecce (€2.80, 45 minutes, two daily), as well as towns throughout the Salento. Most leave from Via Bastioni Carlo V, in front of the train station.

TRAIN

The train station has regular services to the following destinations:

Bari from €8.40, one hour

Lecce from €2.80, 30 minutes

Milan from €99.50, 8½ to 11 hours

Rome from €70, eight to twelve hours

Taranto from €4.90, one hour

❶ Getting Around

Major and local car-rental firms are represented at the airport. To reach the airport by bus,

PUGLIA, BASILICATA & CALABRIA BRINDISI

take the STP-run **Cotrap** bus (☑ 800 232042; www.stpbrindisi.it; single ticket €1) from Via Bastoni Carlo V.

A free **minibus** connects the train station and old ferry terminal with Costa Morena. It departs two hours before boat departures. You'll need a valid ferry ticket.

Southern & Western Salento

The Penisola Salentina, better known simply as Salento, is hot, dry and remote, retaining a flavour of its Greek past. It stretches across Italy's heel from Brindisi to Taranto and down to Santa Maria di Leuca. Here the lush greenery of Valle d'Itria gives way to flat, ochre-coloured fields hazy with wildflowers in spring, and endless olive groves.

Galatina

POP 27,300

With a charming historic centre, Galatina, 18km south of Lecce, is at the core of the Salentine Peninsula's Greek past. It is almost the only place where the ritual *tarantismi* (spider music) is still practised. The tarantella folk dance evolved from this ritual, and each year on the feast day of St Peter and St Paul (29 June), it is performed at the (now deconsecrated) church.

◎ Sights

Basilica di Santa Caterina d'Alessandria CHURCH

(⊙8am-12.30pm & 4.30-6.45pm Apr-Sep, 8am-12.30pm & 3.45-5.45pm Oct-Mar) Most people come to Galatina to see the incredible 14th-century Basilica di Santa Caterina d'Alessandria. Its interior is a kaleidoscope of frescoes and is absolutely beautiful, with a pure-white altarpiece set against the frenzy of frescoes. It was built by the Franciscans, whose patron was Frenchwoman Marie d'Enghien de Brienne.

Married to Raimondello Orsini del Balzo, the Salentine's wealthiest noble, Marie had plenty of cash to splash on interior decoration. The gruesome story goes that Raimondello (who is buried here) climbed Mount Sinai to visit relics of Santa Caterina (St Catherine). Kissing the dead saint's hand, he bit off a finger and brought it back as a holy relic.

It is not clear who the artists Marie employed really were; they could have been itinerant painters down from Le Marche and Emilia or southerners who'd absorbed the latest Renaissance innovations on trips north. Bring a torch.

🛏 Sleeping

Samadhi AGRITURISMO

(☑0836 60 02 84; www.agricolasamadhi.com; Via Stazione 116; r with/without bathroom €119/99; ❄️🛜♨️) 🍃 Soothe the soul with a stay at Samadhi, located around 7km east of Galatina in tiny Zollino. It's on a 10-hectare organic farm and the owners are multilingual. As well as ayurvedic treatments and yoga courses, there's a vegan restaurant offering organic meals. Check the website for upcoming retreats and courses.

ℹ Getting There & Away

FSE runs frequent trains between Lecce and Galatina (€2.10, 30 minutes), and Galatina and Zollino (€1, eight minutes).

Otranto

POP 5540

Bloodied and bruised by an infamous Turkish massacre in 1480, Otranto's story is best told in its amazing cathedral where the bones of 813 martyrs are displayed in a glass case behind the altar. Less macabre is the cathedral's other jaw-dropper, its medieval mosaic floor that rivals the famous early Christian mosaics of Ravenna in its richness and historical significance.

Lying deep in Italy's stiletto, Otranto has back-heeled quite a few invaders over the centuries and been brutally kicked by others – most notably the Turks. Sleuth around its compact old quarter and you can peel the past off in layers – Greek, Roman, Turkish and Napoleonic. These days the town is a generally peaceful place, unless you're fighting for beach space at the height of summer.

◎ Sights

★Cathedral CATHEDRAL

(☑0836 80 27 20; Piazza Basilica; ⊙7am-noon daily, plus 3-7pm Apr-Sep, 3-6pm Oct-Mar) Mosaics, skulls, crypts and biblical-meets-tropical imagery: Otranto's cathedral is like no other in Italy. The church was built by the Normans in the 11th century, though it's been given a few facelifts since. Covering the entire floor is its pièce de résistance, a vast 12th-century mosaic of a stupendous tree of life balanced on the back of two elephants.

The mosaic was created by a young monk called Pantaleone in 1165, whose vision of heaven and hell encompassed an amazing (con)fusion of the classics, religion and plain old superstition, including Adam and Eve, Diana the huntress, Hercules, King Arthur, Alexander the Great, and a menagerie of monkeys, snakes and sea monsters.

Beguiled by the well-preserved floor, most people forget to look up at the beautiful wooden coffered ceiling.

The beauty of the floor contrasts sharply with the ghoulishly fascinating **Cappella Mortiri** (Chapel of the Dead), where the bones and skulls of 813 Otranto martyrs beheaded by the invading Turks peer out of seven tall glass cases. The stone upon which the grisly deed was allegedly carried out is preserved behind the altar.

If the bones haven't freaked you out, the church also has a dungeon-like crypt to explore.

Castello Aragonese Otranto CASTLE
(www.castelloaragoneseotranto.it; Piazza Castello; adult/child €2/free; ⊕9am-1pm & 3-7pm) This squat, thick-walled fort, with the Charles V coat of arms above the entrance, has great views from the ramparts. There are some faded original murals and original cannon-balls on display.

Chiesa di San Pietro CHURCH
(Via San Pietro; ⊕10am-noon & 3-6pm) Vivid Byzantine frescoes decorate the interior of this church, which was being restored at the time of writing. Follow the signs from Castello Aragonese Otranto; if it's closed, ask for the key at the cathedral.

🏃 Activities

There are some great beaches north of Otranto, especially **Baia dei Turchi**, with its translucent blue water. South of Otranto a spectacular rocky coastline makes for an impressive drive down to Castro. To see what goes on underwater, **Scuba Diving Otranto** (⊕0836 80 27 40; www.scubadiving.it; Via Francesco di Paola 43) offers day or night dives as well as introductory courses and diving courses.

🛏 Sleeping

Balconcino d'Oriente B&B $
(⊕0836 80 15 29; www.balconcinodoriente.com; Via San Francesco da Paola 71; d €60-120, tr €80-150; P 📶) This B&B has an African–Middle Eastern theme throughout with colourful bed linens, African prints, Moroccan lamps

and orange colour washes on the walls. The downstairs restaurant serves traditional Italian meals (€20 to €24).

★**Palazzo Papaleo** HOTEL $$
(⊕0836 80 21 08; www.hotelpalazzopapaleo.com; Via Rondachi 1; r €97-249; P 📶 @ 🛜) 🖉 Located next to the town cathedral, this sumptuous hotel was the first to earn the EU Eco-label in Puglia. Aside from its ecological convictions, the hotel has magnificent rooms with original frescoes, exquisitely carved antique furniture and walls washed in soft greys, ochres and yellows. Soak in the panoramic views while enjoying the rooftop spa. The staff are exceptionally friendly.

Palazzo de Mori B&B $$
(⊕0836 80 10 88; www.palazzodemori.it; Bastione dei Pelasgi; s/d €105/140; ⊕Apr-Oct; 📶 @) 🖉 In Otranto's historic centre, this charming B&B serves breakfast on the sun terrace overlooking the port. The rooms are decorated in soothing white on white.

🍴 Eating

La Bella Idrusa PIZZA $
(⊕0836 80 14 75; Via Lungomare degli Eroi; pizzas €5; ⊕7pm-midnight Thu-Tue) You can't miss this pizzeria right by the huge Porta Terra in the historic centre. Despite the tourist-trap location, the food doesn't lack authenticity. And it's not just pizzas on offer: seafood standards are also served.

L'Altro Baffo SEAFOOD $$
(⊕0836 80 16 36; www.laltrobaffo.com; Cenobio Basiliano 23; meals €30-40; ⊕11am-3pm & 6pm-midnight Tue-Sun) This elegant modern restaurant near the castle – on a side street signed towards the cathedral – dishes up seafood with a contemporary twist. Try the raw fish tasting plate or the Otranto classic: *polipo alla pignata* (octopus stewed in a clay pot).

ℹ Information

Tourist Office (⊕0836 80 14 36; Via del Porto; ⊕9am-1pm & 3-7pm) Down in the new port area.

ℹ Getting There & Away

Otranto can be reached from Lecce by FSE train (€3.50, 1¼ hours). It is on a small branch line, which necessitates changing in Maglie and sometimes Zollino too. Services are reduced on Sundays.

PUGLIA, BASILICATA & CALABRIA SOUTHERN & WESTERN SALENTO

DRAMATIC COASTLINE

For a scenic road trip, the drive south from Otranto to Castro takes you along a wild and beautiful coastline. The coast here is rocky and dramatic, with cliffs falling down into the sparkling, azure sea; when the wind is up you can see why it is largely treeless. Many of the towns here started life as Greek settlements, although there are few monuments to be seen. Further south, the resort town of Santa Maria di Leuca is the tip of Italy's stiletto and the dividing line between the Adriatic and Ionian Seas.

Gallipoli

POP 21,100

Like Taranto, Gallipoli is a two-part town: the modern hub is based on the mainland, while the older *centro storico* inhabits a small island that juts out into the Ionian Sea. With a raft of serene baroque architecture usurped only by Lecce, it is, arguably, the prettiest of Salento's smaller settlements.

The old town, ringed by the remains of its muscular 14th-century walls is the best place to linger. It's punctuated by several baroque chapels, a traditional fishing port, a windswept sea drive, and narrow lanes barely wide enough to accommodate a Fiat *cinquecento* (500).

Sights & Activities

Gallipoli has some fine beaches, including the Baia Verde, just south of town. Nature enthusiasts will want to take a day trip to Parco Regionale Porto Selvaggio, about 20km north – a protected area of wild coastline with walking trails amid the trees and diving off the rocky shore.

Cattedrale di Sant'Agata   CATHEDRAL
(Via Antonietta de Pace; ⊙ hours vary) On the island, Gallipoli's 17th-century cathedral is a baroque beauty that could compete with anything in Lecce. Not surprisingly, Giuseppe Zimbalo, who helped beautify Lecce's Santa Croce basilica, worked on the facade. Inside, it's lined with paintings by local artists.

Frantoio Ipogeo   HISTORIC SITE
(☎ 338 1363063; Via Antonietta de Pace 87; admission €1.50; ⊙ 10am-noon) This is only one of some 35 olive presses buried in the tufa rock below the town. It was here, between the 16th and early 19th centuries, that local workers pressed Gallipoli's olive oil, which was then stored in one of the 2000 cisterns carved beneath the old town.

Museo Civico   MUSEUM
(☎ 0833 26 42 24; Via Antonietta de Pace 108; admission €1; ⊙ 10am-12.30pm Tue-Sun, plus 3.30-6pm Tue, Thu, Sat & Sun) Founded in 1878, this dusty museum is a 19th-century time capsule featuring fish heads, ancient sculptures, a 3rd-century-BC sarcophagus and other weird stuff.

Farmacia Provenzana   HISTORIC BUILDING
(Via Antonietta de Pace; ⊙ 8.30am-12.30pm & 4.30-8.30pm Sun-Fri) A beautifully decorated pharmacy dating from 1814.

Sleeping

Insula   B&B $
(☎ 366 3468357; www.bbinsulagallipoli.it; Via Antonietta de Pace 56; s €40-80, d €60-150; ⊙ Apr-Oct; ❈ @) A magnificent 15th-century building houses this memorable B&B. The five rooms are all different but share the same princely atmosphere with exquisite antiques, vaulted high ceilings and cool pastel paintwork.

Hotel Palazzo del Corso   HOTEL $$$
(☎ 0833 26 40 40; www.hotelpalazzodelcorso.it; Corso Roma 145; r from €239; P ❈ @ 🛜 ≋) This beautiful luxury hotel is actually in the new town, but is worth forking out for if you fancy a bit of regal treatment. There's a fantastic terrace complete with a small swimming pool, a gym, and large comfortable rooms that have enough defining features (carpets, interesting furniture, wall paintings) to prevent them from looking too corporate.

Eating

Caffè Duomo   CAFE $
(Via Antonietta de Pace 72; desserts €9; ⊙ 7.30am-1am) For good Gallipoli *spumone* (layered ice cream with candied fruit and nuts) and refreshing *granite* (ices made with coffee, fresh fruit or locally grown pistachios and almonds), head to Caffè Duomo.

La Puritate   TRATTORIA $$$
(☎ 0833 26 42 05; Via S Elia 18; meals €45; ⊙ 12.30-3pm & 8-11.30pm) *The* place for fish in the old town, with large windows and sea views. Follow the practically obligatory seafood antipasti with delicious *primi* (first

courses). Anything involving fish is good, especially the prawns, swordfish and tuna. It's popular and quite formal. Reservations are recommended.

ℹ️ Information

Tourist Office (☑ 0833 26 25 29; Via Antonietta de Pace 86; ⊙ 8am-9pm summer, 8am-1pm & 4-9pm Mon-Sat winter) Near the cathedral in the old town.

ℹ️ Getting There & Away

FSE buses and trains head direct to Lecce (€4.20, one hour, four daily).

Taranto

POP 193,100

The once splendiferous Greek-Spartan colony of Taras is, today, a city of two distinct parts – a mildewed *centro storico* on a small artificial island protecting a lagoon (the Mar Piccolo), and a swankier new city replete with wide avenues laid out in a formal grid. The contrast between the two is sudden and sharp: the diminutive old town with its muscular Aragonese castle harbours a downtrodden, vaguely abandoned air, while the larger new city is busier, plusher and bustling with commerce.

Not generally considered to be on the tourist circuit, Taranto is rimmed by modern industry, including a massive steelworks, and is home to Italy's second biggest naval base after La Spezia. Thanks to an illustrious Greek and Roman history, it has been bequeathed with one of the finest Magna Graecia museums in Italy. For this reason alone, it's worth a stopover.

👁️ Sights

Taranto's medieval town centre is one of southern Italy's least-dressed-up-for-tourism historic quarters. It is perched on the small narrow island dividing the Mar Piccolo (Small Sea) and the Mar Grande (Big Sea). This odd geography means that blue sea and sky surround you wherever you go.

⭐ Museo Nazionale Archeologico di Taranto
MUSEUM

(☑ 099 453 21 12; www.museotaranto.it; Via Cavour 10; adult/reduced €5/2.50; ⊙ 8.30am-7.30pm) In the new town is one of Italy's most important archaeological museums, exploring ancient Taras. It houses, among other artefacts, the largest collection of Greek terracotta figures in the world. Also on exhibit are fine

collections of 1st-century-BC glassware, classic black-and-red Attic vases and stunning jewellery, such as a 4th-century-BC bronze and terracotta crown.

Cathedral
CATHEDRAL

(Via Duomo; ⊙ 8am-noon & 4.30-7.30pm) The 11th-century cathedral is one of Puglia's oldest Romanesque buildings and an extravagant treat. It's dedicated to San Cataldo, an Irish monk who lived and was buried here in the 7th century; the **Capella di San Cataldo** is a baroque riot of frescoes and polychrome marble inlay.

Castello Aragonese
CASTLE

(☑ 099 775 34 38; www.castelloaragonese taranto.it; Piazza Castello; ⊙ 9.30am-10pm) **FREE** Guarding the swing bridge that joins the old and new parts of town, this impressive 15th-century structure was once a prison and is currently occupied by the Italian navy, which has restored it. Multilingual and free guided tours are led by naval officers throughout the day. Opposite are the two remaining columns of the ancient **Temple of Poseidon** (Piazza Castello).

✨ Festivals & Events

Le Feste di Pasqua
RELIGIOUS

Taranto is famous for its Holy Week celebrations – the biggest in the region – when bearers in Ku Klux Klan–style robes carry icons around the town. There are three processions: the Perdoni, celebrating pilgrims; the Addolorata (lasting 12 hours but covering only 4km); and the Misteri (even slower at 14 hours to cover 2km).

🛏️ Sleeping

Affittacamere Sparta
B&B $

(☑ 329 2345262; www.bebsparta.it; Via Principe Amedeo 5; s €45-55, d €65-70, tr €80-85; ✳️ 🛜) These meticulously refurbished apartments are arranged on the ground floor of this otherwise utilitarian building on the western edge of the new town. The decor is ultra-comfortable with kitchenettes, power showers and mood lighting. Clever Greek-Sparta touches provide interesting design accents. Vouchers are provided for a light Italian breakfast in a cafe around the corner.

Hotel Akropolis
HOTEL $$

(☑ 099 470 41 10; www.hotelakropolis.it; Vico Seminario 3; s/d €105/145; ✳️ @ 🛜) A rare ray of light in the crumbling old town, this

Taranto

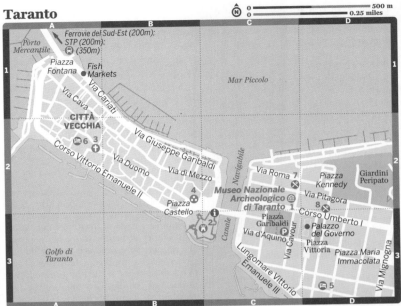

PUGLIA, BASILICATA & CALABRIA SOUTHERN & WESTERN SALENTO

Taranto

◎ **Top Sights**
1 Museo Nazionale Archeologico
  di Taranto...C2

◎ **Sights**
2 Castello Aragonese C3
3 Cathedral A2
4 Temple of Poseidon...............................B2

🛏 **Sleeping**
5 Affittacamere Sparta D3
6 Hotel Akropolis......................................A2

✗ **Eating**
7 Trattoria al Gatto Rosso C2
8 Trattoria-Pizzeria Amici Miei...............D2

converted medieval *palazzo* has been made into a hotel with a heavy Greek theme. Improbably (considering the grungy surroundings), there are 13 stylish cream-and-white rooms, beautiful original maiolica-tiled floors and tremendous views from the rooftop terrace.

The downstairs bar and restaurant is enclosed in stone, wood and glass, and has atmospheric curtained alcoves.

✗ Eating & Drinking

★ **Trattoria-Pizzeria
Amici Miei**   PIZZA, ITALIAN **$**
(☏ 099 400 44 70; Via Ciro Giovinazzi 18; meals €18-22; ⊙ noon-3pm & 7-11pm) The aptly named Amici Miei (my friends) is suitably friendly and renowned for its mega-sized portions that don't scrimp on taste. On top of all that, the warm homemade bread is divine, the wine measures are exceedingly generous, and staff sometimes serve complimentary dishes of freshly fried chips!

Trattoria al Gatto Rosso   TRATTORIA **$$**
(☏ 099 452 98 75; www.ristorantegattorosso.com; Via Cavour 2; meals €30-35; ⊙ noon-3pm & 7.30-11pm Tue-Sun) A relaxed and unpretentious trattoria with a real touch of class – heavy tablecloths, deep wine glasses and the like. It is located in the new town and is very popular with discerning business types.

ℹ Information

Taranto splits neatly into three. The old town is on a tiny island, lodged between the northwest port and train station and the new city to the southeast. Italy's largest steel plant occupies the city's entire western half. The grid-patterned new city contains the banks, and most hotels and restaurants. The **tourist office** (☏ 099 453

23 97; Corso Umberto I 113; ⊙ 9am-3pm) is at the side of the Castello Aragonese.

❶ Getting There & Around

BUS
Buses heading north and west depart from Porto Mercantile. **FSE** (☑ 080 546 21 11; www.fseonline.it) buses go to Bari (€5.80, 1¾ to 2¼ hours, frequent). Infrequent **SITA** (☑ 899 325204; www.sitabus.it) buses leave for Matera (€5.20, 1¾ hours, one daily). **STP** (☑ 080 975 26 19; www.stpspa.it) and FSE buses go to Lecce (€5.80, two hours, four daily).

Marozzi (☑ 080 5799 0111; www.marozzivt.it) has express services serving Rome's Stazione Tiburtina (€43, six hours, three daily). **Autolinee Miccolis** (☑ 099 470 44 51; www.miccolis-spa.it) serves Naples (€23, four hours, three daily) via Potenza (€15, two hours).

The bus **ticket office** (⊙ 6am-1pm & 2-7pm) is at Porto Mercantile.

TRAIN
Trenitalia and FSE trains go to the following destinations:

Bari €8.40, 1¼ hours, frequent
Brindisi €4.90, one hour, frequent
Rome from €50.50, six hours, five daily

AMAT (☑ 099 452 67 32; www.amat.taranto.it) buses run between the train station and the new city.

BASILICATA

Basilicata has an otherworldly landscape of tremendous mountain ranges, dark forested valleys and villages so melded with the rock faces that they seem to have grown there. Its isolated yet strategic location on routes linking ancient Rome to the eastern Byzantine empire has seen it successively invaded, pillaged, plundered, abandoned and neglected.

In the north the landscape is a fertile zone of gentle hills and deep valleys – once covered in thick forests, now cleared and cultivated with wheat, olives and grapes. The purple-hued mountains of the interior are impossibly grand and a wonderful destination for hikers and naturalists, particularly the soaring peaks of the Lucanian Apennines and the Parco Nazionale del Pollino.

On the coast, Maratea is one of Italy's most chic seaside resorts. However, Matera is Basilicata's star attraction, the famous *sassi* (former cave dwellings) of the city presiding over a rugged landscape of ravines and grottoes. Its ancient cave dwellings tell a tale of poverty, hardship and struggle, and its history is best immortalised in writer Carlo Levi's superb book *Christ Stopped at Eboli* – a title suggesting Basilicata was beyond the hand of God, a place where pagan magic still existed and thrived.

Today, Basilicata is attracting a slow but steadily increasing trickle of tourists. For those wanting to experience a raw and unspoilt region of Italy, Basilicata's remote atmosphere and wild landscape will appeal.

History
Basilicata spans Italy's instep with slivers of coastline touching the Tyrrhenian and Ionian Seas. It was known to the Greeks and Romans as Lucania (a name still heard today) after the Lucani tribe who lived here as far back as the 5th century BC. The Greeks also prospered, settling along the coastline at Metapontum and Erakleia, but things started to go wrong under the Romans, when Hannibal, the ferocious Carthaginian general, rampaged through the region.

In the 10th century, the Byzantine Emperor Basilikòs (976–1025) renamed the area, overthrowing the Saracens in Sicily and the south and reintroducing Christianity. The pattern of war and overthrow continued throughout the Middle Ages as the Normans, Hohenstaufens, Angevins and Bourbons constantly tussled over its strategic location, right up until the 19th century. As talk of the Italian unification began to gain ground, Bourbon-sponsored loyalists took to Basilicata's mountains to oppose political change. Ultimately, they became the much-feared bandits of local lore who make scary appearances in writings from the late 19th and early 20th centuries. In the 1930s, Basilicata was used as a kind of open prison for political dissidents – most famously the painter, writer and doctor Carlo Levi – sent into exile to remote villages by the fascists.

Matera
POP 60,500 / ELEV 405M
Stand in the right spot at a viewpoint overlooking Matera's huddled *sassi*, and it's not difficult to imagine you've been teleported back to the Holy Land circa 100 BC. At once epic and cinematic, the 'Città Sotterranea', as it's known, perches on the upper reaches of the steep-sided Gravina gorge and its timeless urban landscape has often been used to evoke biblical scenes in films and TV.

The old town, with its unique *sassi*, is split into two sections – the Sasso Barisano and the Sasso Caveoso – separated by a ridge upon which sits Matera's gracious *duomo* (cathedral). The houses' rock-grey facades once hid grimy, filthy abodes, but since the 1980s, Matera has been a city on the rebound filled with an increasing number of cafes and restaurants, and primed for tourism. With 9000 years of continuous human habitation, the place hides layer upon layer of history.

History

Matera is said to be one of the world's oldest towns, dating back to the Palaeolithic Age and inhabited continuously for around 7000 years. The simple natural grottoes that dotted the gorge were adapted to become homes, and an ingenious system of canals regulated the flow of water and sewage. In the 8th century the caves became home to Benedictine and Basilian monks; the earliest cave paintings date from this period.

The prosperous town became the capital of Basilicata in 1663, a position it held until 1806 when the power moved to Potenza. In the decades that followed, an unsustainable increase in population led to the habitation of unsuitable grottoes – originally intended as animal stalls – even lacking running water. The dreadful conditions fostered a tough and independent spirit: in 1943, Matera became the first Italian city to rise up against German occupation.

By the 1950s more than half of Matera's population lived in the *sassi*, typical caves sheltering families with an average of six children. The infant mortality rate was 50%. In his poetic and moving memoir, *Christ Stopped at Eboli,* Carlo Levi describes how children would beg passers-by for quinine to stave off the deadly malaria. Such publicity finally galvanised the authorities into action and in the late 1950s about 15,000 inhabitants were forcibly relocated to new government housing schemes.

◉ Sights & Activities

The two *sasso* districts – the more restored, northwest-facing **Sasso Barisano** and the more impoverished, northeast-facing **Sasso Caveoso** – are both extraordinary, riddled with serpentine alleyways and staircases, and dotted with frescoed *chiese rupestri* (cave churches) created between the 8th and

13th centuries. Today Matera contains some 3000 habitable caves.

The *sassi* are accessible from several points. There's an entrance off Piazza Vittorio Veneto, or take Via delle Beccherie to Piazza del Duomo and follow the tourist itinerary signs to enter either Barisano or Caveoso. Sasso Caveoso is also accessible from Via Ridola.

For a great photograph, head out of town for about 3km on the Taranto–Laterza road and follow signs for the *chiese rupestri*. This takes you up on the Murgia Plateau to the belvedere, from where you have fantastic views of the plunging ravine and Matera.

◉ Sasso Barisano

Chiesa di Madonna delle Virtù & Chiesa di San Nicola del Greci　　CHURCH
(Via Madonna delle Virtù; ⊘10am-1.30pm Mon-Fri, 10am-1.30pm & 3-6pm Sat & Sun) **FREE** This monastic complex is one of the most important monuments in Matera and is composed of dozens of caves spread over two floors. Chiesa di Madonna delle Virtù was built in the 10th or 11th century and restored in the 17th century. Above it, the simple Chiesa di San Nicola del Greci is rich in frescoes. The complex was used in 1213 by Benedictine monks of Palestinian origin.

★**Chiesa San Pietro Barisano**　　CHURCH
(Piazza San Pietro Barisano; adult/reduced €3/2, joint ticket with Chiesa di Santa Lucia alle Malve & Chiesa di Santa Maria d'Idris €6/4.50; ⊘10am-7pm Apr-Oct, 10am-2pm Nov-Mar) Below this church is an ancient honeycomb of niches where corpses were placed for draining, while at the entrance level are 15th- and 16th-century frescoes. The empty frame of the altarpiece graphically illustrates the town's troubled recent history: the church was plundered when Matera was partially abandoned in the 1960s and '70s.

◉ Sasso Caveoso

Chiesa di San Pietro Caveoso　　CHURCH
(Piazza San Pietro Caveoso; ⊘Mass 7pm Mon-Sat, 11am & 7pm Sun) **FREE** The only church in the *sassi* not dug into the tufa rock, Chiesa di San Pietro Caveoso was originally built in 1300 and has a 17th-century Romanesque-baroque facade.

Chiesa di Santa Maria d'Idris　　CHURCH
(Piazza San Pietro Caveoso; adult/reduced €3/2, joint ticket with Chiesa San Pietro Barisano & Chiesa

Matera

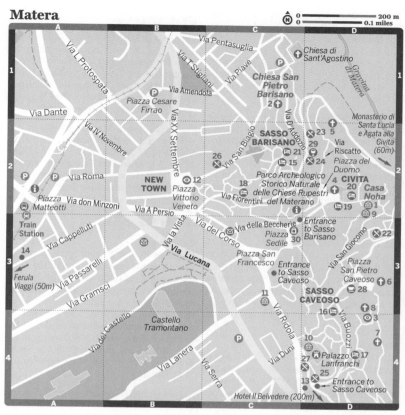

Matera

◎ Top Sights
1 Casa Noha...................................... D2
2 Chiesa San Pietro Barisano................. C1

◎ Sights
3 Casa-Grotta di Vico Solitario............... D4
4 Cathedral... D2
5 Chiesa di Madonna delle Virtù &
   Chiesa di San Nicola del Greci........... D2
6 Chiesa di San Pietro Caveoso............. D3
7 Chiesa di Santa Lucia alle Malve......... D4
8 Chiesa di Santa Maria d'Idris.............. D3
9 Museo della Scultura
   Contemporanea.............................. D2
10 Museo Nazionale d'Arte Medievale
   e Moderna della Basilicata................ D4
11 Museo Nazionale Ridola..................... C3
12 Palombaro Lungo.............................. B2

⊕ Activities, Courses & Tours
13 Altieri Viaggi................................... D4
14 Ferula Viaggi.................................... A3

⊜ Sleeping
15 Hotel in Pietra................................. C2
16 Il Vicinato....................................... D3
17 La Dolce Vita B&B............................ D4
18 Locanda di San Martino..................... C2
19 Palazzo Gattini................................ D2
20 Palazzo Viceconte............................ D2
21 Sassi Hotel..................................... C2

⊗ Eating
22 Baccanti... D3
23 Le Botteghe.................................... D2
24 Oi Marì... D2
25 Soul Kitchen.................................... D4
26 Stone... C2
27 Terrazza Rivelli................................ D4

⊕ Drinking & Nightlife
28 Keiv.. D3
29 Vicolo Cieco.................................... D2

⊕ Shopping
30 Geppetto.. C3

di Santa Lucia alle Malve €6/4.50; ⊙ 10am-1pm & 2.30-7pm Tue-Sun Apr-Oct, 10.30am-1.30pm Tue-Sun Nov-Mar) Dug into the Idris rock, this church has an unprepossessing facade, but the narrow corridor communicating with the recessed church of San Giovanni in Monterrone is richly decorated with 12th- to 17th-century frescoes.

Chiesa di Santa Lucia alle Malve   CHURCH
(Rione Malve; adult/reduced €3/2, joint ticket with Chiesa San Pietro Barisano & Chiesa di Santa Maria d'Idris €6/4.50; ⊙ 10am-1pm & 2.30-7pm Apr-Oct, 10.30am-1.30pm Tue-Sun Nov-Mar) Built in the 8th century to house a Benedictine convent, this church has a number of 12th-century frescoes, including an unusual breastfeeding Madonna.

Casa-Grotta di Vico Solitario   HISTORIC SITE
(admission €2; ⊙ 9.30am-late) For a glimpse of life in old Matera, visit this historic *sasso* off Via Bruno Buozzi. There's a bed in the middle, a loom, a room for manure and a section for a pig and a donkey. You also have access to a couple of neighbouring caves: in one, a black-and-white film depicts gritty pre-restoration Matera.

**Museo della Scultura
Contemporanea**   MUSEUM
(MUSMA; ☑ 366 9357768; www.musma.it; Via San Giacomo; adult/reduced €5/3.50; ⊙ 10am-2pm Tue-Sun, plus 4-8pm Sat & Sun Apr-Sep, 10am-2pm Tue-Sun Oct-Mar) Housed in Palazzo Pomarici, MUSMA is a fabulous contemporary sculpture museum. The setting – deeply recessed caves and frescoed palace rooms – is extraordinary and the works themselves absorbing. You can also book a tour to visit the **Cripta del Peccato Originale** (Crypt of Original Sin), which is located 7km south of Matera and has well-preserved frescoes from the late 8th century. It's known as the Sistine Chapel of the cave churches and the frescoes depict dramatic Old Testament scenes.

★**Casa Noha**   MUSEUM
(☑ 0835 33 54 52; Recinto Cavone 9; suggested donation €4; ⊙ 10am-6pm Wed-Sun) Buffing itself up for its European Capital of Culture status in 2019, Matera opened this brilliant multimedia exhibit in February 2014. Hosted in several rooms of a 16th-century family home, it relates the sometimes painful social history of the town and its *sassi*, warts and all. The presentation is made using films projected onto various walls and lasts approximately 20 minutes.

◉ New Town

The focus of the new town is Piazza Vittorio Veneto, an excellent, bustling meeting point for a *passeggiata*. It's surrounded by elegant churches and richly adorned *palazzi* with their backs to the *sassi*: an attempt by the bourgeois to block out the shameful poverty the *sassi* once represented.

**Museo Nazionale d'Arte Medievale
e Moderna della Basilicata**   MUSEUM
(☑ 0835 31 42 35; Palazzo Lanfranchi; adult/reduced €2/1; ⊙ 9am-8pm Thu-Tue) The stars of the show here are Carlo Levi's paintings, including the panoramic mural *Lucania '61* depicting peasant life in biblical Technicolor. There's also some centuries-old sacred art from the *sassi*.

Cathedral   CATHEDRAL
(Piazza del Duomo) Set high up on a spur between the two natural bowls of the *sassi*, the subdued, graceful exterior of the 13th-century Puglian-Romanesque cathedral makes the neo-baroque excess within all the more of a surprise. The ornate capitals, sumptuous chapels and tons of gilding were getting an extensive renovation at last visit. Pediments mounted on the cathedral's altars came from the Greek temples at Metaponto.

Museo Nazionale Ridola   MUSEUM
(☑ 0835 31 00 58; Via Ridola 24; adult/reduced €2.50/1.25; ⊙ 9am-8pm Tue-Sun, 2-8pm Mon) This impressive collection includes local Neolithic finds and some remarkable Greek pottery, such as the *Cratere Mascheroni*, a huge urn more than 1m high.

Palombaro Lungo   HISTORIC SITE
(Piazza Vittorio Veneto; guided tour €3; ⊙ 10am-1pm & 3-6pm) Being a troglodyte city, much of Matera's beauty is obscured in caves or underground, including this giant cistern, which is, arguably, as magnificent as a subterranean cathedral. Lying under the city's main square with arches carved out of the existing rock, it is mind-boggling in its scale and ingenuity. Multilingual guides explain its conception and history. Tours last 25 minutes.

☞ Tours

There are plenty of official guides for the *sassi* – try www.sassiweb.it.

MATERA ON THE REBOUND

Recently named 2019 European City of Culture, Matera has taken huge strides in burying the unpleasant ghosts of its past. In the 1950s and '60s, the town and its ancient cave-houses were ingloriously considered to be the shame of Italy, a giant slum where malaria was rampant and a desperate populace subsisted on or below the breadline. After years of political squabbling, Matera's inhabitants were eventually evacuated (some forcibly) and resettled in a burgeoning new town higher up the gorge. Neglected and uncared for, the old town and its *sassi* (former cave dwellings) fell into a steep decline. By the 1980s old Matera was a virtual ghost town, an unholy mess of unlivable abodes.

Help came with a three-pronged attack of film-making, tourism and Unesco intervention. Italian director, Pier Paolo Pasolini was one of the first to put Matera on the map, making use of the town's biblical landscapes in his 1964 movie, *The Gospel According to St Matthew*. The success of the film and its eerie backdrops inspired others, including Hollywood heavyweights such as Mel Gibson, who arrived in Matera in 2004 to film *The Passion of the Christ*.

Celluloid fame led to a trickle of curious tourists and this, in turn, fuelled an increasing desire among Italians to clean up the once dilapidated *sassi* and showcase their historical value for future generations. In 1993, Unesco gave the town an extra boost when it named Matera's *sassi* and rupestrian churches a World Heritage Site. Progress has been rapid since. Bars and restaurants now inhabit once abandoned cave-houses and meticulous restoration work has saved ancient frescoes from almost certain decay.

Priming itself for 2019, Matera is in the process of restoring its 13th-century cathedral. In 2014 the town also opened a new interactive museum, Casa Noha, which tells the story of Matera's recent past in blunt, uncensored detail, and the *sassi* provided a backdrop in 2015 for the remaking of the movie *Ben Hur*, starring Morgan Freeman and Jack Huston.

Ferula Viaggi TOUR

(☎ 0835 33 65 72; www.ferulaviaggi.it; Via Cappelluti 34; ☺ 9am-1.30pm & 3.30-7pm Mon-Sat) Excellent and informative guided tours of the *sassi*, plus tours that include tastings or cookery courses, and also hiking and cycling tours into the Parco della Murgia Materana. Ferula Viaggi also runs Bike Basilicata, which rents bikes and helmets, and supplies a road book and map so you can head off on your own.

Altieri Viaggi TOUR

(www.altieriviaggi.it; Via Ridola 61) Runs 50-minute tours in an Ape Calessino (auto rickshaw) around the *sassi* for €15, plus plenty of other trips, including hiking.

🎊 Festivals & Events

Sagra della Madonna della Bruna RELIGIOUS

(☺ 2 Jul) The colourful Procession of Shepherds parades ornately decorated papier-mâché floats around town. The finale is the *assalto al carro,* when the crowd descends on the main cart and tears it to pieces.

Gezziamoci MUSIC

(www.onyxjazzclub.it; ☺ last week Aug) This jazz festival happens in the *sassi* and surrounding Parco della Murgia Materana.

🛏 Sleeping

La Dolce Vita B&B B&B $

(☎ 0835 31 03 24; www.ladolcevitamatera.it; Rione Malve 51; r €80; ☞) ⊘ This delightful, ecofriendly B&B in Sasso Caveoso has self-contained apartments with solar panels and recycled rainwater for plumbing. Accommodation is cool, comfortable and homey. Owner Vincenzo is passionate about Matera and is a mine of information on the *sassi*.

Il Vicinato B&B $

(☎ 0835 31 26 72; www.ilvicinato.com; Piazzetta San Pietro Caveoso 7; s/d €60/80; ❄☞) This B&B enjoys a great, easy-to-find location. Rooms are decorated in clean modern lines, with views across to Idris rock and the Murgia Plateau. As well as the standard rooms, there's a room with a balcony, and a small apartment, each with an independent entrance.

EXPLORING MATERA'S GORGE

In the picturesque landscape of the Murgia Plateau, the **Matera Gravina** cuts a rough gouge in the earth, a 200m-deep canyon pockmarked with abandoned caves and villages and roughly 150 mysterious *chiese rupestri* (cave churches). The area is protected as the **Parco della Murgia Materana**, an 80-sq-km wild park formed in 1990 and, since 2007, included in Matera's Unesco World Heritage Site. You can hike from the *sassi* into the gorge; steps lead down from the parking place near the **Monasterio di Santa Lucia** (Via Madonna delle Virtù). At the bottom of the gorge you have to ford a river and then climb up to the **belvedere** (Taranto–Laterza road) on the other side; this takes roughly two hours.

Cave churches accessible from the belvedere include San Falcione, Sant'Agnese and Madonna delle Tre Porte. The belvedere is connected by road to the **Jazzo Gattini visitor centre** (⏹ 0835 33 22 62; ⏲ 9.30am-1pm Nov-Mar, 9.30am-2.30pm & 4-6.30pm Apr-Oct) encased in an old sheepfold. Guided hikes can be organised here plus walks to the nearby Neolithic village of **Murgia Timone**. For longer forays into the park, including a long day trek to the town of Montescaglioso, consider a guided hike with **Ferula Viaggi** (p139).

Beware: paths and river crossings in the park can be treacherous during and after bad weather.

Sassi Hotel — HOTEL $

(⏹ 0835 33 10 09; www.hotelsassi.it; Via San Giovanni Vecchio 89; s/d €70/90; ❄ @) The first hotel in the *sassi* is set in an 18th-century rambling edifice in Sasso Barisano with some rooms in caves and some not. Singles are small but doubles are gracefully furnished. The balconies have superb views of the cathedral.

★ Hotel Il Belvedere — HOTEL $$

(⏹ 0835 31 17 02; www.hotelbelvedere.matera.it; Via Casalnuovo 133; d from €130; ☎) Looks can be deceptive – especially in Matera. This cave boutique looks unremarkable from its streetside perch on the edge of the Sasso Caveoso, but you'll feel your jaw start to drop as you enter its luxurious entrails and spy the spectacle of Old Matera sprawling below a jutting terrace. Cavernous rooms sport mosaics, mood lighting and curtained four-poster beds.

Hotel in Pietra — BOUTIQUE HOTEL $$

(⏹ 0835 34 40 40; www.hotelinpietra.it; Via San Giovanni Vecchio 22; s/d/ste from €50/115/185; ❄ @ ☎) The lobby of this hotel is set in a former 13th-century chapel complete with soaring arches, while the eight rooms combine soft golden stone with the natural cave interior. Furnishings are Zen-style with low beds, and the bathrooms are super stylish and include vast sunken tubs.

Locanda di San Martino — HOTEL $$

(⏹ 0835 25 66 00; www.locandadisanmartino.it; Via Fiorentini 71; d €89-200; ❄ ☎ ❄) The main lure of this Sasso Caveoso hotel is its Roman-themed spa complete with swimming pool in a subterranean cave. Cave accommodation, with niches and rustic brick floors, is set around a warren of cobbled paths and courtyards. The spa costs an extra €10 for guests, €20 for nonguests.

Palazzo Viceconte — HOTEL $$

(⏹ 0835 33 06 99; www.palazzoviceconte.it; Via San Potito 7; d €95-140, ste €139-350; ❄ @ ☎) You won't have trouble spotting the palatial features at this 15th-century *palazzo* near the cathedral with superb views of the *sassi* and gorge. The hotel is elegantly furnished and the rooftop terrace has panoramic views. Be king (or queen) for a day (or more) amid the courtyards, salons, frescoed ceilings and antiques.

★ Palazzo Gattini — HOTEL $$$

(⏹ 0835 33 43 58; www.palazzogattini.it; Piazza del Duomo 13; d/ste €260/390; ⓟ ❄ @ ☎ ❄) Setting a high standard and living up to it, the Gattini is the former palatial home of Matera's most noble family and the city's plushest hotel. If the erstwhile nobility could see the palace's 20 luxuriously refurbished rooms today, they'd probably give enthusiastic nods of approval. Beautiful stone walls combine with expensive fittings and expansive common areas, including a spa, restaurant, terrace and coffee shop.

✖ Eating

Terrazza Rivelli ITALIAN $
(📞 0835 31 26 13; Via Ridola 47; meals €15-20; ⏱ 11.30am-3.30pm & 7-11.30pm Wed-Mon) There are two terraces here – one out front and one on the roof – plus seating in several semiformal but relaxed dining rooms inside. Food is typical southern Italian with some Puglian influences, such as *orecchiette*. Waiters get you off to a good start with a basket of classic Basilicata bread – possibly the finest in all Italy.

Oi Marì PIZZA $
(📞 0835 34 61 21; Via Fiorentini 66; pizzas from €5; ⏱ 8.30pm-11.45pm daily, plus 1-3pm Sat & Sun) In Sasso Barisano, this lofty and convivial cavern is styled as a Neapolitan pizzeria. It has a great, cheery atmosphere with excellent, substantial pizzas to match, as well as *primi* of the day.

Stone INTERNATIONAL $
(📞 0835 33 99 68; Via San Biagio 23; meals €20-24; ⏱ 7pm-6am) Stone is where you go to find young company or late-night grub (or both). Cavernous (like everywhere in Matera), its brightly lit interior has been given a lounge-lizard makeover with suspended glass floors and luxuriant furnishings.

The noise level rises as the night progresses, but there are plenty of alcoves if you wish to escape the TV soccer, loquacious DJs and out-of-town trendies clustered around the aperitif buffet. The food is good (you can't go wrong with the pizza), but the cocktails are better.

Le Botteghe TRATTORIA $
(📞 0835 34 40 72; www.lebotteghematera.it; Piazza San Pietro; meals €18.50-23; ⏱ 1-2.30pm & 8-11.30pm Thu-Tue) In Sasso Barisano, this is a classy but informal restaurant set in arched whitewashed rooms. Try delicious local specialities like *fusilli mollica e crusco* (pasta and fried bread with local sweet peppers).

★ Soul Kitchen MODERN ITALIAN $$
(📞 0835 31 15 68; www.ristorantesoulkitchen.it; Via Casalnuovo 27; meals €30-35; ⏱ 12.15-2.45pm & 7.15-11.15pm Fri-Wed) If you thought Basilicata was somehow lagging behind the rest of Italy in the food stakes, you clearly haven't been to Soul Kitchen. New in 2013, this cavernous restaurant with sharp colour accents (grab a pew on the mezzanine) epitomises Matera's ambitious drive to reinvent its image. Dishes are recognisably Basilicatan, but

with modern twists, and are presented with artistic aplomb.

Baccanti TRADITIONAL ITALIAN $$$
(📞 0835 33 37 04; www.baccantiristorante.com; Via Sant'Angelo 58-61; meals €50; ⏱ 1-3.30pm & 8-11.30pm Tue-Sat, 1-4pm Sun) As classy as a cave can be. The design is simple glamour against the low arches of the cavern, while the dishes are delicate and complex, using local ingredients, and the gorge views are sublime.

Drinking & Nightlife

★ Vicolo Cieco WINE BAR
(📞 338 8550984; Via Fiorentini 74; ⏱ 11am-3am) Matera's new hipster inclinations are on show at this wine-bar cum cafe in a typical cave-house off Sasso Barisano's main drag. The decor is whimsical to say the least – picture retro jukeboxes, a wall-mounted Scalextric track, chairs cut in half and glued to the wall in the name of art, and a knife-and-fork chandelier! The wine and music selections are excellent and there are also great snacks (cheese boards and *panini*).

Keiv CAFE, BAR
(Via Bruno Ruccini 184; ⏱ 8.30am-2am) The new cooler face of the *sassi* is evident at this cafe that metamorphoses into a lounge bar in the early evening. Giant mirrors decorated by local artists enlarge a comfortable space where DJs spin discs on Friday and Saturday nights.

🛍 Shopping

Geppetto CRAFTS
(Piazza Sedile 19; ⏱ 9.30am-1pm & 3.30-8pm) This craft shop stands out amongst the tawdrier outlets selling tufa lamps and tiles. Its speciality is the *cuccù*, a brightly painted ceramic whistle in the shape of a cockerel, which was once prized by Matera's children. The whistles were traditionally considered a symbol of good luck and fertility.

ℹ Information

The maps *Carta Turistica di Matera* and *Matera: Percorsi Turistici* (€1.50), available from various travel agencies, bookstores and hotels around town, describe a number of itineraries through the *sassi* and the gorge.

Basilicata Turistica (www.aptbasilicata.it) The official tourist website has useful information on history, culture, attractions and sights.

Hospital (📞 0835 25 31 11; Via Montescaglioso) About 1km southeast of the centre.

Parco Archeologico Storico Naturale delle Chiese Rupestri del Materano (☐ 0835 33 61 66; www.parcomurgia.it; Via Sette Dolori; ◷ 9.30am-6.30pm) For info on Parco della Murgia Materana.

Police Station (☐ 0835 37 81; Via Gattini)

Post Office (Via Passarelli; ◷ 8am-6.30pm Mon-Fri, to 12.30pm Sat)

Sassiweb (www.sassiweb.it) Another informative website on Matera.

Tourist Office (Piazza Matteotti 2; ◷ 9am-8pm Mon & Wed-Fri, 9am-7pm Tue, 10am-7pm Sat) Matera's main tourist office is next to the exit for the underground train station.

ⓘ Getting There & Away

BUS

The bus station is north of Piazza Matteotti, next to the subterranean train station.

Grassani (☐ 0835 72 14 43; www.grassani.it) Serves Potenza (€5.50, 1½ hours, four daily). Buy tickets on the bus.

Marino (www.marinobus.it) Runs two services daily to Naples (€22, 4½ hours).

Marozzi (☐ 06 225 21 47; www.marozzivt. it) Runs three daily buses to Rome (€34, 6½ hours). A joint SITA and Marozzi service leaves daily for Siena, Florence and Pisa, via Potenza. Advance booking is essential.

Pugliairbus (☐ 080 580 03 58; http://pugliair bus.aeroportidipuglia.it) Operates a service to Bari airport (€6, 1¼ hours, four daily).

SITA (☐ 0835 38 50 07; www.sitabus.it) Goes to Taranto (€5.70, two hours, six daily) and Metaponto (€2.90, one hour, up to five daily) and many small towns in the province. Buy tickets from newspaper kiosks on Piazza Matteotti.

TRAIN

Ferrovie Appulo-Lucane (FAL; ☐ 0835 33 28 61; http://ferrovieappulolucane.it) runs regular trains (€4.90, 1½ hours, 12 daily) and buses (€4.90, 1½ hours, six daily) to Bari. For Potenza, take a FAL bus to Ferrandina and connect with a Trenitalia train, or head to Altamura to link up with FAL's Bari–Potenza run.

Metaponto

In stark contrast to the dramatic Tyrrhenian coast, Basilicata's Ionian coast is a listless, flat affair dotted with large tourist resorts. A brief respite is provided by the Greek ruins at Metaponto (known as Metapontum to the Greeks), which, with their accompanying museums, bring alive the enormous influence of Magna Graecia in southern Italy.

While the modern town of Metaponto is pretty grim, the two main archaeological sites and the local museum are well worth a visit. The sites have proven particularly valuable to archaeologists who, by studying their undisturbed ruins, have managed to map the entire ancient urban plan. Settled by Greeks in the 8th and 7th centuries BC, Metaponto's most famous resident was Pythagoras, who founded a school here after being banished from Crotone (in Calabria) in the 6th century BC. After Pythagoras died, his house and school were incorporated into the Temple of Hera (known as the Tavole Palatine), whose elegantly ruined columns remain.

◉ Sights

★**Tavole Palatine**　　ARCHAEOLOGICAL SITE
(Palatine Tables; ◷ 9am-1hr before sunset) **FREE** The remains of the **Temple of Hera** – 15 columns and sections of pavement – are Metaponto's most impressive sight. They're known as the Tavole Palatine (Palatine Tables), since knights, or paladins, are said to have gathered here before heading to the Crusades. The ruins are 3km north of town, just off the highway – to find them, follow the slip road for Taranto onto the SS106.

Museo Archeologico Nazionale　　MUSEUM
(☐ 0835 74 53 27; Via Aristea 21; admission €2.50; ◷ 9am-8pm Tue-Sun, 2-8pm Mon) This small but important museum looks like it could do with a good dusting; nevertheless, the artefacts from the nearby Greek ruins of Metaponto are well laid out.

Parco Archeologico　　ARCHAEOLOGICAL SITE
(◷ 9am-1hr before sunset) **FREE** Not to be confused with the Tavole Palatine, the Parco Archeologico is a larger, if less impressive collection of Metaponto ruins that contains the remains of a Greek theatre and the Doric **Tempio di Apollo Licio**.

The park is 2km northeast of the Museo Archeologico Nazionale – from the museum, walk in a straight line down Via Aristea, pass through the town square and go straight ahead at the traffic circle.

ⓘ Getting There & Away

SITA buses run from Matera to Metaponto (€2.90, one hour, up to five daily). The town is also on the Taranto–Reggio train line with connections to Potenza (€5.75, 1½ hours) and Naples (€13.85, four hours).

Potenza

POP 68,600 / ELEV 819M

Basilicata's regional capital, Potenza, has been ravaged by earthquakes (the last in 1980) and, as the highest town in the Basilicata region, it broils in summer and shivers in winter. You may find yourself passing through as it's a major transport hub.

Potenza's few sights are in the old centre, at the top of the hill. To get there, take the elevators from Piazza Vittorio Emanuele II. The ecclesiastical highlight is the **cathedral**, erected in the 12th century and rebuilt in the 18th. The elegant Via Pretoria, flanked by a boutique or two, makes a pleasant traffic-free stroll, especially during the *passeggiata*.

In central Potenza, **B&B Al Convento** (☑ 097 12 55 91; Largo San Michele Arcangelo 21; s/d €55/80; 🅿 @ 🛜) is a great accommodation choice housing a mix of polished antiques and design classics.

The town centre straddles a high ridge, east to west. To the south lie the main Trenitalia and Ferrovie Appulo-Lucane train stations, connected to the centre by buses 1 and 10.

Grassani (☑ 0835 72 14 43) has buses to Matera (€5.30, 1½ hours, four daily). **SITA** (☑ 0971 50 68 11; www.sitabus.it) has daily buses to Melfi, Venosa and Maratea. Buses leave from Via Appia 185 and also stop near the Scalo Inferiore Trenitalia train station. **Liscio** (☑ 097 15 46 73; www.autolineeliscio.it) buses serve various routes including Rome (€24, 4½ hours, three daily).

There are regular train services from Potenza to Foggia (from €6, 2¼ hours), Salerno (from €6, 1¾ hours) and Taranto (from €8.20, two hours). For Bari (from €10.50, four hours, four daily), take the **Ferrovie Appulo-Lucane** (☑ 0971 41 15 61; http://ferrovie appulolucane.it) train at Potenza Superiore station.

Appennino Lucano

The Appennino Lucano (Lucanian Apennines) bite Basilicata in half like a row of jagged teeth. Sharply rearing up south of Potenza, they protect the lush Tyrrhenian coast and leave the Ionian shores gasping in the semi-arid heat. The area is protected by the **Parco Nazionale Dell'Appennino Lucano**, the newest of Italy's 24 national parks, inaugurated in 2007.

ℹ SOUTHERN SUNDAYS

True to Mediterranean tradition, Sunday remains a day of rest in southern Italy, turning many smaller settlements into ghost towns. Shops close, some restaurants take at least part of the day off, and many bus routes and some train routes don't function at all. Unless you have access to your own transport, this is a good day to stay put in a larger city, veg on a beach, or go for a long walk in the countryside.

Aside from its sharp mountain terrain, the park's most iconic site is the Roman ruins of Grumentum, 75km south of Potenza just outside the town of Grumento Nova. The **Parco Archeologico di Grumentum** (admission incl museum €2.50; ⊙ 9am-1hr before sunset) is sometimes known as Basilicata's 'Little Pompeii'. The large site contains remains of a theatre, an amphitheatre, Roman baths, a forum, two temples and a *domus* with mosaic floors. There's also an interesting **museum** (☑ 0975 6 50 74; admission incl archaeological site €2.50; ⊙ 9am-8pm Tue-Sun, 2-8pm Mon).

Castelmezzano & Pietrapertosa

The two mountaintop villages of Castelmezzano (elevation 985m) and Pietrapertosa (elevation 1088m), ringed by the Lucanian Dolomites are spectacular. They are Basilicata's highest villages and are often swathed in cloud, making you wonder why anyone would build here – in territory best suited to goats.

Castelmezzano is surely one of Italy's most theatrical villages: the houses huddle along an impossibly narrow ledge that falls away in gorges to the Caperrino river. Pietrapertosa is even more amazing: the **Saracen fortress** at its pinnacle is difficult to spot as it is carved out of the mountain.

You can 'fly' between these two dramatic settlements courtesy of **Il Volo dell'Angelo** (The Angel Flight; ☑ Castelmezzano 0971 98 60 42, Pietrapertosa 0971 98 31 10; www.volodellangelo. com; singles €35-40, couples €63-72; ⊙ May-Sep), two heart-in-mouth ziplines where you are supended, belly down, in a cradle harness, and whizzed via cables across an abyss. The Peschiera line that runs between Castelmezzano and Pietrapertosa is one of the world's longest (1452m) and fastest (120km/h). Daredevils only!

You can spend a night in Pietrapertosa at a delightful B&B, **La Casa di Penelope e Cirene** (☑0971 98 30 13; Via Garibaldi 32; d from €70). Dine at the authentic Lucano restaurant **Al Becco della Civetta** (☑0971 98 62 49; www.beccodellacivetta.it; Vicolo I Maglietta 7; meals €25; ☺Wed-Mon) in Castelmezzano, which also offers traditionally furnished, simple whitewashed rooms (doubles €80).

You'll need your own vehicle to visit Castelmezzano and Pietrapertosa.

Basilicata's Western Coast

Resembling a mini Amalfi, Basilicata's Tyrrhenian coast is short but sweet. Squeezed between Calabria and Campania's Cilento peninsula, it shares the same beguiling characteristics: hidden coves and pewter sandy beaches backed by majestic coastal cliffs. The SS18 threads a spectacular route along the mountains to the coast's star attraction: the charming seaside settlements of Maratea.

Maratea

POP 5220

Contrasting sharply with Basilicata's rugged isolated interior, Maratea is the antithesis of the rest of the region. This disparate collection of placid coastal villages inhabits a narrow 32km-long strip on the Tyrrhenian Sea sandwiched between Calabria and Campania. Embellished with lush vegetation, sheltered coves and well-tended cliff-side villages, Maratea's latent joys are not dissimilar to those on the Amalfi – but there are fewer people enjoying them (and notably fewer non-Italians). Climb endless steps to lofty viewpoints, poke around ancient hilltop churches (44 of them), sip cappuccinos in diminutive drop-dead-gorgeous piazzas, and watch the sun render the sea turquoise, blue and aquamarine.

🛈 Orientation

What is usually referred to as Maratea is actually a collection of small settlements split into several parts, some of them walkable if you're relatively fit and the weather cooperates. Maratea's main train station sits roughly in the middle.

The Porto is clustered around a small harbour and is about a 10-minute walk below the station (towards the sea). The 'village' of Fiumicello is in the same direction, but reached by turning right rather than left once you've passed under the railway bridge. The main historic centre, known as Maratea Borgo, is perched in the hills behind. A bus leaves every 30 minutes or so from the station, or you can walk up a series of steps and paths (approximately 5km; the town is always visible). It has plenty of cafes and places to eat. The Marina di Maratea is located 5km south along the coast and has its own separate train station. The village of Acquafredda is 8km in the other direction, kissing the border of Campania.

👁 Sights & Activities

The deep green hillsides that encircle this tumbling conurbation offer excellent walking trails, providing a number of easy day trips to the surrounding hamlets of Acquafredda and Fiumicello, with its small sandy beach. The **tourist office** (☑0973 03 03 66; Piazza Vitolo 1; ☺8am-2pm & 3-6pm) in Maratea Borgo's main square dispenses an excellent map.

Statue of Christ the Redeemer　　STATUE

The symbol of Maratea and viewable from multiple vantage points along the coast is this 22m-high statue of Christ with his arms outstretched (completed in 1965). Slightly smaller than the similar Christ the Redeemer statue in Rio de Janeiro, this one is made of concrete with a Carrara marble covering and sits atop 644m-high Monte San Biagio.

A dramatic winding asphalt road leads to the top, although it's more fun to walk the steep path (# 1) that starts off Via Cappuccini in Maratea Borgo.

The statue faces inland towards the **Basilica di San Biagio** opposite.

Maratea Superiore　　RUIN

FREE The ruins of the original settlement of Maratea, supposedly founded by the Greeks, are situated at a higher elevation than the current village on a rocky escarpment just below the Christ the Redeemer statue. Abandoned houses with trees growing in their midst have long been given over to nature.

Marvin Escursioni　　BOAT TOUR

(☑338 8777899; Porto di Maratea; half-day boat trips €25) Operator based in the Porto di Maratea offering half-day boat tours (morning or afternoon) that include visits to surrounding grottoes and coves.

Sleeping

★**Locanda delle Donne Monache** HOTEL $$
(☑0973 87 74 87; www.locandamonache.com; Via Mazzei 4; r €130-310; ☺Apr-Oct; P☀@🛜🏊) Overlooking the medieval *borgo*, this exclusive hotel is in a converted 18th-century convent with a suitably lofty setting. It's a hotchpotch of vaulted corridors, terraces and gardens fringed with bougainvillea and lemon trees. The rooms are elegantly decorated in pastel shades and – bonus – there's a panoramic outdoor pool and tempting offers of cooking classes.

Hotel Villa Cheta Elite HOTEL $$
(☑0973 87 81 34; www.villacheta.it; Via Timpone 46; r €140-264; ☺Apr-Oct; P☀🛜) Set in an art nouveau villa at the entrance to the hamlet of Acquafredda, this hotel is like a piece of plush Portofino towed several hundred kilometres south. Enjoy a broad terrace with spectacular views, a fabulous restaurant and large rooms where antiques mix seamlessly with modernities. Bright Mediterranean foliage fills sun-dappled terraced gardens.

Eating

★**La Caffetteria** CAFE $
(Piazza Buraglia; panini from €4; ☺7.30am-2am summer, to 10pm winter) The outdoor seating at this delightful cafe in Maratea Borgo's central piazza is ideal for dedicated people-watching. The cafe serves homemade snacks throughout the day.

Lanterna Rossa SEAFOOD $$
(☑0973 87 63 52; Porto; meals €40; ☺10.30am-3.30pm & 7.30pm-midnight Wed-Mon Feb-Dec) Head for this terrace overlooking the port to dine on exquisite seafood. Highly recommended is the signature dish, *zuppa di pesce* (fish soup). The Bar del Porto sits beneath it serving ice cream and coffee.

Il Sacello MODERN ITALIAN $$$
(☑0973 87 61 39; Via Mazzei 4; meals €30-50; ☺12.30-2.30pm & 7.30-10.30pm) High-flying fine dining, quite literally, as you overlook the red rooftops of Maratea Borgo and the lovely swimming pool beautifying this restaurant, which is part of the Locanda delle Donne Monache hotel. The food is Italian fare given a modern touch. Try the rabbit with *cavatelli*, the beef tartare or the sweeter-than-sweet desserts including *cannoli*.

ℹ Getting There & Around

Maratea is easily accessed via the coastal train line. InterCity and regional trains on the Rome–Reggio line stop at Maratea train station. Some slower trains stop at Marina di Maratea.

Local buses (€1.10) connect the coastal towns and Maratea train station with Maratea Borgo, running more frequently in summer. Some hotels offer pick-ups from the station.

CALABRIA

If a Vespa-riding, siesta-loving, chaotically unadorned version of Italy still exists, you'll probably find it in Calabria, the 'toe' that kicks Sicily into the Tyrrhenian Sea. Scarred by recurrent earthquakes and lacking a Matera or Lecce to give it high-flying tourist status, this is a land of throwbacks and traditions, sheltered by craggy mountains and burdened with a long history of poverty, Mafia activity and emigration (the few travellers you do meet are often Americans retracing family roots). If you're only going to visit Italy once in your life, it's unlikely that Calabria will be top of your list. But if you're intent on seeing a candid and uncensored version of *la dolce vita* that hasn't been dressed up for tourist consumption, look no further *ragazzi*.

Calabria's gritty cities are of patchy interest. More alluring is its attractive Tyrrhenian coastline dotted with some surprisingly picturesque towns and villages (Tropea and Scilla stand out). The mountainous centre is dominated by three national parks, none of them particularly well-explored. Easily the region's biggest snare are its Greek artefacts collected from ruins, archaeological sites and ancient shipwrecks and catalogued in some truly impressive museums.

History

Traces of Neanderthal, Palaeolithic and Neolithic life have been found in Calabria, but the region only became internationally important with the arrival of the Greeks in the 8th century BC. They founded a colony at what is now Reggio di Calabria. Remnants of this colonisation, which spread along the Ionian coast with Sibari and Crotone as the star settlements, are still visible. However, the fun didn't last for the Greeks and in 202 BC the cities of Magna Graecia all came under Roman control. The Romans did irreparable

PARCO NAZIONALE DEL POLLINO

Italy's largest national park, the **Pollino National Park** (www.parcopollino.it), straddles Basilicata and Calabria and covers 1960 sq km. It acts like a rocky curtain separating the region from the rest of Italy and has the richest repository of flora and fauna in the south.

The park's most spectacular areas are **Monte Pollino** (2248m), **Monti di Orsomarso** (1987m) and the canyon of the **Gole del Raganello**. The mountains, often snowbound, are blanketed by forests of oak, alder, maple, beech, pine and fir. The park is most famous for its ancient *pino loricato* trees, which can only be found here and in the Balkans. The oldest specimens reach 40m in height.

The park has a varied landscape, from deep river canyons to alpine meadows, and is home to rare stocks of roe deer, wild cats, wolves, birds of prey (including the golden eagle and Egyptian vulture) and the endangered otters, *Lutra lutra*.

Good hiking maps are scarce. *The Carta Excursionistica del Pollino Lucano* (scale 1:50,000), produced by the Basilicata tourist board, is a useful driving map. The large-scale *Parco Nazionale del Pollino* map shows all the main routes and includes some useful information on the park, its flora and fauna and the park communities. Both maps are free and can be found in local tourist offices.

Your own vehicle is useful in Pollino. However, from the north there's a daily **SLA Bus** (☑ 0973 2 10 16; www.slasrl.it) between Naples and Rotonda, while **SAM Autolinee** (☑ 0973 66 21 06; www.samautolinee.com) buses operate around some of Basilicata's Pollino villages.

Basilicata

In Basilicata the park's main centre is **Rotonda** (elevation 626m), which houses the official park office, **Ente Parco Nazionale del Pollino** (☑ 0973 66 93 11; Via delle Frecce Tricolori 6; ☺8am-2pm Mon-Fri, plus 3-5.30pm Mon & Wed). Interesting villages to explore include the unique Albanian villages of **San Paolo Albanese** and **San Costantino Albanese**. These isolated and unspoilt communities fiercely maintain their mountain culture and the Greek liturgy is retained in the main churches. For local handicrafts visit the town of **Terranova di Pollino** for wooden crafts, **Latronico** for alabaster and **Sant'Arcangelo** for wrought iron.

---

geological damage destroying the countryside's handsome forests. Navigable rivers became fearsome *fiumare* (torrents) dwindling to wide, dry, drought-stricken river beds in high summer.

Calabria's fortified hilltop communities weathered successive invasions by the Normans, Swabians, Aragonese and Bourbons, and remained largely undeveloped. Although the 18th-century Napoleonic incursion and the arrival of Garibaldi and Italian unification inspired hope for change, Calabria remained a disappointed, feudal region and, like the rest of the south, was racked by malaria. A by-product of this tragic history was the growth of banditry and organised crime. Calabria's Mafia, known as the 'ndrangheta (from the Greek for heroism or virtue), inspires fear in the local community, but tourists are rarely the target of its aggression. For many, the only answer has been to get out and, for at least a century, Calabria has seen its young people emigrate in search of work.

Northern Tyrrhenian Coast

The good, the bad and the ugly line the region's western seashore.

The Autostrada del Sole (A3) is one of Italy's great coastal drives. It twists and turns through mountains, past huge swathes of dark-green forest and flashes of cerulean-blue sea. But the Italian penchant for cheap summer resorts has taken its toll here and certain stretches are blighted by shoddy hotels and soulless stacks of flats.

In the low season most places close. In summer many hotels are full, but you should have an easier time with the camping sites.

Praia a Mare

POP 6820

Praia a Mare, which lies just short of the border with Basilicata, is the start of a stretch of wide, pebbly beach that continues south for about 30km to Cirella and Diamante.

The chalet-style **Picchio Nero** (☑ 0973 9 31 70; www.hotelpicchionero.com; Via Mulino 1; s/d incl breakfast €65/78; 🅿) in Terranova di Pollino, with its Austrian-style wooden balconies and recommended restaurant, is a popular hotel for hikers. It's family run, cosy and friendly, has a small garden and can help arrange excursions.

Two highly recommended restaurants include **Luna Rossa** (☑ 0973 9 32 54; Via Marconi 18; meals €35; ⊙ Thu-Tue) in Terranova di Pollino – where creative local specialities are rustled up simply and with real flair in a rustic wood-panelled building providing breathtaking views – and **Da Peppe** (☑ 0973 66 12 51; Corso Garibaldi 13; meals €25-35; ⊙ noon-3pm & 7.30-11pm Tue-Sun) in Rotonda, which uses wonderful local meat and woodland products such as truffles and mushrooms.

Calabria

Civita was founded by Albanian refugees in 1746. Other towns worth visiting are **Castrovillari**, with its well-preserved 15th-century Aragonese castle, and **Morano Calabro** (look up the beautiful MC Escher woodcut of this town). Naturalists should also check out the wildlife museum **Centro Il Nibbio** (☑ 0981 3 07 45; Vico Il Annunziata 11; admission €4; ⊙ 10am-1pm & 4-8pm summer, 10am-1pm & 3-6pm winter) in Morano, which explains the Pollino ecosystem.

White-water rafting down the spectacular Lao river is popular in the Calabrian Pollino. **Centro Lao Action Raft** (☑ 0985 2 14 76; www.laoraft.it; Via Lauro 10/12) in Scalea can arrange rafting trips as well as canyoning, trekking and mountain-biking. **Ferula Viaggi** (p139) in Matera runs mountain-bike excursions and treks into the Pollino.

The park has a number of *agriturismi*. Tranquil **Agriturismo Colloreto** (☑ 347 3236914; www.colloreto.it; s/d €28/56), near Morano Calabro, is in a remote rural setting, gorgeous amid rolling hills. Rooms are comfortable and old-fashioned with polished wood and flagstone floors. Also in Calabria, **Locanda di Alia** (☑ 0981 4 63 70; www.alia.it; Via letticelle 55; s/d €90/120; 🅿❄✷) in Castrovillari offers bungalow-style accommodation in a lush green garden; it's famous for an outstanding restaurant, where you can sample delectable local recipes featuring peppers, pork, figs, anise and honey.

This flat, leafy grid of a town sits on a wide pale-grey beach, looking out to an intriguing rocky chunk off the coast: the **Isola di Dino**.

Just off the seafront is the **tourist office** (☑ 0985 7 25 85; Via Amerigo Vespucci 6; ⊙ 8am-1pm), which has information on the Isola di Dino sea caves. Alternatively, expect to pay around €5 for a guided tour from the old boys who operate off the beach.

Autolinee Preite (☑ 0984 41 30 01; www.autoservizipreite.it) operates buses to Cosenza (€5.40, two hours, 10 daily). **SITA** (☑ 0971 50 68 11; www.sitabus.it) goes north to Maratea and Potenza. Regular trains also pass through for Paola and Reggio di Calabria.

Aieta & Tortora

Precariously perched, otherworldly Aieta and Tortora must have been difficult to reach pre-asphalt. **Rocco** (☑ 0973 2 29 43; www.roccobus.it) buses serve both villages, 6km and 12km from Praia respectively. Aieta is higher than Tortora and the journey

constitutes much of the reward. When you arrive, walk up to the 16th-century **Palazzo Spinello** at the end of the road and take a look into the ravine behind it – it's a stunning view.

Diamante

POP 5400

This fashionable seaside town, with its long promenade, is central to Calabria's famous *peperoncino* (chilli), the conversation-stalling spice that so characterises the region's cuisine. In early September a hugely popular **chilli-eating competition** takes place. Diamante is also famed for the bright murals that contemporary local and foreign artists have painted on the facades of the old buildings. For the best seafood restaurants, head for the seafront at Spiaggia Piccola.

Autolinee Preite (☑ 0984 41 30 01; www.autoservizipreite.it) buses between Cosenza and Praia a Mare stop at Diamante.

Paola

POP 16,900

Paola is worth a stop to see its holy shrine. The large pilgrimage complex is above a sprawling small town where the dress of choice is a tracksuit and the main activity is hanging about on street corners. The 80km of coast south from here to Pizzo is mostly overdeveloped and ugly. Paola is the main train hub for Cosenza, about 25km inland.

Watched over by a crumbling castle, the **Santuario di San Francesco di Paola** (☑ 0982 58 25 18; ☉ 6am-1pm & 2-6pm) FREE is a curious, empty cave with tremendous significance to the devout. The saint lived and died in Paola in the 15th century and the sanctuary that he and his followers carved out of the bare rock has attracted pilgrims for centuries. The cloister is surrounded by naive wall paintings depicting the saint's truly incredible miracles. The original church contains an ornate reliquary of the saint. Also within the complex is a modern basilica, built to mark the second millennium. Black-clad monks hurry about.

There are several hotels near the train station, but you'll be better off staying in towns further north along the coast.

Cosenza

POP 69,800 / ELEV 238M

Cosenza epitomises the unkempt charm of southern Italy. It is a no-nonsense workaday town where tourists are incidental and local life, with all its petty dramas, takes centre stage. The modern city centre is a typically chaotic Italian metro area that serves as a transport hub for Calabria and a gateway to the nearby mountains of Sila National Park. The old town, stacked atop a steep hill, has a totally different atmosphere. Time-warped and romantically dishevelled, its dark weathered alleys are full of drying clothes on rusty balconies, old curiosity shops and the freshly planted shoots of an arty renaissance.

◎ Sights

In the new town, pedestrianised Corso Mazzini provides a pleasant respite from the chaotic traffic and incessant car honking. The thoroughfare serves as an **open-air museum** with numerous sculptures lining the *corso*, including *Saint George and the Dragon* by Salvador Dalí.

In the old town, head up the winding, charmingly dilapidated Corso Telesio, which has a raw Neapolitan feel to it and is lined with ancient tenements and antiquated shopfronts, including shops housing an instrument maker and a Dickensian shoe mender. The side alleys are a study in urban decay. At the top, the 12th-century **cathedral** (Piazza del Duomo; ☉ 8am-noon & 3-7.30pm) was rebuilt in restrained baroque style in the 18th century. In a chapel off the north aisle is a copy of an exquisite 13th-century Byzantine Madonna.

Head further along the *corso* to Piazza XV Marzo, an appealing square fronted by the Palazzo del Governo and the handsome neoclassical **Teatro Rendano** (Piazza XV Marzo).

From Piazza XV Marzo, follow Via Paradiso, then Via Antonio Siniscalchi for the route to the down-at-heel Norman **castle** (Piazza Frederico II), left in disarray by several earthquakes. It's closed for restoration, but the view merits the steep ascent.

Cosenza's culture is low-key, but you can piece bits of it together at the recently refurbished **Galeria Nazionale** (Via G V Gravina; ☉ 10am-6pm Tue-Sun) FREE, with its Renaissance-baroque art from the Neapolitan school. Close by, the new-ish **Museo dei Brettii e degli Enotri** (www.museodei brettiiedeglienotri.it; Salita S Agostino 3; admission €3; ☉ 9am-1pm & 4.30-7.30pm Tue-Fri, 10am-1pm & 4.30-7.30pm Sat & Sun) is essentially an archaeological museum displaying finds from the Bronze Age–Enotri culture and the Brettii people who founded Cosenza in the 4th century BC.

🛏 Sleeping

B&B Via dell'Astrologo B&B $

(☑ 338 9205394; www.viadellastrologo.com; Via Rutilio Benincasa 16; r €60-95; 🖢) A gem in the historic centre, this small B&B is tastefully decorated with polished wooden floors, white bedspreads and good-quality artwork. Brothers Mario and Marco, the venue's owners, are a mine of information on Cosenza and Calabria in general.

Royal Hotel HOTEL $

(☑ 0984 41 21 65; www.hotelroyalsas.it; Viale delle Medaglie d'Oro 1; s/d/tr €55/65/75; 🅿 ❄ @ 🖢) Probably the best all-round hotel, the Royal is a short stroll from Corso Mazzini and has just moved digs to a brand new building. Rooms are fresh and businesslike, if a little bland.

Hotel Excelsior
HOTEL **$**

(☑ 0984 47 43 83; www.htlexcelsior.it; Piazza Matteotti; s/d/tr €50/70/90; ❄@🖤) One of the few decent central options, the Excelsior has an old-school feel, although regular renovations have kept the place comfortable and up to date.

🍴 Eating

Gran Caffè Renzelli
CAFE **$**

(Corso Telesio 46; cakes from €1.20; ⊙7am-9pm Mon-Sat) This venerable cafe behind the *duomo* has been run by the same family since 1803 when the founder arrived from Naples and began baking gooey cakes and desserts. Sink your teeth into *torroncino torrefacto* (a confection of sugar, spices and hazelnuts) or *torta telesio* (made from almonds, cherries, apricot jam and lupins).

L'Osteria degli Amici
ITALIAN **$$**

(☑ 0984 79 58 93; Via Trento 49; meals €22-28; ⊙11am-3pm & 7pm-midnight) There's no sea in Cosenza, but the seafood is, ironically, rather good at this venerable small restaurant just off the city's main pedestrian street. With Sicily so close you can't go wrong with the *linguine alle vongole* (pasta and clams, a Sicilian speciality).

Ristorante Calabria Bella
CALABRIAN **$$**

(☑ 0984 79 35 31; www.ristorantecalabriabella. it; Piazza del Duomo; meals €25; ⊙12.30-3pm & 7.15pm-midnight) Traditional Calabrian cuisine, such as *grigliata mista di carne* (mixed grilled meats), is regularly dished up at this cosy restaurant in the old town.

ℹ️ Orientation

The main drag, Corso Mazzini, runs south from Piazza Bilotti (formerly known as Piazza Fera), near the bus station, and intersects Viale Trieste before meeting Piazza dei Bruzi. Head further south and cross the Busento river to reach the old town.

ℹ️ Getting There & Around

AIR

Lamezia Terme airport (Sant'Eufemia Lamezia, SUF; ☑ 0968 41 43 33; www.sacal.it; Cosenza), 63km south of Cosenza, at the junction of the A3 and SS280 motorways, links the region with major Italian cities. The airport is served by Ryanair, easyJet and charters from northern Europe. A shuttle leaves the airport every 20 minutes for the airport train station, where there are frequent trains to Cosenza (€5.80, one hour).

BUS

The main **bus station** (☑ 0984 41 31 24) is northeast of Piazza Bilotti. Services leave for Catanzaro (€4.80, 1¾ hours, eight daily) and towns throughout La Sila. **Autolinee Preite** (☑ 0984 41 30 01; www.autoservizipreite.it) has buses heading daily along the north Tyrrhenian coast; **Autolinee Romano** (☑ 0962 2 17 09; www.autolineeromano.com) serves Crotone as well as Rome and Milan.

TRAIN

Stazione Nuova (☑ 0984 2 70 59) is about 2km northeast of the centre. Regular trains go to Reggio di Calabria (from €14.60, 2¾ hours) and Rome (from €52.40, four to six hours), both usually with a change at Paola, and Naples (from €16.90, three to four hours), as well as most destinations around the Calabrian coast.

Regular buses link the centre and the main train station, although they follow a roundabout route.

Parco Nazionale della Sila

'La Sila' is a big landscape, where wooded hills create endless rolling views. It's dotted with small villages and cut through with looping roads that make driving a test of your- digestion.

It's divided into three areas covering 130 sq km: the Sila Grande, with the highest mountains; the strongly Albanian Sila Greca (to the north); and the Sila Piccola (near Catanzaro), with vast forested hills.

The highest peaks, covered with tall Corsican pines, reach 2000m – high enough for thick snow in winter. This makes it a popular skiing destination. In summer the climate is coolly alpine, spring sees carpets of wildflowers and there's mushroom hunting in autumn. At its peak is the Bosco di Gallopani (Forest of Gallopani). There are several beautiful lakes, the largest of which is Lago di Cecita o Mucone near Camigliatello Silano. There is also plenty of wildlife here, including the light-grey Apennine wolf, a protected species.

During August, Sila in Festa takes place, featuring traditional music. Autumn is mushroom season, when you'll be able to frequent mushroom festivals, including the Sagra del Fungo in Camigliatello Silano.

👁️ Sights & Activities

La Sila's main town, San Giovanni in Fiore (1049m), is named after the founder of its beautiful medieval abbey. Today, the abbey houses a home for the elderly and the **Museo Demologico** (☑0984 97 00 59; Abbazia Forense; admission €1.50; ⊘8.30am-6.30pm, closed Sun Oct-May) exhibiting tools from the town's strong artisan culture. The attractive old centre is famous for its Armenian-style handloomed carpets and tapestry; you can visit the studio and shop of carpet maker **Domenico Caruso** (☑0984 99 27 24; www.scuolatappeti.it; Via A Gramsci 195).

A popular ski-resort town with 6km of slopes, **Camigliatello Silano** (1272m) looks much better under snow. A few lifts operate on Monte Curcio, about 3km to the south. Around 5.5km of slopes and a 1500m lift can be found near **Lorica** (1370m), on gloriously pretty Lago Arvo – the best place to camp in summer.

Scigliano (620m) is a small hilltop town located west of the Sila Piccola section of the park and 75km south of Cosenza; it has a superb B&B.

🛏 Sleeping

★**B&B Calabria**   B&B **$**
(☑349 8781894; www.bedandbreakfastcalabria.it; Via Roma 9, Frazione Diano, Scigliano; s/d/t/q €35/60/75/80; ⊘Apr-Nov) This B&B in the mountains has five comfortable rooms, all with separate entrances. Owner Raffaele is a great source of information on the region and can recommend places to eat, visit and go hiking. Rooms have character and clean modern lines and there's a wonderful terrace overlooking endless forested vistas. Mountain bikes available.

The B&B is west of the national park in the village of Scigliano, about an hour south of Cosenza by train.

Hotel Aquila & Edelweiss   HOTEL **$$**
(☑0984 57 80 44; www.hotelaquilaedelweiss.com; Viale Stazione 15, Camigliatello Silano; s/d €80/120; P❋@) This three-star hotel in Camigliatello Silano has a stark and anonymous exterior but it's in a good location and the rooms are cosy and comfortable.

Park Hotel 108   HOTEL **$$**
(☑0521 64 81 08; www.hotelpark108.it; Via Nazionale 86, Lorica; r €95-135; P🛜) Situated on the hilly banks of Lago Arvo, surrounded by dark-green pines. The rooms here are decorated in classic bland-hotel style – but who cares about decor with views like this!

 ## 🛍 Shopping

La Sila's forests yield wondrous wild mushrooms, both edible and poisonous.

Antica Salumeria Campanaro   FOOD
(Piazza Misasi 5, Camigliatello Silano) Sniff around the Antica Salumeria Campanaro; it's a temple to all things fungoid, as well as an emporium of fine meats, cheeses, pickles and wines.

ⓘ Information

Good-quality information in English is scarce. You can try the national park **visitors centre** (☑ 0984 53 71 09) at Cupone, 10km from Camigliatello Silano, or the **Pro Loco tourist office** (☑ 0984 57 81 59; Via Roma; ⊘ 9.30am-12.30pm & 3.30-6.30pm Wed-Mon) in Camigliatello Silano. A useful internet resource is the official park website (www.parcosila.it). The people who run B&B Calabria in the park are extremely knowledgeable and helpful.

For a map, you can use *La Sila: Carta Turistico-Stradale ed Escurionistica del Parco Nazionale* (€7). *Sila for 4* is a miniguide in English that outlines a number of walking trails in the park. The map and booklet are available at tourist offices.

ⓘ Getting There & Away

You can reach the park's two main hubs, Camigliatello Silano and San Giovanni in Fiore, via regular Ferrovie della Calabria buses from Cosenza or Crotone.

Ionian Coast

With its flat coastline and wide sandy beaches, the Ionian coast has some fascinating stops from **Sibari** to **Santa Severina**, with some of the best beaches on the coast around **Soverato**. However, the coast has borne the brunt of some ugly development and is mainly a long, uninterrupted string of resorts, thronged in the summer months and shut down from October to May.

It's worth taking a trip inland to visit Santa Severina, a spectacular mountain-top town, 26km northwest of Crotone. The town is dominated by a Norman castle and is home to a beautiful Byzantine church.

Le Castella

This town is named for its impressive 16th-century Aragonese **castle** (admission €3; ⊘9am-midnight summer, 9am-1pm & 3-6pm winter), a vast edifice linked to the mainland by a short causeway. The philosopher Pliny said that Hannibal constructed the first tower. Evidence shows it was begun in the 4th century BC, designed to protect Crotone in the wars against Pyrrhus.

Le Castella is south of a rare protected area, **Capo Rizzuto**, along this coast, rich not only in nature but also in Greek history. For further information on the park, try www.riservamarinacaporizzuto.it.

With around 15 campgrounds near Isola di Capo Rizzuto to the north, this is the Ionian coast's prime camping area. Try **La Fattoria** (☑ 0962 79 11 65; Via del Faro; camping 2 people, car & tent €23, bungalow €60; ☺ Jun-Sep), 1.5km from the sea. Otherwise, **Da Annibale** (☑ 0962 79 50 04; Via Duomo 35; s/d €50/70; P ✸ @ ☎) is a pleasant hotel in town with a splendid fish **restaurant** (meals €30; ☺ noon-3pm & 7.30-11pm).

For expansive sea views dine at bright and airy **Ristorante Micomare** (☑ 0962 79 50 82; www.ristorantemicomare.it; Via Vittoria 7; meals €20-25; ☺ noon-3pm & 7.30-11pm).

Gerace

POP 2830

A spectacular medieval hill town, Gerace is worth a detour for the views alone – on one side the Ionian Sea, on the other, dark, interior mountains. About 10km inland from Locri on the SS111, it has Calabria's largest Romanesque **cathedral**. Dating from 1045, later alterations have not robbed it of its majesty.

For a taste of traditional Calabrian cooking, the modest and welcoming **Ristorante A Squella** (☑ 0964 35 60 86; Viale della Resistenza 8; meals €20) makes for a great lunchtime stop that serves reliably good dishes, specialising in seafood and pizzas. Afterwards you can wander down the road and admire the views.

Further inland is **Canolo**, a small village seemingly untouched by the 20th century. Buses connect Gerace with Locri and also Canolo with Siderno, both of which link to the main coastal railway line.

Parco Nazionale dell'Aspromonte

Most Italians think of the **Parco Nazionale dell'Aspromonte** (www.parcoaspromonte.gov.it) as a hiding place used by Calabrian kidnappers in the 1970s and '80s. It's still rumoured to contain 'ndrangheta strongholds,

but as a tourist you're unlikely to encounter any murky business. The national park, Calabria's second-largest, is startlingly dramatic, rising sharply inland from Reggio. Its highest peak, **Montalto** (1955m), is dominated by a huge bronze statue of Christ and offers sweeping views across to Sicily.

Subject to frequent mudslides and carved up by torrential rivers, the mountains are nonetheless awesomely beautiful. Underwater rivers keep the peaks covered in coniferous forests and ablaze with flowers in spring. It's wonderful walking country and the park has several colour-coded trails.

Extremes of weather and geography have resulted in some extraordinary villages, such as **Pentidàttilo** and **Roghudi**, clinging limpet-like to the craggy, rearing rocks and now all but deserted. It's worth the drive to explore these eagle-nest villages. Another mountain eyrie with a photogenic ruined castle is **Bova**, perched at 900m above sea level. The drive up the steep, dizzying road to Bova is not for the faint-hearted, but the views are stupendous.

Maps are scarce. Try the **national park office** (☑ 0965 74 30 60; www.parcoaspromonte.gov.it; Via Aurora; ☺ 9am-1pm Mon-Fri, plus 3-5pm Tue & Thu) in **Gambarie**, the Aspromonte's main town and the easiest approach to the park. The roads are good and many activities are organised from here – you can ski and it's also the place to hire a 4WD; ask around in the town.

It's also possible to approach from the south, but the roads aren't as good. The co-operative **Naturaliter** (☑ 347 3046799; www.naturaliterweb.it), based in **Condofuri**, is an excellent source of information, and can help arrange walking and donkey treks and place you in B&Bs throughout the region. **Co-operativa San Leo** (☑ 347 3046799), based in Bova, also provides guided tours and accommodation. In Reggio di Calabria, you can book treks and tours with **Misafumera** (☑ 0965 67 70 21; www.misafumera.it; Via Nazionale 306d; weeklong treks €260-480).

Hotel Centrale (☑ 0965 170 00 43; www.hotelcentrale.net; Piazza Mangeruca 22; s/d incl half-board €60/70; P ✸ ☎) in Gambarie is a large, all-encompassing place reminiscent of a ski hotel in the Italian Dolomites. It has a decent restaurant, a comprehensive modern spa, recently renovated wood-finished rooms and the best cafe in town. It's located right at the bottom of the ski lift.

To reach Gambarie, take ATAM (p154) city bus 319 from Reggio di Calabria (€1, 1½ hours, up to six daily). Most of the roads inland from Reggio eventually hit the SS183 road that runs north to the town.

Reggio di Calabria

POP 185,900

Port, transport nexus and the main arrival and departure point for Sicily, Reggio is an ostensibly unimpressive city with one big get-out-of-jail card: its fabulous national museum, which guards some of the finest artefacts of Magna Graecia you're ever likely to see.

The city's mishmash of architecture is a result of its geographic placement in a major earthquake zone. The last big quake in 1908 triggered a tsunami that claimed over 100,000 lives. By Italian standards, little of historical merit remains, although the *lungomare* sea drive, with its views of smouldering Mt Etna across the Messina Strait, is, arguably, one of the most animated places in Italy for an evening *passeggiata*.

Despite struggles with civic corruption and infiltration from the 'ndrangheta (Calabrian mafia), Reggio has bravely attempted to improve its image in recent years with plans to rehabilitate its port and waterfront (as yet unrealised). Fortunately, there's no need to rehabilitate the food. Reggio hides some of Calabria's best salt-of-the-earth restaurants. You can work up an appetite for them by hiking in the nearby Parco Nazionale dell'Aspromonte, or exploring the coastline at nearby seaside escapes along the Tyrrhenian and Ionian coasts.

◎ Sights

★ **Museo Nazionale di Reggio Calabria** MUSEUM

(☑0965 81 22 55; www.archeocalabria.benicul turali.it; Piazza de Nava 26; adult/reduced €5/3; ◎9am-8pm) Emerging from an interminable renovation (since 2009), southern Italy's finest museum is now partly reopened. More importantly it is displaying what are probably the world's finest examples of ancient Greek sculpture: the Bronzi di Riace, two extraordinary bronze statues discovered on the seabed near Riace in 1972 by a snorkelling chemist from Rome.

You'll have to stand for three minutes in a decontamination chamber (an experience in itself) to see the bronzes, but, after four years in 'storage', they don't disappoint. Larger than life, they depict the Greek obsession with the body; inscrutable, determined and fierce, their perfect form is more godlike than human. The finest of the two has ivory eyes and silver teeth parted in a faint *Mona Lisa* smile. No one knows who they are – whether human or god – and even their provenance is a mystery. They date from around 450 BC; it's believed they're the work of two artists.

In the same room as the bronzes is the 5th-century-BC bronze *Philosopher's Head*, the oldest-known Greek portrait in existence. Also on display are impressive exhibits from Locri, including statues of Dioscuri falling from his horse.

Most of the rest of the exhibits were still locked away as of early 2015. Phone ahead for the latest information. Admission prices could change.

⌖ Sleeping

Finding a room should be easy, even in summer, since most visitors pass straight through en route to Sicily.

B&B Casa Blanca B&B $

(☑347 9459210; www.bbcasablanca.it; Via Arcovito 24; s €50-60, d €70-90, apt €105-120; ❄⑉) A little gem in Reggio's heart, this 19th-century *palazzo* has spacious rooms gracefully furnished with romantic white-on-white decor. There's a self-serve breakfast nook, a small breakfast table in each room and two apartments available. Great choice.

Hotel Continental HOTEL $

(☑0965 81 21 81; www.hotelcontinentalrc.it; Via Vincenzo Florio 10; r from €59; ℗❄⑉) Right next to the port, the Continental does a brisk trade in overnight travellers bound for Sicily. The decor holds no surprises, but the service is exceedingly polite and professional. A breakfast buffet can be procured for an extra €6.

✕ Eating & Drinking

Cèsare GELATERIA $

(Piazza Indipendenza; ◎6am-1am) The most popular gelateria in town is in a modest green kiosk at the end of the *lungomare* (seafront promenade).

★ **La Cantina del Macellaio** TRATTORIA $$

(☑0965 2 39 32; www.lacantinadelmacellaio.com; Via Arcovito 26; meals €25; ◎7.30-11.30pm Mon-Sat, noon-3pm & 8-11pm Sun) One of the best

Reggio di Calabria

restaurants in Calabria with epic risotto (with apple and almonds), *ragù* (meat and tomato sauce) and grilled veal. The mostly Calabrian wines are equally impressive, as is the service.

Caffe Matteotti CAFE
(www.caffematteotti.it; Corso Vittorio Emanuele III 39; ⊙7am-2am Tue-Sun) The stylish white tables and chairs on the terrace here offer sea views with your *aperitivi*. This is also a prime people-watching spot.

ℹ️ Information

Walk northeast along Corso Garibaldi for the tourist office, shopping and other services. The *corso* has long been a de facto pedestrian zone during the ritual *passeggiata*.

Hospital (☑ 0965 39 71 11; Via Melacrino)
Police Station (☑ 0965 41 11 11; Corso Garibaldi 442)
Post Office (Via Miraglia 14)

Reggio di Calabria

◉ Top Sights

1 Museo Nazionale di Reggio
  Calabria C2

🛏 Sleeping

2 B&B Casa Blanca B4
3 Hotel Continental C1

🍴 Eating

4 Cèsare C2
  La Cantina del Macellaio .... (see 2)

🍷 Drinking & Nightlife

5 Caffe Matteotti C2

ℹ️ Transport

  Meridiano .... (see 6)
6 Stazione Marittima C1
  Uscita Lines .... (see 6)

🛈 ONWARD TO SICILY

Reggio di Calabria is the gateway to Sicily and its main port, Messina. There are also boats to the Aeolian Islands.

Note that there are two main departure ports for Sicily: the Stazione Marittima in Reggio di Calabria, and the ferry port in the town of Villa San Giovanni, 14km north of Reggio and easily accessible by train.

The main car ferry from Reggio's Stazione Marittima is operated by **Meridiano** (☎0965 81 04 14; www.meridianolines.net), which runs a dozen ferries a day on weekdays (three to four on weekends). Ferries run either to Messina or Tremestieri (8km south of Messina). The crossing takes 25 to 30 minutes; cars cost €10 and foot passengers €1.50.

The other main ferry company is **Uscita Lines** (☎0965 2 95 68; www.uscitalines.it), which runs passenger-only boats to Messina (€3.50) and the Aeolian Islands, including Stromboli (€41.70) and Vulcano (€22.10).

The car ferries from Villa San Giovanni are run by **Caronte & Tourist** (☎800 627414; www.carontetourist.it). There are 36 crossings a day. Cars cost €37 and foot passengers €3.50. The crossing is a speedy 20 minutes. This is also the port used by Trenitalia's train-ferry; carriages are pulled directly onto the ferry.

Tourist Information Kiosk (Viale Genovese Zerbi; ⊗9am-noon & 4-7pm) There are also information kiosks at both the airport (☎0965 64 32 91; airport; ⊗9am-5pm) and the Stazione Centrale (☎0965 2 71 20; Stazione Centrale; ⊗9am-5pm).

🛈 Getting There & Away

AIR
Reggio's **airport** (REG; ☎0965 64 05 17; www.aeroportodellostretto.it) is at Ravagnese, about 5km south. It has Alitalia flights to Rome, Milan and Turin.

BUS
Most buses terminate at the Piazza Garibaldi bus station, in front of the Stazione Centrale. Several different companies operate to towns in Calabria and beyond. Regional trains are more convenient than bus services to Scilla and Tropea.

ATAM (☎800 433310; www.atam-rc.it) Serves the Aspromonte Massif, with bus 127 to Gambarie (€1.10, 1½ hours, six daily).

Lirosi (☎0966 5 79 01) Serves Rome (€36, eight hours, two daily).

CAR & MOTORCYCLE
The A3 ends at Reggio, via a series of long tunnels. If you are continuing south, the SS106 hugs the coast around the 'toe', then heads north along the Ionian Sea.

TRAIN
Trains stop at **Stazione Centrale** (☎0965 89 20 21), the main train station at the town's southern edge. Of more use to ferry foot passengers and those visiting the Museo Nazionale is the Stazione Lido, near the harbour. There are frequent trains to Milan (from €156, 10 hours), Rome (from €61, 7½ hours) and Naples (from €39, four hours). Regional services run along the coast to Scilla and Tropea, and also to Catanzaro and less frequently to Cosenza and Bari.

🛈 Getting Around

Orange local buses run by ATAM cover most of the city including regular buses between the port and Piazza Garibaldi outside Stazione Centrale. The Università–Aeroporto bus 27 runs from Piazza Garibaldi to the airport and vice versa (15 minutes, hourly). Buy your ticket at ATAM offices, tobacconists or news stands.

Southern Tyrrhenian Coast

North of Reggio, along the coast-hugging Autostrada del Sole (A3), the scenery rocks and rolls to become increasingly beautiful and dramatic, if you can ignore the shoddy holiday camps and unattractive developments that sometimes scar the land. Like the northern part of the coast, it's mostly quiet in winter and packed in summer.

Scilla
POP 5160

In Scilla, cream-, ochre- and earth-coloured houses cling on for dear life to the jagged promontory, ascending in jumbled ranks to the hill's summit, which is crowned by a castle and, just below, the dazzling white confection of the **Chiesa Arcipretale Maria Immacolata**. Lively in summer and serene in low season, the town is split in two by the tiny port. The fishing district of Scilla Chianalea, to the north, harbours small hotels and restaurants off narrow lanes, lapped by the sea. It can only be visited on foot.

Scilla's high point is a rock at the northern end, said to be the lair of Scylla, the mythical six-headed sea monster who drowned sailors as they tried to navigate the Strait of Messina. Swimming and fishing off the town's glorious white sandy beach is somewhat safer today. Head for **Lido Paradiso** from where you can squint up at the castle while sunbathing on the sand.

◉ Sights

Castello Ruffo
CASTLE
(☑0956 70 42 07; admission €1.50; ⊘8.30am-7.30pm) An imposing hilltop fortress, this castle has at times been a lighthouse and a monastery. It houses a *luntre,* the original boat used for swordfishing, and on which the modern-day *passarelle* (a special swordfish-hunting boat equipped with a 30m-high metal tower) is based.

⌷ Sleeping

Le Piccole Grotte
B&B $
(☑338 2096727; www.lepiccolegrotte.it; Via Grotte 10; d €90-120; ❄☎) In the picturesque Chianalea district, this B&B is housed in a 19th-century fisher's house beside steps leading to the crystal-clear sea. Rooms have small balconies facing the cobbled alleyway or the sea. The same people run **La Locandiera** (☑0965 75 48 81; www.lalocandiera.org; Via Zagari 27; d €60-100; ❄☎), another sea-facing B&B just around the corner.

Hotel Principe di Scilla
HOTEL $$
(☑0965 70 43 24; www.ubais.it; Via Grotte 2; ste €150-180; ❄☎) Get lulled to sleep by the sound of lapping waves in this grand old family residence on Scilla's seafront. Two suits of armour guard the front door, while inside, six individually themed suites are stuffed with countless antiques.

✖ Eating & Drinking

Bleu de Toi
SEAFOOD $$
(☑0965 79 05 85; www.bleudetoi.it; Via Grotte 40; meals €30-35; ⊘noon-3pm & 8pm-midnight Wed-Mon) Soak up the atmosphere in the Chianalea district at this little restaurant. It has a terrace over the water and excellent seafood dishes, including Scilla's renowned swordfish.

Dali City Pub
BAR
(Via Porto; ⊘noon-midnight) On the beach in Scilla town, this popular bar has a Beatles tribute corner (appropriately named the Cavern) and has been going strong since 1972.

ℹ Getting There & Away

Scilla is on the main coastal train line. Frequent trains run to Reggio di Calabria (€2.40, 30 minutes). The train station is a couple of blocks from the beach.

Capo Vaticano

There are spectacular views from this rocky cape, with its beaches, ravines and limestone sea cliffs. Birdwatchers' spirits should soar. Around 7km south of Tropea, Capo Vaticano has a lighthouse, built in 1885, which is close to a short footpath from where you can see as far as the Aeolian Islands. Capo Vaticano beach is one of the balmiest along this coast.

Tropea

POP 6780

Tropea, a puzzle of lanes and piazzas, is famed for its captivating prettiness, dramatic position and sunsets the colour of amethyst. It sits on the Promontorio di Tropea, which stretches from Nicotera in the south to Pizzo in the north. The coast alternates between dramatic cliffs and icing-sugar-soft sandy beaches, all edged by translucent sea. Unsurprisingly, hundreds of Italian holidaymakers descend here in summer. If you hear English being spoken, it is probably from Americans visiting relatives: enormous numbers left the region for America in the early 20th century.

Despite the mooted theory that Hercules founded the town, it seems this area has been settled as far back as Neolithic times. Tropea has been occupied by the Arabs, Normans, Swabians, Anjous and Aragonese, as well as being attacked by Turkish pirates. Perhaps they were all after the town's famous red onions, so sweet they can be turned into marmalade.

◉ Sights

Cathedral
(⊘6.30-11.30am & 4-7pm) The beautiful Norman cathedral has two undetonated WWII bombs near the door: it's believed they didn't explode due to the protection of the town's patron saint, Our Lady of Romania. A

FOOTPRINTS OF MAGNA GRAECIA

Long before the Romans colonised Greece, the Greeks were colonising southern Italy. Pushed out of their homelands by demographic, social and political pressures, the nebulous mini-empire they created between the 8th and 3rd centuries BC was often referred to as Magna Graecia by the Romans in the north. Many Greek-founded cities were located along the southern coast of present-day Puglia, Basilicata and Calabria. They included (west to east) Locri Epizephiri, Kroton, Sybaris, Metapontum and Taras (now Taranto).

Magna Graecia was more a loose collection of independent cities than a coherent state with fixed borders, and many of these cities regularly raged war against each other. The most notable conflict occurred in 510 BC when the athletic Krotons attacked and destroyed the hedonistic city of Sybaris (from which the word 'sybaritic' is derived).

Magna Graecia was the 'door' through which Greek culture entered Italy influencing its language, architecture, religion and culture. Though the cities were mostly abandoned by the 5th century AD, the Greek legacy lives on in the Griko culture of Calabria and the Salento peninsula, where ethnic Greek communities still speak Griko, a dialect of Greek.

Remnants of Magna Graecia can be seen in numerous museums and architectural sites along Calabria's Ionian coast.

Sibari

Museo Archeologico Nazionale delle Sibaritide (☑ 0981 7 93 91; Via Casoni, Casa Blanca; admission €2; ☉ 9am-7.30pm Tue-Sun) Founded around 730 BC and destroyed by the Krotons in 510 BC, Sybaris was rebuilt twice: once as Thuni by the Greeks in 444 BC, and again in 194 BC by the Romans who called it Copia. Evidence of all three cities can be seen at this archaeological site and its museum located 5km southeast of the modern beach resort of Sibari. Serious flooding affected the site in 2013, meaning the park suffers periodic closures. Check ahead.

Crotone

Museo Archeologico Nazionale di Crontone (☑ 0962 90 56 25; Via Risorgimento 120, Crotone; admission €2; ☉ 9am-7pm Tue-Sun) Founded in 710 BC, the powerful city state of Kroton was known for its sobriety and high-performing Olympic athletes. Crotone's museum is located in the modern town, while the main archaeological site is at Capo Colonna, 11km to the southeast.

Locri

Museo Nazionale di Locri Epizephiri (☑ 0964 39 00 23; admission €4; ☉ 9am-7pm Tue-Sun) Situated 3km south of modern-day Locri, the Greek colony of Locri Epizephiri was founded in 680 BC and abandoned in the 5th century AD. The archaeological site is large and quite overgrown, although the attached museum is better curated. Reliefs from the on-site **Temple of Marasà** depicting Dioscuri falling from his horse are on display at the **Museo Nazionale di Reggio Calabria** (p152).

Byzantine icon of the Madonna (1330) hangs above the altar – she is also credited with protecting the town from the earthquakes that have pumelled the region.

Santa Maria dell'Isola CHURCH
The town overlooks Santa Maria dell'Isola, a medieval church with a Renaissance make over, which sits on its own rocky little island, although centuries of silt have joined it to the mainland.

🛏 Sleeping

★ **Donnaciccina** B&B $$
(☑ 0963 6 21 80; www.donnaciccina.com; Via Pelliccia 9; s €55-120, d €70-170, apt €112-240; ❋ @ 🛜) Overlooking the main *corso,* this delightful B&B has retained a tangible sense of history with its carefully selected antiques, canopy beds and terracotta tiled floors. There's also a self-catering apartment perfectly positioned on the cliff overlooking the sea, and a chatty parrot in reception.

Residenza il Barone   B&B $$

(☑ 0963 60 71 81; www.residenzailbarone.it; Largo Barone; ste €140-200; ❄ @ 🛜) This graceful *palazzo* has six suites decorated in masculine neutrals and tobacco browns, with dramatic modern paintings by the owner's brother adding pizazz to the walls. There's a computer in each suite and you can eat breakfast on the small roof terrace with views over the old city and out to sea.

✖ Eating

Al Pinturicchio   TRADITIONAL ITALIAN $

(☑ 0963 60 34 52; Via Dardona, cnr Largo Duomo; meals €16-22; ⊙ 7.30pm-midnight) Recommended by the locals, this restaurant in the old town has a romantic ambience, candlelit tables and a menu of imaginative dishes.

Osteria del Pescatore   SEAFOOD $

(☑ 0963 60 30 18; Via del Monte 7; meals €20-25; ⊙ 7.30pm-midnight Thu-Tue) Swordfish (*spada*) is a speciality on this part of the coast and it rates highly on the menu at this simple seafood place tucked away in the backstreets.

ℹ Information

Tourist Office (☑ 0963 6 14 75; Piazza Ercole; ⊙ 9am-1pm & 4-8pm) In the old town centre.

ℹ Getting There & Away

Trains run to Pizzo-Lamezia (€2.40, 30 minutes, 12 daily), Scilla (€4.60, 1¼ hours, frequent) and Reggio (from €6.40, 1¾ hours, frequent). **SAV** (☑ 0963 6 11 29) buses connect with other towns on the coast.

Pizzo

POP 9240

Stacked high up on a sea cliff, pretty little Pizzo is the place to go for *tartufo*, a death-by-chocolate ice-cream ball, and to see an extraordinary rock-carved grotto church. It's a popular and cheerful tourist stop. Piazza della Repubblica is the epicentre, set high above the sea with great views. Settle here at one of the many gelateria terraces for an ice-cream fix.

⊙ Sights

Chiesa di Piedigrotta   CAVE

(admission €2.50; ⊙ 9am-1pm & 3-7.30pm) The Chiesa di Piedigrotta is an underground cave full of carved stone statues. It was carved into the tufa rock by Neapolitan ship-

wreck survivors in the 17th century. Other sculptors added to it and it was eventually turned into a church. Later statues include the less-godly figures of Fidel Castro and John F Kennedy. It's a bizarre, one-of-a-kind mixture of mysticism, mystery and kitsch. Buy tickets at the restaurant above the cave.

Chiesa Matrice di San Giorgio   CHURCH

(Via Marconi) In town, the 16th-century Chiesa Matrice di San Giorgio, with its dressed-up Madonnas, houses the tomb of Joachim Murat, the French-born former king of Naples, brother-in-law of Napoleon and well-known European dandy.

Castello Murat   CASTLE

(☑ 0963 53 25 23; adult/reduced €2.50/1.50; ⊙ 9am-1pm & 3pm-midnight Jun-Sep, 9am-1pm & 3-7pm Oct-May) This neat little 15th-century castle is named for Joachim Murat, supporter of Napoleon Bonaparte. He was captured in Pizzo and sentenced to death for treason in 1815. Inside the castle, you can see his cell and the details of his grisly end by firing squad, which is graphically illustrated with waxworks. Although Murat was the architect of enlightened reforms, the locals showed no great concern when he was executed.

🛏 Sleeping & Eating

Armonia B&B   B&B $

(☑ 0963 53 33 37; www.casaarmonia.com; Via Armonia 9; s/d without bathroom €45/60; @) Run by the charismatic Franco in his 18th-century family home, this B&B has a number of rooms (with shared bathroom). The sea views are spectacular.

Ristorante Don Diego di Pizzo   PIZZA $

(☑ 340 892 44 69; www.dondiegoristorante.com; Via M Salomone 243; meals €20-25; ⊙ noon-3pm & 7pm-midnight Wed-Mon) Fantastic views from a panoramic terrace and food to match. The restaurant is particularly known for its pizza.

ℹ Getting There & Away

Pizzo is just off the major A3 autostrada. There are two train stations. Vibo Valentia-Pizzo is located 4km south of town on the main Rome–Reggio di Calabria line. A bus service connects you to Pizzo. Pizzo-Lamezia is south of the town on the Tropea–Lamezia Terme line. Shuttle buses (€2) connect with trains or you can walk for 20 minutes along the coast road.

Surprises of the South

In the Mezzogiorno, the sun shines on a magical landscape: dramatic cliffs and sandy beaches fringed with turquoise seas; wild rocky mountains and gentle forested slopes; rolling green fields and flat plains. Sprinkled throughout are elegant *palazzi* (mansions), *masserias* (working farms), ancient cave-dwellings and gnome-like stone huts.

Promontorio del Gargano

Along with its charming seaside villages, sandy coves and crystalline blue waters, the Gargano (p110) is also home to the Parco Nazionale del Gargano. It's perfect for hikers, nature trippers and beach fiends alike.

Valle d'Itria

In a landscape of rolling green hills, vineyards, orchards and picture-pretty fields, conical stone huts called *trulli* sprout from the ground en masse in the Disneyesque towns of Alberobello (p117) and Locorotondo (p119).

Salento

In Salento, hot, dry plains covered in wildflowers and olive groves reach towards the gorgeous beaches and waters of the Ionian and Adriatic Seas. It's the unspoilt 'heel' of Italy, with Lecce (p122) as its sophisticated capital.

Matera

The ancient cave city of Matera (p135) has been inhabited since Palaeolithic times. Explore the tangled alleyways, admire frescoes in rock churches, and sleep in millennia-old *sassi* (former cave dwellings).

Parco Nazionale dell'Aspromonte

In this wild park (p151), narrow roads lead to hilltop villages such as spectacularly sited Bova. Waterfalls, wide riverbeds, jagged cliffs and sandstone formations form the backdrop to a landscape made for hiking.

1. Promontorio del Gargano 2. Conical *trulli* houses, Alberobello, Valle d'Itria 3. View over Matera 4. Basilica di Santa Croce (p122), Lecce, Salento

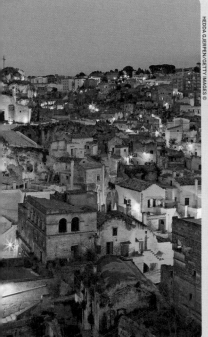

Sicily

Includes ➡

Palermo	164
Cefalù	176
Lipari	179
Vulcano	183
Salina	184
Stromboli	188
Taormina	190
Catania	194
Syracuse	201
Noto	208
Modica	211
Ragusa	212
Agrigento	214
Marsala	218
Trapani	219

Best Places to Eat

➡ Ferro di Cavallo (p171)

➡ A Putia delle Cose Buone (p206)

➡ Osteria Antica Marina (p198)

➡ Ristorante Crocifisso (p210)

Best Places to Stay

➡ Pensione Tranchina (p223)

➡ Henry's House (p206)

➡ Hotel Signum (p185)

Why Go?

More of a sugar-spiked espresso than a milky cappuccino, Sicily rewards visitors with an intense, bittersweet experience. Overloaded with art treasures and natural beauty, undersupplied with infrastructure, and continuously struggling against Mafia-driven corruption, Sicily's complexities sometimes seem unfathomable. To really appreciate this place, come with an open mind – and a healthy appetite. Despite the island's perplexing contradictions, one factor remains constant: the high quality of the cuisine.

After 25 centuries of foreign domination, Sicilians are heirs to an impressive cultural legacy, from the refined architecture of Magna Graecia to the Byzantine splendour and Arab craftsmanship of the island's Norman cathedrals and palaces. This cultural richness is matched by a startlingly diverse landscape that includes bucolic farmland, smouldering volcanoes and kilometres of island-studded aquamarine coastline.

When to Go
Palermo

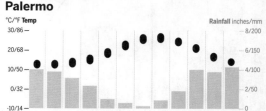

Easter Colourful religious processions and marzipan lambs in every bakery window.

May Wildflowers, dreamy coastal walking and Syracuse's festival of classic drama.

Sep Warm weather and seaside fun without summer prices.

History

Sicily's most deeply ingrained cultural influences originate from its first inhabitants – the Sicani from North Africa, the Siculi from Latium (Italy) and the Elymni from Greece. The subsequent colonisation of the island by the Carthaginians (also from North Africa) and the Greeks, in the 8th and 6th centuries BC respectively, compounded this cultural divide through decades of war when powerful opposing cities struggled to dominate the island.

Although part of the Roman Empire, Sicily didn't truly come into its own until after the Arab invasions of AD 831. Trade, farming and mining were all fostered under Arab influence and Sicily soon became an enviable prize for European opportunists. The Normans, desperate for a piece of the pie, invaded in 1061 and made Palermo the centre of their expanding empire and the finest city in the Mediterranean.

Impressed by the cultured Arab lifestyle, King Roger squandered vast sums on ostentatious palaces and churches, and encouraged a hedonistic atmosphere in his court. But such prosperity – and decadence (Roger's grandson, William II, even had a harem) – inevitably gave rise to envy and resentment and, after two centuries of pleasure and profit, the Norman line was extinguished. The kingdom passed to the austere German House of Hohenstaufen with little opposition from the seriously eroded and weakened Norman occupisers.

In the centuries that followed, Sicily passed to the Holy Roman Emperors, Angevins (French) and Aragonese (Spanish) in a turmoil of rebellion and revolution that continued until the Spanish Bourbons united Sicily with Naples in 1734 as the Kingdom of the Two Sicilies. Little more than a century later, on 11 May 1860, Giuseppe Garibaldi planned his daring and dramatic unification of Italy from Marsala on Sicily's western coast.

Reeling from this catalogue of colonisers, Sicilians struggled in poverty-stricken conditions. Unified with Italy, but no better off, nearly one million men and women emigrated to the USA between 1871 and 1914 before the outbreak of WWI.

Ironically, the Allies (seeking Mafia help in America for the re-invasion of Italy) helped in establishing the Mafia's stranglehold on Sicily. In the absence of suitable administrators, they invited the undesirable *mafioso* (Mafia boss) Don Calógero Vizzini to do the job. When Sicily became a semi-autonomous region in 1948, Mafia control extended right to the heart of politics and the region plunged into a 50-year silent civil war. It only started to emerge from this after the anti-Mafia maxi-trials of the 1980s, in which Sicily's revered magistrates Giovanni Falcone and Paolo Borsellino hauled hundreds of Mafia members into court, leading to important prosecutions.

The assassinations of Falcone and Borsellino in 1992 helped galvanise Sicilian public opposition to the Mafia's inordinate influence, and while organised crime lives on, the thuggery and violence of the 1980s has diminished. A growing number of businesses refuse to pay the extortionate protection money known as the *pizzo*, and there continue to be important arrests, further encouraging those who would speak out against the Mafia. On the political front, anti-Mafia crusaders currently serve in two of the island's most powerful positions: Palermo mayor Leoluca Orlando and Sicilian governor Rosario Crocetta. Nowadays the hot topics on everyone's mind are the island's continued economic struggles and Sicily's role as the gateway for the flood of immigrants from northern Africa.

❶ Getting There & Away

BOAT

Regular car and passenger ferries cross the strait between Villa San Giovanni (Calabria) and Messina, while hydrofoils connect Messina with Reggio di Calabria.

Sicily is also accessible by ferry from Naples, Genoa, Civitavecchia, Salerno, Cagliari, Malta and Tunisia. Prices rise between June and September, when advanced bookings may also be required.

ROUTE	ADULT FARE FROM (€)	DURATION (HRS)
Civitavecchia–Palermo	63	14
Genoa–Palermo	68	21
Malta–Pozzallo	33	1¾
Naples–Catania	42	11
Naples–Palermo	53	10
Naples–Trapani	94	7
Reggio di Calabria–Messina	3.50	35min
Tunis–Palermo	42	11

Ferries to Genoa; Livorno

Ferries to Naples

Ferries to Cagliari

Ustica

Tyrrhenian Sea

Ferries to Cagliari

Falcone-Borsellino

Mondello

Riserva Naturale dello Zingaro

Scopello

Trapani • **Erice**

Monreale • ① **Palermo**

Marettimo

Birgi Airport

Favignana

③ **Segesta**

Egadi Islands

Marsala

•Corleone

A29

Mazara del Vallo

Selinunte

Sciacca•

SS189

Agrigento • *Valley of the Temples*

Mediterranean Sea

Pantelleria

Ferries to Pelagic Islands

Sicily Highlights

① Joining the ranks of impeccably dressed opera-goers at elegant Teatro Massimo in **Palermo** (p164).

② Climbing Europe's most active volcano in the afternoon, and returning to buzzing nightlife in **Catania** (p194).

③ Marvelling at the majesty of the Doric temple in **Segesta** (p223).

④ Watching international stars perform against Mt Etna's breathtaking backdrop at summer festivals in **Taormina** (p190).

Stromboli

Ferries to
Naples

Panarea

Malfa
Alicudi Filicudi   Salina   Santa Marina Salina
                Quattropani
                 Lipari   Canneto
Aeolian Islands ⑤
                Vulcano

Rosarno

Gioia Tauro

Bagnara
Calabra

Milazzo   A20 Messina   Villa San   CALABRIA
                                Giovanni
                                        Gambarie

Cefalù   Roghudi
  ⑧   A20   A18   Condofuri   Bova
        Canneto
Tyrrhenian Coast
  ⑨ Castelbuono   Mélito di   Bova
Parco Naturale   Monti Nebrodi   Porto Salvo Marina
Regionale delle
  Madonie   Linguaglossa ④ Taormina
Polizzi   Petralia   Parco
Generosa Sottana   Naturale   Mt Etna
                        dell'Etna   (3329m)
  A19   Rifugio
                                   Sapienza
Enna   Nicolosi

⊙Caltanissetta   ② Catania
                                 ✈Fontanarossa
Villa Romana   Piazza   Ionian Coast
del Casale ⑦ Armerina

                SS194   Golfo di
              Monti Iblei   Augusta
        SS514

Gela   SS287   ⑥ Syracuse
        ⊙Comiso Airport
  Golfo di
   Gela   Vittòria   Ionian
                                    Sea
        ⊙Ragusa
        ⊙Modica   Noto⊙

                        ⑨
                    Riserva
                   Naturale di
        ⊙Pozzallo Vendicari

                        Ferries to
                         Malta

⑤ Observing Stromboli's
volcanic fireworks and hiking
to your heart's content on the
stunningly scenic **Aeolian
Islands** (p178).

⑥ Stepping back in time

at an ancient Greek theatre
performance in **Syracuse**
(p201).

⑦ Admiring prancing wild
beasts and dancing bikini-clad
gymnasts on the mosaic floors

of **Villa Romana del Casale**
(p213).

⑧ Being dazzled by
Byzantine mosaics and
splendid coastal sunsets in
Cefalù (p176).

AIR

A number of airlines fly direct to Sicily's four international airports – Palermo (PMO), Catania (CTA), Trapani (TPS) and Comiso (CIY) – although many still require a transfer in Rome or Milan. Alitalia (www.alitalia.com) is the main Italian carrier, while **Ryanair** (www.ryanair.com) is the leading low-cost airline serving Sicily.

BUS

SAIS Trasporti (www.saistrasporti.it) runs long-haul services to Sicily from Rome and Naples.

TRAIN

For travellers originating in Rome and points south, InterCity trains cover the distance from mainland Italy to Sicily in the least possible time, without a change of train. If coming from Milan, Bologna or Florence, your fastest option is to take the ultra-high-speed Frecciarossa as far as Naples, then change to an InterCity train for the rest of the journey.

All trains enter Sicily at Messina, after being transported by ferry from Villa San Giovanni at the toe of Italy's boot. At Messina, trains branch west along the Tyrrhenian coast to Palermo, or south along the Ionian coast to Catania.

❶ Getting Around

AIR

Alitalia offers direct flights to the offshore islands of Pantelleria (from Palermo and Trapani) and Lampedusa (from Palermo and Catania).

BUS

Bus services within Sicily are provided by a variety of companies. Buses are usually faster if your destination involves travel through the island's interior; trains tend to be cheaper (and sometimes faster) on the major coastal routes. In small towns and villages tickets are often sold in bars or on the bus.

CAR & MOTORCYCLE

Having your own vehicle is advantageous in the interior, where public transit is often slow and limited. Autostradas connect the major cities and are generally of good quality, especially the A18 and A20 toll roads, running along the Ionian and Tyrrhenian coasts, respectively. Even so, the island's highways have suffered some high-profile problems in recent years – most notably the landslide-induced collapse of a key section of the A19 between Catania and Palermo in April 2015 (still under repair at the time of research). Drive defensively; the Sicilians are some of Italy's most aggressive drivers, with a penchant for overtaking on blind corners, holding a mobile phone in one hand while gesticulating wildly with the other!

TRAIN

Sicily's train service is very efficient along the north and east coasts. Services to towns in the interior tend be infrequent and slow, although if you have the time the routes can be very picturesque. InterCity trains are the fastest and most expensive, while the *regionale* is the slowest.

PALERMO

POP 657,000

Palermo is a city of decay and of splendour and – provided you can handle its raw energy, deranged driving and chaos – has plenty of appeal. Unlike Florence or Rome, many of the city's treasures are hidden, rather than scrubbed up for endless streams of tourists.

At one time an Arab emirate and seat of a Norman kingdom, Palermo became Europe's grandest city in the 12th century, then underwent another round of aesthetic transformations during 500 years of Spanish rule. The resulting treasure trove of palaces, castles and churches has a unique architectural fusion of Byzantine, Arab, Norman, Renaissance and baroque gems.

While some of the crumbling *palazzi* (mansions) bombed in WWII are being restored, others remain dilapidated; turned into shabby apartments, the faded glory of their ornate facades is just visible behind strings of brightly coloured washing. The evocative history of the city remains very much part of the daily life of its inhabitants, and the dusty web of backstreet markets in the old quarter has a Middle Eastern feel.

The flip side is the modern city, a mere 15-minute stroll away, parts of which could be neatly jigsawed and slotted into Paris, with a grid system of wide avenues lined by seductive shops and handsome 19th-century apartments.

◎ Sights & Activities

Via Maqueda is the main street, running north from the train station, changing names to Via Ruggero Settimo as it passes the landmark Teatro Massimo, then finally widening into leafy Viale della Libertà north of Piazza Castelnuovo, the beginning of the city's modern district.

◎ Around the Quattro Canti

The busy intersection of Corso Vittorio Emanuele and Via Maqueda is known as the **Quattro Canti**. Forming the civic heart of

Palermo, this crossroads divides the historic nucleus into four traditional quarters – Albergheria, Capo, Vucciria and La Kalsa.

★Fontana Pretoria   FOUNTAIN

This huge and ornate fountain, with tiered basins and sculptures rippling in concentric circles, forms the centrepiece of **Piazza Pretoria**, a spacious square just south of the Quattro Canti. The city bought the fountain in 1573; however, the flagrant nudity of the provocative nymphs proved too much for Sicilian church-goers attending Mass next door, and they prudishly dubbed it the Fountain of Shame.

La Martorana   CHURCH

(Chiesa di Santa Maria dell'Ammiraglio; Piazza Bellini 3; adult/reduced €2/1; ⊙9.30am-1pm & 3.30-5.30pm Mon-Sat, 9-10.30am Sun) On the southern side of Piazza Bellini, this luminously beautiful 12th-century church was endowed by King Roger's Syrian emir, George of Antioch, and was originally planned as a mosque. Delicate Fatimid pillars support a domed cupola depicting Christ enthroned amid his archangels. The interior is best appreciated in the morning, when sunlight illuminates magnificent Byzantine mosaics.

Chiesa Capitolare di San Cataldo   CHURCH

(Piazza Bellini 3; admission €2.50; ⊙9.30am-12.30pm & 3-6pm) This 12th-century church in Arab-Norman style is one of Palermo's most striking buildings. With its dusky-pink bijou domes, solid square shape, blind arcading and delicate tracery, it illustrates perfectly the synthesis of Arab and Norman architectural styles. The interior, while more austere, is still beautiful, with its inlaid floor and lovely stone-and-brickwork in the arches and domes.

⊙ Albergheria

Southwest of the Quattro Canti is Albergheria, a rather shabby, rundown district once inhabited by Norman court officials, now home to a growing number of immigrants who are attempting to revitalise its dusty backstreets. The top tourist draws here are the Palazzo dei Normanni (Norman Palace) and its exquisite chapel, both at the neighbourhood's far western edge.

★Palazzo dei Normanni & Cappella Palatina   PALACE, CHAPEL

(www.fondazionefedericosecondo.it; Piazza Indipendenza 1; adult/reduced Fri-Mon €8.50/6.50, Tue-Thu €7/5; ⊙8.15am-5.40pm Mon-Sat, to 1pm Sun, Royal Apartments closed Tue-Thu, chapel closed 9.45-11.15am Sun) This venerable palace dates to the 9th century but owes its current look (and name) to a major 12th-century Norman makeover, during which spectacular mosaics were added to its **Royal Apartments** and priceless jewel of a chapel, the Cappella Palatina. Designed by Roger II in 1130, the chapel glitters with stunning gold mosaics, its aesthetic harmony further enhanced by the inlaid marble floors and wooden *muqarnas* ceiling, a masterpiece of Arabic-style honeycomb carving that reflects Norman Sicily's cultural complexity.

The chapel is Palermo's top tourist attraction. Note that queues are likely, and that you'll be refused entry if you're wearing shorts, a short skirt or a low-cut top. The top level of the palace's three-tiered loggia houses Sicily's regional parliament and the Royal Apartments, including the mosaic-lined Sala dei Venti, and Sala di Ruggero II, King Roger's magnificent 12th-century bedroom. These latter attractions are only open to visitors Friday through Monday.

Chiesa di San Giovanni degli Eremiti   CHURCH

(☑091 651 50 19; Via dei Benedettini 16; adult/reduced €6/3; ⊙9am-6pm Mon-Sat, 9am-1pm Sun) This remarkable, five-domed remnant of Arab-Norman architecture occupies a magical little hillside in the middle of an otherwise rather squalid neighbourhood. Surrounded by a garden of citrus trees, palms, cacti and ruined walls, it's built atop a mosque that itself was superimposed on an earlier chapel. The peaceful Norman cloisters outside offer lovely views of the Palazzo dei Normanni.

★Mercato di Ballarò   MARKET

(⊙7am-7pm Mon-Sat, to 1pm Sun) Snaking for several city blocks southeast of Palazzo dei Normanni is Palermo's busiest street market, which throbs with activity well into the early evening. It's a fascinating mix of noises, smells and street life, and the cheapest place for everything from Chinese padded bras to fresh produce, fish, meat, olives and cheese – smile nicely for a taste.

⊙ Capo

Northwest of Quattro Canti is the Capo neighbourhood, another densely packed web of interconnected streets and blind alleys.

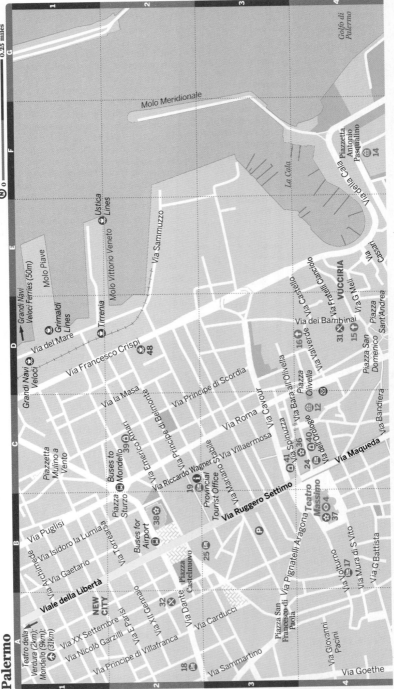

SICILY

Palermo

500 m
0.25 miles

Golfo di
Palermo

Molo Meridionale

Piazzetta
Antonio
Pasqualino
14

La Cala

Via della Cala

Via Cassari

VUCCIRIA

Via Sammuzzo

Via Fratelli Cianciolo

Via G Meli

Piazza
Sant'Andrea

31 × 15

Molo Vittorio Veneto

Ustica
Lines

Grandi Navi
Veloci Ferries (50m);

Molo Plave

Via dei Bambinai

16

Via Valverde

Via Castello

Piazza San
Domenico

Grimaldi
Lines

Tirrenia

Via del Mare

Via Francesco Crispi

48

Via la Masa

Via Principe di Scordia

Via Emerico Amari

Via Roma

Piazza
Olivella

Via Bara all'Olivella

12

Via Bandiera

Grandi Navi
Veloci

Via Principe di Belmonte

Via Cavour

Via Spinuzza

40 36

24

Via dell'Orologio

Via Maqueda

Buses to
Mondello

39

Via Riccardo Wagner

Via Mariano Stabile

Via Villaermosa

41

Piazzetta
Mulino a
Vento

Via Puglisi

Piazza
Sturzo

Provincial
Tourist Office

19

Via Ruggero Settimo

Teatro
Massimo

37

4

Via Archimede

Via Isidoro la Lumia

Buses for
Airport

38

Via Torrearsa

Via Pignatelli Aragona

Via Francesco di Paola

Via Volturno

17

Via Gaetario

25

Piazza
Castelnuovo

Piazza San
Francesco di
Paola

Via Mura di S Vito

Viale della Libertà

NEW
CITY

Via Dante

Via Carducci

Via Giovanni
Pacini

Via XX Settembre

Via Nicolò Garzilli

Via E Parisi

Via XII Gennaio

32

18

Via Principe di Villafranca

Via Sammartino

Via G Battista

Via Goethe

Teatro della
Verdura (2km);
Mondello (9km);
(31km)

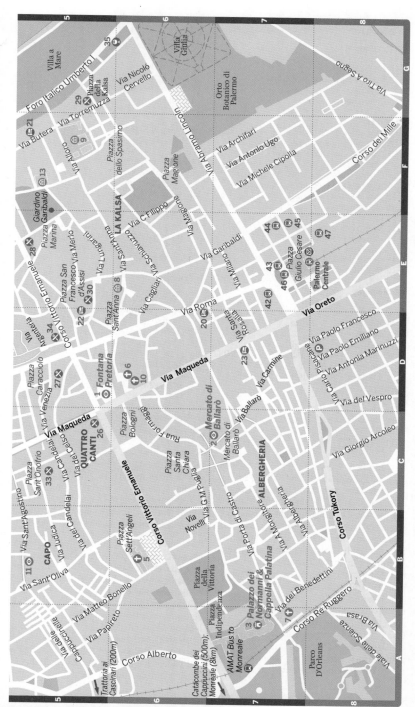

Palermo

⊚ Top Sights
1 Fontana Pretoria.................................D5
2 Mercato di Ballarò..............................C7
3 Palazzo dei Normanni & Cappella
   Palatina..A7
4 Teatro Massimo.................................B4

◎ Sights
5 Cattedrale di Palermo.........................B6
6 Chiesa Capitolare di San Cataldo.........D6
7 Chiesa di San Giovanni degli
   Eremiti...A7
8 Galleria d'Arte Moderna......................E6
9 Galleria Regionale della Sicilia.............F5
10 La Martorana...................................D6
11 Mercato del Capo.............................B5
12 Museo Archeologico Regionale...........C4
13 Museo dell'Inquisizione......................F5
14 Museo Internazionale delle
   Marionette......................................F4
15 Oratorio di San Domenico..................D4
16 Oratorio di Santa Cita.......................D4

⊜ Sleeping
17 A Casa di Amici B&B..........................B4
18 A Casa di Amici Hostel.......................A2
19 B&B Amélie.....................................C2
20 B&B Panormus.................................D6
21 Butera 28.......................................F5
22 Grand Hotel Piazza Borsa..................D5
23 Hotel Orientale.................................D7
24 Massimo Plaza Hotel.........................C4
25 Palazzo Pantaleo..............................B3

⊗ Eating
26 Bisso Bistrot....................................C5
27 Ferro di Cavallo...............................D5

28 Francu U Vastiddaru...........................E5
29 Friggitoria Chiluzzo............................G5
30 Osteria Ballarò.................................E5
31 Osteria Mangia & Bevi........................D4
32 Pasticceria Cappello..........................A2
33 Pizzeria Frida..................................C5
34 Trattoria Il Maestro del Brodo.............D5

⊙ Drinking & Nightlife
35 Kursaal Kalhesa...............................G6

⊙ Entertainment
36 Cuticchio Mimmo..............................C4
37 Teatro Massimo.................................B4
38 Teatro Politeama Garibaldi..................B2

⊙ Shopping
39 Gusti di Sicilia..................................C2
40 Il Laboratorio Teatrale........................C4
41 Le Ceramiche di Caltagirone................C3
   Miniature Alfio Ferlito.................(see 40)

⊙ Transport
   AST..(see 45)
42 AST Bus to Monreale..........................E7
   Autoservizi Tarantola..................(see 45)
43 Bus to Airport & Local Buses...............E7
44 Cuffaro..E7
45 Intercity Bus Stop.............................E7
46 Local Buses Ticket Kiosk.....................E7
47 Piazzetta Cairoli Bus
   Terminal..E8
   SAIS Autolinee...........................(see 47)
   SAIS Trasporti............................(see 45)
   Salemi.......................................(see 47)
   Segesta.....................................(see 45)
48 Siremar...D2

Cattedrale di Palermo   CATHEDRAL
(www.cattedrale.palermo.it; Corso Vittorio Emanuele; cathedral free, tombs €1.50, treasury €2, roof €5, all-inclusive ticket €7; ⊙royal tombs, treasury & roof 9am-4pm Mon-Sat, tombs only 9am-1pm Sun) A feast of geometric patterns, ziggurat crenellations, maiolica cupolas and blind arches, Palermo's cathedral has suffered aesthetically from multiple reworkings over the centuries, but remains a prime example of Sicily's unique Arab-Norman architectural style. The interior, while impressive in scale, is essentially a marble shell whose most interesting features are the royal Norman tombs (to the left as you enter) and treasury, home to Constance of Aragon's gem-encrusted 13th-century crown. For panoramic city views, climb to the cathedral's roof.

Mercato del Capo   MARKET
Capo's street market, running the length of Via Sant'Agostino, is a seething mass of colourful activity during the day, with vendors selling fruit, vegetables, meat, fish, cheese and household goods of every description.

Catacombe dei Cappuccini   CATACOMB
(www.catacombepalermo.it; Piazza Cappuccini; adult €3, child under 8yr free; ⊙9am-1pm & 3-6pm) These catacombs house the mummified bodies and skeletons of some 8000 Palermitans who died between the 17th and 19th centuries. Earthly power, gender, religion and professional status are still rigidly distinguished, with men and women occupying separate corridors, and a first-class section set aside for virgins. From Piazza Indipendenza, it's a 15-minute walk.

◉ Vucciria

Once a notorious den of Mafia activity, the Vucciria retains a grungy, authentic edge. In the evenings, it becomes a mecca for bar-hopping and seriously down-to-earth street food. It's also home to some of Palermo's finest baroque artwork.

Museo Archeologico Regionale
MUSEUM

(☑091 611 68 05; www.regione.sicilia.it/beniculturali/salinas; Piazza Olivella 24) This splendid, wheelchair-accessible museum has been undergoing renovations since 2010, with no dependable reopening date in sight. Situated in a Renaissance monastery surrounding a gracious courtyard, it houses some of Sicily's most valuable Greek and Roman artefacts, including the museum's crown jewel, a series of original decorative friezes from the temples at Selinunte.

Oratorio di Santa Cita
CHAPEL

(www.ilgeniodipalermo.com; Via Valverde; admission €4, joint ticket incl Oratorio di San Domenico €6; ☺9am-2pm Mon-Sat Nov-Mar, to 6pm Apr-Oct) This 17th-century chapel showcases the breathtaking stuccowork of Giacomo Serpotta, who famously introduced rococo to Sicilian churches. Note the elaborate *Battle of Lepanto* on the entrance wall. Depicting the Christian victory over the Turks, it's framed by stucco drapes held by hundreds of naughty cherubs modelled on Palermo's street urchins. Serpotta's virtuosity also dominates the side walls, where sculpted white stucco figures hold gilded swords, shields and a lute, and a golden snake (Serpotta's symbol) curls around a picture frame.

Oratorio di San Domenico
CHAPEL

(www.ilgeniodipalermo.com; Via dei Bambinai 2; admission €4, joint ticket incl Oratorio di Santa Cita €6; ☺9am-2pm Mon-Sat Nov-Mar, to 6pm Apr-Oct) Dominating this small chapel is Anthony Van Dyck's fantastic blue-and-red altarpiece, *The Virgin of the Rosary with St Dominic and the Patronesses of Palermo*. Van Dyck completed the work in Genoa in 1628, after leaving Palermo in fear of the plague. Also gracing the chapel are Giacomo Serpotta's amazingly elaborate stuccoes (1710–17), vivacious and whirling with figures. Serpotta's name meant 'lizard' or 'small snake', and he often included these signature reptiles in his work; see if you can find one!

◉ La Kalsa

Due to its proximity to the port, La Kalsa was subjected to carpet bombing during WWII, leaving it derelict and rundown. Mother Teresa considered it akin to the shanty towns of Calcutta and established a mission here. Certain areas of La Kalsa, especially the part nearest the Quattro Canti, have undergone extensive renovation in recent years – for example, the former stock exchange has been converted into a high-end hotel. However, the neighbourhood still feels scruffy around the edges, with a decaying ambience that some will find intriguing, others off-putting.

Galleria Regionale della Sicilia
MUSEUM

(Palazzo Abatellis; ☑091 623 00 11; www.regione.sicilia.it/beniculturali/palazzoabatellis; Via Alloro 4; adult/reduced €8/4; ☺9am-6.30pm Tue-Fri, to 1pm Sat & Sun) Housed in the stately 15th-century Palazzo Abatellis, this fine museum features works by Sicilian artists from the Middle Ages to the 18th century. Its greatest treasure is *Triunfo della Morte* (Triumph of Death), a magnificent fresco in which Death is represented as a demonic skeleton mounted on a wasted horse, brandishing a wicked-looking scythe while leaping over his hapless victims.

Galleria d'Arte Moderna
MUSEUM

(☑091 843 16 05; www.galleriadartemodernapalermo.it; Via Sant'Anna 21; adult/reduced €7/5; ☺9.30am-6.30pm Tue-Sun) This lovely, wheelchair-accessible museum is housed in a sleekly renovated 15th-century *palazzo*, which metamorphosed into a convent in the 17th century. Divided over three floors, the wide-ranging collection of 19th- and 20th-century Sicilian art is beautifully displayed. There's a regular program of modern-art exhibitions here, as well as an excellent bookshop and gift shop. English-language audio guides cost €4.

Museo dell'Inquisizione
MUSEUM

(Piazza Marina 61; adult/reduced palace or prison €5/2.50, both €7.50/5; ☺10am-6pm) Housed in the lower floors and basements of the 14th-century Palazzo Chiaromonte Steri, Palermo's newest museum offers a chilling but fascinating look at the legacy of the Inquisition in Palermo. Thousands of 'heretics' were detained here between 1601 and 1782; the honeycomb of former cells has been painstakingly restored to reveal multiple layers of their graffiti and artwork (religious and otherwise). Excellent guided visits of the prison and the palace itself are available in English with advance notice.

Museo Internazionale delle
Marionette
MUSEUM

(☎091 32 80 60; www.museomarionettepalermo.it; Piazzetta Antonio Pasqualino 5; adult/reduced €5/3; ⏰9am-1pm & 2.30-6.30pm Mon-Sat) This whimsical museum houses over 3500 marionettes, puppets, glove puppets and shadow figures from Palermo, Catania and Naples, as well as from further-flung places such as Japan, Southeast Asia, Africa, China and India. Occasional puppet shows (adult/child €10/5) are staged on the museum's top floor in a beautifully decorated traditional theatre complete with hand-cranked music machine.

◉ New City

North of Piazza Giuseppe Verdi, Palermo elegantly slips into cosmopolitan mode. Here you'll find fabulous neoclassical and art nouveau buildings hailing from the last golden age of Sicilian architecture, along with late-19th-century mansion blocks lining the broad boulevard of Viale della Libertà.

★ Teatro Massimo
THEATRE

(☎tour reservations 091 605 32 67; www.teatromassimo.it; Piazza Giuseppe Verdi; guided tours adult/reduced €8/5; ⏰9.30am-5.30pm) Palermo's grand neoclassical opera house took over 20 years to complete and has become one of the city's iconic landmarks. The closing scene of *The Godfather: Part III*, with its visually stunning juxtaposition of high culture, crime, drama and death, was filmed here. Guided 25-minute tours are offered throughout the day in English, Spanish, French and Italian.

🎊 Festivals & Events

Festino di Santa Rosalia
RELIGIOUS

(U Fistinu; www.santarosaliapalermo.it; ⏰10-15 Jul) Palermo's biggest annual festival celebrates patron saint Santa Rosalia, beloved for having saved the city from a 17th-century plague. The most colourful festivities take place on the evening of 14 July, when the saint's relics are paraded aboard a grand chariot from the Palazzo dei Normanni through the Quattro Canti to the waterfront, where fireworks and general merriment ensue.

🛌 Sleeping

Budget options can be found around Via Maqueda and Via Roma in the vicinity of the train station. Midrange and top-end hotels are concentrated further north. Parking usually costs an extra €10 to €15 per day.

★ B&B Amélie
B&B €

(☎091 33 59 20; www.bb-amelie.it; Via Prinicipe di Belmonte 94; s €40-60, d €60-80, tr €90-100; ❄@ 🤖) On a pedestrianised New City street a stone's throw from Teatro Politeama, the affable, multilingual Angela has converted her grandmother's spacious 6th-floor flat into a cheery B&B. Rooms are colourfully decorated, and the corner triple has a sunny terrace. Angela, a native Palermitan, generously shares her local knowledge and serves a tasty breakfast featuring homemade cakes and jams.

★ Palazzo Pantaleo
B&B €

(☎091 32 54 71; www.palazzopantaleo.it; Via Ruggero Settimo 74h; s/d/ste €80/100/140; 🅿🤖) Offering unbeatable comfort and a convenient location, Giuseppe Scaccianoce's classy B&B occupies the top floor of an old *palazzo* half a block from Piazza Politeama, hidden from the busy street in a quiet courtyard with free parking. Five rooms and one spacious suite feature high ceilings, marble, tile or wooden floors, soundproof windows and modern bathrooms.

Hotel Orientale
HOTEL €

(☎091 616 57 27; www.albergoorientale.191.it; Via Maqueda 26; s €30-40, d €40-60, d without bathroom €30-45; ❄🤖) This *palazzo*'s grand marble stairway and arcaded courtyard, complete with motor scooters, potted plants and strung-up washing, provide an evocative introduction to Palermo's most atmospherically faded old-school budget hotel. Breakfast is served under the lovely frescoed ceiling in the library. The Ballarò market and train station are both just around the corner.

A Casa di Amici Hostel
HOSTEL €

(☎091 765 46 50; www.acasadiamici.com; Via Dante 57; dm €14-23, d €40-70; ❄🤖) Vibrant, friendly and filled with artwork left by former guests, this funky hostel-cum-guesthouse is a great choice. Beds are in mixed or single-sex dorms, or in several imaginatively decorated, music-themed rooms, complemented by a kitchen and yoga room. Multilingual owner Claudia provides helpful

SICILIAN PUPPET THEATRE

Since the 18th century, the Opera dei Pupi (traditional Sicilian puppet theatre) has been enthralling adults and children alike. The shows are a mini theatrical performance with some puppets standing 1.5m high – a completely different breed from the glove puppet popular in the West. These characters are intricately carved from beech, olive or lemon wood with realistic-looking features; flexible joints ensure they have no problem swinging their swords or beheading dragons.

Effectively the soap operas of their day, Sicilian puppet shows expounded the deepest sentiments of life – unrequited love, treachery, thirst for justice and the anger and frustration of the oppressed. The swashbuckling tales centre on the legends of Charlemagne's heroic knights, Orlando and Rinaldo, with an extended cast including the fair Angelica, the treacherous Gano di Magonza and forbidding Saracen warriors. Good puppeteers are judged on the dramatic effect they can create – lots of stamping feet and a gripping running commentary – and on their speed and skill in directing the battle scenes. See a perfromance at **Cuticchio Mimmo** (p173) or **Piccolo Teatro dei Pupi** (p207).

maps and advice, and also runs the **A Casa di Amici B&B** (⌂091 58 48 84; www.acasadi amici.com; Via Volturno 6; s €20-40, d €40-60; ❄☏) behind Teatro Massimo.

B&B Panormus B&B €
(⌂091 617 58 26; www.bbpanormus.com; Via Roma 72; s €45-70, d €60-83, tr €75-120; ❄☏) Popular for its keen prices, charming host and convenient location between the train station and the Quattro Canti, this B&B offers five high-ceilinged rooms decorated in elegant Liberty style, each with double-glazed windows, flat-screen TV and a private bathroom down the passageway.

Butera 28 APARTMENT €€
(⌂333 3165432; www.butera28.it; Via Butera 28; apt per day €70-180, per week €450-1200; ❄☏⊞) Delightful multilingual owner Nicoletta rents 11 comfortable apartments in the 18th-century Palazzo Lanzi Tomasi, the last home of Giuseppe Tomasi di Lampedusa, author of *The Leopard*. Units range from 30 to 180 sq metres, most sleeping a family of four or more. Four apartments face the sea, most have laundry facilities and all have well-equipped kitchens.

Massimo Plaza Hotel HOTEL €€
(⌂091 32 56 57; www.massimoplazahotel.com; Via Maqueda 437; r €100-250; ℗❄☏) Boasting a prime location along Palermo's newly pedestrianised Via Maqueda, this older hotel is a Palermo classic. Seven of the 15 rooms boast full-on views of the iconic Teatro Massimo across the street. The included breakfast (continental or American) can be delivered directly to your room at no extra charge, and enclosed parking costs €15 per day.

Grand Hotel Piazza Borsa HOTEL €€€
(⌂091 32 00 75; www.piazzaborsa.com; Via dei Cartari 18; s €126-199, d €169-219, ste €370-813; ℗❄@☏) Grandly situated in Palermo's former stock exchange, this four-star hotel encompasses three separate buildings housing 127 rooms. Nicest are the high-ceilinged suites with jacuzzis and windows facing Piazza San Francesco. Parking costs €18 per 24-hour period.

✖ Eating

Sicily's ancient cuisine is a mixture of spicy and sweet flavours, epitomised in the aubergine-based *caponata* and the Palermitan classic *bucatini con le sarde* (hollow tube-shaped noodles with sardines, wild fennel, raisins, pine nuts and breadcrumbs). Cakes, marzipan confections and pastries are all works of art – don't miss the ubiquitous and sinfully delicious *cannoli* (tubes of pastry filled with sweetened ricotta).

Restaurants rarely start to fill up before 9pm. For cheap eats, visit Palermo's markets, wander the tangle of alleys east and south of Teatro Massimo, or spend a Saturday evening snacking with locals at the street food carts in Piazza Caracciolo in the Vucciria district.

Many places close on Sunday, especially in the evening.

★ Ferro di Cavallo TRATTORIA €
(⌂091 33 18 35; www.ferrodicavallopalermo.it; Via Venezia 20; meals €15-17; ☉11.30am-3.30pm Mon-Sat, plus 7.45-11.30pm Wed-Sat) Tables line the footpath and caricatures of the owners beam down from bright-red walls at this cheerful family-run trattoria near the

DON'T MISS

PALERMO'S STREET FOOD

If you were taught that it was bad manners to eat in the street, you can break the rule in good company here. The mystery is simply how Palermo is not the obesity capital of Europe given just how much eating goes on! Palermitans are at it all the time: when they're shopping, commuting, discussing business, romancing...basically at any time of the day. What they're enjoying is the *buffitieri* – little hot snacks prepared at stalls and meant to be eaten on the spot.

Kick off the morning with *pane e panelle*, Palermo's famous chickpea fritter sandwich – great for vegetarians and a welcome change from a sweet custard-filled croissant. If you like, ask for it with a few *crocchè*, potato croquettes flavoured with fresh mint, also cheekily nicknamed *cazzilli* (little penises). Then again, you might want to go for some *sfincione* (a spongy, oily pizza topped with onions and caciocavallo cheese). In summer, locals also enjoy a freshly baked brioche filled with ice cream or *granite* (crushed ice mixed with fresh fruit, almonds, pistachios or coffee).

From 4pm onwards the snacks become decidedly more carnivorous and you may just wish you hadn't read the following translations: how about some barbecued *stigghiola* (goat intestines filled with onions, cheese and parsley), for example? Or a couple of *pani ca meusa* (bread rolls stuffed with ricotta and/or sautéed beef spleen)? You'll be asked if you want your roll *schietta* (single) or *maritata* (married). If you choose *schietta*, the roll will only have ricotta in it before being dipped into boiling lard; choose *maritata* and you'll get the beef spleen as well.

You'll find street food stalls all over town. Classic spots include Piazza Caracciolo in the Vucciria district, **Francu u Vastiddaru** (Corso Vittorio Emanuele 102; sandwiches €1.50-3.50; ⊘ 8am-late) and **Friggitoria Chiluzzo** (Piazza della Kalsa; sandwiches €1.50-2; ⊘ 8.30am-3pm Mon-Sat) in the Kalsa, and the no-name *pane e panelle* cart on Piazza Carmine in Ballarò market.

If you want expert guidance, check out the low-key guided tours offered by **Palermo Street Food** (www.palermostreetfood.com) and **Streat Palermo** (www.streatpalermo. it). Both offer the chance to wander Palermo's backstreets with a knowledgeable local guide, stopping for a taste (or two or three) at the city's most authentic hang-outs.

Quattro Canti. Nothing costs more than €8 on the straightforward à la carte menu. It's a great place to try Sicilian classics like *pasta con le sarde* (pasta with sardines, pine nuts, raisins and wild fennel); save room for the excellent *cannoli* (€2).

★ **Trattoria Ai Cascinari** SICILIAN €
(☑ 091 651 98 04; Via d'Ossuna 43/45; meals €20-25; ⊘ 12.30-2.30pm Tue-Sun, plus 8-10.30pm Wed-Sat) Yes, it's a bit out of the way, but this friendly neighbourhood trattoria, 1km north of the Cappella Palatina, is a long-standing Palermitan favourite, and deservedly so. It's especially enjoyable on Sunday afternoons, when locals pack the labyrinth of back rooms, as waiters perambulate non-stop with plates of scrumptious seasonal antipasti, fresh seafood and desserts from Palermo's beloved Pasticceria Cappello.

★ **Pasticceria Cappello** PASTICCERIA €
(www.pasticceriacappello.it; Via Giosuè Carducci 22; desserts from €2; ⊘ 7.30am-9.30pm Thu-Tue) One of Palermo's finest bakeries, Cappello is famous for its *setteveli* (seven-layer chocolate-hazelnut cake), invented here and now copied all over Palermo. Its display case brims with countless other splendid pastries and desserts, including the *delizia di pistacchio* (a pistachio cake topped with creamy icing and a chocolate medallion) and treats such as *cannoli* and *sfogliatelle*.

Bisso Bistrot BISTRO €
(☑ 328 1314595, 091 33 49 99; Via Maqueda 172; meals €14-17; ⊘ 9am-midnight Tue-Sun) Frescoed walls, high ceilings and reasonably priced appetisers, *primi* and *secondi* greet diners at this historic Liberty-style bookstore at the northwest corner of the Quattro Canti, recently converted into a classy but casual bistro. Lunch and dinner menus range from traditional Sicilian pasta, meat and fish dishes to sardine burgers, with cafe service in the mornings and afternoons.

Pizzeria Frida PIZZA €
(www.fridapizzeria.it; Piazza Sant'Onofrio 37; pizzas €4.50-11; ⊘ 7.30pm-midnight, closed Tue) With

footpath tables under umbrella awnings on a low-key Capo piazza, this local favourite makes pizzas in a variety of shapes, including *quadri* (square pizzas) and *vulcanotti* (named after famous volcanoes and looking the part). Toppings include Sicilian specialities like tuna, capers, pistachios, mint, aubergines and ultra-fresh ricotta.

Osteria Mangia & Bevi
SICILIAN €

(☑ 091 507 39 43; www.osteriamangiaebevi.it; Largo Cavalieri di Malta 18; meals €19-29; ⊘ 1-3pm & 8-11pm Tue-Sun) Despite its somewhat contrived aesthetics – waiters clad in traditional Sicilian *coppole* (caps), checked shirts and suspenders – this Capo district eatery with pavement seating delivers delicious spruced-up renderings of humble Sicilian classics, including the trademark *mangia e bevi* (grilled green onions wrapped in bacon) and *pasta fritta* (pasta with tomato sauce, Parmesan and breadcrumbs served in little frying pans).

★ Trattoria Il Maestro del Brodo
TRATTORIA €€

(☑ 091 32 95 23; Via Pannieri 7; meals €22-31; ⊘ 12.30-3.30pm Tue-Sun, plus 8-11pm Fri & Sat) This no-frills trattoria in the Vucciria offers delicious soups, an array of ultrafresh seafood and a sensational antipasto buffet (€8) featuring a dozen-plus homemade delicacies: *sarde a beccafico* (stuffed sardines), aubergine *involtini* (roulades), smoked fish, artichokes with parsley, sun-dried tomatoes, olives and more.

Osteria Ballarò
SICILIAN €€

(☑ 091 791 01 84; www.osteriaballaro.it; Via Calascibetta 25; meals €30-45; ⊘ 12.15-3.15pm & 7-11.30pm) A hot new foodie address, this classy restaurant-cum-wine bar marries an atmospheric setting with fantastic island cooking. Bare stone columns, exposed brick walls and vaulted ceilings set the stage for delicious seafood *primi,* local wines and memorable Sicilian *dolci* (sweets). Reservations recommended. For a faster eat, you can snack on street food at the bar or take away from the hole-in-the-wall counter outside.

☐ Drinking & Nightlife

Palermo's liveliest clusters of bars can be found along Via Chiavettieri in the Vucciria neighbourhood (just northwest of Piazza Marina) and in the Champagneria district east of Teatro Massimo, centred on Piazza Olivella, Via Spinuzza and Via Patania.

Higher-end bars and dance venues are concentrated in the newer part of Palermo. In summer, many Palermitans decamp to Mondello by the sea.

Kursaal Kalhesa
BAR

(☑ 091 616 00 50; www.facebook.com/kursaalkalhesa; Foro Umberto I 21; ⊘ 6.30pm-1am Tue-Sun) Recently reopened after a restyling, Kursaal Kalhesa has long been a noted city nightspot. Touting itself as a restaurant, wine bar and jazz club, it draws a cool, in-the-know crowd who come to hang out over *aperitivi*, dine alfresco or catch a gig under the high vaulted ceilings. It's in a 15th-century *palazzo* on the city's sea walls.

☆ Entertainment

The daily paper *Il Giornale di Sicilia* has a listing of what's on. Another excellent resource is www.balarm.it.

Teatro Massimo
OPERA

(☑ box office 091 605 35 80; www.teatromassimo.it; Piazza Giuseppe Verdi) Ernesto Basile's six-tiered art-nouveau masterpiece is Europe's third-largest opera house and one of Italy's most prestigious, right up there with La Scala in Milan and La Fenice in Venice. With lions flanking its grandiose columned entrance and an interior gleaming in red and gold, it stages opera, ballet and music concerts from September to June.

Cuticchio Mimmo
THEATRE

(☑ 091 32 34 00; www.figlidartecuticchio.com; Via Bara all'Olivella 95; ⊘ 6.30pm Sat & Sun Sep-Jul) This puppet theatre is a charming low-tech choice for children (and adults), staging traditional shows with fabulous handcrafted puppets.

Teatro di Verdura
PERFORMING ARTS

(☑ 091 765 19 63; Viale del Fante 70; ⊘ mid-Jun–Sep) A summer-only program of ballet and music in the lovely gardens of the Villa Castelnuovo, about 6km north of the city centre. Take Viale della Libertà to Viale Diana to Viale del Fante. There's a delightful open-air bar that opens during shows.

Teatro Politeama Garibaldi
PERFORMING ARTS

(☑ 091 607 25 11; Piazza Ruggero Settimo; ⊘ Oct-Jun) This grandiose theatre is a popular venue for opera, ballet and classical music, staging afternoon and evening concerts. It's home to Palermo's symphony orchestra, the **Orchestra Sinfonica Siciliana** (☑ 091 607 25 32; www.orchestrasinfonicasiciliana.it).

Shopping

Via Bara all'Olivella is good for arts and crafts.

Il Laboratorio Teatrale HANDICRAFTS
(Via Bara all'Olivella 48-50; ⊘10am-1pm & 4-7pm Tue-Sat) A true artists' workshop, this enchanting space is where the Cuticchio family constructs puppets for its famous theatre across the street. High-quality puppets dating from the late 1800s to the present are displayed here, and are available for purchase by serious enthusiasts.

Miniature Alfio Ferlito ARTS
(☑ 339 5416016; Via Bara all'Olivella 60; ⊘9am-1pm & 4-7pm Mon-Sat) Working out of his appropriately tiny shop, artisan Alfio Ferlito crafts beautiful miniature renditions of houses, furniture, people, traditional Sicilian horse-drawn carts and more.

Le Ceramiche di Caltagirone CERAMICS
(www.leceramichedicaltagirone.it; Via Cavour 114; ⊘9am-1pm & 4-8pm Mon-Sat, 9am-1pm Sun) This little shop near Teatro Massimo specialises in tiles and pottery from Caltagirone, the ceramics capital of southeastern Sicily. There's a good selection from a variety of artists, even if prices are a bit higher than you'd pay at the source.

Gusti di Sicilia FOOD & DRINK
(www.gustidisicilia.com; Via Emerico Amari 79; ⊘8.30am-11pm Mon-Sat, 8.30am-2pm & 6-11pm Sun) Whether for gifts or personal souvenirs, this is a stellar spot to stock up on beautifully packaged Sicilian edibles, from tins of tuna to jars of *caponata*, capers and marmalade to bottles of wine and olive oil to unexpected treasures like *pasta con le sarde* sauce.

Information

EMERGENCY
For an ambulance, call ☑ 118 or ☑ 091 666 55 28.

Questura (☑ 091 21 01 11; Piazza della Vittoria 8) Main police station.

MEDICAL SERVICES
Ospedale Civico (☑ 091 666 11 11; www. arnascivico.it; Piazza Nicola Leotta) Emergency facilities.

TOURIST INFORMATION
Municipal Tourist Office (☑ 091 740 80 21; promozioneturismo@comune.palermo.it; Piazza Bellini; ⊘8.30am-6.30pm Mon-Sat) The most reliable of Palermo's city-run information booths. Others at Piazza Castelnuovo, the Port of Palermo and Mondello are only intermittently staffed, with unpredictable hours.

Provincial Tourist Office (☑ 091 58 51 72; informazionituristiche@provincia.palermo.it; Via Principe di Belmonte 92; ⊘8.30am-2pm & 2.30-7pm Mon-Fri, to 6pm Sat) On a pedestrianised street in the New City.

Tourist Information – Falcone-Borsellino Airport (☑ 091 59 16 98; ⊘8.30am-7.30pm Mon-Fri, 8.30am-6pm Sat) Downstairs in the arrivals hall.

Getting There & Away

AIR
Falcone-Borsellino Airport (☑ 091 702 02 73; www.gesap.it) is at Punta Raisi, 31km west of Palermo.

Alitalia flies from Palermo to destinations throughout Europe. Several cut-rate carriers also offer flights to/from Palermo, including Ryanair, Volotea, Vueling and easyJet. Falcone-Borsellino is the hub airport for regular domestic flights to the islands of Pantelleria and Lampedusa.

BOAT
The ferry terminal is located just east of the corner of Via Francesco Crispi and Via Emerico Amari.

Grandi Navi Veloci (GNV; ☑ 091 58 74 04, 010 209 45 91; www.gnv.it; Calata Marinai d'Italia) Runs ferries from Palermo to Civitavecchia, Genoa, Naples and Tunis.

Grimaldi Lines (☑ 081 49 64 44, 091 611 36 91; www.grimaldi-lines.com; Via del Mare) Twice-weekly ferries from Palermo to Salerno (from €55, 10 to 12 hours) and Tunis (from €42, 11 to 14 hours).

Siremar (☑ 091 749 33 15; www.siremar.it; Via Francesco Crispi 118) Car ferries (€18.35, three hours, one daily) and hydrofoils (€23.55, 1½ hours, two daily) from Palermo to Ustica.

Tirrenia (☑ 344 0920924; www.tirrenia.it; Calata Marinai d'Italia) Ferries to Cagliari (from €49, 12 hours, Saturday only) and Naples (from €52, 10 hours, daily).

Ustica Lines (☑ 092 387 38 13; www.ustica lines.it; Molo Vittorio Veneto) From late June to early September, operates one daily hydrofoil to Lipari (€39.80, four hours), Stromboli (€55.20, 5¼ hours) and other points in the Aeolian Islands.

BUS
Offices for all bus companies are located within a block or two of Palermo Centrale train station. The two main departure points are the **Piazzetta Cairoli bus terminal** (Piazzetta Cairoli), just

Your receipt
Estes Valley Library

Customer ID: **********3292**

Items that you checked out

Title: Lonely Planet Southern Italy
ID: U190302120448
Due: Friday, February 3, 2023

Total items: 1
Account balance: $0.00
Checked out: 5
Overdue: 0
Hold requests: 0
Ready for pickup: 0
1/13/2023 4:40 PM

Visit our village-wide catalog:
catalog.estesvalleylibrary.org

Checkouts renew automatically!
Up to 2 times
excluding non-renewable items

WORTH A TRIP

AROUND PALERMO

A few kilometres outside Palermo's city limits, the beach town of Mondello and the dazzling cathedral of Monreale are both worthwhile day trips. Just offshore, Ustica makes a great overnight or weekend getaway.

Mondello's long, sandy beach became fashionable in the 19th century, when people came to the seaside in their carriages, prompting the construction of the huge art nouveau pier that still graces the waterfront. Most of the beaches near the pier are private (two sun loungers and an umbrella cost €10 to €20); however, there's a wide swath of public beach opposite the centre of town with all the requisite pedaloes and jet skis for hire. Given its easygoing seaside feel, Mondello is an excellent base for families. To get here, take bus 806 (€1.40, 30 minutes) from Piazza Sturzo in Palermo.

Cattedrale di Monreale (☑ 091 640 44 03; Piazza del Duomo; admission to cathedral free, north transept €2, terrace €2; ◷ 8.30am-12.45pm & 2.30-5pm Mon-Sat, 8-10am & 2.30-5pm Sun), in the hills 8km southwest of Palermo, is considered the finest example of Norman architecture in Sicily, incorporating Norman, Arab, Byzantine and classical elements. Inspired by a vision of the Virgin, it was built by William II in an effort to outdo his grandfather Roger II, who was responsible for the cathedral in Cefalù and the Cappella Palatina in Palermo. The interior, completed in 1184 and executed in shimmering mosaics, depicts 42 Old Testament stories. Outside the cathedral, the **cloister** (adult/reduced €6/3; ◷ 9am-6.30pm Mon-Sat, 9am-1pm Sun) is a tranquil courtyard with a tangible oriental feel. Surrounding the perimeter, elegant Romanesque arches are supported by an exquisite array of slender columns alternately decorated with mosaics. To reach Monreale, take AMAT bus 389 (€1.40, 35 minutes, every 1¼ hours) from Piazza Indipendenza in Palermo or AST's Monreale bus (one way/return €1.90/3, 40 minutes, hourly Monday to Saturday) from in front of Palermo Centrale train station.

The 8.7-sq-km island of **Ustica** was declared Italy's first marine reserve in 1986. The surrounding waters are a playground of fish and coral, ideal for snorkelling, diving and underwater photography. To enjoy Ustica's wild coastline and dazzling grottoes without the crowds try visiting in June or September. There are numerous dive centres, hotels and restaurants on the island, as well as some nice hiking. To get here from Palermo, take the once-daily car ferry (€18.35, three hours) or the faster, twice-daily hydrofoils (€23.55, 1½ hours) operated by **Siremar** (p174). For more details on Ustica, see Lonely Planet's *Sicily* guide.

south of the train station's eastern entrance, and **Via Paolo Balsamo**, due east of the train station.

AST (Azienda Siciliana Trasporti; ☑ 091 680 00 32; www.aziendasicilianatrasporti.it; New Bus Bar, Via Paolo Balsamo 32) Services to southeastern destinations including Ragusa (€13.50, four hours, four daily Monday to Saturday, two on Sunday).

Autoservizi Tarantola (☑ 092 43 10 20; New Bus Bar, Via Paolo Balsamo 32) Buses from Palermo to Segesta (one way/return €7/11.20, 80 minutes, three daily).

Cuffaro (☑ 091 616 15 10; www.cuffaro.info; Via Paolo Balsamo 13) Services to Agrigento (€9, two hours, three to eight daily).

SAIS Autolinee (☑ 091 616 60 28; www.sais autolinee.it; Piazza Cairoli) To/from Catania (€15, 2¾ hours, eight to 10 daily) and Messina (€16, 2¾ hours, three to six daily).

SAIS Trasporti (☑ 091 617 11 41; www.saistrasporti.it; Via Paolo Balsamo 20) Thrice-weekly overnight service to Rome (€37, 12 hours).

Salemi (☑ 091 772 03 47; www.autoservizi salemi.it; Piazza Cairoli) Several buses daily to Marsala (€9.40, 2½ hours) and Trapani's Birgi airport (€11, 1¾ hours).

Segesta (☑ 091 616 79 19; www.segesta.it; Piazza Cairoli) Services to Trapani (€8.60, two hours, at least 10 daily). Also sells Interbus tickets to Syracuse (€12, 3¼ hours, two to three daily).

CAR & MOTORCYCLE

Palermo is accessible on the A20-E90 toll road from Messina and the A19-E932 from Catania via Enna. Trapani and Marsala are also easily accessible from Palermo by motorway (A29), while Agrigento and Palermo are linked by the SS121, a good state road through the island's interior.

In April 2015, a viaduct on the A19 auto-strada between Palermo and Catania collapsed, disrupting traffic between Sicily's two major cities. As this book went to press, crews were at work repairing the damage, but the 17km-long section of the highway between Scillato and Tremonzelli (62km to 79km southeast of Palermo) remained closed indefinitely, with traffic diverted onto the much slower SS643 through Polizzi Generosa. Until repairs on the A19 are complete, the train remains a more direct and efficient way to travel between Palermo and Catania.

Most major auto hire companies are represented at the airport. You'll often save money by booking your rental online before leaving home. Given the city's chaotic traffic and expensive parking, and the excellent public transit from Palermo's airport, you're generally better off postponing rental car pick-up until you're ready to leave the city.

TRAIN

From Palermo Centrale station, just south of the centre at the foot of Via Roma, regular trains leave for Messina (from €11.80, 2¾ to 3½ hours, hourly), Agrigento (€8.30, 2¼ hours, eight to 10 daily) and Cefalù (€5.15, 45 minutes to one hour, hourly). There are also three to six direct trains daily to Catania (€12.50, 2¾ hours), plus InterCity trains to Reggio di Calabria, Naples and Rome.

ⓘ Getting Around

TO/FROM THE AIRPORT

Prestia e Comandè (ⓘ 091 58 63 51; www.prestiaecomande.it) runs a half-hourly bus service from the airport to the centre of town (one way/return €6.30/11), with stops outside Teatro Politeama Garibaldi (35 minutes) and Palermo Centrale train station (50 minutes). Buses are parked to the right as you exit the airport arrivals hall. Buy tickets at the kiosk adjacent to the bus stop. Return journeys to the airport run with similar frequency, picking up at the same points.

A slower option is the twice-hourly Trinacria Express train (€5.80, one hour) from Punta Raisi station (just downstairs from the arrivals hall) to Palermo Centrale.

A taxi from the airport to downtown Palermo costs €40 to €45.

BUS

Palermo's orange, white and blue city buses, operated by **AMAT** (ⓘ 848 800817, 091 35 01 11; www.amat.pa.it), are frequent but often crowded and slow. The free map handed out at Palermo tourist offices details all the major bus lines; most stop at the train station. Tickets, valid for 90 minutes, cost €1.40 if pre-purchased from *tabaccheria* (tobacconists) or AMAT booths, or €1.80 on board the bus. A day pass costs €3.50.

Three small buses – Linea Gialla, Linea Verde and Linea Rossa (€0.52 for 24-hour ticket) – operate in the narrow streets of the *centro storico* (historic centre) and can be useful if you're moving between tourist sights.

CAR & MOTORCYCLE

Driving is frenetic in the city and best avoided, if possible. Use one of the staffed car parks around town (€12 to €20 per day) if your hotel lacks parking.

TYRRHENIAN COAST

The coast between Palermo and Milazzo is studded with popular tourist resorts attracting a steady stream of holidaymakers, particularly between June and September. The best of these is Cefalù, a resort second only to Taormina in popularity. Just inland lie the two massive natural parks of the Madonie and Nebrodi mountains.

Cefalù

POP 14,300

This popular holiday resort wedged between a dramatic mountain peak and a sweeping stretch of sand has the lot: a great beach; a truly lovely historic centre with a grandiose cathedral; and winding medieval streets lined with restaurants and boutiques. Avoid the height of summer when prices soar, beaches are jam-packed and the charm of the place is tainted by bad-tempered drivers trying to find a car park.

◎ Sights

★**Duomo di Cefalù**   CATHEDRAL
(ⓘ 092 192 20 21; Piazza del Duomo; ◎8am-7pm Apr-Sep, 8am-5pm Oct-Mar) Cefalù's cathedral is one of the jewels in Sicily's Arab-Norman crown, only equalled in magnificence by the Cattedrale di Monreale and Palermo's Cappella Palatina. Filling the central apse, a towering figure of Christ All Powerful is the focal point of the elaborate Byzantine mosaics

CEFALÙ'S BACKYARD PLAYGROUND

Due south of Cefalù, the 40,000-hectare **Parco Naturale Regionale delle Madonie** incorporates some of Sicily's highest peaks, including the imposing Pizzo Carbonara (1979m). The park's wild, wooded slopes are home to wolves, wildcats, eagles and the near-extinct ancient Nebrodi fir trees that have survived since the last ice age. Ideal for hiking, cycling and horse trekking, the park is also home to several handsome mountain towns, including **Castelbuono**, **Petralia Soprana** and **Petralia Sottana**.

The region's distinctive rural cuisine includes roasted lamb and goat, cheeses, grilled mushrooms and aromatic pasta with *sugo* (meat sauce). A great place to sample these specialities is **Nangalarruni** (☑ 0921 67 14 28; www.hostariananangalarruni.it; Via delle Confraternite 10; fixed menus €25-35; ⊙ 12.30-3pm & 7-10pm, closed Wed winter) in Castelbuono.

For park information, contact the Ente Parco delle Madonie in **Cefalù** (p178) or **Petralia Sottana** (☑ 0921 68 40 11; Corso Paolo Agliata 16; ⊙ 8am-2pm & 3-7pm Mon-Fri, 3-7pm Sat, 10.30am-1pm & 4.30-7pm Sun).

Bus service to the park's main towns is limited; to fully appreciate the Madonie, you're better off hiring a car for a couple of days.

– Sicily's oldest and best preserved, predating those of Monreale by 20 or 30 years.

La Rocca VIEWPOINT
(adult/child €4/2; ⊙ 8am-7pm May-Sep, 9am-4pm Oct-Apr) Looming over the town, this imposing rocky crag is the site where the Arabs built their citadel, occupying it until the Norman conquest in 1061 forced them down to the port below. To reach the summit, follow signs for Tempio di Diana from the corner of Corso Ruggero and Vicolo Saraceni. The 30- to 45-minute route climbs the **Salita Saraceno**, a winding staircase, through three tiers of city walls before emerging onto rock-strewn upland slopes with spectacular coastal views.

🏃 Activities

Cefalù's crescent-shaped beach, just west of the medieval centre, is lovely, but in the summer get here early to find a patch for your umbrella and towel. You can escape with a boat tour along the coast during the summer months with agencies along Corso Ruggero, including **Visit Sicily Tours** (☑ 339 2284053, 0921 92 50 36; www.visitsicilytours.com; Corso Ruggero 83; half-day boat tour adult/child €30/15) (right next door to the tourist office).

🛏 Sleeping

Dolce Vita B&B €
(☑ 0921 92 31 51; www.dolcevitabb.it; Via Bordonaro 8; s €25-60, d €45-110) This popular B&B has one of the loveliest terraces in town, complete with deck chairs overlooking the sea and a barbecue for those warm balmy

evenings. Rooms are airy and light, with comfy beds, though the staff's lackadaisical attitude can detract from the charm.

Scirocco Bed & Breakfast B&B €
(☑ 0392 644 41 31; www.sciroccobeb.com; Piazza Garibaldi 8; s €30-60, d €60-90; ❄ 🔕) Convenient location and spectacular views are the two big selling points at this relatively new B&B halfway between the train station and the cathedral. Friendly Romanian owner Nicole offers four comfortable and bright upper-floor guest rooms, crowned by a rooftop terrace that's perfect for watching the sun set over the Tyrrhenian Sea or monitoring cafe life on Piazza Garibaldi directly below.

Hotel Kalura HOTEL €€
(☑ 0921 42 13 54; www.hotelkalura.com; Via Vincenzo Cavallaro 13; s €55-109, d €79-189, 4-person apt €115-249; 🅿 ❄ @ 🏊 🛗) East of town on a rocky outcrop, this German-run, family oriented hotel has its own pebbly beach, restaurant and fabulous pool. Most rooms have sea views, and the hotel staff can arrange loads of activities, including mountain biking, hiking, canoeing, pedalos, diving and dance nights. It's a 20-minute walk into town.

🍴 Eating & Drinking

★ **Ti Vitti** SICILIAN €€
(☑ 0921 92 15 71; www.ristorantetivitti.com; Via Umberto I 34; meals €35-45; ⊙ noon-3pm & 6.30-11pm Wed-Mon) Named after a Sicilian card game, this fine restaurant specialises in fresh-from-the-market fish dishes, locally sourced treats such as basilisco mushrooms from the nearby Monte Madonie, and some

of the best *cannoli* you'll find anywhere on the planet. For something more casual, head to its affiliated pizzeria, **Bottega Ti Vitti** (http://bottegativitti.com; Lungomare Giardina 7; pizza, salads & burgers €5-10; ⏱10am-midnight, closed Tue Nov-Apr), whose waterfront setting is perfect for sunset *aperitivi*.

Locanda del Marinaio   SEAFOOD €€
(⏰0921 42 32 95; Via Porpora 5; meals €30-40; ⏱noon-2.30pm & 7-11pm Wed-Mon) Fresh seafood rules the chalkboard menu at this excellent new eatery along the old town's main waterfront thoroughfare. Depending on the season, you'll find dishes such as red tuna carpaccio with toasted pine nuts, shrimp and zucchini on a bed of velvety ricotta, or grilled octopus served with thyme-scented potatoes, all accompanied by an excellent list of Sicilian wines.

La Galleria   SICILIAN, CAFE €€
(⏰0921 42 02 11; www.lagalleriacefalu.it; Via Mandralisca 23; meals €25-40; ⏱12.30-3pm & 7-11pm Fri-Wed) This is about as hip as Cefalù gets. Functioning as a restaurant, cafe and occasional gallery space, La Galleria has an informal vibe, a bright internal courtyard and an innovative menu that mixes standard *primi* and *secondi* with a range of all-in-one dishes (€14 to €16) designed to be meals in themselves.

❶ Information

Ente Parco delle Madonie (⏰0921 92 33 27; www.parcodellemadonie.it; Corso Ruggero 116; ⏱8am-6pm Mon-Sat) Knowledgeable staff supply information about the Parco Naturale Regionale delle Madonie.

Hospital (⏰0921 92 01 11; www.fondazione sanraffaelegiglio.it; Contrada Pietrapollastra) On the main road out of town in the direction of Palermo.

Questura (⏰0921 92 60 11; Via Roma 15)

Tourist Office (⏰0921 42 10 50; strcefalu@ regione.sicilia.it; Corso Ruggero 77; ⏱9am-8pm Mon-Sat) English-speaking staff, lots of leaflets and good maps.

❶ Getting There & Away

The best way to get to and from Cefalù is by rail. Hourly trains go to Palermo (€5.15, 45 minutes to 1¼ hours) and virtually every other town on the coast.

AEOLIAN ISLANDS

The Aeolian Islands are a little piece of paradise. Stunning cobalt sea, splendid beaches, some of Italy's best hiking and an awe-inspiring volcanic landscape are just part of the appeal. The islands also have a fascinating human and mythological history that goes back several millennia; the Aeolians figured prominently in Homer's *Odyssey,* and evidence of the distant past can be seen everywhere, most notably in Lipari's excellent archaeological museum.

The seven islands of Lipari, Vulcano, Salina, Panarea, Stromboli, Alicudi and Filicudi

MILAZZO: GATEWAY TO THE AEOLIAN ISLANDS

DESTINATION	COST (€) HYDROFOIL/FERRY	DURATION HYDROFOIL/FERRY
Alicudi	29/20	3¼ / 6hr
Filicudi	24/18	2½ / 5hr
Lipari	16/13	50min / 2hr
Panarea	18/14	2¼ / 5hr
Salina	19/15	1¾ / 3¼hr
Stromboli	22/17	2¾ / 6hr
Vulcano	15/12	45min / 1½hr

Most ferries to the Aeolian Islands run from Milazzo. To reach Milazzo's ferry terminal, you have a few options: from Milazzo's train station, take AST local bus 5 (€1.20, 10 minutes, at least hourly); from Catania's Fontanarossa airport, take a **Giuntabus** (⏰090 67 57 49, 090 67 37 82; www.giuntabustrasporti.com) express bus (€15, two hours, two to four daily) or book a shuttle (€25, two hours, reservation required) with **Alibrando** (⏰090 928 85 85; www.eolie booking.com/navetta). In addition, Giuntabus offers direct bus service from Messina Centrale train station (€4.20, 50 minutes, hourly Monday through Saturday, six on Sunday). All will drop you just outside Milazzo's ferry terminal.

are part of a huge 200km volcanic ridge that runs between the smoking stack of Mt Etna and the threatening mass of Vesuvius above Naples. Collectively, the islands exhibit a unique range of volcanic characteristics, which earned them a place on Unesco's World Heritage list in 2000. The islands are mobbed with visitors in July and August, but out of season things remain delightfully tranquil.

ⓘ Getting There & Away

Both **Ustica Lines** (www.usticalines.it) and **Siremar** (www.siremar.it) run hydrofoils year-round from Milazzo, the mainland city closest to the islands. Almost all boats stop first at Vulcano and Lipari, then continue to the ports of Santa Marina and/or Rinella on Salina island. Beyond Salina, boats either branch off east to Panarea and Stromboli, or west to Filicudi and Alicudi. Ustica Lines also operates limited year-round service to the islands from Messina and Reggio Calabria.

Ustica Lines and Siremar's hydrofoil schedules complement each other nicely, with one company or the other providing service nearly hourly to the main islands of Vulcano, Lipari and Salina. Frequency of service on all routes increases in the summer. Note that hydrofoils are sometimes cancelled due to heavy seas.

Both Siremar and **NGI Traghetti** (☑090 928 40 91; www.ngi-spa.it) also run car ferries from Milazzo to the islands; they're slightly cheaper, but slower and less regular than the hydrofoils.

Additional seasonal services include Ustica Lines hydrofoils from Palermo (once daily late June to early September), Siremar ferries from Naples (twice weekly April to September) and **SNAV** (☑081 428 55 55; www.snav.it) hydrofoils from Naples (daily July to early September, plus weekends in June).

ⓘ Getting Around

BOAT

Siremar and Ustica Lines both operate year-round, inter-island hydrofoil services. Siremar also offers inter-island ferry links. Ticket offices with posted timetables can be found close to the docks on all islands.

CAR & SCOOTER

You can take your car to Lipari, Vulcano or Salina by ferry, or garage it at Milazzo or Messina on the mainland from €12 per day. The islands are small, with narrow, winding roads. You'll often save money (and headaches) by hiring a scooter on site, or better yet, exploring the islands on foot.

ⓘ FERRYING TO THE AEOLIANS FROM NAPLES

An atmospheric way to reach the Aeolians is via the twice weekly ferry from Naples. Set off at 8pm and you'll awake to the sight of a smoking Stromboli at dawn. Comfortable private cabins with bunk beds, writing desk and hot showers cost only a bit extra (€85 for a single cabin versus €55 for a standard seat, or €141 versus €111 for two people), and full meals (including *cannoli*!) are served on board at reasonable prices. The boat continues beyond Stromboli to Panarea, Salina, Lipari and Vulcano.

Lipari

POP 11,200 / ELEV 602M

Lipari is the Aeolians' thriving hub, both geographically and functionally, with regular ferry and hydrofoil connections to all other islands. Lipari town, the largest urban centre in the archipelago, is home to the islands' only tourist office and most dependable banking services, along with enough restaurants, bars and year-round residents to offer a bit of cosmopolitan buzz. Meanwhile, the island's rugged shoreline offers excellent opportunities for hiking, boating and swimming.

As evidenced by its fine archaeological museum and the multi-layered ruins strewn about town, Lipari has been inhabited for some 6000 years. The island was settled in the 4th millennium BC by Sicily's first known inhabitants, the Stentillenians, who developed a flourishing economy based on obsidian, a glassy volcanic rock. Commerce subsequently attracted the Greeks, who used the islands as ports on the east–west trade route, and pirates such as Barbarossa (or Redbeard), who sacked the city in 1544.

Lipari's two harbours, Marina Lunga (where ferries and hydrofoils dock) and Marina Corta (700m south, used by smaller boats) are linked by a bustling main street, Corso Vittorio Emanuele, flanked by shops, restaurants and bars. Overlooking the colourful snake of day trippers is Lipari's clifftop citadel, surrounded by 16th-century walls.

Lipari Town

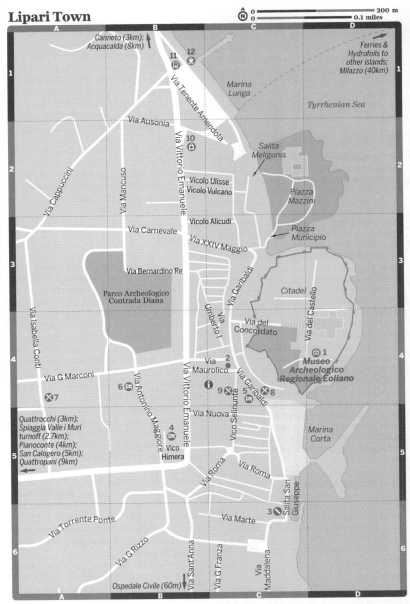

◉ Sights & Activities

★ **Museo Archeologico Regionale Eoliano** MUSEUM

(☏ 090 988 01 74; www.regione.sicilia.it/beniculturali/museolipari; Castello di Lipari; adult/reduced €6/3; ☺ 9am-6.30pm Mon-Sat, 9am-1pm Sun) A must-see for Mediterranean history buffs, Lipari's archaeological museum boasts one of Europe's finest collections of ancient finds. Especially worthwhile are the Sezione Preistorica, devoted to locally discovered artefacts from the Neolithic and Bronze Ages

Lipari Town

◎ **Top Sights**
1 Museo Archeologico Regionale
Eoliano..D4

➌ **Activities, Courses & Tours**
2 Da Massimo/Dolce Vita...................C4
3 Diving Center La Gorgonia C6

🛏 **Sleeping**
4 Diana Brown..B5
5 Enzo Il Negro......................................C4
6 Hotel Oriente.......................................B4

🍴 **Eating**
7 E Pulera...A4
8 Gilberto e Vera C4
9 Kasbah..C4

🛍 **Shopping**
10 La Formagella......................................B2

🚍 **Transport**
11 Guglielmo Urso Local Bus
Stop B1
12 Siremar B1
Siremar & Ustica Lines
Ticket Office ....(see 12)
Ustica Lines ....(see 12)

to the Graeco-Roman era, and the Sezione Classica, whose highlights include ancient shipwreck cargoes and the world's largest collection of miniature Greek theatrical masks.

★**Quattrocchi**   VIEWPOINT
Lipari's best coastal views are from a celebrated viewpoint known as Quattrocchi (Four Eyes), 3km west of town. Follow the road for Pianoconte and look on your left about 300m beyond the turn-off for Spiaggia Valle i Muria. Stretching off to the south, great, grey cliffs plunge into the sea, while in the distance plumes of sinister smoke rise from the dark heights of neighbouring Vulcano.

★**Spiaggia Valle i Muria**   BEACH
Lapped by clean waters and surrounded by sheer cliffs, this dark, pebbly beach on Lipari's southwestern shore is a dramatically beautiful swimming and sunbathing spot. From the signposted turn-off, 3km west of Lipari town towards Pianoconte, it's a steep 15-minute downhill walk; come prepared with water and sunscreen. In good weather, Lipari resident **Barni** (🖂349 1839555, 339 8221583) sells refreshments from his rustic

cave-like beach bar, and provides ultra-scenic boat transfers to and from Lipari's Marina Corta (€5/10 one way/return).

Diving Center La Gorgonia   DIVING
(🖂090 981 26 16; www.lagorgoniadiving.it; Salita San Giuseppe; per dive with rented/personal equipment €50/30, courses €55-750) This outfit offers courses, boat transport, equipment hire and general information about scuba diving and snorkelling around Lipari. See the website for a complete price list.

Eastern Beaches
On Lipari's eastern shore, sunbathers and swimmers head a few kilometres north of Lipari town to bask on **Spiaggia di Canneto**. Further north near the island's abandoned pumice mines is pebbly **Spiaggia della Papesca**, nicknamed **Spiaggia Bianca** for the white pumice dust that used to cover it; residual pumice still gives the sea its limpid turquoise colour.

👉 **Tours**

Numerous agencies in town, including the dependable **Da Massimo/Dolce Vita** (🖂090 981 30 86; www.damassimo.it; Via Maurolico 2), offer boat tours to the surrounding islands. Prices are around €25 for a circuit around Vulcano, €30 for a tour of Salina, €40 to visit Filicudi and Alicudi, €40 for a day trip to Panarea and Stromboli, and €75 to €80 for a late afternoon trip to Stromboli, including a guided hike up the mountain at sunset and a late-night return to Lipari.

🛏 **Sleeping**

Lipari is the Aeolians' best-equipped base for island-hopping, with plenty of places to stay, eat and drink. Note that prices soar in summer; avoid August if possible.

★**Diana Brown**   B&B €
(🖂338 640 75 72, 090 981 25 84; www.diana brown.it; Vico Himera 3; s €30-70, d €40-80, tr €50-100; ❋❀) Tucked down a narrow alley, South African Diana's delightful rooms sport tile floors, abundant hot water and welcome extras such as kettles, fridges, clothes-drying racks and satellite TV. Units downstairs are darker but have built-in kitchenettes. There's a sunny breakfast terrace and solarium with deck chairs, plus a book exchange and laundry service. Optional breakfast costs €5 extra per person.

WORTH A TRIP

COASTAL HIKES

Lipari's rugged northwestern coastline offers excellent walking opportunities. Most accessible is the pleasant hour-long stroll from Quattropani to Acquacalda along Lipari's north shore, which affords spectacular views of Salina and a distant Stromboli. Take the bus to Quattropani (€2.40, 25 minutes), then simply proceed downhill on the main road 5km to Acquacalda, where you can catch the bus (€1.55) back to Lipari.

More strenuous, but equally rewarding in terms of scenery, is the three- to four-hour hike descending steeply from Pianoconte (€1.90, 15 minutes by bus) down past the old Roman baths of Terme di San Calogero to the western shoreline, then skirting the clifftops along a flat stretch before climbing steeply back to Quattropani.

Enzo Il Negro　　　　　　GUESTHOUSE €

(☎090 981 31 63; www.enzoilnegro.com; Via Garibaldi 29; s €40-50, d €60-90; ✻🛜) Family run for decades, this down-to-earth guesthouse near picturesque Marina Corta offers spacious, tiled, pine-furnished rooms with fridges. Two panoramic terraces overlook the rooftops, the harbour and the castle walls.

Hotel Oriente　　　　　　　　HOTEL €

(☎090 981 14 93; www.hotelorientelipari.com; Via Marconi 35; s €40-70, d €60-100; P✻🛜) This centrally located, older hotel will either charm you with its quirkiness or drive you crazy with its clutter. Just 100m west of the centre, its rooms are rather bland and faded, but the common spaces drip with character, from the spacious citrus-filled courtyard, to the eclectically decorated breakfast room and bar, to the in-house museum of antique Sicilian paraphernalia.

🍴 Eating & Drinking

Fish abound in the waters of the archipelago and include tuna, mullet, cuttlefish and sole, all of which end up on local menus. Try *pasta all'eoliana,* a simple blend of the island's excellent capers with olives, olive oil, anchovies, tomatoes and basil.

Bars are concentrated along Corso Vittorio Emanuele and down by Marina Corta.

Gilberto e Vera　　　　　　SANDWICHES €

(www.gilbertoevera.it; Via Garibaldi 22-24; sandwiches €5; ⊙8am-2pm & 4pm-midnight Mar-Nov) This straightforward shop sells two dozen varieties of sandwiches, all costing €5 and served with a smile. Sicilian ingredients such as capers, olives, aubergine and tuna all make frequent appearances. Long opening hours make this the perfect spot to purchase early morning hiking or beach-hopping provisions, or to sip a mid-afternoon or late evening glass of wine on the streetside terrace.

Kasbah　　　　MODERN SICILIAN, PIZZA €€

(☎090 981 10 75; www.kasbahcafe.it; Vico Selinunte 45; pizzas €6-8, meals €30-36; ⊙7-10pm, closed Wed Oct-Apr) Tucked down narrow Vico Selinunte, with a window where you can watch the chefs at work, this place serves everything from fancy pasta, fish and meat dishes to simple wood-fired pizzas (try the Kasbah, with smoked swordfish, rocket, lemon and black pepper). The stylish dining room with its grey linen tablecloths is complemented by a more casual outdoor terrace.

E Pulera　　　　　　　MODERN SICILIAN €€

(☎090 981 11 58; www.pulera.it; Via Isabella Conti; meals €35-45; ⊙7.30-10pm May-Oct) With its serene garden setting, low lighting, artsy tile-topped tables and exquisite food – from tuna carpaccio with blood oranges and capers to *cassata* (sponge cake, ricotta, marzipan, chocolate and candied fruit) served with sweet Malvasia wine for dessert – E Pulera makes an upscale but relaxed choice for a romantic dinner.

🛍 Shopping

La Formagella　　　　　　FOOD & DRINK

(Via Vittorio Emanuele 250; ⊙7.30am-9pm May-Oct, shorter hours rest of year) You simply can't leave the Aeolian Islands without a small pot of capers and a bottle of sweet Malvasia wine. You can get both, along with meats, cheeses and other delicious goodies, at this gourmet grocery-deli just around the corner from the hydrofoil dock.

ℹ️ Information

Corso Vittorio Emanuele is lined with ATMs. The other islands have relatively few facilities, so it's best to sort out your finances here before moving on.

Ospedale Civile (☎090 988 51 11; Via Sant'Anna) First-aid and emergency services.

Police Station (☎090 981 13 33; Via Marconi)

Tourist Office (☎ 090 988 00 95; infopointeo lie@regione.sicilia.it; Via Maurolico 17; ⊙ 9am-1.30pm Mon-Fri, plus 4.30-7pm Mon, Wed & Fri) Lipari's sporadically staffed office provides information covering all of the Aeolian Islands.

ℹ Getting There & Around

BOAT

Lipari is the Aeolians' transport hub. The main port is Marina Lunga, where you'll find a joint **Siremar & Ustica Lines ticket office** (Marina Lunga; ⊙ 5.45-8.30am, 9.30am-2pm & 3-8.30pm) at the head of the hydrofoil jetty. Timetable information is displayed here.

Year-round ferries and hydrofoils serve Milazzo and all the other Aeolian islands; less frequent services include year-round hydrofoils to Messina and ferries to Naples, and summer-only hydrofoil services to Palermo. Websites for **Ustica Lines** (☎ 090 981 24 48; www.usticalines.it) and **Siremar** (☎ 090 981 10 17; www.siremar.it) have complete schedules and price details.

BUS

Autobus Guglielmo Urso (☎ 090 981 10 26; www.ursobus.com/orariursobus.pdf) runs buses around the island roughly hourly from its **bus stop** adjacent to Marina Lunga. The Linea Urbana follows the eastern shoreline, making stops at Canneto (€1.30) and Acquacalda (€1.55), while the Linea Extraurbana climbs to the western highland settlements of Pianoconte (€1.90) and Quattropani (€2.40). Discounts are available for round-trip journeys or multiple rides (six-/10-/20-ride tickets from €7/10.50/20.50).

CAR & MOTORCYCLE

Several places around town rent bicycles (€10 to €15 per day), scooters (€15 to €50) and cars (€30 to €80), including **Da Marcello** (☎ 090 981 12 34; www.noleggiodamarcello.com; Via Sottomonastero) down by the ferry dock.

Vulcano

POP 720 / ELEV 500M

Vulcano is a memorable place, not least because of the vile smell of sulphurous gases. Once you escape the drab and dated tourist centre, Porto di Levante, the island has a delightfully tranquil, unspoilt quality. Beyond the well-marked trail to the looming Fossa di Vulcano, the landscape gives way to rural simplicity with vineyards, birdsong and a surprising amount of greenery. The island is worshipped by Italians for its therapeutic mud baths and hot springs, and its black beaches and weird steaming landscape make for an interesting day trip.

Boats dock at Porto di Levante. To the right, as you face the island, are the mud baths and the small Vulcanello peninsula; to the left is the volcano. Straight ahead is Porto di Ponente, 700m west, where you will find the Spiaggia Sabbia Nera (Black Sand Beach).

🏃 Activities

★ Fossa di Vulcano   WALKING

FREE Vulcano's top attraction is the straight-forward trek up its 391m volcano (no guide required). Start early if possible and bring a hat, sunscreen and water. Follow the signs south along Strada Provinciale, then turn left onto the zigzag gravel track that leads to the summit. It's about an hour's scramble to the lowest point of the crater's edge (290m).

Laghetto di Fanghi   HOT SPRING

(www.geoterme.it; admission €2, incl visit to fara-glione €2.50, shower €1, towel €2.60; ⊙ 7am-7pm mid-Mar–Oct) Backed by a *faraglione* (rock tower) and stinking of rotten eggs, Vulcano's harbourside pool of thick, coffee-coloured sulphurous gloop isn't exactly a five-star beauty farm. But the warm (28°C) mud is considered an excellent treatment for rheumatic pains and skin diseases, and rolling around in it can be fun if you don't mind smelling funny for a few days. Keep the mud away from your eyes and hair, as the sulphur is acidic and can damage the cornea.

Sicily in Kayak   KAYAKING

(☎ 329 5381229; www.sicilyinkayak.com) This outfit offers kayaking tours around Vulcano and the other Aeolians, ranging in length from half a day to an entire week.

Beaches

At Porto di Ponente, on the far side of the peninsula from Porto di Levante, the dramatic and only mildly commercialised black-sand beach of **Spiaggia Sabbia Nera** curves around a pretty bay. It is one of the few sandy beaches in the archipelago. A smaller, quieter black-sand beach, **Spiaggia dell'Asina**, can be found on the island's southern side near Gelso.

🛏 Sleeping & Eating

Unless you're here for the walking and the mud baths, Vulcano is not a great place for an extended stay; the town is pretty soulless and the sulphurous fumes really do smell. However, there are some good options for those who choose to stick around.

Casa Arcada
B&B, APARTMENT €

(☎347 6497633; www.casaarcada.it; Via Provinciale 178; B&B per person €30-55, d apt per week €420-770; ☀🅿) Conveniently located at the volcano's edge, 20m back from the main road between the port and the crater path, this sweet whitewashed complex offers bed and breakfast in five immaculate tile-floored rooms with air-con and mini-fridges, along with weekly rental apartments. The communal upstairs sun terrace affords lovely views up to the volcano and across the water to Lipari.

★ La Forgia Maurizio
SICILIAN €€

(☎339 1379107; Strada Provinciale 45, Porto di Levante; meals €30-35; ⊙noon-3pm & 7-11pm) The owner of this devilishly good restaurant spent 20 winters in Goa, India; Eastern influences sneak into the menu of Sicilian specialities, and several items are vegan- and/or vegetarian-friendly. Don't miss the *liquore di kumquat e cardamom,* Maurizio's homemade answer to *limoncello.* The multicourse tasting menu is an excellent deal at €30 including wine, water and dessert.

❶ Getting There & Around

BOAT
Vulcano is an intermediate stop between Milazzo and Lipari; both Siremar and Ustica Lines run multiple vessels in both directions throughout the day. The trip to or from Lipari takes only 10 minutes, making Vulcano an easy and popular day-trip destination.

CAR & MOTORCYCLE
Nolo Sprint da Luigi (☎347 7600275; http://vulcano-luigi-rent.com; Porto di Levante; bicycle/scooter/car per day from €5/20/40) Rent some wheels from this well-signposted outfit near the port. Multilingual owners Luigi and Nidra offer tips for exploring the island and also rent out an apartment (€40 to €70) in Vulcano's tranquil interior.

Salina

POP 2200 / ELEV 962M

Ah, green Salina! In stark contrast to sulphur-stained Vulcano and lava-blackened Stromboli, Salina's twin craters of Monte dei Porri and Monte Fossa delle Felci – nicknamed *didyme* (twins) by the ancient Greeks – are lushly wooded and invitingly verdant, a result of the numerous freshwater springs on the island.

Wildflowers, thick yellow gorse bushes and serried ranks of grapevines carpet the hillsides in vibrant colours and cool greens, while its high coastal cliffs plunge dramatically towards beaches. The famous Aeolian capers grow plentifully here, as do the grapes used for making Malvasia wine.

◉ Sights & Activities

Pollara
VILLAGE

Don't miss a trip to sleepy Pollara, sandwiched dramatically between the sea and the steep slopes of an extinct volcanic crater on Salina's western edge. The gorgeous beach here was used as a location in the 1994 film *Il postino,* although the land access route to the beach has since been closed due to landslide danger.

★ Monte Fossa delle Felci
HIKING

For jaw-dropping views, climb to the Aeolians' highest point, Monte Fossa delle Felci (962m). The two-hour ascent starts from the **Santuario della Madonna del Terzito,** an imposing 19th-century church at Valdichiesa, in the valley separating the island's two volcanoes. Up top, gorgeous perspectives unfold on the symmetrically arrayed volcanic cones of Monte dei Porri, Filicudi and a distant Alicudi.

Wineries
Outside Malfa there are numerous wineries where you can try the local Malvasia wine. Signposted off the main road, **Fenech** (☎090 984 40 41; www.fenech.it; Via Fratelli Mirabilo 41) is an acclaimed producer whose 2012 Malvasia won awards at five international competitions. Another important Malvasia is produced at the luxurious Capofaro (p185) resort on the 13-acre Tasca d'Almerita estate, between Malfa and Santa Marina.

🛏 Sleeping & Eating

The island remains relatively undisturbed by mass tourism, yet offers some of the Aeolians' finest hotels and restaurants. Accommodation can be found in Salina's three main towns: Santa Marina Salina on the east shore, Malfa on the north shore and Rinella on the south shore, as well as in Lingua, a village adjoining ancient salt ponds 2km south of Santa Marina. Note that many hotels have their own excellent restaurants.

★ **A Cannata** PENSION €€
(☑090 984 31 61; www.acannata.it; Via Umberto, Lingua; r per person incl breakfast €40-90, incl half-board €75-125; 🖥) Newly remodelled in classic Aeolian style, with peach-coloured stucco, cheerful blue doors, and floors clad in gorgeous reproductions of historic tiles, this family-run *pensione* offers 25 spacious units, many (along with the breakfast terrace) overlooking Lingua's picturesque salt lagoon. Don't miss half-board at its Slow Food–acclaimed **restaurant** (☑090 984 31 61; Via Umberto I 13, Lingua; meals €35; ☺12.30-2.30pm & 7.30-10pm), featuring menus built around fresh-caught seafood and home-grown veggies and herbs.

Hotel Mamma Santina BOUTIQUE HOTEL €€
(☑090 984 30 54; www.mammasantina.it; Via Sanità 40, Santa Marina Salina; d €110-190; ☺Apr-Oct; ✳@🖥▨) A labour of love for its architect owner, this boutique hotel has inviting rooms decorated with pretty tiles in traditional Aeolian designs. Many of the sea-view terraces come equipped with hammocks, and on warm evenings the attached restaurant (meals €35 to €40) has outdoor seating overlooking the glowing blue pool and landscaped garden.

★ **Hotel Signum** BOUTIQUE HOTEL €€€
(☑090 984 42 22; www.hotelsignum.it; Via Scalo 15, Malfa; d €150-550, ste €450-700; ✳🖥▨) Hidden in Malfa's hillside lanes is this alluring labyrinth of antique-clad rooms, peach-coloured stucco walls, tall blue windows and vine-covered terraces with full-on views of Stromboli. The attached wellness centre, **Salus Per Aquam** (Wellness Center; ☑090 984 42 22; www. hotelsignum.it; Via Scalo 15, Malfa; admission €30, treatments extra; ☺Apr-Sep), a stunning pool and one of the island's best-regarded restaurants make this the perfect place to unwind for a few days in utter comfort.

Capofaro BOUTIQUE HOTEL €€€
(☑090 984 43 30; www.capofaro.it; Via Faro 3, Malfa; d €190-350, ste €330-690; ☺late Apr-early Oct; ✳@🖥▨) Immerse yourself in luxury at this five-star boutique resort halfway between Santa Marina and Malfa, surrounded by well-tended Malvasia vineyards and a picturesque lighthouse. The 20 rooms all have sharp white decor and terraces looking straight out to smoking

Stromboli. Tennis courts, poolside massages, wine tasting and vineyard visits complete this perfect vision of island chic.

★ **Da Alfredo** SANDWICHES €
(Piazza Marina Garibaldi, Lingua; granite €2.60, sandwiches €9-13; ☺9am-11pm) Salina's most atmospheric option for an affordable snack, Alfredo's place is renowned all over Sicily for its *granite:* ices made with coffee, fresh fruit or locally grown pistachios and almonds. It's also worth a visit for its *pane cunzato* (open-faced sandwiches piled high with tuna, ricotta, aubergine, tomatoes, capers and olives); split one with a friend – they're huge!

🛍 Shopping

Laboratorio di Ceramiche Artistiche CERAMICS
(www.ceramichesalina.it; Via Piccolo Torrente, Malfa; ☺8am-noon & 2-7pm) Gorgeous multicoloured floor tiles, many of them one-of-a-kind historic pieces from the Naples area, are displayed here on shelves, walls and throughout the large gravel courtyard. Overseas shipping can be arranged.

ℹ Information

Banca Nuova Bank with ATM; bear right along the waterfront as you exit the boat docks.

ℹ Getting There & Around

BOAT
Hydrofoils and ferries serve Santa Marina Salina and Rinella from Lipari and the other islands. You'll find ticket offices in both ports.

BUS
CITIS (☑090 984 41 50; www.trasportisalina. it) runs buses every hour or two in the low season (more frequently in summer) from Santa Marina Salina to Lingua and Malfa. In Malfa, make connections for Rinella, Pollara, Valdichiesa and Leni. Fares are €1.90 to €2.90 depending on your destination. Timetables are posted online, and at ports and bus stops.

CAR & MOTORCYCLE
Above Santa Marina Salina's port, **Antonio Bongiorno** (☑338 3791209; www.rentbongiorno.it; Via Risorgimento 222, Santa Marina Salina) rents bikes (per day from €8), scooters (€25 to €30) and cars (€60 to €70). Several agencies in Rinella offer similar services – look for signs at the ferry dock.

Delightful Desserts

From citrus-scented pastries filled with ricotta, to ice cream served on a brioche, to the marzipan fruits piled in every confectioner's window, Sicily celebrates the joys of sugar morning, noon and night.

Multicultural Roots

People from the Arabs to the Aztecs have influenced Sicily's culture of sweets: the former introduced sugar cane; the latter's fiery hot chocolate so impressed the Spaniards that they brought it to Sicily. The land also supplied inspiration, from abundant citrus, almond and pistachio groves to Mt Etna's snowy slopes, legendary source of the first *granita*.

Sweet Sicilian Classics

The all-star list of Sicilian desserts starts with *cannoli*, crunchy pastry tubes filled with sweetened ricotta, garnished with chocolate, crumbled pistachios or a spike of candied citrus. Vying for the title of Sicily's most famous dessert is *cassata*, a coma-inducing concoction of sponge cake, cream, marzipan, chocolate and candied fruit. Feeling more adventurous? How about an *'mpanatigghiu*, a traditional Modican pastry stuffed with minced meat, almonds, chocolate and cinnamon?

A SUGAR-FUELLED ISLAND SPIN

➡ **Pasticceria Cappello** Renowned for its *setteveli*, a velvety seven-layer chocolate cake. (p172)

➡ **Da Alfredo** Dreamy *granite* made with almonds and wild strawberries. (p185)

➡ **Ti Vitti** Divine *cannoli* featuring fresh-from-the-sheep ricotta from the Madonie Mountains. (p177)

➡ **Dolceria Bonajuto** Aztec-influenced chocolate with vanilla and hot peppers. (p211)

➡ **Gelati DiVini** Outlandish ice-cream flavours including Marsala wine, wild fennel and olive oil. (p212)

➡ **Maria Grammatico** Marzipan fruit, almond pastries and toasted-nut *torrone*. (p222)

2

1. Display of marzipan fruit 2. *Cassata siciliana* 3. *Cannoli*
4. Granita made with prickly pear fruit

GILAS/GETTY IMAGES ©

4

JANNHUIZENGA/GETTY IMAGES ©

Stromboli

POP 400 / ELEV 924M

Stromboli's perfect triangle of a volcano juts dramatically out of the sea. It's the only island whose smouldering cone is permanently active, attracting a steady stream of visitors like moths to its massive flame. Volcanic activity has scarred and blackened the northwest side of the island, while the eastern side is untamed, ruggedly green and dotted with low-rise whitewashed houses.

The youngest of the Aeolian volcanoes, Stromboli was formed a mere 40,000 years ago and its gases continue to send up an almost constant spray of liquid magma, a process defined by vulcanologists as *attività stromboliana* (Strombolian activity). The volcano's most dramatic recent activity involved major lava flows that burst forth between June and December 2014, creating a new mass of hardened lava rock below the volcano's northeast crater and cancelling tours to the summit for several months. Several other significant eruptions have occurred in recent years: on 27 February 2007, two new craters opened on the volcano's summit; on 5 April 2003, the village of Ginostra was showered with rocks up to 4m wide; and on 30 December 2002, a tsunami caused damage to Stromboli town, injuring six people and closing the island to visitors for a few months.

Boats arrive at Porto Scari, downhill from the main town of Stromboli at the island's northeastern corner. Accommodation is concentrated within a 2km radius of the port, while San Vincenzo church, the meeting point for guided hikes up the volcano, is a short walk up the Scalo Scari to Via Roma.

◎ Sights & Activities

★ Stromboli Crater   VOLCANO

For nature lovers, climbing Stromboli is one of Sicily's not-to-be-missed experiences. Since 2005 access has been strictly regulated: you can walk freely to 400m, but need a guide to continue any higher. Organised treks depart daily (between 3.30pm and 6pm, depending on the season), timed to reach the summit (924m) at sunset and to allow 45 minutes to observe the crater's fireworks.

The climb itself takes 2½ to three hours, while the descent back to Piazza San Vincenzo is shorter (1½ to two hours). All told, it's a demanding five- to six-hour trek up to the top and back; you'll need to have proper walking shoes, a backpack that allows free movement of both arms, clothing for cold and wet weather, a change of T-shirt, a handkerchief to protect against dust (wear glasses not contact lenses), a torch, 1L to 2L of water and some food. If you haven't got any of these, Totem Trekking (☑ 090 986 57 52; www.totemtrekkingstromboli.com; Piazza San Vincenzo 4; ⊗ 9.30am-1pm & 3.30-7pm) hires out all the necessary equipment, including boots (€6), backpacks (€5), hiking poles (€4), torches (€3) and windbreakers (€5).

★ Sciara del Fuoco Viewpoint   VIEWPOINT

(Trail of Fire) An alternative to scaling Stromboli's summit is the hour-long climb to this viewpoint (400m, no guide required), which directly overlooks the Sciara del Fuoco (the blackened laval scar running down Stromboli's northern flank) and offers fabulous if more distant views of the crater's explosions. Bring plenty of water, and a torch if walking at night. The trail (initially a switchbacking road) starts in Piscità, 2km west of Stromboli's port; halfway up, you can stop for pizza at L'Osservatorio (p189).

La Sirenetta Diving   DIVING

(☑ 347 5961499, 338 8919675; www.lasirenetta diving.it; Via Marina 33; ⊗ Jun–mid-Sep) Offers diving courses and accompanied dives, opposite the beach at La Sirenetta Park Hotel.

Beaches

Stromboli's black sandy beaches are the best in the Aeolian archipelago. The most accessible and popular swimming and sunbathing is at **Ficogrande**, a strip of rocks and black volcanic sand about a 10-minute walk northwest of the hydrofoil dock. Further-flung beaches worth exploring are at **Piscità** to the west and **Forgia Vecchia**, about 300m south of the port.

☞ Tours

Magmatrek (☑ 090 986 57 68; www.magmatrek. it; Via Vittorio Emanuele) has experienced, multilingual vulcanological guides who lead regular treks (maximum group size 20) up to the crater every afternoon (per person €28). It can also put together tailor-made treks for individual groups. Other agencies charging identical prices include **Stromboli Adventures** (☑ 090 98 62 64; www.stromboli adventures.it; Via Vittorio Emanuele), **Quota 900** (☑ 090 98 62 51; www.quota900stromboli.com; Via

Roma) and Il Vulcano a Piedi (☑ 349 2126428, 090 98 61 44; www.ilvulcanoapiedi.it; Via Pizzillo).

Società Navigazione Pippo (☑ 338 9857883, 090 98 61 35; pipponav.stromboli@libero. it; Porto Scari) is among the numerous boat companies at Porto Scari offering 2½-hour daytime circuits of the island (€25), 1½-hour sunset excursions to watch the Sciara del Fuoco from the sea (€20) and evening trips to Ginostra village on the other side of the island for dinner or *aperitivi* (€25).

🛌 Sleeping

Over a dozen places offer accommodation, including B&Bs, guesthouses and fully fledged hotel6ls.

★ Casa del Sole   GUESTHOUSE €
(☑ 090 98 63 00; www.casadelsolestromboli.it; Via Cincotta; dm €25-30, s €30-50, d €60-100) This cheerful Aeolian-style guesthouse is only 100m from a sweet black-sand beach in Piscità, the tranquil neighbourhood at the west end of town. Dorms, private doubles and a guest kitchen all surround a sunny patio, overhung with vines, fragrant with lemon blossoms, and decorated with the masks and stone carvings of sculptor-owner Tano Russo. Call for free pick-up (low season only) or take a taxi (€10) from the port 2km away.

Albergo Brasile   PENSION €
(☑ 090 98 60 08; www.strombolialbergobrasile.it; Via Soldato Cincotta; d €70-90; ☺ Easter-Oct; ❄) About 2km from the boat dock in peaceful Piscità, this laid-back *pensione* has cool, white rooms, a pretty entrance courtyard with lemon and olive trees, and a roof terrace that commands views of the sea and the volcano. Two larger rooms with air-con cost extra. Half-board is sometimes available (and required) in July and August.

🍴 Eating & Drinking

★ L'Osservatorio   PIZZA €
(☑ 338 1097830, 090 945 08 56; pizzas €7-12; ☺ 10.30am-late) Sure, you could eat a pizza in town, but come on – you're on Stromboli! Make the 45-minute, 2km uphill trek west of town to this pizzeria and you'll be rewarded with exceptional volcano views from an expansive panoramic terrace, best after sundown.

La Bottega del Marano   DELI €
(Via Vittorio Emanuele; snacks from €2; ☺ 8.30am-1pm & 4.30-8pm Mon-Sat) The per-

fect source for volcano-climbing provisions or a self-catering lunch, this reasonably priced neighbourhood grocery, five minutes west of the trekking agency offices, has a well-stocked deli case full of meats, cheeses, olives, artichokes and sun-dried tomatoes, plus shelves full of wine and awesomely tasty fresh-baked focaccias.

★ Punta Lena   SICILIAN €€
(☑ 090 98 62 04; Via Marina 8; meals €34-40; ☺ 12.15-2.30pm & 7-10.30pm early May–mid-Oct) For a romantic outing, head to this family run waterfront restaurant with cheerful blue decor, fresh flowers, lovely sea views and the soothing sound of waves lapping in the background. The food is as good as you'll get anywhere on the island, with signature dishes including fresh seafood and spaghetti *alla stromboliana* (with wild fennel, cherry tomatoes and breadcrumbs).

Pardès   WINE BAR
(Via Vittorio Emanuele 81; ☺ 10.30am-2.30pm & 6-10pm mid-Mar–Oct; ☎) This wine bar/cafe has pleasant seating indoors and on an outdoor terrace where you can sip coffee or wine while using its wi-fi (it's one of the few places on the island with reliable internet access).

ⓘ Information

Bring enough cash for your stay on Stromboli. Many businesses don't accept credit cards, and the village's lone ATM on Via Roma is sometimes out of service. Internet access is limited and slow; your best bet for wi-fi is the wine bar/cafe Pardès (p189), five to 10 minutes west of Stromboli's main church.

ⓘ Getting There & Away

Ustica Lines (☑ 090 98 60 03; www.ustica lines.it) and **Siremar** (☑ 090 98 60 16; www. siremar.it) offer hydrofoil service to/from Lipari (€16.80, 50 minutes to 1¾ hours), Salina (€15.50, one hour) and all the other Aeolian islands. Ticket offices for both companies are at Stromboli's port. Siremar also operates one direct early morning hydrofoil from Milazzo (€22.45, 1¼ hours), along with twice weekly ferry service to Naples and the other Aeolians. Another option is to visit Stromboli on an all-inclusive day trip from Lipari.

IONIAN COAST

Magnificent, overdeveloped, crowded – and exquisitely beautiful – the Ionian coast is among Sicily's most popular tourist destinations and home to 20% of the island's population. Moneyed entrepreneurs have built their villas and hotels up and down the coastline, eager to bag a spot on Sicily's version of the Amalfi Coast. Above it all towers the muscular peak of Mt Etna (3329m), puffs of smoke billowing from its snow-covered cone.

Taormina

POP 11,100 / ELEV 204M

Spectacularly situated on a terrace of Monte Tauro, with views westwards to Mt Etna, Taormina is a beautiful small town, reminiscent of Capri or an Amalfi coastal resort. Over the centuries, Taormina has seduced an exhaustive line of writers and artists, aristocrats and royalty, and these days it's host to a summer arts festival that packs the town with international visitors.

Perched on its eyrie, Taormina is sophisticated, chic and comfortably cushioned by some serious wealth – far removed from the banal economic realities of other Sicilian towns. But the charm is not manufactured. The capital of Byzantine Sicily in the 9th century, Taormina is an almost perfectly preserved medieval town, and, if you can tear yourself away from the shopping and sunbathing, it has a wealth of small but perfect tourist sites. Taormina is also a popular resort with gay men.

Be warned that in July and August the town and its surrounding beaches swarm with tourists.

◎ Sights

A short walk uphill from the bus station brings you to Corso Umberto I, a pedestrianised thoroughfare that traverses the length of the medieval town and connects its two historic town gates, Porta Messina and Porta Catania.

★**Teatro Greco**   RUIN

(☑ 0942 2 32 20; Via Teatro Greco; adult/reduced €8/4; ◎ 9am-1hr before sunset) Taormina's premier sight is this perfect horseshoe-shaped theatre, suspended between sea and sky, with Mt Etna looming on the southern horizon. Built in the 3rd century BC, it's the most dramatically situated Greek theatre in the world and the second largest in Sicily (after Syracuse). In summer, it's used to stage international arts and film festivals.

★**Corso Umberto**   AREA

Taormina's chief delight is wandering this pedestrian-friendly thoroughfare, lined with stylish boutiques and Renaissance palaces. Midway down, pause to revel in stunning panoramic views of Mt Etna and the coast from **Piazza IX Aprile** and visit the charming rococo **Chiesa San Giuseppe** (Piazza IX Aprile; ◎ 9am-7pm). Continue west through **Torre dell'Orologio**, the 12th-century clock tower, into **Piazza del Duomo**, home to an ornate baroque fountain (1635) that sports Taormina's symbol, a two-legged centaur with the bust of an angel.

Villa Comunale   PARK

(Parco Duchi di Cesarò; Via Bagnoli Croce; ◎ 9am-midnight summer, 9am-sunset winter) To escape the crowds, wander down to these stunningly sited public gardens. Created by Englishwoman Florence Trevelyan, they're a lush paradise of tropical plants and delicate flowers. There's also a children's play area.

Castelmola   VILLAGE

For eye-popping views of the coastline and Mt Etna, head for this hilltop village above Taormina, crowned by a ruined castle. Either walk (one hour) or take the hourly Interbus service (one way/return €1.90/3, 15 minutes). While you're up here, stop in for almond wine at **Bar Turrisi** (⊘9am-2am), a four-level bar with some rather cheeky decor.

Isola Bella
ISLAND

Southwest of Lido Mazzarò is the minuscule Isola Bella, set in a stunning cove with fishing boats. You can walk here in a few minutes but it's more fun to rent a small boat from Mazzarò and paddle round Capo Sant'Andrea.

🏃 Activities

Lido Mazzarò
BEACH

Many visitors to Taormina come only for the beach scene. To reach Lido Mazzarò, directly beneath Taormina, take the **funivia** (cable car; Via Luigi Pirandello; single ticket/day pass €3/10; ⊘every 15min 8.45am-1.30am Mon, 7.45am-1.30am Tue-Sun). This beach is well serviced with bars and restaurants; private operators charge a fee for umbrellas and deck chairs (usually about €10 per person per day).

Nike Diving Centre
DIVING

(☑339 1961559; www.diveniketaormina.com) Opposite Isola Bella, this dive centre offers a wide range of courses for children and adults.

✨ Festivals & Events

In addition to Taormina's well-established festivals, other recently launched summer cultural events include the **Taormina Opera Festival** (www.taorminafestival.org; ⊘mid-Jul–mid-Sep), **Italian Opera Taormina** (www.italianoperataormina.com; ⊘May-Oct) and **Taormina Lirica** (www.taorminalirica.it; ⊘Jun & Sep).

Taormina FilmFest
FILM

(www.taorminafilmfest.it; ⊘mid-Jun) Hollywood big shots arrive in mid-June for a week of film screenings, premieres and press conferences at the Teatro Greco.

Taormina Arte
PERFORMING ARTS

(www.taormina-arte.com; ⊘Jun-Sep) From June to September, this festival features opera, dance, theatre and music concerts with an impressive list of international names.

🛌 Sleeping

Taormina has plenty of luxurious accommodation although some less expensive places can be found. Many hotels offer discounted parking (from €10) at Taormina's two public parking lots.

Isoco Guest House
GUESTHOUSE €

(☑0942 2 36 79; www.isoco.it; Via Salita Branco 2; s €70-98, d €80-120; ⊘Mar-Nov; ❀@🛜) Charming and well-travelled multilingual owner Michele Scimone runs this welcoming, gay-friendly guesthouse. Each room is dedicated to an artist, from Botticelli to graffiti pop designer Keith Haring. Breakfast is served around a large table on the upstairs patio, while a pair of sunny terraces offer stunning sea views and a hot tub. Multinight or prepaid stays earn the best rates.

Hostel Taormina
HOSTEL €

(☑0942 62 55 05; www.hosteltaormina.com; Via Circonvallazione 13; dm €18-23, r €49-85; ❀🛜) Friendly and laid-back, this year-round hostel occupies a house with pretty tiled floors and a roof terrace commanding panoramic sea views. It's a snug, homey set-up with accommodation in three dorms, a private room and a couple of apartments. There's also a communal kitchen, a relaxed vibe, and the owners go out of their way to help.

Villa Nettuno
PENSION €

(☑0942 2 37 97; www.hotelvillanettuno.it; Via Pirandello 33; s €38-44, d €60-78, breakfast €4; ❀🛜) A throwback to another era, this conveniently located salmon-pink *pensione* has been run by the Sciglio family for seven decades. Its low prices reflect a lack of recent updates, but the pretty gardens, complete with olive trees and potted geraniums, and the sea views from the breakfast terrace, offer a measure of charm you won't find elsewhere at this price.

B&B Le Sibille
B&B €

(☑349 7262862; www.lesibille.net; Corso Umberto 187a; d €70-110, 4-person apt €110-140; ⊘Apr-Oct; @🛜) This B&B wins points for its prime location on Taormina's pedestrian thoroughfare and its rooftop breakfast terrace. Three doubles with small balconies overlooking Corso Umberto are complemented by a pair of modern apartments done up with Ikea furniture and colourfully tiled bathrooms. Light sleepers beware: the street below can get noisy with holidaymakers!

⭐ Hotel Villa Belvedere
HOTEL €€€

(☑094 22 37 91; www.villabelvedere.it; Via Bagnoli Croce 79; d €211-511; ⊘Mar-late Nov; ❀@🛜⊠) Built in 1902, the jaw-droppingly pretty Villa Belvedere was one of the original grand hotels, well-positioned with fabulous views and luxuriant gardens, which are a particular highlight. There is also a swimming pool

Taormina

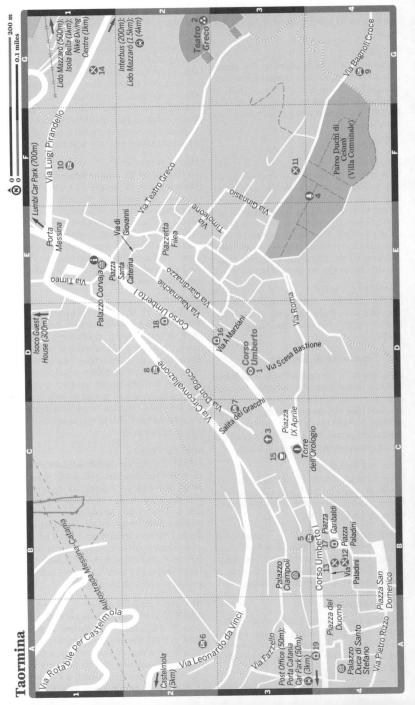

Taormina

◎ Top Sights
 1 Corso Umberto D3
 2 Teatro Greco G2

◎ Sights
 3 Chiesa San Giuseppe C3
 4 Villa Comunale F4

◎ Sleeping
 5 B&B Le Sibille...B3
 6 Casa Cuseni...A2
 7 Casa Turchetti.......................................C3
 8 Hostel Taormina...................................D2
 9 Hotel Villa Belvedere G4
 10 Villa Nettuno...F1

◎ Eating
 11 Andreas F3
 12 La Piazzetta..B4
 13 Tischi Toschi...B4
 14 Trattoria Da Nino................................G1

◎ Drinking & Nightlife
 15 Wunderbar Caffè..................................C3

◎ Shopping
 16 Carlo Mirella Panarello D3
 17 Kerameion..B4
 18 La Torinese...D2
 19 Pafumi...A4

SICILY TAORMINA

with a 100-year-old palm tree rising from a small island in the middle.

Casa Cuseni
B&B €€€

(☑094 22 83 62; www.casacuseni.com; Via Leonardo da Vinci 5; d €150, ste €250) Pre-booking is essential at this early-20th-century villa once frequented by Tennessee Williams, DH Lawrence, Greta Garbo and Bertrand Russell. Dripping with period character and surrounded by a seven-tiered garden with views out to the Ionian Sea and Mt Etna, it was recently opened as a B&B. It's only five minutes from Porta Catania but feels a world apart.

Casa Turchetti
B&B €€€

(☑094 262 50 13; www.casaturchetti.com; Salita dei Gracchi 18/20; d €220-260, junior ste €370; ❄️📶) Every detail is perfect at this painstakingly restored former music school converted to a luxurious B&B, on a back alley only two minutes above Piazza IX Aprile. Vintage furniture and fixtures, handcrafted woodwork and fine homespun sheets all contribute to the elegant feel; above all, guests appreciate the panoramic rooftop terrace, and the warmth of Sicilian hosts Pino and Francesca.

✗ Eating

Eating out in Taormina is expensive, and goes hand in hand with posing. Overpriced, touristy places abound.

★ Tischi Toschi
SICILIAN €€

(☑339 3642088; Via Paladini 3; meals €30-45; ☺1-3pm Tue-Sun, plus 7.30-11.30pm daily) With only eight tables and four people running the show, this family-run, Slow Food–acclaimed trattoria offers a level of creativity and attention to detail that's generally lacking in touristy Taormina. The limited menu of six *primi* and six *secondi* changes regularly based on what's in season, and is filled with regional specialities that you won't find elsewhere.

Add in a charming front patio on a sidestreet staircase and you'll understand why booking is advisable.

La Piazzetta
SICILIAN €€

(☑094 262 63 17; Via Paladini 5; meals €25; ☺closed Mon winter) Tucked into the corner of picturesque Piazza Paladini, this is an agreeable place to enjoy Sicilian classics from *pasta alla Norma* (pasta with basil, aubergine, ricotta and tomato) to fresh fish, all accompanied by a good list of local reds and whites.

Trattoria Da Nino
TRATTORIA €€

(☑0942 2 12 65; www.trattoriadaninotaormina. com; Via Luigi Pirandello 37; meals €25-35; ☺12.30-3pm & 7.30-11pm) Bright and bustling, this place has been in business under the same family ownership for 50 years. Locals and tourists alike flock here for straightforward, reasonably priced Sicilian home cooking, including an excellent *caponata* plus fresh local fish served grilled, steamed, fried, stewed or rolled up in *involtini*.

Andreas
MODERN SICILIAN €€€

(☑0942 2 40 11; Via Bagnoli Croce 88; meals €35-55; ☺1-2.30pm Wed-Sun, plus 8-11pm Tue-Sun) Accomplished chef Andreas Zangerl, a longtime fixture on Taormina's fine-dining scene at venues such as Casa Grugno and Hotel Metropole, opened this classy new restaurant in spring 2015. Culinary delights emerging from his kitchen celebrate the region's seafood, such as the beautifully presented appetiser of tuna prepared seven ways, or the delicious soup of fish, shellfish and wild fennel.

Drinking & Nightlife

Wunderbar Caffè CAFE
(☑ 0942 62 50 32; www.wunderbarcaffe.it; Piazza IX Aprile 7; ☺ 9am-11pm) A Taormina landmark since the *dolce vita* 1960s, this glamorous and achingly expensive cafe has served them all – Tennessee Williams, who liked to watch 'the squares go by', Greta Garbo, Richard Burton and Elizabeth Taylor. With tables spread over the vibrant piazza and white-jacketed waiters taking the orders, it is still very much the quintessential Taormina watering hole.

Shopping

Taormina is a window-shopper's paradise, especially along Corso Umberto. The quality in most places is high but don't expect any bargains.

Carlo Mirella Panarello CERAMICS
(Corso Umberto 122; ☺ 9am-1pm & 4-8.30pm) This eclectic shop is a fun place to browse for citrus-themed ceramics and Sicilian-style *coppole* (caps) in bold, colourful designs.

La Torinese FOOD, WINE
(Corso Umberto 59; ☺ 9.30am-1pm & 4-8.30pm Mon-Sat, 10am-1pm & 5-8.30pm Sun) Stock up on local olive oil, capers, marmalade, honey and wine. Smash-proof bubble wrapping helps to bring everything home in one piece.

Pafumi JEWELLERY
(Corso Umberto 251; ☺ 10am-9pm) Made in Sicily and not sold anywhere off the island, the colourful earrings, bracelets and pendants of the Isola Bella jewellery line are reason enough to browse at this shop near Porta Catania. Other Italian lines are also well represented.

Kerameion CERAMICS
(www.kerameion.com; Corso Umberto 198; ☺ 9am-1pm & 3-8pm Mon-Sat) Three local artists run this shop specialising in colourful Sicilian tiles and made-to-order ceramics.

ⓘ Information

Ospedale San Vincenzo (☑ 094 257 92 97; Contrada Sirina) Downhill, 2km from the centre.
Police Station (☑ 094 261 02 01; Corso Umberto 219)

Tourist Office (☑ 0942 2 32 43; Palazzo Corvaja, Piazza Santa Caterina; ☺ 8.30am-2.15pm & 3.30-6.45pm Mon-Fri year-round, 9am-1pm & 4-6.30pm Sat Apr-Oct, 9am-1pm Sun Jun-Sep) Has plenty of practical information.

ⓘ Getting There & Around

BUS

Bus is the easiest way to reach Taormina. **Interbus** (www.interbus.it; Via Luigi Pirandello) goes to Messina (€4.30, 55 minutes to 1¾ hours, six daily Monday to Saturday, one on Sunday) and Catania (€5.10, 1¼ hours, hourly), the latter continuing to Catania's Fontanarossa airport (€8.20, 1½ hours).

CAR & MOTORCYCLE

Taormina is on the A18 autostrada and the SS114 between Messina and Catania. Driving near the historic centre is a complete nightmare and Corso Umberto is closed to traffic. The most convenient places to leave your car are the **Porta Catania car park** (per 24hr €15), at the western end of Corso Umberto, or the **Lumbi car park** (per 24hr €13.50) north of the centre, connected to Porta Messina (at Corso Umberto's eastern end) by a five-minute walk or a free yellow shuttle bus. Both car parks charge the same rates.

TRAIN

There are frequent trains to and from Messina (€3.95, 45 minutes to 1¼ hours) and Catania (€3.95, 45 minutes to one hour), but the awkward location of Taormina's station (a steep 4km below town) is a strong disincentive. If you arrive this way, catch a taxi (€15) or an Interbus coach (€1.90, 20 minutes, half hourly) up to town.

Catania

POP 296,000

Sicily's second biggest metropolis, Catania is a city of grit and raw energy, a thriving, entrepreneurial centre with a large university and a cosmopolitan urban culture. Yes, it has its rough edges, but it's hard not to love a city with a smiling elephant gracing its central square and gorgeous snowcapped Mt Etna floating on the horizon. Catania is a true city of the volcano, much of it constructed from the lava that poured down the mountain and engulfed the city in Etna's massive 1669 eruption. It is also lava-black in colour, as if a fine dusting of soot permanently covers its elegant buildings, most of which are the work of baroque master Giovanni Vaccarini.

In recent years, Catania has made steady moves to pedestrianise its historic centre, which you'll appreciate as you stroll the streets between Via Crociferi, Via Etnea and Piazza del Duomo, where most of the city's attractions are concentrated.

◉ Sights

If you're visiting multiple attractions or travelling frequently by bus and metro, consider picking up a **Catania Pass** (www.cataniapass.it; 1-/3-/5-day pass individual €12.50/16.50/20, family €23/30.50/38), which offers free museum admissions and unlimited use of public transport.

Piazza del Duomo   SQUARE
A Unesco World Heritage Site, Catania's central piazza is a set piece of contrasting lava and limestone, surrounded by buildings in the unique local baroque style and crowned by the grand Cattedrale di Sant'Agata (p195). At its centre stands **Fontana dell'Elefante** (1736), a naive, smiling black-lava elephant dating from Roman times, surmounted by an improbable Egyptian obelisk. Another fountain at the piazza's southwest corner, **Fontana dell'Amenano**, marks the entrance to Catania's fish market.

★ La Pescheria   MARKET
(Via Pardo; ⊙7am-2pm Mon-Sat) Catania's raucous fish market, which takes over the streets behind Piazza del Duomo every workday morning, is street theatre at its most thrilling. Tables groan under the weight of decapitated swordfish, ruby-pink prawns and trays full of clams, mussels, sea urchins and all manner of mysterious sea life. Fishmongers gut silvery fish and high-heeled housewives step daintily over pools of blood-stained water. It's absolutely riveting. Surrounding the market are a number of good seafood restaurants.

★ Graeco-Roman Theatre & Odeon   RUIN
(Via Vittorio Emanuele II 262; adult/reduced incl Casa Liberti €6/3; ⊙9am-7pm Mon-Sat, to 1.30pm Sun) These twin theatres west of Piazza del Duomo are Catania's most impressive Graeco-Roman ruins. Both are picturesquely sited in the thick of a crumbling residential neighbourhood, with laundry occasionally flapping on the rooftops of vine-covered buildings that appear to have sprouted organically from the half-submerged stage. Adjacent to the main theatre is the **Casa Liberti**, an elegantly restored 19th-century

palazzo with tiled floors and red wallpaper. It now houses two millennia worth of artefacts discovered during excavation of the theatres.

★ Teatro Massimo Bellini   THEATRE
(⊙095 730 61 11; www.teatromassimobellini.it; Via Perrotta 12; guided tours adult/reduced €6/3; ⊙tours 9.30am-noon Tue-Sat) A few blocks northeast of the *duomo*, this gorgeous opera house forms the centrepiece of Piazza Bellini. Square and opera house alike were named after composer Vincenzo Bellini, the father of Catania's vibrant modern musical scene.

Cattedrale di Sant'Agata   CATHEDRAL
(⊙095 32 00 44; Piazza del Duomo; ⊙8am-noon & 4-7pm) Inside the vaulted interior of this cathedral, beyond its impressive marble facade sporting two orders of columns taken from the Roman amphitheatre, lie the relics of the city's patron saint. Consider visiting the **Museo Diocesano** (www.museodiocesanocatania.com; Piazza del Duomo; adult/reduced museum only €7/4, museum & baths €10/6; ⊙9am-2pm Mon, Wed & Fri, 9am-2pm & 3-6pm Tue & Thu, 9am-1pm Sat) next door for access to the Roman baths directly underneath the church and fine views from the roof terrace beneath the cathedral's dome.

Museo Belliniano   MUSEUM
(⊙095 715 05 35; Piazza San Francesco 3; adult/reduced €5/2; ⊙9am-7pm Mon-Sat, to 1pm Sun) One of Italy's great opera composers, Vincenzo Bellini was born in Catania in 1801. The house he grew up in has since been converted into this museum, which boasts an interesting collection of memorabilia, including original scores, photographs, pianos once played by Bellini, and the maestro's death mask.

Castello Ursino   CASTLE
Catania's forbidding 13th-century castle once guarded the city from atop a seafront cliff. However, the 1669 eruption of Mt Etna changed the landscape and the whole area to the south was reclaimed by the lava, leaving the castle completely landlocked. The castle now houses the **Museo Civico** (⊙095 34 58 30; Piazza Federico II di Svevia; adult/reduced €6/3; ⊙9am-6pm Mon-Sat, to 1pm Sun), home to the valuable archaeological collection of the Biscaris, Catania's most important aristocratic family. Exhibits include colossal classical sculpture, Greek vases and some fine mosaics.

Catania

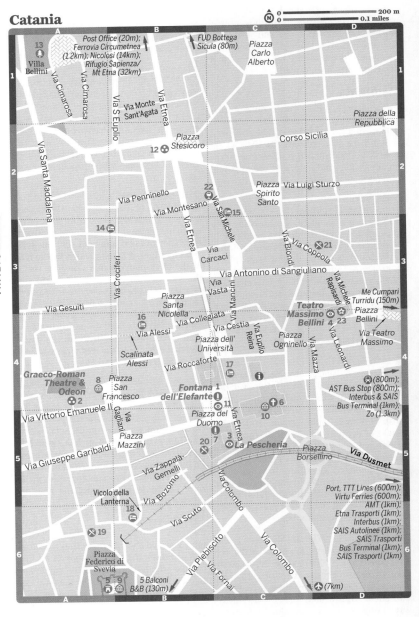

Post Office (20m);
Ferrovia Circumetnea
(1.2km); Nicolosi (14km);
Rifugio Sapienza/
Mt Etna (32km)

FUD Bottega
Sicula (80m)

SICILY CATANIA

Villa Bellini
PARK
(☺8am-8pm) Escape the madding crowd and enjoy the fine views of Mt Etna from these lovely gardens along Via Etnea.

Roman Amphitheatre
RUIN
The modest ruins of this Roman theatre, below street level in Piazza Stesicoro, are worth a quick look.

Catania

◎ Top Sights
1 Fontana dell'Elefante...................................C4
2 Graeco-Roman Theatre &
    Odeon...A4
3 La Pescheria..C5
4 Teatro Massimo Bellini.............................D4

◎ Sights
5 Castello Ursino...A6
6 Cattedrale di Sant'Agata C4
7 Fontana dell'Amenano...........................C5
8 Museo Belliniano.......................................A4
9 Museo Civico...B6
10 Museo Diocesano C4
11 Piazza del Duomo C4
12 Roman Amphitheatre............................B2
13 Villa Bellini..A1

◎ Sleeping
14 B&B Crociferi..B3
15 B&B Faro...C2
16 Il Principe..B4
17 Ostello degli Elefanti.............................C4
18 Palazzu Stidda...B6

◎ Eating
19 Da Antonio..A6
20 Osteria Antica Marina...........................B5
21 Trattoria di De Fiore...............................D3

◎ Drinking & Nightlife
22 Razmataz...C2

◎ Entertainment
23 Teatro Massimo Bellini.........................D4

⚜ Festivals & Events

If visiting Catania in February or early March, don't miss **Carnevale** (www.carnevale acireale.com; ⊘ Feb) in nearby Acireale, one of Sicily's most colourful festivals.

Festa di Sant'Agata   RELIGIOUS
(www.festadisantagata.it; ⊘ 3-5 Feb) In Catania's biggest religious festival (3-5 February), one million Catanians follow the Fercolo (a silver reliquary bust of St Agata) along the main street of the city accompanied by spectacular fireworks.

⊨ Sleeping

Catania is served by a good range of reasonably priced accommodation, making it an excellent base for exploring the Ionian coast and Etna.

★ B&B Crociferi   B&B €
(☑ 095 715 22 66; www.bbcrociferi.it; Via Crociferi 81; d €75-85, tr €100-110, apt €135; 🟦🤝) Perfectly positioned on pedestrianised Via Crociferi, this B&B in a beautifully decorated family home affords easy access to all the attractions of Catania's historic centre. Three palatial rooms (each with private bathroom across the hall) feature high ceilings, antique tiles, frescoes and artistic accoutrements from the owners' travels. There's also a glorious four-bed upstairs apartment with panoramic terrace. Book ahead.

★ Palazzu Stidda   APARTMENT €
(☑ 095 34 88 26; www.palazzu-stidda.com; Vicolo della Lanterna 5; s €40-60, d €70-100, q €130-150; 🤝🏠) Creative, multilingual young hosts Giovanni and Patricia have poured their hearts into creating these three family friendly apartments on a peaceful dead-end alley, with all the comforts of home plus a host of whimsical touches. Each has a flowery mini-balcony, and all are decorated with the owners' artwork, handmade furniture, family heirlooms and vintage finds.

Apartments 2 and 3 each come with a washing machine, kitchen, high chair and stroller, and ample space for a family of four. Apartment 1 is smaller and costs €10 to €20 less. Check the website for seasonal variations in price.

5 Balconi B&B   B&B €
(☑ 095 723 45 34; www.5balconi.it; Via Plebiscito 133; s/d without bathroom €35/50, with air-con €45/60; 🟦🤝) The warm and generous hospitality of British-Sicilian hosts Rob and Cristina more than compensates for the slightly out-of-centre location at this lovingly remodelled antique *palazzo* in a workaday neighbourhood near Castello Ursino. Three high-ceilinged rooms share a pair of bathrooms; breakfast features fresh-baked croissants and organic fruit. Be advised that the street out front gets lots of traffic.

Ostello degli Elefanti   HOSTEL €
(☑ 095 226 56 91; www.ostellodeglielefanti.it; Via Etnea 28; dm €18-24, s €38-40, d €58-70; 🟦🤝) Housed in a 17th-century *palazzo* a stone's throw from the Duomo, this brand-new hostel offers incredible location and value. Three dorms and one private room have frescoed high ceilings and panoramic balconies, with reading lights, USB ports and curtains for every bed. The marble-floored former ballroom doubles as a restaurant-lounge, while

the rooftop terrace-bar offers incomparable Etna vistas.

B&B Faro
B&B €

(☑ 349 4578856; www.bebfaro.it; Via San Michele 26; s/d/tr €50/80/100; ❄ @) Polished wood floors, double-glazed windows, modern bathroom fixtures, antique tiles and bold colours characterise this stylish, artist-owned B&B. Suites can sometimes be booked for the price of a double during slower periods, free bikes are provided for guests' use, and there's a studio downstairs where visiting artists are invited to come and paint.

Il Principe
HOTEL €€

(☑ 095 250 03 45; www.ilprincipehotel.com; Via Alessi 20/26; d €94-174, ste €254-314; ❄ @ ☎) This boutique-style hotel in an 18th-century building features luxurious rooms and two-level suites on one of the liveliest nightlife streets in town (thank goodness for double glazing!). Perks include international cable TV, free wi-fi and fluffy bathrobes to wear on your way to the Turkish steam bath. Check online for special rates.

🍴 Eating

Popular street snacks in Catania include *arancini* (fried rice balls filled with meat, cheese, tomatoes and/or peas) and *seltz* (fizzy water with fresh-squeezed lemon juice and natural fruit syrup). Don't leave town without trying *pasta alla Norma* (pasta with basil, aubergine and ricotta), a Catania original named after Bellini's opera *Norma*.

Da Antonio
TRATTORIA €

(☑ 347 8330636; www.facebook.com/Trattoria DaAntonio; Via Castello Ursino 59; meals €19-25; ⊙ 12.30-2.30pm & 7.30-10pm Tue-Sun) This humble hideaway offers the quintessential trattoria experience: reasonably priced, delicious food served by unpretentious waitstaff. Despite having made inroads onto the tourist radar, it's still the kind of place where well-dressed local families come for Sunday lunch. The menu revolves around local fish, homemade pasta and classic Sicilian desserts featuring ricotta, pistachios, almonds and wild strawberries.

Trattoria di De Fiore
TRATTORIA €

(☑ 095 31 62 83; Via Coppola 24/26; meals €15-25; ⊙ 1-3pm & 7-11pm Tue-Sun) For over 50 years, septuagenarian chef Rosanna has been recreating her great-grandmother's recipes, including the best *pasta alla Norma* you'll taste anywhere in Sicily.

Service is excruciatingly slow, but for patient souls this is a rare chance to experience classic Catanian cooking from a bygone era. Don't miss Rosanna's trademark *zeppoline* (sugar-sprinkled ricotta-lemon fritters) at dessert time.

FUD Bottega Sicula
BURGERS €

(☑ 095 715 35 18; www.fud.it; Via Santa Filomena 35; burgers, panini & pizzas €6-10; ⊙ noon-3pm & 7pm-1am) Sporting pavement seating on trendy Via Santa Filomena, this back-alley eatery epitomises youthful Catania's embrace of 'Sicilian fast food', made with high-quality, locally sourced ingredients (think extra-virgin olive oil, Sicilian cheeses, Nebrodi black pork). With wry humour, every burger, *panino* and pizza on the menu is spelled using Italian phonetics ('cis burgher' for cheeseburger, 'cicchen burgher' for chicken burger etc).

★ Osteria Antica Marina
SEAFOOD €€

(☑ 095 34 81 97; www.anticamarina.it; Via Pardo 29; meals €30-50; ⊙ 1-3pm & 8-11pm Thu-Tue) With a front terrace directly overlooking the fishmongers' stalls in the piazza below, this classy trattoria is *the* place to come for seafood. A variety of tasting menus ranging from €25 to €45 showcase everything from swordfish to scampi, cuttlefish to calamari. All menus start with a dazzling array of fishy appetisers and end with divine lemon sorbet. Reservations are essential.

Me Cumpari Turridu
SICILIAN €€

(☑ 095 715 01 42; Via Ventimiglia 15; meals €27-40; ⊙ 1-2.30pm daily, plus 8-11.30pm Mon-Sat) A quirky little spot that mixes tradition and modernity both in food and decor, this place is a real discovery. Try the ricotta and marjoram ravioli in a pork sauce, or the cannellini with donkey-meat *ragù* (meat and tomato sauce). Vegetarians can opt for the Ustica lentil stew, with broad beans and fennel. Slow Food–recommended.

🍷 Drinking & Nightlife

Not surprisingly for a busy university town, Catania has a reputation for its effervescent nightlife. Areas that bustle with activity after dark include Via Montesano, Via Teatro Massimo, the steps at the western end of Via Alessi, and recent local favourite Via Santa Filomena.

★ Razmataz
BAR

(☑ 095 31 18 93; Via Montesano 17; ⊙ 8.30am-late) Wines by the glass, draught and bottled beer and an ample cocktail list are offered at this delightful wine bar with tables invitingly spread out across the tree-shaded flagstones of a sweet backstreet square. It doubles as a cafe in the morning, but really gets packed with locals from *aperitivo* time onward.

Entertainment

For a current calendar of music, theatre and arts events around Catania, check the website www.lapisnet.it/catania.

Teatro Massimo Bellini   THEATRE
(☑095 730 61 11; www.teatromassimobellini. it; Via Perrotta 12) Catania's premier theatre is named after the city's most famous son, composer Vincenzo Bellini. Sporting the full red-and-gilt look, it stages a year-round season of opera and an eight-month program of classical music from November to June. Tickets, which are available online, start at around €13 and rise to €84 for a first-night front-row seat.

Zo   PERFORMING ARTS
(☑095 816 89 12; www.zoculture.it; Piazzale Asia 6) Part of the very cool Le Ciminiere complex (housed in Catania's former sulphur works), Zo is dedicated to promoting contemporary art and performance. It hosts an eclectic program of events ranging from club nights, concerts and film screenings to art exhibitions, dance performances, installations and theatre workshops. Check the website for upcoming events, many of which are free of charge.

ℹ Information

Ospedale Vittorio Emanuele (☑091 743 54 52; www.policlinicovittorioemanuele.it; Via Plebiscito 628) Has a 24-hour emergency doctor.

Questura (☑095 736 71 11; Piazza Santa Nicolella 8) Police station.

Tourist Office (☑095 742 55 73; www.comune.catania.it; Via Vittorio Emanuele 172; ⊙8am-7.15pm Mon-Sat) Very helpful city-run tourist office.

ℹ Getting There & Away

AIR

Catania's airport, **Fontanarossa** (☑095 723 91 11; www.aeroporto.catania.it), is 7km southwest of the city centre. Alibus 457, operated by **AMT** (☑095 751 91 11; www.amt.ct.it), runs half hourly between 5.30am and midnight from the airport to Catania's central train station (€4, 30 minutes). **Etna Trasporti/Interbus** (☑095 53

03 96; www.interbus.it; Via d'Amico 187) also runs a regular shuttle from the airport to Taormina (€8.20, 1½ hours, hourly 7.45am to 8.45pm). Stops for both buses are to the right as you exit the arrivals hall. All the main car-hire companies are represented at the airport.

BOAT

The ferry terminal is located southwest of the train station along Via VI Aprile.

TTT Lines (☑800 627414, 095 34 85 86; www.tttlines.info) TTT Lines runs nightly ferries from Catania to Naples (from €42, 11 hours).

Virtu Ferries (☑095 703 12 11; www.virtuferries.com) From May through September, Virtu Ferries runs daily ferries from Pozzallo (south of Catania) to Malta (1¾ hours). Fares vary depending on length of stay in Malta (same-day return €85 to €136, open return €113 to €161 depending on the season). Coach transfer between Catania and Pozzallo (€10 each way) adds 2½ hours to the journey.

BUS

All long-distance buses leave from a terminal 250m north of the train station, with ticket offices across the street on Via d'Amico.

Interbus (☑095 53 03 96; www.interbus.it; Via d'Amico 187) runs buses to:
➜ **Piazza Armerina** (€9.20, 1¾ hours, two to four daily)
➜ **Ragusa** (€8.60, two hours, five to 12 daily)
➜ **Syracuse** (€6.20, 1½ hours, hourly Monday to Friday, fewer on weekends)
➜ **Taormina** (€5.10, 1¼ hours, hourly)

SAIS Trasporti (☑090 601 21 36; http://saistrasporti.it; Via d'Amico 181) goes to:
➜ **Agrigento** (€13.40, three hours, nine to 14 daily)
➜ **Rome** (€49, 10½ hours) Overnight service.

Its sister company **SAIS Autolinee** (☑095 53 61 68; www.saisautolinee.it; Via d'Amico 183) runs services to:
➜ **Messina** (€8.40, 1½ hours, hourly)
➜ **Palermo** (€12, 2¾ hours, eight to 10 daily)

CAR & MOTORCYCLE

Catania is easily reached from Messina on the A18 autostrada and from Palermo on the A19 – although travel on the latter was recently disrupted by an April 2015 viaduct collapse (see box p176). From either autostrada, signs for the centre of Catania will bring you to Via Etnea.

TRAIN

From Catania Centrale station on Piazza Papa Giovanni XXIII there are frequent trains.

Messina (€7, 1½ to two hours, hourly)
Palermo (€12.50, three hours, seven daily, three on Sunday)

SICILY CATANIA

Syracuse (€6.35 to €10, 1¼ hours, 10 daily, four on Sunday)

The private Ferrovia Circumetnea (p201) train circles Mt Etna, stopping at towns and villages on the volcano's slopes.

🚉 Getting Around

Several useful AMT city buses (p199) terminate in front of the train station, including buses 1-4 and 4-7 (both running hourly from the station to Via Etnea) and Alibus 457 (station to airport every 25 minutes from 4.40am to midnight). Also useful is bus D, which runs from Piazza Borsellino (just south of the *duomo*) to the local beaches.

Catania's one-line metro currently has only six stops, all on the periphery of town. For tourists, it's mainly useful as a way to get from the central train station to the Circumetnea train that goes around Mt Etna.

A 90-minute ticket for either bus or metro costs €1. A two-hour combined ticket for both costs €1.20.

For drivers, some words of warning: there are complicated one-way systems around the city and the centre is increasingly pedestrianised, which means parking is scarce. Furthermore, there's been a recent increase in organised petty theft from tourists driving through town; if you do drive, keep your doors and windows locked.

For a taxi, call **Radio Taxi Catania** (☑ 095 33 09 66; www.radiotaxicatania.org).

Mt Etna

ELEV 3329M

Dominating the landscape of eastern Sicily and visible from the moon (if you happen to be there), Mt Etna is Europe's largest volcano and one of the world's most active. Eruptions occur frequently, both from the volcano's four summit craters and from its slopes, which are littered with fissures and old craters. The volcano's most devastating eruptions occurred in 1669 and lasted 122 days. Lava poured down Etna's southern slope, engulfing much of Catania and dramatically altering the landscape. The volcano's most destructive recent eruption came in 2002, when lava flows caused an explosion in Sapienza, destroying two buildings and temporarily halting the cable-car service. Less destructive eruptions continue to occur regularly, and locals understandably keep a close eye on the smouldering peak.

Enshrined as a Unesco World Heritage Site in 2013, the volcano is surrounded by the huge **Parco dell'Etna**, the largest un-spoilt wilderness remaining in Sicily. The park encompasses a remarkable variety of environments, from the severe, almost surreal, summit to deserts of lava and alpine forests.

👁 Sights & Activities

The southern approach to Mt Etna presents the easier ascent to the **craters**. The AST bus from Catania drops you off at **Rifugio Sapienza** (1923m) from where the **Funivia dell'Etna** (☑ 095 91 41 41; www.funiviaetna.com; return €35, incl bus & guide €65; ☺ 9am-5.45pm Apr-Nov, to 3.45pm Dec-Mar) cable car runs up the mountain to 2500m. From the upper cable-car station it's a 3½- to four-hour return trip up the winding track to the authorised crater zone (2920m). Make sure you leave enough time to get up *and* down before the last cable car leaves at 4.45pm. You can pay an extra €30 for a guided 4WD tour to take you up from the cable car to the crater zone, but the guides provided by the Funivia tend to be perfunctory at best, and you'll have more freedom to explore if you go it alone.

An alternative ascent is from **Piano Provenzano** (1800m) on Etna's northern flank. This area was severely damaged during the 2002 eruptions, as still evidenced by the bleached skeletons of the surrounding pine trees. To reach Piano Provenzano you'll need a car, as there's no public transport beyond Linguaglossa, 16km away.

👣 Tours

Several Catania-based companies offer private excursions up the mountain.

Gruppo Guide Alpine Etna Sud WALKING
(☑ 095 791 47 55; www.etnaguide.com) The official guide service on Etna's southern flank, with an office just below Rifugio Sapienza.

Gruppo Guide Alpine Etna Nord WALKING
(☑ 095 777 45 02; www.guidetnanord.com) Offers volcano guide service from Linguaglossa on Etna's northern flank.

🛏 Sleeping & Eating

There's plenty of B&B accommodation around Mt Etna, particularly in the small, pretty town of Nicolosi. Contact Nicolosi's tourist information office for a full list.

Agriturismo San Marco AGRITURISMO €
(☑ 389 4237294; www.agriturismosanmarco.com; Rovittello; per person B&B/half-board/full board €35/53/68; 🕸 ❄ 👬) Get back to basics at this

delightful *agriturismo* near Rovittello, on Etna's northern flank. The bucolic setting, rustic rooms, swimming pool, kids' play area and superb country cooking make it a relaxed place to kick back for a couple of days. Call ahead for directions.

Rifugio Sapienza CHALET €

(☑ 095 91 53 21; www.rifugiosapienza.com; Piazzale Funivia; s/d €46/92; ☎) Offering comfortable accommodation with a good restaurant, this place adjacent to the cable car is the closest lodging to Etna's summit.

❶ Information

Catania's downtown tourist office provides information about Etna, as does the Parco dell'Etna office on the mountain's southern flank.

Parco dell'Etna (☑ 095 82 11 11; www.parco etna.ct.it; Via del Convento 45, Nicolosi; ⏰9am-2pm & 4-7.30pm) About 1km from the centre of Nicolosi.

❶ Getting There & Away

BUS

AST (☑ 095 723 05 35; www.aziendasiciliana trasporti.it) runs one bus daily from Catania to Rifugio Sapienza (one way/return €4/6.60, two hours), leaving the car park opposite Catania's train station at 8.15am and arriving at Rifugio Sapienza at 10.15am. The return journey leaves Rifugio Sapienza at 4.30pm, arriving at Catania at 6.30pm.

TRAIN

You can circle Etna on the private **Ferrovia Circumetnea** (FCE; ☑ 095 54 11 11; www.circum etnea.it; Via Caronda 352a, Catania) train line. Catch the metro from Catania's main train station to the FCE station at Via Caronda (metro stop Borgo) or take bus 429 or 432 going up Via Etnea and ask to be let off at the Borgo metro stop.

The train follows a 114km trail around the base of the volcano, providing lovely views. It also passes through many of Etna's unique towns such as Adrano, Bronte and Randazzo. See the website for fares and timetables.

SYRACUSE & THE SOUTHEAST

Home to Sicily's most beautiful baroque towns and Magna Graecia's most magnificent ancient city, the southeast is one of Sicily's most compelling destinations. The classical charms of Syracuse are reason enough to visit, but once you leave the city behind you'll find an evocative checkerboard of river valleys and stone-walled citrus groves dotted with handsome towns.

Shattered by a devastating earthquake in 1693, the towns of Noto, Ragusa and Modica are the superstars here, rebuilt in the ornate and much-lauded Sicilian baroque style that lends the region a cohesive aesthetic appeal. Writer Gesualdo Bufalino described the southeast as an 'island within an island'; indeed, this pocket of Sicily has a remote, genteel air – a legacy of its glorious Greek heritage.

Syracuse

POP 124,000

A dense tapestry of overlapping cultures and civilisations, Syracuse is one of Sicily's most appealing cities. Settled by colonists from Corinth in 734 BC, this was considered to be the most beautiful city of the ancient world, rivalling Athens in power and prestige. Under the demagogue Dionysius the Elder, the city reached its zenith, attracting luminaries such as Livy, Plato, Aeschylus and Archimedes, and cultivating the sophisticated urban culture that was to see the birth of comic Greek theatre.

Arriving in today's drab modern downtown by train or bus, you could be excused for wondering what all the fuss is about. But cross the bridge to the ancient island neighbourhood of Ortygia, and Syracuse's irresistible appeal quickly becomes manifest: in the ancient Greek temple columns peeking out from the baroque walls of Ortygia's cathedral; the throngs of locals and tourists mingling in the reflected evening glow of Piazza del Duomo's vast marble pavements; the flash of fish swimming amidst the papyrus plants in the Fontana Aretusa; and the splash of sunbathers plunging off rocks into the blue Ionian Sea. Adding to the city's magic is Syracuse's annual theatre festival, where classical Greek dramas are staged in one of the Mediterranean's greatest surviving ancient theatres.

Add to this the city's ambitious and enlightened moves towards pedestrian-friendly measures and environmental sustainability (including the 2014 launch of a new fleet of electric minibuses), and you'll begin to understand why this has become Sicily's number one tourist destination. Syracuse is truly a city to savour.

Syracuse

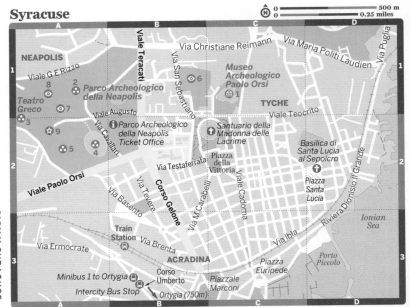

Syracuse

◎ Top Sights
1 Museo Archeologico Paolo Orsi C1
2 Parco Archeologico della Neapolis A1
3 Teatro Greco A2

◎ Sights
4 Anfiteatro Romano A2

5 Ara di Gerone II A2
6 Catacombe di San Giovanni B1
7 Latomia del Paradiso A1
8 Orecchio di Dionisio A1

⊙ Entertainment
9 Fondazione Inda ticket booth A2

◉ Sights

◉ Ortygia

★ Duomo
CATHEDRAL

(Map p818; Piazza del Duomo; adult/reduced €2/1; ⊙9am-6.30pm Mon-Sat Apr-Oct, to 5.30pm Nov-Mar) Built on the skeleton of a 5th-century BC Greek temple to Athena (note the Doric columns still visible inside and out), Syracuse's cathedral became a church when the island was evangelised by St Paul. Its most striking feature is the columned baroque facade (1728–53) added by Andrea Palma after the 1693 earthquake. A statue of the Virgin Mary crowns the rooftop, in the same spot where a golden statue of Athena once served as a beacon to homecoming Greek sailors.

★ Fontana Aretusa
FOUNTAIN

(Map p204) Down the winding main street from the cathedral is this ancient spring, where fresh water still bubbles up just as it did in ancient times when it was the city's main water supply. Legend has it that the goddess Artemis transformed her beautiful handmaiden Aretusa into the spring to protect her from the unwelcome attention of the river god Alpheus.

La Giudecca
AREA

Simply walking through Ortygia's tangled maze of alleys is an atmospheric experience, especially down the narrow lanes of Via Maestranza, the heart of the old guild quarter, and the crumbling Jewish ghetto of Via della Giudecca. At the Alla Giudecca hotel you can visit an ancient Jewish miqwe (Ritual Bath; Map p204; ☎0931 2 22 55; Via Alagona 52; tours in English & Italian €5; ⊙hourly

9am-7pm mid-May–Sep, 11am, noon, 4pm, 5pm & 6pm Oct–mid-May) some 20m below ground level. Blocked up in 1492 when the Jewish community was expelled from Ortygia, the baths were rediscovered during renovation work at the hotel.

Galleria Regionale di Palazzo Bellomo
GALLERY

(Map p204; ☑ 0931 6 95 11; www.regione.sicilia.it/beniculturali/palazzobellomo; Via Capodieci 16; adult/reduced €8/4; ⊗ 9am-7pm Tue-Sat, 9am-1pm Sun) Housed in a 13th-century Catalan-Gothic palace, this art museum's eclectic collection ranges from early Byzantine and Norman stonework to 19th-century Caltagirone ceramics; in between, there's a good range of medieval religious paintings and sculpture.

Museo del Papiro
MUSEUM

(Map p204; ☑ 0931 2 21 00; www.museodelpapiro.it; Via Nizza 14; adult/reduced €5/2; ⊗ 9.15am-2pm Tue-Sun Oct-Apr, 10am-7pm Tue-Sat, 10am-2pm Sun May-Sep) Moved to Ortygia and newly expanded in 2014, this museum exhibits a nice collection of papyrus documents and products, boats and an English-language film about the history of papyrus. The plant grows in abundance around the Ciane River, near Syracuse, and was used to make paper here in the 18th century.

Castello Maniace
CASTLE

(Map p204; admission €2; ⊗ 9am-1.15pm Mon-Sat) Guarding the island's southern tip, Ortygia's 13th-century castle is a lovely place to wander, gaze out over the water and contemplate Syracuse's past glories. It also houses occasional rotating exhibitions.

◉ Mainland Syracuse

★ Parco Archeologico della Neapolis
ARCHAEOLOGICAL SITE

(Map p202; ☑ 0931 6 62 06; Viale Paradiso 14; adult/reduced €10/5, incl Museo Archeologico €13.50/7; ⊗ 9am-6.30pm) For the classicist, Syracuse's real attraction is this archaeological park, with its pearly white 5th-century-BC **Teatro Greco** (Map p202; Parco Archeologico della Neapolis). Hewn out of the rocky hillside, this 16,000-capacity amphitheatre staged the last tragedies of Aeschylus (including *The Persians*), which were first performed here in his presence. In late spring it's brought to life with an annual season of classical theatre.

Beside the theatre is the mysterious **Latomia del Paradiso** (Garden of Paradise; Map p202; Parco Archeologico della Neapolis), a deep, precipitous limestone quarry out of which stone for the ancient city was extracted. Riddled with catacombs and filled with citrus and magnolia trees, it's also where the 7000 survivors of the war between Syracuse and Athens in 413 BC were imprisoned. The **Orecchio di Dionisio** (Ear of Dionysius; Map p202; Latomia del Paradiso, Parco Archeologico della Neapolis), a 23m-high grotto extending 65m back into the cliffside, was named by Caravaggio after the tyrant Dionysius, who is said to have used the almost perfect acoustics of the quarry to eavesdrop on his prisoners.

Back outside this area you'll find the entrance to the 2nd-century **Anfiteatro Romano** (Map p202; Parco Archeologico della Neapolis), originally used for gladiatorial combats and horse races. The Spaniards, little interested in archaeology, largely destroyed the site in the 16th century, using it as a quarry to build Ortygia's city walls. West of the amphitheatre is the 3rd-century-BC **Ara di Gerone II** (Altar of Hieron II; Map p202; Parco Archeologico della Neapolis), a monolithic sacrificial altar to Heron II where up to 450 oxen could be killed at one time.

To reach the park, take Sd'A Trasporti minibus 2 (€0.50, 15 minutes) from Molo Sant'Antonio, on the west side of the main bridge into Ortygia. Alternatively, walking from Ortygia will take about 30 minutes. If driving, park on Viale Augusto (tickets are available at the nearby souvenir kiosks).

★ Museo Archeologico Paolo Orsi
MUSEUM

(Map p202; ☑ 0931 48 95 11; www.regione.sicilia.it/beniculturali/museopaoloorsi; Viale Teocrito 66; adult/reduced €8/4, incl Parco Archeologico €13.50/7; ⊗ 9am-6pm Tue-Sat, to 1pm Sun) About 500m east of the archaeological park, this modern museum contains one of Sicily's largest and most interesting archaeological collections. Allow plenty of time to investigate the four sectors charting the area's pre-history, as well as Syracuse's development from foundation to the late Roman period.

Catacombe di San Giovanni
CATACOMB

(Map p202; Largo San Marciano; adult/reduced €8/5; ⊗ 9.30am-12.30pm & 2.30-5.30pm Tue-Sun) A block north of the archaeological museum, this vast labyrinth of 10,000 underground tombs dates back to Roman times.

Ortygia

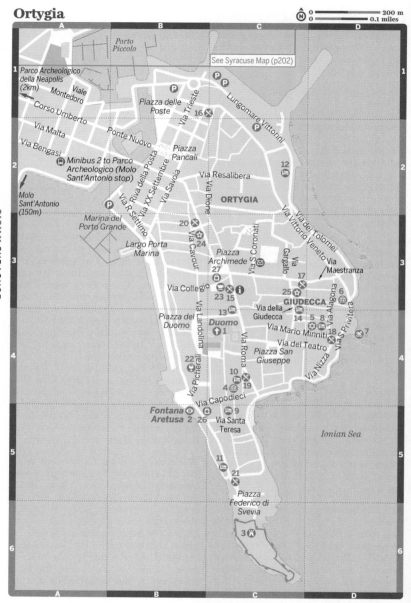

N
0 ————— 200 m
0 ————— 0.1 miles

See Syracuse Map (p202)

Porto Piccolo

Parco Archeologico della Neapolis (2km)

Viale Montedoro

Corso Umberto

Via Malta

Via Bengasi

Piazza delle Poste

Via Trieste

Lungomare Vittorini

Ponte Nuovo

Riva della Posta

Piazza Pancali

Minibus 2 to Parco Archeologico (Molo Sant'Antonio stop)

Molo Sant'Antonio (150m)

Via R Settimo

Via XX Settembre

Via Savoia

Via Resalibera

Via Dione

ORTYGIA

Marina del Porto Grande

Largo Porta Marina

Via Cavour

Piazza Archimede

Via S Coronati

Via Gargallo

Via del Tolomei

Via Vittorio Veneto

Via Maestranza

Via Collegio

Piazza del Duomo

Via Landolina

Duomo

Via della Giudecca

GIUDECCA

Via Mario Minniti

Via Alagona

Via Privitera

Via S Privitera

Via Roma

Piazza San Giuseppe

Via del Teatro

Via Picherali

Via Capodieci

Via Nizza

Fontana Aretusa

Via Santa Teresa

Ionian Sea

Piazza Federico di Svevia

SICILY SYRACUSE

A 30-minute guided tour ushers visitors through the catacombs as well as the atmospheric ruins of the **Basilica di San Giovanni**, Syracuse's earliest cathedral.

Activities

In midsummer, when Ortygia steams like a cauldron, people flock to the beaches south of town at **Arenella** (take bus 23 from Piazza della Posta) and **Fontane Bianche** (bus 21 or 22).

Ortygia

◉ Top Sights
1 Duomo...C4
2 Fontana Aretusa B5

◉ Sights
3 Castello Maniace.............................C6
4 Galleria Regionale di Palazzo
    Bellomo..C4
5 Miqwe...D4
6 Museo del Papiro D3

❸ Activities, Courses & Tours
7 Solarium Forte Vigliena.......................D4

⬛ Sleeping
8 Alla Giudecca..................................D4
9 Aretusa Vacanze.............................C5
10 B&B dei Viaggiatori, Viandanti e
    Sognatori......................................C4
11 Henry's House...................................C5
12 Hotel Gutkowski...............................C2
13 Hotel Roma.......................................C4

14 La Via della Giudecca...........................C4

⬤ Eating
15 A Putia delle Cose Buone......................C3
16 Caseificio Borderi................................B1
17 Don Camillo...C3
18 Il Blu...D4
19 Le Vin De L'Assassin Bistrot................C4
20 Sicilia in Tavola..................................B3
21 Taberna Sveva.....................................C5

⬤ Drinking & Nightlife
22 Barcollo..B4
23 Biblios Cafè...C3

⬤ Entertainment
24 Fondazione Inda ticket office.............B3
25 Piccolo Teatro dei Pupi......................C3

⬤ Shopping
26 Galleria Bellomo.................................B5
27 Massimo Izzo.......................................C3

★ **Solarium Forte Vigliena** SWIMMING
(Map p204) FREE Flanked by the crenellated walls of Forte Vigliena along Ortygia's eastern waterfront, this platform surrounded by flat rocks is a favourite local hang-out for swimming and sunbathing in the summer months.

⚜ Festivals & Events

★ **Ciclo di Rappresentazioni Classiche** THEATRE
(Festival of Greek Theatre; www.indafondazione. org; ⊘mid-May–Jun) Syracuse boasts the only school of classical Greek drama outside Athens, and in May and June it hosts live performances of Greek plays (in Italian) at the Teatro Greco, attracting Italy's finest performers. Tickets (€26 to €60) are available online, from the **Fondazione Inda ticket office** (Map p204; ☑0931 48 72 00; Corso Matteotti 29; ⊘10am-1pm Mon-Sat) in Ortygia or at the **ticket booth** (Map p202; ⊘10am-7pm) outside the theatre.

Festa di Santa Lucia RELIGIOUS
(⊘13 Dec) On 13 December, the enormous silver statue of the city's patron saint wends its way from the cathedral to Piazza Santa Lucia accompanied by fireworks.

⬛ Sleeping

Stay on Ortygia for atmosphere. Cheaper accommodation is located around the train station.

B&B dei Viaggiatori, Viandanti e Sognatori B&B €
(Map p204; ☑0931 2 47 81; www.bedandbreak fastsicily.it; Via Roma 156; s €35-50, d €55-70, tr €75-85, q €100; ✳️🛜) Decorated with verve and boasting a prime Ortygia location, this relaxed B&B exudes a homey boho feel, with books and antique furniture juxtaposed against bright walls. Rooms are colourful and imaginatively decorated, while up top, the sunny roof terrace offers sweeping sea views.

Aretusa Vacanze APARTMENT €
(Map p204; ☑0931 48 34 84; www.aretusavacanze. com; Vicolo Zuccalà 1; d €59-90, tr €70-120, q €105-147; P✳️@🛜) This great budget option, elbowed into a tiny pedestrian street in a 17th-century building, has large rooms and apartments with kitchenettes, computers, wi-fi, satellite TV and small balconies from where you can shake hands with your neighbour across the way.

★ **Hotel Gutkowski** HOTEL €€
(Map p204; ☑0931 46 58 61; www.guthotel.it; Lungomare Vittorini 26; s €60-80, d €75-140; ✳️@🛜) Book well in advance for one of the sea-view rooms at this calmly stylish hotel on the Ortygia waterfront, at the edge of La Giudecca neighbourhood. Rooms are divided between two buildings, both with pretty tiled floors, walls in teals, greys, blues and browns, and

with a minimal style and a mix of vintage and industrial details.

La Via della Giudecca
B&B €€

(Map p204; ☑ 389 6429934, 0931 6 84 46; www.laviadellagiudecca.it; Vicolo III alla Giudecca 4; d €70-120, with sea view €110-140, q €120-150; ❄@🛜) Founded in 2010, this charming, immaculate B&B rose phoenix-like from the ashes of a ruined older structure. Winning amenities include crisp white decor, wood floors, spacious rooms (three with sea-view balconies and several accommodating families), a prime location on a picturesque Giudecca piazza, and the warm reception of the Bellomo family (mother and daughters) who run the place.

Alla Giudecca
HOTEL €€

(Map p204; ☑ 0931 2 22 55; www.allagiudecca.it; Via Alagona 52; d €100-170; ❄@🛜) Located in the old Jewish quarter, this charming hotel boasts 23 suites with warm terracotta-tiled floors, exposed wood beams and lashings of heavy white linen. The communal areas are a warren of vaulted rooms full of museum-quality antiques and enormous tapestries, and feature cosy sofas gathered around huge fireplaces. A few more expensive rooms have sea views.

Hotel Roma
HOTEL €€

(Map p204; ☑ 0931 46 56 30; www.hotelroma siracusa.it; Via Roma 66; d €130-190; P❄@🛜) Within steps of Piazza del Duomo, this *palazzo* has rooms with parquet floors, oriental rugs, wood-beam ceilings and tasteful artwork, plus free bike use, a gym and a sauna.

★ Henry's House
HOTEL €€€

(Map p204; ☑ 0931 2 13 61; http://hotelhenrys house.com; Via del Castello Maniace 68; s €120-160, d €150-230, ste €250-330; ❄🛜) Spy this place from outside and you might mistake it for a private home hosting a party you wish you'd been invited to. Directly overlooking Ortygia's waterfront, with three communal sun terraces perfect for lounging and soaking up the views, this gorgeous 17th-century *palazzo* was lovingly restored by antique collector Signor Corsaro before opening as a hotel in 2014.

The result is by far the nicest new lodging to have sprouted on Ortygia in recent years, with superb customer service provided by gregarious English-speaking brothers Francesco and Alberto, newly returned from London to help their father run the place. If you're in a mood to splurge, spring for one of the two upstairs suites (one has a terrace, both enjoy full-on views of the water).

Eating

Ortygia is the best place to eat. Its narrow lanes are chock-full of trattorias, restaurants, cafes and bars, and while some are obvious tourist traps, there are plenty of quality options in the mix. Most places specialise in seafood.

Sicilia in Tavola
SICILIAN €

(Map p204; ☑ 392 4610889; Via Cavour 28; meals €20-30; ⊙12.30-2.30pm & 7.30-10.30pm Tue-Sun) One of the longest established and most popular eateries on Via Cavour, this tiny trattoria has built its reputation on delicious homemade pasta and seafood. To taste both at once, try the *fettuccine allo scoglio* (pasta ribbons with mixed seafood). Adding to the fun is a bustling atmosphere and the cheerful clutter that adorns the wooden walls. Reservations recommended.

Caseificio Borderi
SANDWICHES €

(Map p204; Via Emanuele de Benedictis 6; sandwiches €5; ⊙6am-5.30pm Mon-Sat) No visit to Syracuse's market is complete without a stop at this colourful cheese shop near Ortygia's far northern tip. Veteran sandwich-master Andrea Borderi stands out front with a table full of cheeses, olives, greens, herbs, tomatoes and other fixings and engages in non-stop banter with customers while creating free-form sandwiches big enough to keep you fed all day.

★ A Putia delle Cose Buone
SICILIAN €€

(Map p204; ☑ 0931 44 92 79; www.aputiadelle cosebuone.it; Via Roma 8; meals €21-33; ⊙1-3pm & 7-11pm) From the garden gnomes greeting you at the door to the benches draped in colourful pillows, this lovely place feels welcoming from the word go. Then there's the food: creative, reasonably priced Sicilian dishes that make ample use of local seafood, veggies and extra-virgin olive oil (labelled EVO on the menu). Salads, vegan and vegetarian options also abound.

★ Le Vin De L'Assassin Bistrot
MEDITERRANEAN €€

(Map p204; ☑ 0931 6 61 59; Via Roma 115; meals €30-45; ⊙7.30-11pm Tue-Sun year-round, plus 12.30-2.30pm Sun Oct-May) Bringing a sophisticated touch to Ortygia's dining scene, this stylish restaurant takes an original French twist on Sicilian ingredients. The friendly Sicilian owner, Saro, spent years in Paris and is generous with advice on the plethora of offerings scrawled on the chalkboard nightly, including Breton oysters, impeccably dressed salads, a host of meat and fish mains, and creamy, chocolatey desserts.

Il Blu
SICILIAN €€

(Map p204; www.ristoranteilblu.it; Via Nizza 50; meals €25-30; ⊙noon-4pm & 6pm-3am Apr-Oct, shorter hours Nov-Mar) With its cosy front porch opposite Ortygia's waterfront, this is a great place for *aperitivi* after a dip in the sea. But it really shines at mealtimes, when owner Sebastian whips up two *primi* and two fresh-from-the-water seafood dishes daily according to his whim; think pasta with pistachios, capers, garlic and cherry tomatoes, or tuna steak with wild strawberries.

Taberna Sveva
SICILIAN €€

(Map p204; ☑0931 2 46 63; Piazza Federico di Svevia; meals €28-36; ⊙7-10.30pm nightly Jun-Sep, noon-3pm & 7-10.30pm Thu-Tue Oct-May) Away from the main tourist maelstrom, the charming Taberna Sveva is tucked in a quiet corner of Ortygia. On warm summer evenings the outdoor terrace is the place to sit, with alfresco tables set out on a tranquil cobbled square in front of Syracuse's 13th-century castle. The food is traditional Sicilian, so expect plenty of tuna and swordfish and some wonderful pasta.

★ Don Camillo
MODERN SICILIAN €€€

(Map p204; ☑0931 6 71 33; www.ristorantedoncamillosiracusa.it; Via Maestranza 96; meals €35-50; ⊙12.30-2.30pm & 7.30-10.30pm Mon-Sat) One of Ortygia's most elegant restaurants, Don Camillo specialises in top service, a classy atmosphere and innovative Sicilian cuisine. Try the starter of mixed shellfish in a thick soup of Noto almonds, lick your lips over the swordfish with orange blossom honey and sweet-and-sour vegetables, or savour the divine *tagliata di tonno* (tuna steak) with red pepper 'marmalade'.

 Drinking & Nightlife

Syracuse is a vibrant university town, which means plenty of life on the streets after nightfall. Many places are clustered near Piazza del Duomo.

Barcollo
BAR

(Map p204; Via Pompeo Picherali 10; ⊙7pm-3am) Hidden away in a historic courtyard, this seductive bar has outdoor deck seating and serves *aperitivi* from 7pm to 10pm.

Biblios Cafè
CAFE

(Map p204; www.biblioscafe.it; Via del Consiglio Reginale 11; ⊙11am-3pm & 6pm-midnight Wed-Mon) This beloved bookshop-cafe organises a whole range of cultural activities, including wine-tasting, literary readings, art classes and language courses. It's a great place to drop in any time of day, for coffee, *aperitivi* or just to mingle.

 Entertainment

Piccolo Teatro dei Pupi
THEATRE

(Map p204; ☑328 5326600, 0931 46 55 40; www.pupari.com; Via della Giudecca 17; ⊙shows 4.30pm, 6 times weekly Apr-Oct, fewer Nov-Mar) Syracuse's beloved puppet theatre hosts regular performances; see its website for a calendar. You can also buy puppets at its workshop next door and visit the affiliated puppet museum.

🔒 Shopping

Massimo Izzo
JEWELLERY

(Map p204; www.massimoizzo.com; Piazza Archimede 25; ⊙4-8pm Mon, 9am-1pm & 4-8pm Tue-Sat) The flamboyant jewellery of Messina-born Massimo Izzo is not for the faint-hearted. Featuring bold idiosyncratic designs and made with Sciacca coral, gold and precious stones, his handmade pieces are often inspired by themes close to the Sicilian heart: the sea, theatre and classical antiquity.

Galleria Bellomo
CRAFTS

(Map p204; www.bellomogallery.com; Via Capodieci 15; ⊙10.30am-8pm Mon-Sat, 10.30am-5pm Sun Mar-Oct, closed Sun & lunchtime Nov-Feb) Papyrus paper is the reason to come to this Ortygia gallery near Fontana Aretusa. Here you'll find a range of papery products, including greeting cards, bookmarks and writing paper, as well as a series of watercolour landscapes. Prices start at around €3 for a postcard, rising to hundreds of euros for original works of art.

ℹ Information

Ospedale Umberto I (☑0931 72 40 33; Via Testaferrata 1) Hospital between the centre and Parco Archeologico.

Police Station (☑093 16 51 76; Piazza San Giuseppe) Ortygia's police station.

Tourist Office (Map p204; ☑800 055500, 0931 46 29 46; infoturismo@provsr.it; Via Roma 31; ⊙9am-6.30pm) City maps and lots of good information.

ℹ️ Getting There & Away

Syracuse's train and bus stations are a block apart from each other, halfway between Ortygia and the archaeological park.

BUS

Long-distance buses operate from the bus stop along Corso Umberto, just east of Syracuse's train station.

Interbus (☑ 093 16 67 10; www.interbus.it) runs buses hourly on weekdays (less frequently on weekends) to Catania (€6.20, 1½ hours) and Fontanarossa airport (€6.20, 1¼ hours). Other Interbus destinations include Noto (€3.60, 55 minutes, two to five daily) and Palermo (€13.50, 3¾ hours, two to three daily).

AST (☑ 840 000323; www.aziendasiciliana trasporti.it) offers services to Ragusa (€7.20, 3¼ hours, five daily except Sunday), with intermediate stops in Noto (€4, 55 minutes) and Modica (€6.40, 2¾ hours).

CAR & MOTORCYCLE

The modern A18 and SS114 highways connect Syracuse with Catania and points north, while the SS115 runs south to Noto and Modica. Arriving by car, exit onto the eastbound SS124 and follow signs to Syracuse and Ortygia.

Traffic on Ortygia is restricted; you're better off parking and walking once you arrive on the island. Most convenient is the **Talete parking garage** at Ortygia's northern tip, which charges a 24-hour maximum of €10 (payable by cash or credit card at the machine when you leave). **Molo Sant'Antonio** on the mainland, just across the bridge from Ortygia, is another option.

TRAIN

From Syracuse's **train station** (Via Francesco Crispi), several trains depart daily for Messina (regional/InterCity train €9.70/19.50, 2½ to 3¼ hours) via Catania (€6.35/10, 1¼ hours). Some go on to Rome, Turin and Milan as well as other long-distance destinations. For Palermo, the bus is a better option. There are also local trains from Syracuse to Noto (€3.45, 30 minutes, eight daily except Sunday) and Ragusa (€7.65, two to 2½ hours, two daily except Sunday).

ℹ️ Getting Around

BICYCLE

Syracuse's bike sharing program, **GoBike** (☑ 366 6917046; per day €10, or annual subscription €10, first 30min free, additional hr €1), allows visitors to pick up and return bikes at 12 locations around town. Register and pay fees at any location, including the train station.

BUS

In late 2014, Syracuse's new city government launched an innovative system of gray electric minibuses operated by **Sd'A Trasporti** (www.siracusadamare.it; single ticket/day pass/week pass €0.50/2/7). To reach Ortygia from the bus and train stations, hop aboard bus 1, which loops around the island every half hour or so, making stops at over a dozen convenient locations. To reach Parco Archeologico della Neapolis, take minibus 2 from Molo Sant'Antonio (just west of the bridge to Ortygia). For route maps, see Sd'A Trasporti's website.

Noto

POP 23,800 / ELEV 160M

Flattened by the devastating earthquake of 1693, Noto was grandly rebuilt by its nobles into the finest baroque town in Sicily. Now a Unesco World Heritage Site, the town is especially impressive in the early evening, when its golden-hued sandstone buildings seem to glow with a soft inner light, and at night when illuminations accentuate the beauty of its intricately carved facades. The baroque masterpiece is the work of Rosario Gagliardi and his assistant, Vincenzo Sinatra, local architects who also worked in Ragusa and Modica.

◎ Sights

Two piazzas break up the long Corso Vittorio Emanuele: Piazza dell'Immacolata to the east and Piazza XVI Maggio to the west. The latter is overlooked by the beautiful **Chiesa di San Domenico** and the adjacent **Dominican monastery**, both designed by Rosario Gagliardi. On the same square, Noto's elegant 19th-century **Teatro Comunale** is worth a look. For sweeping views of Noto's baroque splendour, climb to the rooftop terrace at **Chiesa di Santa Chiara** (Corso Vittorio Emanuele; admission €2; ⊙ 9.30am-1pm & 3-7pm) or the *campanile* (bell tower) of **Chiesa di San Carlo al Corso** (Corso Vittorio Emanuele; admission €2; ⊙ 10am-7pm Apr-Oct, 10am-1pm & 3-5pm Nov-Mar).

★ **Cattedrale di San Nicolò**   CATHEDRAL
(Piazza Municipio; ⊙ 9am-1pm & 3-8pm) Pride of place in Noto goes to San Nicolò Cathedral, a baroque beauty that had to undergo extensive renovation after its dome collapsed during a 1996 thunderstorm. The ensuing decade saw the cathedral scrubbed of centuries of dust and dirt before reopening in 2007. Today the dome, with its peachy glow, is once again the focal point of Noto's skyline.

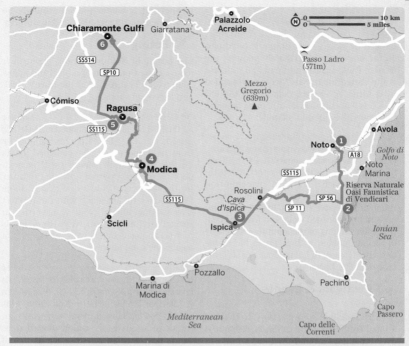

Driving Tour
Baroque Towns

START NOTO
END CHIARAMONTE GULFI
LENGTH 71KM; TWO DAYS

A land of remote rocky gorges, sweeping views and silent valleys, Sicily's southeastern corner is home to the 'baroque triangle', an area of Unesco-listed hilltop towns famous for their lavish baroque architecture. This tour takes in some of the finest baroque towns in Sicily, all within easy driving distance of each other.

Just over 35km south of Syracuse, ① **Noto** is home to what is arguably Sicily's most beautiful street – Corso Vittorio Emanuele, a pedestrianised boulevard lined with golden baroque *palazzi*. From Noto, head 12km south along the SP19 to the ② **Riserva Naturale Oasi Faunistica di Vendicari**, a coastal preserve whose trails, wetlands and beaches are prime territory for walking, bird-watching and swimming. Next, head 23km southwest along the SP56, SP11 and SS115 to ③ **Ispica**, a hilltop town overlooking a

huge canyon, the Cava d'Ispica, riddled with prehistoric tombs. Continuing up the SS115 for a further 18km brings you to ④ **Modica**, a bustling town set in a deep rocky gorge. There's excellent accommodation here and a wealth of great restaurants, so this makes a good place to overnight. The best of the baroque sights are up in Modica Alta, the high part of town, but save some energy for the *passeggiata* (evening stroll) on Corso Umberto I in the lower town.

Next morning, a short, winding, up-and-down drive through rock-littered hilltops leads to ⑤ **Ragusa**, one of Sicily's nine provincial capitals. The town is divided in two – it's the lower town, Ragusa Ibla, that you want, a claustrophobic warren of grey stone houses and elegant *palazzi* that opens up onto Piazza Duomo, a superb example of 18th-century town planning. Although you can eat well in Ragusa, consider lunching in ⑥ **Chiaramonte Gulfi**, a tranquil hilltop town some 20km to the north along the SP10, famous for its olive oil and delicious pork.

Piazza Municipio PIAZZA

About halfway along Corso Vittorio Emanuele is the graceful Piazza Municipio, flanked by Noto's most dramatic buildings. To the north, sitting in stately pomp at the head of Paolo Labisi's monumental staircase is the Cattedrale di San Nicolò, surrounded by a series of elegant palaces. To the left (west) is **Palazzo Landolina**, once home to the powerful Sant'Alfano family.

Palazzo Nicolaci di Villadorata PALACE

(🖉 338 7427022; www.comune.noto.sr.it/palazzonicolaci; Via Nicolaci; admission €4; ◷ 10am-6.30pm) The striking facade of this 18th-century palace features wrought-iron balconies supported by a swirling pantomime of grotesque figures. Inside, the *palazzo's* richly brocaded walls and frescoed ceilings offer an idea of the sumptuous lifestyle of Sicilian nobles, as brought to life in the Giuseppe Tomasi di Lampedusa novel *Il gattopardo* (The Leopard).

🎆 Festivals & Events

Infiorata CARNIVAL

(www.infioratadinoto.it; ◷ mid-May) Noto's big annual jamboree is the Infiorata, celebrated over three days around the third Sunday in May with parades, historical re-enactments and the decoration of Via Corrado Nicolaci with designs made entirely of flower petals.

🛏 Sleeping

Ostello Il Castello HOSTEL €

(🖉 320 8388869; www.ostellodinoto.it; Via Fratelli Bandiera 1; dm €18, d €50-70; 🛜) This hostel directly uphill from the centre offers excellent value for money. Many of the eight- to 16-bed dorms and private rooms (including some with terraces) command fabulous views over the *duomo* and the city's rooftops. Note that reception is closed in the middle of the day.

La Corte del Sole INN €€

(🖉 0931 82 02 10; www.lacortedelsole.it; Contrada Bucachemi, Eloro, Lido di Noto; s €93-114, d €122-196; P❄@🛜♨) Overlooking the green fields of Eloro is this stylish hotel housed in a traditional Sicilian *masseria* (fortified farmhouse). A delightful place to stay, it also offers a range of activities including **cooking lessons** (🖉 0931 82 02 10; www.lacortedel sole.it; Contrada Bucachemi; 3hr lesson per person €70; ◷ 9.30am-12.30pm Tue-Sat) run by the ho-

tel chef and, in winter, tours to study the 80 or so types of wild orchids found in the area.

Eating

The people of Noto are serious about their food, so take time to enjoy a meal and follow it up with a visit to one of the town's excellent ice-cream shops.

★ Caffè Sicilia GELATERIA €

(🖉 0931 83 50 13; Corso Vittorio Emanuele 125; desserts from €2; ◷ 8am-11pm Tue-Sun) Dating from 1892 and especially renowned for its *granite,* this beloved place vies with its next-door neighbour, Dolceria Corrado Costanzo, for the honours of Noto's best dessert shop. Frozen desserts are made with the freshest seasonal ingredients (wild strawberries in springtime, for example), while the delicious *torrone* (nougat) bursts with the flavours of local honey and almonds.

★ Ristorante Crocifisso SICILIAN €€

(🖉 0931 57 11 51; www.ristorantecrocifisso.it; Via Principe Umberto 48; meals €30-40; ◷ noon-3pm & 7.30-11pm Thu-Tue) Up in Noto Alta, this Slow Food–acclaimed restaurant with an extensive wine list is widely regarded as Noto's best. Sicilian classics such as *macco di fave* (broad bean purée with ricotta and toasted breadcrumbs) and *casarecce alla palermitana* (short handmade pasta with sardines and wild fennel) are complemented by juicy roast lamb, Marsala-glazed pork and pistachio- and sesame-crusted tuna.

Il Liberty MODERN SICILIAN €€

(🖉 0931 57 32 26; www.illiberty.com; Via Cavour 40; meals €33-38; ◷ noon-3pm & 7.30-11pm Tue-Sun) Chef Giuseppe Angelino's contemporary spin on Sicilian cuisine is complemented by an excellent local wine list at this attractive eatery with a stone-vaulted dining room and small front terrace. The menu moves from superb appetisers like *millefoglie* – wafer-thin layers of crusty cheese and ground pistachios with minty sweet-and-sour vegetables – to desserts like blood orange *granita*.

❶ Information

Tourist Office (🖉 0931 57 37 79; www.comune.noto.sr.it; Piazza XVI Maggio; ◷ 8am-2pm & 3-8pm Apr-Oct, to 7pm Nov-Mar) Helpful tourist office near the west end of Noto's main thoroughfare.

ⓘ Getting There & Around

BUS

From Largo Pantheon on the eastern edge of Noto's historic centre, AST and Interbus serve Catania (€8.40, 1¾ hours) and Syracuse (€3.60 to €4, 55 minutes). Service is less frequent on Sundays.

TRAIN

Trains run to Syracuse (€3.45, 30 minutes, eight daily except Sunday), but Noto's station is inconveniently located 1km downhill from the centre.

Modica

POP 54,700 / ELEV 296M

A powerhouse in Grecian times, Modica remains a superbly atmospheric town with its medieval and baroque buildings climbing steeply up either side of a deep gorge. The multilayered town is divided into Modica Alta (Upper Modica) and Modica Bassa (Lower Modica). A devastating flood in 1902 resulted in the wide avenues of Corso Umberto and Via Giarrantana (the river was dammed and diverted), which remain the main axes of the town, lined by *palazzi* and tiled stone houses.

◉ Sights

Aside from simply wandering the streets and absorbing the atmosphere, a visit to the extraordinary **Chiesa di San Giorgio** (Corso San Giorgio; ⊙ 8am-1pm & 3.30-7.30pm) is a highlight. This church, Gagliardi's masterpiece, is a vision of pure rococo splendour, a butter-coloured confection perched on a majestic 250-step staircase. Its counterpoint in Modica Bassa is the **Cattedrale di San Pietro** (Corso Umberto I), another impressive church atop a rippling staircase lined with life-sized statues of the Apostles.

⌂ Sleeping

★ **Villa Quartarella**   AGRITURISMO €
(☑ 360 654829; www.quartarella.com; Contrada Quartarella; s €40, d €75-80) Spacious rooms, welcoming hosts and ample breakfasts make this converted villa in the countryside south of Modica an appealing choice for anyone travelling by car. Owners Francesco and Francesca are generous in sharing their love and encyclopaedic knowledge of local history, flora and fauna and can suggest a multitude of driving itineraries in the surrounding area.

B&B Il Cavaliere   B&B €
(☑ 0932 94 72 19; www.palazzoilcavaliere.it; Corso Umberto I 259; d €59-99, ste €89-135; ❄ ☏) Angle for the beautiful front suite with original tiled floors and frescoed ceilings at this classy B&B in a 19th-century *palazzo*, just down from the bus stop on Modica's main strip. Equally charming are the large, high-ceilinged common rooms, including an elegant breakfast room with lovely views of Chiesa di San Giorgio. Standard rooms are less exciting.

✕ Eating & Drinking

Taverna Nicastro   SICILIAN €
(☑ 0932 94 58 84; www.tavernanicastro.it; Via S Antonino 30; meals €18-25; ⊙ 7.30-10pm Tue-Sat) With nearly 70 years of history and a long-standing Slow Food recommendation, this is one of the upper town's most authentic and atmospheric restaurants, and a bargain to boot. The carnivore-friendly menu includes grilled meat, lamb stew, rabbit with mint leaves, capers and olives, and pasta specialities such as ricotta ravioli with pork *ragù*.

ConTrade   MODERN SICILIAN €€
(☑ 0932 94 86 86; Via Clemente Grimaldi 74; meals €27-33; ⊙ noon-3pm & 6.30-11pm, closed Mon or Tue) Run by a husband-wife duo, and decorated with well-stocked wine racks under old stone arches, this recent arrival whips up beautifully presented classics from *caponata* to *cannoli*, interspersed with delicious personal creations such as Nebrodi black pork with mashed potatoes and walnuts. Service can be slow. Closing day varies seasonally.

Rappa Enoteca   WINE BAR
(Corso Santa Teresa 97-99; ⊙ 4.30pm-late Mon-Sat) High ceilings, antique mouldings, tiled floors and chandeliers create a delightful backdrop at this atmospheric *enoteca* in the upper town. Sample a wide range of Sicilian wines, along with cheese and meat platters.

⌂ Shopping

Dolceria Bonajuto   FOOD
(☑ 0932 94 12 25; www.bonajuto.it; Corso Umberto I 159; ⊙ 9am-8.30pm) Sicily's oldest chocolate factory is the perfect place to taste Modica's famous chocolate. Flavoured with cinnamon, vanilla, orange peel and even hot peppers, it's a legacy of the town's Spanish overlords who imported cocoa from their South American colonies.

ℹ️ Information

Tourist Office (📞346 6558227; www.
comune.modica.rg.it; Corso Umberto I 141;
⏰9am-1pm & 3.30-7pm Mon-Sat) City-run
tourist office in Modica Bassa.

ℹ️ Getting There & Away

BUS

AST (📞0932 76 73 01; www.aziendasiciliana
trasporti.it) runs frequent buses Monday to
Saturday from Piazzale Falcone-Borsellino at
the top of Corso Umberto I to Syracuse (€6.40,
2¾ hours), Noto (€4, 1¾ hours) and Ragusa
(€2.70, 30 minutes); on Sunday, service is
limited (two buses each to Noto and Ragusa, no
service to Syracuse).

TRAIN

From Modica's station, 600m southwest of
the centre, there are four trains daily (except
Sunday) to Syracuse (€7, 1½ hours) and three
to Ragusa (€2.25, 25 minutes).

Ragusa

POP 72,800 / ELEV 502M

Like a grand old dame, Ragusa is a dignified and well-aged provincial town. Like
every other town in the region, Ragusa
collapsed after the 1693 earthquake; a
new town called Ragusa Superiore was
built on a high plateau above the original
settlement. But the old aristocracy were
loath to leave their tottering *palazzi* and
rebuilt Ragusa Ibla on the original site.
The two towns were only merged in 1927.

Ragusa Ibla remains the heart and soul
of the town, and has all the best restaurants and the majority of sights. A sinuous bus ride or some very steep and scenic
steps connect the lower town to its modern sister up the hill.

👁️ Sights

Grand churches and *palazzi* line the
twisting, narrow streets of Ragusa Ibla,
interspersed with gelaterie and delightful piazzas where the local youth
stroll and the elderly gather on benches.
Palm-planted Piazza del Duomo, the centre of town, is dominated by the 18th-
century **Cattedrale di San Giorgio** (Piazza Duomo; ⏰10am-12.30pm & 4-6.30pm), with
its magnificent neoclassical dome and
stained-glass windows.

At the eastern end of the old town is the
Giardino Ibleo (⏰8am-8pm), a pleasant

public garden laid out in the 19th century and currently undergoing an extensive
renovation. It's the perfect spot for a picnic lunch.

🛌 Sleeping

L'Orto Sul Tetto B&B €
(📞0932 24 77 85; www.lortosultetto.it; Via
Tenente di Stefano 56; s €45-60, d €70-110;
❄️🌐) This sweet little B&B behind Ragusa's *duomo* offers an intimate experience,
with just three rooms and a lovely roof
terrace where breakfast is served.

Tenuta Zannafondo B&B €
(📞0932 183 89 19; www.tenutazannafondo.
it; Contrada di Zannafondo; d €79; ❄️🌐) Set
amidst olive-sprinkled hillsides lined
with stone walls, this recently converted
19th-century farmstead sits halfway between Ragusa and the coast (a 15-minute
drive from each). Its charm lies in the
tranquil cluster of independent stone-
walled cottages, each with its own little
terrace; two rooms in the main house are
less appealing. Breakfast is included, and
dinner is available on request.

🍴 Eating

⭐**Quattro Gatti** SICILIAN, SLOVAK €
(📞0932 24 56 12; Via Valverde 95; meals €20-
25; ⏰8-11.30pm Tue-Sun) This cosy Sicilian-
Slovak–run eatery near the Giardino Ibleo
serves an amazing four-course fixed-price
menu bursting with fresh, local flavours.
The antipasti spread is especially memorable, as are the seasonally changing specials scribbled on the blackboard up front.
Slovak-inspired offerings such as goulash
and apple strudel round out a menu of Sicilian classics.

Gelati DiVini GELATERIA €
(📞0932 22 89 89; www.gelatidivini.it; Piazza Duomo 20; ice cream from €2; ⏰10am-midnight)
This exceptional gelateria makes wine-
flavoured ice creams like Marsala, passito
and muscat, plus other unconventional
offerings such as pine nut, watermelon,
ricotta, and chocolate with spicy peppers.

A Rusticana TRATTORIA €€
(📞0932 22 79 81; Via Domenico Morelli 4; meals
€20-32; ⏰12.30-3pm & 7.30-10pm Wed-Mon)
Fans of the *Montalbano* TV series will
want to eat here, as it's where scenes
set in the fictional Trattoria San Calogero were filmed. In reality, it's a cheerful,

SICILY'S BEST-PRESERVED ROMAN MOSAICS

Near the town of Piazza Armerina in central Sicily is the stunning 3rd-century Roman **Villa Romana del Casale**, a Unesco World Heritage Site and one of the few remaining sites of Roman Sicily. This sumptuous hunting lodge is thought to have belonged to Diocletian's co-emperor Marcus Aurelius Maximianus. Buried under mud in a 12th-century flood, it remained hidden for 700 years before its magnificent floor mosaics were discovered in the 1950s. Visit out of season or early in the day to avoid the hordes of tourists.

The mosaics cover almost the entire floor (3500 sq metres) of the villa and are considered unique for their narrative style, the range of subject matter and variety of colour – many are clearly influenced by African themes. Along the eastern end of the internal courtyard is the wonderful **Corridor of the Great Hunt**, vividly depicting chariots, rhinos, cheetahs, lions and the voluptuously beautiful Queen of Sheba. Across the corridor is a series of apartments, where floor illustrations reproduce scenes from Homer's *Odyssey*. But perhaps the most captivating of the mosaics is the so-called **Room of the Ten Girls in Bikinis**, with depictions of sporty girls in scanty bikinis throwing a discus, using weights and throwing a ball; they would blend in well on a Malibu beach. These most famous of Piazza Armerina's mosaics were fully reopened to the public in 2013 after years of painstaking restoration and are among Sicily's greatest classical treasures.

Travelling by car from Piazza Armerina, follow signs south of town to the SP15, then continue 5km to reach the villa.

Getting here without a car is more challenging. Buses operated by **Interbus** (p199) from Catania (€9.20, 1¾ hours) or **SAIS** (☑ 093 568 01 19; www.saisautolinee.it) from Enna (€3.60, 40 minutes) run to Piazza Armerina; from here catch a local bus (€1, 30 minutes, May to September only) or a taxi (€20) the remaining 5km.

boisterous trattoria whose generous portions and relaxed vine-covered terrace ensure a loyal clientele. The food is defiantly *casareccia* (home-style), so expect no-frills pasta and uncomplicated cuts of grilled meat.

Ristorante Duomo　　　MODERN SICILIAN €€€
(☑0932 65 12 65; www.cicciosultano.it; Via Capitano Bocchieri 31; lunch menus €45-59, dinner tasting menus €120-190; ⊗noon-3pm Tue-Sat, plus 7.30-11pm Mon-Sat) Widely regarded as one of Sicily's finest restaurants, Duomo comprises a cluster of small rooms outfitted like private parlours behind its stained-glass door, ensuring a suitably romantic ambience for chef Ciccio Sultano's refined creations. The menu abounds in classic Sicilian ingredients such as pistachios, fennel, almonds and Nero d'Avola wine, combined in imaginative and unconventional ways. Booking is essential.

🛈 Information

Tourist Office (☑366 8742621; infotourist. ibla@comune.ragusa.gov.it; Piazza della Repubblica; ⊗9am-7pm Mon-Fri, to 2pm Sat

& Sun) Ragusa Ibla branch of the municipal tourist office.

🛈 Getting There & Around

BUS

Long-distance and municipal buses share a terminal on Via Zama in the upper town. Buy tickets at the Interbus/Etna kiosk in the main lot or at cafes around the corner. **Interbus** (www.interbus.it) runs to Catania (€8.60, two hours, five to 12 daily). **AST** (☑0932 68 18 18; www.aziendasicilianatrasporti.it) serves Syracuse (€7.20, 2¾ to 3¼ hours, three daily except Sunday) with intermediate stops in Modica (€2.70, 30 minutes) and Noto (€6, 2¼ hours).

Monday through Saturday, AST's city buses 11 and 33 (€1.10) run hourly between the Via Zama bus terminal and Giardino Ibleo in Ragusa Ibla. On Sundays, bus 1 makes a similar circuit.

TRAIN

From the station in the upper town, there's one direct train daily except Sunday to Syracuse (€7.65, two hours) via Noto (€5.75, 1½ hours).

CENTRAL SICILY & THE MEDITERRANEAN COAST

Central Sicily is a land of vast panoramas, undulating fields, severe mountain ridges and hilltop towns. Moving towards the Mediterranean, the perspective changes, as ancient temples jostle for position with modern high-rise apartments outside Agrigento, Sicily's most lauded classical site and also one of its busier modern cities.

Agrigento

POP 59,100 / ELEV 230M

Agrigento does not make a good first impression. Seen from a distance, the modern city's rows of unsightly apartment blocks loom incongruously on the hillside, distracting attention from the splendid Valley of the Temples below, where the ancient Greeks once built their great city of Akragas. Never fear: once you get down among the ruins, their monumental grace becomes apparent, and it's easy to understand how this remarkable complex of temples became Sicily's pre-eminent travel destination, first put on the tourist map by Goethe in the 18th century.

Three kilometres uphill from the temples, Agrigento's medieval core is a pleasant place to pass the evening after a day exploring the ruins. The intercity bus and train stations are both in the upper town, within a few blocks of Via Atenea, the main street of the medieval city.

◉ Sights

◉ Valle dei Templi

★**Valley of the Temples** ARCHAEOLOGICAL SITE
(Valle dei Templi; www.parcovalledeitempli.it; adult/reduced €10/5, incl Museo Archeologico €13.50/7; ⊙8.30am-7pm year-round, plus 8-10pm Mon-Fri, 8-11pm Sat & Sun mid-Jul–mid-Sep) Sicily's most enthralling archaeological site encompasses the ruined ancient city of Akragas, highlighted by the stunningly well-preserved **Tempio della Concordia** (Temple of Concord), one of several ridge-top temples that once served as beacons for homecoming sailors. The 1300-hectare park, 3km south of Agrigento, is split into eastern and western zones. Ticket offices with car parks are at the park's eastern edge and along the main road dividing the eastern and western zones.

★**Museo Archeologico** MUSEUM
(☑0922 40 15 65; Contrada San Nicola 12; adult/reduced €8/4, incl Valley of the Temples €13.50/7; ⊙9am-7pm Tue-Sat, 9am-1pm Sun & Mon) North of the temples, this wheelchair-accessible museum is one of Sicily's finest, with a huge collection of clearly labelled artefacts from the excavated site. Noteworthy are the dazzling displays of Greek painted ceramics and the awe-inspiring reconstructed telamon, a colossal statue recovered from the nearby Tempio di Giove.

◉ Medieval Agrigento

Chiesa di Santa Maria dei Greci CHURCH
(www.cattedraleagrigento.com; Salita Santa Maria dei Greci; ⊙10am-1pm Mon-Sat) This small church stands on the site of a 5th-century Doric temple dedicated to Athena. Inside are some badly damaged Byzantine frescoes, the remains of a Norman ceiling and traces of the original Greek columns.

Monastero di Santo Spirito CONVENT
(☑0922 2 06 64; www.monasterosantospirito ag.org; Calle Santo Spirito 9) At the top of a set of steps off Via Atenea, this convent was founded by Cistercian nuns around 1290. A handsome Gothic portal leads inside, where the nuns are still in residence, praying, meditating and baking heavenly sweets, including *cuscusu* (sweet couscous made with local pistachios), *dolci di mandorla* (almond pastries) and *conchiglie* (shell-shaped sweets filled with pistachio paste). Press the doorbell and say *'Vorrei comprare qualche dolce'* ('I'd like to buy a few sweets').

☞ Tours

Associazione Guide Turistiche Agrigento WALKING TOUR
(☑345 8815992; www.agrigentoguide.org) Agrigento's official tour guide association offers guided visits of the Valley of the Temples, Agrigento and the surrounding area in English and eight other languages.

✦ Festivals & Events

Sagra del Mandorlo in Fiore CULTURAL
(⊙Feb) This 11-day folk festival spans two weekends in February, when the Valley of the Temples is cloaked in almond blossoms.

⬔ Sleeping

Fattoria Mosè AGRITURISMO €
(☑0922 60 61 15; www.fattoriamose.com; Via Mattia Pascal 4a; r per person €48, incl breakfast/half-board €58/81;) If Agrigento's urban jungle's got you down, head for this authentic

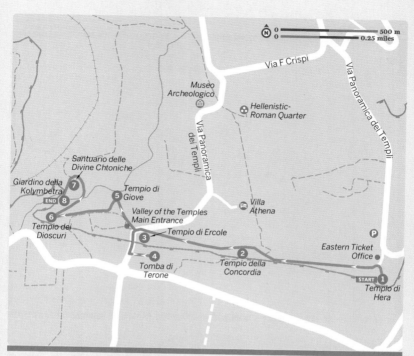

Archaeological Walking Tour
Valley of the Temples

START TEMPIO DI HERA
END GIARDINO DELLA KOLYMBETRA
LENGTH 3KM; THREE HOURS

Begin your exploration in the so-called Eastern Zone, home to Agrigento's best-preserved temples. From the eastern ticket office, a short walk leads to the 5th-century BC ① **Tempio di Hera**, perched on the ridgetop. Though partly destroyed by an earthquake, the colonnade remains largely intact, as does a long sacrificial altar. Traces of red are the result of fire damage likely dating to the Carthaginian invasion of 406 BC.

Next descend past a gnarled 500-year-old olive tree and a series of Byzantine tombs to the ② **Tempio della Concordia** (p214). This remarkable edifice, the model for Unesco's logo, has survived almost entirely intact since its construction in 430 BC, partly due to its conversion into a Christian basilica in the 6th century, and partly thanks to the shock-absorbing, earthquake-dampening qualities of the soft clay underlying its hard rock foundation.

Further downhill, the ③ **Tempio di Ercole** is Agrigento's oldest, dating from the end of the 6th century BC. Down from the main temples, the miniature ④ **Tomba di Terone** dates to 75 BC. Cross the pedestrian bridge into the Western Zone, stopping first at the ⑤ **Tempio di Giove**. This would have been the world's largest Doric temple had its construction not been interrupted by the Carthaginian sacking of Akragas. A later earthquake reduced it to the crumbled ruin you see today. Lying flat on his back amid the rubble is an 8m-tall telamon (a sculpted figure of a man with arms raised), originally intended to support the temple's weight. It's actually a copy; the original is in Agrigento's archaeological museum.

Take a brief look at the ruined 5th-century BC ⑥ **Tempio dei Dioscuri** and the 6th-century BC complex of altars and small buildings known as the ⑦ **Santuario delle Divine Chtoniche**, before ending your visit in the ⑧ **Giardino della Kolymbetra**, a lush garden in a natural cleft near the sanctuary.

Agrigento

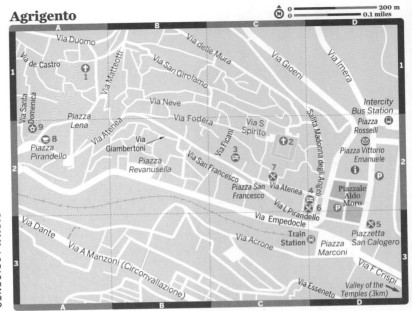

Agrigento

⦿ **Sights**
1 Chiesa di Santa Maria dei Greci.......... A1
2 Monastero di Santo Spirito C2

⬛ **Sleeping**
3 Camere a Sud.....................................C2
4 PortAtenea D2

⊗ **Eating**
5 Kalòs...D3
6 Sal8..D2
7 Trattoria Concordia C2

◉ **Drinking & Nightlife**
8 Caffè Concordia.................................A2

✪ **Entertainment**
9 Teatro Pirandello A2

organic *agriturismo* 6km east of the Valley of the Temples. Four suites, six self-catering apartments and a pool offer ample space to relax. Guests can opt for reasonably priced dinners (including wine) built around the farm's organic produce, cook for themselves or even enjoy cooking courses on site.

PortAtenea   B&B €
(☏ 349 0937492; www.portatenea.com; Via Atenea, cnr Via C Battisti; s €39-50, d €59-75, tr €79-95; ❋ 🛜) This five-room B&B wins plaudits for

its spacious, well-appointed rooms, its panoramic roof terrace overlooking the Valley of the Temples, and its convenient location at the entrance to the Old Town, just a stone's throw from the train and bus stations.

Camere a Sud   B&B €
(☏ 349 6384424; www.camereasud.it; Via Ficani 6; r €60-70; ❋ @ 🛜) This lovely B&B in the medieval centre has three guest rooms decorated with style and taste – traditional decor and contemporary textiles are matched with bright colours and modern art. Breakfast is served on the terrace in the warmer months.

Villa Athena   HISTORIC HOTEL €€€
(☏ 092 259 62 88; www.hotelvillaathena.it; Via Passeggiata Archeologica 33; r €281-432, ste €408-842; 🅿 ❋ @ 🛜 ☈) With the Tempio della Concordia lit up in the near distance and palm trees lending an exotic *Arabian Nights* feel, this historic five-star hotel in an aristocratic 18th-century villa offers the ultimate luxury experience. The cavernous Villa Suite, floored in antique tiles with a free-standing jacuzzi and a vast terrace overlooking the temples, might well be Sicily's coolest hotel room.

✗ Eating & Drinking

On a hot day, nothing refreshes like a chilled glass of almond milk, made from Agrigento's famous almonds mixed with sugar, water and a hint of lemon rind; the classic place to try it is at **Caffè Concordia** (Piazza Pirandello 36; ☺6am-9.30pm Tue-Sat) near Teatro Pirandello.

Trattoria Concordia
TRATTORIA €
(☑0922 2 26 68; Via Porcello 8; meals €18-30; ☺noon-3pm & 7-10.30pm Mon-Fri, 7-11pm Sat) Rough stone walls and wood-beamed ceilings lend a cosy atmosphere to this quintessential family run trattoria, tucked up a side alley in the Old Town. Traditional Sicilian starters (frittata, sweet-and-sour aubergine, ricotta and olives) are complemented by tasty grilled fish and meats.

Sal8
INTERNATIONAL €
(☑0922 66 19 90; Via Cesare Battisti 8; meals €15-25; ☺noon-11pm) Creative and reasonably priced light meals complement a good drinks list at this newly opened wine bar near the entrance to Via Atenea. Depending on the chef's whim, expect anything from sushi to seafood *tagliatelle* to tapas with a Sicilian twist – think shrimp and broad bean cakes or *panelle* (chickpea fritters) served with sparkling wine.

★ Kalòs
MODERN SICILIAN €€
(☑092 22 63 89; www.ristorantekalos.it; Piazzetta San Calogero; meals €28-45; ☺12.30-3pm & 7-11pm Tue-Sun) For fine dining, head to this 'smart' restaurant just outside the historic centre. Five cute tables on little balconies offer a delightful setting to enjoy homemade pasta *all'agrigentina* (with fresh tomatoes, basil and almonds), grilled lamb chops, citrus shrimp or *spada gratinata* (baked swordfish covered in breadcrumbs). Superb desserts, including homemade *cannoli* and almond *semifreddi*, round out the menu.

☆ Entertainment

Teatro Pirandello
THEATRE
(☑0922 59 02 20; www.teatroluigipirandello.it; Piazza Pirandello; tickets €18-23) This city-run theatre is Sicily's third largest, after Palermo's Teatro Massimo and Catania's Teatro Massimo Bellini. Works by local hero Luigi Pirandello figure prominently. The program runs from November to early May.

❶ Information

Ospedale San Giovanni di Dio (☑0922 44 21 11; Contrada Consolida) North of the centre.

Police Station (☑0922 48 31 11; Piazza Vittorio Emanuele 2)

Tourist Office (☑800 236837; www.provincia.agrigento.it; Piazzale Aldo Moro 1; ☺8.30am-1pm & 2.30-7pm Mon-Fri, 8.30am-1pm Sat) In the provincial government building.

❶ Getting There & Away

BUS
The intercity bus station and ticket booths are located on Piazza Rosselli. **Cuffaro** (☑091 616 15 10; www.cuffaro.info) operates eight buses to Palermo (€9, two hours) Monday to Friday, six on Saturday and three on Sunday. **Autoservizi Camilleri** (☑0922 47 18 86; www.camilleriargentoelattuca.it) also runs to Palermo one to five times daily. **SAL** (Società Autolinee Licata; ☑0922 40 13 60; www.autolineesal.it) offers direct service to Palermo's Falcone-Borsellino airport (€12.60, 2¾ hours, three to four departures Monday to Saturday). **Lumia** (☑0922 2 04 14; www.autolineelumia.it) has departures to Trapani and its Birgi airport (€11.90, three to four hours, three daily Monday to Saturday, one on Sunday), while **SAIS Trasporti** (☑092 22 93 24; www.saistrasporti.it) runs buses to Catania (€13.40, three hours, 10 to 14 daily).

CAR & MOTORCYCLE
The SS189 links Agrigento with Palermo, while the SS115 runs along the coast, northwest towards Trapani and southeast to Syracuse.

Driving in the medieval town is near impossible due to all the pedestrianised streets. There's metered parking at the train station and free parking along Via Esseneto just below.

TRAIN
From Agrigento Centrale station (Piazza Marconi), direct trains run regularly to Palermo (€8.30, two hours, seven to 10 daily). Service to Catania (€10.40 to €17.60, 3¼ to 5¼ hours) is less frequent and requires a change of trains. For other destinations, you're better off taking the bus.

❶ Getting Around

TUA (Trasporti Urbani Agrigento; ☑0922 41 20 24; www.trasportiurbaniagrigento.it) runs buses down to the Valley of the Temples from the Intercity Bus Station, stopping in front of the train station en route. Take bus 1, 2 or 3 (tickets €1.20 from tobacconists, €1.70 on board) and get off at either the museum or the main entrance to the temples (between the Tempio di Giove and the Tempio di Ercole). The Linea Verde (Green Line) departs every 50 minutes from the train station, running the length of Via Atenea and looping through the medieval town centre.

WESTERN SICILY

Directly across the water from North Africa and still retaining vestiges of the Arab, Phoenician and Greek cultures that once prevailed here, western Sicily has a bit of the Wild West about it. There's plenty to stir the senses, from Trapani's savoury fish couscous, to the dazzling views from hilltop Erice, to the wild coastal beauty of Riserva Naturale dello Zingaro.

Marsala

POP 82,300

Best known for its sweet dessert wines, Marsala revolves around its lovely, elegant core of stately baroque buildings within a perfect square of walls. To the east and north lie less attractive modern outskirts that gradually peter out into the surrounding vineyards.

The city was originally founded by Phoenician escapees from the Roman onslaught at nearby Mozia. Not wanting to risk a second attack, they fortified their new home with 7m-thick walls, ensuring that it was the last Punic settlement to fall to the Romans. In AD 830 it was conquered by the Arabs, who gave it its current name, Marsa Allah (Port of God).

It was here in 1860 that Giuseppe Garibaldi, leader of the movement for Italian unification, landed in his rickety old boats with his 1000-strong army – a claim to fame that finds its way into every tourist brochure.

◉ Sights & Activities

For a taste of local life, take a stroll at sunset around pretty **Piazza della Repubblica**, heart of the historic centre.

Museo Archeologico Baglio Anselmi
MUSEUM

(✆ 0923 95 25 35; Lungomare Boeo; adult/reduced €4/2; ⊙ 9am-8pm Tue-Sat, 9am-1.30pm Mon) Marsala's finest treasure is the partially reconstructed remains of a Carthaginian *liburna* (warship) sunk off the Egadi Islands during the First Punic War. Displayed alongside objects from its cargo, the ship's bare bones provide the only remaining physical evidence of the Phoenicians' seafaring superiority in the 3rd century BC, offering a glimpse of a civilisation extinguished by the Romans.

Whitaker Museum
MUSEUM

(✆ 0923 71 25 98; www.fondazionewhitaker.it; adult/child €9/5; ⊙ 9.30am-1.30pm & 2.30-6.30pm Apr-Oct, 9am-3pm Nov-Mar) This museum on San Pantaleo island, 10km north of Marsala, houses a unique collection of Phoenician artefacts assembled over decades by amateur archaeologist Joseph Whitaker. Its greatest treasure (recently returned to Sicily after two years at London's British Museum and Los Angeles' Getty) is *Il giovinetto di Mozia,* a 5th-century-BC Carthaginian-influenced marble statue of a young man.

To get here, drive or bike to the Mozia dock 10km north of Marsala and catch one of the half-hourly, 10-minute ferries operated by **Mozia Line** (✆ 338 7860474, 0923 98 92 49; www.mozialine.com; adult/reduced €5/2.50; ⊙ 9.15am-6.30pm).

Cantine Florio
WINERY

(✆ 0923 78 11 11; www.duca.it/cantineflorio; Via Vincenzo Florio 1; tours €10; ⊙ wine shop 9am-1pm & 3.30-6pm Mon-Fri, 9.30am-1pm Sat, English-language tours 3.30pm Mon-Fri, 10.30am Sat year-round, plus 11am Mon-Fri Apr-Oct) These venerable wine cellars just east of town open their doors to visitors to explain the Marsala-making process and the fascinating history of local viticulture. Afterwards visitors can sample the goods in Florio's spiffy tasting room (tastes of two Marsalas and a moscato, accompanied by hors d'oeuvres, are included in the tour price). Take bus 16 from Piazza del Popolo. Other producers in the same area include Pellegrino, Donnafugata, Rallo, Mavis and Intorcia.

🛏 Sleeping & Eating

★ Il Profumo del Sale
B&B €

(✆ 0923 189 04 72; www.ilprofumodelsale.it; Via Vaccari 8; d €50-60; 🛜) Perfectly positioned in Marsala's historic city centre, this lovely B&B offers three attractive rooms – including a palatial front unit with cathedral views from its small balcony – enhanced by welcoming touches like almond cookies, fine soaps and ample breakfasts featuring homemade bread and jams. Sophisticated owner Celsa is full of helpful tips about Marsala and the surrounding area.

Hotel Carmine
HOTEL €€

(✆ 0923 71 19 07; www.hotelcarmine.it; Piazza Carmine 16; s €75-105, d €105-130; P ✳ @ 🛜) This lovely hotel in a converted 16th-century monastery has elegant rooms (especially numbers 7 and 30), with original blue-and-gold majolica tiles, stone walls, antique furniture and lofty beamed ceilings. Enjoy your cornflakes in the baronial-style breakfast room with its historic frescoes and over-the-top chandelier, or sip your drink by the roaring fireplace in winter. Modern perks include a rooftop solarium.

★ San Lorenzo Osteria
SICILIAN €€

(SLO; ✆ 0923 71 25 93; Via Garraffa 60; meals €25-35; ⊙ 7.30-10.30pm Wed-Mon; 🛜) With roots as a wedding-catering business, this stylish eatery is a class act all round – from the ever-changing menu of fresh seafood scrawled daily on the blackboard to the interior's sleek modern lines to the gorgeous presentation of the food. The stellar wine list features some local choices you won't find elsewhere.

Assud MODERN SICILIAN €€
(☑ 0923 71 66 52; www.assud.eu; Via Armando Diaz 66; meals €25-35; ☺ noon-3pm & 6.30-11pm Tue-Sun) Good wines accompany the short but sweet menu at this newcomer straddling Marsala's historic walls. The nightly evolving mix of inventive antipasti, *primi* and *secondi* (three to four in each category) might include anything from seafood couscous to a *tris di arancine* (three reimagined versions of Sicily's classic rice balls, filled respectively with meat, aubergine and ricotta, and squid ink).

ⓘ Information

Tourist Office (☑ 0923 71 40 97, 0923 99 33 38; ufficioturistico.proloco@comune.marsala. tp.it; Via XI Maggio 100; ☺ 8.30am-1.30pm & 3-8pm Mon-Fri, 8.30am-1.30pm Sat) Spacious office with comfy couches right off the main square; provides a wide range of maps and brochures.

ⓘ Getting There & Away

From Marsala, bus operators include **Lumia** (www.autolineelumia.it), which goes to Agrigento (€10.10, 2¾ hours, one to three daily), and **Salemi** (☑ 0923 98 11 20; www.autoservizisalemi. it) to Palermo (€11, 2½ hours, at least 11 daily).

Train is the best way to get to Trapani (€3.45, 30 minutes, 10 Monday through Saturday, four on Sunday).

Selinunte

The **ruins of Selinunte** (☑ 0924 4 62 77; adult/reduced €6/3; ☺ 9am-6pm Apr-Oct, 9am-4pm Nov-Mar) are the most impressively sited in Sicily. The huge city was built in 628 BC on a promontory overlooking the sea, and over two and a half centuries became one of the richest and most powerful in the world. It was destroyed by the Carthaginians in 409 BC and finally fell to the Romans in about 350 BC, at which time it went into rapid decline and disappeared from history. The city's past is so remote that the names of the various temples have been forgotten and they are now identified by the letters A to G, M and O. The most impressive, **Temple E**, has been partially rebuilt, its columns pieced together from their fragments with part of its tympanum. Many of the carvings, particularly from **Temple C**, are now in the archaeological museum in Palermo. They

are on a par with the Parthenon marbles and clearly demonstrate the high cultural levels reached by Greek colonies in Sicily.

The ticket office and entrance to the ruins is located near the eastern temples. Try to visit in spring when the surroundings are ablaze with wildflowers.

For overnight stays, **Sicilia Cuore Mio** (☑ 0924 4 60 77; www.siciliacuoremio.it; Via della Cittadella 44; d €68-95; ☏ ⓟ) is a lovely B&B with an upstairs terrace overlooking both the ruins and the sea. Guests enjoy breakfast (including homemade jams, *cannoli* and more) on a shady patio bordered by olive trees. Escape the touristy and mediocre restaurants near the ruins by heading for **Lido Zabbara** (☑ 0924 4 61 94; Via Pigafetta; buffet per person €12), a beachfront place in nearby Marinella di Selinunte with good grilled fish and a varied buffet. You could also drive 15km east to **Da Vittorio** (☑ 0925 7 83 81; www.ristorantevittorio.it; Porto Palo; meals €30-45) in Porto Palo, another great place to enjoy seafood, sunset and the sound of lapping waves.

Selinunte is midway between Agrigento and Trapani, about 10km south of the junction of the A29 and SS115 near Castelvetrano. **Autoservizi Salemi** (☑ 0924 8 18 26; http://autoservizisalemi.it/tratte/selinunte) runs five to seven buses daily from Selinunte to Castelvetrano (€2, 25 to 35 minutes), where you can make onward bus connections with **Lumia** (www.autolineelumia.it) to Agrigento (€8.60, two hours), or train connections to Marsala (€3.95, 35 to 45 minutes), Trapani (€5.75, 1¼ hours) and Palermo (€7.65, 2½ hours).

Trapani

POP 70,600

The lively port city of Trapani makes a convenient base for exploring Sicily's western tip. Its historic centre is filled with atmospheric pedestrian streets and some lovely churches and baroque buildings, although the heavily developed outskirts are rather bleak. The surrounding countryside is beautiful, ranging from the watery vastness of the **Saline di Trapani**, coastal salt ponds interspersed with windmills south of town, to the rugged mountainous shoreline to the north. Once situated at the heart of a powerful trading network that stretched from Carthage to Venice, Trapani's sickle-shaped spit of land hugs the precious harbour, nowadays busy with a steady stream of tourists and traffic to and from Pantelleria and the Egadi Islands.

Sights

The narrow network of streets in Trapani's historic centre remains a Moorish labyrinth, although it takes much of its character from the fabulous 18th-century baroque of the Spanish period. Especially appealing is pedestrianised Corso Vittorio Emanuele, punctuated by the huge **Cattedrale di San Lorenzo** (Corso Vittorio Emanuele; ⊙ 8am-4pm), with its baroque facade and stuccoed interior, and flanked at its eastern end by another baroque confection, the **Palazzo Senatorio** (cnr Corso Vittorio Emanuele & Via Torrearsa). The best time to stroll here is in the early evening (around 7pm) when the *passeggiata* is in full swing. Several other fine examples of baroque architecture can be found along Via Garibaldi.

Chiesa del Purgatorio CHURCH
(⌨ 0923 56 28 82; Via San Francesco d'Assisi; voluntary donation requested; ⊙ 7.30am-noon & 4-7pm Mon-Sat, 10am-noon & 4-7pm Sun) Just off the *corso* in the heart of the city, this church houses the impressive 18th-century *Misteri*, 20 life-sized wooden effigies depicting the story of Christ's Passion, which take centre stage during the city's dramatic Easter Week processions every year. Panels in English, Italian, French and German explain the story behind each figure.

Museo Nazionale Pepoli MUSEUM
(⌨ 0923 55 32 69; www.comune.trapani.it/turismo/pepoli.htm; Via Conte Pepoli 180; adult/reduced €6/3; ⊙ 9am-5.30pm Mon-Sat, 9am-12.30pm Sun) In a former Carmelite monastery, this museum houses the collection of Conte Pepoli, who devoted his life to salvaging Trapani's local arts and crafts, most notably the garish coral carvings – once all the rage in Europe before Trapani's offshore coral banks were decimated. The museum also has a good collection of Gagini sculptures, silverwork, archaeological artefacts and religious art.

Egadi Islands ISLANDS
The islands of **Levanzo**, **Favignana** and **Marettimo** make a pleasant day trip from Trapani. For centuries the lucrative tuna industry fuelled the islands' economy, but overfishing of the surrounding waters means that the Egadi survive primarily on income from tourists who come to cycle, walk, dive or simply enjoy the relaxed pace of life. Siremar and Ustica Lines both run year-round hydrofoil service to the islands. The best range of meals and accommodation can be found on Favignana.

The islands' single greatest tourist attraction is Levanzo's **Grotta del Genovese**, a cave decorated with Mesolithic and Neolithic artwork, including a famous image of a prehistoric tuna. Marettimo offers off-the-beaten-track seclusion and excellent walking trails.

Festivals & Events

I Misteri RELIGIOUS
(www.processionemisteritp.it) Sicily's most venerated Easter procession is a four-day festival of extraordinary religious fervour. Nightly processions, bearing life-sized wooden effigies, make their way through the old quarter to a specially erected chapel in Piazza Lucatelli. The high point is on Good Friday when the celebrations reach fever pitch.

Sleeping

The most convenient – and nicest – place to stay is in Trapani's pedestrianised historic centre, just north of the port.

Ai Lumi B&B B&B €
(⌨ 0923 54 09 22; www.ailumi.it; Corso Vittorio Emanuele 71; s €40-70, d €70-100, tr €90-125, q €100-150; ❉ 🖧) Housed in an 18th-century *palazzo*, this centrally located B&B offers 13 rooms of varying size. Best are the spacious apartments (numbers 32, 34 and 35), with kitchenettes and balconies overlooking Trapani's most elegant pedestrian street. Upstairs apartment 23 is also lovely, with a private balcony reached by a spiral staircase. Guests get discounts at the hotel's atmospheric restaurant next door.

Albergo Maccotta HOTEL €
(⌨ 0923 2 84 18; www.albergomaccotta.it; Via degli Argentieri 4; s €30-40, d €55-75, breakfast per person €3; ❉ @ 🖧) This unassuming hotel in the centre of the Old Town offers clean and neat rooms. There's no atmosphere to speak of, but prices are reasonable, the location is quiet and there's satellite TV in every room.

Eating

Sicily's Arab heritage and Trapani's unique position on the sea route to Tunisia have made couscous (or *'cuscusu'* as they sometimes spell it around here) a local speciality. It's also the centrepiece of annual festivals including nearby San Vito Lo Capo's well-established **Cous Cous Fest** (www.couscousfest.it; ⊙ mid-late Sep) and Trapani's recently launched **Cuscusu** (⊙ late May).

La Rinascente PASTICCERIA €
(⌨ 0923 2 37 67; Via Gatti 3; cannoli €2; ⊙ 9am-1.30pm & 3-7pm Mon, Tue, Thu & Fri, 7.30am-2pm Sat & Sun) When you enter this bakery through the side door, you'll feel like you've

CANNOLI 101

Sugary treats can quickly become an obsession in Sicily. Among them, nothing compares to *cannoli*, the crown jewel of Sicilian sweets. Here's what you need to know:

➡ *Cannoli* are meant to be eaten with your fingers, even in a fancy restaurant. Leave the knife and fork behind, grasp that little sugary beauty between thumb and forefinger, and crunch away to your heart's content!

➡ *Cannoli* is actually the plural form, so if you just want one, ask for *'un cannolo'*. Of course, you could be excused for wanting two or more, in which case *'cannoli'* works just fine!

➡ A truly good *cannolo* will be filled on the spot with fresh ricotta. Don't go for the prefilled shells piled high in airport cafes and other tourist hang-outs. Left to sit for too long, the shell gets soggy, which defeats the whole crunchy beauty of the *cannoli* experience.

A few great places to try *cannoli*: **Ti Vitti** (p177), **Me Cumpari Turriddu** (p198), **Kalòs** (p217), **Pasticceria Cappello** (p172), **La Rinascente** (p220).

barged into someone's kitchen – and you have! Thankfully, owner Giovanni Costadura's broad smile will quickly put you at ease, as will a taste of his homemade *cannoli*, which he'll create for you on the spot.

⭐ **Osteria La Bettolaccia**   SICILIAN **€€**
(☑ 0923 2 16 95; www.labettolaccia.it; Via Enrico Fardella 25; meals €30-45; ⏱ 12.45-3pm Mon-Fri, plus 7.45-11pm Mon-Sat) Unwaveringly authentic, this perennial Slow Food favourite just two blocks from the ferry terminal is the perfect place to try *cous cous con zuppa di mare* (couscous with mixed seafood in a spicy fish sauce, with tomatoes, garlic and parsley). In response to its great popularity, the dining room was recently expanded, but it's still wise to book ahead.

Al Solito Posto   SICILIAN **€€**
(☑ 0923 2 45 45; www.trattoria-alsolitoposto.com; Via Orlandini 30; meals €25-35; ⏱ 1-3pm & 8-11pm Mon-Sat) A 15-minute walk east of the centre, this local favourite is a well-deserved wearer of the Slow Food badge. Service can be a bit surly, but the food is superb, from *primi* such as *busiate con pesto alla trapanese* (corkscrew-shaped pasta with a sauce of almonds, garlic and tomatoes) to super-fresh seafood *secondi* (don't miss the local tuna in May and June) to the creamy-crunchy homemade *cannoli*. Book ahead.

ℹ Orientation

Trapani's city centre sits on a sickle-shaped peninsula jutting west into the Mediterranean from the Sicilian mainland. The ferry and hydrofoil ports straggle along Via Ammiraglio Staiti at the peninsula's southern edge. Just a couple of blocks inland (to the north), Corso Vittorio

Emanuele marks the heart of the pedestrianised centre, with its handsome baroque churches and *palazzi*. The bus and train stations lie about 1km east of the centre.

ℹ Information

Ospedale Sant'Antonio Abate (☑ 0923 80 91 11; www.asptrapani.it; Via Cosenza 82) Five kilometres east of the centre.

Questura (☑ 0923 59 81 11; Piazza Vittoria Veneto 1) Trapani's main police station.

Tourist Office (☑ 0923 54 45 33; www. trapaniwelcome.it; Piazzetta Saturno; ⏱ 9am-4.30pm Mon & Thu, 9am-1pm Tue, Wed & Fri) Just north of the port, Trapani's tourist office offers city maps and information.

ℹ Getting There & Around

Egatours (☑ 0923 2 17 54; www.egatourviaggi. it; Via Ammiraglio Staiti 13), a travel agency opposite the port, offers one-stop shopping for bus, plane and ferry tickets.

AIR

Trapani's small **Vincenzo Florio Airport** (TPS; Birgi Airport; ☑ 0923 61 01 11; www.airgest.it) is 17km south of town at Birgi. **Ryanair** (www. ryanair.com) offers direct flights to two dozen Italian and European cities, while Alitalia flies to the Mediterranean island of Pantelleria. **AST** (Azienda Siciliana Trasporti; ☑ 0923 2 10 21; www.astsicilia.it; Via Virgilio 20) operates hourly buses from 5.30am to 11.30pm connecting the airport with downtown Trapani (€4.90, 45 minutes).

BOAT

Ferry ticket offices are inside Trapani's ferry terminal, opposite Piazza Garibaldi. Hydrofoil ticket offices are 350m further east along Via Ammiraglio Staiti.

Ustica Lines (☑ 0923 87 38 13; www.usticalines.it; Via Ammiraglio Staiti) and **Siremar** (☑ 0923 2 49 68; www.siremar.it; Via Ammiraglio Staiti) both operate hydrofoils year-round to the Egadi Island ports of Favignana (€12, 25 to 40 minutes), Levanzo (€12, 25 to 40 minutes) and Marettimo (€19, 1¼ hours). Ustica Lines also offers summer-only Saturday morning hydrofoil services to Ustica (€33, 2½ hours) and Naples (€99, seven hours).

Siremar offers year-round ferry service to Pantelleria (from €30, six to seven hours) and the Egadi Islands (Favignana €8.20, one to 1½ hours; Levanzo €8.20, one to 1½ hours; Marettimo €13.10, three hours). **Traghetti delle Isole** (☑ 0923 2 17 54; www.traghettidelleisole.it) also sails to Pantelleria five times weekly from June through September.

BUS

Intercity buses arrive and depart from the terminal 1km east of the centre (just southeast of the train station).

Segesta (☑ 0923 2 84 04; www.buscenter.it) runs express buses to Palermo (€9.60, two hours, hourly). Board at the bus stop across the street from Egatours or at the bus station.

Lumia (☑ 0923 2 17 54; www.autolineelumia.it) buses serve Agrigento (€11.90, 2¾ to 3¾ hours, one to three daily).

ATM (☑ 0923 55 95 75; www.atmtrapani.it) operates two free city buses (No 1 and 2), which make circular trips through Trapani, connecting the bus station, the train station and the port.

CAR & MOTORCYCLE

To bypass Trapani's vast suburbs and avoid the narrow streets of the city centre, follow signs from the A29 autostrada directly to the port, where you'll find abundant paid parking along the broad waterside avenue Via Ammiraglio Staiti, within walking distance of most attractions.

TRAIN

From Trapani's station on Piazza Umberto I, Trenitalia offers efficient connections to Marsala (€3.45, 30 minutes, 10 Monday to Saturday, five on Sunday). There are also three direct but slow daily trains to Palermo (€10.40, 3¾ hours).

Erice

POP 28,800 / ELEV 751M

One of Italy's most spectacular hill towns, Erice combines medieval charm with astounding 360-degree views. Erice sits on the legendary Mt Eryx (750m); on a clear day, you can see Cape Bon in Tunisia. Wander the medieval tangle of streets interspersed with churches, forts and tiny cobbled piazzas. The town has a seductive history as a centre for the cult of Venus. Settled by the mysterious Elymians, Erice was an obvious abode for the goddess of love, and the town followed the peculiar ritual of sacred prostitution, with the prostitutes themselves accommodated in the Temple of Venus. Despite countless invasions, the temple remained intact – no guesses why. Erice's tourist infrastructure is excellent. Posted throughout town, you'll find bilingual (Italian–English) informational displays along with town maps providing suggested walking routes.

◉ Sights

The best views can be had from **Giardino del Balio**, which overlooks the turrets and wooded hillsides south to Trapani's saltpans, the Egadi Islands and the sea. Looking north, there are equally staggering views of San Vito Lo Capo's rugged headlands.

Castello di Venere CASTLE
(☑ 339 8974843; www.fondazioneericearte.org/castellodivenere.php; Via Castello di Venere; adult/reduced €5/2.50; ⊙ 10am-1hr before sunset daily Apr-Oct, 10am-4pm Sat & holidays Nov-Mar) The Norman Castello di Venere was built in the 12th and 13th centuries over the Temple of Venus, long a site of worship for the ancient Elymians, Phoenicians, Greeks and Romans. The views from up top, extending to San Vito Lo Capo on one side and the Saline di Trapani on the other, are spectacular. To arrange midweek visits in winter, phone at least 24 hours in advance.

🛏 Sleeping & Eating

Hotels, many with their own restaurants, are scattered along Via Vittorio Emanuele, Erice's main street. After the tourists have left, the town has a beguiling medieval air.

Erice has a tradition of *dolci ericini* (Erice sweets) made by the local nuns. There are numerous pastry shops in town, the most famous being **Maria Grammatico** (☑ 0923 86 93 90; www.mariagrammatico.it; Via Vittorio Emanuele 14; pastries from €2; ⊙ 9am-10pm May, Jun & Sep, to 1am Jul & Aug, to 7pm Oct-Apr), revered for its *frutta martorana* (marzipan fruit) and almond pastries. If you like what you taste, you can even stick around and take cooking classes from Signora Grammatico herself!

Hotel Elimo HOTEL €€
(☑ 0923 86 93 77; www.hotelelimo.it; Via Vittorio Emanuele 75; s €80-110, d €90-130, ste €150-170; 🌫🗟) Communal spaces at this atmospheric historic house are filled with tiled beams,

SICILY'S OLDEST NATURE RESERVE

Saved from development and road projects by local protests, the tranquil **Riserva Naturale dello Zingaro** is the star attraction on the Golfo di Castellammare, halfway between Palermo and Trapani. Founded in 1981, this was Sicily's first nature reserve. Zingaro's wild coastline is a haven for the rare Bonelli's eagle along with 40 other species of bird. Mediterranean flora dusts the hillsides with wild carob and bright yellow euphorbia, and hidden coves, such as Capreria and Marinella Bays, provide tranquil swimming spots. The main entrance to the park is 2km north of the village of Scopello. Several walking trails are detailed on maps available free at the entrance or downloadable from the park website. The main 7km trail along the coast passes by the visitor centre and five museums documenting everything from local flora and fauna to traditional fishing methods.

Once home to tuna fishers, tiny **Scopello** now mainly hosts tourists. Its port, 1km below town and reachable by a walking path, has a picturesque **beach** (www.tonnaradi-scopello.com; admission €3; ⊘9am-7pm) backed by a rust-red *tonnara* (tuna-processing plant) and dramatic *faraglioni* (rock towers) rising from the water.

Pensione Tranchina (☑0924 54 10 99; www.pensionetranchina.com; Via Diaz 7, Scopello; B&B per person €36-48, half-board per person €55-75; ❄️🐾) is the nicest of several places to stay and eat clustered around the cobblestoned courtyard at Scopello's village centre. Friendly hosts Marisin and Salvatore offer comfortable rooms, a roaring fire on chilly evenings and superb home-cooked meals featuring local fish and home-grown fruit and olive oil. For drinks at sunset, head for the scenic back terrace at nearby **Bar Nettuno** (Baglio Scopello 1; ⊘9am-late).

marble fireplaces, intriguing art, knick-knacks and antiques. The bedrooms are more mainstream, although many (along with the hotel terrace and restaurant) have breathtaking vistas south and west towards the Saline di Trapani, the Egadi Islands and the shimmering sea.

ℹ️ Information

The main **tourist office** (☑348 6912335; www.facebook.com/EriceTourism; Porta Trapani; ⊘2-6pm Mon, 10am-2pm & 3-6pm Tue-Sat, 10am-2pm Sun) is adjacent to Porta Trapani (Erice's old town gate); there's another branch 100m up the street at the **Enoteca Comunale** (☑0923 86 93 88; Via Conte Agostino Pepoli 11).

ℹ️ Getting There & Away

AST (p221) runs five buses daily (three on Sunday) between Erice and Trapani's bus terminal (€2.90, 45 minutes). Alternatively, catch the **funicular** (Funivia; ☑0923 86 97 20, 0923 56 93 06; www.funiviaerice.it; one way/return €5.50/9; ⊘1-8pm Mon, 8.10am-8pm Tue-Fri, 10am-10pm Sat, 10am-8pm Sun) opposite the car park at the foot of Erice's Via Vittorio Emanuele; the 10-minute descent drops you in Trapani near Ospedale Sant'Antonio Abate, where you can catch local bus 21 or 23 (€1.40) into the centre of Trapani.

Segesta

ELEV 304M

Set on the edge of a deep canyon in the midst of wild, desolate mountains, the 5th-century BC **ruins of Segesta** (☑0924 95 23 56; adult/reduced €6/3; ⊘9am-4pm Oct-Mar, 8.30am-1hr before sunset Apr-Sep) are a magical site. On windy days the 36 giant columns of its magnificent temple are said to act like an organ, producing mysterious notes.

The city, founded by the ancient Elymians, was in constant conflict with Selinunte in the south, whose destruction it sought with dogged determination and singular success. Time, however, has done to Segesta what violence inflicted on Selinunte; little remains now, save the **theatre** and the never-completed **Doric temple**, the latter dating from around 430 BC and remarkably well preserved. A shuttle bus (€1.50) runs every 30 minutes from the temple entrance 1.5km uphill to the theatre.

Tarantola (☑0924 3 10 20) runs four daily buses to Segesta from Trapani (one way/return €4/6.60, 45 minutes), plus three daily buses from Via Balsamo near Palermo's train station (one way/return €7/11.20, 1¼ hours); all buses stop just outside the entrance to the archaeological site. If driving, exit the A29dir at Segesta and follow signs 1.5km uphill to the site.

Understand Southern Italy

SOUTHERN ITALY TODAY.....................226

High unemployment, asylum seekers and Calabrian crime on the rise: it's a testing time for the land of the midday sun.

HISTORY 228

Courted, betrayed, loved and abused: southern Italy's biography reads like that of a stunning, tragic diva.

THE SOUTHERN WAY OF LIFE 241

In equal measure proud, rueful, gregarious and suspicious, Italy's *meridionali* (southerners) are as contradictory as they are intriguing and complex.

THE MAFIA 246

Drugs, rackets and bloody vendettas: welcome to the sunny south's dark side.

THE SOUTHERN TABLE.......................248

Southern Italy is an edible fantasy; loosen your belt and prepare for the feed of your life.

ART & ARCHITECTURE 256

From pagan temples and holy frescoes to tongue-in-cheek contemporary statements, the south is a seasoned culture vulture.

Southern Italy Today

Singing about his native Naples in the song *Napule è,* the late musician Pino Daniele muses, *'Napule è nu sole amaro'* (Naples is a bitter sun). This irony could easily encompass the whole of Italy's Mezzogiorno (land of the midday sun). A region justifiably famous for its cultural cachet and natural splendour, southern Italy is also one of the European Union's problem children. In the face of soaring unemployment and suffocating corruption, an ever-growing number of *meridionali* (southern Italians) are questioning their region's future.

Best on Film

Il Postino (*The Postman;* Michael Radford; 1994) Exiled poet Pablo Neruda brings poetry and passion to a drowsy southern Italian isle and a misfit postman.

Matrimonio all'italiana (*Marriage, Italian-Style;* Vittorio De Sica; 1964) Sophia Loren and Marcello Mastroianni join forces in this comedy about a cynical businessman and his shrewd Neapolitan mistress.

Cinema Paradiso (Giuseppe Tornatore; 1988) A bittersweet tale about a director who returns to Sicily and rediscovers his true loves: the girl next door and the movies.

Best in Print

The Italians (Luigi Barzini; 1964) A revealing look at Italian culture beyond the well-worn clichés.

Christ Stopped at Eboli (Carlo Levi; 1945) Bitter-sweet recollections from a writer exiled by fascists to a mountain village in Basilicata.

Midnight in Sicily (Peter Robb; 1996) A disturbing yet fascinating portrait of postwar Sicily.

The Silent Duchess (Dacia Maraini; 1992) A feminist-flavoured historical novel set in 18th-century Palermo.

Wanted: Work

Italy's economic headache continues to pound strongest in the south. While the national unemployment rate hovered at just over 12% in 2015, the rate was closer to 22% in Campania, 21% in Puglia and 23% in Calabria and Sicily. The figures are especially grim for the young. Calabria and Puglia are two of the 10 worst areas for youth unemployment in Europe according to the European Union's bureau of statistics (Eurostat), with an unemployment rate of almost 60% in both regions.

The toxic cocktail of high unemployment and taxes, low salaries and rampant cronyism has become intolerable for a growing number of Italians. A staggering 94,000 of them moved abroad in 2013, close to double the number for 2007. And this is just the official figure, accounting only for those who officially registered a new address. The actual figure is estimated to be two to three times higher.

The increase has been especially sharp among those aged between 20 and 40, desperate to forge careers in the more robust economies of northern Europe, Britain and beyond. Dubbed the 'lost generation', they are part of the so-called brain drain; an exodus of highly qualified Italian graduates and professionals leaving behind a rapidly ageing population increasingly in need of a young, capable workforce.

Seeking Asylum

As more Italians head for the departure gates, an ever-growing number of asylum seekers are piling onto boats in North Africa, bound for Europe. Roughly 62,000 migrants arrived in Italy by sea in the first half of 2015, with an estimated 1800 dying en route. Most are fleeing war, persecution and abject poverty in sub-Saharan Africa and the Middle East, placing their lives in the hands of unscrupulous smugglers who cram them onto unseaworthy vessels for the journey north. According to the Italian Navy, over 200,000 people have crossed the Mediterranean to Italy since 2014, while official estimates put the number of migrants waiting to attempt the journey at one million.

Of those who do not perish at sea, many land on the tiny Italian island of Lampedusa. Wedged between Italy and Libya, a mere 113km off the Tunisian coast, the island forms one end to what is now Europe's busiest sea migration route. Incessant media images of desperate arrivals and bodies at sea have become a PR nightmare for an island heavily reliant on tourism.

While most migrants continue their journey north to other European countries, many do seek asylum in Italy; almost 65,000 in 2014 according to Eurostat. Those who do stay inevitably face other challenges in a country where jobs are in short supply, corruption is rife and xenophobic sentiments are increasingly common.

Rise of the 'ndrangheta

Also on the ascent is the 'ndrangheta, which continues to tighten its grip on Italy and other parts of the world. Calabria's home-grown mafia is now the country's most powerful organised-crime syndicate, turning over €50 billion in profit annually. Shrewd ties with Mexican and South American drug cartels have allowed it to become the dominant player in the transatlantic cocaine trade, and the Calabrian port of Gioia Tauro is now the main entry point for illicit drugs into Italy.

Though Calabria remains the 'ndrangheta's base, its reach extends far beyond its borders, with cells in northern Italy, other EU countries, the United States and beyond. In 2015, a joint investigation by Australia's Fairfax media and ABC (Australian Broadcasting Corporation) exposed the group's growing influence in Australia. In the same year, the owner of a pizzeria in Queens, New York, was arrested for allegedly assisting the 'ndrangheta to smuggle cocaine into the US. The owner, Gregorio Gigliotti, had acted as the 'ndrangheta's go-between with New York's Genovese crime family, reflecting the Calabrian mafia's wish to strengthen ties with local American crime groups, both old and new. Gigliotti's wife and son were also arrested.

In Calabria itself, the 'ndrangheta continues to strangle economic development. Government funds set aside for projects such as wind farms regularly end up in the pockets of corrupt officials. Meanwhile, the group's laundering of dirty money has allowed it to quietly and effectively integrate into the mainstream Italian economy. In 2014, a string of arrests revealed the mafia's infiltration of Expo Milano 2015, which included the rigging of contracts for public works.

COMBINED POPULATION: **17.02 MILLION (2015)**

COMBINED SIZE: **83,733 SQ KM**

HIGHEST POINT: **MT ETNA, SICILY (3329M)**

NUMBER OF UNESCO WORLD HERITAGE SITES: **15**

AVERAGE CUPS OF COFFEE PER PERSON PER YEAR: **600**

if Italy were 100 people

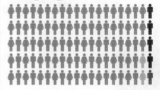

93 would be Italian
4 would be Albanian & Eastern European
1 would be North African
2 would be Others

belief systems
(% of population)

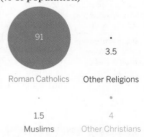

91 — Roman Catholics
3.5 — Other Religions
1.5 — Muslims
4 — Other Christians

population per sq km

NAPLES   LOS ANGELES   ITALY

⚦ ≈ 201 people

History

Some northern Italians dismiss the country's south as the land of *terroni* (peasants) – the backward sibling to Italy's salubrious north. Yet the south is terribly ancient, its history tracing back some 8000 years; writer Carlo Levi called it 'that other world…which no-one may enter without a magic key'. Magical it may be, but there has been plenty to regret – invasions, feudalism and a centuries-long scourge of malaria that stunted the south's development. Venture here and expect to have your preconceptions of modern Italy challenged.

The Early Years

Southern Italy has been active for a very long time. The first inhabitant we know of is the Altamura Man, currently wedged in the karst cave of Lamalunga, Puglia, and slowly becoming part of the crystal concretions that surround him. He's about 130,000 years old.

Fast forward to around 7000 BC, when the Messapians, an Illyrian-speaking people from the Balkans, were settling down in the Salento and around Foggia. Alongside them, other long-gone tribes such as the Daunii in the Gargano, the Peucetians around Taranto and the Lucanians in Basilicata were starting to develop the first settled towns – by 1700 BC there is evidence that they were beginning to trade with the Mycenaeans from mainland Greece and the Minoans in Crete.

The first evidence of an organised settlement on Sicily belongs to the Stentillenians, who came from the Middle East and settled on the island's eastern shores sometime between 4000 and 3000 BC. But it was the settlers from the middle of the second millennium BC who radically defined the island's character and whose early presence helps us understand Sicily's complexities. Thucydides (c 460–404 BC) records three major tribes: the Sicanians, who originated either in Spain or North Africa and settled in the north and west (giving these areas their Eastern flavour); the Elymians from Greece, who settled in the south; and the Siculians (or Sikels), who came from the Calabrian peninsula and spread out along the Ionian Coast.

Archaeological Treasures

....

Museo Archeologico Nazionale, Naples

....

Museo Archeologico Paolo Orsi, Syracuse

....

Museo Archeologico, Agrigento

....

Museo Archeologico Regionale Eoliano, Lipari, Aeolian Islands

TIMELINE	c 200,000–9000 BC	3000–1000 BC	750–600 BC
	As long ago as 700,000 BC, Palaeolithic humans like the Altamura Man lived precarious lives in caves. Painted caves like the Grotta dei Cervi bear testimony to this period.	The Bronze Age reaches Italy courtesy of the Mycenaeans of Eastern Europe. The use of copper and bronze marks a leap in sophistication, accompanied by a more complex social organisation.	The Greeks begin establishing cities all over southern Italy and Sicily, including Naxos and Syracuse in Sicily, and Cumae, Sybaris, Croton, Metaponto, Eraklea and Taras in southern Italy.

Magna Graecia

Following the earlier lead of the Elymians, the Chalcidians landed on Sicily's Ionian Coast in 735 BC and founded a small settlement at Naxos. They were followed a year later by the Corinthians, who built their colony on the southeastern island of Ortygia, calling it Syracoussai (Syracuse). The Chalcidians went further south from their own fort and founded a second town called Katane (Catania) in 729 BC, and the two carried on stitching towns and settlements together until three-quarters of the island was in Hellenic hands.

On the mainland, the Greeks' major city was Taras, which dominated the growing region now known as Magna Graecia (Greater Greece). They exploited its harbour well, trading with Greece, the Near East and the rich colonies in Sicily and so built up a substantial network of commerce. Their lucrative business in luxury goods soon made them rich and powerful; by the 4th century BC, the population had swelled to 300,000 and city life was cultured and civilised.

Although few monuments survive, among them the ambitious temples of Paestum in Campania and Selinunte in Sicily, the Greek era was a golden age for the south. Art and sculpture, poetry, drama, philosophy, mathematics and science were all part of the cultural life of Magna Graecia's cities. Exiled from Crotone (Calabria), Pythagoras spent years in Metapontum and Taras; Empedocles, Zeno and Stesichorus were all home-grown talents.

But despite their shared Greekness, these city-states' deeply ingrained rivalries and parochial politics undermined their civic achievements, ultimately leading to damaging conflicts like the Peloponnesian War (431–399 BC), fought by the Athenians against the Peloponnesian League (led by Sparta). Although Syracuse fought successfully against the attacking Athenian forces, the rest of Sicily was in a constant state of civil war. In 409 BC this provided the perfect opportunity for the powerful city-state of Carthage (in modern-day Tunisia) to seek revenge for its humiliation in 480 BC, in which Carthaginian mercenaries, commanded by Hamilcar, were defeated by the crafty Greek tyrant Gelon. Led by Hamilcar's bitter but brilliant nephew Hannibal, the Carthaginians wreaked havoc in the Sicilian countryside, completely destroying Selinunte, Himera, Agrigento and Gela. The Syracusans were eventually forced to surrender everything to Carthage except the site of Syracuse itself.

During the 4th century, the mainland's Greek colonies came under increasing pressure from other powers with expansionist ambitions. The Etruscans began to move south towards the major port of Cumae in Campania and then the Samnites and Sabines started to capture the highlands of the Appenines in Basilicata. Unable to unite and beat off the

HISTORY MAGNA GRAECIA

> **Graeco-Roman Greats**
> ....
> *Pompeii & Herculaneum, Campania*
> ....
> *Paestum, Campania*
> ....
> *Selinunte, Sicily*
> ....
> *Segesta, Sicily*
> ....
> *Valley of the Temples, Agrigento, Sicily*

> Get to grips with the history, peoples and wars of Ancient Greece by logging on to www.ancientgreece.com, which gives potted histories of all the key characters and places. It also has an online bookstore.

264–146 BC	280 BC–AD 109	AD 79	300–337
The Punic Wars rage between the Romans and the Carthaginians. In 216 BC Hannibal inflicts defeat on the Romans at Cannae, but the Romans go on to ultimately defeat the Carthaginians in 146 BC.	The Romans build the Via Appia and then the Via Appia Traiana. The Via Appia Traiana covered 540km and enabled travellers to journey from Rome to Brindisi in 14 days.	Mt Vesuvius showers molten rock and ash upon Pompeii and Herculaneum. Pliny the Younger later describes the eruption in letters; the towns are only rediscovered in the 18th century.	After a series of false starts, the Roman Empire is divided into Eastern and Western halves just east of Rome. In 330 Constantine moves the imperial capital to Byzantium and refounds it as Constantinople.

growing threat, the Greeks had little choice but to make a Faustian pact with the Romans, long-standing admirers of the Greeks and seemingly the perfect allies. It was a partnership that was to cost them dearly; by 270 BC the whole of southern Italy was under Roman control.

Eastern Influences

Roman control of southern Italy was to set the tone for centuries to come. While they turned the Bay of Naples into a holiday hot spot for emperors and built the Via Appia (280–264 BC) and later the Via Appia Traiana (AD 109) – the first superhighway to the south from Rome – the Romans also stripped the southern landscape of its trees, creating just the right conditions for the malarial scourge that the region would face centuries hence. Then they parcelled up the land into huge *latifondi* (estates) that they distributed among a handful of wealthy Romans, who established a damaging agricultural monoculture of wheat to feed the Roman army. Local peasants, meanwhile, were denied even the most basic rights of citizenship.

Despite the Romans' attempts at Latinising the region, this period actually had the effect of reinforcing Eastern influences on the south. As it was, the Romans admired and emulated Greek culture, the locals in cities like Neapolis (modern-day Naples) continued to speak Greek, and the Via Appia made Puglia the gateway to the East. In AD 245 when Diocletian came to power, he determined that the empire was simply too vast for good governance and split it in two. When Constantine came to power in AD 306, the groundwork was already established for an Eastern (Byzantine) Empire and a Western Empire – in AD 324 he officially declared Constantinople the capital of Nova Roma.

With southern Italy's proximity to the Balkans and the Near East, Puglia and Basilicata were exposed to a new wave of Eastern influence, bringing with it a brand-new set of Christian beliefs. This new wave of influence would officially reach Sicily in AD 535, when the Byzantine general Belisarius landed an army on the island's shores. Despite falling to the Visigoths in AD 470 after more than 700 years of Roman occupation, the island's population was still largely Greek, both in language and custom. The Byzantines were eager to use Sicily as a launching pad for the retaking of the lands owned by the combined forces of Arabs, Berbers and Spanish Muslims, collectively known as the Saracens, but their dreams were not to be realised.

In AD 827 the Saracen army landed at Mazara del Vallo, in Sicily. Palermo fell in AD 831, followed by Syracuse in AD 878. Under them, churches were converted to mosques and Arabic was implemented as the common language. At the same time, much-needed land reforms were introduced and trade, agriculture and mining were fostered. New crops were intro-

> It is commonly said that there is less Italian blood running through modern Sicilian veins than there is Phoenician, Greek, Arabic, Norman, Spanish or French.

> The Arabs introduced spaghetti to Sicily; 'strings of pasta' were documented by the Arab geographer Al-Idrissi in Palermo in 1150.

476	827–965	1059	1130
The last western emperor, Romulus Augustulus, is deposed. Goths, Ostrogoths and Byzantines tussle over the spoils of the empire.	A Saracen army lands at Mazaradel Vallo in Sicily in 827. The island is united under Arab rule and Palermo becomes the second-largest city in the world after Constantinople.	Pope Nicholas II and Norman mercenary Robert Guiscard sign a concordat at Melfi, making Robert duke of Apulia and Calabria. Robert agrees to rid southern Italy of Saracens and Byzantines.	Norman invader Roger II is crowned king of Sicily, a century after the Normans landed in southern Italy; a united southern Italian kingdom is created.

IMPERIAL INSANITY

Bribes? *Bunga bunga* parties? Spare a thought for the ancient Romans, who suffered their fair share of eccentric leaders. We salute some of the empire's wackiest, most ruthless and downright kinkiest rulers.

Tiberius (ruled AD 14–37) With a steady governing hand but prone to depression, Tiberius had a difficult relationship with the Senate and withdrew in his later years to Capri, where, they say, he devoted himself to drinking, orgies and fits of paranoia.

Gaius (Caligula; ruled AD 37–41) 'Little Shoes' made grand-uncle Tiberius look tame. Sex – including with his sisters – and gratuitous, cruel violence were high on his agenda. He emptied the state's coffers and suggested making a horse consul before being assassinated.

Nero (ruled AD 54–68) Augustus' last descendant, Nero had his pushy stage mother murdered, his first wife's veins slashed, his second wife kicked to death and his third wife's ex-husband killed. The people accused him of playing the fiddle while Rome burned to the ground in AD 64.

Diocletian (ruled AD 284–305) Dalmatian-born Diocletian had little time for the growing cult of Christianity. He ordered the burning of churches and sacred scriptures, and had Christians thrown to wild beasts in a grisly public spectacle. One of them was Naples' patron saint, San Gennaro, slaughtered at Pozzuoli's Solfatara Crater.

duced, including citrus trees, date palms and sugar cane, and a system of water supply and irrigation was developed. Palermo was chosen as the capital of the new emirate and, over the next 200 years, it became one of the most splendid cities in the Arab world.

Pilgrims & Crusaders

Ever since Puglia and Basilicata's colonisation by the Greeks, multifarious myths had established themselves in the region – many were related to the presence of therapeutic waters and the practice called *incubatio*, a rite whereby one had to sleep close to a holy place to receive revelations from a deity. In its early days, the cult of the Archangel Michael was mainly a cult of healing forces based on the saint's revelations. It started to gain currency in the early 5th century but it wasn't until the arrival of the Lombards in the 7th century that it really began to take off.

Sweeping down from the north, the Lombards found in St Michael a mirror image of their own pagan deity, Wodan. In Michael, they saw similar characteristics: the image of a medieval warrior, a leader of celestial armies. There is little doubt that their devotion to the saint was instrumental in their easy conversion to Catholicism, as they repeatedly

Messages could be shot around the Roman Empire in days or weeks. At wayside inns, dispatch riders would have a bite and change mounts. The Romans even devised a type of odometer, a cogwheel that engaged with the wheel of a chariot or other vehicle.

1215	1224	1270–1500	1516
Frederick II is crowned Holy Roman Emperor in Aachen where he symbolically re-inters Charlemagne's body in a silver and gold reliquary. He takes the cross and vows of a crusader.	The Università degli Studi di Napoli Federico II is founded in Naples. The oldest state university in the world, its alumni include Catholic theologian and philosopher Thomas Aquinas.	The French Angevins and Spanish Aragonese spend the best part of two centuries fighting over southern Italy. Instability, warfare, the Black Death and overtaxation strangle the region's economic development.	Holy Roman Emperor Charles V of Spain inherits southern Italy. The region is strategically important to Spain in its battle with France. Charles invests in defences in cities like Lecce.

Best Places for Arab-Norman Flavour

Cappella Palatina, Palazzo dei Normanni, Palermo

Chiesa Capitolare di San Cataldo, Palermo

Cattedrale, Palermo

Duomo, Cefalù

restored and enlarged the Monte Sant'Angelo shrine, making it the most important centre of the cult in the western world. Soon the trail of pilgrims along the Via Traiana became so great that the road was nicknamed the Via Sacra Langobardorum (Holy Road of the Lombards), and dozens of churches, hostels and monasteries were built to accommodate the pilgrims along the way.

Another group of pilgrims in this region were the Normans. Ruling over northern France, they arrived in southern Italy in the 10th century, initially en route from Jerusalem, and later as mercenaries attracted by the money to be made fighting for the rival principalities and against the Muslim Saracens in Sicily. By 1053, after six years of mercenary activity, Robert Guiscard (c 1015–85), the Norman conquistador, had comprehensively defeated the combined forces of the Calabrian Byzantines, the Lombards and the papal forces at the Battle of Civitate. Having established his supremacy, Robert turned his attentions to expanding the territories under his control. To achieve this, he had to negotiate with the Vatican. In return for being invested with the titles of duke of Apulia and Calabria in 1059, Robert agreed to chase the Saracens out of Sicily and restore Christianity to the island. He delegated this task – and promised the island – to his younger brother Roger I (1031–1101), who landed his troops at Messina in 1061, capturing the port by surprise. In 1064, Roger tried to make good on his promise and take Palermo, but was repulsed by a well-organised Saracen army; it wasn't until Robert arrived in 1072 with substantial reinforcements that the city fell into Norman hands. Impressed by the island's cultured Arab lifestyle, Roger shamelessly borrowed and improved on it, spending vast amounts of money on palaces and churches and encouraging a cosmopolitan atmosphere in his court.

By 1130 most of southern Italy, including Sicily, was in Norman hands and it was only a question of time before the prosperous duchy of Naples gave in to the inevitable. It did so in 1139 – the Kingdom of the Two Sicilies was thus complete.

Kingdom in the Sun is John Julius Norwich's wonderful romp through the Norman invasions of the south, leading to their spectacular takeover of Sicily.

The Wonder of the World

Frederick II, king of Sicily and Holy Roman Emperor, presided over one of the most glamorous periods of southern history. The fact that he came to wield such power and wear Charlemagne's crown at all is one of those unexpected quirks of history.

He inadvertently inherited the crown of Sicily and the south from his mother Constance (the posthumous daughter of Roger I) in 1208 after William II died childless; the crown to the Holy Roman Empire came to him through his father, Henry VI, the son of Frederick Barbarossa. The union of the two crowns in 1220 meant that Frederick II would rule over lands covering Germany, Austria, the Netherlands, Poland, the Czech Re-

1600	1647	1714	1737
Naples is Europe's biggest city, boasting a population of over 300,000. Among its growing number of residents is renegade artist Caravaggio, who arrives in 1606.	Gross mismanagement causes the southern Italian economy to collapse. In Naples, the Masaniello Revolt breaks out over heavy taxes. Revolt spreads to the provinces and peasant militias rule the countryside.	The end of the War of the Spanish Succession forces the withdrawal of Spanish forces from Lombardy. The Spanish Bourbon family establishes an independent Kingdom of the Two Sicilies.	Naples' original Teatro San Carlo is built in a swift eight months. Designed by Giovanni Antonio Medrano, it was rebuilt in 1816 after a devastating fire.

public, Slovakia, southern France, southern Italy, the rich Kingdom of Sicily and the remnants of the Byzantine world.

It was a union that caused the popes much discomfort. For while they wanted and needed an emperor who would play the role of temporal sword, Frederick's wide-reaching kingdom all but encircled the Papal States and his belief in the absolute power of monarchy gave them grave cause for concern.

Like Charlemagne before him, Frederick controlled a kingdom so vast that he could realistically dream of reviving the fallen Roman Empire – and dream he did. Under his rule, Sicily was transformed into a central-ised state playing a key commercial and cultural role in European affairs, and Palermo gained a reputation as the continent's most important city; most of the northern Italian city-states were brought to heel. In 1225 he went on to marry Jolanda of Brienne and gained the title of King of

BORN TO RUMBLE

In the late 10th century, Norman fighters began to earn a reputation across Europe as fierce and tough mercenaries. As inheritance customs left younger sons disadvantaged, younger brothers were expected to seek their fortunes elsewhere – and seek they did, with remarkable success.

According to one legend, Norman involvement in southern Italy began in 1013 at the shrine of St Michael at Monte Sant'Angelo, when Latin rebel Meles, chaffing under Byz-antine authority, invited the Normans to serve him as mercenaries. By 1030 what had begun as an offer of service in return for booty became a series of unusually successful attempts at wresting control from local warlords.

At the forefront of the Italian conquests were the Hauteville brothers: the eldest Wil-liam 'Bras de Fer' (Iron Arm; c 1009–46), who controlled Puglia, and Robert Guiscard (the Cunning; c 1015–85), who rampaged over Calabria and southern Campania. By 1053, after six years of incessant fighting, Robert had defeated the combined forces of the Calabrian Byzantines, the Lombards and the papal forces at Civitate.

Up to this point the Normans (as mercenaries) had fought both for and against the pa-pacy as their needs had required. But Robert's relationship with the Vatican underwent a radical transformation following the Great Schism of 1054, which resulted in a complete break between the Byzantine and Latin churches. In their turn, the popes saw in the Normans a powerful potential ally, and so in 1059 Pope Nicholas II and Robert signed a concord at at Melfi, which invested Robert with the titles of Duke of Apulia (including Basilicata) and Calabria. In return, Robert agreed to chase the Byzantines and Saracens out of southern Italy and Sicily and restore the southern kingdom to papal rule.

Little would the pope suspect that Roger would go on to develop a territorial monar-chy and become a ruler who saw himself as detached from the higher jurisdiction of both Western and Eastern emperors – or even the pope himself.

1752	1798–99	1805	1814–15
Work commences on the Palazzo Reale in Ca-serta, north of Naples. Commissioned by Charles VII of Bourbon and designed by Luigi Vanvitelli, the palace would be larger than Versailles.	Napoleon invades Italy and occupies Rome. Ferdinand I sends an army to evict them, but his troops flee. The French counter-attack and take Naples, estab-lishing the Partheno-pean Republic.	Napoleon is proclaimed king of the newly constituted Kingdom of Italy, comprising most of the northern half of the country. A year later, he retakes the Kingdom of Naples.	After Napoleon's fall the Congress of Vienna is held to re-establish the balance of power in Europe. The result for Italy is largely a return of the old occupying powers.

Jerusalem, making him the first Roman emperor to bear that title. In 1228 the Crusade he launched was not only nearly bloodless, but it saw the return of the shrines of Jerusalem, Nazareth and Bethlehem to the Christian fold.

As well as being a talented statesman, he was also a cultured man, and many of his biographers see in him the precursor of the Renaissance prince. Few other medieval monarchs corresponded with the sages of Judaism and Islam; he also spoke six languages and was fascinated by science, nature and architecture. He even wrote a scholarly treatise on falconry during one of the long, boring sieges of Faenza, and Dante was right to call him the father of Italian poetry.

Yet despite his brilliance, his vision for an international empire was incompatible with the ambitions of the papacy and he struggled throughout his reign to remain on good terms with increasingly aggressive popes. Finally, in 1243, Pope Innocent IV proclaimed him deposed, characterising him as a 'friend of Babylon's sultan' and a heretic. At the same time the northern Italian provinces were straining against his centralised control and years of war and strategising were finally taking their toll. Only in Puglia, his favourite province throughout this reign, did Frederick remain undisputed master.

In December 1250, after suffering a bout of dysentery, he died suddenly in Castel Fiorentino near Lucera. His heirs, Conrad and Manfred, would not survive him long. Conrad died of malaria four years later in Lavello in Basilicata, and Manfred was defeated at the Battle of Benevento in 1266 by Charles of Anjou, the pope's pretender to the throne. Two years later another battle took the life of Manfred's 15-year-old nephew and heir, Conradin, who was publicly beheaded in Naples.

By 1270 the brilliant Hohenstaufen period was officially over. And while Frederick's rule marked a major stage in the transformation of Europe from a community of Latin Christians under the headship of two competing powers (pope and emperor) to a Europe of nation-states, he had failed to leave any tangible legacies. The following ruling family, the Angevins, did not make the same mistake: Naples' Castel Nuovo (built by Charles of Anjou in 1279) and Castel Sant'Elmo (constructed by Robert of Anjou in the early 14th century) remain two of the city's iconic landmarks.

Sicily's Inglorious Slide

Under the Angevins, who succeeded the German Hohenstaufens, Sicily was weighed down by onerous taxes, religious persecution of the island's Muslim population was the order of the day and Norman fiefdoms were removed and awarded to French aristocrats. On Easter Monday 1282, the city of Palermo exploded in rebellion. Incited by the alleged rape of a lo-

Steven Runciman's *Fall of Constantinople 1453* provides a classic account of this bloody episode in Crusade history. It manages to be academically sound and highly entertaining at the same time.

For a wide-ranging general site on Italian history, check out www.arcaini.com. It covers everything from prehistory to the postwar period, and includes a brief chronology to the end of the 20th century.

1848	1860	1861	1880–1915
European revolts spark rebellion in Italy. The Bourbons are expelled from Sicily but retake it in a rain of fire that earns Ferdinand II the epithet 'Re Bomba' (King Bomb).	In the name of Italian unity, Giuseppe Garibaldi lands with 1000 men, the Red Shirts, in Sicily. He takes the island and lands in southern Italy.	By the end of the Franco-Austrian War (1859–61), Vittorio Emanuele II controls Lombardy, Sardinia, Sicily, southern Italy and parts of central Italy, and is proclaimed king of a newly united Italy.	People vote with their feet; millions of impoverished southerners embark on ships for the New World, causing a massive haemorrhage of the most able-bodied and hardworking southern male youths.

cal girl by a gang of French troops, peasants lynched every French soldier they could get their hands on. The revolt spread to the countryside and was supported by the Sicilian nobility, who had formed an alliance with Peter of Aragon. Peter had landed at Trapani with a large army and was proclaimed king. For the next 20 years, the Aragonese and the Angevins were engaged in the War of the Sicilian Vespers – a war that was eventually won by the Spanish.

By the end of the 14th century, Sicily had been thoroughly marginalised. The eastern Mediterranean was sealed off by the Ottoman Turks, while the Italian mainland was off limits on account of Sicily's political ties with Spain. As a result, the Renaissance passed the island by, reinforcing the oppressive effects of poverty and ignorance. Even Spain lost interest in its colony, choosing to rule through viceroys. By the end of the 15th century, the viceroy's court was a den of corruption, and the most influential body on the island became the Catholic Church (whose archbishops and bishops were mostly Spaniards). The Church exercised draconian powers through a network of Holy Office tribunals, otherwise known as the Inquisition.

Reeling under the weight of state oppression, ordinary Sicilians demanded reform. Unfortunately, their Spanish monarchs were preoccupied by the Wars of the Spanish Succession and Sicily was subsequently passed around for decades from European power to European power like an unwanted Christmas present. Eventually the Spanish reclaimed the island in 1734, this time under the Bourbon king Charles III of Sicily (r 1734–59).

> Between January and August of 1656, the bubonic plague wiped out about half of Naples' 300,000-plus inhabitants and much of the economy. The city would take almost two centuries to reach its pre-plague headcount again.

The Bourbon Paradox

Assessment of Bourbon rule in southern Italy is a controversial topic. Many historians consider it a period of exploitation and stagnation. Others, more recently, have started to re-evaluate the Kingdom of the Two Sicilies, pointing out the raft of positive reforms Charles III implemented. These included abolishing many noble and clerical privileges, curtailing the legal rights of landowners within their fiefs and restricting ecclesiastical jurisdiction at a time when the Church was reputed to own almost a third of the land within the kingdom.

Naples had already begun prospering under the rule of Spanish viceroy Don Pedro de Toledo (1532–53), whose building boom attracted some of Italy's greatest artistic talent. Under Charles, the city became one of the great capital cities of Europe, attracting hundreds of aristocratic travellers. On top of this, Charles was a great patron of architecture and the arts. During his reign Pompeii and Herculaneum (both destroyed in the AD 79 eruption of Mt Vesuvius) were discovered and the Archaeological Museum in Naples was founded. He was responsible for the Teatro San

1889	1908	1915	1919
Raffaele Esposito invents 'pizza margherita' in honour of Queen Margherita, who takes her first bite of the Neapolitan staple on a royal visit to the city.	On the morning of 28 December, Messina and Reggio di Calabria are struck by a 7.5-magnitude earthquake and a 13m-high tsunami. More than 80,000 lives are lost.	Italy enters WWI on the side of the Allies to win Italian territories still in Austrian hands after Austria's offer to cede some of the territories is deemed insufficient.	Former socialist journalist Benito Mussolini forms a right-wing militant group, the *Fasci Italiani di Combattimento* (Italian Combat Fasces), precursor to his Fascist Party.

236

HISTORY THE BOURBON PARADOX

Carlo, the largest opera house in Europe, and he built the huge palaces of Capodimonte and Caserta. Some subsequent Bourbon monarchs also made positive contributions, such as Ferdinand II (1830–59), who laid the foundations for modern industry, developing southern harbours, creating a merchant fleet and building the first Italian railway line and road systems, such as the dramatic Amalfi drive for example.

But where Charles might rightfully claim a place among southern Italy's outstanding rulers, later Bourbon princes were some of the most eccentric and pleasure-seeking monarchs in Europe. Charles' son, Ferdinand I (1751–1825), was by contrast venal and poorly educated. He spent his time hunting and fishing, and he delighted in the company of the *lazzaroni*, the Neapolitan underclass. He much preferred to leave the business of government to his wife, the ambitious and treacherous Archduchess Maria Carolina of Austria, whose main aim was to free southern Italy from Spanish influence and secure a rapprochement with Austria and Great Britain. Her chosen administrator was the English expatriate Sir John Acton, who replaced the long-serving Tanucci, a move that was to mire court politics in damaging corruption and espionage.

When the French Revolution broke out in 1789, Maria Carolina was initially sympathetic to the movement, but when her sister Marie Antoinette was beheaded, she became fanatically Francophobic. The following French invasion of Italy in 1799, and the crowning of Napoleon as king in 1800, jolted the south out of its Bourbon slumbers. Although Napoleonic rule was to last only 14 years, this brief flirtation with republicanism was to awaken hopes of an independent Italian nation. Returning to his beloved Naples in 1815, Ferdinand, who was once so at ease with his subjects, was now terrified of popular revolution and became determined to exert his absolute authority. Changes that had been made by the Bonapartist regime were reversed, causing widespread discontent. Revolutionary agitators sprang up everywhere, and the countryside, now full of discharged soldiers, became more lawless than ever.

Yet there was no putting the genie back in the bottle. The heavy-handed tactics of Ferdinand II only exacerbated the situation, and in 1848 Sicily experienced a violent revolt that saw the expulsion of the Bourbons from the island. Although the revolt was crushed, Ferdinand's response was so heavy-handed that he earned himself the nickname 'Re Bomba' (King Bomb) after his army mercilessly shelled Messina. From such a promising beginning, the last decades of Bourbon rule were so oppressive that they were almost universally hated throughout liberal Europe. The seeds had well and truly been sown for the Risorgimento (Resurgence), which would finally see the whole peninsula united into a modern nation-state.

The exodus of southern Italians to North and South America between 1880 and WWI is one of the great mass movements of a population in modern times. By 1927, 20% of the Italian population had emigrated.

1922	1927	1934	1940
Mussolini and his Fascists stage a march on Rome in October. Doubting the army's loyalty, a fearful King Vittorio Emanuele III entrusts Mussolini with the formation of a government.	A study released by the Italian government puts the number of Italian citizens living abroad at around 9.2 million. Southern Italians make up over 60% of the Italian diaspora.	Screen siren Sophia Loren is born, and spends her childhood living in Pozzuoli and Naples. Her break would come in 1951, as an extra in Mervyn LeRoy's film *Quo Vadis*.	Italy enters WWII on Nazi Germany's side and invades Greece in October. Greek forces counter-attack and enter southern Albania. Germany saves Italy in March–April 1941 by overrunning Yugoslavia and Greece.

The Kingdom of Death

Although not commonly acknowledged, the widespread presence of malaria in the Italian peninsula during the 19th and 20th centuries is one of the most significant factors in the social and economic development (or lack of it) of the modern country. An endemic as well as an epidemic disease, it was so enmeshed in Italian rural society that it was widely regarded as the Italian national disease. Even the word itself – malaria – comes from the Italian *mal aria* (bad air), as it was originally thought that the disease was caused by a poisoning of the air as wet earth dried out during the heat of summer.

The scale of the problem came to light in the decades following Italian unification in 1861. Out of 69 provinces only two were found to be free of malaria; in a population of 25 million people, at least 11 million were permanently at risk of the disease. Most famously, Giuseppe Garibaldi, one of the founding fathers of modern Italy, lost both his wife, Anita, and a large number of troops to the disease. Thus stricken, Garibaldi urged the newly united nation to place the fight against malaria high on its list of priorities.

In the dawning era of global competition, Italian farming was dangerously backward. As a predominantly grain-producing economy, it was tragically ironic that all of Italy's most fertile land was in precisely the zones – coastal plains and river valleys – where malaria was most intense. To survive, farm workers had to expose themselves to the disease. Unfortunately, disease in turn entailed suffering, days of absence and low productivity.

More significantly, although malaria ravaged the whole peninsula, it was pre-eminently an affliction of the south, as well as the provinces of Rome and Grosseto in the centre. Of all the regions, six were especially afflicted – Abruzzo, Basilicata, Calabria, Lazio, Puglia and Sardinia – earning the south the lugubrious epithet 'the kingdom of death'. Furthermore, Giovanni Battista Grassi (the man who discovered that mosquitoes transmit malaria) estimated that the danger of infection in the south was 10 times greater than in northern Italy.

No issue illustrates the divide between the north and south of the country quite so vividly as the malaria crisis. The World Health Organization defines malaria in the modern world as a disease of poverty that distorts and slows economic growth. In the case of the Italian south, malaria was a significant factor in the underdevelopment of the region at a critical time in its history. Malarial fever thrives on exploitative working conditions, substandard housing and diet, war and ecological degradation, and Italy's south had certainly had its fair share by the early 20th century. As late as 1918, the Ministry of Agriculture reported that

History of the Italian People, by Giuliano Procacci, is one of the best general histories of the country in any language. It covers the period from the early Middle Ages until 1948.

Edward Gibbon's *History of the Decline and Fall of the Roman Empire* is the acknowledged classic work on the subject of the empire's darker days. Try the abridged single-volume version.

1943	1944	1946	1950
King Vittorio Emanuele III sacks Mussolini. He is replaced by Marshall Badoglio, who surrenders after Allied landings in southern Italy. German forces free Mussolini.	Mt Vesuvius explodes back into action on 18 March. The eruption is captured on film by United States Army Air Forces personnel stationed nearby.	Italians vote in a national referendum in June to abolish the monarchy (by about 12.7 million votes to 10.7 million) and create a republic. The south is the only region to vote against the republic.	The *Cassa per il Mezzogiorno* is established to help fund public works and infrastructure in the south. Poor management and corruption sees at least one-third of the money squandered.

'malaria is the key to all the economic problems of the South'. Against this background of regional inequality, the fever became an important metaphor deployed by *meridionalisti* (southern spokesmen) such as Giustino Fortunato (1848–1932) and Francesco Nitti (1868–1953) to describe the plight of the south and to demand redress. Nitti attributed the entirety of southern backwardness to this single factor.

Between 1900 and 1907, the Italian parliament passed a series of laws establishing a national campaign – the first of its kind in the world – to eradicate or at least control the disease. But it was to take the best part of half a century to bring malaria under control, as two world wars and the fascist seizure of power in 1922 were to overwhelm domestic policies, causing the program to stall and then collapse entirely amid military defeat and occupation.

Final victory against the disease was only achieved following the end of WWII, when the government was able to re-establish public-health infrastructures and implement a five-year plan, which included the use of a new pesticide, DDT, to eradicate malaria. The designation of 'malarial zone' was only officially lifted from the entire peninsula in 1969.

The Southern Question

The unification of Italy meant sudden and dramatic changes for all the southern provinces. The huge upsurge in *brigantaggio* (banditry) and social unrest throughout the last decades of the 19th century was caused by widespread disillusionment about the unification project. Though remembered as a leading figure in the push towards unification, it was never the intention of 19th-century Italian statesman Camillo Benso, Count of Cavour, to unify the whole country. Even later during his premiership, Cavour favoured an expanded Piedmont rather than a united Italy.

For southerners, it was difficult to see the benefits of being part of this new nation-state. Naples was stripped of its capital-city status; the new government carried away huge cash reserves from the rich southern Italian banks; taxes went up and factories closed as new tariff policies, dictated by northern interests, caused a steep decline in the southern economy. Culturally, southerners were also made to feel inferior; to be southern or 'Bourbon' was to be backward, vulgar and uncivilised.

After WWI the south fared a little better, experiencing slow progress in terms of infrastructure projects like the construction of the Puglian aqueduct, the extension of the railways and the improvement of civic centres like Bari and Taranto. But Mussolini's 'Battle for Wheat' – the drive to make Italy self-sufficient in food – compounded many of the southern problems. It destroyed even more valuable pastureland by turning it over to the monoculture of wheat, while reinforcing the parlous state of the southern peasantry, who remained uneducated, disenfranchised, land-

The Nazis took Naples in 1943, but were quickly forced out during the *quattro giornate di Napoli* (four days of Naples), a series of popular uprisings between 26 and 30 September. These paved the way for the Allies to enter the city on 1 October.

Between 1944 and 1946 the German Wehrmacht systematically sabotaged the pumping systems that drained Italy's marshes and confiscated quinine from the Department of Health. The ensuing malaria epidemic proved as deadly as any WWI ground offensive.

1950s–60s	1980	1999	2003
Soaring unemployment causes another mass migration of about two million people from the south to the factories of northern Italy, Europe and Australia.	At 7.34pm on 25 November, a 6.8 Richter scale earthquake strikes Campania. The quake kills almost 3000 people and causes widespread damage; the city of Naples also suffers damage.	Brindisi becomes a strategic base for the Office of the UN and the World Food Programme. The disused military airport's hangars are converted into storage space for humanitarian aid.	Sicilian *mafioso* Salvatore 'Totò' Riina is arrested in Palermo. Nicknamed 'The Beast', the 'boss of bosses' had ordered the bombing death of antimafia magistrates Giovanni Falcone and Paolo Borsellino.

HISTORY ON SCREEN

Il Gattopardo (The Leopard; Luchino Visconti; 1963) A Sicilian aristocrat grapples with the political and social changes heralded by the 19th-century Risorgimento (reunification period).

Le quattro giornate di Napoli (The Four Days of Naples; Nanni Loy; 1962) Neapolitan courage shines through in this film about the famous popular uprisings against the Nazis in September 1943.

Il resto di niente (The Remains of Nothing; Antonietta De Lillo; 2003) Eleonora Pimental de Fonesca, heroine of the ill-fated Neapolitan revolution of 1799, is the protagonist in this tale.

Salvatore Giuliano (Francesco Rosi; 1963) A neorealist classic about the murder of Sicily's very own modern Robin Hood.

less and at high risk of malaria. To escape such a hopeless future, many of them packed their bags and migrated to North America, northern Europe and Australia, starting a trend that was to become one of the main features of post-WWII Italy.

In the 1946 referendum that established the Italian Republic, the south was the only region to vote no. In Naples, 80% voted to keep the monarchy. Still, change moved on apace. After the wreckage of WWII was cleared – especially that caused by Allied air raids in Sicily and Naples – the *Cassa per il Mezzogiorno* reconstruction fund was established to bring the south into the 20th century with massive, cheap housing schemes and big industrial projects like the steel plant in Taranto and the Fiat factory in Basilicata. Yet constant interference by the Mafia in southern Italy's economy did much to nullify the efforts of Rome to reduce the gap between the prosperous north and the poor south. The disappearance of large amounts of cash eventually led the central government to scrap the *Cassa per il Mezzogiorno* fund in 1992.

Clean Hands, Dirty Politics

Hitting the headlines that same year was the *Tangentopoli* (Bribesville) scandal, which exposed the breadth and depth of institutionalised kickbacks and bribes in Italy (the country's modus operandi since WWII). Although it was largely focused on the industrial north of Italy, the repercussions of the widespread investigation into graft (known as *Mani pulite*, or Clean Hands) were inevitably felt in southern regions like Sicily and Campania, where politics, business and organised crime were longtime bedfellows.

Denis Mack Smith produced one of the most penetrating works on Il Duce in his biography *Mussolini*. It explores the life and career of the Italian dictator and his influence on Adolf Hitler.

2003	2004–05	2005	2010
The Campania government launches Progetto Vesuvia in an attempt to clear Mt Vesuvius' heavily populated lower slopes. The €30,000 offered to relocate is rejected by most in the danger zone.	Tension between rival Camorra clans explodes on the streets of suburban Naples. In only four months, almost 50 people are gunned down in retribution attacks.	Nichi Vendola, representing the Communist Refoundation Party, is elected president of Puglia. He is the first gay communist to be elected president of a southern Italian region.	Local youths in Rosarno, Calabria, shoot air rifles at African migrants returning from work in January. About 2000 migrants subsequently clash with locals in two days of violent rioting.

The scandal eventually brought about the demise of the Democrazia Cristiana (DC; Christian Democrats), a centre-right Catholic party that appealed to southern Italy's traditional conservatism. Allied closely with the Church, the DC promised wide-ranging reforms while at the same time demanding vigilance against godless communism. It was greatly aided in its efforts by the Mafia, which ensured that the local DC mayor would always top the poll. The Mafia's reward was *clientelismo* (political patronage) that ensured it was granted favourable contracts.

In the meantime, things were changing in regard to how many southern Italians viewed the Mafia, thanks in no small part to Sicilian investigating magistrates Paolo Borsellino and Giovanni Falcone. The duo contributed greatly to turning the climate of opinion against the Mafia on both sides of the Atlantic, and made it possible for ordinary citizens to speak about and against the Mafia more freely. When they were tragically murdered in the summer of 1992, it was a great loss for Italy and Sicily, but it was these deaths that finally broke the Mafia's code of *omertà* (silence).

Although much has happened since it was written, Paul Ginsborg's *A History of Contemporary Italy: Society and Politics 1943–1988* remains one of the single most readable and insightful books on postwar Italy.

2011	2013	2015	2015
Thousands of boat people fleeing the revolutionary chaos in northern Africa land on the island of Lampedusa. Italy grants 30,000 refugees temporary visas, creating tension with France.	On 4 March, Naples' much-loved Città della Scienza (City of Science) museum is destroyed in an arson attack. The crime is widely blamed on the Camorra, with the mayor tweeting 'Naples is under attack'.	After lengthy delays, Naples' showcase Municipio metro station opens to the public, featuring unearthed ancient ruins and a specially commissioned video-painting by Israeli artist Michal Rovner.	Police in Sicily arrest 39 individuals and seize assets worth around €10m in May as part of a crackdown on a trio of Palermo mafia gangs. Among those held is a municipal police commissioner.

The Southern Way of Life

The Mezzogiorno, or land of the midday sun, is more than haunting ruins, poetic coastlines and peeling *palazzi* (mansions). Its true protagonists are the *meridionali* (southern Italians), whose character and nuances echo a long, nail-biting history of dizzying highs and testing lows. To understand the southern psyche is to understand the complexities and contradictions that have moulded Italy's most misunderstood half.

Dreams & Diasporas
Emigration to Immigration

Severe economic problems in the south following Italy's unification and after each of the world wars led to massive emigration as people searched for a better life in northern Italy, northern Europe, North and South America, and Australia. Between 1880 and 1910, more than 1.5 million Sicilians alone left for the US, and in 1900 the island was the world's main area of emigration. In Campania, a staggering 2.7 million people left the motherland between 1876 and 1976.

Today, huge numbers of young Italians, often the most educated and ambitious, continue to move abroad. According to official estimates, almost 136,000 Italians aged 20 to 40 left the country between 2010 and 2014. This brain-drain epidemic is fuelled by a debilitatingly high national youth unemployment rate – around 44% in mid-2015. Adding insult to injury is Italy's entrenched system of patronage and nepotism, which commonly makes landing a job more about who you know than what you know. For southern Italians, the standard of education available is often another contributing factor. A commonly held belief that southern universities aren't up to scratch sees many parents send their children north or overseas to complete their studies. While some return after completing their master's degree, many become accustomed to the freedom and opportunities found in their host city or country and tend to stay.

And yet, somewhat ironically, southern Italy has itself become a destination for people searching for a better life. Political and economic upheavals in the 1980s brought new arrivals from central and eastern Europe, Latin America and North Africa, including Italy's former colonies in Tunisia, Somalia and Ethiopia. More recently, waves of Chinese, Filipino and Sri Lankan immigrants have given Italian streetscapes an Asian twist.

From a purely economic angle, these new arrivals are vital for the country's economic health. Without immigrant workers to fill the gaps left in the labour market by pickier locals, Italy would be sorely lacking in tomato sauce and shoes. From hotel maids on the Amalfi Coast to fruit pickers on Calabrian farms, it is often immigrants who take the low-paid service jobs that keep Italy's economy afloat. Unfortunately, their vulnerability has sometimes led to exploitation, with several reported cases of farmhands being paid below-minimum wages for back-breaking work.

A one-man 'Abbott & Costello', Antonio de Curtis (1898–1967), aka Totò, famously depicted the Neapolitan *furbizia* (cunning). Appearing in more than 100 films, including *Miseria e nobiltà* (Misery & Nobility; 1954), his roles as a hustler living on nothing but quick wits would guarantee him cult status in Naples.

The North–South Divide

In his film *Ricomincio da tre* (I'm Starting from Three; 1980), acting great Massimo Troisi comically tackles the problems faced by southern Italians forced to head north for work. The reverse scenario is tackled in the more recent comedy *Benvenuti al Sud* (Welcome to the South; 2010), in which a northern Italian postmaster is posted to a small southern Italian town, bullet-proof vest and prejudices in tow. Slapstick aside, both films reveal Italy's very real north–south divide. While the north is celebrated for its fashion empires and moneyed metropolises, Italy's south is a PR nightmare of high unemployment, crumbling infrastructure and Mafia arrests. At a deep semantic level, the word *meridionale* (southern Italian) continues to conjure a string of unflattering words and images.

From the Industrial Revolution to the 1960s, millions of southern Italians fled to the industrialised northern cities for factory jobs. As the saying goes, '*Ogni vero Milanese ha un nonno Pugliese*' (Every true Milanese has a Pugliese grandparent). For many of these domestic migrants, the welcome north of Rome was anything but warm. Disparagingly nicknamed *terroni* (peasants), many faced discrimination on a daily basis, from everyone from landlords to baristas. While such overt discrimination is now practically nonexistent, historical prejudices linger. Many northerners resent their taxes being used to 'subsidise' the 'lazy', 'corrupt' south – a sentiment well exploited by the right-wing, Milan-based Lega Nord (Northern League) party.

Yet negative attitudes can work both ways. Many southerners view their northern compatriots as just a little *freddi* (cold) and uptight. As one 30-something employee at Lecce University reveals: 'Many friends of mine are desperate to return after a few years spent in northern Italy or abroad. They find life too isolated and anonymous'.

> Today, people of Italian origin account for more than 40% of the population in Argentina and Uruguay, more than 10% in Brazil, more than 5% in Switzerland, the US and Venezuela, and more than 4% in Australia and Canada.

The Southern Psyche

Beautiful Family, Beautiful Image

Family is the bedrock of southern Italian life, and loyalty to family and friends is usually non-negotiable. As Luigi Barzini (1908–84), author of *The Italians,* noted, 'A happy private life helps tolerate an appalling public life'. This chasm between the private arena and the public one is a noticeable aspect of the southern mentality, and has evolved over years of intrusive foreign domination. Some locals mightn't think twice about littering their street, but step inside their home and you'll get floors clean enough to eat from. After all, you'd never want someone dropping in and thinking you're a *zingaro* (gypsy), right?

Maintaining a *bella figura* (beautiful image) is very important to the average southerner, and how you and your family appear to the outside world is a matter of honour, respectability and pride. As Alessio explains: 'In the south, you are better than your neighbour if you own more and better things. This mentality is rooted in the past, when you really did need to own lots of things to attain certain social roles and ultimately sustain your family'. Yet *fare bella figura* (making a good impression) goes beyond a well-kept house; it extends to dressing well, behaving modestly, performing religious and social duties and fulfilling all essential family obligations. In the context of the extended family, where gossip is rife, a good image protects one's privacy.

> Any self-respecting Italian bookshelf features one or more Roman rhetoricians. To *fare la bella figura* (make a good impression) among academics, trot out a phrase from Cicero or Horace (Horatio), such as 'Where there is life there is hope' or 'Whatever advice you give, be brief'.

It's Not What You Know...

In Europe's most ancient, entrenched bureaucracy, strong family ties are essential to getting things done. Putting in a good word for your son, niece or grandchild isn't just a nice gesture, but an essential career boost. According to Italy's Ministry of Labour, over 60% of Italian firms rely on personal introductions for recruitment. Indeed, *clientelismo* (nepotism) is as much a part of the Italian lexicon as *caffè* (coffee) and *tasse* (taxes); a fact satirised in Massimiliano Bruno's film *Viva L'Italia* (2012), about a crooked, well-connected senator who secures jobs for his three children, among them a talentless TV actress with a speech impediment. The Italian film industry itself came under attack in 2012 when newspaper *Il Fatto Quotidiano* accused several members of the Italian Academy (which votes for the prestigious David di Donatello film awards) of having conflicts of interest. As the satirist Beppe Severgnini wryly comments in his book *La Bella Figura: A Field Guide to the Italian Mind*, 'If you want to lose an Italian friend or kill off a conversation, all you have to say is "On the subject of conflicts of interest..." If your interlocutor hasn't disappeared, he or she will smile condescendingly.'

A Woman's Place

'In Sicily, women are more dangerous than shotguns', said Fabrizio (Angelo Infanti) in *The Godfather*. 'A woman at the window is a woman to be shunned', proclaimed the writer Giovanni Verga in the 19th century. And 'Women are too stupid to be involved in the complex world of finance', decided a judge when faced with a female Mafia suspect in the 1990s. As in many places in the Mediterranean, a woman's position in southern Italy has always been a difficult one. In the domestic sphere, a mother and wife commands the utmost respect within the home. She is considered the moral and emotional compass for her family; an omnipresent role model and the nightmare of newly wedded wives. In the public sphere, however, her role has less commonly been that of a protagonist.

But times are changing. Only two generations ago, many southern men and women were virtually segregated. In many cases, women would only go out on Saturdays, and separate beaches for men and women were

John Turturro's film *Passione* (2010) is a *Buena Vista Social Club*–style exploration of Naples' rich and eclectic musical traditions. Spanning everything from folk songs to contemporary tunes, it offers a fascinating insight into the city's complex soul.

THE SOUTHERN WAY OF LIFE THE SOUTHERN PSYCHE

THROUGH SOUTHERN EYES

Meet Alessio, a 30-something Sicilian expat. Born into a close-knit family near Catania, he studied physics in Florence before moving to Bonn to complete a PhD in astrophysics...and to start a career as a culinary consultant. Every Easter and Christmas, he makes the 2276km journey back home to catch up with family and friends, and to sink his teeth into a steaming *arancino* (a deep-fried, stuffed rice ball; his favourite homeland snack). Alessio's story is not unusual in a part of Italy so bitter-sweetly defined by emigration, nostalgia and tradition. Alessio muses: 'A deep part of my personality and feelings are based in the south. Even though I am happy and grateful for what I have obtained abroad, I often feel homesick. The bucolic life spent enjoying the sun with family and friends, eating, drinking and singing, Sicilian hills in the background, is an image that haunts me. I think this is true for many expats.'

Perhaps more uniquely southern is the love/hate dynamic underlying this relationship. As Alessio explains: 'In Germany, there's a sense of personal civic responsibility. In southern Italy, suspicion of strangers has stifled this collective feeling from developing.' The other obstacle is a stubborn sense of personal pride and vanity. 'Too often in the south, doing something that's civic minded – like picking rubbish off the street or not using your car to help reduce pollution – leaves you open to mockery from others, who see your action as a sign of weakness.' There is genuine regret in Alessio's voice: 'It's frustrating to think that a society so rich in culture and traditions, so warm-hearted, could do much more for itself if it only learned to trust and cooperate.'

Yet, things are changing. Both the internet and travel are helping to shape a generation more aware of, and open to, foreign ideas. Online communities are allowing people once socially or ideologically isolated to connect with others, to share experiences and develop new ways of tackling old problems. Alessio is hopeful: 'Words like "integration" and "openness" are becoming more meaningful in the south. Slowly, people are becoming more aware of the common ground they share. With this awareness, we can hopefully build a brighter, collectively minded future.'

THE OLD PROVERBIAL

They might be old clichés, but proverbs can be quite the cultural revelation. Here are six of the south's well-worn best:

➡ *Cu si marita, sta cuntentu nu jornu, Cu' ammazza nu porcu, sta cuntentu n'annu* (Sicilian). Whoever gets married remains happy for a day, whoever butchers a pig remains happy for a year.

➡ *Aprili fa li ciuri e li biddizzi, l'onuri l'avi lu misi ri maju* (Sicilian). April makes the flowers and the beauty, but May gets all the credit.

➡ *A chi troppo s'acàla 'o culo se vede* (Neapolitan). He who kowtows too low bares his arse.

➡ *Cu va 'n Palermu e 'un viri Murriali, sinni parti sceccu e tonna armali* (Sicilian). Whoever goes to Palermo and doesn't see Monreale goes there a jackass and returns a fool.

➡ *Quannu la pulice se vitte a la farina, disse ca era capu mulinaru* (Pugliese). When the flea found itself in the flour, it said it was the master miller.

➡ *Lu mericu piatusu fa a chiaja virminusa* (Sicilian). A compassionate doctor makes the wound infected.

common. Dating would often involve a chaperone, whether it be the young woman's brother, aunt or grandmother. These days, more and more unmarried southern women live with their partners, especially in the cities. Improvements in educational opportunities and more liberal attitudes mean that the number of women with degrees and successful careers is growing. In its 2014 Gender Gap Index, the Organisation for Economic Co-operation and Development (OECD) revealed that entry rates into higher education in Italy were 74% for women, compared to 52% for men.

Yet true gender equality remains an unattained goal, both in southern Italy and the country as a whole. The World Economic Forum's 2014 Global Gender Gap Report ranked Italy 69th worldwide in terms of overall gender equality, up from 71st position in 2013. It ranked 114th in female economic participation and opportunity, 62nd in educational attainment and 37th in political empowerment.

According to the OECD, only 47% of Italian women are in the workforce, compared to 72% in Sweden, 69% in Germany and 60% in France. Statistics released by Italy's national bureau of statistics (Istat) indicate that the potential earnings of Italian women is half that of their male counterparts, reflecting both lower employment rates and pay. Though successful Italian businesswomen do exist – among them Poste Italiane chairperson Luisa Todini and Eni president Emma Marcegaglia – almost 95% of public company board members in Italy remain male, and of these, approximately 80% of them are older than 55.

Italian women fare no better on the domestic front. OECD figures reveal that Italian men spend 103 minutes per day cooking, cleaning or caring, less than a third as long as Italian women, who spend an average of 326 minutes per day on what the OECD labels unpaid work.

Turkish-Italian director Ferzan Özpetek explores the clash of southern tradition and modernity in his film *Mine vaganti* (Loose Cannons; 2010), a situation comedy about two gay brothers and their conservative Pugliese family.

The Sacred & the Profane

While almost 80% of Italians identify as Catholics, only around 15% of Italy's population regularly attends Sunday Mass. Yet, the Church continues to exert considerable influence on public policy and political parties, especially those of the centre- and far-right. Furthermore, religious festivals and traditions continue to play a major role in southern Italian life. Every town has its own saint's day, celebrated with music, special events, food and wine. Indeed, these religious festivals are one of the best ways into the culture of the south. Cream of the crop is Easter, with lavish weeklong events to mark Holy Week. People pay handsomely for the privilege and prestige of carrying the various back-breaking decorations around the town.

Pilgrimages and a belief in miracles remain a central part of the religious experience. You will see representations of Padre Pio – the Gargano saint who was canonised for his role in several miraculous recoveries – in churches, village squares, pizzerias and private homes everywhere. Around eight million pilgrims visit his shrine every year. Three times a year, thousands cram into Naples' Duomo to witness their patron saint San Gennaro's blood miraculously liquefy in the phial that contains it. When the blood liquefies, the city is considered safe from disaster. Another one of Naples' holy helpers is Giuseppe Moscati (1880–1927), a doctor who dedicated his life to serving the city's poor. According to the faithful, the medic continues to heal from up above, a dedicated section inside the city's Chiesa del Gesù Nuovo heaving with *ex-voti* (including golden limbs) offered in thanks for miraculous recoveries.

Still, the line between the sacred and the profane remains a fine one in the south. In *Christ Stopped at Eboli*, his book about his stay in rural Basilicata in the 1930s, writer-painter-doctor Carlo Levi wrote: 'The air over this desolate land and among the peasant huts is filled with spirits. Not all of them are mischievous and capricious gnomes or evil demons. There are also good spirits in the guise of guardian angels.'

While the mystical, half-pagan world Levi describes may no longer be recognisable, ancient pagan influences live on in daily southern life. Here, curse-deterring amulets are as plentiful as crucifix pendants, the most famous of which is the iconic, horn-shaped *corno*. Adorning everything from necklines to rear-view mirrors, this lucky charm's evil-busting powers are said to lie in its representation of the bull and its sexual vigour. A rarer, but by no means extinct, custom is that of Naples' 'o Scartellat. Usually an elderly man, he'll occasionally be spotted burning incense through the city's older neighbourhoods, clearing the streets of bad vibes and inviting good fortune. The title itself is Neapolitan for 'hunchback', as the task was once the domain of posture-challenged figures. According to Neapolitan lore, touching a hunchback's hump brings good luck...which beats some of the other options, among them stepping in dog poop and having wine spilt on you accidentally.

Italy's culture of corruption and *calcio* (football) is captured in *The Dark Heart of Italy*, in which English expat author Tobias Jones wryly observes, 'Footballers or referees are forgiven nothing; politicians are forgiven everything'.

THE SOUTHERN WAY OF LIFE THE SOUTHERN PSYCHE

CALCIO (FOOTBALL): THE OTHER RELIGION

Catholicism may be Italy's official faith, but its true religion is *calcio*. On any given weekend from September through to May, you'll find millions of *tifosi* (football fans) at the *stadio* (stadium), glued to the TV, or checking the score on their mobile phone. In Naples' Piazzetta Nilo, you'll even find an altar to Argentine football star Diego Maradona, who elevated the city's Napoli team to its most successful era in the 1980s and early 1990s.

It's no coincidence that in Italian *tifoso* means both 'football fan' and 'typhus patient'. When the ball ricochets off the post and slips fatefully through the goalie's hands, when half the stadium is swearing while the other half is euphorically shouting 'Gooooooooooooool!', 'fever pitch' is the term that comes to mind.

Indeed, nothing quite stirs Italian blood like a good (or a bad) game. Nine months after Neapolitan Fabio Cannavaro led Italy to victory in the 2006 World Cup, hospitals in northern Italy reported a baby boom. In February the following year, rioting at a Palermo–Catania match in Catania left one policeman dead and around 100 injured. Blamed on the Ultras (a minority group of hard-core football fans), the violence shocked both Italy and the world, leading to a temporary ban of all matches in Italy, and increased stadium security.

Yet, the same game that divides also unites. You might be a Juventus-loathing Bari supporter on any given day, but when national team *Azzurri* (the Blues) bag the World Cup, you are nothing but a heart-on-your-sleeve *italiano*. In his book *The 100 Things Everyone Needs to Know About Italy*, Australian journalist David Dale writes that Italy's 1982 World Cup win 'finally united twenty regions which, until then, had barely acknowledged that they were part of the one country'.

The Mafia

To many outside Italy, the Mafia means Sicily's Cosa Nostra, seared into popular culture thanks to Francis Ford Coppola's classic film *The Godfather*. In reality, Cosa Nostra has three other major partners in crime: Campania's Camorra, Calabria's 'ndrangheta and Puglia's Sacra Corona Unita. Apt at everything from loaning money at astronomical interest rates to trafficking narcotics, arms and people, these four criminal networks produce a staggering annual profit estimated at around €100 billion.

Origins

The concept of the *mafioso* dates back to the late 15th century, when Sicily's rent-collecting *gabellotti* (bailiffs) employed small gangs of armed peasants to help them solve 'problems'. Soon robbing large estates, the bandits struck fear and admiration into the peasantry, who were happy to support efforts to destabilise the feudal system. They became willing accomplices, protecting the outlaws, and although it was another 400 years before crime became 'organised', the 16th and 17th centuries witnessed a substantial increase in the activities of brigand bands. The peasants' loyalty to their own people resulted in the name Cosa Nostra (Our Thing). The early Mafia's way of protecting itself from prosecution was to become the modern Mafia's most important weapon: the code of silence, or *omertà*.

In 2011, police seized an adult tiger from the estate of murdered Sacra Corona Unita boss Lucio Vetrugno. Kept in a cage for 16 years, the giant feline had come in handy for intimidating Vetrugno's enemies. The tiger was subsequently transferred to an animal park in Bologna.

In the 1860s, a band of Sicilians exiled to Calabria began forming their own organised gangs, planting the seeds for the 'ndrangheta. For almost a century, these gangs remained a local menace, known for extortion, racketeering and rural banditry. But it was the murder of a local godfather in 1975 that sparked a bloody gang war, transforming the organisation and creating a rebellious faction infamous for holding northern Italian businessmen to ransom. With its profits invested in narcotics, the 'ndrangheta would transform itself into Italy's most powerful Mafia entity.

The powerful Camorra reputedly emerged from the criminal gangs operating among the poor in late-18th-century Naples. The organisation had its first big break after the failed revolution of 1848. Desperate to overthrow Ferdinand II, pro-constitutional liberals turned to *camorristi* to help garner the support of the masses – the Camorra's political influence was sealed. Dealt a serious blow by Mussolini, the organisation would get its second wind from the invading Allied forces of 1943, which turned to the flourishing underworld as the best way to get things done. The black market thrived and the Camorra slowly began to spread its roots again.

In turn, the Camorra would give birth to the Sacra Corona Unita (Sacred United Crown), created by Camorra boss Raffaele Cutolo in the 1970s to gain access to Puglia's seaports. Originally named the Nuova Grande Camorra Pugliese, it gained its current name in the early 1980s after its Pugliese members cut ties with Campania and strengthened their bond with Eastern Europe's criminal networks.

Toxic Profits

The combined annual revenue of Italy's four main mafia organisations is equal to 10% of Italy's entire GDP and greater than that of the country's largest legitimate corporation, multinational oil and gas company Eni. This is a far cry from the days of roguish characters bullying shopkeepers into paying the *pizzo* (protection money). As journalist Roberto Saviano writes in his Camorra exposé *Gomorra:* 'Only beggar Camorra clans inept at business and desperate to survive still practice the kind of monthly extortions seen in Nanni Loy's film *Mi manda Picone*'.

The top money-spinner is drugs and king of the trade is the 'ndrangheta. According to Italian police, the Calabrian mafia controls between 60% and 80% of Europe's cocaine market. Combined with its other activities – which include the illegal trading of arms and disposal of hazardous waste – the organisation pulls in an estimated €56 billion annually.

Illegal waste disposal is also one of the Camorra's biggest profit generators. According to the Italian environmentalist association Legambiente, the Camorra has illegally dumped, buried or burned close to 10 million tons of garbage in Campania since 1991. Alarmingly, this includes highly toxic waste, collected from northern Italian and foreign manufacturers lured by the cut-price rates of Camorra-owned waste-disposal companies. Abnormally high rates of cancer and congenital malformations of the nervous and urinary systems have led medical journal *Lancet Oncology* to nickname an area in Naples' northeast hinterland 'the triangle of death'.

Mafia-affiliated loan sharks commonly offer struggling businesses cash with an average interest rate of 10%. An estimated 50% of shops in Naples are run with Camorra money. Mafia profits are often reinvested globally in legitimate real estate, credit markets and businesses in what is known as 'the Invisible Mafia'.

Backlash of the Brave

Despite the Mafia's ever-expanding reach, the war against it soldiers on, with frequent police crackdowns and arrests. Notable recent successes include the capture of fugitive Camorra boss Pasquale Scotti in 2015, convicted in absentia of over 20 murders and arrested in Brazil after 30 years on the run. In the same year, authorities arrested 160 alleged members of the 'ndrangheta, an operation hailed as being of 'unprecedented importance' by Italy's top prosecutor, Franco Roberti. The operation also seized €100 million in assets belonging to the organisation, including luxury cars, trucks, businesses and a block of 200 flats close to the northern Italian city of Parma.

The assassination of Sicilian anti-Mafia judges Giovanni Falcone and Paolo Borsellino in 1992 sparked particularly intense anti-Mafia sentiment throughout Italy. In 1994, Paolo Borsellino's sister Rita cofounded the group Libera (www.libera.it), whose member organisations were permitted to transform properties seized from the Mafia into agricultural cooperatives, *agriturismi* (farm-stay accommodation) and other legitimate enterprises. Equally encouraging has been the establishment of Addiopizzo (www.addiopizzo.org), a Sicilian organisation encouraging consumers to support businesses that have said 'no' to Mafia extortion.

MAFIA MOVIES

Gomorra (Matteo Garrone; 2009) An award-winning Camorra exposé based on Roberto Saviano's best-selling book.

The Godfather Trilogy (Francis Ford Coppola; 1972–90) Marlon Brando plays an old-school mobster in this Oscar-winning saga.

Mi manda Picone (Picone Sent Me; Nanni Loy; 1983) A cult comedy about a small-time hustler embroiled in Naples' seedy underworld.

In nome della legge (In the Name of the Law; Pietro Germi; 1949) A young judge is sent to a Mafia-riddled Sicilian town in this neorealist film, co-written by Federico Fellini.

The Southern Table

Blessed with sun, mineral-rich soils and the salty goodness of the Mediterranean, southern Italy was always destined for culinary glory. Waves of migration have flavoured the pot – the Greeks supplied the olives, the Arabs brought the pine nuts, eggplants, almonds, raisins and honey, and the Spanish came with tomatoes. The end result is a larder bursting with buxom vegetables, glistening fish, spicy meats and decadent sweets. Peckish? Read on for a crash course in southern gluttony.

The Simple Things

Picture it: wood-fired bread drizzled in extra-virgin olive oil, sprinkled with ripe *pomodori* (tomatoes) and fragrant *basilico* (basil). The flavours explode in your mouth. From the char-grilled crunch of the bread to the sweetness of the tomatoes, it's a perfect symphony of textures and flavours.

In many ways, *pane e pomodoro* (bread and tomatoes) captures the very soul of the southern Italian kitchen. Down here, fresh produce is the secret and simplicity is the key. Order grilled fish and chances are you'll get exactly that. No rich, overbearing sauces...just grilled fish with a wedge of lemon on the side. After all, it's the freshness of the fish you should be savouring, right?

This less-is-more approach is a testament to the south's impoverished past. Pasta made without eggs, bread made from hard durum wheat, wild greens scavenged from the countryside are all delicious, but their consumption was driven by necessity. The tradition of *sopratavola* (raw vegetables such as fennel or chicory eaten after a meal) arose because people could not afford fruit. That of *sottaceti* (vegetables cooked in vinegar and preserved in jars with olive oil) is part of the waste-not, want-not philosophy.

In the end, it was the simple goodness of this *cucina povera* (poor man's cuisine) that would make it the darling of health-conscious foodies.

> Tomatoes were not introduced to Italy until the 16th century, brought from the Americas. The word *pomodoro* literally means 'golden apple'.

Regional Focus

In reality, southern Italian cuisine encompasses the culinary traditions of five regions: Campania, Puglia, Basilicata, Calabria and Sicily. They might share similarities, but they are all distinctly unique. So raise your fork to the following appetite-piquing regional fortes.

Campania

Perfect Pizza

It was in Naples that the city's most famous *pizzaiolo* (pizza chef), Raffaele Esposito, invented the classic pizza margherita. Esposito was summoned to fire up a treat for a peckish King Umberto I and his wife Queen Margherita on a royal visit in 1889. Determined to impress the Italian royals, Esposito based his creation of tomato, mozzarella and basil on the red, white and green flag of the newly unified Italy. The resulting topping met with the queen's approval and was subsequently named in her honour.

Pizza purists claim that you really can't top Esposito's classic combo when made by a true Neapolitan *pizzaiolo*. Not everyone is in accordance and Italians are often split between those who favour the thin-crust Roman variant, and those who go for the thicker Neapolitan version. Whatever your choice, the fact remains that the pizza they make in Naples is nothing short of superb. It's also a brilliant cheap feed – these giant discs of bubbling perfection often start from €3 or €4.

According to the official, nonprofit Associazione Verace Pizza Napoletana (Real Neapolitan Pizza Association), genuine Neapolitan pizza dough must be made using highly refined type 00 wheat flour (a small dash of type 0 is permitted), compressed or natural yeast, salt, and water with a pH level between 6 and 7. While a slow-speed mixer can be used for kneading the dough, only hands are allowed to form the *disco di pasta* (pizza base), which should not be thicker than 3mm. The pizza itself should be cooked at 485°C (905°F) in a double-domed, wood-fired oven using oak, ash, beech or maple timber.

Don't believe the hype about espresso: one diminutive cup packs less of a caffeine wallop than a large cup of French-pressed or American-brewed coffee, and leaves drinkers less jittery.

THE SOUTHERN TABLE REGIONAL FOCUS

The Cult of Caffè

According to the Neapolitans, it's the local water that makes their coffee stronger and better than any other in Italy. While the magic formula is up for debate, there's no doubting that Naples brews the country's thickest, richest, most unforgettable espresso. Indeed, coffee plays a venerable role in Neapolitan cultural identity. Celebrated Neapolitan folk songs include *'O cafè* (Oh, coffee) and *A tazza 'e cafè* (The cup of coffee), while Italian design company Alessi pays tribute to the city's distinctive, stove-top coffee maker with its own *Caffettiera napoletana* (Neapolitan coffee maker), designed by prolific Neapolitan artist Riccardo Dalisi.

Locals still favour the Arabica and Robusta blends that deliver a dense crema, higher caffeine jolt, longer shelf life and, crucially, a price point everyone can afford. Chances are you'll be savouring it on your feet. In Naples, as in the rest of Italy, drinking coffee at a bar is usually a moment to pause, but rarely linger. It's a stand-up swirl and gulp, and an exchanged *buongiorno* or *buona sera* with the barista, and a hop back onto the street. But don't be fooled – the speed with which it's consumed does not diminish the importance of its quality.

Magnificent Mozzarella

So you think the cow's-milk mozzarella served in Capri's *insalata caprese* (a salad made of mozzarella, tomato, basil and olive oil) is delicious? Taste Campania's porcelain-white *mozzarella di bufala* (buffalo-milk mozzarella) and you'll move onto an entirely different level of deliciousness. Best eaten when freshly made that morning, its delicate, sweet flavour and luscious texture is nothing short of a revelation. Made using the milk of black water buffalo reared on the plains surrounding Caserta and Paestum, you'll find it served in trattorias (informal restaurants) and restaurants across the region. Indeed, you'll also find it dished up at dedicated mozzarella eateries, among them Muu Muzzarella Lounge (p54) in Naples and Inn Bufalito (p81) in Sorrento.

For a comprehensive yet easy-to-use guide to Italian cooking, hunt down Marcella Hazan's award-winning *Essentials of Classic Italian Cooking* (1992), which incorporates two of her cult-status cookbooks.

Bought fresh from *latterie* (dairies), it comes lukewarm in a plastic bag filled with a slightly cloudy liquid, the run-off from the mozzarella making. Fresh mozzarella should have an elastic consistency; a tight, smooth surface; and no yellowish marks or spots. Sliced, it should appear grainy, layered, and seeping pearls of milky whey.

While its most common form is round and fresh, *mozzarella di bufala* also comes in a twisted, plait form *(treccia)*, as well as smoked *(affumicata)*. Its most decadent variation is *burrata,* a mozzarella filled with a wickedly buttery cream. *Burrata* itself was invented in the neighbouring region of Puglia; the swampy fields around Foggia are famed for their buffalo-milk goodness.

Puglia, Basilicata & Calabria

Desirable Virgins

Campania and Sicily may produce a few impressive olive oils, but southern Italy's *olio* (oil) heavyweight is Puglia. The region produces around 40% of Italy's olive oil, much of it from the region's north. Indeed, Puglia is home to an estimated 50 to 60 million olive trees, and some of these gnarled, silver-green icons are said to be over 1000 years old.

While Pugliese oil is usually made up of two types of olives – faintly bitter coratina (from Corato) and sweet, fat ogliarola (from around Cima di Bitonto) – there is no shortage of common olive varieties. Among these are cellina di nardò, frantoio, leccino, peranzana, garganica, rotondella, cima di bitonto and cima di mola. The European Union itself formally recognises five Denomination of Origin of Production (DOP) areas in Puglia in order to protect the unique characteristics of each terroir: Collina di Brindisi DOP, Dauno DOP, Terra d'Otranto DOP, Terra di Bari DOP and Terre Tarentine DOP. While sweet fruitiness characterises the oils from Collina di Brindisi, Dauno DOP oils are noted for their aromatic, well-rounded nature. Ancient growing regions define both the Terra di Bari DOP and Terra d'Otranto DOP oils, the former known for their clear colour and almond notes, the latter for their darker green hue and fresh herb aroma. Last but not least are Terre Tarentine DOP oils, known for their greenish-yellow colouring, medium bitterness and light spiciness.

Whatever the origin, the best oil is made from olives that are picked and rushed to the mill, as olives that are left for too long after harvesting quickly become acidic. Pugliese farmers traditionally harvest the easy way: by letting the olives drop into nets, rather than paying for labour-intensive harvesting by hand. This means the olives are too acidic and the oil has to be refined, often taken north to mix with higher quality, costlier oils. That said, more and more places in the south produce stunning oils at low prices; you can buy it at local farms such as organic Il Frantoio (p118).

The Beauty of Bread

Puglia's celebrated olive oils are a fine match for the region's equally lauded *pane* (bread). Indeed, eating a meal in Puglia or neighbouring Basilicata without bread is like playing tennis without a racquet – it is essential for wiping up the sauce (a practise fondly called *fare scarpetta*, 'to make a little shoe'). Puglia's wood-fired variety is the stuff of legend, usually made from hard durum wheat (like pasta), with a russet-brown crust, an eggy-golden interior and a distinctively fine flavour. The best comes from Altamura, where it's thrice-risen, getting even better with time.

Many of Puglia's and Basilicata's recipes call for breadcrumbs, among them summery spaghetti with oven-roasted tomatoes, breadcrumbs and garlic, and fusilli pasta with tomato, breadcrumbs and *crusco* (a dried, sweet pepper unique to Basilicata). Across in Calabria, breadcrumbs and pasta meet in classics like spaghetti with anchovies and chilli. The breadcrumbs themselves are made from stale bread – in Italian, it's *pane rafferme* (firmed-up bread), which is a much more glass-half-full way of looking at it.

Another southwest staple is *friselli,* dried bagel-shaped rolls born out of practicality, ideal for labourers on the move. Douse them in water to soften and then dress with tomatoes, olive oil and oregano. Just leave a little room for bagel-shaped *taralli,* hard little savoury biscuits that make for a tasty snack. In Bari they're traditionally plain, in Taranto they're sprinkled with fennel seeds and in Lecce they're sexed-up with a touch of chilli.

Sicily

To Market, To Market

Only Naples' Mercato di Porta Nolana can rival the sheer theatricality and gut-rumbling brilliance of Sicily's *mercati* (markets). Loud, crowded and exhilarating, these alfresco larders are a Technicolor testament to the importance of fresh produce in daily life. To watch the hard-to-please hagglers bullying vendors into giving them precisely what they want is to understand that quality really matters here. And it's these people, the *nonne* (grandmothers) and *casalinghe* (homemakers), who keep the region's culinary traditions alive.

Two of the most atmospheric markets are Palermo's Mercato del Capo and Catania's La Pescheria, their souk-like laneways crammed with glistening tuna and swordfish, swaying sausages and tubs of olives and pungent cheeses. Look out for pistachios from Bronte, almonds from Noto, and *caciocavallo,* one of southern Italy's most renowned cheeses. Don't panic: despite the name 'horse cheese', it's made from cow's milk. It has a distinctive gourd-shaped, pale-mustard exterior, and the name is thought to have arisen either because it was once made from mare's milk, or because it would be hung from the horse's back when transported. When it's young, it tastes *dolce* (sweet); after two month's ageing, it's *piccante* (spicy) or *affumicato* (smoked).

La Dolce Vita

From *gelso di melone* (watermelon jelly) and *buccellati* (little pies filled with minced fruit), to *biscotti regina* (sesame-coated biscuits) and *cassatelle* (pouches of dough stuffed with sweetened ricotta and chocolate), Sicilians have a way with sugar that verges on the pornographic. Down here, *pasticcerie* (pastry shops) are culinary sex shops, leading taste buds into temptation. Ditch the guilt, you're not alone – Sicilians normally migrate from restaurant tables to the nearest pastry shop for a coffee and cake at the bar.

It was the Saracens who first brought sugar cane to Sicily, a novelty that would help kindle the island's passion for sweets. Sicily's legendary

Antonio Carluccio's *Southern Italian Feast: More than 100 Recipes Inspired by the Flavour of Southern Italy,* is a splendid collection to inspire you to get busy in the kitchen.

THE SOUTHERN TABLE REGIONAL FOCUS

THE BIG FORK MANIFESTO

The year was 1987. McDonald's had just begun their expansion into Italy, and lunch outside the bun seemed to be fading into fond memory. Enter Carlo Petrini and a handful of other journalists from the small Piedmontese town of Bra, in northern Italy. Determined to buck the trend, these *neoforchettoni* ('big forks', or foodies) created a manifesto. Published in the like-minded culinary magazine *Gambero Rosso,* the manifesto declared that a meal should be judged not by its speed, but by the pure pleasure it offers.

The organisation they founded would soon become known worldwide as Slow Food. Its mission: to reconnect artisanal producers with enthusiastic, educated consumers. The movement has taken root, with more than 100,000 members in 150 countries – not to mention Slow Food *agriturismi* (farm-stay accommodation), restaurants, farms, wineries, cheesemakers and revitalised farmers markets across Italy.

While traditions in the south remain stronger than in Italy's north, the Slow Food Movement does its bit to prevent their disappearance and to promote interest in food, taste and the way things are produced. For more information, see www.slowfood.com.

cassata (a coma-inducing concoction of sponge cake, ricotta, marzipan, chocolate and candied fruit) comes from the Arabic word *qas'ah* (a reference to the terracotta bowl used to shape the cake), while *cannolo* (a pastry shell with a sweet ricotta filling) originates from *canna* (cane, as in sugar cane).

The Arabs also kick-started the Sicilian mania for all things icy – *granite* (flavoured crushed ice), *cassata* ice cream, gelato (ice cream) and *semifreddo* (literally 'semifrozen'; a cold, creamy dessert). The origins of ice cream lie in the Arab *sarbat* (sherbet), a concoction of sweet fruit syrups chilled with iced water, later developed into *granite* (where crushed ice was mixed with anything from fruit juice to coffee and almond milk) and *cremolata* (fruit syrups chilled with iced milk), the forerunner to gelato.

Homemade gelato (*gelato artiginale*) is sold at cafes and bars across the island, and is truly delicious. *Granite* are sometimes topped with fresh whipped cream, or you could try it like a Sicilian – first thing in the morning in a brioche.

Southern Staples
Pasta: Fuel of the South

In the 1954 cult film *Un americano a Roma* (An American in Rome), a US-obsessed Alberto Sordi snubs a plate of pasta in favour of an unappetising 'American-style' concoction. It only takes a few mouthfuls before Sordi thinks better of it, plunging into the pasta with unbridled passion. It's hard not to follow Sordi's lead.

A standard *primo* (first course) on menus across the south, pasta is not only delicious, it's often a filling meal in itself. Your waiter will understand and there is usually no pressure to order a *secondo* (second course). The south's knack for pasta dishes is hardly surprising given that it was here that pasta first hit Italy, introduced to Sicily by Arab merchants in the Middle Ages. It was to be a perfect match. Southern Italy's sunny, windy disposition was just right for producing *pasta secca* (dry pasta), while the foodstuff's affordability and easy storage made it handy in the face of hardship. It's no coincidence that *pasta fresca* (fresh pasta) has, traditionally, been more prevalent in Italy's more affluent north.

Arriving from Sicily, *pasta secca* took off in a big way in Campania, especially after the 1840 opening of Italy's first pasta plant in Torre Annunziata, a town on the Bay of Naples. Not that Torre Annunziata was Campania's first pasta-making hub. Some 30km southeast of Naples, small-town Gragnano has been making pasta since the 17th century. Gragnano's main street was specifically built along the sun's axis so that the pasta put out to dry by the town's *pastifici* (pasta factories) would reap a full day's sunshine. To this day, *pasta di Gragnano* enjoys an air of exclusivity.

And while *pasta secca* may be the dominant form of pasta on southern plates, the Mezzogiorno is not without its fresh pasta icons. The most famous is arguably Puglia's *orecchiette* (meaning 'little ears'), best savoured in dishes such as *orecchiette con cime di rapa* (with turnip tops) and *orecchiette con pomodori e ricotta forte* (with tomato sauce and strong ricotta).

Eat Your Greens...Purples, Reds & Yellows

Vegetables across the world must loathe their southern Italian counterparts. Not only do they often look more beautiful, they're prepared with a know-how that turns them into culinary protagonists. Take the humble *melanzana* (eggplant or aubergine), glammed up in the punchy *melanzane ripiene al forno* (baked eggplant stuffed with olives, capers and

While it's perfectly normal to order 'a biscotti' or 'a cannoli' back home in Sydney or New York, these are actually plural forms in Italian; use the singular form *'un biscotto'* or *'un cannolo'* when in Italy – unless, of course, you're seriously famished.

Less is more: most of the recipes in Ada Boni's classic *The Talisman Italian Cookbook* have fewer than 10 ingredients, yet the flavours of her mozzarella and anchovy *crostini* or Sicilian-style *caponatina* are anything but simple.

tomatoes) and decadent *parmigiana melanzane* (batter-fried eggplant layered with parmesan, mozzarella, ham and tomato sauce). Another version, simply named *parmigiana,* does the same for *carciofi* (globe artichokes). Campania's *pomodoro San Marzano* (San Marzano plum tomato) is one of the world's most lauded tomatoes. Grown in the shadow of Mt Vesuvius, its low acidity and intense, sweet flavour make a perfect *conserva di pomodoro* (tomato concentrate). It's this sauce that adorns so many of Naples' signature pasta dishes, including the colourfully named *spaghetti alla puttanesca* (whore's spaghetti).

Ironically, southern Italy's sophisticated flair with vegetables is firmly rooted in centuries of deprivation and misery. The food of the poor, the so-called *mangiafoglie* (leaf eaters), was largely based on the *verdure* (vegetables) grown under the nourishing southern sun, from artichokes and courgettes (zucchini), to tomatoes and peppers. Hardship and sunshine helped develop celebrated antipasto staples like *zucchine fritte* (pan-fried courgettes) and *peperoni sotto aceto* (marinated pickled

The word *melanzane* (eggplant or aubergine) comes from 'mela insane', meaning crazy apple. In Latin it was called *solanum insanum* as it was thought to cause madness.

FESTIVE FAVOURITES

In Italy, culinary indulgence is the epicentre of any celebration and major holidays are defined by their specialities. Lent is heralded by Carnevale (Carnival), a time for *sanguinaccio* (blood pudding made with dark chocolate and cinnamon), *chiacchiere* (fried biscuits sprinkled with icing sugar) and Sicily's *mpagnuccata* (deep-fried dough tossed in soft caramel).

If you're in southern Italy around 19 March (St Joseph's Feast Day), expect to eat *zeppole* (fritters topped with lemon-scented cream, sour cherry and dusting sugar) in Naples and Bari, and *crispelle di riso* (citrus-scented rice fritters dipped in honey) in Sicily.

Lent specialities like Sicilian *quaresimali* (hard, light almond biscuits) give way to Easter binging with the obligatory lamb, *colomba* (dove-shaped cake) and *uove di pasqua* (foil-wrapped chocolate eggs with toy surprises inside). The dominant ingredient at this time is egg, also used to make traditional regional specialities like Naples' legendary *pastiera* (shortcrust pastry tart filled with ricotta, cream, candied fruits and cereals flavoured with orange water).

If you're in Palermo around late October, before the festival of Ognissanti (All Souls' Day), you will see plenty of stalls selling the famous *frutti della Martorana,* named after the church that first began producing them. These marzipan biscuits, shaped to resemble fruits (or whatever takes the creator's fancy), are part of a Sicilian tradition that dates back to the Middle Ages.

Come Christmas, it's time for stuffed pasta, seafood dishes and national staples like Milan's *panettone* (yeasty, golden cake studded with raisins and dried fruit), Verona's simpler, raisin-free *pandoro* (yeasty, star-shaped cake dusted with vanilla-flavoured icing sugar) and Siena's *panforte* (chewy, flat cake made with candied fruits, nuts, chocolate, honey and spices). It's at this time that Neapolitans throw caution (and scales) to the wind with *raffioli* (sponge and marzipan biscuits), *struffoli* (tiny fried pastry balls dipped in honey and sprinkled with colourful candied sugar) and *pasta di mandorla* (marzipan), while their Sicilian cousins toast the season with *cucciddatu* (ring-shaped cake made with dried figs, nuts, honey, vanilla, cloves, cinnamon and citrus fruits). Not that the Sicilians stop there, further expanding waistlines with Yuletide *buccellati* (dough rings stuffed with minced figs, raisins, almonds, candied fruit and/or orange peel, especially popular around Christmas).

Of course, it's not all about religion. Some Italian holidays dispense with the spiritual premise and are all about the food. During spring, summer and early autumn, towns across Italy celebrate *sagre,* the festivals of local foods in season. You'll find a *sagra della melanzana* (aubergine) in Campania, *del pomodoro* (tomatoes) in Sicily and *della cipolla* (onion) in Puglia (wouldn't want to be downwind of that one). For a list of *sagre,* check out www.prodottitipici.com/sagre (in Italian).

peppers), as well as celebrated Sicilian dishes like *peperonata in agridolce* (a stew of red, green and yellow peppers, onions, pine nuts, raisins and capers). Onions feel the love in Puglia's moreish *calzone pugliese* (onion pie), while legumes see the light in the region's broad bean and chicory puree; 'a dish to die for' according to celebrity chef, restaurateur and food writer Antonio Carluccio.

The Vine Revival

Winemaking in the south dates back to the Phoenicians. The Greeks introduced Campania to its now-famous Greco (Greek) grape, and dubbed the south 'Enotria' (Wineland). Yet, despite this ancient viticulture, oenophiles had often dismissed local *vini* (wines) as little more than 'here for a good time, not a long time' drops. A case in point is wine critic Burton Anderson, who in his *Wine Atlas of Italy* (1990) wrote that Campania's noteworthy winemakers could be 'counted on one's fingers'.

Anderson would need a few more hands these days. In little more than two decades, southern Italy has transformed itself into one of the world's hottest in-the-know wine regions, with renewed pride in native varieties and stricter, more modern winemaking practices.

Campania

Lauded producers such as Feudi di San Gregorio, Mastroberardino, Villa Matilde, Pietracupa and Terredora have returned to their roots, cultivating ancient grape varieties like the red Aglianico (thought to be the oldest cultivated grape in Italy) and the whites Falanghino, Fiano and Greco (all growing long before Mt Vesuvius erupted in AD 79). Keeping them company is a growing list of reputable organic and biodynamic wineries, among them Terre Stregate, I Cacciagalli, Colli di Lapio and Cautiero.

Taurasi, a full-bodied Aglianico wine, sometimes known as the Barolo of the south, is one of southern Italy's finest labels. One of only four in the region to carry Italy's top quality rating, DOCG (Denominazione di Origine Controllata e Garantita; Controlled and Guaranteed Denomination of Origin), it goes perfectly with barbequed and boiled meats. The other three wines to share this honour are Aglianico del Taburno, a full-bodied red from the Benevento area, as well as Fiano di Avellino and Greco di Tufo, both whites and both from the Avellino area.

Other vino-producing areas include the Campi Flegrei (home to DOC-labelled Piedirosso and Falanghina vines), Ischia (whose wines were the first to receive DOC status) and the Cilento region, home to the DOC Cilento bianco (Cilento white) and to the Aglianico Paestum. Mt Vesuvius' most famous drop is the Lacryma Christi (Tears of Christ), a blend of locally grown Falanghina, Piedirosso and Coda di Volpe grapes.

Puglia & Basilicata

The different characteristics of these regions' wines reflect their diverse topography and terroir. In Puglia, there are vast, flat acreages of vineyards, while Basilicata's vineyards tend to be steep and volcanic.

It's the Pugliese reds that gain most plaudits. The main grapes grown are the Primitivo (a clone of the zinfandel grape), Negroamaro, Nero di Troia and Malvasia. The best Primitivi are found around Manduria, while Negroamaro reaches its peak in the Salento, particularly around Salice, Guagnano and Copertino. The two grapes are often blended to derive the best from the sweetness of Primitivo and the slightly bitter, wilder edge of Negroamaro.

Almost all Puglia reds work perfectly with pasta, pizza, meats and cheeses. Puglia whites have less cachet; however, those grown on the Murge, particularly Locorotondo and Martina, are good, clean, fresh-

The average Italian adult consumes around 42 litres of wine per year – a sobering figure compared with the 100 litres consumed on average back in the 1950s. Somewhat surprisingly, the world's top consumers of wine live in the Vatican City (74 litres per person).

Although some producers find these official Italian classifications unduly costly and creatively constraining, the DOCG (Denominazione di Origine Controllata e Garantita) and DOC (Denominazione di Origine Controllata) designations are awarded to wines that meet regional quality-control standards.

tasting wines, while those from Gravina are a little weightier. They are all excellent with fish.

In Basilicata, the red wine of choice is made from the Aglianico grape, the best being produced in the Vulture region. It is the volcanic terroir that makes these wines unique and splendid. Basilicata, like Puglia, has seen a renaissance in recent years with much inward investment, such as that of oenologist Donato d'Angelo at his eponymous winery at Rionero in Vulture.

Sicily

Sicily is one of the largest wine-producing regions in Italy, yet few Sicilian wines are well known beyond the island.

The most common varietal is Nero d'Avola, a robust red similar to Syrah or Shiraz. Vintages are produced by numerous Sicilian wineries, including Planeta (www.planeta.it), which has four estates around the island; Donnafugata (www.donnafugata.it) in Western Sicily; Azienda Agricola COS (www.cosvittoria.it) near Mt Etna; and Azienda Agricola G Milazzo (www.milazzovini.com) near Agrigento. Try Planeta's Plumbago and Santa Cecilia labels, Donnafugata's Mille e una Notte, COS' Nero di Lupo and Milazzo's Maria Costanza and Terre della Baronia Rosso.

Local cabernet sauvignons are less common but worth sampling; the version produced by Tasca d'Almerita at its Regaleali estate in Caltanissetta province is particularly highly regarded (the estate also produces an excellent Nero d'Avola under its Rosso del Conte label).

The Sangiovese-like Nerello Mascalese and Nerello Cappuccio are used in the popular Etna Rosso DOC, a dark-fruited, medium-bodied wine that pairs perfectly with lamb and goat's-milk cheeses.

There is only one Sicilian DOCG, Cerasuolo di Vittoria, a blend of Nero d'Avola and Frappato grapes.

While Sicily's *vini rossi* (red wines) are good, the region's real forte are its *bianchi* (whites), including those produced at Abbazia Santa Anastasia near Castelbuono, and Fazio Wines near Erice, Tasca d'Almerita and Passopisciaro. Common white varietals include Carricante, chardonnay, Grillo, Inzolia, Cataratto, Inzolia, Cataratto, Grecanico and Corinto. Look out for Tasca d'Almerita's Nozze d'Oro Inzolia blend, Fazio's Catarratto Chardonnay, Abbazia Santa Anastasia's chardonnay blends, and Passopisciaro's Guardiola Chardonnay.

Equally impressive are Sicily's dessert wines. Top billing goes to Marsala's sweet wine; the best labels are Florio and Pellegrino. Italy's most famous Moscato (muscat) is the Passito di Pantelleria from the island of the same name. Deep-amber in colour, its taste is an extraordinary melange of apricots and vanilla.

The annual *Italian Wines*, produced by the Gambero Rosso, is considered to be the bible of Italian vino, offering plenty of information about southern wines and wineries. You can buy it at many Italian bookstores or online at www.gamberorosso.it.

THE SOUTHERN TABLE THE VINE REVIVAL

Art & Architecture

Southern Italy is Western Europe's cultural attic – a dusty repository filled to the rafters with ancient temples and statues, exotic mosaics, brooding castles, vainglorious frescoes and innovative installations. It's an overwhelming heap, so why not start with the undisputed highlights?

Art

Classical Splendour

The Greeks had settled many parts of Sicily and southern Italy as early as the 8th century BC, naming it Magna Graecia (Greater Greece) and building great cities such as Syracuse and Taranto. These cities were famous for their magnificent temples, many of which were decorated with sculptures modelled on, or inspired by, masterpieces by Praxiteles, Lysippus and Phidias.

The Greek colonisers were equally deft at ceramics, adorning vases with painted scenes from daily life, mythology and Greek theatre. Some of the most vivid examples are the 4th-century-BC phylax vases, with larger-than-life characters and costumes that depict scenes from phylax plays, a type of ancient southern-Italian farce.

Visit www.exibart. com (in Italian) for up-to-date listings of art exhibitions throughout Italy, as well as exhibition reviews, articles and interviews.

In art, as in so many other realms, the Romans looked to the Greeks for examples of best practice, and sculpture, architecture and painting flourished during their reign. Yet, the art produced in Rome was different in many ways from the Greek art that influenced it. Essentially secular, it focused less on harmony and form and more on accurate representation, mainly in the form of sculptural portraits. Innumerable versions of Pompey, Titus and Augustus all show a similar visage, proving that the artists were seeking verisimilitude in their representations, and not just glorification.

Wealthy Roman citizens also dabbled in the arts, building palatial villas and adorning them with statues looted from the Greek world or copied from Hellenic originals. You'll find many fine examples in Syracuse's Museo Archeologico Paolo Orsi, including the celebrated *Venere Anadiomene,* a 1st-century Roman copy depicting a voluptuous goddess of love. Status-conscious Romans didn't stop there, lavishing floors with mosaics and walls with vivid frescoes. Outstanding mosaics continue to enthrall at Sicily's Villa Romana del Casale, Pompeii, Herculaneum and Naples' Museo Archeologico Nazionale. Pompeii itself claims the world's largest ancient wall fresco, a recently restored wonder inside the Villa dei Misteri.

The Glitter of Byzantine

In 330, Emperor Constantine, a convert to Christianity, made the ancient city of Byzantium his capital and renamed it Constantinople. The city became the great cultural and artistic centre of Christianity and it remained so up to the time of the Renaissance, though its influence on the art of that period was never as fundamental as the art of ancient Rome.

Artistically, the Byzantine period was notable for its extraordinary mosaic work and – to a lesser extent – its painting. Its art was influenced by the decoration of the Roman catacombs and the early Christian churches, as well as by the Oriental Greek style, with its love of rich decoration and luminous colour.

As a major transit point on the route between Constantinople and Rome, Puglia and Basilicata were exposed to Byzantine's Eastern aesthetics. Indeed, the art that most encapsulates these regions is its 10th- and 11th-century Byzantine frescoes, hidden away in locked chapels dotted across their expanse. There is an incredible concentration in Matera, the most fantastic of which include the monastic complex of Chiesa di Madonna delle Virtù & Chiesa di San Nicola dei Greci. Impressive examples in Puglia include the lively frescoes inside Otranto's Chiesa di San Pietro.

In Sicily, Byzantine, Norman and Saracen influences fused to create a distinct regional style showcased in the mosaic-encrusted splendour of Palermo's Cappella Palatina inside the Palazzo dei Normanni, not to mention the cathedrals of Monreale and Cefalù.

Giotto & the 'Rebirth' of Italian Art

Italy's Byzantine painters were apt with light and shade, but it would take Florentine painter Giotto di Bondone (c 1266–1337) to break the spell of conservatism and venture into a new world of naturalism. Giotto is best known for his frescoes in Padua and Assisi, but faded fragments of his work survive in Naples' Castel Nuovo and Basilica di Santa Chiara.

Giotto and the painters of the Sienese School introduced many innovations in art: the exploration of perspective and proportion, a new interest in realistic portraiture and the beginnings of a new tradition of landscape painting. The influx of Eastern scholars fleeing Constantinople in the wake of its fall to the Ottoman Turkish Muslims in 1453 prompted a renewed interest in classical learning and humanist philosophy. Coupled with the increasingly ambitious, competitive nature of northern Italy's city states, these developments would culminate in the Renaissance.

Centred in Florence in the 15th century, and Rome and Venice in the 16th century, the Renaissance was slower to catch on in southern Italy, which was caught up in the power struggles between its French and Spanish rulers. One of the south's few Renaissance masters was Antonello da Messina (1430–79), whose luminous works include *The Virgin Annunciate* (1474–77) in Palermo's Galleria Regionale della Sicilia and *The Annunciation* (1474) in Syracuse's Galleria Regionale di Palazzo Bellomo.

Bad Boys & the Baroque

With the advent of the baroque, it was the south's time to shine. Under 17th-century Spanish rule, Naples was transformed into Europe's biggest city. Swelling crowds and counter-Reformation fervour sparked a building boom, with taller-than-ever *palazzi* (mansions) and showcase churches sprouting up across the city. Ready to adorn these new landmarks was a brash, arrogant and fiery league of artists, ditching Renaissance restraint for baroque exuberance.

The main influence on 17th-century Neapolitan art was Milanese-born Caravaggio (1573–1610). A controversial character, he escaped to Naples in 1606 after killing a man in Rome; although he only stayed for a year, his impact on the city was huge. Caravaggio's dramatic depiction of light and shade, his supreme draughtsmanship and his naturalist style had an electrifying effect on the city's younger artists. One look at Caravaggio's *Flagellazione* (Flagellation; 1607–10) in Naples' Museo Nazionale di Capodimonte, his *Le sette opere di Misericordia* (Seven Acts of Mercy; c 1607) in the Pio Monte della Misericordia, or his swan song *Martirio*

EH Gombrich's seminal work *The Story of Art*, first published in 1950, gives a wonderful overview of the history of Italian art.

Italy's dedicated art police, the Comando Carabinieri Tutela Patrimonio Culturale, tackles the looting of Italy's priceless heritage. It's estimated that over 100,000 ancient tombs have been ransacked by *tombaroli* (tomb raiders) alone; the contents are often sold to private and public collectors around the world.

STARS OF NEAPOLITAN BAROQUE

Michelangelo Merisi da Caravaggio (1573–1610) Bridging Mannerism and the baroque, Caravaggio injected raw emotion and foreboding shadow. His greatest masterpiece is the multi-scene *La sette opere di Misericordia* (Seven Acts of Mercy; 1607), appearing in Naples' Pio Monte della Misericordia.

Giuseppe de Ribera (1591–1652) Though Spanish born, most of this bullying painter's finest work was created in southern Italy, including his dramatic *St Jerome* (1626) and *Apollo and Marsyas* (c 1637), both in the Museo Nazionale di Capodimonte.

Cosimo Fanzago (1591–1678) This revered sculptor, decorator and architect cut marble into the most whimsical forms, producing luscious, inlaid spectacles. Naples' Certosa di San Martino aside, his beautiful high altar in Naples' Chiesa di San Domenico Maggiore is not to be missed.

Mattia Preti (1613–99) Dubbed 'Il Cavaliere Calabrese' (The Calabrian Knight), Preti infused thunderous, apocalyptic scenes with a deep, affecting humanity. Seek out his *Feast of Absalom* (c 1670) in the Museo Nazionale di Capodimonte.

Luca Giordano (1632–1705) Affectionately nicknamed Luca fa presto (Luca does it quickly) for his dexterous ways with a brush. Fabulous frescoes aside, his canvassed creations include *Apollo and Marsyas* (c 1660) in the Museo Nazionale di Capodimonte.

Francesco Solimena (1657–1747) Lavish and grandiose compositions define this icon's work. One of his best is the operatic fresco *Expulsion of Eliodoro from the Temple* (1725) in Naples' Chiesa del Gesù Nuovo.

Giuseppe Sanmartino (1720–93) Arguably the finest sculptor of his time, Sanmartino's ability to breathe life into his creations won him a legion of fans, including the bizarre alchemist prince, Raimondo di Sangro. Don't miss his *Cristo velato* (Veiled Christ) in Di Sangro's Cappella Sansevero, Naples.

di Sant'Orsola (Martyrdom of St Ursula) in the city's Galleria di Palazzo Zevallos Stigliano and you'll understand why.

One of Caravaggio's greatest fans was artist Giuseppe (or Jusepe) de Ribera (1591–1652), whose combination of shadow, colour and gloomy naturalism is brilliantly executed in his masterpiece, *Pietà* (1637), which is hanging in Naples' Certosa di San Martino. Merciless to the extreme, Lo Spagnoletto (The Little Spaniard, as Ribera was known) reputedly won a commission for the Cappella del Tesoro in Naples' Duomo by poisoning his rival Domenichino (1581–1641), as well as wounding the assistant of a second competitor, Guido Reni (1575–1642). The Duomo would be adorned with the frescoes of a number of rising stars, among them Giovanni Lanfranco (1582–1647) and Luca Giordano (1632–1705).

A fledging apprentice to Ribera, Naples-born Giordano found great inspiration in the brushstrokes of Mattia Preti (1613–99). By the second half of the 17th century, Giordano would become the single most important artist in Naples. His finest fresco, the *Triumph of Judith,* decorates the treasury ceiling of the Certosa di San Martino's church.

In *M: The Man Who Became Caravaggio*, Peter Robb gives a passionate personal assessment of the artist's paintings and a colourful account of Caravaggio's life, arguing he was murdered for having sex with the pageboy of a high-ranking Maltese aristocrat.

Architecture

Ancient Legacies

One word describes the buildings of ancient southern Italy: monumental. The Greeks invented the architectural orders (Doric, Ionic and Corinthian) and used them to great effect in once-mighty cities like Akragas (modern-day Agrigento), Catania and Syracuse. More than two millennia later, the soaring temples of Segesta, Selinunte, the Valley of the Temples and Paestum confirm not only the ancient Greeks' power, but also their penchant for harmonious proportion. This skill also underscored their sweeping theatres, the finest of which still stand in Syracuse, Taormina and Segesta.

Having learned a few valuable lessons from the Greeks, the Romans refined architecture to such a degree that their building techniques, designs and mastery of harmonious proportion underpin most of the world's architecture and urban design to this day. In Brindisi, a brilliant white column marks one end of the Via Appia – the ancient cross-country road connecting Rome to east-coast Brindisi. In Pozzuoli, they erected the Anfiteatro Flavio, the empire's third-largest arena and the very spot where Roman authorities had planned to feed San Gennaro to hungry bears. (In the end, they opted to behead the Christian at the nearby Solfatara Crater.)

Medieval Fusion

Following on from Byzantine architecture and its mosaic-encrusted churches was Romanesque, a style that found four regional forms in Italy: Lombard, Pisan, Florentine and Sicilian Norman. All displayed an emphasis on width and the horizontal lines of a building rather than height, and featured church groups with *campaniles* (bell towers) and baptisteries that were separate fom the church. Surfacing in the 11th century, the Sicilian Norman style encompassed an exotic mix of Norman, Saracen and Byzantine influences, from marble columns to Islamic-inspired pointed arches to glass tesserae detailing. Clearly visible in the two-toned masonry and 13th-century bell tower of Amalfi's Cattedrale di Sant'Andrea, one of the greatest examples of the form is the cathedral of Monreale, just outside Palermo.

With the 12th and 13th centuries came the Gothic aesthetic. The Italians didn't embrace this style as enthusiastically as the French, Germans and Spanish did. Its flying buttresses, grotesque gargoyles and over-the-top decorations were just too far from the classical ideal that was (and still is) bred in the Italian bone. This said, the Gothic style did leave its mark in southern Italy, albeit in the muted version encapsulated by Naples' Chiesa di San Lorenzo Maggiore and Chiesa di San Domenico Maggiore, and Palermo's Palazzo Bellomo. The south's most striking Gothic icon, however, is Puglia's Castel del Monte; its Italianate windows, Islamic floor mosaics and Roman triumphal entrance attest to the south's flair for absorbing foreign influence.

Baroque: The Golden Age

Just as Renaissance restraint redefined Italy's north, the wild theatricality of 17th- and 18th-century baroque revamped the south. Encouraging the makeover was the Catholic Church, for whom baroque's awe-inducing qualities were the perfect weapon against the Reformation and its less-is-more philosophy. Deploying swirls of frescoes, gilt and polychromatic marble, churches like Naples' Chiesa del Gesù Nuovo and Chiesa di San Gregorio Armeno turned Catholicism into a no-holds-barred extravaganza.

Inlaid marble would become a dominant special effect, adorning everything from tombs and altars to floors and entire chapel walls. The form's undisputed master was Cosimo Fanzago (1591–1678), an occasionally violent sculptor whose masterpieces would include Naples' Certosa di San Martino's church, a mesmerising kaleidoscope of colour, geometry and arresting precision.

In Puglia's Salento region, *barocco leccese* (Lecce baroque) saw the style reach extraordinary new heights. Local limestone was carved into lavish decorative detail around porticoes, windows, balconies and loggias, themselves crowned with human and zoomorphic figures as well as a riot of gargoyles, flora, fruit, columns and cornices. The leading

One of the few well-known female artists of the Italian Renaissance was Artemisia Gentileschi (1593–1652), whose style is reminiscent of Caravaggio's. One of her most famous paintings, the intensely vengeful *Judith and Holofernes*, hangs inside Naples' Museo Nazionale di Capodimonte.

For a Blast of Baroque

Lecce, Puglia

Noto, Sicily

Catania, Sicily

Naples, Campania

MODERN MOVEMENTS

Of the many movements that shaped Italy's 20th-century art scene, few match the radical innovation of Arte Povera (Poor Art). Emerging from the economic and political instability of the 1960s, its artists aimed to blur the boundary between art and life. Using everyday materials and mediums ranging from painting and photography to installations, they created works that put the viewer at the centre, triggering personal memories and associations. The movement would ultimately pave the way for contemporary installation art. Its leading practitioners included Mario Merz (1925–2003), Luciano Fabro (1936–2007) and Giovanni Anselmo (b 1934), the latter's sculptures inspired by the geological forces of Stromboli. Another icon of the scene is the Greek-born Jannis Kounellis (b 1936), whose brooding installations often focus on the disintegration of culture in the modern world. Naples' MADRE contains a fine collection of Kounellis' creations, as well as other Arte Povera works. Among the wittiest is Michelangelo Pistoletti's *Venere degli stracci* (Venus of the Rags), in which a Greek goddess contemplates a pile of modern hand-me-downs.

Reacting against Arte Povera's conceptual tendencies was the 'Transavanguardia' movement of the late 1970s and 1980s, which refocussed attention on painting and sculpture in a traditional (primarily figurative) sense. Among its leading artists are Mimmo Paladino (b 1948) and Francesco Clemente (b 1952). Both of these Campanian artists are represented in Naples' Novecento a Napoli, a museum dedicated to 20th-century southern Italian art.

exponents of the style were Gabriele Riccardi (1524–82) and Francesco Antonio Zimbalo (1567-1631), but it was Francesco's grandson Giuseppe Zimbalo (1620-1710), nicknamed Lo Zingarello (The Little Gypsy), who was its most exuberant disciple. Among his greatest designs is the upper facade of Lecce's Basilica di Santa Croce.

It would take an earthquake in 1632 to seal Sicily's baroque legacy. Faced with destruction, ambitious architects set to work rebuilding the towns and cities of the island's southeast, among them Noto, Modica and Ragusa. Grid-patterned streets were laid and spacious piazzas were lined with confident, curvaceous buildings. The result was a highly idiosyncratic *barocco siciliano* (Sicilian baroque), best known for its cheeky stone *putti* (cherubs), wrought-iron balustrades and grand external staircases. Equally idiosyncratic was the use of dramatic, centrally placed church belfries, often shooting straight above the central pediment. Two of the finest examples are Ragusa's Cattedrale di San Giorgio and Modica's Chiesa di San Giorgio, both designed by the prolific Rosario Gagliardi (1698-1762).

Sicily's most celebrated baroque architect, however, would be Giovanni Battista Vaccarini (1702-68). Trained in Rome, Vaccarini would dedicate three decades of his life to rebuilding earthquake-stricken Catania, using the region's volcanic black rock to dramatic effect in Piazza del Duomo. His reputation would see him join forces with Neapolitan star architect Luigi Vanvitelli (1700-73) in the creation of Italy's epic baroque epilogue: the Reggia di Caserta, 30km north of Naples.

Survival Guide

DIRECTORY A–Z....262

Accommodation........ 262

Customs
Regulations............ 264

Discount Cards......... 264

Electricity 265

Embassies &
Consulates 265

Food 265

Gay & Lesbian
Travellers.............. 265

Health................. 266

Insurance.............. 267

Internet Access......... 267

Legal Matters 267

Maps.................. 267

Money................. 267

Post.................. 268

Public Holidays......... 268

Safe Travel............. 268

Telephone 269

Time 270

Tourist Information 270

Travellers with
Disabilities............. 271

Visas.................. 271

Volunteering 272

Women Travellers....... 272

TRANSPORT........273

GETTING THERE
& AWAY 273

Entering the Country.....273

Air 273

Land 274

Sea 275

GETTING AROUND.......276

Air 276

Bicycle 276

Boat 277

Bus 277

Car & Motorcycle.......277

Local Transport.........278

Train 278

LANGUAGE 281

Glossary............... 285

Directory A–Z

Accommodation

Accommodation in Italy's south is ever improving and increasingly varied. Hotels and *pensioni* (guesthouses) make up the bulk of the offerings, covering everything from cheap sleeps near the train station to trendy art hotels and five-star legends with ocean views. Youth hostels, camping grounds and an ever-increasing number of B&Bs are a boon for the euro-economisers, while *agriturismi* (farm stays) and *masserie* (southern Italian farms or estates) allow you to live out your bucolic Italian fantasies. Capturing the imagination still more are the options to stay in everything from castles to convents and monasteries.

➡ Where applicable, our accommodation reviews list minimum to maximum high-season rates. Where indicated, half-board means breakfast and either lunch or dinner; full board is breakfast, lunch and dinner.

➡ Some hotels, in particular the lower-end places, barely alter their prices throughout the year. In low season there's no harm in bargaining for a discount, especially if you intend to stay for several days.

➡ Hotels usually require that reservations be confirmed with a credit-card number. No-shows will be docked a night's accommodation.

➡ The high season is during July and August, though prices peak again around Easter and Christmas. It's essential to book in advance during these periods. Conversely, prices drop between 30% and 50% in low season. In the winter months (November to Easter) many places, particularly on the coast, completely shut down. In the cities and larger towns accommodation tends to remain open all year. The relative lack of visitors in these down periods means you should have little trouble getting a room in those places that do stay open.

➡ Most hotels offer breakfast, though this can vary from bountiful buffets to more modest offerings of pastries, packaged yoghurt and fruit. The same is true of B&Bs, where morning food options can sometimes be little more than pre-packaged *cornetti* (Italian croissants), biscuits, jam, coffee and tea.

Agriturismi, Masserie & B&Bs

An *agriturismo* (*agriturismi* in the plural) is accommodation on a working farm, where you'll usually be able to sample the produce. Traditionally families simply rented out rooms in their farmhouses; it's still possible to find this type of lodging, although many *agriturismi* have now evolved into sophisticated accommodation. There are several Italian guidebook directories devoted solely to *agriturismi*, or try www.agriturismo.it or www.agriturismo.net (also good for self-catering apartments and villas).

Unique to southern Italy, *masserie* are large farms or estates, usually built around a fortified watchtower, with plenty of surrounding accommodation to house workers and livestock. Many have been converted into luxurious hotels, *agriturismi* or holiday apartments. A *masseria* isn't necessarily old: sometimes new buildings built around similar principles are called *masserie*.

B&Bs are a burgeoning sector of the southern accommodation market and can be found in both urban

OFFBEAT ACCOMMODATION

Looking for something out of the ordinary? Southern Italy offers a number of sleeping options that you won't find anywhere else in the world.

➡ Down near Italy's heel, rent a **trullo**, one of the characteristic whitewashed conical houses of southern Puglia.

➡ Ancient **sassi** (cave dwellings) have found new life as boutique hotels in otherworldly Matera, a Unesco World Heritage–listed town in the southern region of Basilicata.

➡ In Naples, spend a night or two slumbering in the **aristocratic palazzo** of a powerful Bourbon bishop. Now the **Decumani Hotel de Charme** (☏ 081 551 81 88; www.decumani. it; Via San Giovanni Maggiore Pignatelli 15; s €99-124, d €99-164; ✳ @ ☎; Ⓜ Università), the property comes complete with a sumptuous baroque salon.

and rural settings. Options include everything from restored farmhouses, city *palazzi* (mansions) and seaside bungalows to rooms in family houses. Tariffs for a double room cover a wide range, from about €60 to €140. For more information, contact B&B Italia (www.bbitalia.it).

Camping

Italians go camping with gusto and most camping facilities in Campania, Puglia, Calabria and Sicily (less so in Basilicata, where camping options are few and far between) include swimming pools, restaurants and supermarkets. With hotel prices shooting up in July and August, campgrounds can be a splendid option, especially given that many have enviable seaside locations.

Charges often vary according to the season, peaking in July and August, when accommodation should be booked well in advance. Typical high-season prices range from €10 to €20 per adult, up to €12 for children aged under 12, and from €5 to €25 for a site.

Many campgrounds offer the alternative of bungalows or even simple, self-contained flats. In high season, some only offer deals for stays of a week or longer.

Most campgrounds operate only in high season, which is roughly April to October (in many cases June to September only).

Lists of campgrounds are available from local tourist offices or online – try www. campeggi.com, www.camping.it or www.italcamping.it.

Convents & Monasteries

Some Italian convents and monasteries let out cells or rooms as a modest revenue-making exercise and happily take in tourists, while others only take in pilgrims or people who are on a spiritual retreat. Many impose a fairly early curfew, but prices tend to be quite reasonable.

A useful if ageing publication is Eileen Barish's *The Guide to Lodging in Italy's Monasteries*. A relatively more recent book on the same subject is Charles M Shelton's *Beds and Blessings in Italy: A Guide to Religious Hospitality*. Other resources can assist you in your search:

Monastery Stays (www.monasterystays.com) A well-organised online booking centre for monastery and convent stays.

In Italy Online (www.initaly. com/agri/convents.htm) Offers a list of monastery and convent accommodation across the country, as well as a general holiday itinerary planning service.

Chiesa di Santa Susana (www. santasusanna.org/coming ToRome/convents.html) This American Catholic church in Rome has searched out convent and monastery accommodation options around the country

and posted a list on its website. Note that some places are just residential accommodation run by religious orders and not necessarily big on monastic atmosphere. The church doesn't handle bookings; to request a spot, you'll need to contact each individual institution directly.

Hostels

Ostelli per la gioventù (youth hostels) are run by the Associazione Italiana Alberghi per la Gioventù (www.aighostels. com), affiliated with Hostelling International (www.hi hostels.com). A valid HI card is required in all associated youth hostels in Italy. You can get this in your home country or direct at many hostels.

A full list of Italian hostels, with details of prices, locations and so on, is available online or from hostels throughout the country. Nightly rates in basic dorms vary from around €15 to €40, which usually includes a buffet breakfast. You can often get lunch or dinner for an extra €10 or so. Many hostels also offer singles/doubles (for around €30/50) and family rooms.

A growing contingent of independent hostels offer alternatives to HI hostels. Many are barely distinguishable from budget hotels. One of many hostel websites is www.hostelworld.com.

Hotels & Pensioni

There is often little difference between a *pensione* (guesthouse) and an *albergo* (hotel). However, a *pensione* will generally be of one- to three-star quality and has traditionally been a family-run operation, while an *albergo* can be awarded up to five stars. *Locande* (inns) long fell into much the same category as *pensioni,* but the term has become trendy in some parts and reveals little about the quality of a place. *Affittacamere* are rooms for rent in private houses. They are generally simple affairs.

Quality can vary enormously and the official star system gives limited clues. One-star hotels/*pensioni* tend to be basic and usually do not offer private bathrooms. Two-star places are similar but rooms will generally have a private bathroom. Three-star options usually offer reasonable standards. Four- and five-star hotels offer facilities such as room service, laundry and dry-cleaning.

Prices are highest in major tourist destinations. A *camera singola* (single room)

costs from around €30. A *camera doppia* (twin beds) or *camera matrimoniale* (double room with a double bed) will cost from around €50.

Tourist offices usually have booklets with local accommodation listings. Many hotels are also signing up with (steadily proliferating) online accommodation-booking services. You could start your search at any of the following:

All Hotels in Italy (www.hotels italyonline.com)

Hotels web.it (www.hotelsweb.it)

In Italia (www.initalia.it)

Villas

Numerous agencies offer villa accommodation in southern Italy – often in splendid rural locations not far from enchanting medieval towns or Mediterranean beaches. Operators include the following.

Cuendet (www.cuendet.com) One of the old hands in this business; offers properties across the country.

Ilios Travel (www.iliostravel.com) UK-based company with villas and apartments in Campania and Sicily.

Long Travel (www.long-travel.co.uk) Specialises in Puglia, Sicily, Sardinia and other southern areas.

Think Sicily (www.thethinking traveller.com/thinksicily) Strictly Sicilian properties.

Customs Regulations

Within the European Union you are entitled to tax-free prices on fragrances, cosmetics and skincare; photographic and electrical goods; fashion and accessories; and gifts, jewellery and souvenirs where they are available and if there are no longer any allowance restrictions on these tax-free items.

On leaving the EU, non-EU residents can reclaim value-added tax (VAT) on expensive purchases.

Duty-Free Allowance

spirits & liqueurs	1L
wine	4L (or 2L of fortified wine)
perfume	60mL
cigarettes	200
other goods	up to €300/430 (travelling by land/sea)

Discount Cards

Free admission to many galleries and cultural sites is available to youth under 18 and seniors over 65 years old; in addition, visitors aged between 18 and 25 often qualify for a discount. In some cases, these discounts only apply to EU citizens.

If travelling to Naples and Campania, consider buying a **Campania Artecard** (www.

YOUTH, STUDENT & TEACHER CARDS

CARD	WEBSITE	COST	ELIGIBILITY
European Youth Card (Carta Giovani)	www.eyca.org; www.cartagiovani.it	€10	under 30yr
International Student Identity Card (ISIC)	www.isic.org	US$25, UK£12, €13	full-time student
International Teacher Identity Card (ITIC)		US$25, UK£12, €10-18	full-time teacher
International Youth Travel Card (IYTC)		US$25, UK£12, €13	under 31yr

campaniaartecard.it), which offers free public transport and free or reduced admission to many museums and archaeological sites.

Electricity

Electricity in Italy conforms to the European standard of 220V to 230V, with a frequency of 50Hz. Wall outlets typically accommodate plugs with two or three round pins.

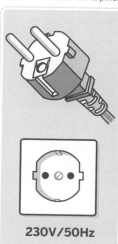

230V/50Hz

230V/50Hz

Embassies & Consulates

Most countries have an embassy in Rome, where passport enquiries should be addressed. South of the capital, you'll find some honorary consulates in several major cities.

Australian Embassy (☑emergencies 800 877790, info 06 85 27 21; www.italy.embassy.gov.au; Via Antonio Bosio 5, Rome; ☺9am-5pm Mon-Fri)

Canadian Embassy (☑06 85 44 41; www.canadainternational.gc.ca/italy-italie; Via Zara 30, Rome)

French Embassy (☑06 68 60 11; www.ambafrance-it.org; Piazza Farnese 67, Rome)

French Consulate (☑081 598 07 11; www.ambafrance-it.org; Via Francesco Crispi 86, Naples; Ⓜ Amedeo)

German Embassy (☑06 49 21 31; www.rom.diplo.de; Via San Martino della Battaglia 4, Rome)

German Consulate (☑081 248 85 11; www.neapel.diplo.de; Via Francesco Crispi 69, Naples)

Irish Embassy (☑06 585 23 81; www.ambasciata-irlanda.it; Villa Spada, Via Giacomo Medici 1, Rome)

Netherlands Embassy (☑06 3228 6001; www.olanda.it; Via Michele Mercati 8, Rome)

New Zealand Embassy (☑06 853 75 01; www.nzembassy.com/italy; Via Clitunno 44, Rome)

UK Embassy (☑06 4220 0001; ukinitaly.fco.gov.uk; Via XX Settembre 80a, Rome)

UK Consulate (☑081 423 89 11; ukinitaly.fco.gov.uk; Via dei Mille 40, Naples)

US Embassy (☑06 4 67 41; italy.usembassy.gov; Via Vittorio Veneto 121, Rome)

US Consulate (☑081 583 81 11; italy.usembassy.gov; Piazza della Repubblica 2, Naples; Ⓜ Mergellina)

US Consulate (☑091 30 58 57; italy.usembassy.gov; Via Vaccarini 1, Palermo)

Food

For detailed information on eating in Southern Italy, see Eat & Drink Like a Local (p26) and The Southern Table (p248).

Gay & Lesbian Travellers

Although homosexuality is legal in Italy, attitudes in the south remain largely conservative and overt displays of affection by homosexual couples could attract consternation and unpleasant responses.

You'll find gay scenes in Naples, Catania and Taormina (the last mostly in the summer), and to a lesser extent in Palermo and Bari.

Online resources include the following Italian-language websites:

Arcigay (www.arcigay.it) Bologna-based national organisation for the LGBTI community.

Circolo Mario Mieli (www.mariomieli.org) Rome-based cultural centre that organises debates, cultural events and social functions, including Gay Pride.

Coordinamento Lesbiche Italiano (CLR; www.clrbp.it) The national organisation for lesbians, holding regular conferences and literary evenings.

Gay.it (www.gay.it) Website featuring LGBT news, feature articles and gossip.

Pride (www.prideonline.it) National monthly magazine of art, music, politics and gay culture.

Health

Recommended Vaccinations

No jabs are required to travel to Italy. The World Health Organization (WHO), however, recommends that all travellers should be covered for diphtheria, tetanus, measles, mumps, rubella and polio, as well as hepatitis B.

Health Insurance

Italy has a public health system that is legally bound to provide emergency care to everyone. EU nationals are entitled to reduced-cost, sometimes free, medical care with a European Health Insurance Card (EHIC), available from your home health authority; non-EU citizens should take out medical insurance.

If you do need health insurance, make sure you get a policy that covers you for the worst possible scenario, such as an accident requiring an emergency flight home. Find out in advance if your insurance plan will make payments directly to providers or reimburse you later for overseas health expenditures.

It's also worth finding out if there is a reciprical arrangement between your country and Italy. If so, you may be covered for essential medical treatment and some subsidised medications while in Italy. Australia, for instance, has such an agreement; carry your Medicare card.

Availability of Health Care

Good health care is readily available throughout southern Italy, although public hospitals tend to be less impressive the further south you travel. Pharmacists can give you valuable advice and sell over-the-counter medication for minor illnesses. They can also advise you when more specialised help is required and point you in the right direction. In major cities you are likely to find English-speaking doctors or a translator service available.

Pharmacies generally keep the same hours as other shops, closing at night and on Sundays. However, a handful remain open on a rotation basis (*farmacie di turno*) for emergency purposes. These are usually listed in newspapers. Closed pharmacies display a list of the nearest ones open.

If you need an ambulance anywhere in Italy, call ☎118. For emergency treatment, head straight to the *pronto soccorso* (casualty) section of a public hospital, where you can also get emergency dental treatment.

Environmental Hazards

Italian beaches are occasionally inundated with jellyfish. Their stings are painful, but not dangerous. Dousing them in vinegar will deactivate any stingers that have not fired. Calamine lotion, antihistamines and analgesics may reduce the reaction and relieve pain.

Italy's only dangerous snake, the viper, is found throughout Puglia and Basilicata. To minimise the possibility of being bitten, always wear boots, socks and long trousers when walking through undergrowth where snakes may be present. Don't put your hands into holes and crevices, and be careful when collecting firewood. Viper bites do not cause instantaneous death and an antivenin is widely available in pharmacies. Keep the victim calm and still, wrap the bitten limb tightly, as you would for a sprained ankle, and attach a splint to immobilise it.

Always check all over your body if you have been walking through a potentially tick-infested area. Ticks can cause skin infections and other more serious complications such as Lyme disease and tick-borne encephalitis. If a tick is found attached, press down around the tick's head with tweezers, grab the head and gently pull upwards. Avoid pulling the rear of the body as this may squeeze the tick's gut contents through the attached mouth into the skin, increasing the risk of infection and disease. Lyme disease begins with the spreading of a bull's-eye rash at the site of the bite, accompanied by fever, headache, extreme fatigue, aching joints and muscles, and severe neck stiffness. If untreated, symptoms usually disappear, but disorders of the nervous system, heart and joints can develop later. Treatment works best early in the illness: medical help should be sought. Symptoms of tick-borne encephalitis include blotches around the bite, which is sometimes pale in the middle, and head-

TRAVEL HEALTH WEBSITES

The following government websites offer up-to-date travel advisories.

Australia www.smartraveller.gov.au

Canada travel.gc.ca/travelling/health-safety

New Zealand www.safetravel.govt.nz

UK www.gov.uk/foreign-travel-advice

USA travel.state.gov

aches, stiffness and other flu-like symptoms (as well as extreme tiredness) appearing a week or two after the bite. Again, medical help must be sought.

Leishmaniasis is a group of parasitic diseases transmitted by sandflies and found in coastal parts of Puglia. Cutaneous leishmaniasis affects the skin and causes ulceration and disfigurement; visceral leishmaniasis affects the internal organs. Avoiding sandfly bites by covering up and using repellent is the best precaution.

Insurance

A travel-insurance policy to cover theft, loss and medical problems is a very good idea. It may also cover you for cancellation or delays to your travel arrangements. Paying for your ticket on a credit card can often provide limited travel accident insurance and you may be able to reclaim the payment if the operator doesn't deliver. Ask your credit-card company what it will cover.

Worldwide travel insurance is available at www. lonelyplanet.com/travel-insurance. You can buy, extend and claim online anytime – even if you're already on the road.

Internet Access

Some cities and towns offer public wi-fi hot spots, though to use them you will generally need to register online using a credit card or an Italian mobile number. An easier option (no need for a local mobile number) is to head to a cafe or bar offering free wi-fi.

Most hotels, B&Bs, hostels and *agriturismi* offer free wi-fi to guests, though signals can vary in quality. There will usually be at least one fixed computer for guest use.

Legal Matters

Southern Italy is relatively safe and the average tourist will only have a brush with the law if robbed by a bag-snatcher or pickpocket.

Police

If you run into trouble in Italy, you're likely to end up dealing with the *polizia statale* (state police) or the *carabinieri* (military police). The former wear powder blue trousers with a fuchsia stripe and a navy blue jacket, the latter wear black uniforms with a red stripe and drive dark blue cars with a red stripe. The table below outlines Italian police organisations and their jurisdictions.

Polizia statale (state police)	thefts, visa extensions and permits
Carabinieri (military police)	general crime, public order and drug enforcement
Vigili urbani (local traffic police)	parking tickets, towed cars
Guardia di finanza	tax evasion, drug smuggling
Corpo forestale	environmental protection

Drugs & Alcohol

➡ If you're caught with what the police deem to be a dealable quantity of hard or soft drugs, you risk prison sentences of between six and 20 years. Possession for personal use may result in a fine, depending on the type of drug and quantity possessed.

➡ The legal limit for blood-alcohol when driving is 0.05%; random breath tests do occur.

Maps

The city maps provided by Lonely Planet, combined with the good, free local maps available at most Italian tourist offices, will be sufficient for many travellers. For more-specialised maps, browse the good selection at national bookshop chain Feltrinelli (www.lafeltrinelli. it), or consult the websites listed here.

Touring Club Italiano (TCI; www.touringclub.com) Italy's largest map publisher operates shops around Italy and publishes decent 1:500,000 and 1:200,000 maps of Italy (€11.90 and €19.90 respectively), plus a series of 15 regional maps at 1:200,000 (€7.90 each) and an exhaustive series of walking guides with maps, co-published with the Club Alpino Italiano (CAI).

Stanfords (www.stanfords. co.uk) Excellent UK-based shop that stocks many useful maps, including cycling maps.

Omni Resources (www.omni map.com) US-based online retailer with an impressive selection of Italian maps, including cycling and hiking maps.

Money

Italy's currency is the euro. The seven euro notes come in denominations of €500, €200, €100, €50, €20, €10 and €5. The eight euro coins are in denominations of €2 and €1, and 50, 20, 10, five, two and one cents.

Credit & Debit Cards

➡ ATMs (called 'Bancomat') are widely available throughout Italy and most will accept cards tied into the Visa, MasterCard, Cirrus and Maestro systems.

➡ Cards are good for payment in most hotels, restaurants, shops, supermarkets and tollbooths. Major cards such as Visa, MasterCard, Eurocard, Cirrus and Eurocheques are widely accepted. Amex is also recognised, though less common.

→ Let your bank know when you are going abroad, in case they block your card when payments from unusual locations appear.

→ Check any charges with your bank. Most banks charge a foreign exchange fee (usually around 1% to 3%) as well as a transaction charge of around 1%.

If your card is lost, stolen or swallowed by an ATM, you can telephone toll-free to have an immediate stop put on its use:

→ **Amex** ☑800 928391
→ **Diners Club** ☑800 393939
→ **MasterCard** ☑800 789525
→ **Visa** ☑800 819014

Changing Money

You can change money in banks, at post offices or in a *cambio* (exchange office). Post offices and banks tend to offer the best rates; exchange offices keep longer hours, but watch for high commissions and inferior rates.

Have your passport or some form of photo ID available when exchanging money.

Taxes & Refunds

A value-added tax of 22%, known as IVA (*Imposta di Valore Aggiunto*), is slapped onto just about everything in Italy. If you are a non-EU resident and spend more than €155 (€154.94 to be exact!) on a purchase, you can claim a refund when you leave. The refund only applies to purchases from affiliated retail outlets that display a 'Tax Free' sign. When you make your purchase, ask for a tax-refund voucher, to be filled in with the date of your purchase and its value. When you leave the EU, get this voucher stamped at customs and take it to the nearest tax-refund counter where you'll get an immediate refund,

either in cash or charged on your credit card. For more information, see www.tax refund.it.

Tipping

Tipping is not generally expected or demanded in Italy as it is in some other countries. This said, a discretionary tip for good service is appreciated in some circumstances. Use the following table as a guide.

PLACE	SUGGESTED TIP
restaurant	10-15%, if service charge (*servizio*) not included
bar	€0.10-0.20 if drinking at bar, 10% for table service
porter, maid, room service (top-end hotel)	€4
taxi	round up to the nearest euro

Post

Poste Italiane (☑80 31 60; www.poste.it), Italy's postal system, is reasonably reliable.

Francobolli (stamps) are available at post offices and authorised tobacconists (look for the big white-on-black 'T' sign). Since letters often need to be weighed, what you get at the tobacconist for international airmail will occasionally be an approximation of the proper rate. Tobacconists keep regular shop hours.

Postal Rates & Services

The cost of sending a letter by *via aerea* (airmail) depends on its weight, size and where it is being sent. Most people use *posta prioritaria* (priority mail), Italy's most

efficient mail service. Postage rates depend on weight and destination: rates are listed at www.poste.it/post-ali/estero/prioritaria.shtml (in Italian).

Public Holidays

Most Italians take their annual holiday in August, with the busiest period occurring around 15 August, known locally as Ferragosto. As a result, many businesses and shops close for at least part of that month. Settimana Santa (Easter Holy Week) is another busy holiday period for Italians.

National public holidays include the following:

Capodanno (New Year's Day) 1 January

Epifania (Epiphany) 6 January

Pasquetta (Easter Monday) March/April

Giorno della Liberazione (Liberation Day) 25 April

Festa del Lavoro (Labour Day) 1 May

Festa della Repubblica (Republic Day) 2 June

Ferragosto (Feast of the Assumption) 15 August

Festa di Ognisanti (All Saints' Day) 1 November

Festa dell'Immacolata Concezione (Feast of the Immaculate Conception) 8 December

Natale (Christmas Day) 25 December

Festa di Santo Stefano (Boxing Day) 26 December

Safe Travel

Despite mafia notoriety, southern Italy is not a dangerous place and the biggest threat you face is from faceless pickpockets and bag-snatchers. The following tips will help ensure a safe and happy stay:

→ Leave valuables in your hotel room and never leave them in your car.

OPENING HOURS

➡ We have listed high-season opening hours for each review; hours will generally decrease in the shoulder or low seasons. In coastal resort areas, many hotels and restaurants close during the winter, reopening around Easter.

➡ 'Summer' hours generally refer to the period from April to September or October. 'Winter' hours generally refer to the period from October or November to March.

➡ The opening hours of museums, galleries and archaeological sites vary enormously. As a rule, museums close on Monday, but from June to September many sights open daily.

BUSINESS TYPE	STANDARD HOURS	NOTES
banks	8.30am-1.30pm & 2.45-3.45 or 4.30pm Mon-Fri	Exchange offices usually keep longer hours.
central post offices	8am-7pm Mon-Fri, 8.30am-noon Sat	Smaller branches often close at 2pm on weekdays.
restaurants	noon-2.30pm or 3pm & 7.30-11pm or midnight	Kitchen often shuts an hour earlier than final closing time; most places close at least one day a week.
cafes & bars	7.30am-8pm	Some venues remain open until 1am or 2am.
clubs	10pm-4am or 5am	May open earlier if they have eateries on the premises; things don't get seriously shaking until after midnight.
shops	9am-1pm & 3.30-7.30pm (or 4-8pm) Mon-Sat	In larger cities, larger chains and supermarkets may stay open at lunchtime or on Sundays.

➡ If carrying a bag or camera, wear the strap across your body and away from the road – moped thieves can swipe a bag and be gone in seconds.

➡ Be vigilant for pickpockets in crowded areas, including at train stations and ferry terminals, on buses and in markets (especially those in Naples, Palermo and Catania).

➡ Never buy electronics, including mobile phones, from market vendors – one common scam sees the boxes filled with bricks.

➡ Always report thefts to the police within 24 hours, and ask for a statement, otherwise your travel insurance company won't pay out.

Telephone

Directory Enquiries

National and international phone numbers can be requested at ☑1254 (or online at 1254.virgilio.it).

Domestic Calls

➡ Italian telephone area codes all begin with 0 and consist of up to four digits. The area code is followed by a number of anything from four to eight digits. The area code is an integral part of the telephone number and must always be dialled, even when calling from next door.

➡ Mobile-phone numbers begin with a three-digit prefix such as ☑330.

➡ Toll-free (free-phone) numbers are known as *numeri verdi* and usually start with ☑800.

➡ Nongeographical numbers start with ☑840, ☑841, ☑848, ☑892, ☑899, ☑163, ☑166 or ☑199.

➡ Some six-digit national rate numbers are also in use (such as those for Alitalia, rail and postal information).

➡ As elsewhere in Europe, Italians choose from a host of providers of phone plans and rates, making it difficult to make generalisations about costs.

International Calls

➡ The cheapest options for calling internationally are free or low-cost computer programs/smartphone apps such as Skype and Viber.

➡ Another cheap option is to call from a private call centre, or from a payphone with an international calling card.

➡ International calling cards, sold at newsstands and tobacconists, offer cheaper call rates. They can be used at public telephones. Dial ☑00 to get out of Italy, then the relevant country and area codes, followed by the telephone number.

➡ To call Italy from abroad, dial the international access number, Italy's country code (☑39) and then the area code of the location you want, including the leading 0.

Mobile Phones

➔ Italian mobile phones operate on the GSM 900/1800 network, which is compatible with the rest of Europe and Australia but not always with the North American GSM or CDMA systems – check with your service provider.

➔ Most smartphones are multiband, meaning that they are compatible with a variety of international networks. Before bringing your own phone to Italy, check with your service provider to make sure it is compatible, and beware of calls being routed internationally (very expensive for a 'local' call).

➔ If you have a GSM dual-, tri- or quad-band phone that you can unlock (check with your service provider), it can cost as little as €10 to activate a prepaid (*prepagato*) SIM card in Italy. TIM (Telecom Italia Mobile; www.tim.it), Wind (www.wind.it) and Vodafone (www.vodafone.it) all offer SIM cards and have retail outlets across town. All SIM cards must be registered in Italy, so make sure you have a passport or ID card with you when you buy one.

➔ You can easily top up your Italian SIM with a recharge card (*ricarica*), available from most tobacconists, some bars, supermarkets and banks.

Payphones & Phonecards

You can still find public payphones around Italy. Most work and most take telephone cards (*schede telefoniche*), although you'll still find some that accept coins or credit cards. You can buy phonecards (€5, €10 or €20) at post offices, tobacconists and newsstands.

Time

➔ Italy is one hour ahead of GMT. When it is noon in London, it is 1pm in Italy.

➔ Daylight savings time, when clocks are moved forward one hour, starts on the last Sunday in March and ends on the last Sunday in October.

➔ Italy operates on a 24-hour clock.

Tourist Information

The quality of tourist offices varies dramatically. One office might have enthusiastic staff, another might be indifferent. Most offices offer a plethora of brochures, maps and leaflets, even if they're uninterested in helping in any other way. Outside major cities and international tourist areas, it's fairly unusual for the staff to speak English.

Four tiers of tourist office exist: local, provincial, regional and national.

Local & Provincial Tourist Offices

Despite their different names, provincial and local offices offer similar services. All deal directly with the public and most will respond to written and telephone requests for information. Staff can usually provide a city map, lists of hotels and information on the major sights. In larger towns and major tourist areas, English is generally spoken.

Main offices are generally open Monday to Friday; some also open on weekends, especially in urban areas or during peak summer season. Affiliated information booths (at train stations and airports, for example) may keep slightly different hours.

Regional Tourist Authorities

Regional offices are generally more concerned with planning, budgeting, marketing and promotion than with offering a public information service. However, they still

---

PRACTICALITIES

➔ **Smoking** Banned in all enclosed public spaces.

➔ **Newspapers** If your Italian is up to it, try the following newspapers: *Corriere della Sera*, the country's leading daily, and its southern spin-off *Corriere del Mezzogiorno*; or *La Repubblica*, a centre-left daily.

➔ **Radio** Tune into state-owned Italian RAI-1, RAI-2 and RAI-3 (www.rai.it), which broadcast throughout Italy and abroad. The plethora of contemporary music stations include Radio Kiss Kiss (www.kisskiss.it).

➔ **Television** Channels include state-run RAI-1, RAI-2 and RAI-3 (www.rai.it). The main commercial stations (mostly run by Silvio Berlusconi's Mediaset company) include Canale 5 (www.mediaset.it/canale5), Italia 1 (www.mediaset.it/italia1), Rete 4 (www.mediaset.it/rete4) and La 7 (www.la7.it).

➔ **Weights & Measurements** Metric.

TOURIST OFFICES

OFFICE NAME	DESCRIPTION	MAIN FOCUS
Azienda di Promozione Turistica (APT)	main provincial tourist office	information on the town and its surrounding province
Azienda Autonoma di Soggiorno e Turismo (AAST) or Informazione e Assistenza ai Turisti (IAT)	local tourist office in larger towns and cities	town-specific information only (bus routes, museum opening times etc)
Pro Loco	local tourist office in smaller towns and villages	similar to AAST and IAT

maintain some useful websites. In some cases you'll need to look for the Tourism or Turismo link within the regional site.

Basilicata (www.aptbasilicata.it)

Calabria (www.turiscalabria.it)

Campania (www.incampania.com)

Puglia (www.viaggiareinpuglia.it)

Sicily (www.regione.sicilia.it/turismo)

Tourist Offices Abroad

The Italian National Tourist Office (www.enit.it) maintains offices in 23 cities on five continents. Contact information for all offices can be found on the website.

Travellers with Disabilities

Italy is not an easy country for travellers with disabilities and getting around can be a problem for wheelchair users. Even a short journey in a city or town can become a major expedition if cobblestone streets have to be negotiated. Although many buildings have lifts, they are not always wide enough for wheelchairs. Not an awful lot has been done to make life for the hearing/vision impaired easier.

The Italian National Tourist Office in your country may be able to provide advice on Italian associations for travellers with disabilities and information on what help is available.

If travelling by train, ring the national helpline ☏199

303060 to arrange assistance (available 6.45am to 9.30pm daily). Airline companies should be able to arrange assistance at airports if you notify them of your needs in advance. Alternatively, contact ADR Assistance (www.adrassistance.it) for assistance at Fiumicino or Ciampino airports. Some taxis are equipped to carry passengers in wheelchairs; ask for a taxi with a *sedia a rotelle* (wheelchair).

Italy's official tourism website (www.italia.it) offers a number of links for travellers with disabilities. Another online resource is Lonely Planet's Travel for All community on Google+, worth joining for information sharing and networking.

Accessible Italy (www.accessibleitaly.com) A San Marino–based company that specialises in holiday services for people with disabilities. This is the best first port of call.

Sage Traveling (www.sagetraveling.com) A US-based agency offering advice and tailormade tours to help mobility-impaired travellers in Europe.

Visas

➡ Italy is one of the 15 signatories of the Schengen Convention, an agreement whereby participating countries abolished customs checks at common borders. EU citizens do not need a Schengen tourist visa to enter Italy. Nationals

of some other countries, including Australia, Canada, Israel, Japan, New Zealand, Switzerland and the USA, do not need a tourist visa for stays of up to 90 days. To check the visa requirements for your country, see www.schengenvisainfo.com/tourist-schengen-visa.

➡ All non-EU and non-Schengen nationals entering Italy for more than 90 days or for any reason other than tourism (such as study or work) may need a specific visa. See vistoperitalia.esteri.it or contact an Italian consulate for details.

Permesso di Soggiorno

➡ Non-EU citizens planning to stay at the same address for more than one week are supposed to report to the police station to receive a *permesso di soggiorno* (a permit to remain in the country). Tourists staying in hotels are not required to do this.

➡ A *permesso di soggiorno* only really becomes a necessity if you plan to study, work (legally) or live in Italy. The exact requirements, such as specific documents, are always subject to change. Updated requirements can be found at www.poliziadistato.it (click on the English tab and follow the links).

➡ EU citizens do not require a *permesso di soggiorno*.

Volunteering

Concordia International Volunteer Projects (www.concordiavolunteers.org.uk) Short-term community-based projects covering the environment, archaeology, the arts and more. You might find yourself working as a volunteer on a restoration project or in a nature reserve.

European Youth Portal (europa.eu/youth) Has various links suggesting volunteering options across Europe. Navigate to the Volunteering page and then narrow down the search to Italy.

World Wide Opportunities on Organic Farms (www.wwoof.it) For a membership fee of €35 this organisation provides a list of farmers and growers looking for volunteer workers.

Women Travellers

The most common source of discomfort for solo women travellers in southern Italy is harassment. Local men are rarely shy about staring at women and this can be disconcerting, especially if the staring is accompanied by the occasional *'ciao bella'*. In many places, local Lotharios will try it on with exasperating insistence. Foreign women are particular objects of male attention. Usually, the best response to undesired advances is to ignore them. If that doesn't work, politely tell your interlocutors you're waiting for your *marito* (husband) or *fidanzato* (boyfriend) and, if necessary, walk away. Avoid becoming aggressive as this may result in an unpleasant confrontation. In most cases, passersby will assist if you are in distress.

On crowded buses some men may attempt to grope female passengers. Either keep your back to the wall or make a loud fuss if someone tries to touch you. A loud *'Che schifo!'* (How disgusting!) will usually do the trick. You can report incidents to the police, who are required to press charges.

Transport

GETTING THERE & AWAY

A plethora of airlines links Italy to the rest of the world, and an extensive network of intra-European and domestic flights provide easy access to many southern Italian destinations. Good rail and/or bus services connect most of southern Italy's major cities and towns, while car and passenger ferries operate to ports throughout the Mediterranean.

Flights, tours and rental cars can be booked online at www.lonelyplanet.com/bookings.

Entering the Country

➡ European Union and Swiss citizens can travel to Italy with their national identity card alone. All other nationalities must have a valid passport and may be required to fill out a landing card (at airports).

➡ By law you are supposed to have your passport or ID card with you at all times. You'll need one of these documents for police registration every time you check into a hotel.

➡ In theory there are no passport checks at land crossings from neighbouring countries, but random customs controls do occasionally still take place between Italy and Switzerland.

Air

Airports & Airlines

Italy's main intercontinental gateways are Rome's **Leonardo da Vinci Airport** (Fiumicino; ☑ 06 6 59 51; www.adr.it/fiumicino) and Milan's **Malpensa Airport** (MXP; ☑ 02 23 23 23; www.milanomalpensa-airport.com). Both are served by nonstop flights from around the world. Venice's **Marco Polo Airport** (VCE; ☑ flight information 041 260 92 60; www.veniceairport.it) is also served by a handful of intercontinental flights.

Most direct flights into southern Italy are domestic or intra-European, so you may need to change in Rome, Milan or Venice if arriving from outside Europe.

Handy airports in southern Italy include the following:

Capodichino Airport, Naples (www.aeroportodinapoli.it) Connections include London (Gatwick, Stansted and Luton), Paris (Charles de Gaulle and Orly) and Berlin (Schönefeld). Airlines include Alitalia, British Airways, Lufthansa and easyJet. Seasonal connections to New York (JFK).

Karol Wojtyła Airport, Bari (www.aeroportidipuglia.it) Flights include London (Gatwick and Stansted), Paris (Orly and

CLIMATE CHANGE & TRAVEL

Every form of transport that relies on carbon-based fuel generates CO_2, the main cause of human-induced climate change. Modern travel is dependent on aeroplanes, which might use less fuel per kilometre per person than most cars but travel much greater distances. The altitude at which aircraft emit gases (including CO_2) and particles also contributes to their climate change impact. Many websites offer 'carbon calculators' that allow people to estimate the carbon emissions generated by their journey and, for those who wish to do so, to offset the impact of the greenhouse gases emitted with contributions to portfolios of climate-friendly initiatives throughout the world. Lonely Planet offsets the carbon footprint of all staff and author travel.

Beauvais), Berlin (Schönefeld), Cologne, Istanbul, Munich and Prague. Airlines include Alitalia, British Airways, Turkish Airways, Ryanair, easyJet, Germanwings and Wizzair.

Brindisi-Salento Airport (www.aeroportidipuglia.it) Destinations include London (Gatwick and Stansted), Paris (Orly), Geneva, Eindhoven, Zurich, Munich and Barcelona. Airlines include Alitalia, easyJet, Germanwings, Ryanair, Air Berlin and Vueling.

Lamezia Terme Airport, Cosenza (www.sacal.it) Destinations include London (Stansted), with seasonal routes including Zurich, Brussels, Berlin, Tel Aviv and Toronto. Airlines include Alitalia, Ryanair and Germanwings.

Falcone-Borsellino Airport, Palermo (www.gesap.it) European connections include London (Gatwick and Stansted), Paris (Charles de Gaulle, Orly and Beauvais), Marseilles, Madrid, Vienna, Frankfurt, Berlin (Schönefeld and Tegel), Amsterdam, Brussels and Stockholm. Inter-continental flights to Tunis, New York and Seoul. Airlines include Alitalia, Ryanair, easyJet, Austrian Airlines, Norwegian Air Shuttle and Korean Air.

Fontanarossa Airport, Catania (www.aeroporto.catania.it) Destinations include London (Gatwick and Luton), Manchester, Paris (Charles de Gaulle and Orly), Geneva, Zurich, Cologne, Berlin (Tegel), Barcelona and Istanbul. Airlines include Alitalia, Air Berlin, Lufthansa, easyJet, Germanwings and Turkish Airways.

Vincenzo Florio Airport, Trapani (www.airgest.it) Ryanair operates direct flights to a handful of European destinations, including Paris (Beauvais) and Frankfurt.

Tickets

The internet is the easiest way of locating and booking reasonably priced seats.

Full-time students and those aged under 26 may qualify for discounted fares at agencies such as **STA Travel** (www.statravel.com). Many of these fares require a valid International Student Identity Card (ISIC).

Land

Reaching southern Italy overland involves travelling the entire length of Italy, which can either be an enormous drain on your time or, if you have plenty to spare, a wonderful way of seeing the country. Buses are usually the cheapest option, but services are less frequent and considerably less comfortable than the train.

Border Crossings

Aside from the coast roads linking Italy with France and Slovenia, border crossings into Italy mostly involve tunnels through the Alps (open year-round) or mountain passes (seasonally closed or requiring snow chains). The list below outlines the major points of entry.

Austria From Innsbruck to Bolzano via A22/E45 (Brenner Pass); Villach to Tarvisio via A23/E55.

France From Nice to Ventimiglia via A10/E80; Modane to Turin via A32/E70 (Fréjus Tunnel); Chamonix to Courmayeur via A5/E25 (Mont Blanc Tunnel).

Slovenia From Sežana to Trieste via SR58/E70.

Switzerland From Martigny to Aosta via SS27/E27 (Grand St Bernard Tunnel); Lugano to Como via A9/E35.

Regular trains on two western lines connect Italy with France (one along the coast and the other from Turin into the French Alps). Trains from Milan head north into Switzerland and on towards the Benelux countries. Further east, two main lines head for the main cities in Central and Eastern Europe. Those crossing the Brenner Pass go to Innsbruck, Stuttgart and Munich. Those crossing at Tarvisio proceed to Vienna, Salzburg and Prague. The main international train line to Slovenia crosses near Trieste.

Bus

Buses are the cheapest overland option to Italy, but services are less frequent, less comfortable and significantly slower than the train. Useful companies include the following.

Eurolines (www.eurolines.com) A consortium of coach companies with offices throughout Europe. Italy-bound buses head to Milan, Venice, Florence and Rome, from where Italian train and bus services continue south.

Marozzi (www.marozzivt.it) Connects Rome to Bari several times weekly.

Miccolis (www.miccolis-spa. it) Runs daily services from Naples, Caserta and Salerno to Campania to towns and cities in Basilicata and Puglia, including Matera, Metaponto, Taranto, Brindisi, Lecce and Gallipoli.

Marino (www.marinobus.it) Runs daily services from Naples to Bari, Brindisi, Matera, Lecce and Gallipoli.

Liscio (www.autolineeliscio. it) Connects Potenza to Rome, Naples, Salerno, Florence, Siena and Perugia. Also connects Rome to Matera.

BUS PASSES

Eurolines offers a low-season **bus pass** (www.eurolinespass.com) valid for 15/30 days that costs €375/490 (reduced €315/405) in high season and €225/340 (reduced €195/265) in low season. This pass allows unlimited travel between 53 European cities, including Milan, Venice, Florence and Rome.

Lirosi (www.lirosilinee.com) Connects Reggio di Calabria and Villa San Giovanni to numerous Italian cities and towns, including Rome, Perugia, Milan, Como, Turin and Aosta.

SAIS (www.saistrasporti.it) Operates long-haul services to Sicily from numerous centres, including Rome, Naples and Bari.

Car & Motorcycle
CONTINENTAL EUROPE

➡ Every vehicle travelling across an international border should display a nationality plate of its country of registration.

➡ Always carry proof of vehicle ownership and evidence of third-party insurance. If driving an EU-registered vehicle, your home-country insurance is sufficient. Ask your insurer for a European Accident Statement (EAS) form, which can simplify matters in the event of an accident. The form can also be downloaded online at cartraveldocs. com/european-accident-statement.

➡ A European breakdown assistance policy is a good investment and can be obtained through the Automobile Club d'Italia (ACI; ☑ 803 116, from a foreign mobile 800 116 800; www. aci.it).

➡ Italy's scenic roads are tailor-made for motorcycle touring, and motorcyclists swarm into the country every summer. With a motorcycle you rarely have to book ahead for ferries and can enter restricted-traffic areas in cities. Crash helmets and a motorcycle licence are compulsory.

➡ The US-based Beach's Motorcycle Adventures (www.bmca.com) offers a number of two-week tours from April to October, with destinations including Sicily. For campervan and motor-home hire, check IdeaMerge (www. ideamerge.com).

UK
You can take your car to Italy, via France, by ferry or via the Channel Tunnel (www. eurotunnel.com). The latter runs 49 daily crossings (35 minutes) between Folkestone and Calais in the high season.

For breakdown assistance, both the AA (www.theaa.com) and the RAC (www.rac.co.uk) offer comprehensive cover in Europe.

Train
➡ The comprehensive European Rail Timetable (UK£15.99), updated monthly, is available for purchase online at www. europeanrailtimetable. co.uk, as well as at a handful of bookshops in the UK and continental Europe (see the website for details).

➡ Reservations on international trains to/ from Italy are always advisable, and sometimes compulsory. Some international services include transport for private cars. Consider taking long journeys overnight, as the supplemental fare for a sleeper costs substantially less than Italian hotels.

➡ Within Italy, direct trains run from Milan, Florence and Rome to Naples, Reggio di Calabria and to Messina, Sicily. Trains to Sicily are transported from the mainland by ferry from Villa San Giovanni, just north of Reggio di Calabria. From Messina, services continue on to Palermo, Catania and other provincial Sicilian capitals.

➡ From both Rome and Milan, high-velocity Freccia trains run to Naples and Salerno. Those travelling from Venice will usually need to change trains in Bologna. Trains to Puglia and Basilicata usually require at least one change along Italy's main north–south route.

UK
High-velocity passenger train Eurostar (www.eurostar. com) travels between London and Paris, or London and Brussels. Alternatively, you can get a train ticket that includes crossing the Channel by ferry.

For the latest fare information on journeys to Italy, contact International Rail (www.internationalrail.com).

Sea

Multiple ferry companies connect southern Italy with countries throughout the Mediterranean. Many routes only operate in summer, when ticket prices also rise. During this period, all routes are busy and you need to book several weeks in advance. Fares to Greece are generally more expensive from Bari than those available from Brindisi, although unless you're planning on travelling in the Salento, Bari is the more convenient port of arrival and also has better onward links for bus and train travel. Prices for vehicles vary according to their size.

The helpful website www. directferries.co.uk allows you to search routes and compare prices between the numerous international ferry companies servicing Italy. Another useful resource for ferries from Italy to Greece is www.ferries.gr.

International Ferry Companies Serving Southern Italy

Adria Ferries (www.adria ferries.com)

Anek Lines (www.anekitalia.com)

Grandi Navi Veloci (GNV; www. gnv.it)

Grimaldi Lines (www.grimaldi-lines.com)

Jadrolinija (www.jadrolinija.hr)

Montenegro Lines (www.monte-negrolines.net)

SNAV (www.snav.it)

INTERNATIONAL FERRY ROUTES FROM SOUTHERN ITALY

DESTINATION COUNTRY	DESTINATION PORT(S)	ITALIAN PORT(S)	COMPANY
Albania	Durrës	Bari	Ventouris, Adria Ferries
Croatia	Dubrovnik	Bari	Jadrolinija
Greece	Igoumenitsa, Patras	Brindisi	Grimaldi Lines
Greece	Corfu, Igoumenitsa, Patras	Bari	Superfast, Anek Lines
Malta	Valletta	Pozzallo, Catania	Virtu Ferries
Montenegro	Bar	Bari	Montenegro Lines
Tunisia	Tunis	Palermo	GNV
Tunisia	Tunis	Palermo, Salerno	Grimaldi Lines

Superfast (www.superfast.com)

Ventouris (www.ventouris.gr)

Virtu Ferries (www.virtuferries.com)

GETTING AROUND

Unless you're a masochist, avoid driving in larger centres such as Naples, Bari, Lecce, Palermo and Catania, where anarchic traffic and parking restrictions will quickly turn your holiday sour. Beyond these urban centres, however, having your own car is the easiest way to get around Italy's south. Buses and trains will get you to most of the main destinations, but they are run by a plethora of private companies, which makes buying tickets and finding bus stops a bit of a bind. Furthermore, the rail network in Salento is still of the narrow-gauge variety, so trains chug along at a snail's pace.

Your own vehicle will give you the most freedom to stray off the main routes and discover out-of-the-way towns and beaches. This is particularly the case in the Parco Nazionale del Cilento e Vallo di Diano in Campania, the Pollino National Park in Basilicata, the Salento in Puglia and throughout much of rural Sicily.

This said, it's also worth considering the downside of driving. Aside from the negative environmental impact, petrol prices are notoriously high, less-travelled roads are often poorly maintained and popular routes (including Campania's Amalfi Coast, the SS16 connecting Bari and the Salento in Puglia, and Sicily's Ionian and Tyrrhenian coastal routes) can heavy traffic during holiday periods and throughout the summer.

Air

A number of international airlines compete with the country's national carrier, **Alitalia** (www.alitalia.com), among them Italy's **Meridiana** (www.meridiana.it) and cut-rate foreign companies **Ryanair** (www.ryanair.com) and **easyJet** (www.easyjet.com).

Useful search engines for comparing multiple carriers' fares (including those of cut-price airlines) are www.skyscanner.com, www.kayak.com and www.azfly.it. Airport taxes are factored into the price of your ticket.

Bicycle

Cycling may be more popular in northern Italy, but it can be just as rewarding south of Rome. Cyclo-trekking is particularly popular in the Murgia and the Promontorio del Gargano in Puglia. Cycling is also very popular in the Salentine cities of Lecce, Galatina, Gallipoli and Otranto, with more challenging itineraries in Basilicata's Parco Nazionale del Pollino and on Sicily's hilly terrain.

Avoid hitting the pedal in large cities like Naples and Palermo, where unruly traffic makes cycling a veritable death wish. Cycling along the Amalfi Coast is another bad idea (think blind corners and sheer drops). Bikes are prohibited on the autostradas.

Bikes can be wheeled onto regional trains displaying the bicycle logo. Simply purchase a separate bicycle ticket, valid for 24 hours (€3.50). Certain international trains, listed on Trenitalia's 'Bike on Board' page, also allow transport of assembled bicycles for €12, paid onboard. Bikes dismantled and stored in a bag can be taken for free, even on night trains. Most ferries also allow free bicycle passage.

Bikes are available for hire in most towns. City bikes start at €10/50 per day/week; mountain bikes cost a bit more.

If you fancy seeing the south on a two-wheeler the following reputable organisations offer advice and/or guided tours:

Cyclists' Touring Club (www.ctc.org.uk) This UK organisation can help you plan your tour or organise a guided tour. Membership costs £41.50 (£27 for seniors, £18 for under-18s).

Puglia in Bici (www.pugliainbici. com) A reputable outfit offering bike rental and tailor-made itineraries throughout Puglia.

Gargano Bike Holidays (www. garganobike.com) Specialises in cultural and scenic mountain bike tours exploring the Gargano on half-day to five-day adventures.

Boat

Craft Domestic *navi* (large ferries) service Campania and Sicily, while *traghetti* (smaller ferries) and *aliscafi* (hydrofoils) service the Bay of Naples islands, the Amalfi Coast, the Isole Tremiti in Puglia and the Aeolian Islands off Sicily's north coast. Most services are pared back between October and Easter, and some are suspended altogether during this period. Most ferries carry vehicles; hydrofoils do not.

Routes Ferries for Sicily leave from Naples, as well as from Villa San Giovanni and Reggio di Calabria. The main points of arrival in Sicily are Palermo, Catania, Trapani and Messina.

Timetables and tickets Comprehensive website Direct Ferries (www.directferries.co.uk) allows you to search routes, compare prices and book tickets for ferry routes in Italy.

Overnight ferries Travellers can book a two- to four-person cabin or a poltrona, which is an airline-type armchair. Deck class (which allows you to sit/sleep in lounge areas or on deck) is available only on some ferries.

Bus

Numerous companies provide bus services in southern Italy, from meandering local routes to fast and reliable intercity connections. Buses are usually priced competitively with the train and are often the only way to get to smaller towns. If your destination is not on a main train line (trains tend to be cheaper on major routes), buses are usually a faster way to get around – this is especially true for the Salento in Puglia, Basilicata and for inland Calabria and Sicily.

Services are provided by a variety of companies. While these can be frequent on weekdays, they are reduced considerably on Sundays and holidays – runs between smaller towns often fall to one or none. Keep this in mind if you depend on buses as it is easy to get stuck in smaller places, especially at the weekends.

It's usually possible to get bus timetables (*orari*) from local tourist offices and the bus companies' websites. In larger cities most of the intercity bus companies have ticket offices or sell tickets through agencies. In villages and even some good-size towns, tickets are sold in bars – just ask for *biglietti per il pullman* – or on the bus itself.

Advance booking, while not generally required, is a good idea in the high season for overnight or long-haul trips.

Car & Motorcycle

Italy has an extensive privatised network of autostradas, represented on road signs by a white 'A' followed by a number on a green background. The main north–south link is the Autostrada del Sole (the 'Motorway of the Sun'), which extends from Milan to Reggio di Calabria (called the A1 from Milan to Naples, and the A3 from Naples to Reggio di Calabria). The east–west A16 links Naples to Canosa di Puglia. From here, it becomes the A14, shooting southeast to Bari and continuing south to Taranto. From Bari, the SS16 is the main arterial route to the Salento; in summer this can have heavy traffic.

There are several additional road categories, listed below in descending order of importance.

Strade statali (state highways) Represented on maps by S or SS. They vary from toll-free, four-lane highways to two-lane main roads. The latter can be extremely slow, especially in mountainous regions.

Strade regionali (regional highways connecting small villages) Coded SR or R.

Strade provinciali (provincial highways) Coded SP or P.

Strade locali (local roads) Often not even paved or mapped.

For information in English about distances, driving times and fuel costs, see en.mappy. com. Additional information, including traffic conditions and toll costs, is available at www.autostrade.it.

Automobile Associations

The **Automobile Club d'Italia** (ACI; ☏803 116, from a foreign mobile 800 116 800; www.aci.it) is a driver's best resource in Italy and offers 24-hour roadside emergency service. Foreigners do not have to join but instead pay a per-incident fee.

Driving Licence

All EU driving licences are recognised in Italy. Travellers from other countries should obtain an International Driving Permit (IDP) through their national automobile association.

Fuel & Spare Parts

Italy's petrol prices vary from one service station (*benzinaio, stazione di servizio*) to another. At the time of writing, lead-free gasoline (*senza piombo*; 95 octane) was averaging €1.57 per litre, with diesel (*gasolio*) costing €1.37 per litre.

Spare parts are available at many garages or via the 24-hour ACI motorist assistance number, ☏803116 (or ☏800 116800 if calling with a non-Italian mobile phone number).

Hire

➡ Pre-booking via the internet often costs less than hiring a car in Italy. Online booking agency **Rentalcars.com** (www. rentalcars.com) compares the rates of numerous car-rental companies.

➡ Renters must generally be aged 21 or over, with a credit card and home-country driving licence or IDP.

➡ Consider hiring a small car, which will reduce your fuel expenses and help you negotiate narrow city lanes and tight parking spaces.

➡ Check with your credit-card company to see if it offers a Collision Damage Waiver, which covers you for additional damage if you use that card to pay for the car.

Multinational car-rental agencies include the following:

Auto Europe (www.autoeurope. com)

Avis (www.avis.com)

Budget (www.budget.com)

Europcar (www.europcar.com)

Hertz (www.hertz.it)

Maggiore (www.maggiore.it)

Sixt (www.sixt.com)

MOTORCYCLES

➡ Agencies throughout Italy rent motorbikes, ranging from small Vespas to larger touring bikes. Prices start at around €35/150 per day/week for a 50cc scooter, or upwards of €80/400 per day/week for a 650cc motorcycle.

➡ A licence is not required to ride a scooter under 50cc, but you should be aged 14 or over and you cannot carry passengers or ride on an autostrada. To ride a motorcycle or scooter up to 125cc, you must be aged 16 or over and have a licence (a car licence will do). For motorcycles over 125cc you need a motorcycle licence.

➡ Do not venture onto the autostrada with a bike of less than 150cc.

Road Rules

Before getting behind the wheel, it's worth acquainting yourself with the country's road rules. Here are some of the most essential:

➡ Cars drive on the right side of the road and overtake on the left.

➡ Seat belt use (front and rear) is mandatory.

➡ Give way to cars entering an intersection from a road on your right, unless otherwise indicated.

➡ In the event of a breakdown, a warning triangle is compulsory, as is the use of an approved yellow or orange safety vest if you leave your vehicle. Recommended accessories include a first-aid kit, spare-bulb kit and fire extinguisher.

➡ The blood alcohol limit is 0.05%; for drivers under 21 and those who have had their licence for less than three years, it's zero.

➡ Some cities, including Naples, ban nonresidents from driving in the *centro storico* (historic centre). Fines can be steep.

➡ Speed limits for cars are 130km/h on autostradas; 110km/h on other main highways; 90km/h on secondary, non-urban roads; and 50km/h in built-up areas.

➡ The speed limit for mopeds is 40km/h.

➡ Helmets are required on all two-wheeled transport.

➡ Motorbikes can enter most restricted traffic areas in Italian cities, and traffic police generally turn a blind eye to motorcycles or scooters parked on footpaths.

➡ Headlights are compulsory day and night for all vehicles on autostradas, and are

advisable for motorcycles, even on smaller roads.

Local Transport

Bus & Underground Trains

Every city or town of any size has an efficient *urbano* (urban) and *extraurbano* (suburban) system of buses. Services are generally reduced on Sundays and holidays. Naples and Catania also have a metro system.

Purchase bus and metro tickets before boarding. Validate bus tickets on-board and metro tickets at the station turnstile. Tickets can be bought from a *tabaccaio* (tobacconist), newsstands, ticket booths or dispensing machines at bus stations and in underground stations, and usually cost around €1 to €1.80. Some cities offer good-value 24-hour or daily tourist tickets.

Taxi

You can catch a taxi at the ranks outside most train and bus stations, or simply telephone for a radio taxi. Note that radio taxi meters start running from when you've called rather than when you're picked up.

Charges vary somewhat from one region to another. Most short city journeys cost between €10 and €15. Generally, no more than four people are allowed in one taxi.

Train

Trains in Italy are relatively cheap compared with other European countries, and the better train categories are fast and comfortable.

Trenitalia (☑892021; www. trenitalia.com) is the partially privatised, state train system that runs most services. Its privately owned competitor **Italo** (☑060708; www.italotreno.it) runs high-velocity trains

Train Routes

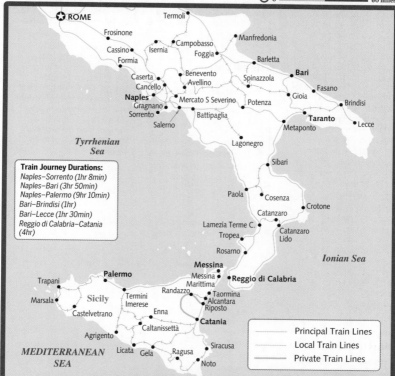

Train Journey Durations:
Naples–Sorrento (1hr 8min)
Naples–Bari (3hr 50min)
Naples–Palermo (9hr 10min)
Bari–Brindisi (1hr)
Bari–Lecce (1hr 30min)
Reggio di Calabria–Catania (4hr)

Principal Train Lines
Local Train Lines
Private Train Lines

---

on two lines: one between Turin and Salerno, and one between Venice and Naples.

Italy operates several types of trains:

Regionale/interregionale Slow and cheap, stopping at all or most stations.

InterCity (IC) Faster services operating between major cities.

Alta Velocità (AV) State-of-the-art, high-velocity trains, including Frecciarossa, Frecciargento, Frecciabianca and Italo trains. Speeds of up to 300km/h and connections to the major Italian cities. More expensive than InterCity express trains, but journey times cut by almost half.

As with the bus services, there are a number of private train lines operating through-

out Italy's south, including the following:

Circumvesuviana (www.eavsrl.it) Links Naples and Sorrento, stopping at Ercolano (Herculaneum) and Pompeii.

Ferrovia Cumana (www.eavsrl.it) Connects Naples to the Campi Flegrei to the west. Stops include Pozzuoli.

Ferrotramviaria (www.ferrovienordbarese.it) Services towns in Puglia's Terra di Bari, including Bitonto, Ruvo di Puglia, Andria and Barletta. Replacement bus service operates Sundays.

Ferrovie Appulo Lucane (www.fal-srl.it) Links Bari province with Basilicata, including stops at Altamura, Matera and Potenza. Replacement buses on Sundays.

Ferrovie del Sud-Est (www.fseonline.it) The main network

covering Puglia's Murgia towns and the Salento, servicing tourist hot spots like Castellana Grotte, Alberobello, Martina Franca, Lecce, Gallipoli and Otranto. Replacement buses on Sundays.

Ferrovia Circumetnea (www.circumetnea.it) A 114km line connecting the towns around the base of Mt Etna in Sicily. No service on Sundays.

Classes & Costs

➡ Prices vary according to the class of service, time of travel and how far in advance you book. Most Italian trains have 1st- and 2nd-class seating; a 1st-class ticket typically costs from a third to a half more than the 2nd-class ticket.

➡ Travel on Trenitalia's InterCity and Alta Velocità

(Frecciarossa, Frecciargento, Frecciabianca) trains means paying a supplement, determined by the distance you are travelling and included in the ticket price. If you have a standard ticket for a slower train and end up hopping on an IC train, you'll have to pay the difference on-board. (You can only board an Alta Velocità train if you have a booking, so the problem does not arise in those cases.)

➡ Validate train tickets in the green machines (usually found at the head of rail platforms) just before boarding. Failure to do so usually results in a fine.

Reservations

➡ Reservations are obligatory on Alta Velocità trains. Otherwise they're not required on other train lines and, outside of peak holiday periods, you should be fine without them. Reservations can be made on the Trenitalia and Italo websites, at railway station counters and self-service ticketing machines, or through travel agents.

➡ Both Trenitalia and Italo offer a variety of advance purchase discounts. Basically, the earlier you book, the greater the saving. Discounted tickets are limited, and refunds and changes are highly restricted. For all ticket options and prices, see the Trenitalia and Italo websites.

Language

Standard Italian is taught and spoken throughout Italy. Regional dialects are an important part of identity in many parts of the country, but you'll have no trouble being understood anywhere if you stick to standard Italian, which we've also used in this chapter.

The sounds used in spoken Italian can all be found in English. If you read our coloured pronunciation guides as if they were English, you'll be understood. The stressed syllables are indicated with italics. Note that ai is pronounced as in 'aisle', ay as in 'say', ow as in 'how', dz as the 'ds' in 'lids', and that r is a strong and rolled sound. Keep in mind that Italian consonants can have a stronger, emphatic pronunciation – if the consonant is written as a double letter, it should be pronounced a little stronger, eg *sonno son*·no (sleep) versus *sono so*·no (I am).

BASICS

Hello.	*Buongiorno.*	bwon·*jor*·no
Goodbye.	*Arrivederci.*	a·ree·ve·*der*·chee
Yes./No.	*Sì./No.*	see/no
Excuse me.	*Mi scusi.* (pol)	mee *skoo*·zee
	Scusami. (inf)	*skoo*·za·mee
Sorry.	*Mi dispiace.*	mee dees·*pya*·che
Please.	*Per favore.*	per fa·*vo*·re
Thank you.	*Grazie.*	*gra*·tsye
You're welcome.	*Prego.*	*pre*·go

WANT MORE?

For in-depth language information and handy phrases, check out Lonely Planet's *Italian Phrasebook*. You'll find it at **shop.lonelyplanet.com**, or you can buy Lonely Planet's iPhone phrasebooks at the Apple App Store.

How are you?		
Come sta/stai? (pol/inf)		*ko*·me sta/stai
Fine. And you?		
Bene. E lei/tu? (pol/inf)		*be*·ne e lay/too
What's your name?		
Come si chiama? (pol)		*ko*·me see *kya*·ma
Come ti chiami? (inf)		*ko*·me tee *kya*·mee
My name is ...		
Mi chiamo ...		mee *kya*·mo ...
Do you speak English?		
Parla/Parli inglese? (pol/inf)		*par*·la/*par*·lee een·*gle*·ze
I don't understand.		
Non capisco.		non ka·*pee*·sko

ACCOMMODATION

campsite	*campeggio*	kam·*pe*·jo
guesthouse	*pensione*	pen·*syo*·ne
hotel	*albergo*	al·*ber*·go
youth hostel	*ostello della gioventù*	os·*te*·lo de·la jo·ven·*too*
Do you have a ... room?	*Avete una camera ...?*	a·*ve*·te *oo*·na *ka*·me·ra ...
double	*doppia con letto matrimoniale*	*do*·pya kon *le*·to ma·tree·mo·*nya*·le
single	*singola*	*seen*·go·la
How much is it per ...?	*Quanto costa per ...?*	*kwan*·to *kos*·ta per ...
night	*una notte*	*oo*·na *no*·te
person	*persona*	per·*so*·na
air-con	*aria condizionata*	*a*·rya kon·dee·tsyo·*na*·ta
bathroom	*bagno*	*ba*·nyo
window	*finestra*	fee·*nes*·tra

DIRECTIONS

Where's ...?
Dov'è ...? do·ve ...

What's the address?
Qual'è l'indirizzo? kwa·le leen·dee·ree·tso

Could you please write it down?
Può scriverlo, pwo skree·ver·lo
per favore? per fa·vo·re

Can you show me (on the map)?
Può mostrarmi pwo mos·trar·mee
(sulla pianta)? (soo·la pyan·ta)

EATING & DRINKING

What would you recommend?
Cosa mi consiglia? ko·za mee kon·see·lya

What's the local speciality?
Qual'è la specialità kwa·le la spe·cha·lee·ta
di questa regione? dee kwe·sta re·jo·ne

Cheers!
Salute! sa·loo·te

That was delicious!
Era squisito! e·ra skwee·zee·to

Please bring the bill.
Mi porta il conto, mee por·ta eel kon·to
per favore? per fa·vo·re

I'd like to	*Vorrei*	vo·ray
reserve a	*prenotare un*	pre·no·ta·re oon
table for ...	*tavolo per ...*	ta·vo·lo per ...
(eight) o'clock	*le (otto)*	le (o·to)
(two) people	*(due) persone*	(doo·e) per·so·ne

I don't eat ...	*Non mangio ...*	non man·jo ...
eggs	*uova*	wo·va
fish	*pesce*	pe·she
nuts	*noci*	no·chee

Key Words

bar	*locale*	lo·ka·le
bottle	*bottiglia*	bo·tee·lya
breakfast	*prima colazione*	pree·ma ko·la·tsyo·ne
cafe	*bar*	bar
dinner	*cena*	che·na
drink list	*lista delle bevande*	lee·sta de·le be·van·de
fork	*forchetta*	for·ke·ta
glass	*bicchiere*	bee·kye·re
knife	*coltello*	kol·te·lo

lunch	*pranzo*	pran·dzo
market	*mercato*	mer·ka·to
menu	*menù*	me·noo
plate	*piatto*	pya·to
restaurant	*ristorante*	ree·sto·ran·te
spoon	*cucchiaio*	koo·kya·yo
vegetarian	*vegetariano*	ve·je·ta·rya·no

Meat & Fish

beef	*manzo*	man·dzo
chicken	*pollo*	po·lo
herring	*aringa*	a·reen·ga
lamb	*agnello*	a·nye·lo
lobster	*aragosta*	a·ra·gos·ta
mussels	*cozze*	ko·tse
oysters	*ostriche*	o·stree·ke
pork	*maiale*	ma·ya·le
prawn	*gambero*	gam·be·ro
salmon	*salmone*	sal·mo·ne
scallops	*capasante*	ka·pa·san·te

shrimp	gambero	gam·be·ro
squid	calamari	ka·la·ma·ree
trout	trota	tro·ta
tuna	tonno	to·no
turkey	tacchino	ta·kee·no
veal	vitello	vee·te·lo

Fruit & Vegetables

apple	mela	me·la
beans	fagioli	fa·jo·lee
cabbage	cavolo	ka·vo·lo
capsicum	peperone	pe·pe·ro·ne
carrot	carota	ka·ro·ta
cauliflower	cavolfiore	ka·vol·fyo·re
cucumber	cetriolo	che·tree·o·lo
grapes	uva	oo·va
lemon	limone	lee·mo·ne
lentils	lenticchie	len·tee·kye
mushroom	funghi	foon·gee
nuts	noci	no·chee
onions	cipolle	chee·po·le
orange	arancia	a·ran·cha
peach	pesca	pe·ska
peas	piselli	pee·ze·lee
pineapple	ananas	a·na·nas
plum	prugna	proo·nya
potatoes	patate	pa·ta·te
spinach	spinaci	spee·na·chee
tomatoes	pomodori	po·mo·do·ree

Other

bread	pane	pa·ne
butter	burro	boo·ro
cheese	formaggio	for·ma·jo
eggs	uova	wo·va
honey	miele	mye·le
jam	marmellata	mar·me·la·ta

Signs

Closed	Chiuso
Entrance	Entrata/Ingresso
Exit	Uscita
Men	Uomini
Open	Aperto
Prohibited	Proibito/Vietato
Toilets	Gabinetti/Servizi
Women	Donne

noodles	pasta	pas·ta
oil	olio	o·lyo
pepper	pepe	pe·pe
rice	riso	ree·zo
salt	sale	sa·le
soup	minestra	mee·nes·tra
soy sauce	salsa di soia	sal·sa dee so·ya
sugar	zucchero	tsoo·ke·ro
vinegar	aceto	a·che·to

Drinks

beer	birra	bee·ra
coffee	caffè	ka·fe
juice	succo	soo·ko
milk	latte	la·te
red wine	vino rosso	vee·no ro·so
tea	tè	te
water	acqua	a·kwa
white wine	vino bianco	vee·no byan·ko

EMERGENCIES

Help!
Aiuto! a·yoo·to

Leave me alone!
Lasciami in pace! la·sha·mee een pa·che

I'm lost.
Mi sono perso/a. (m/f) mee so·no per·so/a

Call the police!
Chiami la polizia! kya·mee la po·lee·tsee·a

Call a doctor!
Chiami un medico! kya·mee oon me·dee·ko

Where are the toilets?
Dove sono i do·ve so·no ee
gabinetti? ga·bee·ne·tee

I'm sick.
Mi sento male. mee sen·to ma·le

SHOPPING & SERVICES

I'd like to buy ...
Vorrei comprare ... vo·ray kom·pra·re ...

I'm just looking.
Sto solo guardando. sto so·lo gwar·dan·do

Can I look at it?
Posso dare un'occhiata? po·so da·re oo·no·kya·ta

How much is this?
Quanto costa questo? kwan·to kos·ta kwe·sto

It's too expensive.
È troppo caro. e tro·po ka·ro

There's a mistake in the bill.
C'è un errore nel conto. che oo·ne·ro·re nel kon·to

ATM	Bancomat	ban·ko·mat
post office	ufficio postale	oo·*fee*·cho pos·*ta*·le
tourist office	ufficio del turismo	oo·*fee*·cho del too·reez·mo

TIME & DATES

What time is it?
Che ora è? ke o·ra e

It's (two) o'clock.
Sono le (due). so·no le (*doo*·e)

Half past (one).
(L'una) e mezza. (*loo*·na) e me·dza

in the morning	di mattina	dee ma·*tee*·na
in the afternoon	di pomeriggio	dee po·me·*ree* jo
in the evening	di sera	dee se·ra
yesterday	ieri	ye·ree
today	oggi	o·jee
tomorrow	domani	do·*ma*·nee

Monday	lunedì	loo·ne·dee
Tuesday	martedì	mar·te·dee
Wednesday	mercoledì	mer·ko·le·dee
Thursday	giovedì	jo·ve·dee
Friday	venerdì	ve·ner·dee
Saturday	sabato	sa·ba·to
Sunday	domenica	do·me·nee·ka

TRANSPORT

boat	nave	na·ve
bus	autobus	ow·to·boos
ferry	traghetto	tra·*ge*·to
metro	metro- politana	me·tro· po·lee·*ta*·na
plane	aereo	a·e·re·o
train	treno	tre·no

bus stop	fermata dell'autobus	fer·*ma*·ta del ow·to·boos
ticket office	biglietteria	bee·lye·te·*ree*·a
timetable	orario	o·*ra*·ryo
train station	stazione ferroviaria	sta·*tsyo*·ne fe·ro·*vyar*·ya

... ticket	un biglietto ...	oon bee·*lye*·to
one way	di sola andata	dee so·la an·*da*·ta
return	di andata e ritorno	dee an·*da*·ta e ree·*tor*·no

Numbers

1	uno	*oo*·no
2	due	*doo*·e
3	tre	tre
4	quattro	kwa·tro
5	cinque	*cheen*·kwe
6	sei	say
7	sette	se·te
8	otto	o·to
9	nove	*no*·ve
10	dieci	dye·chee
20	venti	ven·tee
30	trenta	tren·ta
40	quaranta	kwa·*ran*·ta
50	cinquanta	cheen·*kwan*·ta
60	sessanta	se·san·ta
70	settanta	se·*tan*·ta
80	ottanta	o·*tan*·ta
90	novanta	no·*van*·ta
100	cento	*chen*·to
1000	mille	mee·lel

Does it stop at ...?
Si ferma a ...? see fer·ma a ...

Please tell me when we get to ...
Mi dica per favore quando arriviamo a ... mee dee·ka per fa·*vo*·re kwan·do a·ree·*vya*·mo a ...

I want to get off here.
Voglio scendere qui. vo·lyo shen·de·re kwee

I'd like to hire a ...	Vorrei noleggiare una ...	vo·ray no·le·*ja*·re oo·na ...
bicycle	bicicletta	bee·chee·*kle*·ta
car	macchina	ma·kee·na
motorbike	moto	mo·to

bicycle pump	pompa della bicicletta	pom·pa de·la bee·chee·*kle*·ta
child seat	seggiolino	se·jo·lee·no
helmet	casco	kas·ko
mechanic	meccanico	me·*ka*·nee·ko
petrol	benzina	ben·dzee·na
service station	stazione di servizio	sta·*tsyo*·ne dee ser·vee·tsyo

Is this the road to ...?
Questa strada porta a ...? kwe·sta stra·da por·ta a ...

Can I park here?
Posso parcheggiare qui? po·so par·ke·*ja*·re kwee

GLOSSARY

abbazia – abbey

agriturismo – farm-stays

(pizza) al taglio – (pizza) by the slice

albergo – hotel

alimentari – grocery shop

anfiteatro – amphitheatre

aperitivo – pre-dinner drink and snack

APT – Azienda di Promozione Turistica; local town or city tourist office

autostrada – motorway; highway

battistero – baptistry

biblioteca – library

biglietto – ticket

borgo – archaic name for a small town, village or town sector

camera – room

campo – field; also a square in Venice

cappella – chapel

carabinieri – police with military and civil duties

Carnevale – carnival period between Epiphany and Lent

casa – house

castello – castle

cattedrale – cathedral

centro storico – historic centre

certosa – monastery belonging to or founded by Carthusian monks

chiesa – church

chiostro – cloister; covered walkway, usually enclosed by columns, around a quadrangle

cima – summit

città – town; city

città alta – upper town

città bassa – lower town

colonna – column

comune – equivalent to a municipality or county; a town or city council; historically, a self–governing town or city

contrada – district

corso – boulevard

duomo – cathedral

enoteca – wine bar

espresso – short black coffee

ferrovia – railway

festa – feast day; holiday

fontana – fountain

foro – forum

funivia – cable car

gelateria – ice-cream shop

giardino – garden

golfo – gulf

grotta – cave

isola – island

lago – lake

largo – small square

lido – beach

locanda – inn; small hotel

lungomare – seafront road/ promenade

mar, mare – sea

masseria – working farm

mausoleo – mausoleum; stately and magnificent tomb

mercato – market

monte – mountain

necropoli – ancient name for cemetery or burial site

nord – north

nuraghe – megalithic stone fortress in Sardinia

osteria – casual tavern or eatery

palazzo – mansion; palace; large building of any type, including an apartment block

palio – contest

parco – park

passeggiata – traditional evening stroll

pasticceria – cake/pastry shop

pensione – guesthouse

piazza – square

piazzale – large open square

pietà – literally 'pity' or 'compassion'; sculpture, drawing or painting of the dead Christ supported by the Madonna

pinacoteca – art gallery

ponte – bridge

porta – gate; door

porto – port

reale – royal

rifugio – mountain hut; accommodation in the Alps

ristorante – restaurant

rocca – fortress

sala – room; hall

salumeria – delicatessen

santuario – sanctuary; 1. the part of a church above the altar; 2. an especially holy place in a temple (antiquity)

sassi – literally 'stones'; stone houses built in two ravines in Matera, Basilicata

scalinata – staircase

scavi – excavations

sestiere – city district in Venice

spiaggia – beach

stazione – station

stazione marittima – ferry terminal

strada – street; road

sud – south

superstrada – expressway; highway with divided lanes

tartufo – truffle

tavola calda – literally 'hot table'; pre-prepared meals, often self-service

teatro – theatre

tempietto – small temple

tempio – temple

terme – thermal baths

tesoro – treasury

torre – tower

trattoria – simple restaurant

Trenitalia – Italian State Railways; also known as Ferrovie dello Stato (FS)

trullo – conical house in Perugia

vaporetto – small passenger ferry in Venice

via – street; road

viale – avenue

vico – alley; alleyway

villa – town house; country house; also the park surrounding the house

Behind the Scenes

SEND US YOUR FEEDBACK

We love to hear from travellers – your comments keep us on our toes and help make our books better. Our well-travelled team reads every word on what you loved or loathed about this book. Although we cannot reply individually to postal submissions, we always guarantee that your feedback goes straight to the appropriate authors, in time for the next edition. Each person who sends us information is thanked in the next edition – the most useful submissions are rewarded with a selection of digital PDF chapters.

Visit **lonelyplanet.com/contact** to submit your updates and suggestions or to ask for help. Our award-winning website also features inspirational travel stories, news and discussions.

Note: We may edit, reproduce and incorporate your comments in Lonely Planet products such as guidebooks, websites and digital products, so let us know if you don't want your comments reproduced or your name acknowledged. For a copy of our privacy policy visit lonelyplanet.com/privacy.

OUR READERS

Many thanks to the travellers who used the last edition and wrote to us with help-ful hints, useful advice and interesting anecdotes:

Anastasie Martin, Ann Thomas, David Place, Greg Thompson, Javeed Taher, Laurent Ruhl-mann, Lisa Micklewright , Oron Frenkel, Ruth Ryder, Sergiy Sumnikov, Ted Garland

AUTHOR THANKS

Cristian Bonetto

As always, *grazie infinite* to my 'Re e Regina di Napoli', as well as to Alfonso Sperandeo, Andrea Maglio, Susy Galeone and La Paran-za, Bonnie Alberts, Luca Coda and Harriet Driver, Alfredo Cefalo and Malgorzata Gajo, Giancarlo Di Maio, Gigi Crispino and Valentina Vellusi. At Lonely Planet, a big thanks to Anna Tyler for the commission and to my diligent co-writers Helena Smith, Brendan Sainsbury and Gregor Clark.

Gregor Clark

Grazie mille to the many dozens of people who shared their love and knowledge of Sicily with me, especially Angela, Francesco and Matilde in Palermo. Love and special thanks to my father, Henry Clark, who first showed me the wonders of Sicily. Back in Vermont, big hugs to Gaen, Meigan and Chloe, who always make coming home the best part of the trip.

Brendan Sainsbury

Thanks to all the untold bus drivers, coffee baristas, pasta makers, museum curators and innocent bystanders who smoothed the path during my research. Special thanks to my wife, Liz, and nine-year-old son, Kieran, for their company on the road.

ACKNOWLEDGMENTS

Climate map data adapted from Peel MC, Finlayson BL & McMahon TA (2007) 'Updated World Map of the Koppen-Geiger Climate Classification', Hydrology and Earth System Sciences, 11, 1633-44

Illustration pp74-5 by Javier Martinez Zarracina

Cover photograph: Vieste, Puglia; Matt Munro/Lonely Planet

THIS BOOK

This 3rd edition of Lonely Planet's *Southern Italy* guidebook was researched and written by Cristian Bonetto, Gregor Clark, Brendan Sainsbury and Helena Smith. This guidebook was produced by the following:

Destination Editor
Anna Tyler

Product Editors
Briohny Hooper, Alison Ridgway

Senior Cartographer
Anthony Phelan

Book Designer
Wendy Wright

Assisting Editors Melanie Dankel, Helen Koehne, Chris Pitts

Cover Researcher Naomi Parker

Thanks to Liz Abbott, Andi Jones, Elizabeth Jones, Claire Murphy, Karyn Noble, Samantha Russell-Tulip, Dianne Schallmeiner, Lauren Wellicome, Tony Wheeler

Index

A

accommodation 16, 262-4,
   see also individual
   locations
   language 281
Acquacalda 182
activities 20-1, *see also*
   individual activities
Aeolian Islands 11, 178-
   90, **11**
   beaches 181, 183, 188
   hiking 182, 183, 184, 188
   travel to/from 154,
   178, 179
   travel within 179
Agrigento 10, 214-17,
   216, **10**
agriturismi 262
Agropoli 96
Aieta 147
air travel
   to/from Southern Italy
   273-4
   within Southern Italy 276
Albanian towns 146-7
Alberobello 11, 117-19,
   11, **159**
Alicudi 189
Amalfi 87-9
Amalfi Coast 12, 83-96, **13**
Appennino Lucano 143-4
archaeological sites &
   ruins 228
   Campi Flegrei 59, 99, **98**
   Catania 195
   Crotone 156
   Herculaneum 70-1, 99, **99**
   Locri 156
   Paestum 95, 99, **98**
   Parco Archeologico della
   Neapolis 203
   Pompeii 9, 72-8, 99, **76**,
   8, **98-9**

Map Pages **000**
Photo Pages **000**

Segesta 223-4
Selinunte 219
Sibari 156
Valley of the Temples 214,
   215, **215**
Villa Jovis 61
Villa Romana del Casale
   213
architecture 18, 258-60
area codes 15, 269-70
art 256-8
art galleries, *see museums*
   & galleries
asylum seekers 226-7
ATMs 17, 267

B

Bacoli 59
Baia 59
bargaining 17
Bari 101, 104-7, **104**
baroque architecture 18,
   259-60
baroque art 257-8
basilicas, *see churches &*
   cathedrals
Basilicata 34, 100, 135-45,
   146-7, **102-3**
   climate 100
   driving tour 108, **108**
   food 28, 112
   highlights 100, 102-3
   history 135, 156
   travel seasons 100
Bay of Naples 60-70
B&Bs 262-3
beaches 19
   Aeolian Islands 181,
   183, 188
   Amalfi Coast 87
   Bay of Naples 67
   Calabria 146, 150, 155
   Campania 82, 91
   Ischia 67
   Lipari 181
   Mondello 175

Otranto 131
Palermo 175, 177
Procida 69
Promontorio del
   Gargano 111
Sicily 191, 204-5
Stromboli 188
Syracuse 204
Taormina 191
Vulcano 183
bicycle travel, *see cycling*
Blue Grotto 64
boat travel
   to/from Southern Italy
   275-6
   within Southern Italy 277
books 226
border crossings 274
Bourbon rule 235-6
Bova 151
bread 250-1
Brindisi 127-30, **128**
budget 15
buffitieri 172
bus travel
   local transport 278
   to/from Southern Italy
   274-5
   within Southern Italy 277
business hours 15, 143, 269
Byzantine art 256-7

C

Calabria 34, 100, 145-57,
   102-3
   climate 100
   driving tour 108, **108**
   food 28, 112
   highlights 100, 102-3
   history 145-6, 156
   travel seasons 100
   travel to/from 154
calcio 245
Camigliatello Silano 150
Campania 33, 36-97, **38-9**
   accommodation 36

   climate 36
   food 27-8, 36
   highlights 38-9
   travel seasons 36
Campi Flegrei 59, 99, **98**
camping 263
cannoli 186, 221, **186**
Canolo 151
Capo Vaticano 155
Capraia 116
Capri 10, 60-6, **62**, **11**
   accommodation 63-5
   activities 63
   drinking & nightlife 65-6
   food 65
   hiking 65
   shopping 66
   sights 61-3
   tourist information 66
   travel to/from 66
   travel within 66
car travel
   driving tours 108, 132,
   209, **108**, **209**
   to/from Southern Italy 275
   within Southern Italy
   277-8
Caravaggio 257-8
cartapesta 126
Casamicciola Terme 68
Caserta 60
Castel del Monte 110
Castelmezzano 143-4
Castrovillari 147
catacombs 51, 52, 99
Catania 194-200, **196**, **2**
   accommodation 197-8
   drinking & nightlife 198-9
   entertainment 199
   festivals & events 197
   food 198
   medical services 199
   tourist information 199
   travel to/from 176,
   199-200
   travel within 200

cathedrals, *see* churches & cathedrals
caves
Grotta Azzurra 64
Grotta dello Smeraldo 88
Grotte di Castelcivita 97
Grotte di Castellana 117
Grotte di Pertosa 97
Naples 51
Promontorio del Gargano 111
Cefalù 176-8
cell phones 14, 270
ceramics 91
Certosa e Museo di San Martino 45-6
Cetara 91
Chiaia 69
Chiaramonte Gulfi 209
children, travel with 31-2
Christmas 21, 46
churches & cathedrals
Basilica di San Nicola 105
Basilica di Santa Caterina d'Alessandria 130
Basilica di Santa Chiara 37, 40
Basilica di Santa Croce 122
Cappella Sansevero 40-1
Cattedrale di Monreale 175
Cattedrale di Sant' Andrea 87
Duomo (Naples) 42-3
Duomo (Salerno) 91, 93
Lecce 124
Ciclo di Rappresentazioni Classiche 205
Civita 147
climate 14, 20-1, *see also individual locations*
climate change 273
coffee 28, 249
Condofuri 151
consulates 265
cooking courses 125
Corricella 69
Cosenza 148-9
Costiera Amalfitana, *see* Amalfi Coast
Costiera Cilentana 96-7
costs 15
credit cards 17, 267-8
Croatia 109
Crotone 156
cucina povera 112
culture 226-7, 241-5

currency 14, 267
customs regulations 264
cycling 276-7

D
dangers, *see* safety
Diamante 147
Diocletian 231
disabilities, travellers with 271
discount cards 264-5
diving
Capri 63
Ischia 67
Lipari 181
Otranto 131
Praiano 87
Promontorio del Gargano 111
Punta Campanella 82
San Domino 116
Stromboli 188
Taormina 191
drinking 26-30, 254-5
drinks, *see* coffee, wine
driving, *see* car travel
driving licences 277
driving tours
Puglia, Calabria & Basilicata 108, 132, **108**
Sicily 209, **209**
drugs, possession of 267
Duomo (Naples) 42-3
Duomo (Salerno) 91, 93

E
economy 226-7, 241
Egadi Islands 189, 220
electricity 265
embassies 265
emergencies 15
language 283
environmental hazards 266-7
Erchie 91
Ercolano 70-2
Erice 222-3
etiquette 17, 29
events 20-1
exchange rates 15

F
Favignana 220
ferry travel 275-6, 277
Festival della Valle d'Itria 21
festivals 20-1, *see also individual locations*
food 253

theatre 205
wine 51-2
Filicudi 189
film 226
history 239
Mafia, the 247
fishing platforms 114
food 13, 18, 26-30, 248-55, 265, **12**, *see also individual locations*
buffitieri 172
cannoli 186, 221, **186**
cooking courses 125
cucina povera 112
language 282
Sicilian desserts 186-7, **186**, **187**
Slow Food movement 251
football 56, 245
Foresta Umbra 115
Furore 87

G
Gaius 231
Galatina 130
Gallipoli 132-3
Gambarie 151
Gargano Peninsula, *see* Promontorio del Gargano
gay travellers 265-6
Gerace 151
Giotto di Bondone 257
Gothic architecture 259
Greece, travel to/from 109
Greek colonisation 156
Grotta Azzurra 64
Grotte di Castellana 117

H
haggling 17
health 266-7
Herculaneum 70-1, 99, **99**
hiking
Aeolian Islands 182, 183, 184, 188
Amalfi Coast 85
Basilicata 140, 146-7
Calabria 146-7, 151
Capri 65
Puglia 115
Sicily 200, 223
history 19, 228-40, *see also individual locations*
early settlers 228
film 239
Greek settlement 229

Holy Roman Empire 232-4
Lombards 231-2
Mafia, the 240
malaria 237-8
Normans 232, 233
prehistoric inhabitants 228
Roman settlement 230
Sicily 234-5
Tangentopoli scandal 239-40
unification 238-9
WWI 238
WWII 238-9
holidays 268
hot springs 183

I
Il Volo dell'Angelo 143
immigration 226-7, 271-2, 273
insurance
car 275
health 266
travel 267
internet access 267
internet resources 15
Ionian coast 150-1, 190-201
Ischia 66-9
islands 19
Isole Tremiti 115-16
Ispica 209
Italian language 14, 17, 281-5
itineraries 22-5

J
jellyfish 266

L
La Notte della Taranta 21
Lampedusa 189
Lampione 189
language 14, 17, 281-5
Latronico 146
Le Castella 150-1
Lecce 13, 122-7, **123**, **13**, **19**, **159**
accommodation 125
courses 125
drinking 126-7
food 125-6
medical services 127
sights 122, 124-5
travel to/from 127
legal matters 267
leishmaniasis 267

lesbian travellers 265-6
Levanzo 220
Linosa 189
Lipari 179-83, **180**
literature 226
local transport 278
Locorotondo 118, 119-20
Locri 156
Lorica 150
Lucanian Apennines 143-4
lyme disease 266

M
Mafia, the 161, 240, 246-7
Maggio dei Monumenti 20, 51
Magna Graecia 156
Maiori 91, **5**
malaria 237-8
maps 267
Maratea 144-5
Marettimo 220
Marina del Cantone 82-3
Marina di Chiaiolella 69
markets 251
Marsala 218-19
Martina Franca 120-1
masserias 118, 262
Matera 12, 135-42, 158, **137, 10, 158**
accommodation 139-40
activities 136-8
drinking & nightlife 141
festivals & events 139
food 141
history 136, 139
medical services 141
shopping 141
sights 136-8
tourist information 141-2
tours 138-9
travel to/from 142
Matera Gravina 140
measures 270
medical services 266
medieval towns 18
Messina, travel to/from 154
Metaponto 142
Milazzo 178
Minori 91
mobile phones 14, 270
Modica 211-12

monasteries
accommodation 263
Certosa di San Giacomo 61
Certosa di San Lorenzo 97
Certosa e Museo di San Martino 45-6
Complesso Monumentale di Santa Chiara 37, 40
Monastero di Santo Spirito 214
Museo Nazionale di Capodimonte 50
Mondello 175
money 14, 15, 17, 264-5, 267-8
Monreale 175
Monte Sant'Angelo 113-14
Morano Calabro 147
motorcycle travel 275, 277-8
mozzarella 249
Mt Etna 12, 200-1, **12**
Mt Vesuvius 70, 72, 73
museums & galleries
Certosa e Museo di San Martino 45-6
MADRE 43
Museo Archeologico Nazionale 43
Museo del Palazzo Reale 47
Museo Nazionale di Reggio Calabria 152
Palazzo Reale di Capodimonte 47, 50

N
Naples 9, 33, 36, 37-60, **40, 44, 48-9, 9**
accommodation 36, 52-3
climate 36
discount cards 42
drinking & nightlife 55-6
entertainment **56**
festivals & events 51-2
food 27-8, 36, 53-5
history 37
itineraries 41
medical services 57
shopping 56-7
sights 37, 40-50, 51
tourist information 57
tours 51
travel seasons 36
travel to/from 57-8
travel within 56, 59-60
national parks & reserves
Foresta Umbra 115

Parco Naturale Regionale delle Madonie 177
Parco Nazionale del Cilento e Vallo di Diano 96-7
Parco Nazionale del Pollino 146-7
Parco Nazionale della Sila 149-50
Parco Nazionale dell' Aspromonte 151-2
Riserva Naturale dello Zingaro 223
nativity scenes 46
'ndrangheta, the 146, 227
Nero 231
newspapers 270
Nocelle 88
Noto 208, 210-11

O
olive oil 250
opening hours 15, 143, 269
opera
Naples 56
Palermo 170, 173
Opera dei Pupi 171
Ostuni 118, 121-2
Otranto 130-1
outdoor activities 18-19, *see also individual activities*

P
Paestum 94-6, 99, **98**
palaces
Castel del Monte 110
Palazzo dei Normanni 165
Palazzo Reale 47
Reggia di Caserta 60
Villa Rufolo 90
Palermo 164-76, **166-7**
accommodation 170-1
climate 160
drinking & nightlife 173
entertainment 173
festivals & events 170
food 171-3
medical services 174
shopping 174
sights 164-5, 168-70
tourist information 174
travel seasons 160
travel to/from 174-6
travel within 176
Panarea 189
Pantelleria 189
Paola 148

papier-mâché 126
Parco Archeologico della Neapolis 203
Parco Naturale Regionale delle Madonie 177
Parco Nazionale del Cilento e Vallo di Diano 96-7
Parco Nazionale del Pollino 146-7
Parco Nazionale della Sila 149-50
Parco Nazionale dell' Aspromonte 151-2, 158
passports 271-2, 273
pasta 252
pasticcerie 251-2
Pelagic Islands 189
pensioni 264
Pentidàttilo 151
Peschici 114-15
phonecards 270
Piano Provenzano 200
Pianoconte 182
Piazza Armerina 213
pickpockets 268-9
Pietrapertosa 143-4
pizza 248-9, **19**
Pizzo 157
planning 16-17
budgeting 15
calendar of events 20-1
children, travel with 31-2
climate 14, 20-1
first time travellers 16-17
internet resources 15
itineraries 22-5
Southern Italy basics 14-15
Southern Italy's regions 33-4
travel seasons 14, 20-1
weather 14, 20-1
police 267
politics 226-7
Pollara 184
Pompeii 9, 72-8, 99, **76, 8, 74-5, 98, 99**
accommodation 78
food 78
sights 73-8
tourist information 78
tours 73
travel to/from 78
population 227
Positano 83-7, **84, 13**
postal services 268
Potenza 143
Pozzuoli 59
Praia a Mare 146-7

Praiano 85, 87
presepe napoletano 46
Procida 69-70
Promontorio del Gargano 110-15, 158, **158**
public holidays 268
public transport 278
Puglia 34, 100, 101-35, **102-3**
  climate 100
  driving tours 108, 132, **108**
  food 28, 112
  highlights 100, 102-3
  history 101, 156
  travel seasons 100
  travel to/from 109
puppet shows 171, 173, 174

Q
Quattropani 182

R
radio 270
rafting 147
Ragusa 212-13
Ravello 89-91
Ravello Festival 21
Reggia di Caserta 60
Reggio di Calabria 152-4, **153**
religion 227, 244-5
Renaissance, the 257
Riserva Naturale dello Zingaro 223
road rules 278
Roghudi 151
Romanesque architecure 259
Rotonda 146, 147

S
safety 268-9
  car travel 278
Salento 130-5, 158

Salerno 91-4, **92**
Salina 184-5
San Costantino Albanese 146
San Domino 116
San Nicola 116
San Paolo Albanese 146
Santa Severina 150
Sant'Agata sui Due Golfi 82
Sant'Arcangelo 146
Santuario di San Michele 113
sassi 136, 139
Scigliano 150
Scilla 154-5
Scopello 223
Segesta 223-4
Selinunte 219
Settimana Santa 20
Sibari 156
Sicily 34, 160-224, **162-3**
  accommodation 160
  climate 160
  driving tours 209, **209**
  food 29, 160, 186-7, **186-7**
  highlights 162-3
  history 161, 234-5
  travel seasons 160
  travel to/from 154, 161, 164
  travel within 164, 176
skiing 150
Slow Food movement 251
smoking laws 270
snakes 266
soccer 56, 245
Sorrento 78-82, **79**
Soverato 150
Stromboli 188-90, **11**
Syracuse 201-8, **202**, **204**
  accommodation 205-6
  activities 204-5
  drinking & nightlife 207
  entertainment 207

  festivals & events 205
  food 206-7
  medical services 207
  shopping 207
  sights 202-4
  tourist information 207
  travel to/from 208
  travel within 208

T
Taormina 190-4, **192**
Taranto 133-5, 156, **134**
taxes 14, 268
taxis 278
Teatro Massimo 170, 173
Teatro San Carlo 56
telephone services 14, 269-70
Terranova di Pollino 146, 147
theft 268-9
thermal springs 183
Tiberius 231
ticks 266
time 14, 270
tipping 17, 268
Tortora 147
tourist information 270-1
tours, *see* driving tours, walking tours, *individual locations*
trabucchi 114
train travel 275, 278-80
Trani 107-10
transport 15, 273-80
  language 284
Trapani 219-22
travel to/from Southern Italy 273-6
travel within Southern Italy 276-80
trekking, *see* hiking
Tropea 155-7
trulli 116, 117, 119, **11**, **159**
TV 270

U
underground train travel 278
unemployment 226
Ustica 175

V
vacations 268
vaccinations 266
Valle d'Itria 116-22, 158
Valley of the Temples 214, 215, **215**
vegetables 252-4
Vieste 110-13, **3**
Vietri sul Mare 91
Villa Romana del Casale 213
Villa Rufolo 90
Villa San Giovanni 154
visas 14, 271-2
volcanoes
  Mt Etna 200-1
  Mt Vesuvius 72
  Stromboli 188
  Vulcano 183
volunteering 272
Vulcano 183-4

W
walking, *see* hiking
walking tours 215
weather 14, 20-1, *see also individual locations*
websites 15
weights 270
wine 51-2, 254-5
  Aeolian Islands 184
  Malfa 184
  Marsala 218
women in Southern Italy 243-4
women travellers 272
WWI 238
WWII 238-9

Map Legend

Sights

- Beach
- Bird Sanctuary
- Buddhist
- Castle/Palace
- Christian
- Confucian
- Hindu
- Islamic
- Jain
- Jewish
- Monument
- Museum/Gallery/Historic Building
- Ruin
- Shinto
- Sikh
- Taoist
- Winery/Vineyard
- Zoo/Wildlife Sanctuary
- Other Sight

Activities, Courses & Tours

- Bodysurfing
- Diving
- Canoeing/Kayaking
- Course/Tour
- Sento Hot Baths/Onsen
- Skiing
- Snorkelling
- Surfing
- Swimming/Pool
- Walking
- Windsurfing
- Other Activity

Sleeping

- Sleeping
- Camping

Eating

- Eating

Drinking & Nightlife

- Drinking & Nightlife
- Cafe

Entertainment

- Entertainment

Shopping

- Shopping

Information

- Bank
- Embassy/Consulate
- Hospital/Medical
- Internet
- Police
- Post Office
- Telephone
- Toilet
- Tourist Information
- Other Information

Geographic

- Beach
- Gate
- Hut/Shelter
- Lighthouse
- Lookout
- Mountain/Volcano
- Oasis
- Park
- Pass
- Picnic Area
- Waterfall

Population

- Capital (National)
- Capital (State/Province)
- City/Large Town
- Town/Village

Transport

- Airport
- Border crossing
- Bus
- Cable car/Funicular
- Cycling
- Ferry
- Metro station
- Monorail
- Parking
- Petrol station
- Subway station
- Taxi
- Train station/Railway
- Tram
- Underground station
- Other Transport

Note: Not all symbols displayed above appear on the maps in this book

Routes

- Tollway
- Freeway
- Primary
- Secondary
- Tertiary
- Lane
- Unsealed road
- Road under construction
- Plaza/Mall
- Steps
- Tunnel
- Pedestrian overpass
- Walking Tour
- Walking Tour detour
- Path/Walking Trail

Boundaries

- International
- State/Province
- Disputed
- Regional/Suburb
- Marine Park
- Cliff
- Wall

Hydrography

- River, Creek
- Intermittent River
- Canal
- Water
- Dry/Salt/Intermittent Lake
- Reef

Areas

- Airport/Runway
- Beach/Desert
- Cemetery (Christian)
- Cemetery (Other)
- Glacier
- Mudflat
- Park/Forest
- Sight (Building)
- Sportsground
- Swamp/Mangrove

OUR STORY

A beat-up old car, a few dollars in the pocket and a sense of adventure. In 1972 that's all Tony and Maureen Wheeler needed for the trip of a lifetime – across Europe and Asia overland to Australia. It took several months, and at the end – broke but inspired – they sat at their kitchen table writing and stapling together their first travel guide, *Across Asia on the Cheap*. Within a week they'd sold 1500 copies. Lonely Planet was born.

Today, Lonely Planet has offices in Franklin, London, Melbourne, Oakland, Beijing and Delhi, with more than 600 staff and writers. We share Tony's belief that 'a great guidebook should do three things: inform, educate and amuse'.

OUR WRITERS

Cristian Bonetto

Coordinating Author, Naples & Campania Despite his northern Italian background, espresso-guzzling Cristian is an ardent fan of the country's sunbaked south. A one-time writer of farce and TV drama, the Melbourne-born writer is hooked on the region's penchant for intensity, irony and extremes. Cristian has both lived and holidayed in the *Bel paese* (Beautiful Country), his musing on the country's food, culture and inimitable style appearing in newspapers, magazines and websites across the globe. To date, Cristian has contributed to over 30 Lonely Planet guides, including *Italy, Naples & the Amalfi Coast, Venice & The Veneto, New York City, Denmark,* and *Singapore*. You can follow Cristian's globe-trotting adventures on Twitter (@CristianBonetto) and Instagram (rexcat75).

Gregor Clark

Sicily Gregor caught the Italy bug at age 14 while living in Florence with his professor dad, who took him to see every fresco, mosaic and museum within a 1000km radius. He's lived in Florence and Le Marche, huffed and puffed across the Dolomites while researching LP's *Cycling Italy* and contributed to three previous editions of this guide. A lifelong polyglot with a Romance Languages degree, Gregor has written for Lonely Planet since 2000, with an emphasis on Mediterranean Europe and Latin America.

Brendan Sainsbury

Puglia, Basilicata & Calabria An expat Brit from Hampshire, England, now living near Vancouver, Canada; Brendan has covered Italy five times for Lonely Planet reporting on 16 of its 20 regions. For this edition he suffered horizontal rain in Matera and spent three minutes in a decontamination chamber in Reggio di Calabria. When not scribbling research notes for Lonely Planet in countries such as Cuba, Peru, Spain and Canada, Brendan likes to run up mountains, strum his flamenco guitar, and experience the pain and occasional pleasure of following Southampton Football Club.

Contributing Writer

Helena Smith contributed to the Naples & Campania chapter.

Published by Lonely Planet Publications Pty Ltd
ABN 36 005 607 983
3rd edition – March 2016
ISBN 978 1 74321 687 3
© Lonely Planet 2016   Photographs © as indicated 2016
10 9 8 7 6 5 4 3 2 1
Printed in China

Although the authors and Lonely Planet have taken all reasonable care in preparing this book, we make no warranty about the accuracy or completeness of its content and, to the maximum extent possible, disclaim all liability arising from its use.